Born in Chatham, Kent, **HENRY STEDMAN** has been writing guidebooks for almost a quarter of a century now and is the author or co-author of a dozen titles, including Trailblazer's *Coast to Coast Path*, *Hadrian's Wall Path*, *Dales Way*, and all three books in the South-West Coast Path series as well as *The Bradt Guide to Palestine* and the Rough Guides to *Indonesia* and *Southeast Asia*. Travel remains his abiding love, a passion surpassed only by his obsession with Kilimanjaro – an obsession that has seen him climb all the routes several times, as well as collect books, maps and other paraphernalia about it. He also maintains a website dedicated to climbing it (🖳 www.climbmountkilimanjaro.com), leads groups up the mountain and runs the trekking company, Kilimanjaro Experts.

When not travelling, Henry lives near Hastings in England, writing, editing and putting on weight. Friends describe him as living proof that almost anyone can climb Kilimanjaro.

Author

Kilimanjaro – the trekking guide to Africa's highest mountain

First edition 2003; **this fifth edition 2018, reprinted with amendments 2021**

Publisher Trailblazer Publications 🖳 www.trailblazer-guides.com
The Old Manse, Tower Rd, Hindhead, Surrey, GU26 6SU, UK

British Library Cataloguing in Publication Data
A catalogue record for this book is available from the British Library

ISBN 978-1-905864-95-9

Editor: Clare Weldon
Cartography: Nick Hill   **Layout**: Daniel McCrohan & Bryn Thomas
Proof-reading: Daniel McCrohan   **Index**: Jane Thomas

A request

The author and publisher have tried to ensure that this guide is as accurate and up to date
as possible. However, things change quickly in this part of the world. Agencies come and
go, trails are re-routed, prices rise and ... well, rise some more, governments are toppled
and glaciers shrink. If you notice any changes or corrections for the next edition of this
guide, please email Henry Stedman at 🖳 henry@climbmountkilimanjaro.com.
You can also contact Trailblazer via 🖳 www.trailblazer-guides.com. Those persons
making a significant contribution will be rewarded with a free copy of the next edition,
an acknowledgement in that edition and Henry's undying gratitude.

Acknowledgements

See p402 for a list of those who contributed to this edition.

Warning: mountain walking can be dangerous

Please read the notes on when to go (pp15-16), health and fitness (pp53-8) and on safe
trekking (pp260-72). Every effort has been made by the author and publisher to ensure
that the information contained herein is as accurate and up to date as possible. However,
they are unable to accept responsibility for any inconvenience, loss or injury sustained by
anyone as a result of the advice and information given in this guide.

Updated information will, as always, be available on:
🖳 **www.climbmountkilimanjaro.com**

Photos – Front cover and **this page**: Looking towards Kilimanjaro
from the crater of Mount Meru.
Previous page: Kilimanjaro as seen from Moshi, the nearest town to the mountain.
Overleaf: The final 100m to Uhuru Peak – just keep going!

Printed in China; print production by D'Print (☎ +65-6581 3832), Singapore

Kilimanjaro

THE TREKKING GUIDE TO
AFRICA'S HIGHEST MOUNTAIN

also includes MOUNT MERU & guides to
Arusha, Moshi, Marangu, Nairobi & Dar es Salaam

HENRY STEDMAN

TRAILBLAZER PUBLICATIONS

Contents

PART 8: MOUNT MERU

PART 9: TRAIL GUIDE AND MAPS

PART 10: THE SUMMIT

APPENDICES

Contents

IN THIS EDITION

For this fifth edition we have, of course, given everything a thorough update, including our guides to the cities and towns and our reviews of the trekking agencies. The main change between the previous edition and this one is that we have collected the trekking agency reviews – which were previously scattered across several chapters depending on their location – and given them their own chapter; by doing so, we hope that we have made the task of comparing the agencies a little easier. For this fifth edition we have also walked routes again to satisfy ourselves that our descriptions are still accurate; and once again, we've called upon the services of Karen Valenti at KPAP (see pp26-9) to help us tackle the problem of porter mistreatment.

We do, of course, also welcome updates, criticisms and suggestions from readers on *any* aspect of the book.

🖳 www.climbmountkilimanjaro.com – the website!

The website that was set up in 2007 to accompany this book is still going strong. It was designed to keep our readers informed of the latest news and developments on the mountain; if we discover something major has changed since the publication of the book, this is where you can find out all about it. This is also the place to find out about park-fee increases, rule changes in the national park and all the tragedies and triumphs that occur on the mountain. If you need to get in touch with us then the email address on the website – henry@climbmountkilimanjaro.com – is your best bet; and unless we're out trekking, we usually respond within 24 hours.

❑ **The six golden rules for ascending Kilimanjaro safely and successfully**
● **Walk slowly** Emulate the deliberate, careful tread of an elderly, cautious elephant. Or a jaunty tortoise.
● **Drink plenty** Aim for at least three litres per day. Water, not beer.
● **Eat well** Don't worry, it's very unlikely you'll gain weight on your trek, so tuck in!
● **Take as long as you can** Six days minimum, seven better, eight best!
● **Climb up to high altitude before you arrive** If you've got a mountain in your back garden, now's the time to climb it.
● **Choose your trekking company carefully** To make the task simpler, check out our reviews of the trekking agencies beginning on p75.

INTRODUCTION

Kilimanjaro is a snow covered mountain 19,710 feet high, and is said to be the highest mountain in Africa. Its western summit is called the Masai 'Ngà'je Ngài', the House of God. Close to the western summit there is the dried and frozen carcass of a leopard. No one has explained what the leopard was seeking at that altitude.

Ernest Hemingway in the preamble to *The Snows of Kilimanjaro*

On 13 August, 2014, Karl Egloff of Switzerland stood at Umbwe Gate on the southern slopes of Africa's greatest mountain, Kilimanjaro. We can imagine the scene that day, for it's one that's repeated there every day of the year. There would be the noisy, excitable hubbub as porters, guides and rangers packed, weighed, re-packed and re-weighed all the equipment; the quiet murmur of anticipation from Karl's fellow trekkers as they stood on the threshold of the greatest walk of their lives; maybe there was even a troop of blue monkeys crashing through the canopy, or the scarlet flash of a turaco's underwing as it glided from tree to tree, surveying the commotion below.

Herr Egloff's main goal that day was no different from the ambitions of his fellow trekkers: he wanted to reach the summit. Unlike them, however, Karl planned to forego many of the features that make a walk up Kili so special. Not for him the joys of strolling lazily through the mountain's four main eco-zones, pausing frequently to admire the views or examine the unique mountain flora. Nor did Egloff want to experience the blissful evenings spent scoffing popcorn, sharing stories and gazing at the stars with his fellow trekkers. Nor, for that matter, was he looking forward to savouring the wonderful *esprit de corps* that builds between a trekker and his or her crew as they progress, day by day, up the mountain slopes; a sense of camaraderie that grows with every step until, exhausted, they stand together at the highest point in Africa.

It is these experiences that make climbing Kilimanjaro so unique and so special. Yet Karl had chosen to eschew all of them because, for reasons best known to himself, he had decided to *run* up the mountain. Which is exactly what he did, completing the entire route from gate to summit in an incredible 4 hours and 56 minutes – on an ascent trail that

> **Karl Egloff ran to the summit in an incredible 4 hours and 56 minutes**

takes the average trekker anywhere from four to six days to complete! For an encore he then ran all the way back down to Mweka Gate, and in doing so set another record for the fastest ascent and descent of Kilimanjaro, completing the round trip in just 6 hours and 42 minutes.

A mountain for eccentrics

Barking mad though Karl's exploits may have been, in his defence it must be said that he isn't exactly alone in taking an unorthodox approach to tackling Kilimanjaro. Take the Crane cousins from England, for example, who cycled up to the summit, surviving on Mars bars that they'd strapped to their handlebars.

Douglas Adams reached the summit wearing an 8ft rubber rhinoceros costume

Or the anonymous Spaniard who, in the 1970s, drove up to the summit on a motorbike. Or what about Douglas Adams, author of *The Hitchhikers' Guide to the Galaxy*, who in 1994 reached the summit for charity while wearing an 8ft rubber rhinoceros costume. Not to mention the many people who have got to the top and celebrated their achievement by stripping off, posing for summit photos wearing nothing but suncream and a smile. There's also a team of trekkers who, in 2012, climbed barefoot! Just recently I heard about a group of climbers from the Middle East who tried and failed to get to the top riding camels; and I've just watched a YouTube TV interview with an Irishman who's planning to scale the mountain with a washing machine strapped to his back. And who can forget the (possibly apocryphal) story of the man who walked *backwards* to the summit in order to get into the *Guinness Book of Records* – only to find out, on his return to the bottom, that he had been beaten by somebody who had done exactly the same thing just a few days previously.

And that's just the ascent; for coming back again we've had skiing, a method first practised by Walter Furtwangler way back in 1912; snowboarding, an activity pioneered on Kili by Stephen Koch in 1997; and even paragliding, first attempted by a team back in January 2013.

Don't be fooled

Cyclists, skiers, bikers, boarders and backward walkers: it's no wonder, given the sheer number of people who have climbed Kili over the past century and the

... these stories of successful expeditions ... also serve to obscure the tales of suffering and tragedy that are just as frequent

ways in which they've done so, that so many people believe climbing Kili is a doddle. And you'd be forgiven for thinking the same.

You'd be forgiven – but you'd also be wrong. Whilst these stories of successful expeditions tend to receive a lot of coverage, they also serve to obscure the tales of suffering and tragedy that are just as frequent. To give you just one example: for all the coverage of the Millennium celebrations, when over 7000 people stood on the slopes of Kilimanjaro during New Year's week – with 1000 on New Year's Eve alone – little mention was made of the fact that well over a third of all the people who took part in those festivities failed to reach the summit, or indeed get anywhere near it. Or that another 33 had to be rescued. Or that, in the space of those seven days, three people died.

Below: Marching through the everlastings east of the Saddle, with Kibo in the background.

INTRODUCTION

The Breakfast or Barranco Wall is the nearest that trekkers get to actual 'climbing' but don't worry, it's not difficult to scramble up and is actually a lot of fun.

The reason why most of these attempts were unsuccessful is altitude sickness, brought about by a trekker climbing too fast and not allowing his or her body time to acclimatise to the rarified air. Karl Egloff didn't just set a record by climbing Kilimanjaro in under five hours; he also, unwittingly, set a bad example.

For once, statistics give a reasonably accurate impression of just how difficult climbing Kili can be. According to the park authorities, almost one in four people who climb up Kilimanjaro fail to reach even the crater. They also admit to there being a couple of deaths per annum on Kilimanjaro – though independent observers put that figure nearer six or seven.

There's no doubt the joys of climbing Kili are manifold; unfortunately, so are the ways in which it can destroy you. Because the simple truth is that Kilimanjaro is a very big mountain and, like all big mountains, it's very adept at killing off the unprepared, the unwary or just the plain unlucky. The fact that the Maasai call the mountain the 'House of God' seems entirely appropriate, given the number of people who meet their Maker every year on Kili's slopes.

At one stage we were taking a minute to complete thirty-five small paces. Altitude sickness had already hit the boys and two were weeping, pleading to pack up. All the instructors with the exception of Lubego and myself were in a bad way. They were becoming violently ill. It was becoming touch and go. The descent at one stage was like a battlefield. Men, including the porters, lying prone or bent up in agony. Tom and Swato though very ill themselves rallied the troops and helped manhandle the three unconscious boys to a lower altitude.

From the logbook of **Geoffrey Salisbury**, who led a group of blind African climbers up Kilimanjaro, as recorded in *The Road to Kilimanjaro* (1997).

The high failure and mortality rates speak for themselves: despite appearances to the contrary, climbing Kilimanjaro is no simple matter.

'Mountain of greatness'

But whilst it isn't easy, it *is* achievable. After all, no technical skill is required to reach the summit of Africa's highest mountain beyond the ability to put one

foot in front of the other; because, unless you go out of your way to find a particularly awkward route, there is no actual *climbing* involved at all – just lots and

No technical skill is required to reach the summit of Africa's highest mountain

lots of walking. Thus, anyone above the age of 10 (the minimum legal age for climbing Kilimanjaro) *can*, with the right attitude, a sensible approach to acclimatisation, a half-decent pair of calf muscles and lots of warm clothing, make it to the top. Even vertigo sufferers are not excluded, there being only one or two vertical drops on any of the regular trekking routes that will have you scrabbling in your rucksacks for the Imodium.

Simply put, Kilimanjaro is for everyone. Again, statistics can back this up: with the youngest successful summiteer aged just seven and the oldest, the venerable American Dr Fred Distelhorst, aged 88, it's clear that Kili conquerors come in all shapes and sizes. Amongst their number there are a few who have managed to overcome enormous personal disabilities on their way to the summit. Virtually every year there is at least one group of blind trekkers who, incredibly, make it to the top by using the senses of touch and hearing alone. There's also Bern Goosen, who has managed to manoeuvre his wheelchair to the summit *twice*, in 2003 and 2007; Erica Davis of Carlsbad, who became the first woman to do so, in 2011; Spencer West, who lost his legs at the age of five due to a rare genetic disorder but on 2012 managed to ascend entirely on his hands; and Kyle Maynard, who on January 15, 2012, became the first quadruple amputee to climb Mount Kilimanjaro without assistance, by crawling to the summit in just 10 days.

It is this 'inclusivity' that undoubtedly goes some way to explaining Kilimanjaro's popularity, a popularity that saw 47,232 people on the mountain in the 2015-16 season, thereby confirming Kili's status as the most popular of the so-called 'Big Seven', the highest peaks on each of the seven continents.

The sheer size of it must be another factor behind its appeal. This is the Roof of Africa, a massive massif 60km long by 80km wide with an altitude that reaches to a fraction under 6km above sea level. Writing in 1924, one of the pio-

Below: Walking down from Kibo Huts towards the Saddle, with Mawenzi in the distance.

neers of the coffee industry in Moshi, Charles Dundas, claimed that he once saw Kilimanjaro from a point over 120 miles away. This enormous monolith is big enough to have its own weather systems (note the plural) and, furthermore, to influence the climates of the countries that surround it.

The aspect presented by this prodigious mountain is one of unparalleled grandeur, sublimity, majesty, and glory. It is doubtful if there be another such sight in this wide world.
Charles New, the first European to reach the snow-line on Kilimanjaro, from his book
Life, Wanderings, and Labours in Eastern Africa (1873).

But size, as they say, isn't everything, and by themselves these bald figures fail to fully explain the allure of Kilimanjaro. So, instead, we must look to attributes that cannot be measured by theodolites or yardsticks if we are to understand the appeal of Kilimanjaro.

In particular, there's its beauty. When viewed from the plains of Tanzania, Kilimanjaro conforms to our childhood notions of what a mountain should look like: high, wide and handsome, a vast triangle rising out of the flat earth, its sides sloping exponentially upwards to the satisfyingly symmetrical summit of Kibo; a summit that rises imperiously above a thick beard of clouds and is adorned with a glistening bonnet of snow. Kilimanjaro is not located in the crumpled mountain terrain of the Himalayas or the Andes. Where the mightiest mountain of them all, Everest, just edges above its neighbours – and looks less impressive because of it – Kilimanjaro stands proudly alone on the plains of Africa. The only thing in the neighbourhood that can even come close to looking it in the eye is Mt Meru, over 60km away to the south-west and a good 1329m/4360ft smaller. The fact that Kilimanjaro is located smack bang in the

heart of the sweltering East African plains, just a few degrees (330km/205 miles) south of the equator, with lions, giraffes, and all the other celebrities of the safari world running around its base, only adds to its charisma.

Then there's the scenery on the mountain itself. So massive is Kilimanjaro that to climb it is to pass through **four seasons in four days**, from the sultry rainforests of the lower reaches through to the windswept heather and moorland

> **So massive is Kilimanjaro that to climb it is to pass through four seasons in four days**

of the upper slopes, the alpine desert of the Saddle and Shira Plateau and on to the arctic wastes of the summit. There may be about 124 higher mountains on the globe but there can't be many that are more beautiful, or more tantalising.

In sitting down to recount my experiences with the conquest of the "Ethiopian Mount Olympus" still fresh in my memory, I feel how inadequate are my powers of description to do justice to the grand and imposing aspects of Nature with which I shall have to deal.

Hans Meyer, the first man to climb Kilimanjaro, in his book
Across East African Glaciers – an Account of the First Ascent of Kilimanjaro (1891)

Nor is it just tourists who are entranced by Kilimanjaro; the mountain looms large in the Tanzanian psyche too. Just look at their supermarket shelves. The nation's favourite lager is called Kilimanjaro. There's Kilimanjaro coffee (grown on the mountain's fertile southern slopes), Kilimanjaro tea (ditto), Kilimanjaro mineral water (bottled on its western side) and Kilimanjaro honey (again, sourced from the mountain). While on billboards lining the country's highways, Tanzanian models smoke their cigarettes in its shadow and cheerful roly-poly housewives compare the whiteness of their laundry with the mountain's glistening snows. And to pay for all of these things you might just use an

old Tanzanian Ts2000 note which just happens to have, on its reverse side, a lion posing in front of the distinctive silhouette of Africa's highest mountain.

It was perhaps no surprise, therefore, that when Tanganyikans won their independence from Britain in 1961, one of the first things they did was plant a torch on its summit; a torch that the first president, Julius Nyerere, declared would '...shine beyond our borders, giving hope where there was despair, love where there was hate, and dignity where before there was only humiliation.'

To the Tanzanians, Kilimanjaro is clearly much more than just a very large mountain separating them from their neighbour Kenya. It's a symbol of their freedom and a potent emblem of their country. And given the tribulations and hardships willingly suffered by thousands of trekkers on Kili each year – not to mention the money they spend for the privilege of doing so – the mountain obviously arouses some pretty strong emotions in non-Tanzanians as well.

Climbing up Kilimanjaro will be one of the hardest things you ever do. But it will also, without a doubt, be one of the most rewarding.

Whatever the emotions provoked in you by this wonderful mountain, and however you plan to climb it, we wish you well. Because even if you choose to walk rather than run, leave the bicycle at home and forego the pleasures of wearing a latex rhino outfit, climbing up Kilimanjaro will still be one of the hardest things you ever do.

But it will also, without a doubt, be one of the most rewarding.

We were in an amiable frame of mind ourselves and, notwithstanding all the toil and trouble my self-appointed task had cost me, I don't think I would that night have changed places with anybody in the world. **Hans Meyer** on the evening after reaching the summit, as recorded in *Across East African Glaciers – an Account of the First Ascent of Kilimanjaro* (1891)

The experience of climbing Kilimanjaro affected me so powerfully that, for a long time afterward, if I caught myself saying 'I'm not a person who likes to do that activity, eat that food, listen to that music,' I would automatically go out and do what I imagined what I didn't like. Generally I found I was wrong about myself – I liked what I thought I didn't like. And even if I didn't like the particular experience, I learned I liked having new experiences. **Michael Crichton**, taken from *Travels* (1988), a collection of essays about his worldwide wanderings.

❑ Star gazing

Having decided when to go you may wish to refine your dates still further by timing your walk so that on the final push to the summit, which is usually conducted at night, you will be walking under the brightness of a **full moon**. The weather is said to be more stable at this time, too – though, of course, the night sky is less spectacular when it's a full moon as fewer stars are visible to the naked eye. For this reason, stargazers may wish to try to coincide their trip at a time near the new moon, when the sky is at its darkest and the stars at their clearest. Or they may want to climb when there's a major astronomical happening; the views of the night sky from Kili are, after all, quite exceptional.

It's good to know that it isn't just the costs of climbing Kilimanjaro that are astronomical; the rewards can be too.

INTRODUCTION

When to go

The two main trekking seasons for Kilimanjaro correspond with the mountain's two dry seasons (an imprecise term, the weather being often inclement during these periods too) namely January to mid-March and June to October. Of course you can walk in the rainy season but not only is there a much higher chance of walking **The two main trekking seasons are January to mid March and June to October.** in the rain, your views of Kibo and Mawenzi are likely to be obscured by thick cloud and you may be trudging through thigh-high snow to the summit. Indeed, several agencies even suspend their operations in April and May, deciding that any trek is foolhardy at this time and the rewards for the trekkers considerably less. Curiously, however, Christmas and New Year, when the weather is far from perfect, are actually amongst the most popular times to go. (You can read peoples' experiences of climbing during the rainy season in the box on pp144-5.)

As to the relative merits of the two trekking seasons, the differences are small though significant. The **January to March** season tends to be colder and

DAR ES SALAAM

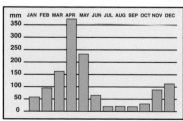

Average rainfall (mm)

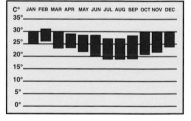

Average max/min temp (°C)

ARUSHA

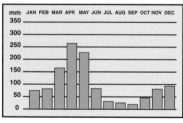

Average rainfall (mm)

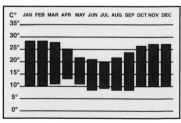

Average max/min temp (°C)

For statistics and graphs on the weather on Kilimanjaro, see pp143-6.

Mount Meru, seen from Arusha. At 4566m, Meru is the perfect warm-up trek (see pp274-85).

there is a much greater chance of snow on the path at this time. The days, however, are often clearer, with only the occasional brief shower. It is usually an exceptionally beautiful time to climb and is often a little quieter than the other peak season of **June to October**, which coincides to a large degree with the main academic holidays in Europe and the West. In this latter season the clouds tend to hang around the tree-line following the heavy rains of March to May. Once above this altitude, however, the skies are blue and brilliant and the chance of precipitation is minimal (though still present).

Although the June to October season tends to be busier, this is not necessarily a disadvantage. For example, if you are planning on travelling by yourself to Tanzania but wish, for the sake of companionship or simply to cut down on costs, to join up with other travellers for the trek, the high visitor numbers in the June to October peak season will give you the best chance of doing this. And even if you do crave solitude when you walk, it can still be found on the mountain during this peak season. The trails are long, so you can usually find vast gaps between trekkers to allow you to walk in peace; a couple of the routes – Umbwe, for example, or the two trails across the Shira Plateau – are quieter than others; indeed Umbwe seldom has more than one or two groups on it at any one time. And besides, Kilimanjaro is just so huge that its presence will dwarf your fellow trekkers to the point where they become, if you wish them to be, quite unnoticeable.

For what it's worth, our favourite times to be on Kilimanjaro are February to mid-March, when the crowds are fewer, the skies clearer and there's less snow than in January; and also late September through October, for much the same reasons. Other factors that you may want to consider when deciding the exact date of your trek is whether your final push to the summit will coincide with a full moon (see p14); and whether to go mid-week, when the number of people starting their trek should be lower (as many people like to start at the weekend to minimise the amount of time they need to take off work). But having said all that, you may choose to climb on a particular day in order to be on the summit on your birthday/anniversary etc – and that, we think, is as good a reason as any.

● **(Opposite)** **Top**: Strolling through the forest at the start of the Umbwe Route, the quietest of all the routes on Kilimanjaro. **Bottom left**: The equipment rental shop at Marangu Gate. **Right**: A traditional Chagga dwelling in Marangu village.
● **(Overleaf)** **Top**: Looking west back from Kili towards Mount Meru. **Centre, left to right**: **1**. Guide Salvatore taking a break at the top of the Barranco Wall. **2**. Preparing lunch for trekkers at Karanga Camp. **3**. The toughest job on the mountain is that of the porters (see pp26-9). **Bottom left**: Camping on the Rongai Route with the broken summit of Mawenzi in the background. **Right**: The giant groundsel 'forest' above Barranco Campsite.

PLANNING YOUR TRIP

With a group or on your own?

INDEPENDENT TREKKING NOT AN OPTION

In 1991, the park authorities made it compulsory for all trekkers to arrange their walk through a licensed agency. Furthermore, they insist that all trekkers must be accompanied throughout their walk by a guide supplied by the agency. Even after these laws were introduced, for a while it was still feasible to sneak in without paying and many were the stories of trekkers who managed to climb Kilimanjaro independently, tales that were often embellished with episodes of encounters with wild animals and even wilder park rangers.

Fortunately, the authorities have tightened up security and clamped down on non-payees, so these tedious tales are now few in number. Don't try to climb Kilimanjaro without a guide or without paying the proper fees. It's very unlikely you'll succeed and all you're doing is freeloading – indeed, stealing isn't too strong a word – from one of the poorest countries in the world. Yes, climbing Kilimanjaro is expensive. But the costs of maintaining a mountain that big are high. Besides, whatever price you pay, trust us, it's worth it.

WITH FRIENDS . . .

So you have decided to climb Kilimanjaro, and have thus taken the first step on the path that leads from the comfort and safety of your favourite armchair to the untamed glory of the Roof of Africa. The second step on this path is to consider with whom you wish to go.

This may not be as straightforward as it sounds, because Kilimanjaro breaks friendships as easily as it breaks records. The tribulations suffered by those who dare to pit themselves against the mountain wear down the most even of temperaments, and relationships are often the first to suffer. Idiosyncrasies in your friend's behaviour that you previously thought endearing now simply become irritating, while the most trivial of differences between you and your chum could lead to the termination of a friendship that, before you'd both ventured onto its slopes, you thought was as steadfast and enduring as the mountain itself. Different levels of stamina, different levels

---

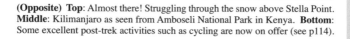

(**Opposite**) **Top**: Almost there! Struggling through the snow above Stella Point. **Middle**: Kilimanjaro as seen from Amboseli National Park in Kenya. **Bottom**: Some excellent post-trek activities such as cycling are now on offer (see p114).

of desire to reach the top, different attitudes towards the porters and guides, even differences in your musical tastes or the colour of your socks: on Kilimanjaro these things, for some reason, suddenly matter.

Then there's the farting. It is a well-known fact that the regular breaking of wind is a sure sign that you are acclimatising satisfactorily (for more about acclimatisation, see pp260-70); while the onset of a crushing headache, combined with loss of sleep and a consequent loss of humour, are all classic symptoms suffered by those struggling to adapt to the rarified atmosphere. Problems occur, of course, when two friends acclimatise at different rates: ie, the vociferous and joyful flatulence of Friend A is simply not appreciated by Friend B, who has a bad headache, insomnia and an ill-temper. Put the two parties together in a remote, confined space, such as that provided by a two-man tent on the slopes of a cold and lonely mountain, and you have an explosive cocktail that can blow apart even the strongest of friendships.

It rained terrible all night, and we put most of the Wachaga porters in our tent. It was rather distressing to the olfactory nerves ... At 4am a leopard visited us but did not fancy our scent.
Peter MacQueen, *In Wildest Africa* (an account of an expedition of 1907, published in 1910)

Of course, the above is just one possible scenario. It may be that both of you adapt equally well/badly to the new conditions and can draw pleasure/comfort from each other accordingly. People from Northern Europe seem particularly good at making the best of the windy conditions: while researching the first edition of this book we encountered a party of four Germans holding a farting competition, and one particularly talented Dutch pair who even managed a quick game of Name that Tune. (It probably won't surprise you to know that all but one of the participants in these events was male.)

And there are plenty of advantages in going with a friend too. There's the companionship for a start. It's also cheaper, because you'll probably be sharing rooms, which always cuts the cost, and if you are planning on booking your climb after you've arrived in Tanzania your bargaining position is so much stronger if there are two of you. Having a companion also cuts the workload, enabling, for example, one to run off and find a room while the other looks after the luggage. It also saves your being paired with someone you don't know when you book with an agency; someone who may snore or blow off more violently than your friend ever would. And, finally, if you *do* both make it to the top, it's good to know there will be somebody to testify to your achievements upon your return.

Climbing Kili with a companion has its problems, but there's no doubting the extra pleasure that can be gained as well. As the graffiti on the walls of the Kibo Huts tells us: '*What does not break us makes us stronger*'. If you are planning on travelling with a friend this, perhaps, should be your motto for the trek.

. . . OR ON YOUR OWN?

Those without friends, or at least without friends willing to climb a mountain with them, should not be too concerned. For one thing, you'll never truly be on your own, simply because the park authorities forbid you from climbing without a guide (see p17) and you'll probably need at least one other crew member to act as porter/cook. Furthermore, planning to go on your own means you can

arrange **the trek that you want**; you choose the trail to follow, the time to go and for how long; the pace of the walk, the number of rest-stops, when to go to bed – these are all your decisions, and yours alone. You are the boss; you have nobody else's feelings to consider but your own.

If you want to join a group trek, for companionship or simply to make the expedition cheaper (a private trek for one person is always the most expensive option), that's not a problem. You can book your trek in your home country with a tour operator (they nearly always insist on a minimum number of participants before the trek goes ahead); or you can book with a company in Tanzania and ask to be put with other trekkers (which will often happen anyway, unless you specifically say otherwise).

Furthermore, even if it does transpire that you are walking alone, you can always meet other trekkers at the campsite in the evening if you so desire.

Trekking by yourself is fun and not the lonely experience many imagine; unless, of course, you enjoy the bliss of solitude and *want* to be alone. That's the beauty of walking solo: everything is up to you.

Budgeting

The most significant cost of your holiday, unless you opt for a few days at one of Tanzania's top-of-the-range safari lodges (US$8000-plus per night for a four-person cottage at Singita Serengeti is the most mind-boggling rate I've heard for a night's accommodation though there are probably other, even higher ones), is the walk itself. With the introduction of a sales tax on park fees in July 2016, those already sky-high trek prices soared even further into the stratosphere. Set aside US$1200-plus for the *absolute cheapest* budget trek (though double this is more usual); more if you plan on taking more than the minimum – and thus not recommended – five days, or if you're ascending by the Lemosho/Shira or Rongai routes (which both have higher transport charges). You will also need to plan to spend more on your trek if you insist on walking without other trekkers. Once on the mountain, however, you won't need to pay for anything else throughout the trek (save, of course, for tips for the crew at the end – see p23-4), especially as the rangers at the huts and campsites along the way are no longer allowed to sell drinks and snacks.

Away from the mountain and the other national parks, by far the most expensive place in Tanzania is Zanzibar. Elsewhere, you'll find transport, food and accommodation, the big three day-to-day expenses of the traveller's life, are pretty cheap in Tanzania and particularly in Moshi and Arusha – it's just unfortunate that Zanzibar and the national parks are pretty much all most visitors want to see of the country!

ACCOMMODATION

Basic tourist accommodation starts at around £6.50/US$8. You can get cheaper, non-tourist accommodation but this is often both sleazy and unhygienic and

should be considered only as a last resort. We have not reviewed these cheap hotels in the book. At the other end of the spectrum, there are hotel rooms and luxury safari camps going for anything up to US$8000 or more per night in the high season. Note that if you've booked your trek from home, you'll get at least a couple of nights' accommodation included in your package.

FOOD

Food can be dirt cheap if you stick to the street sellers who ply their wares at all hours of the day – though dirt is often what you get on the food itself too, with hygiene standards not always the highest. Still, even in a clean and decent tourist restaurant the bill should still be only around Ts20,000-30,0000 (£7-10.50/US$9-13.50) and in a local place it can be as little as a dollar or two. On the trek, meals will be included in the package.

TRANSPORT

Public transport is cheap in Tanzania, though it could be said you get what you pay for: dilapidated buses, potholed roads, inadequate seating and narcoleptic drivers do not a pleasant journey make, but this is the reality of public transport, Tanzanian style. Then again, at US$1-1.50 per hour for local buses and Coasters (the local minibuses that ply the route between Arusha and Moshi; see p233), it seems churlish to complain. That said, given the appalling number of accidents on Tanzanian roads (at one time it was said that road accidents were the third biggest killer in the country, with only AIDS and malaria killing more), if your budget can stretch a little further consider spending more on transport: extra safety and comfort are available on the luxury buses, and at only a slightly higher price. Airport transfers and transfers to the mountain should be included in your trek package.

THE TREK: WHY IS IT ALL SO EXPENSIVE?

With little change from US$1300 for even the cheapest trek, it cannot be denied that climbing Kili is a relatively expensive walk, particularly when compared to other famous treks (prices for an all-inclusive trek on the Inca Trail, for example, start at around US$500); with no refund available to those who fail either, even if you are forced to give up after only a few minutes on the mountain, at first sight this trek can seem very bad value too – though to those who successfully reach the summit, of course, the sense of achievement and the enjoyment of the trek makes almost any amount seem worth it.

To give you some idea of where your money goes, the following is a breakdown of fees, wages and other outgoings incurred on the trek, while the box on p22 is an example of the expenses for an average trek. Don't forget that, in addition to the official costs outlined below, there is also the matter of **tips** (see p23).

Park fees
- **Rescue fee** US$20
- **Conservation fee (formerly Park Entry fee)** US$70 per day
- **Hut fee (Marangu Route only)** US$60 per night

● **Camping fee (all routes except Marangu Route)** US$50 per night
● **Crew fees** US$2 per trip
All these fees are then subject to 18% VAT.

Take a quick look at these figures; already you can see just why the cost of climbing Kilimanjaro is so high. Even if you took the quickest (and thus not recommended) five-day/four-night yomp up the Marangu Route, your park fees alone still come to US$719.80 plus porter/guide entrance fees. See p22 for how much a typical trek could cost.

Other costs

The following are the other major expenses involved in an expedition up Kilimanjaro. Note that, unlike park fees, with all of the following the more people in your group, the lower the per-person charge.

Wages (per trip) Wages vary from company to company, of course. Tanzania National Parks (TANAPA) set the following minimum wages way back in 2009; though as I write this eight years later they are still not being rigidly enforced. The figures they came up with were as follows:

● **Porters** US$10 per day   ● **Assistant guides and cooks** US$15 per day
● **Guides** US$20 per day

❏ **Discounts on park fees**
Children are not only allowed on Kili but, it seems, given the hefty discounts offered to under-16s by the park authorities, they are positively encouraged to climb.

For example, where adults are forced to pay a whopping US$70 per day in Conservation fees, those **under 16 years old** are obliged to pay US$20 per day – and those **under five years of age** don't have to pay anything! The story is similar with the Camping fees (US$10 per night for under 16s and free for under 5s as opposed to US$50 per night for adults) and the Marangu Route's Hut fees (US$5 per night for under 16s and free for under 5s as opposed to the US$60 adults' fee). Once all these fees have been subjected to the 18% VAT, this makes for a considerable reduction on the overall price. For example, on a seven-day Machame trek, once the VAT has been added to all fees, under 16s pay a colossal US$696.20 less. If you're travelling with someone under 16, make sure your company passes these discounts on in full – there is no reason why they shouldn't because, let's face, it'll be you and not the child who's going to be paying.

Nor is it just the under-16s who are entitled to a decent reduction in the park fees. Firstly, **those who hold a valid resident's permit for East Africa** are, under the new regime, supposed to get a 50% reduction on *every* park fee compared to non-residents; you'll need to show either the paper document or the relevant stamp in your passport as proof. Diplomatic ID or a diplomatic passport are also accepted. **East African passport holders** do even better, with their Conservation fees set at just Ts10,000 per day, while Camping fees are Ts10,000 per night (or it's Ts5000 per night in the huts on the Marangu Route). This means that they enjoy discounts on the regular fees of at least US$100 per day off the non-residents' fees.

Do make sure, however, if you're an East African passport holder, or a resident, or under 16, that you furnish your agency with the necessary proof well before your trek, in order that they can apply for these discounts. It will definitely be worth it!

❑ AN EXAMPLE: THE MACHAME TREK

A 7-day Machame trek for one person, taking one guide, one assistant guide, one cook and four porters (and assuming they're paid the TANAPA recommended wage) would cost as follows:

Park fees

Rescue fee	US$20.00
Conservation fee (US$70 x 7 days)	US$490.00
Camping fee (US$50 x 6 nights)	US$300.00
Porter/guide entrance fees (US$2 x 7)	US$14.00
TOTAL	US$824 + 18% VAT = **US$972.32**

Wages

Four porters (assuming a wage of US$10 per day)	US$280.00
Assistant guide (assuming US$15 per day)	US$105.00
Cook (assuming US$15 per day)	US$105.00
Guide (assuming US$20 per day)	US$140.00
TOTAL	**US$630.00**

Food

One person plus crew	**US$235.00**

Transport

Estimate per person	**US$70.00**
GRAND TOTAL	**US$1,907.32**

Obviously if there are more of you some costs, such as food, wages and transport, can be divided between the group, thus making it cheaper. Nevertheless, the above example gives you an idea of just how quickly the costs add up. Any excess over these costs goes straight to the agency but they have significant costs of their own, including an annual licence fee of US$2000 plus VAT. Remember, too, when working out your budget, to add on **tips** for your crew; see opposite for details.

However, while TANAPA were adamant that these wages would be observed by all the companies on the mountain and the companies themselves signed written agreements to this effect, many porters are still being paid as little as Ts8,000 (less than US$4) because the more devious companies simply make up their own dollar/shilling exchange rates.

Transport to/from the mountain A litre of premium diesel at the time of writing cost Ts1925. According to one company's price schedule, the cost of transport from Arusha to Machame is around Ts150,000, (just under US$70), for Marangu it's Ts200,000 (US$90), Lemosho Ts300,000 (US$135) and Rongai Ts400,000 (US$180). Of course, the per-person charge may change dramatically if there are enough of you that you need to hire a second vehicle for your crew.

Food on the mountain Your total bill has to cover not only *your* food but the food of the porters and guides too. One agency boss told me that, as a rough estimate, the food (including cooking fuel) for one person plus crew on a seven-day climb is US$150, though the per person cost drops significantly as more people join the trek.

TIPPING

Like a herd of elephants on the African plains, the subject of tipping is a bit of a grey area. What is certain is that, in addition to the cost of booking your trek, you will also need to shell out tips to your crew at the end. The gratuity system on Kilimanjaro follows the American style: that is to say, a tip is not so much a bonus to reward particularly attentive service or honest toil as a mandatory payment to subsidise the poor wages the porter and guides receive. In other words, **tipping is obligatory**.

To anybody born outside North America this compulsory payment of gratuities seems to go against the very spirit of tipping. Nevertheless, it is very hard to begrudge the guides and porters a decent return for their labours – and depriving your entourage of their much-needed gratuities is not the way to register your protest against this system.

As to the **size of the remuneration**, there are no set figures or formulas, though we do urge you to let your conscience instruct you on this matter as much as your wallet. Some of the most detailed advice I have found is on the KPAP (Kilimanjaro Porters Assistance Project) website (🖥 www.kiliporters .org), which suggests that a fair reward for a porter's work – ie the sum of wages and tips – should be Ts28,000 per day. So what you pay depends to a large degree on what the company you are climbing with is already paying in wages to the porters. Once you've established that, you then just need to add enough to bring the total per diem rate to Ts28,000.

This means, of course, that if the company you're with *is* a KPAP partner and already paying their minimum wage of Ts20,000, then you only need to bring a little more to bring it up to the Ts28,000 rate. If you're with a company that pays only Ts8000 – yes unbelievably some still do – then you'll have to pay Ts20,000 per day in tips. **In other words, a KPAP company may charge slightly more for their treks, but this is offset by the reduction in tips you are asked to pay.**

Most decent companies will now provide guidelines to their clients to help them negotiate the tricky topic of tipping. But just in case they don't, and to simplify matters, we suggest doing the following: **bring about US$400 for tips in a mixture of large and small denomination notes to Tanzania**. This doesn't mean you will hand this entire amount over – most people give around US$250-350 – but it means you're pretty much covered for any eventuality. You can then discuss with your fellow trekkers how to divide up the total tips and who should get what. (Note there is one exception to this rule: **if you're trekking by yourself in a private group for one, you should really bring nearer US$500-600.**)

Having collected all the tip money together, the usual form is to hand out the individual shares to each porter and guide in turn. **Do not hand all your tips to the guide** unless you are happy that the distribution of the tips will be fair and honest; sadly, no matter how much respect and affection you have towards your guide, often he'll end up trousering most of it.

Finally, I am obliged to Hassan, a guide at Mauly Tours, who accosted me halfway up the Breakfast Wall on the Machame Route to tell me to write, in bold, the following: **that the figures we have quoted above are correct for 2017.** If you're trekking in 2018, ask your trekking agency, or KPAP, for the latest recommended tips, or add on another 5-10 per cent to the above figures to allow for inflation; and thereafter, for every subsequent year, add 5-10 per cent onto the figures. **What you mustn't do is use the figures in this book as an excuse for bringing a lower tip, as people have been known to do.**

The above are mere guidelines; you may wish to alter them if you feel, for example, a certain porter is deserving of more than his normal share or if your trek was particularly difficult.

The crew

PORTERS

My guide was as polite as Lord Chesterfield and kindly as the finest gentleman of the world could be. So I owe much to the bare-footed natives of this country, who patiently for eight cents a day bear the white man's burden. **Peter MacQueen** *In Wildest Africa* (1910)

The wages may have gone up – a porter today could earn almost US$10 per day if the minimum wages were enforced – and all now have footwear of some description. But the opinion expressed back at the beginning of the 20th century by the intrepid MacQueen is much the same as that voiced by thousands of trekkers at the beginning of the 21st.

These men (and the ones hired by trekkers are nearly always male, though female porters are occasionally seen on the mountain) never fail to draw both gratitude and, with the amount they carry and the minimum of fuss they make about it, admiration from the trekkers who hire them. Ranging in age from about 18 (the minimum legal age, though some look a good deal younger) to 50 (and occasionally beyond this), porters are amongst the hardest workers on Kilimanjaro. To see them traipsing up the mountain, water in one hand, cooker in another, rucksack on the back and picnic table on the head, is staggering to behold. And though they are supposed to carry no more than 20kg (plus 5kg of their own luggage), many, desperate for work in what is an over-supplied market, manage to bypass the weight checks at the gates to carry much more.

And if that isn't enough, while at the end of the day the average trekker spends his or her time at camp moaning about the hardships they are suffering – in between cramming down mouthfuls of popcorn while clasping a steaming hot cup of tea – these hardy individuals are putting up the tents, helping with the preparation of the food, fetching more water and generally making sure that every trekker's whim is, within reason, catered for.

Yet in spite of appearances, porters are not indestructible. Though they rarely climb to the summit themselves, several still die each year on the slopes

of Kilimanjaro. The most common cause of death, perhaps unsurprisingly given the ragged clothes many wear, is exposure. For this reason, if you see a porter dozing by the wayside and it's getting a bit late, put aside your concerns about depriving him of some much needed shut-eye and wake him up: many are the tales of porters who have perished on Kilimanjaro because they took forty winks and then couldn't find their way to camp in the dark. It's this kind of horror story that has caused so much concern over recent years and led to the formation of organisations such as the Kilimanjaro Porters Assistance Project (see pp26-7).

How many . . .
Of course, you don't need to worry about this question as your agency will determine how many porters each expedition employs. Nevertheless, it's worth examining how they work this out as so many trekkers are surprised (and often horrified) when they discover how many porters are going to be climbing with them. As a general rule, the larger the number of trekkers, the fewer porters per person are required and, if you take the Marangu Route (where no tent is needed), you can probably get away with as few as two per trekker. On other routes, where tents are necessary, around three porters or more per person is the norm.

Sound a lot? Well, remember that in addition to carrying your rucksack, all your food and camping equipment needs to be lugged up the mountainside too, as well as all those items (eg cooking and medical equipment for the group, possibly a portable toilet too) that are not exclusively yours but from which you will doubtless derive some benefit.

Those looking to save every last shilling often ask the agency to cut down on the number of porters. But this is neither easy nor particularly worthwhile, given that the cost of a porter's wages is a relatively minor part of the overall cost. What's more, you're also tempting the agency to overload each porter in order to reduce their total number – leading to the kind of illegal practices described on pp26-7. So, in general, accept the agency's recommendations as to the number of porters on your expedition and make sure that they're not overloaded. You could always offer to carry your own backpack, of course, but from our observations the people who do this tend to have more trouble acclimatising and thus have a lower chance of reaching the summit. (Nevertheless, there are certain companies that arrange 'alpinist' style climbs where, for a lower price than their regular treks, you carry some of your own luggage; see box p89.)

Finally, if the prospect of having someone else carry your luggage up makes you feel a little less, well, virile, you may like to know that the great Count Teleki – see p161 – took no fewer than 65 porters up the mountain with him!

. . . and how much?
The porters' wages are paid by your agency. All you need to worry about is how much to give them as a **tip** (see p23) at the end of the trek. Given the privations they suffer over the course of an average expedition and the often desultory wages they earn in return, their efforts to extract as much money as possible from the over-privileged *mzungu* (Swahili for 'white person') are entirely forgivable. One elaborate yet surprisingly common method is for the porters to pretend there are more of them than there actually are; which, given the large numbers of

porters running around each campsite and the fact you don't actually walk with them on the trail, is a lot easier to achieve than you may think. It's a technique hinted at by John Reader in his excellent 1982 book *Kilimanjaro*:

I hired four porters for part of my excursion on Kilimanjaro. The fourth man's name was Stephen, or so the other three told me. I never met Stephen himself. Our gear seemed to arrive at each campsite without his assistance and I am not aware that he ever spent a night

❏ **A PORTER'S LOT IS NOT A HAPPY ONE**

Nobody should underestimate the achievement of reaching the summit of Kilimanjaro. For five days or so you've dragged yourself up around 4000m of vertical height, through four different seasons, on terrain that may be as alien to you as the moon. Imagine then, trying to do the same trek while eating only one square meal a day, with nothing but a pair of secondhand plimsolls on your feet and tatty cast-offs for clothes; that your days on the mountain are spent carrying up to 30kg on your back or head, while your nights are spent sharing a draughty four-man tent with up to nine other people, often with no ground mats and inadequate sleeping bags. And that, should anything go wrong – which, given the conditions you're expected to work in, they very well might – there'll be no insurance to cover you.

Imagine, furthermore, climbing not out of desire to be on Africa's highest mountain, but out of necessity; for if you don't submit yourself to these deprivations you won't be able to fund yourself through college (which costs about US$350 per year) or feed your children. Imagine, too, that your reward for putting up with such conditions is somewhere around Ts13,500 (US$6) per day (the average wage for porters in 2016); and that, out of this, you have to pay for your transport to and from the mountain (Ts4500 each way from Arusha to Marangu Gate, though it's much more if you're heading to Rongai, of course), your food whilst on the mountain (which is why you eat only once a day) and you may even have to bribe the guide (at least Ts10,000-20,000) in order to be allowed on the mountain in the first place. No wonder you often end up relying on tips from tourists in order to take home any money from your labours – tips that, if you're unlucky, may end up in the pocket of that same guide you bribed in order to get a job in the first place.

Such is the lot for many porters on Kilimanjaro: a precarious existence that, at best, involves hardship and indignity, and at worst can lead to death, as happens to porters several times per year on the mountain. It is these kinds of conditions that various organisations are now trying to improve. Foremost amongst these, without a doubt, is KPAP.

THE KILIMANJARO PORTERS ASSISTANCE PROJECT (KPAP)

Registered at the beginning of 2003, KPAP (🖥 www.kiliporters.org) is an initiative of the American-based International Mountain Explorers Connection (IMEC; 🖥 www.mountainexplorers.org), which fights for porters' rights worldwide including those working in other trekking hotspots such as Nepal. With offices (open roughly Mon-Sat 8am-4pm, and sometimes on Sunday too) just round the corner from the Coffee Shop in Moshi, KPAP has been run for the past few years with both passion and considerable courage by American Karen Valenti. Largely thanks to her commitment, KPAP remains by some distance the most effective organisation working on behalf of porters.

According to their manifesto, the organisation's focus is on improving the working conditions of the porters on Kilimanjaro. They do this in several main ways:

with us. I was assured that he was engaged elsewhere on tasks essential to the success of my journey, but I occasionally wondered whether Stephen actually existed. I was particularly aggrieved when he failed to collect his pay in person at the end of the trip. The other guides collected it for him. They also collected his tip.

The practice is common enough to have been given a name – *kirunje*, which is Swahili for 'shadow'. This sort of thing shouldn't happen if you're with a rep-

● Making available appropriate climbing gear for any mountain crew to borrow. KPAP has a couple of wardrobes full of good-quality trekking gear, much of it donated by American skiing companies and couriered over by trekkers. For a returnable deposit (which can be anything from a school certificate to a mobile-phone charger) the porter can borrow for free items of clothing such as fleeces, boots etc.
● Educating the climbers and general public on proper porter treatment
● Encouraging climbers to select a climbing company with responsible practices towards their crew
● Assisting climbing companies with implementing procedures that ensure fair and ethical treatment of their porters

The partnership scheme
KPAP tries to encourage the trekking agencies to improve the way they treat their crew via the '**Partner for Responsible Travel**' scheme. Established in 2006, the Partner Program was created to recognise and highlight those tour operators committed to fair treatment of the mountain crew.

Despite what several trekking companies may tell you, there is no charge to become a KPAP partner. Instead, in order to join the scheme companies have to conform to certain guidelines issued by KPAP. These include directives on porters' wages (which KPAP have said has to be a minimum of **Ts20,000 per day**), a limit on the amount the porters are required to carry, the amount of food and water they receive on the mountain, what the sleeping conditions are like and how they are treated in the event of an accident or sickness. You may have noticed that several of these guidelines, such as the amount the porters are allowed to carry (20kg) and the wages a porter should be paid (US$10) are already covered by KINAPA's own rules. Unfortunately, KINAPA does a poor job in enforcing them. True, the bags are weighed at every gate to make sure the porter isn't over-burdened – but the practice of bribery is as widespread on the mountain as it is elsewhere in Tanzania, and it doesn't take much for a guide to hand over a few thousand shillings to a warden to persuade him to record incorrectly what the scales are saying. Similarly, while KINAPA have set a minimum wage of US$10 per day for the porters, those companies – and they are the majority – who want to pay their porters less than this merely use a different exchange rate to the usual market one – which is why many porters end up with Ts10,000 (US$5) or less per day.

So it's left to KPAP to try to enforce the rules properly. In order to be considered as a partner, the trekking agency not only has to adhere to KPAP's guidelines but also has to allow KPAP to monitor them, too, to make sure they stick to them. If the trekking agency manages to fulfil all these criteria the benefits, in terms of increased marketing opportunities and the extra demand that comes from being known as a Partner for Responsible Travel, are considerable.

There are several ways in which KPAP monitors their partner companies but the most effective way is the 'investigative porter' method, in which the partner company allows an undercover worker on *all* of their climbs. (*continued overleaf*)

PLANNING YOUR TRIP

utable company but it's a good idea anyway to **make sure you meet your team at the start of the trail before you set off**. This will help to prevent this sort of scam and it's good manners too. While at the end, to ensure each porter gets his fair share, dish the tips out yourself – *do not* give them to your guide to hand them out on your behalf unless you are sure your agency has systems in place to prevent the guide pocketing it all for himself; see the box below for why this is so.

❏ **A PORTER'S LOT IS NOT A HAPPY ONE**

(*continued from p27*) This porter has been trained by KPAP to report back on the treatment meted out to the crew on each trek. This has proved to be a highly effective way of monitoring how well a partner company is treating their staff. If the company fails to meet the standards set by KPAP on the trek, they are advised on where they failed and how they can improve; if they continue to slip up, however, then they will be forced to leave the Partnership scheme altogether.

We genuinely believe KPAP to be the only organisation that properly monitors what is happening on the mountain, and as such their opinions should be relied upon to an even greater extent than more established campaign groups such as Tourism Concern. KPAP is a fantastic charity, working on a shoestring and fighting for the rights of porters, despite opposition from several large agencies and even the authorities.

So how can you help?
The most straightforward way to help the campaign for the better treatment of porters is to **book your trek with a KPAP partner company**. This is a surefire way that your crew will be treated fairly by their employers. You may be persuaded by the spiel on a company's website that drones on about how altruistic they are and how well they treat their porters. But if they aren't KPAP partners, you need to ask yourself: why not? Why aren't they prepared to subject themselves to the scrutiny of an independent body like KPAP? It's free, after all. What are they hiding? And having asked yourself why they aren't KPAP partners – you then need to ask them. They will doubtless come out with all sorts of excuses and a few may denigrate the work of KPAP and even slander them. Several may try to hoodwink you and say that they are actually partners or are in the process of becoming one, when the reality is they have no intention of doing so. For this reason it's **vital you visit the KPAP website** (🖳 kiliporters.org) to find out the latest list of KPAP partners. You can also contact Karen (karen@kiliporters.org) to ask about a specific company and see if their claims actually contain any truth.

What if, for some reason, you're not on a trek organised by a KPAP partner? While this list is extensive, if you can do any of the following it would be a help:

● 1 **Make sure your porters are outfitted with appropriate clothing** Porters need adequate footwear, socks, waterproof jackets and trousers (pants), gloves, hats, etc. They are also required by the park authorities to have a torch and sunglasses. Clothing can be borrowed for free at the KPAP office in Moshi; make sure porters know this.

● 2 **Fair wages should be paid to the porters** See p27 for the minimum wages KINAPA are proposing to introduce and enforce. Ask your porters how much they are paid and if it includes food. Showing that you care about such things will encourage all operators and guides to treat their porters fairly.

● 3 **Make sure porters have proper food and water** If they are required to purchase their own food, wages should be increased accordingly.

Please note that however much money and equipment you lavish on them at the end, the porters' reaction will usually be the same. Simply put, porters are not above play-acting, in the same way that the sea is not above the sky. On being given their gratuity some porters will grimace, sigh, tut, shake their head, roll their eyes in disgust and stare at the money in their hand with all the enthusiasm and gratitude of one who has just been handed a warm jar of the contents

● **4 Check the weights of porters' loads** Kilimanjaro National Park has a maximum carrying weight per porter of 25kg, which includes the porter's personal gear which is assumed to be 5kg. Thus the load they carry for the company should not exceed 20kg. If you can, be there at the weighing of the luggage at the start of the trek to make sure no funny business is going on.

If additional porters need to be hired, do ensure that the tour company is paying each porter their full wage when you return.

● **5 Count the number of porters every day** Know the number of people in your crew. After all, you are paying for them. If there are any missing, ask where they are. If they've been sent down the mountain, ask why, and whether they will still receive both a fair wage and their share of the tips.

● **6 Make sure your porters are provided with proper shelter** Where no shelter is available (ie on all routes other than Marangu), porters need proper accommodation: that means their own tents and sleeping bags.

● **7 Ensure your porters are given the tips you intend for them** Give your tips to the guide and you run the risk that they won't pass on the full amount to your crew. Tipping directly to each individual crew member ensures they receive their fair share. Or, ensure that your tour company has a transparent method of distributing tips.

● **8 Make sure any sick or injured porters are properly cared for** Porters deserve the same standard of care as their clients. Sick or injured porters need to be sent back with someone who speaks their language and understands the problem.

● **9 Get to know your porters and thank them** Some porters speak English and will appreciate your making an effort to speak with them. The Swahili word *pole* (pronounced 'polay') – which translates as 'I'm sorry for you' – shows respect for porters after a hard day carrying your bags. *Ahsante* ('asantay') means 'Thank you'.

● **10 Report any instances of abuse or neglect** To both the trekking agency concerned and, more importantly, to KPAP on 🖳 info@kiliporters.org.

● **11 Complete the post-climb survey** This is perhaps the most important and easiest thing you can do. Before heading off up the mountain, pick up a questionnaire from the KPAP office in Moshi or the website (🖳 www.kiliporters.org), as this will remind you of what to look out for on the mountain. By providing KPAP with your feedback regarding the tour company's treatment of its staff, they will be able to share with the company any problem areas that need to be corrected.

Further details
● **Kilimanjaro Porters Assistance Project (KPAP)** 🖳 kiliporters.org
● **International Mountain Explorers Connection** 🖳 mountainexplorers.org IMEC is the umbrella organisation of which KPAP is a part
● **International Porter Protection Group (IPPG)** 🖳 ippg.net

of the Barranco Camp toilets. Several of the more talented ones may even manage a few tears.

Nevertheless, providing you have paid a reasonable tip (and for guidance over what is the correct amount, see pp23-4), don't fall for the melodramatics but simply thank them warmly for all their endeavours over the course of the trek. Once they realise your conscience remains unpricked it will all be handshakes and smiles and, having pocketed the money, they'll soon trot off happily enough.

❏ The remarkable Mr Lauwo

Mzee Yohana Lauwo, the porter guide who accompanied the first Europeans up the Kilimanjaro Mountain a century ago, was the centre of attention in a commemorative ceremony in Moshi on Friday. Mzee Lauwo, now over 118 years, was presented with a prize in cash. The Deputy Minister for Lands, Natural Resources and Tourism, Ndugu Chabanga Hassan Dyamwalle, suggested that Mzee Lauwo also be given a house to be built in his own village.

The ambassador to the Federal Republic of Germany (FRG) to Tanzania, Christel Steffler, presented Mzee Lauwo with a letter which expressed gratitude for his service in cementing German-Tanzanian relations. She said it was high time porters and guides were given the recognition they deserved for their work.

Press cutting from a local newspaper,
found stuck on the wall of Kibo Hotel, Marangu

In 1989, celebrations for the centenary of Hans Meyer's first-ever ascent of Kilimanjaro were organised. As the committee in charge of arranging the festivities looked at some old photos taken at around the time of Meyer's ascent, the members were struck by the similarity of one of the locals pictured to a very elderly man who still lived in Marangu village. That man was Mr Yohana Kinyala Lauwo, known to his friends and family as Kinyala. Could it really be that somebody who was on Meyer's conquest of Kilimanjaro was actually still alive?

The committee decided to visit Mr Lauwo in the hope that he would be able to tell them whether it was him in those photos or not. Unfortunately, when they pointed to the person in the photographs, even Mr Lauwo was rather vague as to whether it was really him. While claiming to have climbed Kili at least three times before World War I – and, according to the legend that grew up around him, for seventy years in total – he did not recall either Meyer or Purtscheller. He did, however, remember an expedition involving a 'Dutch doctor' that he worked on, the experience perhaps being particularly memorable as he didn't wear shoes for the entire eight days! Could Mr Lauwo's memory be slightly hazy on this matter and the Dutch doctor actually be a German one?

The committee certainly thought so and not only decided that 'Kinyala' was part of the team that climbed Kili with Meyer but even claimed, using other evidence that they had come by, that he was the main guide who led them up!

Their story about how Lauwo became the head guide on the most-celebrated climb of Kilimanjaro goes something like this: in 1889 the Germans were beginning to build highways in the area to assert and secure their domination over the region, coercing the local village chiefs into supplying the labour to work on the roads. Kinyala was one of those who tried to avoid being enlisted but he was arrested and taken to the local chief or *Mangi*, Marealle, for punishment. As luck would have it, however, Meyer and Purtscheller arrived at the same time at the court of Mangi

GUIDES

If portering is the first step on the career ladder of Kilimanjaro, it is the guides who stand proudly on the top rung. Ornithologist, zoologist, botanist, geologist, tracker, astronomer, butler, manager, doctor, linguist and teacher, a good guide will be all of these professions rolled into one. With luck, over the course of the trek they'll also become your friend.

The metamorphosis from porter to guide is a lengthy one. Having served an

Marealle to ask for porters and guides to help with their expedition.

Tall, lithe, loose-limbed and from the mountain village of Marangu, Kinyala Lauwo fitted the bill as a mountain guide, his relative youth notwithstanding. He would have known at least the lower slopes of Kili very well for the forest would have been a happy hunting ground for collecting honey, plants for medicine, colobus monkey skins for ceremonial clothing and ivory for trading with the Swahili traders from the coast.

But can we be certain all this is true and, more importantly, that the elderly Mr Lauwo who resided in Marangu all his life is the same man in the photos taken from Meyer's time? And was he really the main guide? And if so, how far up did he go with them? To the summit?

Unfortunately, Meyer himself is very unhelpful on this matter, for while he was full of admiration for the guides he hired on the coast of Tanzania and refers to them throughout his account, he only briefly mentions a local Chagga guide – and never by name. This could be due to the contempt with which Meyer clearly felt for this guide:

As on a former occasion (1887), our guide tried hard to persuade us to camp in this very inviting neighbourhood, although it was still comparatively early; but now, as then, I turned a deaf ear to all his representations, and after a short rest pushed onward and upward to where the forest loomed ahead. The guide protested volubly and forcibly, and capered about like a madman; but we paid no heed to his frantic demonstrations, and left him to follow when he should have danced himself back to his ordinary senses.

It is, of course, highly unlikely we'll ever find out whether Kinyala really was part of that first successful climb of Kili; and if he was, we'll probably never know in what capacity he served – and if it was as the head guide, how far he actually ventured up the mountain with them. There are those who seem convinced by his claim; while others will always view the evidence that backs up his claim as circumstantial at best. They will also, not unreasonably, point to the fact that if Mr Lauwo really did climb as an 18 year old with Meyer's team back in 1889, he would have been around 125 years old when he died in 1996, which means that he would have set all kinds of longevity records!

But even if it isn't true, there seems little doubt that Mr Lauwo did work as a guide for many decades (if not quite the 70 years that is claimed), beginning at a time when the locals wore little more than blankets to protect them from the cold. Furthermore, he isn't the only person in his family who took part in a famous ascent of Kili; by chance a nephew of Mr Lauwo's, Emmanuel Petro Minja, guided Lieutenant Alexander Nyirenda on his trek towards the summit on December 9, 1961, and carried the torch that the lieutenant was supposed to have placed at Uhuru Peak to celebrate Tanzania's independence (see p167).

apprenticeship by lugging luggage, a few talented and ambitious ones are eventually promoted to the position of **summit porter**. In addition to carrying their fair share of equipment, they are also expected to perform many of the duties of a fully fledged guide. This includes, most painfully of all, escorting trekkers on that final, excruciating push to the summit, as well as carrying the client's daypack if they are struggling.

From there the next logical step is to become a fully fledged guide. Standing between them and a licence is a period of intensive training conducted by the park authorities, KINAPA (Kilimanjaro National Park Authorities). What typically happens is this: every few years, KINAPA contact all the major agencies, asking them to nominate their most talented and ambitious porters for a 'training camp'. This training camp lasts around a month and includes various courses hosted by experts in their fields, including lessons on caring for the mountain environment, customer care, first aid, how to spot the symptoms of altitude sickness in trekkers and, just as importantly, what to do about it.

Towards the end of the month the trainees are expected to climb to the summit en masse to prove their fitness for the job. At Uhuru Peak, the very highest point in Africa, a warden hands out pieces of paper to each successful summiteer with a code written on it. That code allows the recipient to enter into the final exam; without it, they can't complete the course.

At the last intake, around 1300 applicants attended the training camp, with about 700 qualifying. Those who successfully graduate are ranked either as a full route guide or as an assistant guide and are given different licences accordingly. They are now free to tout themselves around the agencies looking for work. While a few of the better guides are snapped up by the top agencies and work exclusively for them, the majority are freelance and have to actively seek work in what is already an over-supplied market. This explains why a newly qualified guide will probably have to settle for being an **assistant guide** in order to secure work. For this he'll receive a higher wage than a porter (and a summit porter) and a commensurately greater proportion of the tips – though not as much as he would receive if leading the climb himself. Note that I say 'he' as the majority of guides are male. But there are, in fact, at least four female guides working on Kilimanjaro at the moment, as well as around fifty female porters; see p79 for those companies that employ female guides.

Getting to Kilimanjaro

One of the gladdest moments in life, methinks is the departure upon a distant journey into unknown lands. Shaking off with one mighty effort the fetters of habit, the leaden weight of routine, the cloak of many cares and the slavery of home, man feels once more happy... The blood flows with the fast circulation of childhood ... afresh dawns the morn of life.
Diary entry of **Richard Burton** (the explorer, not the actor), 2 December 1856

BY AIR

Tanzania has four major international airports: Dar es Salaam, Zanzibar, Mwanza and Kilimanjaro. The latter, as you may expect, is the most convenient for Kilimanjaro, standing only 43km away from the mountain town of Moshi and 50km from Arusha. Information about international flights to and from KIA (the acronym for Kilimanjaro International Airport, though the three-letter international airport code is JRO) can be found on p387.

It used to be the case that only a few airlines served Kilimanjaro. The resulting lack of competition meant that airfares for flights in and out of JRO were relatively high – to such an extent that many trekkers would fly into Nairobi instead and catch a bus down in order to save themselves hundreds of dollars. The situation has improved recently, however, with the introduction of regular services from Flydubai, Turkish Airlines and Qatar Airways, as well as local services from the budget African airline Fastjet, adding to those companies – KLM, Ethiopian Airlines, Kenyan Airways and local operators Precision – that already have Kilimanjaro on their flight roster. So, while Nairobi (Kenya) and to a lesser extent Dar es Salaam remain the main regional hubs and airfares to these destinations can sometimes be lower, the saving is seldom sizeable and nowadays most people prefer to fly direct to Kilimanjaro, particularly as Nairobi and Dar are a minimum of six and ten hours away respectively by bus from Arusha.

You will find brief guides in this book to Dar es Salaam (pp192-9) as well as Nairobi (pp200-9) and Kilimanjaro International Airport (p210-11).

From the UK
A flight to Kilimanjaro from London with KLM via Amsterdam will set you back a minimum of £550, or £750 in the July-August high season, though depending on when you book your tickets – and from whom – the fare may well rise to £1100 or more. Though KLM are perhaps the most reliable and direct, there are usually cheaper flights with the other airlines. For example, in January 2017 I was able to book a flight for the end of March from Heathrow to Kilimanjaro for just £303 return with Kenyan Airlines, whose flights are as direct to JRO as KLM's. To get the best deals, it pays to be flexible with your dates, begin your search several months in advance and shop around. To help you, there are a number of 'price-comparison' websites specialising in flights of

which you'll probably already be aware, perhaps the most popular being **Skyscanner** (🖳 skyscanner.net) and **Cheapflights** (🖳 cheapflights.co.uk); both of these give a summary of flight prices to your destination from several different agents, enabling you to choose the cheapest.

Other online agencies to recommend are **DialAFlight** (🖳 dialaflight.com), **Netflights** (🖳 netflights.com), **Expedia** (🖳 expedia.co.uk), **lastminute** (🖳 lastminute.com), **TravelUp** (🖳 travelup.co.uk) and **Travel Trolley** (🖳 traveltrolley.co.uk). High-street travel agents (all of which have a considerable online presence too) include **STA Travel** (☎ 0333-321 0099; 🖳 statravel.co.uk), **Flight Centre** (☎ 0800-587 0058; 🖳 flightcentre.co.uk) and **Trailfinders** (☎ 020-7368 1200; 🖳 trailfinders.com), all with branches countrywide.

From North America

Skyscanner (🖳 skyscanner.com) are again probably the first place to look for cheap flights as they compare different travel agencies to find the lowest fares. Otherwise, try **Flight Center** (USA 🖳 flightcenter.com; Canada 🖳 flightcentre.ca), **Travel Cuts** (Canada 🖳 travelcuts.com) and **STA Travel** (🖳 statravel.com).

From Australia and New Zealand

Skyscanner (🖳 skyscanner.com.au) also operate Down Under and are a good place to start your search for cheap tickets. Also try **Flight Centre** (Aus 🖳 flightcentre.com.au; NZ 🖳 flightcentre.co.nz) and **STA Travel** (Aus 🖳 statravel.com.au; NZ 🖳 statravel.co.nz).

OVERLAND

A big country lying at the heart of East Africa, Tanzania has borders with many countries including Burundi, Kenya, Malawi, Mozambique, Rwanda, Uganda and Zambia.

There are several border crossings between Tanzania and **Burundi** including a sailing on the venerable old *MV Liemba* that traditionally journeys to Kigoma, cutting across the northern corner of Lake Tanganyika from the Burundi capital Bujumbura. The last time we checked it was running twice a month on a Wednesday afternoon, taking 44 hours to Zambia. However, it's important to check on the current situation with regard to both the state of the *Liemba* – it's often out of action – and the security situation in Burundi. If the boat's out of action, you can always catch a Taqwa or Tawfiq bus from Dar to Lusaka, spending a night at the border settlement of Tunduma before continuing on the next day to the Zambian capital. Both journeys last about 12-14 hours.

The borders with **Rwanda** (at the Rusumo crossing), **Uganda** (most commonly crossed at Mutukula, north-west of Bukoba), **Mozambique** (over the Unity Bridge across the Ruvuma), **Malawi** (Songwe River Bridge) and **Kenya** (see p209 for details on the border crossing at Namanga; Tarakea, north-east of Kili, is about to become an official crossing point for tourists too) are all relatively straightforward and served by public buses.

Tanzania and Zambia are also linked by express train, running twice weekly between Dar es Salaam and Kapiri Mposhi via Mbeya.

The routes up Kilimanjaro

GETTING TO THE MOUNTAIN

This book aims to take you from your armchair to the summit of Africa's highest mountain. If you've booked your climb already, then your agency should have arranged your lift from the airport to your hotel – and will also have arranged the subsequent transport from your hotel to the mountain.

However, from the gates to the summit, it's all down to you – and there won't be any transport available to you (at least, none heading upwards) from now on. Because, of course, this is where the walking begins...

GETTING UP THE MOUNTAIN   [See colour map inside back cover]

Kilimanjaro has two main summits. The higher one is **Kibo**, the glacier-clad circular summit that stars on all the pictures of Kilimanjaro; the second summit is spiky **Mawenzi**, to its east. While the latter is impossible to conquer without knowledge of advanced climbing techniques and no small amount of courage, it is possible to *walk* up to the top of Kibo at a height of 5895m above sea level. This is the aim of almost every trekker on Kilimanjaro.

Look down at Kilimanjaro from above and you should be able to count **seven paths** trailing like ribbons up the sides of the mountain. Five of these are ascent-only paths (ie you can only walk *up* the mountain on them; you are not allowed to come down on these trails); one, Mweka, is a descent-only path, and one, the Marangu Route, is both an ascent and descent trail. At around 4000m these trails meet up with a path that loops right around the Kibo summit. This path is known as the Kibo Circuit, though it's often divided into two halves known as the Northern and Southern circuits. From the Kibo Circuit, only three paths lead up the slopes to the summit itself.

For a *brief* description of the trails and a look at their relative merits, read on; for a map, see inside back cover, while for further details check out the **full trail descriptions**, beginning on p286. Note that some trekking agencies vary the routes slightly, particularly those routes that cross the Shira Plateau, though any agency worth its salt will provide you with a detailed itinerary so you can check exactly which path you'll be taking each day.

Ascending Kilimanjaro: the options

There are six ascent trails leading up to the foot of Kibo peak. These are (running anti-clockwise, beginning with the westernmost trails): the **Shira Plateau Route**, **Lemosho Route**, **Machame Route**, **Umbwe Route**, **Marangu Route** and, running from the north-eastern side, the **Rongai (Loitokitok) Route**. Each of these eventually meets with a path circling the Kibo cone, a path known as either the **Northern Circuit** or the **Southern Circuit** depending on which side of the mountain you are.

Just three trails lead up to the Crater Rim from the Kibo Circuit: the **Western Breach Route** (aka the **Arrow Glacier Route**), **Barafu Route** and the nameless third path which runs up from Kibo Huts to Gillman's Point, which we have always called the **Kibo Huts Route**. Which of these you take to the summit will depend upon which path you took to get this far: the Shira, Lemosho, Machame and Umbwe routes can use either the difficult Western Breach Route or the easier (but longer) Barafu Route, while the Marangu and Rongai trails use the Kibo Huts Route. You can deviate from this rule – and many of the larger agencies make a habit of doing so – and design your own combination of trails but you may require permission from KINAPA and the agencies may well charge more to organise such a trek.

The minimum number of days for each route is written below. **Note these refer to the total time it takes from the gate to the summit and back down again to the designated exit gate. This descent is assumed to take a day and a half** whatever the route you take; so, assuming you climbed to the summit during the night and arrived at the peak at dawn, you'll begin to descend from the summit soon after sunrise and, all being well, you'll reach the gate at around lunchtime the next day. **Note, too, that when we say 'minimum', we mean it – treks typically last at least a day longer than these minimum durations to allow people time to acclimatise and thus improve their chances of reaching the summit.**

A brief description of each of the six main trails follows:

The Marangu Route (minimum 5 days: 3½ days for the ascent, plus 1½ days for the descent)
The oldest and once the most popular trail on the mountain, the Marangu Route also has the dubious honour of having the lowest success rate for getting trekkers to the summit. This is presumably because it is one of the three routes where you can pay to be on the mountain for just five days – where other routes require you to pay for a minimum of six. It is also the one that comes closest (though not very) to the trail Hans Meyer took in making the first successful assault on the summit. Furthermore it is the only ascent trail where camping is not necessary, indeed not allowed, with trekkers sleeping in dormitory huts along the way. From Kibo Huts, trekkers climb up to the summit via Gillman's Point. The trail should take a minimum of five days and four nights to complete, though an extra night is usually taken after the second day to allow trekkers more time to acclimatise.

Though beautiful, the main disadvantage with this route is that you descend on the same route as you ascended. See p286 for the full description of this trek including maps and altitude profiles.

The Machame Route (minimum 6 days: 4½ days for the ascent, plus 1½ days for the descent)
The Machame Route has now overtaken Marangu as the most popular trail. Though widely regarded as more difficult than the Marangu Route, the success rate on this trail is higher, possibly because it is a day longer at six days and five nights (assuming you take the Barafu Route to the summit), which gives trekkers more time to acclimatise; most trekkers also

take an extra acclimatisation day near the Karanga Valley (thereby making it seven days in total). You can also take the more difficult Western Breach Route though this shortens the trek by a day or two; it would thus be wise to build in acclimatisation days if taking this option.

See p306 for a full description of this trek including maps and altitude profiles.

The Shira Plateau and Lemosho Routes (minimum 6 days: 4½ days for the ascent, plus 1½ days for the descent)

Both of these routes run from west to east across the centre of the Shira Plateau. The **Shira Plateau Route** is the original plateau trail though it seldom sees trekkers these days, with much of it now a 4WD track used mainly by emergency vehicles. Walkers embarking on this trail often begin their trek above the forest in the moorland zone. After traversing the plateau the trekker has several choices. Firstly, one can climb Kibo via the Western Breach/Arrow Glacier Route; follow this route and you can expect the trek to last a total of six days and five nights. Or you can take the longer and easier Barafu Route, which extends the trek by a day to around seven days, or eight days if extra overnight stops on the plateau and around the Karanga Valley are taken. A third option, and one that both African Walking Company and Nature Discovery – the two companies that utilise the Shira Trail most frequently – adopt, is to head round the northern side of Kibo on the Northern Circuit and reach the summit via Gillman's Point. Again, a trekker on this route should take eight days to complete this trek.

The **Lemosho Route** (aka the **Lemosho Glades Route**) improves on the Shira Plateau Route by starting below the Shira Ridge, thus providing trekkers with a walk in the forest at the trek's start, giving them more time to acclimatise and enabling them to enjoy, in this author's opinion, the best forest on the mountain. As with the Shira Plateau Route, you can ascend Kibo either by the Western Breach or by the Barafu Route – allow five nights for the former (though this is *too fast* for such a long trail) or a recommended seven nights for the latter – or opt to head round the Northern Circuit, another seven-night/eight-day climb.

Note: It's common for trekking agencies to refer to the Lemosho Route as the Shira Route, which is of course confusing. If you have already booked your 'Shira' trek and want to know what route you will actually be taking, one way to check is to see where your first night's campsite will be; if it's the Big Tree Campsite – Mti Mkubwa in Swahili – it's actually the Lemosho Route you'll be following.

See p324 for the full descriptions of these treks including the maps and altitude profiles.

The Rongai Route (minimum 5 days: 3½ days for the ascent, plus 1½ days for the descent)

This is the only trail to approach Kibo from the north. Indeed, the original trail began right against the Kenyan border, though recently it shifted eastwards and now starts at the Tanzanian town of **Loitokitok** after which the new trail has been named (though everybody still refers to it as the Rongai Route; it is also sometimes called the **Nalemuru**

Route, after the nearby river). For the final push to the summit, trekkers take the Kibo Huts Route, joining it either at the huts themselves or just below Hans Meyer Cave, after spending the penultimate night at School Huts. In theory the trek can be completed in five days and four nights though really you need six or even seven, especially if taking the detour to camp beneath Mawenzi peak which adds a day.

Turn to p351 for the full description of this trek, including the maps and the altitude profiles.

❏ The topography of Kilimanjaro

And surely never monarch wore his royal robes more royally than this monarch of African mountains, Kilimanjaro. His foot rests on a carpet of velvety turf, and through the dark green forest the steps of his throne reach downward to the earth, where man stands awestruck before the glory of his majesty. Art may have colours rich enough to fix one moment of this dazzling splendour, but neither brush nor pen can portray the unceasing play of colour – the wondrous purples of the summit deepening as in the Alpine afterglow; the dull greens of the forest and the sepia shadows in the ravines and hollows, growing ever darker as evening steals on apace; and last, the gradual fading away of all, as the sun sets, and over everything spreads the grey cloud-curtain of the night. It is not a picture but a pageant – a king goes to his rest.
Hans Meyer *Across East African Glaciers* (1891)

Kilimanjaro is not only the highest mountain in Africa, it's also one of the biggest volcanoes on the entire planet, covering an area of approximately 388,500 hectares. In this area are three main peaks that betray its origins as the offspring of three huge volcanic eruptions.

The oldest and lowest peak, known as **Shira**, lies on the western edge of the massif. This is the least impressive of the three summits, being nothing more than a heavily eroded ridge, 3962m tall at its highest point, **Johnsell Point**. This ridge is, in fact, merely the south-western rim of the original Shira crater, the northern and eastern sides being covered by later material from Kibo (see p137). The Shira Ridge separates the western slopes from the **Shira Plateau**. This large rocky plateau, 6200ha in size, is one of Kilimanjaro's most intriguing features. It is believed to be the *caldera* (a collapsed crater) of the first volcano that was subsequently 'filled in' by lava from later eruptions which then solidified and turned to rock.

The plateau rises gently from west to east until it reaches the youngest and main summit, **Kibo**. This is the best-preserved crater on Kilimanjaro. Michael Crichton describes it as looking 'safe, matronly. More like a breast than a mountain.' The description is perhaps not entirely accurate; I can't remember in my (admittedly limited) experience ever encountering a woman with a boob that shape, especially one which, if it was to really resemble Kili, would have to be crowned with an inverted nipple. But we do get his point, for its gently voluptuous slopes do look 'safe' and welcoming, especially when compared to its spiky neighbour, Mawenzi (see below).

If you study Kibo's southern lip you'll find that it is slightly higher than the rest of the rim; and the highest point on this southern lip is **Uhuru Peak** – at 5895m the highest point in Africa and the goal of just about every Kilimanjaro trekker.

Kibo is the only one of the three summits which is permanently covered in snow or ice, thanks to the large **glaciers** that cover much of its surface. Kibo is also the one peak that really does look like a volcanic crater; indeed, there are three concentric craters on Kibo. Within the inner **Reusch Crater** (1.3km in diameter) you can still

The Umbwe Route (minimum five days: 3½ days for the ascent, plus 1½ days for the descent) The hardest and statistically the least popular trail (Shira probably comes a close second in the unpopularity stakes but its figures tend to be lumped together with those of Lemosho), the Umbwe Route is also, in my opinion, the most beautiful. The trek involves a tough vertical slog up Kili's southern slopes, in places using the tree roots as makeshift rungs on a ladder. Having reached the Southern Circuit, trekkers traditionally continue north-west to tackle Kibo from the west and the more difficult Arrow

---

see signs of volcanic activity, including fumaroles, the smell of sulphur and a third crater, the **Ash Pit**, measuring 130m deep by 140m wide.

The outer **Kibo Crater** (1.9 by 2.7km) is not a perfect, unbroken circle. There are gaps in the circumference where the walls have been breached by lava flows; the most dramatic of these is the **Western Breach**, through which some climbers gain access to the summit each year. The crater has also subsided a little over time, leading to a landslide 100,000 years ago that created the **Barranco** on Kibo's southern side. On the whole, though, Kibo's slopes are gentle, allowing trekkers as well as mountaineers to reach the summit. (For more on the Kibo summit, see p382)

Separating Kibo from Kilimanjaro's second peak, Mawenzi, is the **Saddle**, at 3600ha the largest area of high-altitude tundra in tropical Africa. This really is a beautiful, eerie place — a dusty desert almost 5000m above sea level, featureless except for the occasional parasitic cone dotted here and there, including the **Triplets**, **Middle Red** and **West Lava Hill**, all running south-east from the south-eastern side of Kibo. (A *parasitic cone* is a mini cone on the slopes of a volcano caused by a later, minor eruption; amazingly, there are said to be some 250 parasitic cones on Kilimanjaro!)

Nothing could be more marked than the contrast between the external appearance of these two volcanoes – Kibo, with the unbroken, gradual slopes of the typical volcanic cone – Mawenzi with its bewildering display of many-coloured lavas and its fantastically carved outlines, the result of long ages of exposure, combined with the tendency of its component rocks to split vertically rather than horizontally. The hand of time has left its impress upon Kibo too, but the havoc it has wrought is not to be detected at a distance. **Hans Meyer** *Across East African Glaciers* (1891)

Seen from Kibo, **Mawenzi**, the second summit, looks less like a crater than a single lump of jagged, craggy rock emerging from the Saddle. This is merely because its western side also happens to be its highest and hides everything behind it. Walk around Mawenzi, however, and you'll realise that this peak is actually a horseshoe shape, with only the northern side of the crater having been eroded away. Its sides too steep to hold glaciers, there is no *permanent* snow or ice on Mawenzi, and the gradients are enough to dissuade all but the bravest and most technically accomplished climbers.

Mawenzi's highest point is Hans Meyer Peak at 5149m but so shattered is this summit, and so riven with gullies and fractures, that there are a number of other distinctive peaks including Purtscheller Peak (5120m) and South Peak (4958m). There are also two deep gorges, the Great Barranco and Lesser Barranco, scarring its north-eastern face.

Few people know this but Kilimanjaro does actually have a crater lake. **Lake Chala** (aka Jala) lies some 30km to the south-east, lying right across the Tanzanian and Kenyan border, and is said to be up to 2½ miles deep.

For details on how exactly Kilimanjaro came to be this shape, see pp137-41.

Glacier/Western Breach Route, though you can also head east round to Barafu and approach the summit from there. The entire walk up and down takes a minimum of five days though this is far too rapid; six or seven days is much more sensible for acclimatisation purposes.

See p364 for the full description of this trek including the maps and altitude profiles.

Descending Kilimanjaro: the designated descents

In an attempt to control the number of people walking on each trail, and thus limit the amount of soil erosion on some of the more popular routes, KINAPA introduced regulations regarding the descent routes and which ones you are allowed to take. In general, the main rule is as follows: those ascending Kilimanjaro from the west, south-west or south (ie by taking the Machame, Umbwe, Lemosho or Shira Plateau routes) must take as their descent route the **Mweka** trail; whereas if you have climbed the mountain from the south-east or north (ie on the Marangu or Rongai/Loitokitok trails) you must descend by the **Marangu Route**.

Those trekkers who wish to **deviate from these rules** should first seek permission from KINAPA; begin making contact with them well in advance of your trek as the process can take a long time.

See p372 for the full descriptions of these descent routes including maps and altitude profiles.

PLANNING YOUR TRIP

❏ **Day trips**

If for some reason you cannot climb all the way to the top but nevertheless wish to experience the pleasure of walking on Africa's biggest and most beautiful mountain, it is possible to enter the park for one day only. There are some advantages in doing this. It's safer for one thing, for few will get beyond 3000m altitude in one day so altitude sickness shouldn't be an issue. With no camping or rescue fees, porters' wages or food to pay, it will work out much cheaper too: Factor in US$70 per day entry fee, plus a wage for the compulsory guide, transport to and from the mountain and a packed lunch, and the whole package can cost as little as US$100. And as well as being wonderfully pleasant, if you're fit and start out early enough there's no reason why you can't climb above the treeline to the heathland, thereby covering two vegetation zones and giving yourself a good chance of a reasonably unhindered view of Kibo and Mawenzi. There are even designated picnic spots on the way.

Marangu Gate has a **3-hour nature loop** through the cloud forest, which is lovely and from which you can descend either via the trekkers' trail or the less scenic but faster porters' route. There are also a number of seldom-visited waterfalls in the area. The ambitious can attempt to reach the Mandara Huts (p294) and descend again in one day. Furthermore, just 15 minutes beyond the Mandara Huts – through a small patch of forest alive with monkeys – is Maundi Crater (p294), with excellent views of Kibo and Mawenzi to the north-west and the flat African plains stretching away to the east.

The other place where day trips are allowed is on the Shira Plateau, where your chances of spotting big game are much greater (though still very, very small). However, the time taken in getting to the park gate on this western side deters most day-trippers.

What to take

CLOTHES

The best head-gear for all weathers is an English sun-helmet, such as are supplied by Messrs. Silver & Co., London; while a soft fez or smoking cap should be kept for wearing in the shade – one with flaps for drawing down over the ears on a cold night to be preferred.
Hans Meyer *Across East African Glaciers* (1891)

According to his book *Life, Wanderings, and Labours in Eastern Africa*, when Charles New attempted to climb Kili in 1861 he took 13 porters, all of whom were completely naked. New and his crew became the first to reach the mountain's snow-line, which is a rather creditable effort considering their lack of suitable apparel. Assuming your goal is to reach more than just snow, however, you will need to make sure you (and indeed your porters) are appropriately attired for the extreme conditions.

The fact that you will be paying porters to carry your rucksack does, to some degree, make packing simpler – allowing you to concentrate on warmth rather than weight. However, packing for warmth does not mean packing lots of big jumpers. The secret to staying warm is to **wear lots of layers**. Not only does this actually make you warmer than if you just had one single, thick layer – the air trapped between the layers heats up and acts as insulation – but it also means you can peel off the layers one by one when you get too warm and put them on again one by one when the temperature drops.

A suitable mountain wardrobe would include:

● **Walking boots** Mountaineering boots (ie ones with stiff soles that take a crampon) are unnecessary unless you're taking an unusual route or trekking in the low season when crampons may be required. If you're not, a decent pair of trekking boots will be fine.

The important thing about boots is comfort, with enough toe room: on the ascent up Kibo you might be wearing an extra pair or two of socks, and on the descent your toes will be shoved into the front of the boots with every downhill step. Remember these points when trying on trekking boots in the shop. Make sure they are also sturdy, waterproof, durable and high enough to provide support for your ankles. Finally, ensure you break them in *before* you go to Tanzania, so that if they do give you blisters, you can recover before you set foot on the mountain.

● **Socks** Ahhh, the joy of socks ... a couple of thick thermal pairs and some regular ones should be fine; you may stink but you'll be comfortable too, which is far more important. Some people walk in one thick and one thin pair of socks, changing the thin pair regularly, rinsing them out in the evening and tying them to their pack to dry during the day.

● **Thermal underwear** The value of thermal underwear lies in the way it draws

moisture (ie your sweat) away from your body. A thermal vest and long-johns are sufficient.

● **Regular underwear** You won't need to wear thermals every day – indeed, many people save them just for the summit night. Most of the time your regular undies are fine. Women will probably feel the benefit of sports bras rather than regular ones – they're certainly more comfy, so I'm told.

● **Fleece** Fleeces are light, pack down small, dry quickly and can be very, very warm. Take at least two: one thick 'polar' one and one of medium thickness and warmth. Make sure that you can wear the thinner one over all the T-shirts and shirts you'll be taking, and that you can wear your thick one over all of these – you'll probably need to on the night-walk up Kibo.

● **Trousers** Don't take jeans, which are heavy and difficult to dry. Instead, take a couple of pairs of trekking trousers, preferably one light and one heavy.

● **Sunhat** One reader wrote in to say that, because he wears glasses, a baseball cap or similar was much more useful than a regular sunhat as it kept the rain off his spectacles. This is a good idea but do make sure you have something to cover the back of your neck too. Whatever you choose, headgear is essential as it can be hot and dazzling on the mountain ...

● **Woolly/fleecy hat** ... but it can also be very cold. Brightly coloured bobble hats can be bought very cheaply in Moshi; or, better still, invest in one of those **balaclavas** which you can usually find on sale in Moshi, which look a bit like a miniature knitted pizza oven but which will protect your face from the biting summit wind.

● **Bandanna (aka 'buff')** For keeping the dust out of your face when walking on the Saddle, to use as an ear-warmer on the final night, and to mop the sweat from your brow on those exhausting uphill climbs. Also useful for blocking out odours when using the public toilets at the campsites.

● **Gloves** Preferably fleecy; many people wear a thin thermal under-glove too.

● **Down jacket** Not necessary if you have enough fleeces but nevertheless wonderfully warm, light, compact – and expensive. Make sure it is large enough to go over all your clothes.

❏ **Where to buy your trekking gear (UK)**
These are the best online retailers I've found for buying clothes and equipment for Kilimanjaro:

● **Field & Trek.com** (🖳 fieldandtrek.com) One of the cheaper options and with a big stock.
● **GO Outdoors** (🖳 gooutdoors.co.uk) Probably Field & Trek.com's biggest rival; prices not usually as cheap but with a wider selection of (usually) better quality stuff.
● **BananaFingers** (🖳 bananafingers.co.uk) A climbing specialist, really, but cheap and with excellent service. Unfortunately descriptions of their merchandise are sometimes a bit brief, so my advice is to browse the other sites first to find out exactly what it is you want to buy, then look to see if it's cheaper with BananaFingers.
● **Alpine trek** (🖳 alpinetrek.co.uk) An excellent selection of brands that are hard to find elsewhere.

● **Rainwear** While you are more likely to be rained on during the walk in the forest, where it should still be warm, once you've got your clothes wet there will be little opportunity to dry them on the trek – and you will not want to attempt to climb freezing Kibo in wet clothes. A **waterproof jacket** – preferably made from Gore-Tex or a similar breathable material, hopefully with a warm or fleecy lining too, and big enough to go over all your clothes so you can wear it for the night-walk on Kibo – is ideal; **waterproof trousers** are a necessity too. Alternatively, one reader suggests a cheap waterproof **poncho** 'from a dollar store', preferably one that goes over your daypack as well as yourself.

● **Summer clothes** T-shirts and shorts are the most comfortable things to wear under the humid forest canopy. You are strongly recommended to take a shirt with a collar too, to stop the sun from burning the back of your neck.

OTHER EQUIPMENT

Any trekking agency worth its licence will provide a **tent**, as well as **cooking equipment**, **cutlery** and **crockery**. You will still need to pack a few other items, however, if you don't want to return from your trek as a sunburnt, snow-blinded, dehydrated wretch with hepatitis and hypothermia. Some of these items can be bought or rented in Moshi or Arusha. Your agency can arrange equipment rental, which is the most convenient way, though you may well find it slightly cheaper to avoid going through them as they will, of course, take their cut. Note that the following lists concern the trek only; it does not include items necessary for other activities you may have planned on your holiday, such as binoculars for your safari or a bucket and spade for Zanzibar.

Before buying or renting all of the following, check to see what your agency will supply as part of their trekking package. Many will provide mattresses and water purifiers, for example, which will save you a little.

Essentials

● **Sleeping bag** The warmest you've got. Four-season and even five-season – yes, such things do exist! – sleeping bags are obviously best but for many people a three-season bag (up to -10°C) is probably the most practical, offering a compromise between warmth and cost; team this with a **thermal fleecy liner**, which is available in camping shops back at home for about £20-30/US$30-45, to provide further insurance against the cold.

● **Sleeping mat** Essential unless you're following the standard Marangu Route as you'll be sleeping in huts. Trekking agencies sometimes supply these – check to see if yours does.

● **Water bottles/Platypus Hoser/Camelbak system** On that final push up Kibo you'll need to carry three litres of water *at the very least*; many people take enough bottles to carry four litres. It's certainly good to take a lot of water, though do remember you've got to carry it with you and four litres of water weighs four kilos.

Make sure your bottles are **thermally protected** or they will freeze on the summit. Regular army-style water bottles are fine, though these days many

trekkers prefer the **Platypus Hoser-style systems** (aka **CamelBaks**), a soft, plastic bladder with a long tube from which you can drink as you walk along. We think they're great and they have several advantages over regular bottles, not the least of which being that they save you fiddling about with bottle tops and you can keep your hands in your pockets while you drink, which is great on the freezing night-time walk to the summit. But while they encourage you to drink regularly, which is good, they discourage you from taking a break, which is bad. What's more, these systems nearly always freeze up on the way to the summit, especially the hose and mouthpiece. One way to avoid this – or at least delay it – is to **blow back into the tube** after you have taken a drink to prevent water from collecting in the tube and freezing. (One reader suggested adding Dioralyte which apparently also helps to delay freezing, though this may in time permanently alter the flavour of your water.) So, if you are going to bring one of these, make sure it's fully insulated – and don't forget to take frequent breaks!

❏ A Kilimanjaro washbag

Hygiene is very, very important on Kilimanjaro. The last thing you want is a stomach bug due to the poor hygiene regime of one of your fellow trekkers – or, indeed, yourself. The trouble is, of course, that opportunities to wash are minimal on the mountain and water is limited the further up you go. Put the following in your washbag, however, and you should be able to maintain some sort of standards:

● **Anti-bacterial handwash** This stuff is very effective and though you won't find it on most kit lists, I think it's essential. Giving some to your cook before he prepares your meals is a good idea too!

● **Moist toilet tissues (Wet-wipes)** For mopping brows, mainly; use several at the end of the day and on most treks it's the closest thing you'll get to a shower on the mountain.

● **Toothbrush and toothpaste** Ensure your dental checks are up to date; if there is one thing more painful than climbing to the summit of Kili, it's climbing to the summit of Kili with toothache.

● **Toilet paper** See p271 for advice on how to dispose of it when you've finished with it.

● **Soap** Though you won't get through much of it on the mountain and your trekking agency should provide some for you.

● **Tampons/sanitary towels**

● **Contraceptives** For those with too much energy. But gentlemen be warned: if she says she has a headache on the mountain, the chances are she *really does have* a headache.

You should also bring a **towel**. The controversy here is over which sort of towel to have. Many just bring one enormous beach towel because they plan to visit Zanzibar after the trek and don't see the point of packing two towels.

At the other extreme there are the tiny so-called 'travel towels', a sort of chamois-cloth affair sold in camping shops and airport lounges the world over. Some people swear by these things but others usually end up swearing at them, finding that they have all the absorbency of your average block of volcanic stone. Nevertheless, we grudgingly admit that they do have their uses on Kilimanjaro, where opportunities to wash anything other than face and hands are minimal. You can dry your towel by attaching it to the outside of your rucksack during the day.

❏ A Kilimanjaro medical kit

According to Meyer, the Chagga treated their cuts and scars with the liberal application of cow dung. We advise, however, that you don't. Instead, if you're going on a cheap trek, take a medical kit with you as few of the budget agencies will have one. (And even if you're going with a more luxurious operator, check to see what they pack in the way of medication, bandages etc.)

A medical kit should include:

● **Antiseptic cream and plasters** For small cuts and grazes.

● **Bandages** Useful for twists and sprains as well as for larger flesh wounds.

● **Compeed** For blisters.

● **Elastic joint supports** For steeper gradients if you have knee/ankle problems.

● **Ice packs** One of my clients brought Koolpaks with him; these turn icy cold when squeezed and shaken and provide great relief for painful joints. Can be bought online, are very reasonable – and are ideal if you know that your knees or ankles will play up on the mountain.

● **Anti-malarials** You won't catch malaria on the mountain but if you're on a course of anti-malarials you should continue taking them. Be warned, however, that there is a belief among many guides that the popular anti-malarial drug Malarone interferes with the efficacy of the anti-altitude sickness drug Diamox. Speak with your guide/doctor to get their opinion on this.

● **Aspirin/Paracetamol** Or other painkillers, though do read the discussion on Acute Mountain Sickness (AMS; see p260) and the medical indications that come with the packet before scoffing these.

● **Imodium** Stops you going when you don't want to, which could come in handy.

● **Rehydrating powders** Such as Dioralyte. Usually prescribed to people suffering from diarrhoea but useful after a hot day's trekking as well.

● **Lip salve or chapstick/vaseline** See under *Highly desirable*, p47.

● **Throat pastilles** Useful, as the dry, dusty air causes many a sore throat.

● **Any current medication you are on** Bring all your needles, pills, lotions, potions and pungent unguents.

● **Diamox** Diamox is the brand name for Acetazolamide, the drug that fights AMS – or at least the symptoms of it (see p261) – and which many people use prophylactically on Kilimanjaro. See the box on p266 to help you decide whether you want to bring a course of these with you.

● **Sterile needles** If you need an injection in Tanzania, insist that the doctor uses your new needles.

Carry everything in a **waterproof bag or case** and keep at least the emergency stuff in your daypack – where hopefully it will lie undisturbed for the trek's duration.

We think **the best combination is to bring both a 'Camelbak' and a regular bottle**, which you should keep insulated by wrapping in a towel or putting inside an old, thick sock inside your daypack, to be retrieved once your Camelbak has frozen (and I've never experienced a climb to the summit where my Camelbak hasn't, eventually, frozen up). Another good tip is to store the bottle upside-down in your daypack; that way, if it too starts to freeze, it will do so from the bottom of the bottle, so you can still drink out of the top.

● **Water purifiers/filter** Essential only if your agency has stated they won't purify your water for you – though most now do. Of the two, **purifying tablets**

such as iodine are more effective as they kill everything in the water, though they taste awful. A cordial will help to mask this taste and you can buy packets of powdered flavouring in the local supermarkets. **Filters** are less effective and more expensive, though the water they produce tastes much better.

There's now a third option, the **SteriPEN** (🖳 www.steripen.com), which kills waterborne microbes by using ultraviolet light. The pen is simple to use: just turn it on, hold it in a litre of water for 30 seconds and ... that's it. I was on the mountain when I first saw one of these in action and I have to say I found it a very impressive bit of kit – to the extent that I now have one of my own. My only quibble is that you can use it on only one litre of water at a time, so it can be awkward if you have, for example, a three-litre bottle.

● **Torch** A **head-torch**, if you have one and don't find it uncomfortable, is far more practical than a hand-held one, allowing you to keep both hands free; on the last night this advantage is pretty much essential, enabling you to keep your hands in your pockets for warmth. It's also pretty essential when going to the toilet after dark too, saving you from juggling toilet roll and torches while squatting and trying to maintain your balance.

● **Sunscreen** High factor (35-40) is essential. That sun is fierce at these altitudes!
● **Sunglasses** Essential for the summit where the light on Kibo can be really painful and damaging and cause snow-blindness.
● **Ice axe/crampons** Ice axes are really useful only if you are taking a highly unusual route on the mountain (ie none of the official ones) where you have to cross glaciers, or, possibly, if you're travelling out of season when snow and ice can be heavy. **Crampons**, too, would be useful on these occasions, though ask your agency first if they will be necessary before bringing them. Otherwise leave them, your snow boots, rope, karabiners and all that other mountaineering gear at home.
● **Glasses/contact lenses** For those who need them, of course. **Contact lenses** are fine but super-expensive ones should be avoided on the final assault to the summit as there's a risk that when the strong cold wind blows across the Saddle the lenses can dry, go brittle very quickly and fall out of your eye. I suggest affordable disposable lenses be worn but that spare **glasses** be carried, especially during the assault on the summit. Obviously you'll need to be extra careful to keep your hands super clean, dry and dust-free when putting in lenses.

Highly desirables
● **Plastic bags** Useful for segregating your wet clothes from the rest of your kit in your rucksack and for collecting rubbish to take off the mountain.
● **Trekking poles** If you've done some trekking before you'll know if you need trekking poles or not; if you haven't, assume you will. While people often use them for the entire trek, poles really come into their own on the descent where they minimise the strain on your knees as you trudge downhill. Telescopic poles can be bought from trekking/camping outfitters in the West, or you can invest in a more local version – a Maasai 'walking stick' – from souvenir shops in Moshi or Arusha.
● **Boiled sweets/chocolate** For winning friends and influencing people. Good

for energy levels too. And morale. If you can bring them from home so much the better; sweets sold in Tanzania may look similar to those at home but they seldom taste the same.

● **Chapstick/lip salve or vaseline** The wind on the summit will rip your sun-burnt lips to shreds. Save yourself the agony by investing in a chapstick, available in strawberry and mint flavours from pharmacists in Moshi and Arusha.

● **She-wee** AKA the Miss Piss, this is for ladies who want to wee without the bother of removing layers or getting out of the tent at night. According to some, the 'female urinal' is cheaper and better. Men, by the way, usually make do with an empty water bottle.

● **Camera and equipment** See box below.

❏ **Cameras and camera equipment**

It's important to prepare properly when it comes to taking a camera on Kilimanjaro. After all, it's likely that your camera will not have spent seven days in constant use before and almost certainly not in the dusty and/or humid conditions one finds on Kili, with its extremes of temperature and weather.

The first thing to do is to make sure you have enough **memory cards**; I take an average of 400-600 shots each time I spend a week on Kilimanjaro and while that's probably a bit extreme, if you like taking photographs you could well match or even surpass these figures. Indeed it may feel as if you've spent the entire trip with your camera attached to your face, such is the frequency with which you find something worth photographing.

Bring at least one **spare set of batteries** and make sure all rechargeable batteries are fully charged before you set off on the mountain. More and more photographic equipment is becoming available for sale in Arusha and, to a lesser extent, Moshi, but I certainly wouldn't rely on them having the battery you require for your camera. And for goodness sake don't forget to bring the **charger**, so you can charge your batteries the night before you head off onto the mountain.

For those with an SLR, regarding **lenses**, I always take a couple of zooms: a wide-angle (around 18mm-135mm) and a telephoto. This latter is far less useful on Kilimanjaro, of course, as panoramic shots of the mountain and stunning wide-angle views are the order of the day; but occasionally it's nice to zoom in on a bird of prey or a particular part of the mountain. A telephoto zoom also comes into its own if you're going on safari after your trek (I suggest a 300mm minimum for this).

Other useful equipment includes: a **polarising filter** to bring out the rich colours of the sky, rocks and glaciers. A **tripod** is useful for those serious about their photography, in order to keep the camera steady and allow for maximum depth of field – though remember, you're the one who's going to have to carry it if you want to use it during the day (though you could ask your agency to provide a porter for this task); a bean-bag, or one of those new, bendy 'gorillas', would be a more portable alternative. One other essential investment is a **camera-cleaning kit**. Your camera goes through a lot of hardship on Kili, not least because of the different vegetation zones you pass through, from the humidity of the forest to the dusty desert of the Saddle. Either buy a ready-made kit from a camera shop or make one yourself by investing in a soft cloth, cotton buds, a blow brush and tweezers.

Many people with expensive SLR cameras also bring a cheap point-and-shoot **compact**; this is not a bad idea, as it doubles your chances of getting some photographic record of your journey.

Usefuls

● **Earplugs** Some porters have stereos and mobile phones and they love advertising this fact by playing the former and speaking into the latter extremely loudly at campsites. A set of earplugs will reduce this disturbance.

● **Gaiters** For every edition of this book we put these in the 'Useful' category; and every edition at least one trekker writes in to tell me that they should be in the 'Essentials' category. I've never worn them on Kili, though I can see the point of them and they are pretty vital if you don't have waterproof trousers as they perform a similar function. To be fair, many of the guides I have trekked with feel naked without them. So it's a matter of preference, really, and they are particularly useful on the slopes of Kibo and the dusty Saddle to prevent small stones from entering one's shoes.

● **Aluminium sheet blanket** Provides extra comfort if your sleeping bag isn't as warm as you thought, though they do cause condensation overnight that can leave your sleeping bag feeling damp.

❑ SHOOTING KILI – VISITING KENYA'S AMBOSELI NATIONAL PARK

It's all Toto's fault. In their chart-topping hit from the 1980s, the lead singer of the Canadian dad-rock outfit crooned the line *'Sure as Kilimanjaro rises like Olympus above the Serengeti'*. To those who know their geography, such a scenario is absurd as you can't, in fact, see Africa's greatest mountain from its greatest national park; one quick look at an atlas will show you that there's actually more than 200 miles separating them. But in singing those lyrics the band unwittingly provided a mental picture, at least for those who've never been to Tanzania, of what the country looks like: that is to say, a foreground filled with the archetypal Serengeti scenery of acacia and fever trees, all set against a backdrop of a bloody great mountain with snow on top.

It is presumably for this reason that this book's publisher, Trailblazer, chose just such a scene for the cover of the first four editions of this book.

Well, surprising as it may seem, this idyllic picture – savannah in the foreground, mountain in the background – *does* actually exist in the real world. Only not in Tanzania. On the Tanzanian side, the slopes are too well watered (most of the rainfall received by Kilimanjaro falls on its southern slopes, remember), and the mountain on this side too densely inhabited as a result, to provide us with the necessary remote acacia-clad landscape.

So instead you have to go round the northern side of Kili, to Kenya and its famous Amboseli National Park, to see the 'classic' Kili view. The plains that skirt this northern side of Kili are much drier than those on the southern side. Indeed, the word 'amboseli' is Maasai for 'dust devil' – the mini tornados of dust that whip across the surface of the park – which gives you some idea of how parched the land skirting the mountain's northern face can be.

But there is some water coming down these northern slopes too. Via several miles of underground channels these waters emerge on the Kenyan plains as large swamps. These swamps attract a lot of animals to the area – including over 900 African elephants as well as wildebeest, giraffe, lion, monkey, zebra, hyena and antelope – and form the centrepiece of Amboseli National Park. And surrounding these swamps is semi-arid bush, a land of acacia and fever tree – perfect, in other words, for a cover shot.

● **Sandals/flip-flops** Useful in the evenings at camp but make sure they are big enough to fit round a pair of thick socks.

● **Candles** But don't use them in the tent and keep them away from everybody else's tent too. Usually supplied by the trekking company for use in the mess tent.

● **Bootlaces/string**

● **Clothes pegs** Useful for attaching wet clothes to the back of rucksacks to allow them to dry in the sun while you walk; a reader wrote in to recommend **binder clips** (also known as bulldog or office clips) as a smaller, stronger alternative.

● **Penknife** Always useful, if only for opening beer bottles at the post-trek party.

● **Matches** As with the penknife, always useful, as any Boy Scout will tell you.

● **Sewing kit** For repairs on the trail.

● **Insulating tape** Also for repairs, this time for shoes, rucksacks, tents etc, and

Unfortunately, taking the right picture is still largely a matter of luck. During our time there, the mountain tended to appear naked only first thing in the morning, before modesty overcame it and it hid behind its screen of clouds. But even when cloud-free, a combination of evaporation, dust and heat haze ensure Kili's summit is indistinct for most of the time. Apparently, this is pretty much the norm – which explains why the blogs I read describing people's experiences in Amboseli all talk about seeing Kilimanjaro, though none actually illustrate their site with a picture to prove it. Because, simply put, the results are usually underwhelming.

I've since been told that August is the best time of year to go to increase your chance of a clear, photogenic view of Kili from this side. But whether this is true or not, I shouldn't be surprised at my lack of success. Whenever I am in Moshi or Marangu and the mountain appears bright and clear, it's enough to send me scurrying up to the roof of the nearest building to take a few shots – for the simple reason, of course, that it doesn't happen very often. So gambling that a two-day safari in Amboseli would reward me with the cover photo I was after was always going to be a long-shot.

Practicalities for visiting Amboseli

A visit to Amboseli is easiest to organise from Kenya – few Tanzanian safari companies offer trips to Kenya parks. Prices start at about US$250-300 for a private two-day trip for one person, including a night at a lodge just outside the park gates. The dry season of July to October is the best time to visit for the swamps provide one of the few sources of water in the region, so lots of game gather in the park at this time. The vegetation is not as thick, so it's easier to spot wildlife in the undergrowth, and there are fewer mosquitoes too. The disadvantages of going at this time is that it's also the busiest time and prices in the lodges are higher as a result.

There's a wide range of accommodation from fairly basic tented camps near Kimana Gate, the main eastern entry point into the park, up to the luxury Tortilis Camp, situated on its own private conservancy to the south of the main reserve. In addition to Kimana, you can also enter the park at Meshanani Gate, 45 minutes from Namanga on the park's western side.

PLANNING YOUR TRIP

as a last resort for mending holes in clothes if you have forgotten your sewing kit or are incapable of using it.

● **Watch** Preferably cheap and luminous for night-time walking.

● **Compass** Not essential, but useful when combined with ...

● **Map** See p388 for a list of our preferred maps; again not essential but will, in combination with a compass, help you to determine where you are on the mountain, and where you're going.

● **GPS receiver** See box below.

● **Whistle** It's difficult to get lost on Kilimanjaro but if you're taking an unusual route – on the northern side of the mountain, for example, or around Mawenzi – a whistle may be useful to help people locate into which ravine you've fallen. The international distress (emergency) signal is six blasts on a whistle.

● **Multi-plug adaptor** Not for Kili, obviously, where there's no power, though could be useful before and after the trek if you're staying in a room with only one socket and you have a camera/GPS/laptop/batteries to recharge.

Luxuries

● **Mobile phone** You can get reception on much of the mountain now – including, so it is said, on the summit. What better place could there be from which to phone friends stuck behind their desks at work on a rainy day back home? The guides and porters know where reception is best at each campsite, so if you're

---

❏ GPS waypoints and phone apps

If you have a handheld GPS (Global Positioning System) receiver you will be able to take advantage of the waypoints marked on the maps and listed on pp396-400 of this book. Essentially a GPS calculates your position on the Earth using a number of satellites and the results should be accurate to a few metres. It is, of course, not essential that you use a GPS; your chances of getting lost on the mountain are very slim, given that you will be accompanied at every step by a guide who may have climbed on your route a hundred times or more.

If you do decide to use a GPS unit in conjunction with this book don't feel that you need to be ticking off every waypoint as you reach it; you'll soon get bored with that method. But if you look at it occasionally – when you stop for lunch, for example – it will give you an idea both of where you are on the trail and also how far you have to go.

You have two ways of inputting the waypoints into your receiver. You can either manually key the nearest waypoint from the list in this book as and when the need arises. Or, much less laboriously and with less margin for keystroke error, download the complete list (but not the descriptions) for free from our website at 🖥 climb mountkilimanjaro.com or from 🖥 trailblazer-guides.com.

If you don't have a designated GPS receiver, you can still record your walk using your phone and one of the **apps** that are available. Apps such as Columbia's **GPS Pal**, which allows you to record your track as well as tag your favourite spots with photos and videos, with elevation, and time taken also recorded; or the simpler **MapMyHike**, which simply logs your hike without any frills. Finally, there's **i.walk**, though this is more of a fitness coaching tool than a GPS and thus is most useful for the months leading up to your Kilimanjaro climb rather when you're on it.

having trouble making contact just ask one or simply follow them. We give general advice on the quality of phone reception at the start of the description for each trail. Remember, too, that batteries last a lot longer if you keep the phone in airline mode. And if you're going to bring one of these then it's a good idea to also bring....

● **Phone battery pack/power bank** Phones have a habit of dying on the mountain; it must be the cold. Revive them with a battery pack – they're portable and cheap and do the business.

● **Hot water bottle** Several people have suggested this and a number of trekking companies now supply them as standard. Get your crew to fill it with hot water before bedtime and use the water in the morning for washing.

● **Pillow** One luxury I have never actually used on the mountain but would love is a pillow; not one of those inflatable travel ones but a proper, plump, goose-down number. Bulky and a pain to carry, of course – but so much nicer than resting one's weary head on a scrunched-up fleece at the end of the day.

● **MP3 players** and **iPods** While some find the idea abhorrent, many trekkers bring their tunes on the trek. There is nothing wrong with a little mountainside music, of course, but do remember that while you may think you've found the perfect soundtrack for climbing up Kili, others may disagree: bring headphones, so as not to disturb.

● **Diary/reading material** A list of appropriate reading matter can be found on pp390-5. Note that more than one client has said that books and other forms of entertainment are essential to while away the hours in camp, whereas others say it's all unnecessary; it depends who you're climbing with, I suppose, and how well you're all getting along.

● **Champagne** For celebrating, of course, though don't try to take it up and open it at the summit – the combination of champagne and altitude sickness could lead to tragedy.

WHAT TO PACK IT IN

You'll need two bags: a **rucksack** – a 70-litre one is the absolute minimum, with 80 litres-plus more practical for carrying all the equipment necessary for most climbs – and a smaller, lighter **daypack**. While trekkers usually spend a long time finding the rucksack that's most comfortable for them, few bother to spend as long when choosing a daypack. However, on Kili it is the porters who traditionally carry your rucksack (usually on their heads, and often inside a rice sack or similar outer layer to protect it from getting wet or damaged), while you will carry your daypack. So make sure you **choose your daypack with care** and that it is both comfortable and durable. It also needs to be big enough to hold everything you may need when walking. See box p52 for a possible list of these things.

A few more points. Firstly, it is not uncommon for bags to be delayed during your flight; indeed, at one point it was estimated that one in seven bags got lost or delayed in transit. (The figures are better now but only just. The Qatar Airways flight from London is particularly notorious due to the short transfer time at Doha.)

❏ **What to put in your daypack**

Normally you will not see your backpack from the moment you hand it to the porter in the morning until lunchtime at least, and maybe not until the end of the day. It's therefore necessary to pack everything you may need during the day in the bag you carry with you. Some suggestions, in no particular order:

● sweets
● water
● water purifiers
● toilet paper and plastic bag for packing used paper to the next camp; see p271 for toilet etiquette
● this book/maps/GPS
● camera and spare batteries
● phone plus battery pack
● sunhat/sunglasses and suncream
● rainwear
● walking sticks/knee supports
● medical kit, including chapstick
● lunch (supplied by your crew)

PLANNING YOUR TRIP

This is why it is imperative that you **wear or carry your boots on the plane**. Your daypack (which you should carry on as hand luggage) should also contain a waterproof coat and anything else you think you may need for your first day on the mountain (camera, medication etc). In other words, pack in the knowledge that you may be on the mountain by the time your main bag arrives in Tanzania. Sleeping bags and mats are probably too bulky to be carried as hand luggage on a flight so you'll have to discuss with your trekking agency/guide about renting this stuff from them, at least until your main pack arrives.

Once your main bag does arrive at its destination (and most delayed bags turn up within 24 hours of their scheduled arrival time), if your trekking company is half-decent they'll fetch it from JRO for you and will then give it to a porter to bring to you on Kili. Bearing this in mind, if you have brought some stuff in your main bag that you *don't* want to take on the mountain with you – a snorkel and fins for your post-Kili trip to Zanzibar, for example – pack this in a separate bag within the main bag. You can then give instructions to the agency on what you'd like removed from the bag and kept safely in their office, and what you want on the mountain. This 'non-Kili' stuff can then be removed by them easily without having to rummage through your entire luggage.

Once you're on the mountain **don't leave valuables in your rucksack**. Though porters are trustworthy on the whole, it's only fair that you do not put temptation in their path; and it saddens me to say that there have been a spate of thefts recently from bags and tents, particularly at Barranco Camp but elsewhere too.

Finally, **put everything in plastic bags** (or **bin bags**) inside your backpack and daypack to keep everything dry.

Fitness, inoculations and insurance

FITNESS

I ascribe the almost perfect health I have always enjoyed in Africa to the fact that I have made every step of my journey on foot, the constant exercise keeping my bodily organs in good order. **Hans Meyer** *Across East African Glaciers* (1891)

There's no need to go overboard with fitness preparations for climbing Kili. The main reason why people fail to reach the summit is altitude sickness rather than lack of necessary strength or stamina. But the trek will obviously be more enjoyable for you the fitter you are, so anything you can do in the way of training can only help (see box p54).

A weekend (or several) of walking would be a good thing to do; it won't improve your fitness to a great degree but it will at least confirm that you can walk for more than a few hours at a time, and for more than one day at a time too. Wear the clothes you plan to take to Kilimanjaro – particularly your boots and socks – and the daypack that you hope to be carrying all the way to the top of Kibo, as well.

INOCULATIONS

Sort out your vaccinations a few months before you're due to fly. Note that in order to enter Tanzania **it is compulsory to have a yellow-fever vaccination if you're coming from a country where the disease is endemic** (even if you were only transiting there, assuming you left the airport in that country for more than 12 hours); see p126 for further details.

In the UK the jab costs about £60-85 including a certificate (from what I understand it's about US$150 in the States though can climb to US$350) to prove you've been vaccinated. Other recommended inoculations include:

● **Typhoid** This disease is caught from contaminated food and water. A single injection lasts for three years. Available on the NHS in the UK. There is also a typhoid vaccine that is combined with one for...

● **Hepatitis A** This debilitating disease of the liver is spread by contaminated water, or even by using cutlery that has been washed in this water. The latest inoculation involves two injections; the first will protect you for a year, the second, taken six to twelve months later, will cover you for 20 years. (These times may vary if you're taking the combined Hep A/typhoid vaccine).

● **Polio** The polio vaccine used to be administered by sugar-lump, making it one of the more pleasant inoculations, though these days it's nearly always injected. The vaccine lasts for ten years and there's a high chance you may

already have been immunised for life if you had a course of inoculations during childhood – which if you were born in the UK after 1958 you probably will have done.

● **Tetanus** Tetanus vaccinations last for ten years and are absolutely vital for visitors to Tanzania. The vaccination is usually given in combination with one for **diphtheria**. Once you've had five injections, you're covered for life. Once again, the chances you were immunised against this for good at childhood is high. If you need a booster, it should last for five years.

● **Meningococcal meningitis** This disease of the brain is often fatal though the vaccination, while not free, is safe, effective and lasts for three to five years.

● **Rabies** If you're spending some time with animals or in the wilderness it's also worth considering having a course of **rabies** injections, consisting of three injections spread over one month, though it isn't pleasant and doesn't prevent you from contracting the disease – it just gives you more time to receive medical help if you do get bitten.

❑ **A fitness regime**

"Though I am tall, I always had secretly defined myself as a physically weak and somewhat sickly person. After climbing Kilimanjaro, I had to acknowledge that I was mentally and physically tough. I was forced to redefine myself. Climbing the mountain was the hardest thing I had ever done, physically, in my life, but I had done it."
Michael Crichton, *Travels* (1988)

When people ask us how fit you need to be to climb Kilimanjaro, we usually reply that you don't need to be especially fit, just *not unfit*. But while altitude sickness is the main reason why people fail to reach the summit – and this can strike you regardless of whether you are fit or not – there's no doubt that you *do* need to be in reasonable condition to tackle Kilimanjaro, and will have a much more pleasant time on the mountain if you are fit and healthy.

For this reason, and to answer the many emails we get from people who want to undertake some sort of fitness regime before their trek, here is a typical daily exercise programme for Kilimanjaro. It should be started about four months (three minimum) before the climb. This should help to reduce body fat, improve aerobic fitness and also strengthen the muscles in the places where it really matters: your legs. We think it helps to concentrate on aerobic exercises one day (say three times a week), alternating with leg-strengthening exercises for the other three days – then follow God's example and rest on the seventh day.

Aerobic exercise

Aerobic exercise is designed to improve oxygen consumption in the body. Thirty minutes to an hour of jogging, cycling, climbing stairs or even just brisk walking are all good aerobic exercises. Aim to exercise at 70% of your maximum heart rate for the best results.

Leg strengthening

Go to any gym and you'll come across plenty of contraptions designed to increase the strength of your calves, thighs, hamstrings and buttocks. These are fine though the usual

Malaria

Malaria is a problem in Tanzania, which is considered one of the highest risk countries in the world. While you are highly unlikely to contract malaria on Kilimanjaro, which is too high and cold for the anopheles mosquito (the species that carries malaria but which is rarely seen above 1200m – much lower than your starting point on Kili), it is rife in coastal areas and on Zanzibar. It's also present in Moshi and, despite an altitude above 1200m, in Arusha too.

When beginning a course of **anti-malarials**, it is very important to begin taking them before you go; that way the drug is established in your system by the time you set foot on Tanzanian soil and it will give you a chance to see if the drug is going to cause a reaction or allergy. Once started, complete the full course, which usually runs for several weeks after you return home.

Which anti-malarial you need depends on which parts of Africa you are visiting and your previous medical history. Your doctor will be able to advise on what drug is best for you. With Tanzania in the highest risk category, the chances are you will be recommended either Lariam (the brand name for mefloquine), Doxycycline or Malarone, which is supposedly free of side effects but expensive.

warnings apply: always read the instructions carefully before using any machine and never be too ambitious and overload the machine with too much weight. Either course of action could lead to serious injury and the cancellation of your trek altogether.

If you don't have access to gym equipment, however, don't worry: there are exercises you can do without the need for machines. **Lunges**, where you take an exaggerated step forward with one leg, dropping your hips as low as possible while keeping your torso upright, are great for thighs, hamstrings and buttocks. A **reverse lunge**, which is the same as a regular lunge only you take a step *backwards*, until your forward thigh (ie the one you didn't take a step backwards with) is parallel to the floor, is also good, particularly for your hamstring. **Calf raises**, where you position yourself with the front half of your feet on a platform, then gently raise and lower yourself on your toes so your heel is alternately higher and lower than the toes, is also useful.

Smoking and other preparations

While the above exercises certainly provide many benefits, we still maintain that nothing is better preparation than **going for a long walk**. A walk provides excellent aerobic exercise, is great for strengthening leg muscles and if the walk is long enough and involves plenty of uphills, can be great for improving stamina too. Find walks in your area or take a walking weekend or walking holiday. You never know, you may even enjoy it as well.

Finally, you could always take up **smoking**. I'd long heard the rumour that smokers have a better chance of reaching the summit, apparently due to the fact that their bodies are used to less oxygen because of the reduced functioning of their lungs – and certainly my experiences of taking smokers up the mountain bear this bizarre idea out. While those of my clients who've led a blameless, tobacco-free life frequently struggle with the altitude, long-term smokers tend to saunter up. Breathless, certainly, and often wheezing – but headache-free and happy.

Of course, we're not seriously suggesting you take up smoking – but it's interesting, isn't it?

> ❏ **High-altitude health**
>
> Before you go, if you suffer from heart or lung problems (such as angina or asthma), high blood pressure or are pregnant, you must visit your doctor to get advice on the wisdom of climbing up Africa's highest mountain; many of the deaths on the mountain are due to pre-existing conditions that have gone undetected before.
>
> The illness you are most likely to suffer from is altitude sickness; indeed, it's a rare trekker on Kilimanjaro who doesn't to some degree. Altitude sickness is caused by the body's inability to adapt quickly enough to the thinner mountain air present at high altitudes. It can be fatal if ignored or left untreated but is also preventable. For a run-down on the causes, symptoms and treatments of altitude sickness, read the section on pp260-9 carefully.
>
> One more thing: if you're planning on relying on it on the mountain, try Diamox (see p266) before you go to make sure you have no severe adverse reaction to it.

Stories of Lariam causing hallucinations, nightmares, blindness and even death have been doing the rounds in travellers' circles for years now but if you feel no adverse reaction – and millions don't – carry on taking it and don't worry.

Of course the best way to combat malaria is not to get bitten at all. A **repellent** with 30% Diethyltoluamide (DEET) worn in the evenings when the anopheles mosquito is active should be effective in preventing bites. Some use it during the day too, when the mosquitoes that carry yellow and dengue fevers are active. There's a new, all-natural repellent out that's apparently as effective as DEET called **PMD**. Effective for up to five hours, it's available in the UK under the brand name Incognito (🖥 lessmosquito.com).

Alternatively, you could just keep covered up with long-sleeve shirts and long trousers, sleep under a **mosquito net** and burn **mosquito coils**; these are available within Tanzania.

Travellers' medical clinics (UK)

For all your jabs, malaria advice and anything else you need to know regarding health abroad, visit your doctor or one of the following clinics:
● **Trailfinders Travel Clinic** (☎ 020-7938 3999; 🖥 trailfinders.com/travelclinic) 194 Kensington High St, London.
● **Nomad Travellers Store and Medical Centre** (☎ 01341 555061; 🖥 nomadtravel.co.uk) has several branches in London as well as Bristol, Manchester, Bath, Birmingham and Cardiff.
● **MASTA** (Medical Advisory Services for Travellers Abroad; 🖥 masta-travelhealth.com) has branches throughout the country.

Also worth looking at is the website of the **US Center for Disease Control** (🖥 cdc.gov); it's packed full of advice and the latest medical news Stateside.

INSURANCE

When buying insurance you must make clear to the insurer that you'll be trekking to the top of a very big mountain. If you are taking an unusual route

and will be using ropes you need to tell them that too. Informing them that you're climbing Kili is usually enough to double the premium and may even exclude you from being covered altogether. But if you don't make this clear and pay the lower premium you'll probably find, should you try to make a claim, you aren't actually covered at all.

Remember to **read the small print** of any insurance policy before buying and shop around, too, for each insurance policy varies slightly from company to company. Details to consider include:
● How much is the deductible if you have to make a claim?
● Can the insurers pay for your hospital bills etc immediately, while you are still in Tanzania, or do you have to wait until you get home?
● How long do you have before making a claim and what evidence do you require (hospital bills, police reports etc)?

Remember the premium for the entire trip will probably double when you mention you are climbing above 4000-5000m, even though you will actually be on the mountain for only a few days. However, you will need to be covered for your entire trip: there are just as many nasty things that can happen – indeed, many more – when off the mountain than on it; theft becomes a much bigger issue too.

One other thing to note. There is a helicopter rescue service of sorts on Kilimanjaro. It might be worth checking to see if your insurance covers this; if not, your trekking company may well offer some sort of helicopter rescue insurance instead which should cost only a few dollars.

For UK residents, the following companies offer insurance that should cover your Kili trek:
● **Big Cat** (🖥 bigcattravelinsurance.com) Their Extreme Activity Pack seems to cover trekking over 4500m, which will be good for Kili and Meru.

❏ My favourite piece of advice on Kilimanjaro

'**WARNING** Due to the rise in the frequency and severity of human-leopard encounters, the Ministry of Tourism, Kilimanjaro Branch, Tanzania, is advising trekkers and anyone else that uses Kilimanjaro for recreational or work-related purposes to take extra precautions while on the mountain.

In particular, we advise that all trekkers wear little bells on their clothing. This will give advanced warning to any leopards that might be close by and thereby prevent you from taking them by surprise. We also advise anyone visiting Kilimanjaro to carry pepper spray with him or her in case of an encounter with a leopard.

Visitors should also be on the watch for any fresh leopard activity, and be able to tell the difference between leopard cub shit and big leopard shit:
Leopard cub shit is smaller and contains lots of berries and fur.
Big leopard shit has bells in it, and smells like pepper.
Enjoy your stay in Tanzania!'

This was sent to me by a friend via Facebook and caught me so much by surprise that I snorted tea out of my nose. Hope it had a similar effect on you. (In case you're wondering, it *is* a joke – leopard-human encounters are pretty much unheard of today.)

● **British Mountaineering Council** (🖳 thebmc.co.uk) Their Alpine & Ski Policy is the one for Kilimanjaro.
● **ihi Bupa** (🖳 ihi.com)
● **Insure and Go** (🖳 www.insureandgo.com) You need to take out their winter sports option which covers trekking up to 6000m.
● **True Traveller** (🖳 truetraveller.com) Their Extreme Adventure pack covers treks over 4500m.
● **World Nomads** (🖳 worldnomads.com)

For American trekkers the following have been recommended by readers:
● **Global Rescue** (🖳 www.globalrescue.com)
● **HTH** (🖳 hthtravelinsurance.com)
● **International Plan** (🖳 internationalplan.com) We sent an email to these people asking if they offered insurance for those climbing Kilimanjaro but failed to get a reply. Still, they were recommended by several clients so it would be worth checking with them.
● **Ripcord** (🖳 ripcordrescuetravelinsurance.com) Specialist rescue and evacuation insurance company, used by Tusker (p100) for their clients.
● **Travel Guard** (🖳 travelguard.com) have an 'Adventure package' upgrade that currently covers trekkers on Kilimanjaro.
● **World Nomads** (🖳 worldnomads.com)

❏ Jambo Bwana – Kilimanjaro's very own theme tune

Jambo, Jambo Bwana,	(Hello, hello sir)
Habari gani,	(How are you?)
Msuri sana,	(I'm very well)
Wageni Wakaribishwa Kilimanjaro,	(Visitors are very welcome to Kilimanjaro)
Hakuna matata!	(No problem!)

Anybody who's spent more than a day or two on the mountain will undoubtedly have heard the guides and porters belting this song out. Indeed, it seems rare to arrive at a campsite these days and not hear it being sung by one expedition or another. By the end of the trek, it's highly likely you'll know all the lyrics and singing along too.

The song was first recorded in 1982 by Them Mushrooms, a Kenyan ensemble formed in the early seventies who used to ply their trade at the luxury beach hotels in Mombasa. The song was written by the band's leader, Teddy Kalanda, though he borrowed heavily from traditional folk tunes around at the time. In the Mushrooms' version there was no mention of Kilimanjaro at all – instead the original song welcomed people to *Kenya yetu*, or 'our Kenya'.

The song proved to be a big hit, selling over 200,000 copies, and was subsequently covered by several other African bands including Mombasa Roots, Safari Sound Band, Khadja Nin and Adam Solomon. Worldwide fame, however, arrived when the German-Caribbean disco outfit Boney M released their version, *Jambo – Hakuna Matata* – though the lyrics were heavily doctored and only the first and last lines of the original survived.

BOOKING YOUR TRIP   2

Welcome to the most boring chapter in the book. Boring but also, perhaps, the most necessary. For alongside your decisions on which friends should come with you, when to climb and what route to take, all of which were covered in the previous chapter, your choice of trekking company will go a long way to determining whether your trek is a safe, successful and happy one... or an unmitigated disaster leading to the breakdown of relationships, divorce, subsequent financial ruin, loss of self-esteem and years of counselling.

So the following pages are devoted to reviewing the companies that offer treks up the mountain. We have divided this chapter into two main sections. The second section deals with the overseas agents but the first and most important half looks at the Tanzanian agents. A brief flick through these pages will lead you to realise that we have written more extensive reviews of Tanzanian companies than for the overseas agents. The reason for this is obvious: **the Tanzanian companies are the ones that are actually going to take you up the mountain**. When a company in the US, UK, Europe etc offers you a trek, all they are doing is acting as middlemen for a Tanzanian company who will be the ones who organise the trek. So no matter what the branding may say on the side of your tent or on the T-shirts that the porters wear, the people inside those T-shirts are not in the employment of the foreign agency through whom you may have booked your trek, but the ground operator that your agent uses to organise and run the expedition.

So, I hear you ask: why not cut out the middleman and book directly with the ground operator? Well, it's a good question and in most instances there are certainly financial benefits with booking directly with a Tanzanian operator; in other words, it's cheaper. That said, there could be some advantages to booking instead with an agent in your home country. The drawbacks and advantages of both options are discussed here.

❏ **Free advice**
Remember that if this chapter is too long and dreary for you, simply get in touch with us via our website 🖳 climbmountkilimanjaro.com, tell us what you're looking for from your trekking company and the budget you have for your trek and we'll do our best to advise you. And we don't even charge!

Who to book with

TANZANIAN OPERATOR vs AN AGENT FROM HOME

This all depends on what the foreign agencies are adding to the package provided by the local ground operator. In many cases they may be adding nothing at all, except perhaps the reassurance that comes from dealing with an agency that you may already know and one that is based in your home country. It may also be easier for you to get compensation from them should something go wrong, and their insurance is likely to be more comprehensive should something go *seriously* wrong on the mountain. Occasionally, some agencies send a North American or European tour leader to work alongside the local guide on each trek, which some people are reassured by; there's a list of the agencies we know that do this in the box on p106. But even assuming they don't, your agency will hopefully have done its homework and checked out the ground operators thoroughly, and flown to Moshi or Arusha to compare a few of them, thus providing you with peace of mind that the Tanzanian agency you'll be climbing with isn't totally terrible.

Another advantage, with UK agencies at least, is that they are required to provide a bond or to join an institution called ABTA which means that, should they fall into financial trouble, their clients' money is safe and will be refunded; other countries may have similar schemes. What's more, the chances are that the English spoken by the agent in your country will be superior to that of the Tanzanian operator, for whom English will be his or her third language (after Swahili and their tribal tongue). Your agent's response may also be more prompt; Tanzanians can sometimes be rather slack at replying to an enquiry.

And then there's the payment. It always feels a lot less, well, *scary*, sending payment to someone in your home country, rather than transferring thousands of dollars to some bloke in deepest, darkest Africa whom you've never even met. And if you pay by credit card, the banking system in Tanzania currently charges somewhere between 3-5% for this – which can easily amount to several hundred dollars in total; pay by credit card with your agent at home and the charges, if they exist at all, are unlikely to be anything like as large.

Booking with a Tanzanian operator

Looking at the other side of the argument, **it will nearly always be cheaper to book directly with a Tanzanian agency**. By doing so, you'll be cutting out the middleman (ie the agency in your country) and removing any fee that he has added to the basic trek cost. **You'll also be dealing directly with those who are actually organising the trek**, and who have a lot of experience on the mountain – rather than somebody who has never climbed Kilimanjaro, indeed may never have been within 5000 miles of the mountain, and when answering your emails must resort to spouting something they were taught at a workshop when training for their job (a role for which they've probably been given the ludicrously inaccurate title of

'trekking expert', 'Kilimanjaro specialist' or some other such nonsense).

And while it may be true that the response of the foreign agent will usually be more prompt, you'll get a more precise reply from a Tanzanian agent who will probably know first-hand how difficult the third day on the Rongai Route is, for example, or how likely it is to rain in September on the Lemosho Route, or what kind of menu you can expect as a vegetarian. Furthermore, many of the agencies actually have a 'Westerner' as one of the owners or managers, and often they'll be the person who answers the emails – so their response to your enquiry may not be that tardy after all, and may be written in English that's every bit as good as yours.

Of course, thanks to the internet you don't even need to wait until you arrive in Tanzania before booking with a local operator: pretty much every agency in Arusha and Moshi now has online-booking services and while it may seem a bit scary sending a four-figure sum to people in East Africa whom you've never met, most companies are used to receiving bookings this way and are trustworthy. What's more, if you go with an agency that's been recommended in this book or by friends, there's no reason why it should be any more risky than if you were booking with an agency in your home country; indeed, there's a slim chance that you might even end up joining a group who *did* book their tour abroad and paid more as a consequence. **Before you do commit to anything, however, do visit our website and drop us a line at henry@climbmountkili manjaro.com to make sure that the company you're interested in is still running and still has a good reputation.** Similarly, if you want to book with a KPAP-partner company, do check out the KPAP website (🖳 kiliporters.org) for the latest list and write to Karen Valenti (🖳 karen@kili porters.org) to find out how well your company is treating its porters.

Before we look in more detail at the Tanzanian agencies, what they offer, and which one could be right for you, let us look at what you can expect to be included in the price of a Kilimanjaro trek – and at what isn't included.

WHAT TO LOOK FOR IN YOUR TREK PACKAGE

So, having done all the necessary research, you've found a suitable agency offering the trek you want for the required duration at an acceptable price. Before you sign on any metaphorical dotted lines, however, you need to be absolutely sure that you know what you're paying for. In other words, **you need to sort out** *exactly* **what is and isn't included in the price of the trek**. Don't just ask what you are getting for your money: ask what you *aren't* getting too – ie what you yourself will need to pay out of your own pocket. Once you have this information you'll get a good idea of exactly how much extra you need to pay in addition to the basic cost of the trek. **The following should be included**:

● All park fees (see p20) and any taxes for you, the porters and guides.
● Hire of porters, assistant guides and guides, their wages and food.
● Food and water for the entire trek. Get a breakdown of exactly how many meals per day you will be getting: normally trekkers are served three main meals per day plus a snack – typically a hot drink with popcorn and biscuits – upon arrival at

camp at the end of the day; see p289 for more details on food on the trek.

● Transport to and from the park at the beginning and end of the trek.

● Hire of camping and cooking gear. If you have brought your own gear, you might be able to persuade the agency to reduce the cost of your trek, though it will be only by a small amount.

● Hire of any equipment – torches, trekking poles, spare water-bottles – that you don't want to bring with you from home. There will probably be a small surcharge for these; just make sure that whatever you agree is included in the contract.

● Any special dietary requirements or other needs, all of which should be stipulated in the contract.

● Any free night's accommodation at the beginning or end of your trek that the trekking company has agreed to cover.

In addition to the above, clients who are booking from abroad and have agreed that transfers from and to Kilimanjaro Airport are included should again make sure that's stipulated in the contract.

Please note: items that are rarely, if ever, included in the package include cigarettes, all drinks except water and hot drinks that accompany meals (and any other beverages that the crew give to you to help you get to the summit or celebrate once you get there) and the tips you dish out to your crew at the end.

One final note: if you're already in Tanzania and dealing with the companies face to face, then you need to **make sure that *everything* the agency has said they will provide, including everything listed above, is specified in a contract**. This is important because, as you are probably aware, a verbal contract is simply not worth the paper it isn't written on. The trekking companies all have standard contracts which should include most of the above but will not include specific things such as the hire of any equipment you need or any free nights' accommodation that you have managed to negotiate into the package. These will need to be written in as well.

Tanzanian agencies

As discussed above, these are the people who actually run the treks. The agencies are often referred to as 'ground operators', particularly by the overseas agents, and it's a term we will sometimes use here too. There are around 300 local companies that offer climbs up Kilimanjaro. The vast majority of them are based in either Moshi or Arusha, though there are a few in Marangu and elsewhere. In all probability, and assuming you booked your trek before you arrived, you won't have any reason to visit the company's offices and so where they are based will have little impact on you, save that the hotel they have booked for you will in all likelihood be located in the same place (ie if you're with a Moshi-based company, your hotel will be in Moshi too, and Arusha-based companies will book you a hotel in Arusha). But if you have decided to hold off booking your trek until you arrive in Tanzania (see p66) then you'll need to choose where to base yourself when shopping for your trek.

Of the 300 or so companies that are licensed to operate on the mountain, we have reviewed 84. We didn't really have any set criteria when deciding which ones to review. These 84 may have earned the right to be included in this book because they are the biggest companies, or the most popular, or the most well-known, or the oldest, or the most ethically minded, or simply the ones our readers have asked us about the most. In fact, if we did have any guidelines when it came to choosing which companies to include, it was that we thought they would be the 84 companies that people would most want to read about.

Writing about 84 may seem like overkill but do remember that **booking with the right agency is perhaps the single most important factor in determining the success or otherwise of your trek**. It is the local agency who supplies all the equipment, builds the menus and buys the food, employs the personnel – guides, cooks, porters etc – who are going to work on the trek, arranges the transport to and from the mountain for you and your crew, books your hotel for before and after the trail, organises and pays for the park fees... and so on, and so on. So take your time choosing your agency. Because unless you are a guide, porter, guidebook writer or just plain daft, climbing Kili will be a once-in-a-lifetime experience – and an expensive one too – so it's important that you get it right.

To save you wading through all 84 reviews, we have also created a table (see pp72-4) that provides you with an overview of these companies. We have organised them into price order, with the cheapest first. The prices in the table (which are *per person* prices) are for a group of four people for a seven-day Machame trek; if you have a bigger group or want a shorter trek then the per person price will be smaller; whereas if your group is smaller, or your trek longer, or the route you choose is further away and thus involves greater transport costs (ie Lemosho or Rongai), then you can expect the per person price to be higher. The last column in the table shows you where you can read each company's reviews.

In addition we've scattered boxes across the following pages that hopefully help you to find the company that suits you best; if you want to carry your own luggage on the mountain, or want to go with an ethical company, or you're looking to book on behalf of a big group, then you'll find boxes that will help you to narrow down your search.

ONLINE REVIEWS vs OUR REVIEWS
Which are more reliable?
It's a fair question: Why have we gone to the trouble of reviewing these agencies when the internet has thousands of reviews from clients on various websites, many of which will be more up-to-date than the ones printed here?

Well, we have two main answers to this. Firstly, as we mention above, we think that choosing the right operator is one of the most important decisions you'll make, so it would be remiss of us to not even attempt to offer you some guidance on this matter. But secondly, we felt compelled to write it because of late we have become rather sceptical about some of the reviews we're seeing online.

Please don't misunderstand us. A genuine, detailed online review can be useful. The people who write these reviews have usually actually climbed with

the company concerned, whereas we may not have done, so they have firsthand experience and a far better knowledge of what it's actually like to climb with them which is invaluable. This is the main limitation of our reviews: we haven't climbed with many of the companies we review.

❏ HOW TO MAKE YOUR TREK CHEAPER – AND HOW NOT TO

Kilimanjaro is an expensive mountain to climb. But there are several ways in which you can make it cheaper. We're not talking about saving a four-figure sum – though with a bit of luck and effort and by following the guidelines listed here, you could save yourself a three-figure one:

● **Bring your friends** Simply put, the larger your group, the lower the per person price – so try to persuade your friends and family to come along too (first insisting, of course, that they all individually buy a copy of this book; and maybe even two each, just to be safe).

● **Join a group** If you're travelling by yourself or with just one or two friends, look to join a public trek; most of the big companies organise these and you'll save yourself a fair bit of cash by opting to join an open, group trek rather than booking a private one.

● **Decide what 'luxuries' you don't need** Don't require a private toilet on Kili? Or a mess tent? Or chairs? Then ask your company if they can leave them behind. It could save you a few dollars.

● **Book your trek in Tanzania** It is possible to just turn up at the airport, get a taxi to Moshi or Arusha (US$50), and begin negotiating with the companies there; see box p66 for more details. Obviously you can do this only if you have the time to wander around Moshi or Arusha and haggle with the trekking companies, but we find that by dealing with them face-to-face you can save a little off the price of your trek.

● **Volunteer with a Tanzanian charity** Trekking companies in Moshi often offer a discount for volunteers who are based in the town.

● **Travel outside of the high season** You won't save much on the mountain by doing this – we know of only one company that varies its prices according to season – but you may well save several hundred dollars by *flying* outside of the busiest months. I very recently booked a flight from Heathrow to Kilimanjaro with Kenyan Airways for just over £300 – the lowest I've ever paid. The flights were for March – which I suppose could be described as a shoulder season, just before the rainy/low season of April and May. That same flight in August is usually at least double that. Many hotels in Tanzania also reduce their prices in the quieter months.

● **Choose your airline carefully** There's a wide variation in airfares and it pays to shop around. Some airlines, such as Ethiopian, charge less because the route they take is lengthy and inconvenient. Others, such as Turkish Airlines, charge less because they touch down at Kilimanjaro Airport at some godforsaken hour in the morning, which means you may have to pay for an extra night's accommodation – thus reducing any money you've saved by flying with them. But Kenyan Airways are usually both cheap and pretty direct, and we've always found their service to be good too. If you fly with an airline such as Turkish, KLM, Qatar or Ethiopian, look to see if they'll include a free stopover at their hub cities (ie Istanbul, Amsterdam, Doha or Addis Ababa respectively). It won't save you any money, but it will at least make the airfare feel like better value, allowing you to enjoy two holidays in one!

● **Haggle** Again, this is easier if you are booking for a large group as your bargaining position is so much stronger (because the companies will be even more desperate for your custom). Don't be shy but don't be too aggressive either, as this just creates a bad feeling and any money you save may come out of the wages of the mountain crew.

The limitations of online reviews

There are several arguments, though, as to why we think an online review may be of limited help. For starters, in all probability it was the reviewer's first and only time on Kili, so he or she has nothing with which to compare it. At the risk

● **Be aware of any discounts on the park fees that you are due** Under 16 years old? East African citizen? Tanzanian resident? Then you're entitled to a significant discount on your park fees (see p21) and there's no reason why this discount shouldn't be passed onto you *in full* by your trekking company. Unfortunately, many of them don't, so make sure you know what you're entitled to and don't accept anything less than the full discount. See p71 and table p72-4 for which companies we found were passing on the 'child discount' in full.

● **Book your safari with the same company** Many trekking companies run first-rate safaris as well and offer a 'climbers' discount' if you book both with them.

● **Look at charity climbs** Some trekking agencies, particularly in the UK, specialise in offering 'charity climbs', where the price of a trek is lower if you manage to collect a certain amount in sponsorship for a charity. How do these companies manage to offer such a low price for their treks? Because some of the sponsorship money you collect goes not to the charity but to the trekking company who invoices them. We personally think it's better to just arrange the trek yourself and then organise your charity fundraising separately. The whole process is more transparent this way and you can then climb with whatever trekking company you want. But while we aren't at all convinced by these charity climb companies, we suppose it is another way of lowering the price you pay.

How not to save money

There are, of course, other ways in which you can make it cheaper but which we *don't* recommend. The following, we think, are not sensible ways of lowering your costs – because by reducing the amount you pay, you may also be reducing your chances of reaching the summit and/or your enjoyment of climbing Africa's highest mountain:

● **Don't carry your own luggage** There are companies that allow trekkers the opportunity of doing this and the trek is slightly cheaper as a result. But the saving is small – essentially it will be equivalent to the wages that would be paid to that porter, which is only US$10 per day even if he is paid the KINAPA minimum. Furthermore, in our experience those that carry their own luggage on the mountain tend to succumb to altitude sickness more than those who don't.

● **Don't take fewer days than you can afford** Sure, if your budget allows you to climb for only six days, then take a six-day climb. But don't opt for a six-day climb if you can actually afford seven; and unless you absolutely have to, don't opt for a five-day trek at all unless you've acclimatised somewhere else beforehand, as we think this is insufficient time for allowing your body to get used to the rarified air.

● **Don't base your choice of company purely on the prices they charge** Companies that charge more for their treks usually do so for a reason: because their equipment is better, their crew more knowledgeable and helpful, their food tastier and healthier, their portions bigger, and their all-round service superior. Sure, there are some that do overcharge, and some who are great value – and in this chapter we try to sift through to point out which companies fall into which category; so read the specifications of every company carefully to find out what they offer and why they charge what they do.

● **Don't scrimp on the tips you give to your crew** Come on, where's your dignity?

of sounding like a braggart, I have now climbed the mountain more than thirty times – so I have. Secondly, as a general rule, clients tend to be happier if they make the summit, and think better about their company as a result; whereas those that don't make it tend to feel less enamoured of their company, and may even blame them for their 'failure' to reach Uhuru Peak, even if that company actually ran a better trek than the one where everyone got to the top. How? Well, as we've pointed out several times, getting to the summit is often a matter of chance and depends to a large degree on whether you acclimatise to the rarified air or not. The company you choose to take you up there can make only a marginal difference to your chances of getting to the summit. Where their expertise and professionalism do come to the fore, however, is when it comes to getting you off the mountain if you aren't acclimatising well. For it's only then that you'll truly be grateful that

---

❏ BOOKING YOUR TREK AFTER YOU'VE ARRIVED IN TANZANIA

The overwhelming majority of trekkers book their Kilimanjaro climb before they arrive in Tanzania (either with a foreign agent or online with a local company). This is sensible – you will have enough on your plate once you get to Tanzania just trying to get to the top of Africa's highest mountain without having to sort out the whole trek beforehand as well. **Booking your trek before you arrive in Tanzania gets rid of the hassle of arranging everything when you arrive**. It depends what kind of package you have booked, of course, but few tour companies will sell you a climb up Kilimanjaro and nothing more. Nearly all will include such things as: airport pick-up and drop-off at the start/end of your trip; accommodation in Arusha, Moshi or Marangu for before and after your trek; sightseeing trips; transport to and from the mountain; and maybe even the odd safari or Zanzibar excursion. Pay them some more and maybe they'll even throw in the flights and insurance and sort out your visas too. With no need to arrange these things yourself, booking from home will save you a considerable amount of time. It also ensures you know exactly when you'll be walking, rather than having to hang around for a few days as you may have to if you wait until you've arrived in Tanzania before organising your trek. Booking in advance of your arrival in Tanzania also means you can plan your trek more precisely months in advance, and ask your agent any questions you may have well before you even arrive in Tanzania.

However, **waiting until you've arrived in Tanzania to book your trek has its advantages too**. You may be able to get your trek cheaper for a start, as you can negotiate face to face. If you've brought dollars in cash then you can avoid the hefty (4-5%) credit card fee or the charge for making a bank transfer. There are other advantages too. If you ask, there should be no reason why you cannot meet the guides and porters before you agree to sign up – and even your fellow trekkers, all of whom have a huge role to play in making your trek an enjoyable one. You can also personally check the tents and camping equipment before booking. Furthermore, the fact that you can book a trek the day before you start (though see the note on p64) gives you greater flexibility, allowing you to alter your plans so that you can pick a day that suits you; whereas when booking with an agency at home you often have to book months in advance, the tour is usually organised to a pretty tight schedule and altering this schedule at a later date may be difficult or even impossible. Another point: while the money you spend on a trek may not be going to the most destitute and deserving of Tanzania's population, at least you know that *all* of it is going to Tanzanians, with little, if any, going into the pockets of a Western company.

you chose a decent company, one with a decent medical kit and excellent evacuation procedures. Unfortunately, the person evacuated may not appreciate what their company has done and may be a bit grumpy that they failed to make the summit. As a result, they'll be less likely to review the company positively, even though in reality they may have saved his or her life. Whereas the person who went to the summit with the bad operator may write a glowing review, not realising that if the situation had been reversed and they, too, had needed to be evacuated, their company may have killed them through incompetence and ignorance. Result: good company gets an average review, bad company gets a positive one.

Trusting the review websites
But as well as casting doubt on the usefulness of the reviews, we're also a little sceptical about how much one can rely on the review websites that host these reviews.

How to book your trek after you've arrived in Tanzania
The best place to look for an agency is either **Arusha**, which has the greatest number of tour and trekking operators, or **Moshi**. A third option, **Marangu**, has a few agencies and only one that we recommend (though it is a good one). Agencies in Dar es Salaam and other Tanzanian towns are usually nothing more than middlemen for the operators in Moshi, Arusha or Marangu: book a tour with an agency in Dar, for example, and the chances are you'll still end up on a trek organised by an agency in Moshi or Arusha, only you would have paid more for it. Furthermore, if you book outside of Arusha or Moshi, you have less chance of inspecting the equipment or meeting your guide before you set off.

The difference between Arusha and Moshi
In general the former is the home of the more established and larger safari companies/trekking agencies. However, perhaps due to its location, the Arusha-based companies tend to concentrate just as much on safaris in the Serengeti, Ngorongoro and Arusha National Park (including climbs up Meru) as they do on treks up Kilimanjaro. Indeed, some just act as middlemen for one of the agencies in Moshi and don't actually arrange Kili treks themselves. Moshi, on the other hand, is a smaller place and one where the agencies tend to focus more on climbing Kilimanjaro than on safaris. It would also be fair to say that the Moshi-based companies tend to be a little cheaper than those in Arusha, and most budget operators have their offices in Moshi. What's more, Moshi is a more convenient place to shop for a trek, given its smaller size and the fact that many of the agents have offices either in the town centre or within walking distance of it. Moshi also has the two biggest and best equipment rental stores for those who need to hire something for their trek.

Reading the above, therefore, it would seem that you should base yourself in Moshi rather than Arusha if you are in the market for a budget trek. And it's true that Moshi captures the lion's share of the Kilimanjaro-trekking business, and some of the trekking companies in this town do a roaring trade. But beware: there is still a fair bit of monkey business going on here too, and you do need to be on your guard against cheetahs.

Before booking with any company, read the general advice given on pp60-2 about dealing with the trekking companies. Note, too, that often agencies lower their costs by hitting the wages of the crew; please, if you are going to book with one of these agencies, at the very least increase the amount in tips you pay your crew to compensate for their lower pay. *(continued overleaf)*

BOOKING YOUR TRIP

Our suspicions were initially raised when we noticed that the companies that rank highly on all of these websites are rarely the ones that feature prominently on the mountain. In other words, if you were to believe these review websites *and nothing else*, then the companies with the highest number of five-star reviews or which are at the top of their rankings should be the best operators on Kilimanjaro. The reality, alas, is that they are often anything but. Because in our experience many of these highly ranked and well-reviewed operators often don't run that many treks, and we rarely see them on the mountain; seldom have a lengthy history or experience of climbing Kilimanjaro; are rarely members of KPAP; and are not, as far as we can tell, doing anything outstanding for their customers. Indeed, often the first and only time we've heard of them is when they appear on these websites!

How can this be? Well, some websites charge the companies that advertise on them, and the companies have to pay more if they wish to feature more prominently. In other words, on some websites greater prominence is not given to the 'best' companies, but merely those that pay the most. But we also know it to be true that some operators are just better at publicising themselves online and using the web to their advantage. These agencies, if they know their clients have had a successful trek, will push them to write a review on one of the websites almost as soon as they come off the mountain. In light of this, don't make the mistake

---

❏ BOOKING YOUR TREK AFTER YOU'VE ARRIVED IN TANZANIA

Dealing with a Tanzanian agency (*continued from p67*)

Wherever you decide to shop for your trek, the golden rule when shopping around is: **stick to agencies that have a TALA licence for trekking** and check that licence thoroughly to ensure it covers trekking. If they don't have a licence, or the one they show you looks a bit suspect, or is out of date, take your business elsewhere.

Other advice includes:

● Decide **what sort of trek** you want, **what route** you wish to take, **how long** you wish to go for, and **with how many people**.

● **Ask other travellers** for their recommendations of a good agency.

● **Contact us** via our website to find out our latest recommendations.

● **Shop around**. Don't sign up with the first agent you talk to but consult other agencies first to compare.

● Read the section on p61 on **what should be included in your trek package** and learn it off by heart (or take this book with you!) so you know what to ask the agency.

● Ask about the **number of people** on your trek and the **number of porters** you'll be taking with you.

● Ask if you can see their **'comments book'**. This is a book where previous clients have written their thoughts on the agency. Some agencies will have one (though it's fair to say in the internet age they are becoming less common, with people often emailing their comments instead; the rule is the same, however: ask to see them!); and if they are any good they will show it to you with little or no prompting. Ask if you can speak with someone who's climbed with them recently, too – this is often an enormous help.

● If you have any **dietary requirements** or other **special needs**, ask them if these will be a problem, if it will cost any more, and how exactly they propose to comply with your requirements. For example, if you are a vegetarian, ask the agent what kind of meals you can expect to receive on the trek.

of thinking that the company with the most 5-star ratings is automatically the best one; all it really means is that they are the best at getting their happy clients to write reviews. Similarly, those that feature at the top of search-engine rankings (Google etc) are there not because they run the best treks; it simply means they are the best at getting themselves to the top of the search engines.

We have also received a couple of emails from people who had had a pretty poor trek but were then offered significant bribes (amounting to several hundred dollars) *not* to write a bad review online. These people refused and decided instead to publicise as much as possible their whole sorry experience, which included writing to us. But does this mean that there are dozens of people who *did take* a bribe and as a consequence never wrote about their experience? We've also heard of at least one instance where a negative review mysteriously disappeared from a website. Neither we nor the reviewer have any idea why this would happen, but it does somewhat make a mockery of the whole system if only positive reviews are allowed, particularly if, as we suspect, complaints from a company about a negative review resulted in its removal.

Using multiple sources
Please understand, we are not saying that you should believe our reviews and nobody else's. After all, as mentioned earlier, we have not climbed with many

---

● Ask to see a print-out of the **day-to-day itinerary** (though some, admittedly, will not have this, all agencies should be able to describe the trekking routes and their itineraries without any problem); if you're negotiating with an agency at the upper end of the market, you may even be able to get a preview of the daily menus.

● If you think you've found a good company, ask to see the **equipment** you will be using and make sure the tent is complete, untorn and that all the zips work.

● Check the **sleeping arrangements**, particularly if you're not trekking with friends but have joined a group: are you going to have a tent to yourself, or are you going to be sharing with somebody you've never met before?

● If you are **alone and on a budget**, ask if it is possible to be put with a group, which should make things cheaper. (This is normally done automatically anyway; indeed, if you are travelling alone and were quoted a very low price, you can expect to be put with another group.)

Following on from the last point, many of the operators at the budget end often band together to lump all their customers into one large trekking group, thereby making it cheaper for them as certain fixed costs can be shared. So don't be surprised if, having signed up with one company, you end up being joined by trekkers who booked with another company. Once again, make sure you know about any arrangements like this *before* you sign anything or hand over any money. And if you want to be on your own, tell them.

Finding that you don't have your own tent but have to share with a stranger is just one of the potential hazards of booking with a budget company. Or rather, it's one of the advantages of paying a bit more and going with a company that won't spring any nasty surprises on you. Sign up with a more expensive company and you should also find that they have better safety procedures and emergency equipment and more knowledgeable guides. So unless money is really tight don't look for the cheapest company but the *best-value* one; hopefully our reviews will help you to decide which agencies offer the best deals.

BOOKING YOUR TRIP

of the agencies we review, unlike nearly everyone who posts online reviews. Given the diktats of limited funds and tight publishing deadlines, we've done as much research as we can; in many cases we've seen the companies operate on the mountain, and we've asked KPAP and other bodies to find out what they know about the company. But we don't for one minute pretend that we are omniscient. Besides, this book was researched in 2017 and the situation does change; though we try to minimise this problem by offering to give you, free of charge, the latest information we have if you write to us (📧 henry@climbmount kilimanjaro.com).

In summary, we think you should look on this chapter as just a useful tool, one of several in your toolbox that you should utilise when deciding on which company to choose; one that can then be supplemented by looking online or asking friends. And hopefully by doing so you'll end up with the company that's right for you; because that is what we all want.

HOW WE RESEARCHED THIS SECTION

As with the previous editions we once again did as much of our research as possible anonymously. In other words, the companies we contacted thought we were just regular punters and had no idea we were researching the next edition of the book. Having first checked out each company's website, the next step was to email them in order to find out a bit more about the service they could provide and what they would charge for it. To do this we invented a fictional family of four (see below), set up an email address for them, and then sent a standard email to each trekking agency. Our research didn't stop there, however. We also asked trekkers we met on Kilimanjaro or in Arusha/Moshi of their experiences; consulted all the letters and emails from climbers that we'd received, in which recommendations and complaints about agencies often featured; and finally, we talked with KPAP (see box pp26-9) to find out how well or badly each company treated and paid their staff on the mountain.

Please bear in mind that **the reviews are our opinions only**. Remember, too, that things change very quickly in this part of the world, so some of the following will inevitably have altered by the time you begin your research. **For the latest advice and information please do not hesitate to get in touch via email** (📧 **henry@climbmountkilimanjaro.com**) and we'll be happy to oblige; and if you have any advice, comments, praise or criticisms about any of the agencies, again, please contact us – we are always delighted to receive them.

How to read the table

In the table the **companies are listed in price order**, with the cheapest first. The price is for a seven-day Machame trek for 4 people, and was given to us by the companies in response to an anonymous email we sent to them in which we pretended to be a family of two adults and two children, with one child 17 years old and one aged 14. Note that sometimes a company would give us a range of prices depending on the standard of the trek; if this was the case then we give all the prices they gave us, and you can read about the differences between these standards in the company's review. Sometimes, a company doesn't actually deal

with the public directly but only through agents. When this is the case, we quote the price provided by one of the company's main agencies – and mark it as such with an asterisk. We note which agent we contacted in the notes below the table.

In two cases – take a bow, African Walking Company and Real Life Adventure Travel – these companies no longer run Machame Route treks so what we have given is a price they charge on another route, and positioned them in the table at a place where we think they would go if they did run treks on Machame.

We also asked all the companies several other questions which form the basis of the other columns in the box:

● **Location** This is where their main office is located. **M** is for Moshi, **A** for Arusha; there are also a few companies that are based in Marangu, Nairobi and elsewhere; we have noted them too. Note that if the company's office is in the centre of town, and thus easy to visit, we have also given their full address in their review. They are also marked on the relevant town plans.

● **Airport transfers** If airport transfers are included in the price then you'll see a tick in this column; if they aren't then the price the company charges for them is noted here too.

● **Accommodation** This column displays the hotel where you'll be staying before and after the hike as part of the overall trek package. If no accommodation is included, then this is denoted by an 'N'. With most/all companies, you can choose to pay a little more and stay in a better class of hotel if you are unhappy with the one in the package.

● **Child discount** This column is worth paying attention to even if you don't have children. Because in many ways, it can be seen as a measure of a company's honesty. If a trekker is under 16, they are entitled to a significant discount off the park fees that, for a seven-day Machame trek, amounts to US$696.20. We admit that it is difficult to calculate this amount exactly, especially with the introduction of 18% VAT in 2016. Nevertheless, there is no reason why any company can't pass this discount on in full to the customer. So if the company offers only a discount of, for example, US$250, then you know that they are making a profit of US$446.20 by not passing on this discount in full. Interestingly, some companies, perhaps desperate for the custom, or who couldn't work out the correct figure, actually offered considerably more than the park fee reduction as a discount! We have noted the amount each company offered as a discount in this column. If there are two amounts, the second figure is what was offered to us *after* we'd complained (again anonymously) that the initial amount (the first figure) was too low.

● **KPAP** This column shows which companies are partners of KPAP, the body that looks after the welfare of porters. If you care about the crew that is going to take you up the mountain then pick a KPAP partner company; see p61.

● **Oxygen** We asked each company if emergency oxygen is included as part of your trek (as we think it should be). A tick means that it is included; if a company does not include it as part of their standard package, then the amount that they charge to have it included is noted in the box.

● **Western Breach** Many companies refuse to work on the Western Breach anymore because, they say, it is too dangerous because of rockfalls. In this column we show those companies that are still willing to take climbers on this route.

TANZANIAN TREKKING AGENCIES TABLE – BY PRICE

Trekking Company Name	Location	Airport Transfers Included	Usual Accommodation	Machame Price (US$)	Child Discount (US$)	KPAP	Oxygen Provided	Western Breach	More Info
Mega Adventures	M	$40 p/v o/w	✗	$1430	$680			✓	p91
Bobby Tours	A	✓	Impala	$1450	$725			✓	p78
Kessy Brothers	M	✓	Sal Salinero	$1465	$642			✓	p86
High Peaks Expeditions	A	✓	Sal Salinero	$1485	$681			✓	p85
MEM Tours	M	✓	Parkview Inn, Bristol Cottages, Leopard Hotel, Sal Salinero ($1400-1700/1600-2100)	$1500-1800	$180		$50	✓	p92
Tanzania Joy	M	✓	Keys	$1500	$400		$70	✓	p98
Homeland	M	✓	Keys	$1580	$316		✓	✓	p85
Maua Adventures	M	✓	Parkview Inn	$1600	$500		✓	✓	p91
dotcom safaris	M	✓	Bristol Cottages	$1600	$700		✓	✓	p80
Trans-Kibo Travels	M	✓	YMCA	$1600	$500		✓	✓	p99
Lava Peaks	M	✓	Altezza Lodge	$1650	$470		$80	✓	p88
Viva Africa	M	✓	Rafiki/Honey Badger	$1655	$650		$50pp	✓	p101
Team Maasai	A	$50 p/v o/w	✗	$1683	$590		$5 per day	✓	p99
Kilimanjaro Heroes Adventures	A&M	✓	Parkview Inn	$1700	$850		✓	✓	p88
Hot Sun	M	✓	Buffalo	$1700	$150/$250		✓	✓	p85
Top Climbers	M	✓	Kili Wonders	$1700	$750		✓	✓	p101
African Spoonbill Tours	M	✓	Keys	$1700	$1000		✓	✓	p75
Popote Africa	M	✓	Parkview Inn, Kili Wonders	$1700	$390		✓	✓	p93
Shidolya	A	$50 p/v	✗	$1725	$440		✓	✓	p96
Sunny Safaris	A	✓	Venus Hotel	$1730	$530		$150	✓	p97
Tro Peaks	M	✓	Panama Garden Resort	$1745	$490		✓	✓	p101
Kilimanjaro Vikings	M	✓	Parkview Inn	$1750	$300		✓	✓	p88
Gladys Adventure	M	✓	Aa, Leopard, Sal Salinero, Kili Wonders	$1755/1845 $1905/2070	$742	✓	✓	✓	p84
Materuni	M	$35 o/w	✗	$1765	$700		$150	✗	p90
Gazelle Adventures	M	✓	Stella Maris	$1779	$165-709		✓	✗	p84

Company	Base	Transfer	Accommodation	Price	Deposit	Hotel	Rev.	Page
Snow Cap Tanzania Tours	Rongai & M	✓	Leopard/Snowcap	$1780	$330/$450	✓	✓	p96
Bryson Adventures	M	✓	Bristol Cottages	$1785	$245/$700	✓	✓	p78
Enosa	M	✓	Kili Wonders, H' Badger, Parkview Altezza	$1800	$700	✓	✓	p82
Milestone Safaris	M	✓	Honey Badger Lodge	$1834	$630	✓	✓	p92
Meru Slopes Tours	A	✓	Arha Tourist Inn	$1850	$300	✓	✓	p91
Kili Treks (1)	A	✓	Outpost	$1855	$655	$50	✓	p87
Tin Tin Tours	M	✓	Nyota B&B	$1875	$675	✓	✓	p99
Shah Tours	M	$80 o/w	Mountain Inn	$1880	$350	$150	✓	p96
Keys	M	✓	Keys	$1922	$567	$140	✓	p86
African Scenic Safaris	M	✗		$1950	$600	✓	✓	p75
Origin Trails	M	✓	Ameg Lodge	$1951	$702	✓	✓	p93
Chagga Tours/Kindoroko	M	✓	Keys, Weru Weru & Kindoroko	$1995/2120/2610	$696.20	$75	✓	p78
Altezza	M	✓	Aishi, Altezza Lodge	$2008	$350	✓	✗	p77
Pristine Trails	M	✓	Leopard/Urban Hostel	$2015/2215/2415	$371	$90	✓	p94
Tanzania Travel Company	A	✓	Tulia	$2025	$686	✓	✓	p98
Nyange Adventures	M & A	✓	Secret Garden	$2050	$550	✓	✓	p92
Kibo Slopes	A & Nairobi	✓	Aishi (1 night)	$2050	$410	✓	✓	p87
Ahsante	M	✓	Weru Weru	$2060	$1160	✓	✓	p77
Zara Tours	M	$20pp o/w	Springlands	$2063	$619	$14pd	✗	p101
Kwetu	A	✓	Outpost	$2084	$847	✓	✓	p88
Easy Travel & Tours	A	✓	Planet Lodge, Karama	$2112	$350	$250	✗	p82
African Zoom Adventure Tours	A	✓	Outpost	$2170	$774	✓	✓	p76
Roy Safaris	A	$85 p/v o/w	✗	$2190	$519	✓	✗	p95
Kili Climb Outfitters	A	$50pp o/w	Kibo Palace	$2230	$180	✓	✓	p87
It Started in Africa	A	✗	✗	$2240	$1120	✓	✓	p85
Tanzania Journeys	M	✓ (from Nairobi too)	Bristol Cottages	$2275/2800	$650	$30pp	✓	p98
Majestic Kilimanjaro	A	✓	Outpost	$2296	$696	✓	✓	p90
Marangu Hotel	Marangu	$85 o/w	✗	$2318	$696	$100 + $36 pd	✓	p90
Kili Treks (2)	M	✓	Kili Wonders	$2370	$500	✓	✓	p87
Climb Kili	A	✓	Summit Safari Lodge	$2375	None	✓	✓	p78

KEY p/v = per vehicle   o/w = one way   pp = per person   pd = per day

TREKKING COMPANY NAME	LOCATION	AIRPORT TRANSFERS INCLUDED	USUAL ACCOMMODATION	MACHAME PRICE (US$)	CHILD DISCOUNT (US$)	KPAP	OXYGEN PROVIDED	WESTERN BREACH	MORE INFO
Duma Explorer	A	$65 o/w	✗	$2399	$530	✓	✓	✗	p80
Kilimanjaro Brothers	M	✓	Parkview Inn	$2400	$500		✓	✓	p88
Team Kilimanjaro	A	✓	Outpost	$2414 ($1803/2235) $696			✓	✓	p99
Big Expeditions	A	✓	Planet Lodge	$2445	$350	✓	✓	✓	p77
Maasai Wanderings	A	$90 o/w	✗	$2460	$300/540		$75	✗	p89
Udare	A	✓	Outpost	$2468	$649	✓	✓	✓	p101
Fair Travel Tanzania	A	✓	Ilboru Lodge/Stella Maris	$2475 inc tips	$744	✓	✓	✓	p82
Detasa	A	✓	3 nights Ilboru	$2500	$250/750		✓	✓	p79
East African Voyage	A	$100 o/w	✗	$2525	$465	✓	✓	✗	p81
Good Earth	A	✓	Planet Lodge	$2525	$420	✓	✓	✓	p84
Serengeti Pride Safaris	A	✓	Planet Lodge	$2530	$696	✓	$50	✓	p96
Trek2Kili	M	✓	Bristol Cottages	$2550	$1275	✓	✓	✓	p100
Tanzania Experience	A	✓	Sal Salinero	$2565	$740		$58pd	✗	p98
Kibo Expeditions	A	✓	Ilboru/Mount Meru Hotel	$2595/3995/4995/5695	$530	✓	✓	✓	p86
Everlasting	A	✓	African Tulip	$2650	$650	✓	✓	✗	p82
TDMC	M/UK	✓	Stella Maris	$2795 *	$700	✓	✓	✗	p98
Kili Zone	A	✓	3 nights Kaliwa Lodge	$2945 **	$475	✓	✓	✗	p87
African Walking Company	A	$87.50 o/w	Moivaro	(7-day Rongai trek $3048)†	$696	✓	✓	✗	p76
Real Life Adventure Travel		✓	Bristol Cottages/Parkview	(8-day Lemosho trek $3400)†	$180/600	✓	$230	✓	p94
Dik Dik	Usa River near A	✓	3 nights at Dik Dik	$3195	$400	✓	$50	✓	p79
Barking Zebra	A	✓	3 nights at Planet Lodge	$3330	$477	✓	✓	✗	p77
Nature Discovery	A	$110 o/w	3 nights at Planet Lodge	$3475 ($2697/2071) $695	$650	✓	✓	✓	p92
Africa VIP Travel	A	✓	3 nights Ilboru/Planet Lodge	$3493	$650	✓	✓	✓	p75
Summit Expeditions &... (SENE)	M	✓	Mbahe in Marangu	$3565	$700	✓	✓	✗	p97
Summits Africa	A	✓	✗	$3595/4153/4420§	$696	✓	✓	✓	p97
Peak East Africa/Intrepid Guerba	M	$130 o/w	Kibo Hotel	$3885	$300	✓	✓	✗	p93
Tusker/Tembo Trails	M	$110 o/w	3 nights at Parkview Inn/Bristol Cottages	$3970	$0/560	✓	✓	✗	p100
Abercrombie & Kent	A	$110 o/w	Arusha Coffee Lodge or Lake Duluti Serena	GB£4368	GB£490	✓	✓	✓	p75
African Environments	A	✓	✗	$6226	$2042	✓	✓	✓	p75

THESE QUOTES SUPPLIED BY AGENTS: *Kandoo (see p106) ** Bush 2 Beach (p87) *Kandoo (see p105) †Embark (p109) ¶Africa Travel Resource (p105) §Aardvark Safaris (p104)

TREKKING AGENCIES IN TANZANIA

Abercrombie & Kent (see UK agencies, p104; **A**) Ground operator of UK-based agency. KPAP partners, with oxygen, airport transfers and accommodation at Lake Duluti Serena included. Prices are in sterling; their current rates for Machame put them close to the top of the list, price-wise, at £4,368pp (over US$5800 using the current exchange rate) with under-16 discount of £490/US$658 (though we had to push them before they gave us this).

● **Summary** The latest foreign tour operator to set up its own trekking operator for Kilimanjaro: safe, reliable and expensive, with treks as luxurious as the mountain allows.

African Scenic Safaris (ASS) (☎ 0783-080 239, 🖳 africanscenicsafaris.com; contact Hostel Hoff, see p243; **M**) Run by the same Australian-Tanzanian couple who operate the highly regarded Hostel Hoff in Moshi, ASS have done pretty brisk business over the past few years thanks to a simple winning formula of keeping their prices low (Machame Route US$1950pp for four people, though oxygen, airport transfers and pre-/post-trek accommodation are all extra) and ethical standards high. They are also KPAP partners. Our only criticisms are that they charge US$140 for a tank of oxygen on each trek (we think it should be compulsory on every trek and included in the price); and their discount for under 16s was US$600 rather than the full US$696. But these are minor quibbles for their treks are well regarded with some extensive and effusive reviews from readers and online.

● **Summary** A likeable bunch doing good work both for their clients and their mountain crew. Perfect for volunteers but also for anyone looking for a reasonable trek that doesn't exploit the mountain crew.

African Spoonbill Tours (☎ 0713-408291, 🖳 africanspoonbilltours.com; Boma Rd, Umpide St, **M**) First, the good points: they were the first to reply to our emails for both this edition and the last one. The price is very reasonable, too, at

US$1700, with the under-16 discount a jaw-dropping US$1000. Bad points? You can't offer such low prices and a high-spec trek (with oxygen, airport transfers and accommodation at Moshi's Keys Hotel) and still pay your porters US$15 per day, as they claim. You just can't. Reviews are also variable, and their reply to our email seemed to be a fairly standard 'template' that they probably send to all their correspondents, and thus didn't address many of the questions we set.

● **Summary** Hard – actually, make that virtually impossible – to believe their claims; we think there are better and more trustworthy agencies in the same price bracket.

Africa VIP Travel (☎ 0732-971 775, 0784 510422; 🖳 africaviptravel.com; **A**) Fairly small company with few treks, though response to our email was considerate and comprehensive and showed a reassuring degree of knowledge. Also include some nice touches in their Kili package, including a pre-trek trip to Arusha National Park, a Gamow bag for Kili and the offer of a day room for your last day in Tanzania before your flight home. Price also includes *three* nights at lovely Ilboru Lodge, and they're also KPAP partners. Given these extras, their rather exorbitant price of US$3493pp seems less unreasonable.

● **Summary** Difficult to judge as organise few treks; rivals in this luxury price bracket are busier and better known so will doubtless get the majority of the market – but we can't see anything wrong with these people.

African Environments (☎ 0784-700 100; 🖳 africanenvironments.com; **A**) Established in 1987, African Environments (AE) are the only company with no Tanzanian ownership (they were founded before this became mandatory). They're a top-of-the-range operator with a history on Kili that's both lengthy and impressive. They were instrumental in pioneering the Lemosho Route, for example (though annoyingly they call it the Shira Route), and remain the No1 specialists on the Western Breach. They were also the first to

equip *all* their expeditions with WFR-trained guides and Gamow hyperbaric bags. Rarely take bookings direct but will arrange a private trek if requested; otherwise, contact one of their agents such as Mountain Madness p111, Wilderness Travel p112 and Mountain Travel Sobek p111. Continuing their trailblazing, they now offer their clients a night or two at their acclimatisation camp on the slopes of Meru before their Shira/Western Breach climbs. Prices are as steep as the mountain itself ($6226pp *excluding* pre- and post-trek accommodation!) though thankfully some of that money filters down to their mountain staff, for they pay some of the best wages on Kili and they are KPAP partners. Child discount was also the highest at US$2042. Criticisms? Well, their responses to our emails were tardy and incomplete – but otherwise you're in very safe hands.

● **Summary** There's no doubting the excellence of their treks but you're better off going via one of their agents if you want prompt attention and/or to join a group trek.

African Walking Company (A) No website or email contact but still one of the biggest operators on the mountain and a favourite with overseas agencies (Africa Travel Resource, Exodus and Gane & Marshall to name but three). They have been through a bit of a dip recently, during which time they stopped being KPAP partners, but they seem to be storming back

(and it is believed that they have approached KPAP again with a view to being partners once more). Specialists on the Shira Route – about which we're not 100 per cent convinced as you miss out on the forest on the ascent – but which, to be fair, does have a high success rate. They are also the first company to have not one but *two* female guides, and are also the first we know about to offer neither the Machame nor the Marangu routes because of these trails' over-popularity.

● **Summary** Uncompromising, reliable and experienced, they don't take bookings directly but only through their agents. Note they are one of only two companies not to offer the Machame Route so their position in the table is a rough estimate of what they would charge based on the prices they set for other routes (their seven-day Rongai Route trek, for example, booked through Africa Travel Resource, was US$3048pp). If you want oxygen to help you climb to the top (as opposed to just have it with you on the trek in case of emergencies) then AWC agency African Travel Resource (see p76) offer this.

African Zoom Adventure Tours (☎ 0732-972218; 🖳 africanzoom.com; A) Small company but one that's experienced, pleasant and polite. Don't do a huge amount of business but there's a lot to like: wholly Tanzanian-owned, KPAP partners, WFR-trained guides and very fair prices of

---

❏ **Best for big groups**
Some companies have developed a reputation over the years for being able to handle large groups of trekkers with aplomb. One such company is **Ahsante** (see p77), thanks in large part to the sizeable groups that get sent over regularly from their European and North American agents. They also have the infrastructure to deal with these big groups. **African Walking Company** (see p76), **Summits Africa** (p97) and **Nature Discovery** (p92), too, seem very adept at handling groups both big and small. There is also **Everlasting Tanzania Travels** (p82) whose business has really suffered following the tragic death of Irishman Ian McKeever, who would bring large groups with him from his native land. Big groups have dried up and the days when Everlasting took 119 people up – believed to be the largest single group ever to attempt the climb, with 117 making it to the top – are just memories now. Nevertheless, the infrastructure is still there, as is the expertise, and they still hold onto their status as KPAP partners; all that's required now is a foreign agent to come along and believe in them again.

US$2170pp, with the under-16 park fee discount given US$774 – more than the expected US$696.20. Only (slight) hesitation is that they've just won a large contract with a big Irish agency – so it will be interesting to see how they'll cope and whether the quality of their other treks will suffer.

● **Summary** Again not many treks so not easy to judge them, but they're certainly fairly priced and worth contacting for those seeking a trek at the lower end of the midrange price spectrum.

Ahsante Tours (☎ 027-2750248; 🖳 ahsantetours.com; Plot 29-A Karanga Drive, **M**) No longer the rock-bottom cheapest but still a reliable operator, their extensive list of overseas agencies that work with them proving their dependability. They were the first company I ever climbed with back in 2001, though they've grown considerably since, with the plush Weru Weru River Lodge part of their portfolio now too. Boss Cuthbert Swai is still something of a Kili obsessive – I've seen pictures of him climbing with his elderly dad, and read newspaper articles about him climbing to the summit with his ten-year-old daughter too. They remain a very good value option, with a good service, excellent guides and many happy customers. Pricewise they hover between budget and midrange, with seven days on Machame US$2060pp including two nights at lovely Weru Weru, with the under-16 discount a whopping US$1160!

● **Summary** One of the better value operators on the mountain, reliable, experienced and decent.

Altezza (☎ 0786-350115, 🖳 altezza.travel; Lema Road, Shanty Town, **M**) Relatively new but already one of the biggest and most popular companies currently operating on Kili. Their website tells you why: it's all in Cyrillic, and the vast majority of their clients are Russians. That said, if you write to them for a quote they will respond (in English) and they're pretty good value at US$2008pp (though under 16s are given only a US$350 discount). Their climb is of a pretty high spec and praised frequently on the internet, with

WFR-trained guides and accommodation at Aishi Machame, near Machame gate, and at their own hotel (see p250) all included.

● **Summary** Quite good, honest and very fairly priced – but unless you're a Russian speaker, there's no real reason to go with them.

Barking Zebra (US ☎ 1-619-213-9712, Tanzania ☎ 0686-760-495, 🖳 barkingzebratours.com; **USA & A**) Few direct bookings as far as we can tell but instead gets most of its business from top US agency RMI Expeditions. Soon to become a KPAP member, we hear, and there's some good points including WFR-trained guides, oxygen and three nights at lovely Planet Lodge. A few concerns: firstly, they have very few treks so reviews are hard to come by. Secondly, they offered only US$477 for the under-16 discount rather than the full US$696; to be honest, I believe this was a mistake rather than anything more mendacious, but it's further evidence of how 'unbusy' they are that they didn't know the correct figure off by heart. And thirdly, if you're going to charge as much as they do (US$3330pp) then you need to tick pretty much every box – and, for the moment, at least, until they get busier, they don't.

● **Summary** Their prices are too high but otherwise they are a fine company with high standards and decent people by all accounts; hopefully by the next edition they'll be much busier and we'll be able to provide a more positive assessment.

Big Expeditions (☎ 0754-203 301, 027-254 8449; 🖳 bigexpeditions.net; Shule Rd, nr Exim Bank, **A**) Around since 2002 but only now grabbing a decent share of the Kili market thanks in large part to their adoption by US outfit Alpine Ascents. Itineraries seem fairly standard but they do try to make themselves slightly different by hosting the best post-trek celebrations of any company at the end of each trek, with a buffet lunch set up on trestle tables at Mweka Gate and musicians, singers and a man in drag leading the dancing. Prices are neither outstandingly cheap nor extortionate at US$2445pp. A couple of gripes: the

child discount of US$350 was only half of what we expected, and they were one of the worst at responding to our emails.

● **Summary** KPAP partners and they have a lot of clients, though we get the feeling they are too occupied with their agency treks to care much about taking individual bookings directly.

Bobby Tours (☎ 0786-110786; 💻 bobby-tours.com; Goliondoi Rd, **A**) Established way back in 1976, very slick and professional company with a whole fleet of 4WDs and the smartest offices on Goliondoi. Kili not their primary focus (they're more renowned for their safaris) but they are surprisingly cheap; indeed, it may be worth asking them how they can be so cheap, where they make their savings and how much they pay their crew. (When we pushed them on this subject they rather unsubtly avoided the subject: "Question: Are you members of KPAP and how much do you pay your porters? Answer: "Our company is 40 years old".) Prices are a very cheap US$1450 per person for four people for seven days on Machame, with under 16s half price (!), a price that includes oxygen on the trek, two nights at Impala and airport transfers.

● **Summary** You have to ask how they can be so cheap and yet still pay their staff a living wage; reviews are decidedly mixed too, with enough negative ones to suggest that you'd be better looking elsewhere.

Bryson Adventures (aka Bryson Heroes; ☎ 0754-318033, 027-275 3154; 💻 brysonheroestours.com; Room 29, NSSF Building, Aga Khan St, **M**) One of the myriad of smallish agencies in the centre of Moshi. Initial contact was impressive and their email was polite, informative and well organised. Prices good too, at US$1785pp including two nights at Moshi's Bristol Cottages (see p248), airport transfers and oxygen. Only caveat is that the discount they offered for under-16s was a paltry US$245 – though when we challenged them on this they then offered us a much more respectable and accurate US$700 off the full price. Reviews we've seen are few and fairly old – though pretty much all positive.

● **Summary** Cheap outfit, not spectacular but not bad. Get the feeling you can bargain with them over the price – though make sure any discount you get doesn't come out of the porters' wages.

Chagga Tours (☎ 0785-482251; 💻 kindorokohotels.com; **M**) No-nonsense, upfront company with links to Moshi's Kindoroko Hotel that offers three different standards of treks: All-Inclusive, McClimb and Reinhold Messner. With the all-inclusive the tips are included, as is a toilet tent on the mountain and you get three nights of pre- and post-trek accommodation at Weru Weru; for the other two you get just two nights at Keys Hotel or Kindoroko, there's no toilet tent and you have to pay the tips yourself. Prices are US$1995/2120/2610pp for Messner, McClimb and All-Inclusive respectively – plus US$75 for oxygen. Curiously, they were pretty much the only ones to offer the exact child discount (down to the nearest cent), which was refreshing.

● **Summary** They make no pretensions to being particularly ethical and reviews are rare and tend to be a little dated; but they seem honest and their prices fair.

Climb Kili (☎ 0754-448 2676, 💻 climbkili.com; **A**) Experienced outfitter with many reviews from happy clients and their own agents in both the UK and America. But we have to say we aren't 100% won over by them. They make big claims on their website about being an ethical company, but when we asked why they weren't with KPAP they proceeded instead to slander them, stating (falsely) that KPAP's boss had been deported (she hasn't been), that the partnership scheme list is out-of-date (it isn't), that KPAP indulges in unethical practices (they don't) and charges people to appear on their website (they don't). To cap it all, when we pressed them on any child discount they could offer us, they wrote that '...the national parks charges the same price for 14 year olds so we offer the same price.' Which again is clearly wrong. True, this may all be down to misunderstandings, misinformation or sheer ignorance rather than anything more malicious – but it leaves a nasty taste in the

❏ Companies with female guides

They're almost as rare as rhinos on Kili, but there are, according to estimates, around half a dozen female guides working on the mountain. Finding out which companies they work for, however, is not easy. From my research I know that **Kili Zone** (see p87) definitely has one female guide, as does **East African Voyage** (p81) and there are two female guides who work for **African Walking Company** (p76).

However, we've now heard of **Pink Safaris** (🖳 pinksafaris.com), the female-guide specialists formerly known as Wilderness with a Woman, which were set up by Glory Thobias, a guide who used to work with top outfitter Nature Discovery. They are still a very small company and you have to dig around the internet a bit to find them, but they are certainly unique and their aims laudable; as they say on their website, they want to 'inspire girls to embrace the tour guide profession' so that they can 'break the barriers of traditions'. Do note that at the time of writing they were struggling for business and did not currently have a TALA licence.

We should also mention the budget Moshi operator **Nyange Adventures** (see p92) who started an NGO a couple of years ago to support females porters (of which there are about 30 working on Kili) in their efforts to become mountain guides. So far they haven't managed to get any licensed – the process of becoming a guide is a lengthy one (see p31) and happens only once every few years – but we'll keep you updated via the website when we hear of any who have graduated through this scheme.

Other than the above companies, we are not sure which other operators, if any, can boast a female guide in their ranks. Given the working conditions on Kili – the lack of privacy, the overcrowded sleeping quarters, the minimal chances to wash properly and the testosterone-wracked macho environment that pervades most expeditions – you can see why most local women wouldn't dream of working on Africa's highest mountain. But as Glory Thobias would no doubt argue, and it needs to be emphasised again here, women guides are just as capable as men when it comes to leading groups on the mountain.

---

mouth nevertheless. Price-wise they charge US$2375pp with accommodation at the obscure Summit Safari Lodge included, and all their guides are WFR-trained and their treks are, by all accounts, pretty good. Note that only the Machame and Lemosho routes are advertised on their website.

● **Summary** Popular and successful but our correspondence leaves us far from convinced.

Destination Tanzania Safaris (aka Detasa; ☎ 0754-669 086; 🖳 detasa.com; **A**) Medium-sized operator founded by two brothers that claim to specialise in Lemosho/Western Breach (though they annoyingly call it the Shira Route). Refuses to touch the Marangu Route but happy to offer Machame, with the price of US$2500 including oxygen, hyperbaric chamber, airport transfers and *three* nights' accommodation at Ilboru Lodge. Certainly the speci-

fication for their treks seems fairly impressive and the price not outrageous, but there are two things that we find rather naughty: a child discount of only US$250 (to be fair, when confronted they were apologetic and offered US$750); and they also lied to us and said they were partners of KPAP – though they aren't. Also have an office in the US (see p109).

● **Summary** Reviews are generally positive but at this price point we think you can get better.

Dik Dik (☎ 027-255 3499; 🖳 dikdik.ch; **A**) You can tell a Dik Dik expedition on the mountain with their smart luggage crates and mountain gear emblazoned with their logo. They claim that they are 'widely acknowledged to be the best Climbing Tour Operator in Tanzania' but they are not quite the force they were. The hotel (see p224) is, admittedly, still lovely. But trek-wise we

found a few flaws. Their reply to our email was just one long pre-written 'advert' for their services and didn't address directly many of the questions we asked them. And secondly we think their treks are overpriced at US$3195pp for four people for seven days on Machame (though this includes three night's accommodation at Dik Dik), and their child discount was just over half of what it should be at US$400. They have also stopped being KPAP partners.

● **Summary** Always worth contacting because of their pedigree and experience but they do seem to be on a bit of a decline.

dotcom safaris (☎ 027-275 4104; 🖳 dotcomsafaris.com; Kaunda St **M**) One of Moshi's older budget outfits, still clinging to survival by offering basic treks at a cheap price, with Machame Route just US$1600pp; commendably, they offered the full US$700 under-16 discount. Two nights at Moshi's decent Bristol Cottages,

transfers and oxygen on the mountain are also included. Their absence from KPAP's partnership program is largely down to the fact that they refuse to raise their prices to pay KPAP's minimum required wages. This review is necessarily brief because it's been a while since we've met or heard from anyone who's climbed with them, so I can't really comment on their service these days.

● **Summary** Cheap and no-frills treks but try to find some recent positive reviews before putting any money down. Alternatively, if you can afford it, pay a little more and go with a KPAP partner company, which tend to have a better reputation for the quality of their treks as well as being nicer to their staff.

Duma Explorer (☎ 0787-079127, 🖳 dumaexplorer.com; **A**) Owned by a local and his American wife, Duma Explorer are one of our favourites. KPAP partners with a lot of experience, a strong commitment to

---

❑ **Best ethical companies**

Many companies bang on for pages on their website about being an ethical company. Some even go as far as setting up organisations and unions for their porters as proof of how much they care for their staff. But at the risk of sounding cynical, you have to wonder why these companies go to these lengths rather than subject themselves to the scrutiny of an independent body such as KPAP? After all, KPAP's services are free and if you become a KPAP partner, you are allowed to put their logo on your website, which can only be good from a commercial perspective.

Given our scepticism about other bodies that claim to oversee the welfare of porters (including the various porters' unions and the Kilimanjaro Association of Tour Operators, or KIATO), we believe KPAP's endorsement – and only KPAP's. And we think that you should too. So if you want to be sure that you're climbing with a company whose mountain crew are being treated fairly, make sure they are KPAP partners. There are three warnings that we need to give here:

● **Don't necessarily believe a company if it tells you that they are members of KPAP**. In our research, the number of companies that weren't partners of KPAP but lied to us and said they were, was at least a dozen. To find out if they truly are or not, visit the KPAP website 🖳 www.kiliporters.org; look for the partners' page and you'll find all current partners there.

● **Don't necessarily believe a company even if it has the KPAP logo on their website**. Again, this is not a cast-iron guarantee that they are a KPAP partner, because they could have just stolen it, or not removed it when they stopped being a partner. Just visit the KPAP website to find out the most up-to-date list.

● **Don't necessarily believe this book!** The list of KPAP partners changes regularly as new companies are added and existing partners fall foul of KPAP's strict standards. So while this book is as up-to-date as possible when it goes to print, and is a good

sustainability, great reviews (one reader wrote that Duma 'exceeded my expectations in every way') and guides that are WFR-trained, they have pretty much everything going for them. Our only gripes are that airport transfers and accommodation are both *not* included in the trek package; and that only US$530 out of the full under-16 discount of US$696 was offered to us. On the plus side they also operate a mobile camp in the Serengeti and have accommodation in Tarangire too.

● **Summary** Looking for a mid-range trek with a decent, ethically minded company, and hoping for a safari afterwards? Duma are one of a handful of companies in this price range that are very, very good – and, at the moment we think they're just about leading the field.

East African Voyage (EAV; ☎ 0732 975143; 🖳 eastafricanvoyage.com; **A**) Founded by a former guide and his wife, a Canadian human rights lawyer, EAV are a great little company that lacks for nothing except, perhaps, more customers. Website, too, could do with a bit of work – it's not very informative, a bit clunky, and some of the pages don't load properly. Surprisingly, given his heritage as a trip leader with African Environments, EAV don't climb on the Western Breach, considering it to be too dangerous. But they're still worth contacting: they're beloved by KPAP, their guides are WFR-trained, their kit is of a high quality, the reviews of their treks are few in number but always positive and their response to our enquiry was eloquent and informative. Furthermore, prices are reasonable at US$2525 including oxygen and Gamow bag – though accommodation and airport transfers are extra, and their under-16 discount was only 50% of the park fees. Interestingly, they are one of the few companies to count a female guide amongst

place to begin your search, the only surefire way to make sure your company is a KPAP partner is to look on KPAP's website.

Four standout companies

Given the fluid nature of the KPAP partners list, I asked Karen Valenti (KPAP's boss) which companies she thinks will be with KPAP for the long term; in other words, which firms actually do seem genuinely to care about the welfare of porters, as opposed to those who have joined it only for commercial reasons, to take advantage of the extra business that comes with having the KPAP logo on their website, but who will struggle to adhere to the KPAP standards.

So, with apologies to those companies that are KPAP partners, have a genuine determination to treat their mountain crews well, and yet are not mentioned here, these are the four companies that Karen cited as the ones that seem genuinely concerned about the treatment of their staff, and who are likely to be with KPAP for the long term. They also score the highest on KPAP's porter surveys. The companies are: **Good Earth**, based in Arusha (see p84); **Nature Discovery/Thomson** of Arusha (see p92); **Fair Travel Tanzania**, also in Arusha (see p82); and **Trek2Kili** of Moshi (see p100).

For budget travellers with a conscience

If you're gung-ho about personal safety and couldn't give a monkey's about how the porters are treated then, yes, it is still possible to get a trek for about US$1200. But for those who have been blessed with some sort of social conscience, these are currently the cheapest members of KPAP. Do check with KPAP before booking, though, as the cheaper companies tend to be the ones that struggle to keep to KPAP's strict guidelines. The companies are: **Snowcap** (see p96); **Gladys Adventure** (p84); **Tin Tin Tours** (p99); **African Scenic Safaris** (p75); and **Origin Trails** (p93).

BOOKING YOUR TRIP

their ranks – another useful selling tool, methinks.

● **Summary** Definitely worth enquiring with if you're after a solid mid-range company.

Easy Travel & Tours (☎ 0686 374363; 🖥 easytravel.co.tz; Boma Rd, **A**) Long-established company located right in the centre of Arusha by New Safari Hotel. Efficient and very busy, more renowned for their safaris though they do seem to be concentrating more on Kili treks these days. Prices are reasonable (US$2112pp) but there are a couple of negatives: the under-16 discount they passed onto us was only US$350, and they charge US$250 for a tank of oxygen – a sum that's high enough, we believe, to persuade some trekkers not to take it. Still, the last we heard is that they are looking to become partners of KPAP, which is a step in the right direction.

● **Summary** Doing a fair bit of Kili business now and about to be adopted by a major Canadian agency, we hear, though reviews of their treks are still few in number – possibly because those who have climbed with them booked with an overseas agency and so had no idea they were actually climbing with Easy. If they can emulate the success of their safari arm on Kili then everyone will win, though it's too early to say this just yet.

Enosa (☎ 0715-223767; 🖥 enosaexpedi tions.com, **M**) Company that, like several others, has managed to secure a fair bit of business by featuring highly on review websites (eg TripAdvisor, safaribookings.com). Good prices (US$1800pp) and the full discount for under 16s was offered within the first paragraph of their reply. Indeed, their whole email was concise but full of sound common-sense.

● **Summary** Not one of the more established companies but plenty of good reviews online suggests they could be worth a punt for those looking below the US$2000 threshold.

Everlasting Tanzania Travels (☎ 0788 835575, 🖥 everlastingtz.com; **A**) Wholly Tanzanian-owned company run by three ex-guides. Has been suffering recently following the sudden death of the Irishman Ian

McKeever who used Everlasting as his ground operator for the large groups that he used to bring over. (Mr McKeever died from a lightning strike on the mountain.) Nevertheless, Everlasting still have a lot going for them: KPAP partners with a strong ethical outlook and a deserved reputation for taking massive groups on Kili – indeed, they hold the record for taking the largest group ever to climb the mountain, with 117 out of the initial 119 making it to the top. Their treks are efficiently run and all guides are WFR trained. Prices firmly in the mid-range at US$2650pp, including two nights at Arusha's expensive African Tulip; after prompting, they confirmed that the under 16 discount would be a healthy US$650.

● **Summary** For large groups, this team's experience and nous has few rivals.

Fair Travel Kilimanjaro We've given this company space in this book purely to emphasise the fact that this is *not* the same company as Fair Travel Tanzania (see below), and are, by all accounts, actually pretty dreadful.

● **Summary** Don't get them confused!

Fair Travel Tanzania (☎ 0786 025886; 🖥 fairtraveltanzania.com; **A**) Is this the future of trekking on Kilimanjaro? Those who care about the welfare of porters would probably like it to be. Fair Travel Tanzania are KPAP partners who describe themselves as a non-profit company, founded by a Swede who won a large amount of money on a TV game show and decided to invest it by setting up Fair Travel. Approaches the whole question of porter welfare from a whole new angle by firstly determining what amount a porter needs each month to maintain a decent standard of living (which they've decided is US$252 per month), then paying them a daily wage, assuming that they work on two treks each month, that will equal this amount. All of which means that the porters on a Fair Travel climb earn US$18 per day in wages – a startling amount when you consider KPAP's own minimum daily wage is a comparatively paltry US$10! It also means that their clients are not obliged to pay any gratuities for their crew and the

❏ Route specialists

Some companies have become associated with certain routes on the mountain. In a couple of instances this is because they actually pioneered the trail; in other cases it is just because they have concentrated on this route for one reason or another. Note that these companies all offer other routes in addition to the one they're associated with; and conversely, there are countless other companies that offer treks on these routes. Just because they're specialists on one particular route doesn't mean it follows that they're particularly expensive: indeed, Snowcap, the pioneers of the Rongai Route, are amongst the cheapest companies on the mountain (and are KPAP partners too!).

Northern Circuit

They may call it the TK Lemosho – and other companies may call it the Alternative Lemosho – but **Team Kilimanjaro** have certainly made this trail more popular since they started offering treks on it about a decade ago, and probably run more treks on this route than any other. **Nature Discovery/Thomson** go one step better, incorporating the Northern Circuit in their **Grand Traverse Trek**, which starts on the Shira Route before then heading off via Moir Huts to Mawenzi Tarn on the Rongai Route!

Rongai

The father of the current boss of **Snowcap** helped to establish and popularise the Rongai Route, built the School Hut/Outbound Hut on the slopes of Kibo, and they own lovely Snowcap Cottages – the only accommodation near the Rongai Gate.

Marangu

The **Marangu Hotel** has been running treks on the oldest established route since the 1930s and continues to be the go-to company for this trail. Originally the treks started at the gates of their lovely hotel (as Michael Crichton illustrates; see p375) but these days, like everyone else, they bus their clients up to the gate.

Shira

While most companies ignore the Shira Trail these days as it's largely a 4WD track, both **African Walking Company** and **Nature Discovery/Thomson** positively promote it, claiming – justifiably, given their success rates – that it is great for acclimatisation.

Umbwe

We love this route and we have a soft-spot for the people that, in our opinion, do more on the Umbwe trail than most. **Summit Expeditions and Nomadic Experiences** (SENE) is run by Simon Mtuy, who took this route up to the summit when breaking the world record for the fastest unassisted ascent of Kilimanjaro, and who promotes the route quite heavily. An honourable mention must also go to **Nature Discovery/Thomson Treks** who also appreciate the trail's charms and run more treks than most on it; and to **Tembo/Tusker Trails** whose unique 360 Route starts off on the Umbwe before bending round the northern side of Kibo.

Lemosho and the Western Breach

Alongside the late Scott Fischer's Mountain Madness company, **African Environments** (AE) helped pioneer both the Lemosho route and the ascent to the summit via the tricky Western Breach. One of AE's former employees, Lema Peter, has set up his own company, **Serengeti Pride Safaris**, that also specialises in this route – and at half the price.

Machame

Such a popular trail, there are no real specialists on the Machame Route; indeed, we should probably mention African Walking Company and Real Life, who are the only two companies who *don't* offer this route.

BOOKING YOUR TRIP

porters don't need to rely on unreliable tips to survive. I think this needs to be emphasised: *on a Fair Travel Tanzania trek you are not obliged to pay any tips.* So while their prices are US$2475pp, in order to compare them fairly with their competitors you need to add on US$200-300 to any quote from another company – that sum being the tips you'll be asked to pay. All of which is very laudable but what is their service like? Well, we love the transparent way they conduct their business, providing potential clients with a breakdown of how their prices are made up. They also offered a very healthy child discount of US$744 (ie more than the full park fee discount). As for the quality of their treks, they make no claim towards luxury but they're pretty standard in that respect, their guides are very good, and the reviews (though few) are almost universally positive.

● **Summary** Their transparency is staggering and the innovative and ethical way they approach their business is worthy of the highest praise. If the fair treatment of porters is high on your wish list then you must send them an enquiry.

Gazelle Adventures (☎ 717 728 967, 💻 gazelleadventures.com; Shule St, **M**) One of the more reliable of the many, many small operators working out of Moshi, Gazelle have been around for about five years now. Hard-working and reliable, with good online reviews, there's little to criticise though little to get too excited about either. Prices are good for those seeking a trek at the cheaper end, with a seven-day Machame trudge costing US$1779pp, though only US$165 of the discount in park fees for under-16s was passed on; when we questioned this they raised it to an impressive US$709. They're certainly not alone in trying to keep part of the park fee discount for themselves – indeed, they're probably in the majority – so it's a tad unfair to single them out on this score.

● **Summary** OK, but not exactly pulling up any trees; still, a fair choice for those looking for a budget climb particularly if you're already in Moshi – their offices are right in the centre.

Gladys Adventure (☎ 0787-111881, 💻 gladysadventure.com; Hill St, **M**) Once the best place to go to rent trekking-gear, now one of the better and busier budget trekking agencies in Moshi. Gladys herself started off trading with trekkers who had finished their trek, offering souvenirs in return for any bits of kit they no longer required. From this, she was able to set up the first and best equipment rental agency in town. Then about five years ago she moved into organising the treks themselves – and seems to be doing a great job in this field too. Gladys herself still runs the show from the office on Moshi's Hill St, just down from the Coffee Shop. Three levels of trek are offered, the differences between them being largely confined to the standard of hotel you stay in before and after the trek. In brief, pre- and post-trek accommodation on the budget climbs (US$1755pp if joining an open-group climb, US$1845pp on a private climb) is at Aa Hotel (see p244), above their office; Leopard Hotel (see p244) is the hotel they use for their mid-range treks (US$1905pp), while Sal Salinero or Kilimanjaro Wonders are the accommodation options for the luxury treks (US$2070pp). KPAP partners, they offered us more than the full child discount of US$742 and we've received good reviews from our readers about their service, with knowledgeable guides and a reassuring focus on the health and wellbeing of their clients.

● **Summary** For budget treks that don't exploit the mountain crew there are few that are better.

Good Earth (☎ 0682-530187; 💻 goodearthtours.com; Arusha Municipality Rd, Plot 1896; Planet Lodge, **M**) A very good option. Their website rightly boasts that they practise responsible tourism, providing scholarships, books, and supplies to local children and financial support to various environmental groups. Also longstanding KPAP partners and regularly come out on top or thereabouts when it comes to treating porters fairly according to KPAP's own rankings. Price-wise they're solidly mid-range, with prices US$2525pp includ-

ing two nights at the lovely Planet Lodge (which they own) and airport transfers. Just two (small) negatives to note: 1) oxygen is an extra US$50 per group; and 2) their response to enquiries can be a little unenthusiastic. This doesn't matter in the great scheme of things, of course – it's how they perform on the mountain rather than in front of a laptop that counts, of course. But while many operators have a *mzungu* (foreigner) on board who can answer the emails, those owned and run entirely by Tanzanians tend to get fewer bookings, regardless of their facility with the English language, purely because they don't know how to write what the client wants to read. But don't let these very minor quibbles put you off, for their treks are fine, the reviews are great and we like them an awful lot.

● **Summary** Regularly cited by KPAP for their exemplary treatment of porters, this lot are a good-hearted bunch with pretty much everything going for them.

High Peaks Expeditions (☎ 0736 210968, 0786 263216; 🖳 highpeaks-expeditions.com; A) Company with a very slick website that came to our attention following their adoption by the large Belgian agency Allibert, who now use them for their climbs. Certainly very cheap – one of only four to sneak under the US$1500pp mark, charging US$1485pp for their seven-day Machame trek; the under-16 discount was also fair but not quite perfect at US$681. Reviews scarce but in their emails they provided us with contact details of people who had recently climbed with them.

● **Summary** Professional approach and attitude, prices very cheap. As with all the 'super-budget' companies, do ask about how much they pay and how well they treat their staff.

Homeland (🖳 homelandadventures.com; M) Undoubtedly cheap treks but we're always put on our guard when a company's website is set up to take credit and debit card payments instantly, especially when they do not provide an office address or even a phone number by which you can contact them! Seem to be one of several little agents with the same business model: set

up an office in Moshi, offer very cheap treks (in this instance US$1580pp, with under 14s getting 20% off, which we calculated to be US$316), bend the truth to tell the customer what he wants to hear regarding porters' wages and treatment in particular (can they really be paying US$20 per day to porters and still make a profit?), then garner as many good reviews online as you can and let the customers pour in.

● **Summary** One of several Moshi outfits all cut from the same cloth, with nothing remarkable to separate any of them. If you're after a cheap trek at the end of your time volunteering in Moshi then this bunch are no better or worse than any of the other budget operators and worth a look.

Hot Sun (☎ 027-275 4037, 🖳 hotsunsafaris.com; Shule St, **M**) Replied to our initial email very promptly, succinctly and, best of all, honestly (admitting, for example, to paying only US$8 per day to their porters; they are not alone in paying below the legal minimum wage for their mountain crew – in fact, they are probably in the majority – but they are one of the few to admit to it). Unfortunately, this was pretty much the last time they impressed us. True, their prices are cheap at US$1700 per person, though their child discount of US$150 (which rose only to US$250 after we'd complained) seems rather light when compared to the US$696 that it should be if they passed on all park fee discounts. Reviews are few and rather out of date now and we get the feeling they're not doing much business, even though their office is close to many of the tourist hotels which you would think would be useful for attracting custom.

● **Summary** They're not the cheapest, they're not partners of KPAP, and while we couldn't judge the treks themselves, having never met one on the mountain nor heard from any of their clients, we suspect that these would be unexceptional too.

It Started in Africa (☎ 0753 224816; 🖳 itstartedinafrica.com; New Safari Hotel Building, Boma Rd, Floor No 3, Room 421, **A**) We've heard more bad stories about this lot than any other company. I was going to

simply ignore them for the book, but then people started to write to us saying that they were considering a climb with them (we believe it's because they rank highly on one of the review websites; the one that we think is the least useful), so we feel it's our duty to warn people. Suffice to say, we've received more than one email from readers saying that they were offered a considerable bribe if they didn't post a negative review online. As we expected, when we contacted them about their climbs they claimed to be partners of KPAP, which of course they are not. So you'll forgive us if we are also sceptical about their claim to have WFR-trained guides; and that the BBC works with them; and that they have a 98 per cent success rate. If you insist on contacting them you'll find they charge US$2240pp for the Machame trek, so they're not even particularly cheap.

● **Summary** For your sanity and safety, steer clear; there are just too many stories/rumours swirling around them for us to believe they're 100% reliable.

Kessy Brothers (☎ 0754-803953; 🖳 kessybrotherstours.co.tz; opposite KNCU Hotel on Old Moshi Road, **M**) If there's one thing this lot are good at, it's self-promotion. Stay in Moshi for more than a day or so and you may well be approached by one of their flycatchers; their adverts are ubiquitous around town too. They're very cheap at US$1465pp for a no-frills trek (ie no mess tent, chairs etc) – though two nights' accommodation, oxygen, airport transfers and even, so they say, kit hire *are* included. Their boast of a 98% success rate seems a little far-fetched, as is their assertion that they pay their porters US$15 per day (we've been told by one reliable source that the real porters' salary is about 20% of that!), and they are most definitely *not* partners of KPAP. But weighed against these gripes is the positive reviews they get both from our readers and online.

● **Summary** Made some dubious claims in their email but for a rock-bottom climb they're worth looking at given the wealth of positive reviews – assuming you can tuck your conscience away and not care about how much they pay their porters.

Keys (see p249 for contact details; Keys Hotel, Uru Rd, **M**) Still very busy Moshi operator that's been going for about 20 years. Offers a refreshingly honest appraisal of the routes on Kili (describing Machame as overcrowded, for example, and talking about the acclimatisation problems on the Marangu Route). Hotel's nice too. However, their claim that they are partners of KPAP is, quite frankly, wrong (and must make KPAP's blood boil) though to be fair we've heard they're paying a good wage these days. Price-wise they charge US$1922pp for Machame, under 16 discount US$567.

● **Summary** Experienced, competent and busy. Their claim to be a KPAP partner (they've still got the KPAP badge on their website too) is naughty and disappointing; though to be fair the last we heard they were looking to be a KPAP partner again; if they do so, and manage to keep their prices low – for their treks are unquestionably good value – we would certainly be happy to endorse them.

Kibo Expeditions (☎ 0782-985640, 0787-378252; 🖳 kiboexpeditions.com; **A**) Company that grew out of the old Kiliwarriors/Taraji outfit. Describes itself as a charitable company and makes a big hoo-ha on its website about its charitable concerns – but not a partner of KPAP as failed to meet the standards when it last applied. Offers four levels of trek, with Explorer level the standard (US$2595), though also offers Expedition (US$3995, includes toilet tent, shower, hot water bottle, Gamow bag, pillow, walk-in tents and solar charging station), All-inclusive (US$4995; same as the Expedition but also includes a personal porter, laundry and drinks at the hotel – and tips) and All-inclusive Plus (US$5695; includes defibrillator too); the quality of the pre- and post-trek accommodation improves through the levels too. The child discount remains the same at US$530.

● **Summary** Many laudable features and we love companies that are brave enough to include tips in some of their treks; but the prices made our eyes water. They need to go back to the drawing-board and work on

their prices if they really want to be a major player.

Kibo Slopes (☎ 020-213 9981; 🖳 kiboslopessafaris.com; Silver Springs Hotel, **A** & **Nairobi**) Smart and professionally run agency and the biggest of those operating out of Kenya. Offer Kilimanjaro treks using their own climbing outfit, Kibo Slopes Tanzania, based in Arusha. Prices are very reasonable at US$2050pp though only *one* night's accommodation is included at the Aishi (p246), and the under-16 discount was just over half of what it should be at US$410.

● **Summary** Not brilliant but they are KPAP partners and, if you have to book your trek with a Kenyan agency, they're the best option.

Kili Climb Outfitters (☎ 0787 491886, 🖳 kiliclimboutfitters.com, **A**) Fairly obscure Arusha-based company, have come to prominence recently due to their activity on a review website where you pay for greater prominence and which they seem to exploit rather well. Talk a good talk on their website and their treks are of a decent specification, with all guides WFR trained, oxygen issued as standard and pre- and post-trek accommodation offered at the very smart Kibo Palace. Given this, their treks are pretty good value at US$2230pp. A couple of red flags: claimed in their email to have met with KPAP to discuss becoming a partner – KPAP deny that any such meeting has taken place; and the discount they offered for under 16s was a paltry US$180 rather than the near US$700 it should be.

● **Summary** Possibly worth keeping an eye on; at the moment there are better options out there but if they manage to adhere to the ambitions and standards they talk about on their website they could be a contender in the future.

Kili Treks (1) (☎ 0754 389885; 🖳 kilitreks.com; **A**) Two companies called Kili Treks, with only a hyphen in one website address to distinguish them. Both OK. This one is pretty much a one-man band, Eligius, who is owner, manager and also the lead guide on most treks. Still, he's built up a fine reputation for providing a good service on and off the mountain, and probably

has the better reputation of the two companies. He's cheap, too, at US$1855pp; oxygen (US$50 per group) is not included. though airport transfers and accommodation at the ever-reliable Outpost Lodge are.

● **Summary** Few treks but very good reviews and a pretty reliable and cheap option for small groups.

Kili Treks (2) (☎ 0754-473515; 🖳 kili-treks.com; **M**) A wholly Tanzanian-owned company established by a former guide of top trekking outfit, Nature Discovery, who also happens to be the first Tanzanian to have climbed Everest! He is now also the vice-president of the Guides Association. They're a small company but a good KPAP partner. Positioned squarely in the mid-range market, with prices US$2370 per person with oxygen, *one* night in the ultra-smart Kili Wonders Hotel and airport transfers included. Took a lot of prompting to get a discount for under 16s, but when we did they offered us US$500.

● **Summary** More ethical but more expensive than their namesake, but again provides very good, highly rated treks and capable of taking large groups. Hard to fault, though child discount was small.

Kili Zone (🖳 kilizone.co.tz, **A**) They have their own website but if you want to elicit any kind of response from them you have to go via agents 🖳 bush2beach.com, which they also own. Can't fault their experience, with all guides (including one woman) having completed at least 100 successful ascents of Kili, and all their cooks have worked for at least ten years on the mountain. Can't fault the treatment of their staff, either, for this KPAP partner is one of the few companies that offers insurance cover for porters, cooks and guides – a welcome innovation. As for the treks themselves, as you'd expect they're very good and they are also the only local company that offers, at a price, the ALTOX oxygen system to help people reach the summit. The hefty price tag of US$2945pp took us by surprise, however, and seems a bit unwarranted, even if it does include three nights at lovely Kaliwa Lodge by Machame Gate. Don't seem to be getting too much work at the moment – and

recent reviews are hard to come by – but that's the only criticism we can make.

● **Summary** We think they could lower their price, and some more recent reviews about their climbs would be reassuring. Nevertheless, a high quality company.

Kilimanjaro Brothers (☎ 0716 958 597; 🖳 kilimanjarobrothers.com; Kilima St, opposite Mawenzi Hospital, **M**) Moshi-based company who, if you were to believe everything on their website, sound amazing – though the reality slightly disappoints. There's nothing particularly bad about them – save, perhaps, the measly wages they pay their porters – but nothing extraordinary either. On their website they make a big song-and-dance about taking the safety of their clients very seriously, with Gamow bags, oxygen and pulse oximeters on every climb and reviews are largely positive. Surprised by how much they charge, however – US$2400 for a 7-day Machame climb puts them firmly in the mid-range bracket, but can't really see what they're offering that justifies this amount.

● **Summary** For this price there are more established and more ethical companies offering superior treks.

Kilimanjaro Heroes Adventures (☎ 0755 227040, ☎ 0716 588188; 🖳 kilimanjaroheroes.com; Kaunda St, opposite Crane Hotel, **A & M**) At first glance this company looks good, with a swish website, offices in both Moshi and Arusha and extremely reasonable prices (US$1700pp was the price we were quoted, though it's advertised as US$2500 on their website); apparently they are willing to drop their prices still further if you bargain with them. The walls of their office in Moshi are smothered with pictures and posters proclaiming all the charity work that they do, too. Unfortunately, however, everything is not quite as rosy as it seems, for they're yet another agency happy to lie about becoming members of KPAP (indeed, according to statistics we have seen they pay some of the worst wages on the mountain). Also, neglected to offer us any children's discount until we prompted them (after which, to be fair, their discount was a generous US$850).

● **Summary** Good specifications for their trek and garner a lot of custom from the overseas volunteers working in Moshi; but very poor wages paid and, for all their front about being an ethical company that supports various charities, we're not so sure.

Kilimanjaro Vikings (☎ 0769-654036; 🖳 kilivikings.com; corner of Kilima and Kahawa St, **M**) Small but one of the slickest at the budget end of the market. Said they were KPAP but aren't, which is cheeky, though they claim to pay the US$10 minimum wage to porters (but then, so does everyone else; the reality, however, rarely bears this out). Prices good at US$1750 for what they provide, child discount of US$300 is less thrilling.

● **Summary** Lots of good online reviews so the treks would seem to be OK, but take everything they claim regarding porter treatment etc with a pinch of salt.

Kwetu Tanzania (☎ 0754 374095, 🖳 kwetutours.com; **A**) Straightforward and upfront, profess an ethical outlook (their director, Dennis, who seems to run the whole operation, works with a California-based charity looking to improve health and education in East Africa). Price is fair at US$2084, with the child discount an impressive US$847 (surprisingly so as they say they're paying US$12 per day to porters; above the KINAPA/KPAP minimum). Unfortunately, without the independent scrutiny of a body such as KPAP these claims are difficult to verify. As their treks are largely booked through their UK agent, IntoAfrica, they have few online reviews (though those of their agent are largely positive).

● **Summary** Fair price and they seem decent and honest; worth writing to if it suits your budget.

Lava Peaks (☎ 0754 590 172; 🖳 lavapeaks.com, **M**) Essentially a one-man band based in Moshi. Ransom Swai was a guide for ten years; in addition to running the company and taking the bookings, he still leads the treks too. Price-wise they're US$1650pp for a seven-day Machame Route for four people; only US$470 of the park fee discount for under 16s was passed on, however. The price includes airport

transfers and two nights at Altezza Lodge (see p250), with oxygen US$80 extra.

● **Summary** A one-man operation but at least that man is a decent one and according to the limited information we have Lava Peaks do a good job.

Maasai Wanderings (☎ 0755-984925; 🖥 maasaiwanderings.com; **A**) Company

established by an Australian woman and her Tanzanian husband. Boast repeatedly on their website about how 'ethical' they are though they are no longer partners of KPAP – that said, we understand that the wage they pay their porters is a very healthy Ts20,000. Also offered us a child discount of just US$300 – around half of what it should be (though they did later

---

❏ IF CARRYING SOME OF YOUR OWN LUGGAGE

A couple of of the more expensive companies on Kili offer a cheaper, stripped-back version of their treks. One of the ways that they pare down their service is by asking clients to carry at least some of their own luggage. They may also not supply a mess tent. In this way, fewer porters are required to service the trek and the company is able to drop the price as a result. Note that, given the paltry wages that porters are paid, the drop in price won't be as large as you probably hope. That said, some of the features of their regular, pricier treks – the stuff that made their prices so expensive in the first place – are often present on their cheaper treks too. For example, if a company has WFR-trained guides on their 'normal' treks, it's highly likely they'll also be present on their budget treks. Similarly, if the company is a KPAP partner, that means that they must obey KPAP's rigid standard on *all* of their treks, including their budget ones. So we think that these pared down budget treks are more for those who just like the idea of challenging themselves by carrying their own luggage, rather than for those who want to save every last penny. We should also point out that, from our observations on the mountain, it appears that those who carry their own luggage seem to have a poorer chance of acclimatising successfully and as such their chances of reaching the summit are diminished too. Though I admit I have little to back up this argument and when I asked the companies below on their thoughts they disagreed, saying that their clients were equally likely to get to the top whatever level of service they were on.

Team Kilimanjaro (p99)
TK run a Lite series of climbs where you agree to carry 12kg of their own luggage and forego the pleasures of a mess tent. They also offer the ascetic-style Superlite, where climbers have to provide and carry all their own food and equipment, make their own way to Arusha from the airport and book their own accommodation. Even cheaper than either of these, TK also run Team Maasai (p99), a budget version of their climbs.

Nature Discovery (p92)
Like TK, ND also run Lite and Superlite versions of their treks, though in this instance they agree to carry the first 8kg of your luggage, so you'll be required to carry only any extra above this figure (for most people this will be about 7kg). On their Superlite version, you also miss out on a dining tent (present on their 'Lite' treks) – and you don't even get pudding! But on all ND treks you do still get WFR-trained guides, a Gamow bag and comprehensive medical kit.

MEM Tours (Moshi Expedition & Mountaineering) (p92)
Offer a 'Budget' version of their already budget 'Deluxe' treks where you have to carry everything but the first 10kg of your own luggage, and no airport transfers or accommodation are included; you save only about US$100 by doing so (though that rises to anywhere between US$200-500 if you're a solo traveller on a private trek, which makes it more worthwhile).

increase it to US$540 after we complained – better, but still less than what it should have been). As for the treks themselves, they are by all accounts well run and organised. Concentrating solely on the Machame Route, (though other routes can be done privately), currently they organise set departures every Sunday (seven days, US$2460pp) with a maximum group size of 12, as well as private treks on other days. Add oxygen (US$75 per cylinder per group), airport transfers (US$90 per vehicle) and accommodation ($160 for a double room in Ahadi Lodge, half-board, is what we were recommended).

● **Summary** Their treks are good by all accounts but if you do approach them, check out all their claims thoroughly; we think their prices are perhaps a little steep, too.

Majestic Kilimanjaro (☎ 0784 393 538; 🖳 majestickilimanjaro.com; **A**) Currently the most successful of the slew of companies set up by current and former Team Kilimanjaro guides. They've certainly got their marketing sorted out and their reply to our enquiry was detailed, comprehensive and managed the tricky feat of answering all questions, including the difficult ones, honestly while still conveying a positive overall impression. For example, they're not partners of KPAP but emphasised that they pay their porters Ts19,000 per day – an impressive amount for a non-KPAP partner. Garnering good reviews from their clients, their treks are priced at a fair US$2,296pp and almost the full amount of the under-16 discount was passed on to us too. Their Australian backers take no income from the business and their half of the profits go to community projects in East Africa – very laudable.

● **Summary** Team Kilimanjaro have always had some of the best guides on the mountain but we've always been uneasy about the wages they pay their porters. If Majestic can continue to emulate the high standards set by TK, while simultaneously offering their porters a better life, and all at a cheaper price, then there's nothing to stop them from overhauling their mentors and hoovering up a large share of the Kili market in the process. Still a young company but worth investigating.

Marangu Hotel (☎ 0717 408615, ☎ 0754 886 092; 🖳 maranguhotel.com; **Marangu**) No company can boast the pedigree and experience of Marangu Hotel, which has been sending climbers up Kilimanjaro since – wait for it – 1932! Always had a good reputation for treating their porters well and clients are not only introduced to their crew at the start of the trek but are encouraged to mix more with them too, resulting in a camaraderie that is absent from treks with other agencies. At the end of the climb the hotel also throws a bit of a party for *every-one* to celebrate. Little wonder they've been partners with KPAP since the organisation's inception. Trek-wise, a Marangu Hotel expedition is fairly easy to spot because of the wooden trekking poles they give to each of their clients for the mountain, and which they can keep afterwards as a souvenir – a nice touch. Price is US$2318pp, with full discount offered for under 16s. Surprisingly, on top of that you need to add on accommodation at their divine hotel (reduced to US$75 per person per night half board for climbers), airport transfers (US$85 per vehicle each way to Marangu) and oxygen (US$100 plus US$36 a day). These extras are the only drawbacks, for reviews from readers and on the net are recent and enthusiastic.

● **Summary** We have always loved this hotel and by all accounts their treks are fine too. Worth enquiring with for any route and there's no better choice for a mid-range Marangu climb (US$1755pp for six days in a party of four, though again with accommodation, transfers and oxygen extra).

Materuni Tours (☎ 0753 069696, 🖳 materunitours.com; corner of Mawenzi Rd and Shule St, **M**) Named after a local waterfall and village, this company was formed by an Australian woman and her partner, a former porter who used to work for African Scenic. Not with KPAP, and if you ask why not they'll give you a lengthy explanation/excuse. But KPAP aside, there's a lot to like about them and they garner enthusiastic reviews from their clients. Claim to pay porters a reasonable Ts16,500 per day and our instinct is to believe them. (That said, we do advise you to ask KPAP

to see if their statistics backs this up.) Prices are cheap, with a seven-day Machame trek US$1765 per person for four people; though airport transfers (US$35 each way), accommodation and oxygen (US$150 for a 7-day trek) are all extra, so headline price is not so impressive as it first seems. Still, they offered the full US$700 discount for under 16s, which leads us to think they're an honest bunch.

● **Summary** If a fair treatment of the crew is important to you then drill down to make sure the standards they espouse are maintained (or opt for a KPAP company, of course, where such things are independently verified); but otherwise they're pretty good.

Maua Adventures (☎ 0783 386 631, 🖳 mauaadventures.com; **M**) Moshi-based company operating out of the owner's front room which, though not the absolute bargain basement, gets a decent slice of business from the hordes of volunteers who want to summit Africa's Highest Mountain before returning home at the end of their trip. Their response to our email was not very helpful, however: saying you're in the process of becoming a partner of KPAP when you're not always creates an atmosphere of distrust, while avoiding the subject of discounts for under-16s, even though we clearly stated we had one in our party, suggests that they're trying to pull a fast one. Still, prices are cheap at US$1600 per person for four people for seven days on Machame (and when we did eventually get a response on this matter, they offered us a US$500 discount for under 16s). Given that this includes two nights at the pleasant ParkView Inn, airport transfers and oxygen, it's very reasonable, though it can't leave much money to pay the wages of their porters. Reviews are few but generally OK.

● **Summary** If you're going to climb with them bring extra money for tips to supplement the meagre wages the company is clearly paying.

Mega Adventures (☎ 0715-820280, 🖳 megaadventurestravel.com; We Travel Hostel, Mawenzi Road, **M**). The cheapest company we found, at least for the particular trek we were enquiring about. The price of US$1430pp for four people for seven

days on Machame earns them their place at the top of the table on p72; commendably, they also offered all but US$10 of the under-16 discount off this price; only MEM Tours' (see p92) low-season budget rate is lower and then you have to carry some of your own luggage. True, airport transfers are excluded but they only charge US$40 for these (US$10 less than normal rate); accommodation is also excluded though seeing as they are based at the We Travel Hostel, one of the nicest and cheapest budget options in town, it's no real hardship. But what are the treks actually like? Unfortunately, none of our readers has to date sent us any reviews of them, and the only reviews we could find were on safari-bookings.com, which we are a little sceptical about. However, we know this company exists; we've met them and they are legit so you will get a trek of some sort – and hopefully by the time you read this there'll be some more reviews on other websites so we can more properly judge their treks.

● **Summary** The cheapest. Obviously the wages they pay to their porters will be low – at these prices, they can't be anything but – but they seem pretty upfront; it's just too early to judge whether their treks are any good – though hopefully there will be more online reviews when you're doing your research that will give you a better idea of their service.

Meru Slopes Tours (☎ 0754 583455, 🖳 meruslopestours.com; Meru House Inn, Sokoine Road, **A**) In-house company of Meru House Inn and Arusha Tourist Inn. Prices are at the budget end (US$1850pp, though with a disappointing US$300 discount for under 16s). Convenient if you're staying at this end of town (in addition to the two hotels above Arusha Backpackers is just over the road) but you should really be choosing your company based on more than just its location and there are better options around. Also claim to be KPAP partners, which they're not, and when we wrote to ask why they aren't on KPAP's website they told us that maybe there was a problem with KPAP's website!

● **Summary** Said they're members of KPAP, when they clearly aren't, so you

have to ask: why book your trek with a company that finds it so easy to lie?

Milestone Safaris (☎ 0767 551190, 🖥 milestonesafaris.com, **M**) Tour-operating arm of Moshi's Honey Badger Lodge, a small outfit but one that offers pretty good private treks. From an ethical standpoint they're very good, supporting various projects in the local community and they're close to being a KPAP partner. As far as their treks go, everything seems to be in order with prices a quite impressively low US$1834pp. We did have to prompt them on what sort of discount they could provide for the under 16s, and when it came it was close to the full amount.

● **Summary** They're not very busy but as far as we can tell they're a decent outfit with their heart in the right place.

Moshi Expedition & Mountaineering (aka **MEM Tours and Safaris**; ☎ 027-275 4234; 🖥 memafrica.com; Station Rd, opposite Nakumatt, **M**) To be fair to MEM they're a fairly slick and professional agency with swish new offices across the road from the former Nakumatt Supermarket. However, their treatment of porters is reputed to be less than exemplary and, strangely, it took us over a month to get any sort of response from them. When we did, they explained that they offer three levels of trek, all of them cheap. At the top is Stellar class, with chemical toilets on the mountain, oxygen, a greater ratio of guides and porters per trekker and two nights in Sal Salinero (see p249). While at the other extreme there's Budget class, with a luggage limit of just 10kg per person (you have to carry anything above this amount yourself) and there's no accommodation or airport transfers included. Prices are US$1700-2100pp depending on the class and, uniquely in my experience, they also offer low-season discounts so you can get a seven-day Machame trek for as little as US$1400pp for four people in April/May – the cheapest price we were quoted. Note, however, that their child discount was a pathetic US$180.

● **Summary** If you can get through to them they offer a lot for a good price, though their piddling child discount is naughty.

Nature Discovery (☎ 0732-971859; 🖥 naturediscovery.com; **A**) Upmarket company, founded and still partly managed by Brits that's been in operation for a quarter of a century now. Working closely with the large safari operator Thomson, this lot are ahead of the pack when it comes to offering high-spec treks. Their safety record and procedures are certainly amongst the best, with WFR-trained guides and a hyperbaric chamber/Gamow bag accompanying every trek, as well as a 'medical porter' who stays with the clients at all times. Their menus, too, are carefully planned and the food can approach gourmet standards. We really like their optional 'add-ons', where for a supplement you can have your own lounge tent complete with inflatable furniture, coffee table and soft flooring, or a proper frame bed (with mattress), or hot showers, or solar-charging kits – or even wi-fi. We also really like the look of their Grand Traverse Tour, an eight-day odyssey that starts on the Shira Plateau and heads east towards Mawenzi Tarn before looping back to School Hut; encompassing the northern/western, eastern and southern sides of the mountain, there is no trek that takes in more of Kili than this one. Group treks are also available. They are also KPAP partners, pay their staff very well (the only porters who are fully clad in Gore-Tex!) and are one of only three companies who employ a designated Porter Welfare Officer. Of course, such a fine service doesn't come cheap – but, nor, refreshingly, is it outlandishly expensive at US$3,475 for their most popular, 'Superior' standard treks, though remember it's extra for pre- and post-trek accommodation and airport transfers or if you want any of the add-ons listed above. They now also offer Lite and Superlite versions of their treks (see p89).

● **Summary** It's hard to find fault with these people and if money is no object then Nature Discovery are, to coin a phrase, the best a man (or woman) can get.

Nyange Adventures (☎ 0717 385304, 🖥 nyangeadventures.com; corner of Swahili St and Industries Rd, **M**, with new offices on Goliondoi Rd, **A**, too)

Impressive budget agency with a lot of clients. One of the very few companies who became a KPAP partner without having to alter their practices significantly – because they were already treating their porters very well. Perhaps this is because founder, Praise, started as a porter himself. Seldom misses a trick when it comes to attracting custom, from advertising group treks in cafés around town to paying the taxi drivers who drive people from the airport to promote their tours too; they also seem to advertise on safaribookings.com. Have their own charming accommodation just outside of Moshi, called Secret Garden, where their clients stay before and after their climbs. Have seen some outstanding reviews for their treks and they're fairly priced at US$2050pp, with the under-16 discount US$650 (though, admittedly, this was only offered after we prompted them).

● **Summary** Amongst the slew of little companies operating in Moshi, Nyange stand out for the standard of their treks and their fair treatment of porters. For a budget trek with a conscience they're definitely worth contacting.

Origin Trails (☎ 0754 276944, 🖳 origin-trails.co.tz, **M**) Fairly new Moshi company, in existence for less than two years, but one whose heritage is impressive. Origin Trails was set up by cheerful local Emanuel whose CV, including several years' work for Summits Africa, is impeccable. This experience has put him in good stead, enabling him to recruit some of his former WFR-trained guides as employees in his new venture (though do check this as a WFR-trained guide can't be guaranteed on every trek). Emanuel himself still leads some of the climbs too. Price-wise they're very good value given the quality of their treks, what is supplied (including sleeping bags and a private toilet) and the fact they're KPAP partners, with the seven-day Machame trek costing US$1951pp for four people and the under-16 price US$702. Clients are usually housed in Moshi's Ameg Lodge (two free nights included), oxygen and airport transfers are also included. Few reviews as they currently operate few treks, but we expect them to be busier in future.

● **Summary** One to watch – small, but very good value.

Peak East Africa/Intrepid Guerba (🖳 peakdmc.com; Kenya and Australia) The relationship is rather confusing between Intrepid Guerba Tanzania (who are the legally registered Tanzania company) and Peak East Africa (which is based in Kenya and Melbourne), though it seems to be the latter who actually organise the treks. They do not take bookings directly but only through Intrepid or one of their agents (including Peregrine and Imaginative Traveller). Concentrate on group treks and turn over a lot of volume, though their refusal to run treks on the Lemosho Route but instead concentrate on the busy routes of Machame and Marangu (as well as Rongai) is a bit disappointing. Prices, too, are a little higher than the average at US$3885, and this doesn't include airport transfers either. When we asked about a discount for our son, they told us that he has to be 15 to climb with them; and when they eventually came up with a discount for him, it was a very disappointing US$300. However, they do use the lovely Kibo Hotel in Marangu to base their climbs, which we think shows imagination, and they offer free kit hire if booked in advance. They're also KPAP partners and by all accounts a decent bunch.

● **Summary** Lots of happy customers but personally we would have expected a little more for the price, and are disappointed by the under-16 discount offered by such an experienced company.

Popote Africa (☎ 0757-190784; 🖳 popoteafrica.com; **M**) One of the more successful of the little companies in Moshi, largely because of good reviews online and successful exploitation of a review website. Their website is slow but otherwise they're slick and good value, with prices US$1700pp, though the under-16 discount was a disappointing US$390.

● **Summary** Popular and good value and worth investigating for a cheaper trek; not members of KPAP so do interrogate them on their treatment of porters, and bring

BOOKING YOUR TRIP

more money for tips to make sure your crew doesn't go short.

Pristine Trails (☎ 0717-100788, ☎ 027-275 4463; 🖥 pristinetrails.com; Ghala Rd, up from the old train station, **M**) Going for almost a decade now, this Moshi-based operation has been garnering good reviews throughout this time and we have become fans. Certainly ticks just about every box: KPAP partners, entirely owned by Tanzanians (though an American woman helps take the bookings and writes excellent, comprehensive responses to all enquiries from potential customers) and provides very good value treks, professionally run by head guides who, pretty much uniquely for a company operating at this end of the market, are all WFR trained! Also own the simple but pleasant and relaxing Moshi Urban (see p249). As for their prices, they advertise three different levels of trek: Standard (seven-day Machame US$2015pp with two nights in Moshi Leopard Hotel, see p244, included but no emergency oxygen on the mountain – that's US$90 extra); Luxury (US$2215pp, two nights at Bristol Cottages, see p248; trek includes oxygen, toilet and pillows); and Exclusive (US$2415pp including two nights at Sal Salinero, see p249; same as Luxury but with shower, sleeping cot, walk-in tents and even daypack porters!). Airport transfers are also included and the under-16 discount was a humungous US$871 off the adult fee! Operate open groups every Monday and will honour the cheaper price that they advertise for these even if only a couple of people sign up.

● **Summary** One of the best companies going and for the price they charge they're hard to beat.

❑ **Companies offering an unusual experience**

With 300 companies operating on Kilimanjaro, you would have thought that the incentive for each company to do something different with their treks – to make themselves 'stand out' – would be rather strong. So it's both surprising and disappointing to find how little one company's service varies from another's. Obviously the rigid rules laid out by KINAPA, the park authorities, are just one mitigating factor as to why so many companies' treks are so alike. But there are a few companies who manage to both obey the rules *and* offer something different. Some of them do so by concocting fantastic routes around the mountain such as **Tusker/Tembo** (p100), whose excellent '360 trek' manages to include the glorious Umbwe trails *and* the Northern Circuit on its way to the summit; for those who want a lengthy, peaceful climb, you won't find better. **Nature Discovery** (p92) deserve a mention here too for their 'Grand Traverse Route' which covers the mountain from west to east *and* north to south – it's the longest of all the routes on the mountain. While we're on the subject of Nature Discovery, they also provide (for a fee) a 'lounge tent' on their climbs that includes heaters, inflatable furniture, a coffee table and even wi-fi.

Other companies manage to separate themselves from the masses by the accommodation they offer before and after the trek. First prize in this category must go to **African Environments** (p75), who have their own acclimatisation camp in Arusha National Park on the slopes of Mount Meru. **Summit Expedition and Nomadic Enterprises** (SENE; see p97) also offer their clients the chance to stay in their B&B-cum-farm at Mbahe, a few kilometres from Marangu Gate – a lovely place to relax, acclimatise and learn about farming on the slopes of Kili. They also offer guided tours of Mbahe and Moshi at the start and end of the trek respectively and are in the process of building cottages near Mweka Gate, where most people finish their trek, which will presumably offer a similar experience as at Mbahe.

All the companies we've mentioned so far, of course, are positioned firmly at the luxury end of the market. But there are some companies that manage to offer their

Real Life Adventure Travel (☎ 0732-972159; 🖳 reallifeadventuretravel.com) Wholly Tanzanian-owned company. Had no joy contacting these people directly so went instead through the only agent of theirs that I know, Embark of the US. KPAP partners, they offer only 8 days on Lemosho (for which they charge US$3400), so their position in the table is based on an estimate of how much they would charge for the Machame Route if they did offer it. Also took an age to get responses to our questions – instead, they spent an awful lot of time boasting of their Kilimanjaro expertise and knowledge, though this knowledge clearly doesn't extend to knowing what the correct child discount was (passing on US$600, having initially said it was US$180). But we're being unfair because these criticisms are the fault of the agent, not the ground operator that we should be reviewing; and

our understanding is that it's a competent company and one that supports a number of charitable projects.
● **Summary** Few treks so difficult to judge but ticks all the boxes; knowledgeable and experienced.

Roy Safaris (☎ 027-250 2115; 🖳 roysa-faris.com; 20 Serengeti Rd, **A**) Safari operator but one that knows what they're doing on Kili, too. Offer only private treks (so if you book with them you won't suddenly find yourself lumped with a larger group). Pretty competent and reasonably priced too at US$2190pp – which is a little surprising given the luxury quality of their hotel. Airport transfers, however, are extra and no accommodation is included, either – even though they own the superb African Tulip, next to their offices on Arusha's Serengeti Road. Climbers are offered rooms here for

clients something different without charging them thousands for the privilege. **Snow Cap Tanzania Tours** (p96) have the lovely Snowcap Cottages near the start of the Rongai Route, which are ideal for those taking that route and looking to acclimatise (as well as anyone coming from Kenya who doesn't want to schlep all the way down to Moshi or Arusha).

The **Marangu Hotel** (p90) is more mid-range and in addition to offering the opportunity to trek with the oldest company still working on the mountain – and stay in one of the oldest hotels in the region too – they also have display cases of old records and documents on Kili that date back to the 1930s. They are willing to let you peruse if you ask; their clients are also given a simple carved wooden walking stick and afterwards their entire mountain crew are often invited to join with their clients in a party in the grounds of the hotel, during which tips are distributed, songs sung and alcohol drunk.

There are a couple of companies that can be distinguished by the crew they employ. **Team Maasai** (p99), as the name suggests, is staffed largely by Maasai, their slender, angular physiques standing out amongst the stockier, squatter forms of the Chagga and other tribes on the mountain. Then there's **Pink Safaris** (p79) which tries to employ female porters, cooks and guides wherever possible and the founder, Glory, is herself a former guide with Nature Discovery. (Please note, however, that this company is still in its infancy and we are not even sure if it has a current TALA licence; for that reason they are not included in this list of reviews.)

Finally, **Big Expeditions** (p77) have managed to carve out a niche for themselves by literally making a song-and-dance about their treks, employing a small band of musicians and dressing up one of their staff in drag to lead a celebratory sing-song in the car park at Mweka Gate to welcome their climbers down, followed by a buffet at the gate; if you're finishing at the same time as the celebrations but didn't climb with Big Expeditions, it can make you feel unappreciated!

BOOKING YOUR TRIP

US$110pp but try to negotiate for a *free* night or two here as part of your package; they may be willing to comply if it means securing your booking.

● **Summary** Safe and competent; manage to get a night or two at the African Tulip included in your package and you've got yourself a bargain.

Serengeti Pride Safaris (☎ 0785-353534, 💻 serengetipridesafaris.com; **A**) Small but likeable joint Tanzanian and American-owned company that has been going for almost a decade now. Email responses are eloquent, thorough and polite and they deserve praise on several fronts: for maintaining standards of safety (their expedition leaders are all WFR-trained and all treks are equipped with a Gamow bag, oxygen and oximeter); the treatment of their crew (they are solid KPAP partners); and the quality of their service (with pre- and post-trek accommodation at the plush Planet Lodge in Arusha and a decent set of online reviews from happy clients). Highly recommended in particular for those who want to climb the Western Breach and sleep in the crater – specialists on this route are hard to come by and the most well-known one, African Environments (see p75), is terrifically expensive; the co-owner of Serengeti Pride, however – who himself used to work as a guide with African Environments and runs his climbs along their lines – has set his prices at less than half of his former employers. For Machame, they charge US$2530 per person, or it's US$2850 for eight days on Lemosho via the Western Breach; add US$250 per person for a private trek on each route.

● **Summary** Well worth investigating, particularly for those looking to take the Western Breach Route up Kibo to the summit.

Shah Tours (☎ 027-275 2370; 💻 kilimanjaro-shah.com; **M**) Family-run and in business for over thirty years. Reliable and reasonable, in part because their rates include two nights at their Mountain Inn (see p250). Those rates are US$1880pp (4 people, 7 days Machame), though the child discount they offered was a relatively miserly US$350. Do watch out for hidden charges, however, with an oxygen tank priced at US$150 and airport transfers extra too. Reviews are positive but tend to be at least two years old; though we haven't heard of any reason to be overly concerned about this.

● **Summary** Unexceptional but cheap-ish and reliable.

Shidolya (☎ 027-254 8506, 💻 shidolya-safaris.com; Room 218, at the end of the corridor on the 2nd floor, Ngorongoro wing, AICC Bldg, **A**) Shidolya have been going for more than 25 years now and remain surprisingly cheap by Arusha standards, with seven-day Machame treks for just US$1725 per person (though the discount they offered for under 16s was only US$440 rather than the full US$696). Note, however, that no airport transfers (US$50 each way) nor pre- or post-trek accommodation is included for this price (they recommend that you stay at Colobus Mountain Lodge by the entrance to Arusha National Park – which is not surprising as they own it; rates are US$50 per climber including dinner and breakfast). Alas, they're another company that claims to be a KPAP partner, even though, according to KPAP themselves, they've never come close to joining and the wages they pay are terrible. Reviews tend to be mixed too.

● **Summary** Undoubtedly cheap and experienced but little else to recommend them.

Snow Cap Tanzania Tours (☎ 0759-114527, ☎ 0786-506249; 💻 snowcap.co.tz; **M**) There are a couple of big reasons to contact Snow Cap. Firstly, by our reckoning, they're one of the cheapest KPAP partners. Secondly, they are also the go-to company if you're interested in the Rongai Route, which they concentrate on more than any other company and which they've done more than any other to popularise. The father of the current owner did so to help the employment prospects on this corner of the mountain, and they also renovated the School Hut, the final hut on the standard Rongai ascent, and built the rather lovely Snowcap Cottages on the Kenyan border by the start of the trek (see p247). Small but very experienced, their treks are very good value (their Machame package is US$1779.50 per person, which includes

two nights half-board at the smart Snowcap Cottages), they have a good heart (the boss, Kenneth, is a genuinely good fellow) and the only negatives we could find was that their child discount was a meagre US$330, and reviews of them online are hard to find.

● **Summary** If you are on a budget but still want to do the right thing by your mountain crew they've got to be worth considering. Also recommended for those on the Rongai Route, and especially if you're coming from Kenya and want to climb the mountain without schlepping all the way to Moshi or Arusha to arrange it.

Summit Expeditions and Nomadic Experience (aka **SENE**; ☎ 027-275 3233, US toll free ☎ 1-866-417-7661; 💻 nomadicexperience.com, **M**) Run by the irrepressible force of personality that is Simon Mtuy – an ultra-racer and the holder of the record for the fastest unaided ascent and descent of Kili (see p168) – SENE just do things slightly differently to everyone else when it comes to tackling Africa's highest mountain and for this they are to be highly praised. Concentrate mainly on the Lemosho Route (which accounts for about 80% of their climbs) though also, refreshingly, run several climbs per year on little-used Umbwe Route. Not cheap – US$3565pp on Machame – though the child discount is the full US$100 per day. Price includes a stay at Simon's lovely farm at Mbahe, 15 minutes' west of Marangu Gate (Simon is also building cottages by Mweka Gate.) A Moshi walking tour and a Mbahe village walking tour are also included – both of which will give you a brief glimpse into the day-to-day lives of the locals. Furthermore, the treks themselves are by all accounts excellent, and we've received some truly glowing reports from delighted trekkers about them. They're partners of KPAP, which makes them one of only a handful of wholly Tanzanian companies that are, and they are also used by several Western agencies who appreciate SENE's ethical and ecologically minded approach to climbing.

● **Summary** We love these people. They're not cheap, but by all accounts their prices are worth it.

Summits Africa (💻 summits-africa.com; **A**) One of the leading companies on the mountain, formed and still run by the son of one of the founders of Hoopoe Adventure – one of the biggest names in climbing and safaris in recent years. Very safety-conscious with WFR-trained guides and oximetry tests for their clients standard on all their climbs. Ethically minded too, having been with KPAP since its inception; they are also one of only three companies to employ a porter welfare officer (Nature Discovery and Fair Travel Tanzania are the others). They run three levels of treks, Standard (lightweight mess tent, table and stools), Luxury (private toilet, sleeping bag and backed chairs rather than stools all included) and VIP (walk-in tents, cots). Reluctant to take direct bookings, preferring instead that you use one of their agents such as Aardvark in the UK (see p104) or Piper & Heath (p111) and Scott Dunn in the US. Contacting their agent Aardvark Safaris, they offered a 'Standard-spec' trek on Machame for seven days for US$3595 (with the child discount US$696), luxury US$4153) and VIP (US$4420).

● **Summary** Very, very good indeed; not quite our favourite of the luxury operators but pretty faultless nevertheless.

Sunny Safaris (☎ 027-250 8184; 💻 sunnysafaris.com; Col Middleton Rd, **A**) Once one of the busier budget agencies but a little quieter now – possibly because their office on Colonel Middleton Road sees far fewer budget travellers than in years gone by when this part of town was Backpacker Central. Smart new shopfront suggests things aren't going so badly for them. Price of US$1730pp for seven days on Machame seems reasonable at first sight, and includes hotel accommodation (at Venus) and airport transfers, while their child discount of US$530 wasn't the worst we'd received (though not the full amount). An oxygen tank is a hefty US$150 on top, though.

● **Summary** More a safari specialist than a Kili one; their correspondence was amongst the briefest and most unhelpful we received. Few climbs and if you are after a budget trek, they are neither the cheapest nor the best.

Tanzania Experience (☎ 0786 961506; 🖥 tanzania-experience.com; **A**) Established and run with significant help from German backers, Tanzania Experience have been operating since 2007 and offer both scheduled departures and private climbs. Price-wise they're pretty average at US$2565pp, though this includes stays at the plush Sal Salinero. Note, however, that oxygen is *not* issued on group climbs, and to hire it is US$58 per day (which works out at a whopping US$406 for a seven-day trek). It *is* free, however, with private climbs and as these usually only cost a little more than the group ones, it's usually better value to opt for one of these. In terms of how they treat their porters, they aren't bad and they're upfront about no longer being KPAP partners – though we are a little sceptical about the claim in their email that they pay more than the KPAP minimum. Treks, too, receive a lot of praise in their reviews.

● **Summary** Fair, honest and offer reliably decent treks.

Tanzania Journeys (☎ 027-275 4296, ☎ 0787 834152; 🖥 tanzaniajourneys.com; **M**) Formed in 2005, Tanzania Journeys boast a UK connection, are friendly and profess an ecological and humanitarian outlook. In response to our email we found this KPAP partner to be honest, well-informed and fairly priced, with Machame seven days US$2275pp for their standard service including two nights B&B in Moshi's Bristol Cottages (see p248) and transfers from either Kilimanjaro Airport or, unusually, Nairobi. Note that oxygen is US$30 per person extra though they have a luxury option too for US$2800 where oxygen, as well as WFR-trained guides, private toilets and Gamow bags are included. The discount in park fees for the under 16 was *almost* passed on in full (minus US$50 or so), which is better than most but not perfect. They've recently poached a big North American agency from a rival so we can expect their operation to expand soon, though hopefully not to the detriment of those who book directly. Service on the mountain is, by all accounts, very good.

● **Summary** We like them and think they're worth contacting for an ethically minded mid-range trek.

Tanzania Joy (☎ 0719-973749; 🖥 tanzaniajoytours.com; First Floor, NSSF Building, Old Moshi Rd **M**) Another central Moshi company that is worth popping into if you're spending the day traipsing around the operators looking for a deal, if only because they're so cheap at US$1500pp. This is pretty much the only thing that lifts them above the ordinary, however. Say they're KPAP partners and pay their porters Ts20,000 per day but the reality is they're not with KPAP and we hear they pay their porters nearer half of what they claim. Good reviews overall so busy and popular – but we don't like it when a company can so blithely lie on certain issues.

● **Summary** Cheap but dishonest in certain areas. Positive appraisals online but if you can't trust the company, why care about the reviews?

Tanzania Travel Company (aka TTC; ☎ 0754-294365; 🖥 tanzaniatravelcompany.com; **A**) Small company run by Tanzanian naturalist Sam Diah that offers, despite the name, safaris all over East Africa. Their Kili treks are rather secondary to their safaris, which is clearly Sam's passion. Claimed in their email to us to be KPAP partners, which they aren't, which is naughty. Also clearly care little for copyright infringement, with some of the text on their website taken from a previous edition of this book. They're not alone in doing that, but if you're copying something wholesale from another source it does suggest a lack of familiarity with the subject, which is a concern. Their prices are US$2025pp for the 7-day Machame; no reduction for children was mentioned initially (though when we enquired why this was so, they then offered all but US$10 of the full discount).

● **Summary** Can't find much to recommend their climbs. Sam should stick to safaris – and you should look elsewhere.

TDMC (☎ +44 (0)1283-711100; 🖥 trekdmc.com; **UK + M**) Large-ish KPAP partner run mostly from Britain (there's no Tanzanian phone number that we could

find) and another that takes bookings only through their agencies. Having climbed with them I found, on the plus-side, the equipment supplied to be very good and food sometimes verging on the excellent. The biggest disappointment, however, was the quality of one or two of their guides on the trek who were distinctly below par given the prices charged by their agencies (US$2795pp, though the full child discount was offered).

● **Summary** Given the bombast on a couple of their agents' websites you'd think that this bunch were the Holy Grail of trekking companies, and they are doing a lot of business; but really need to sort out the quality of their guides if they're going to be anywhere near as good as their agencies boast.

Team Kilimanjaro (☎ 0787-77 5895, 🖥 teamkilimanjaro.com; **A**) No doubting the quality of this well-established company that offers treks on all the routes (although Marangu only reluctantly) including their own take on the Rongai Route and their very popular TK Lemosho Route (see p83). Their guides are, on the whole, amongst the best on the mountain, which has always been their biggest selling point, and the reviews are still pretty universally positive. Slightly concerned about the wages of the porters, however, which are slipping behind their rivals. Price-wise, they're firmly in the mid-range bracket at US$2414pp, with the full under-16 discount passed on to their clients. Note they also provide cheaper versions of their treks, including a Lite version (US$2235pp for seven days on Machame) with no pre- or post-trek accommodation, mess tents or airport transfers, and you have to carry around 12kg; and Superlite (US$1803), where you provide and carry all your own food and equipment too. For even cheaper treks with the same organisation, see Team Maasai, below.

● **Summary** Still a class act with some top-performing guides but do enquire about the treatment and salary of porters when you contact them.

Team Maasai (☎ 0777-123 5895, 🖥 climbkilimanjaro.co; **A**) If the name doesn't give it away, one look at the wordy website of this outfit should provide enough clues that this is an offspring of Team Kilimanjaro – staffed almost exclusively by Maasai from the Ngorongoro and Lake Natron regions (though the guides seldom are). Claim to have the cheapest published prices anywhere on the internet for fully supported climbs (note this is not the same as claiming to have the cheapest prices full stop), with Machame US$1683pp. It's very much a stripped-down service – accommodation in Arusha, airport transfers and oxygen are all extra – and Kilimanjaro isn't the natural home of the Maasai; they prefer the plains below, of course, so the operation can almost be seen as one big social experiment. But the reviews are positive and certainly value for money.

● **Summary** They're reliable, they're cheap and their treks are basic but fine – though the concern we raise in our Team Kilimanjaro review (see above) also applies here.

Tin Tin Tours (☎ 0657 123766, 🖥 tintin-tours.org; Rengua Rd, **M**) Always a lovely surprise finding a budget company that nevertheless tries to maintain some sort of ethical standards. Tin Tin Tours, a small Moshi-based enterprise, is just such a company, a KPAP partner run by the affable Kashenge who started off as a flycatcher in Dar but has since climbed the social ladder to become both a company director and one of the nicest people in town. Their well-liked treks are amongst the cheapest of those offered by KPAP partners, at US$1875pp (with the under 16 discount a decent US$675), including two nights' accommodation at their own small Nyota B&B (see p249). Positive and recent reviews from clients too.

● **Summary** A good little company, recommended for small groups on a budget looking for a company with well-reviewed treks and its heart in the right place. What's not to like?

Trans-Kibo Travels Ltd (☎ 0754-287618; 🖥 transkibo.com; YMCA Building, Kilimanjaro Rd, **M**) Some companies surprise us with their tenacity, and

BOOKING YOUR TRIP

Trans-Kibo Travels is definitely one of these. Still operating out of shabby offices in the YMCA, they manage to survive while other, bigger companies stumble and fall. Price-wise they are only US$1600 per person for four people for seven days on Machame (with under 16s entitled to a US$500 discount), including two nights at the YMCA thrown in as well as oxygen on the climb. In response to our email they told some downright lies – they *aren't* members of KPAP, despite what they may claim and, given their prices, we can't believe they pay a magnificent Ts25,000 per day to their porters either! Struggled to find any online reviews.

● **Summary** Very cheap – when we called into their office anonymously they offered us a six-day Machame trek for US$1259 without any haggling on my part – but you get what you pay for. And in this case, that isn't much.

Trek2Kili (☎ 0788-360715; 💻 trek2kili.com; M) This company is great. Owned and founded in 2010 by easygoing former porter and guide, Azizi, with administrative help from a Canadian woman, this company has everything going for it: a good success rate, great online reviews for their treks, a fine website and a desire, if their emails are anything to go by, to genuinely treat porters well; indeed, they applied to join KPAP before they'd even taken a booking. (And according to KPAP's latest statistics they're pretty much the tops when it comes to treating their porters fairly.) Treks are all led by WFR-trained guides and are justifiably in the mid-range at US$2550pp with two nights' accommodation at Bristol Cottages thrown in. Also offered us an impressive 50% discount for under 16s – significantly more than the US$696.20 reduction in park fees. Has open-group climbs too that they'll run even if they make a loss

● **Summary** We're really impressed by this lot and think they're well worth contacting.

Tembo Trails/Tusker Trail (toll free ☎ 1-800-231-1919, 💻 tusker.com; M) The ground operator may be Tembo Trails but

everybody knows them as **Tusker**, a very successful American company that's been operating for over 40 years now (second only to Marangu Hotel, we believe). No longer partners of KPAP but have set up their own porter support project. Normally sceptical about companies that set up their own porter welfare programs but we're prepared to give Tusker the benefit of any doubt as it has a long history of being at the vanguard of improving the lot of porters (though we still think it's better when a company subjects itself to independent scrutiny on this matter). More disconcerting was their response to our enquiry about discounts for under 16s. Initially there was no mention of it, then after we enquired about this they replied that the cost to them was the same so no discount was due. Eventually we got a discount of US$560 – still not the full whack but better. Nevertheless, a disappointing response for such an experienced outfit. The quality of their treks, however, is beyond reproach. Prices are pretty wince-making at US$3970 per person, though not outlandish given the specifications of the trek, with oxygen, airport transfers, three or four nights accommodation all included, as well as catering on Kili from a properly trained, qualified chef, private toilets, guides who receive amongst the best medical training, and first-rate gear, much of it specifically designed by Tusker themselves. We also like the enthusiasm they clearly demonstrate towards the mountain, with regular interesting and intelligent articles about Kili produced for those who subscribe to their website. They also, uniquely, run a 'Kili360' tour that begins on the Umbwe Route before heading round the northern side of Kibo, aiming for the summit via the Kibo Huts; we like it when companies create new routes – it shows both imagination and a love of the mountain, in our opinion – and one that incorporates the lovely Umbwe Route should be doubly praised.

● **Summary** Still first-rate, a couple of minor quibbles, but always worth enquiring with if you have the financial wherewithal.

Top Climbers (☎ 0765-993193; 🖥 top-climbersexpedition.com; **M**) Cheap and seemingly excellent value, with Machame price just US$1700 with a great child's discount of US$750 and two nights at the lovely Kili Wonders Hotel. How can they do it, we asked? Well, sad to say that, despite their claims, we have seen a report that their treatment of porters is not exactly exemplary – and certainly not as good as they claim. What can't be argued with is that they do get glowing reviews online.

● **Summary** If their treatment of porters is as good as they claim then they're great and we'll wholeheartedly recommend them. If not, and we don't believe they are, then they're only for those who can leave their conscience at the hotel before climbing.

Tro Peaks (☎ 0763-830820; 🖥 tropeaks.com; **M**) Small company offering budget treks, their prices well below two grand at US$1745pp, though only US$490 of the under-16 discount was passed onto us. When we asked if they were with KPAP they told us that they didn't need to be as they were "human being who believe in God and fear on doing against God so we control ourselves and not forced with any institute to do what they want or they think is better". Which is a novel defence. But maybe we should stop being so cynical because the weight of positive reviews online suggest they're doing something right.

● **Summary** We confess we know little about them other than what we've learnt online and from our correspondence. But if you're after a budget trek and plan to fire off emails to several different companies, you may as well fire off one to Tro Peaks too; according to the reviews, you won't regret it.

Udare (☎ 0784-665 115; 🖥 udaresafari.com, 🖥 www.udaresafari.es; **A**) Fairly new Arusha-based outfit, Udare are, for the time being at least, not doing much business but they have one big selling point: their staff, including the mountain guides, are Spanish speakers. Do still take bookings from Anglophone trekkers too, of course, and their correspondence, though in broken English, was thorough and friendly and their prices reasonable and precise at US$2468.

● **Summary** For Spanish speakers only. We can't comment on the treks themselves at the moment as they have had too few climbs to make a judgement but will be interesting to see how they develop. At the time of writing, they are KPAP partners.

Viva Africa Tours (☎ 0758 555554; 🖥 vivaafricatours.com; Uru Road, **M**) Operating out of Rafiki Backpackers, Viva Africa Tours have been grabbing a fairly healthy slice of the budget market recently. Perhaps deservedly so, too, for their prices start at US$1655pp with two nights accommodation at Rafiki Backpackers thrown in; remember to add on US$50 per person if you want oxygen (which you should). Online reviews suggest they're doing a good job though according to research the wage they pay their porters is less than they claim and disappointingly low.

● **Summary** Not bad but if you can afford to pay a little more to sign up with a company that pays a better wage, please do so.

Zara Tours (☎ 0784-451 000, toll-free 1-866-550-4447; 🖥 zaratours.com; Kibo Tower, **M**) Once the biggest operator on the mountain, Zara are no longer the trekking behemoth they once were though they're still gigantic. The loss of at least one big agent and the rise in competition from several other large-scale operators has reduced their power and influence, and they get fewer bookings these days; a situation that the sour faces of the people in their office will do little to change. Still getting good reviews online but proudly announced in their email that they pay their porters US$7 – which is below the minimum set by KINAPA. Prices: US$2063pp, child discount US$619. Airport transfers are US$20pp extra each way, oxygen is US$14 per day, but two nights at Springland are included.

● **Summary** Competent, cheap-ish and their Springlands Hotel is still lovely – but we think there are now better options for the money.

BOOKING YOUR TRIP

Overseas agencies

A run-down of the larger agencies based outside Tanzania who advertise treks up Kilimanjaro follows. Before booking with anybody, you should have a look at *Booking with a Tanzanian operator* on p60 and *What to look for in your trek package* (p61); though their titles would suggest they're not pertinent, they contain useful advice that could also be relevant when dealing with these agents too.

If you contact several of these agencies you'll probably receive a wide range of prices so remember to **ask each agency exactly what is included**; most companies provide airport transfers and a night or two in a hotel but you'll need to check this with any company you approach. Some prices also include return flights from your home country. You should also check each supplier's ethical credentials. A disappointing number of foreign agencies make bold claims about how well they (ie their ground operator) treat their porters, because this is what their Tanzania operator has told them they do. Unfortunately, the foreign agency rarely verifies these claims – so you must.

It is, of course, the job of travel agencies around the world to extol the virtues of the treks they're selling and each company's website groans under the weight of superlatives that they use to describe the service you can expect on your trek and the once-in-a-lifetime experience you can enjoy. But the bottom line is, these foreign agencies usually have very little input into the treks they're booking on your behalf. So if you want to get a good idea of what your trek will *really* be like, ignore the agents' hyperbole and look instead to see which Tanzanian agency is actually running your trek. Of course, many foreign agencies are reluctant to reveal who their Tanzanian ground operator is, though where we have managed to find who the local operator is we have revealed it.

A couple more things: Some of the information given on the websites of these overseas agencies is either out-of-date or just plain wrong. For example, more than one agency says that the Marangu Route is easy or the Machame Route is quiet; at the risk of sounding arrogant, trust *our* descriptions of the trails rather than theirs. Finally, if you are planning on a safari after your trek, take this into account when choosing which agency to book with: often booking a safari and Kilimanjaro trek with the same company will work out cheaper than booking each leg with a separate company.

COUNTRY-BY-COUNTRY RUN-DOWN

In the following section we have separated the foreign agencies into the country where they're based, as most people will either want to book with an agency in their own country or with an agency in Tanzania. That said, there's no reason

why you can't book with an agency in a third country (eg, somebody from the UK booking with a US agent) if you prefer.

TREKKING AGENCIES IN EUROPE

Austria
● **Clearskies Expeditionen und Trekking** (☎ 0512 28 45 61, 🖳 clearskies.at)
● **Hauser Exkursionen** (☎ 1-50 50 34 6, 🖳 hauser-exkursionen.de) – branch of German agency, see opposite
● **Islaverde Reisen eU** (☎ 660 55 52 775, 🖳 islaverde.at)
● **Weltweitwandern** (☎ 0316-58 35 04-0, 🖳 weltweitwandern.at).

Belgium
● **Africa Tours** (☎ 051-70 81 71, 🖳 africa-tours.be)
● **Allibert** (☎ 04-76 45 84 84, 🖳 allibert-trekking.com) Agents for High Peaks Expeditions (see p85)
● **Joker Tourisme** (☎ 015-40 75 58, 🖳 joker.be)
● **Terres d'Aventure** (☎ 02-543 9560, 🖳 terdav.com).

Denmark
● **Frontiers Ltd** (☎ 33 30 88 10, 🖳 frontiertours.dk) Agent for Snowcap (p96)
● **Inter-Travel** (☎ 33 15 00 77, 🖳 intertravel.dk)
● **Marco Polo Tours** (☎ 70 12 03 03, 🖳 marcopolo.dk)
● **Profil Rejser** (☎ 77 33 56 36, 🖳 profilrejser.dk)
● **Tanzania Tours** (☎ 61 70 16 10, 🖳 tanzaniatours.dk) – uses Good Earth (p84)
● **Topas** (☎ 86 89 36 22, 🖳 topas.dk)
● **Trekking Bureauet** (☎ 46 32 05 32, 🖳 trekkingbureauet.dk).

France
● **Allibert** (☎ 04-76 45 50 50, 🖳 allibert-trekking.com)
● **Huwans Club Aventure** (☎ 01-44 32 09 30, 🖳 huwans-clubaventure.fr)
● **Terres d'Aventure** (☎ 01- 70 82 90 00, 🖳 terdav.com).

Germany
● **Chui Tours** (☎ 0611-182490, 🖳 chui-tours.de) uses Tanzanian Journeys (p98)
● **concept reisen** (☎ 030-218 40 53, 🖳 tanzania-reisebuero.de)
● **DAV Summit Club** (☎ 089 64240 196, 🖳 dav-summit-club.de)
● **Elefant Tours** (☎ 0761-611667-0, 🖳 elefant-tours.de)
● **Explorer Fernreisen** (☎ 0211-994901, 🖳 explorer.de)
● **Hauser Exkursionen** (München ☎ 089-2 35 00 60, Berlin ☎ 30 88 67 81 03, 🖳 hauser-exkursionen.de) – currently uses Snowcap (see p96)
● **Macho Porini** (☎ 08-076/97 07, 🖳 www.macho-porini.de)
● **Tansania Erfahren** (🖳 tansania-erfahren.de) Agents for Origin Trails (see p93)
● **Top Mountain Tours** (☎ 8151 444 1914, 🖳 top-mountain-tours.de).

Ireland
● **Earth's Edge** (🖳 earths-edge.com) Provides an Irish tour leader with every trek and uses KPAP partner Africa Zoom (see p76) as their ground operator. A good company with a good heart offering very good treks.

Israel
● **Kosher Treks** (☎ 2-56-33-218, 🖳 kosher treks.com).

Luxembourg
● **Bel Africa** (☎ 6 33 40 57 73, 🖳 bel africa.com).

Netherlands
● **7 Summits** (🖳 7summits.com) Company run by one-man band Harry Kilkstra that specialises in climbs up each of the continents' highest peaks; uses Zara Tours (see p101)

BOOKING YOUR TRIP

● **Explore Tanzania** (☎ 055-533 25 50, 💻 exploretanzania.nl)
● **Himalaya Trekking** (☎ 052-22 41146, 💻 htwandelreizen.nl)
● **Nederlandse Klim en Bergsport Vereniging** (NKBV; ☎ 0348-409521, 💻 nkbv.nl)
● **Riksja Tanzania** (☎ 071-516 2035, 💻 tanzaniaonline.nl) – agent for Tanzania Journeys (see p98)
● **Snow Leopard Adventure Reizen** (☎ 070-388 2867, 💻 snowleopard.nl)
● **SNP Reiswinkel** (☎ 024-327 7000, 💻 snp.nl)
● **Tanzania Specialist** (☎ 174-50-3917, 💻 tanzaniaspecialist.com).

Norway

● **EcoExpeditions** (☎ 90 04 13 30, 💻 ecoexpeditions.no)
● **Explore Travel** (☎ 69 36 18 50, 💻 exploretravel.no)
● **Hvitserk** (☎ 23 21 30 70, 💻 hvitserk.no)
● **Kilroy Travels** (☎ 026 33, 💻 travels.kilroy.no)
● **Tapac Safaris** (💻 tapacsafaris.com) Agents for Everlasting Tanzania (see p82)
● **Uhuru** (☎ 41 02 02 78, 💻 uhuru.no).

Spain

● **A Step Ahead** (💻 astepahead.es)
● **Giroguies** (☎ 972-303 886, 💻 giroguies.com).

Sweden

● **Aventyrsresor** (☎ 08-55 60 69 00, 💻 aventyrsresor.se)
● **Kilroy Travels** (☎ 0771-545769, 💻 travels.kilroy.se).

Switzerland

● **Acapa Tours** (☎ 056-443 32 21, 💻 acapa.ch)
● **Aktivferien AG** (☎ 052-335 13 10, 💻 aktivferien.com)
● **b&b travel** (☎ 44-380 4343, 💻 bandbtravel.ch)
● **Good African Tours** (💻 goodafricantours.com) – uses African Scenic Safaris (see p75)
● **Kaufmann Trekking** (☎ 041-822 00 55, 💻 aktivferien.ch) – agent for Marangu Hotel (see p90)
● **Terres d'Aventure** (☎ 022-518 0513, 💻 terdav.com).

TREKKING AGENCIES IN THE UK

360 Expeditions (☎ 020-7183 4360, 💻 360-expeditions.com) Uses KPAP partner Pristine Trails (see p94) as their ground operator. Currently seems to offer treks on the Lemosho and Rongai routes only – and only a couple of times a year too. Still, a UK tour leader is added to the mountain crew (in addition to the local guides), they hold regular pre-expedition sessions so you can meet your climbing buddies before you go – and prices include airfare.

Aardvark Safaris (Hants ☎ 01980-849 160, London ☎ 0208-1507216, Scotland ☎ 01578-760222, 💻 aardvarksafaris.co.uk) With a name that pretty much guarantees it will always be at the top of any alphabetical list of companies, this agency offers tailor-made trips to Africa and is the main agent for Summits Africa (see p97). Offer Summits' 'Luxury' and VIP services only.

Abercrombie & Kent (☎ 01242-547 760, 💻 abercrombiekent.co.uk) Upmarket holiday company (they have branches in both Harrods and Monaco!) now using their own trekking company – one of the few that do. Concentrate on Machame and Lemosho but can guide on Rongai and Umbwe too.

Acacia Africa (☎ 020-7706 4700, 💻 acacia-africa.com) Africa specialist using Springlands as a base (so it looks like Moshi's Zara Tours, see p101, are the local trekking agency here).

Action Challenge (☎ 020-7609 6695, 💻 actionchallenge.com) 'A specialist organiser of challenge events across the globe', Action Challenge's main business is helping with the organisation of various charity treks and adventures. Runs around 25 group treks per year, with each group size a hefty 20-25 people – too many for some

BOOKING YOUR TRIP

people's tastes, though others will like the feeling of safety that comes with being surrounded by so many kindred spirits. Offer three payment options: you can either pay for it all yourself; pay a deposit then commit to raise a certain amount of sponsorship for a charity of your choice, from which payment for your final balance is taken; or you can opt for a mixture of the first two. A UK trip leader and doctor accompany every trip and the packages include everything, even the flights. Only the Machame, Lemosho and Rongai routes are offered. Currently uses both Big Expedition (see p77) and Ahsante (see p77), we believe.

Africa Odyssey (☎ 020-8704 1216, 💻 africaodyssey.com) Agents for African Walking Company (see p76).

Africa Travel Resource (ATR; ☎ 01306-880770, 💻 africatravelresource.com) The only foreign agency I know that offers, for a price, the ALTOX Personal Oxygen Systems (where two bottles of oxygen are fed through cannulas inserted into the nostrils to help clients to the summit; their advertised summit success rate is 96%, possibly because of this). ATR's website is stuffed with information but can be a little clunky and confusing. Uses African Walking Company. Recommended.

Audley Travel (☎ 01993-838 000, 💻 audleytravel.com) A travel agency with multiple awards to their name that uses Nature Discovery (see p92) as their ground operator, so Lemosho, Machame and Nature Discovery's 'Grand Traverse' (which combines the Shira Plateau Route with the Northern Circuit) are the routes offered. Flights are included.

Charity Challenge (☎ 020-8346 0500, 💻 charitychallenge.com) Arranges expeditions to various places for those looking to raise money for charity. Seems to concentrate on the Lemosho and Rongai routes only. Flights are included. Use Ahsante (see p77) as their Kili ground operator.

Climb Kili (☎ 0800-098 8773, 💻 climbkili.com) UK office of Arusha-based company (see p78).

Different Travel Company (☎ 0788-169 8623, 💻 different-travel.com) Offers trips all over the world including the (very) occasional foray up Kili, using the praiseworthy African Scenic Safaris (see p75).

Dig Deep (Africa) (☎ 0114-275 1790, 💻 digdeep.org.uk) Great little charity working to increase access to water and sanitation in Kenya. Uses KPAP partners African Scenic Safaris and Trek2Kili for their six-day Machame treks.

Discover Adventure (☎ 01722-718 444, 💻 discoveradventure.com) As with many of these charity expedition companies, if you manage to raise a certain amount of sponsorship the money to pay for your climb will come out of it. Currently offer only the Machame Route.

Equatours (☎ 0203-239 3235; 💻 equatours.co.uk) Agent for Big Expeditions (see p77).

Exodus (☎ 0203-131 2941, 💻 exodus.co.uk) Large, long-standing and agents for African Walking Company (see p76). Offer return flights too. Laudably, they also run the Porter Education Project to teach English to the porters during the low season (Apr-June) and have established three schools in the local area to facilitate this.

Explore Worldwide (☎ 01252-883 725, 💻 explore.co.uk) Long-established company offering treks on the Lemosho Route, often in combination with something else such as a four-day safari or three-day Zanzibar jaunt. Prices can include or exclude flights. For Kili they use Ahsante of Moshi (see p77).

Extraordinary Africa (☎ 0207-097 1801, 💻 extraordinary-africa.com) Agent for Nature Discovery offering Machame and Rongai routes.

Gane & Marshall (☎ 01822-600 600, 💻 ganeandmarshall.com) Africa specialists whose co-founder, Jeremy Gane, was one of the organisers behind 2009's successful Comic Relief celebrity climb (a UK television charity fundraiser). Treks offered include regular, open group climbs (ie anyone can join) for eight days on Shira (that's

BOOKING YOUR TRIP

the old Shira Route via the Morum Barrier) and six days on Rongai – though, concerned about acclimatisation, they offer the latter only if you book in combination with a Meru climb or a short 'acclimatisation safari' – a walk in the Ngorongoro Highlands. All other routes are offered. African Walking Company (see p76) are their ground operators. Unfortunately, they are another that still advertises their work with KPAP – though they are not currently partners.

Imaginative Traveller (☎ 01728-862 230, 🖳 imaginative-traveller.com) Runs group treks on the Rongai, Marangu and Machame routes each month as well as a fourteen-day Serengeti and Kilimanjaro trip culminating in a six-day jaunt up the Marangu Route. Uses the charming Kibo Hotel as their base for at least some of their climbs. Seem to use the Intrepid ground operator Peak Tanzania for their treks (see p93).

IntoAfrica (☎ 0114-255 5610, 🖳 intoafrica.co.uk) Advertises fair trade open-group mountain climbs on the Machame Route, the price depending on the number of people in your booking. Support several charity projects and work with Kwetu, see p88.

Intrepid Travel (☎ 0808-274 5111, 🖳 intrepidtravel.com) Offer some humungous overland tours – including a 64-day odyssey between Capetown and Nairobi – as well as Kili climbs on the Rongai, Marangu and Machame routes, with the Kibo Hotel as their base and now operate their own treks via their company Peak Tanzania (see p93).

Jacada Travel (☎ 0203-131 5263, 🖳 jacadatravel.com) Tailor-made luxury trips using Nature Discovery (see p92) for their Kili climbs.

Jagged Globe (☎ 0114-276 3322, 🖳 jagged-globe.co.uk) Serious mountaineering company established more than 30 years ago that arranges eight-day treks on the Lemosho Route (they call it Lemosho Glades), each led by a UK guide; also, refreshingly, offer an Umbwe/Western Breach combination, with a climb up Meru beforehand to aid with acclimatisation. Prior to all their expeditions they host a weekend in North Wales for their clients both for instruction and to meet their fellow trekkers. Uses Moshi's Keys Hotel (see p249) as their suppliers, who aren't (yet) KPAP partners, though Jagged Globe do give away fleeces and waterproof jackets to every porter that works for them on the mountain.

Kandoo Adventures (☎ 01283-499 980, 🖳 kandooadventures.com) Agent for TDMC (see p98).

Kilimanjaro Tours (☎ 0800-081 9014, 🖳 kilimanjarotours.co.uk) Fairly secretive company (there's no real clue as to who they are, where they're based or even who their local operators are); though given that they use Mountain Inn as their Moshi base,

---

❏ **Companies with Western tour leaders**
The following overseas agents always send one of their own representatives to 'lead' the group. As these individuals do not have the necessary licence to actually be in charge of the trek, they work alongside the local guide who, in the eyes of the park authorities, will be the real leader of the trek. The Western representative will also be called something like 'tour leader' to distinguish them from the (local) head guide. These guides vary in quality and experience, of course, though most will have some sort of medical qualification, usually Wilderness First Responder (WFR), and will probably have climbed Kili and several other mountains on numerous occasions before.

In the US, **Rainier** (see p112), **Alpine Ascents** (p108) and **International Mountain Guides** (p109) all send a tour leader to accompany their treks, as do **Earth's Edge** (p103) in Ireland, **Action Challenge** (p104), **360 Expeditions** (p104) and **Mountaineerin** (p107) in the UK, **No Roads Expeditions** in Australia (p113) and **Kauffman** (p104) of Switzerland.

it seems pretty certain that Shah Tours, see p96, are the operators here.

KE Adventure Travel (☎ 01768-773 966, ☐ keadventure.com) Worldwide trekking specialists, established for over thirty years now, running seven-day Rongai, eight-day Lemosho and six-day Machame Route treks, the latter usually combined with a trip up either Mount Meru or, unusually, Mount Kenya. Trekkers are housed at the Mount Meru Hotel.

Monix Adventures (☎ 01747-838909, ☐ monixadventures.com) Agency set up by Rhys Jones, one-time record-holder as the youngest person to climb the Seven Summits. Organises corporate teams, charity fundraisers and private group treks.

Mountaineerin (☎ 01925 812 928, ☐ mountaineerin.com) Offers three or four treks per year on the Machame Route accompanied by a UK tour leader, with Duma (see p80) as the local agents.

Outlook Expeditions (☎ 01248-672760, ☐ outlookexpeditions.com) Company specialising in organising expeditions for schools to various parts of the world. For Kilimanjaro the climb is an eight-day assault on the Machame Route. Also offer a trek up Mount Meru. Uses Duma Explorer (see p80) as their local supplier.

Rainbow Tours (☎ 0203-131 4845, ☐ rainbowtours.co.uk) Smart agency specialising in Africa and Latin America, offering Lemosho and Rongai routes (both scheduled treks and private ones) as well as Mount Meru, with flights included. Trekkers stay in the Moivaro Coffee Lodge before and after the climb and African Walking Company (see p76) are the ground operator.

Safarihub (☎ 0203-174 2238, ☐ safarihub.com) Offers Lemosho/Northern Circuit, Machame, Marangu and Rongai treks with African Scenic Safaris as the local operator.

Tribes Travel (☎ 01473-890499, ☐ tribes.co.uk) Award-winning, eco-friendly, fair-trade company that makes a big song and dance about their expertise on Kilimanjaro. Offer treks on all the routes using different ground operators according to the standard of trek and the budget required.

The Ultimate Travel Company (☎ 0203-811 6830, ☐ theultimatetravelcompany.co.uk) Luxury tour operator offering plenty of trips in Africa, including charity climbs on the Rongai Route with their base at Moivaru Coffee Plantation Lodge. Uses Ahsante (p77) for some of their climbs.

Walks Worldwide (☎ 01962-302 085, ☐ walksworldwide.com) Does pretty much what it says on the tin, offering treks and hikes all over the globe including Shira and Rongai routes – so no surprise that African Walking Company (see p76) are the suppliers here. Safaris and Zanzibar excursions can be added too.

Wayfairer Travel (☎ 0203 143 4293, ☐ wayfairertravel.com) Winning the award for the cleverest company name in this book, ethically minded Wayfairer offer Machame and Lemosho treks, with Fair Travel Tanzania as their local partner.

World Expeditions (☎ 020-8875 5060, ☐ worldexpeditions.co.uk) See p113 (Australia) for more details.

TREKKING AGENCIES IN THE USA

North American trekking agencies tend to quote land cost only.

Adventures in Good Company (☎ 877-439-4042, ☐ adventuresingoodcompany.com) Agency specialising in 'adventure holidays' for women including *very* occasional trips up Africa's highest mountain with the lovely Marangu Hotel (p259) as both their base and their ground operator.

Adventure International (☎ 1-888-664-3865, ☐ adventure-international.com) Using Summits Africa (see p97) as their local outfitter (indeed, one of the guys who founded Summits Africa is also part of Adventure International), so as you'd expect this company offers treks on the

Rongai, Machame and Lemosho routes as well as an 'Ultimate Kilimanjaro' climb – a standard Lemosho climb but with a couple of days in the West Kilimanjaro corridor tacked on at the start and a night in Crater Camp included.

Adventure Life (☎ 406 541 2677, 🖥 adventure-life.com) Offers Machame Route treks using Tanzania Journeys as the ground operator (see p98).

Adventure To Africa (☎ 888 683 4886, 🖥 AdventureToAfrica.com) Offers Machame, Rongai and Lemosho treks including women-only treks.

Adventures Within Reach (☎ 303-500-5047, 🖥 adventureswithinreach.com) Award-winning 'adventure company' now working with Moshi's Tanzania Journeys (see p98). Offers all routes, the itinerary of

their treks being fairly standard and their prices reasonable.

Africa Adventure Consultants (☎ 303-416 6202, 🖥 adventuresinafrica.com) Another multi award-winning company more famous, perhaps, for its Southern and Western Circuit safaris than Kili, though they offer all the routes. Use Nature Discovery (see p92) for their treks.

Africa Travel Resource (☎ 1-313-744-2871 or toll free ☎ 1-888-487 5418, 🖥 africatravelresource.com) American contact of UK company, using African Walking Company for their climbs; see p76.

Alpine Ascents International (☎ 206-378-1927, 🖥 alpineascents.com) Highly regarded, very professional and efficient agency that uses Big Expeditions of Arusha (see p77). All their climbs are accompanied

---

❑ **WHICH NATIONS CLIMB KILI?**

Once again I am very grateful to KINAPA for supplying the most up-to-date statistics available for this edition on which nationalities climb the most. I'm not sure how reliable they are, but they are the best we can get; plus, to be fair, they do seem to conform to my own impression of which nationalities climb the most.

Where are all the trekkers from?

The following are the figures for 2016 – the latest figures available for the mountain:

United States	11,065	Swaziland	784
United Kingdom	5065	Russian Fed	712
Germany	3569	India	645
Australia	2374	Poland	636
Canada	1844	Korea (South)	622
France	1666	Ireland	595
Tanzania	1470	South Africa	547
China	1295	Italy	505
Netherlands	1166	Belgium	461
Denmark	1157	Israel	407
Norway	1038	Switzerland	355
Sweden	960	Austria	251
Spain	959	Singapore	245
Kenya	935	New Zealand	228
British Indian Ocean	905	Other	3979
Japan	792	**Total**	**47,232**

The first thing to note is that there are fewer people climbing now than in the last edition when, in 2012, a total of 57,456 people attempted to reach the summit of Kili. Ever-increasing park fees, the addition of VAT to those park fees, concerns about terrorism (which is unfair on Tanzania, which has seldom been the target of terrorism,

by one of their own mountain guides on the only two routes they offer – Machame and Lemosho.

American Foundation for Children with AIDS (☎ 888-683 8323, 🖵 afcaids.org) Charitable foundation with good ethical principles, arranging climbs through Summit Expeditions and Nomadic Experiences (see p97) to raise money under their 'Climb Up So Kids Can Grow Up' scheme.

Anywhere (☎ 888-456 3212, 🖵 anywhere.com) Uses ground operator Everlasting Tanzania (see p82).

Climb Kili (☎ 1-888-589-1884, 🖵 climbkili.com) American office of Arusha-based company (see p78).

Destination Tanzania Safaris (☎ 1-888-861-6518, 🖵 detasa.com) American office of Arusha-based company (see p79).

Embark Exploration Company (☎ 503-922-1050, 🖵 embarkexplorationco.com) A company that claims it was founded on the slopes of Kili, offering just the Lemosho route with options to take the Western Breach and sleep in the Crater. Uses Real Life Adventures (p94), a KPAP partner.

Global Basecamps (☎ 866-577-2462, 🖵 globalbasecamps.com) Offers 8-day treks on the Machame Route.

Good Earth (☎ 888-776-7173, 🖵 goodearthtours.com) Maryland branch of Arusha-based KPAP partners.

International Mountain Guides (IMG; ☎ 360-569-2609, 🖵 mountainguides.com) Long-established company that's conduct-

---

though its neighbours, and in particular Kenya, certainly have) and a downturn in the economic fortunes of several countries that usually send a lot of trekkers to Kili (such as the UK) have probably all contributed to this decline in visitor numbers. Bad news for those who make their living from the mountain, of course, though some of us will be pleased that there are fewer people climbing – the trekking companies will disagree, but over 57,000 people on the mountain in a year is, we think, just too many.

As for which countries they come from, I suppose these figures hold few surprises for those who know the mountain. In general Americans don't travel as much as Canadians, Europeans and Antipodeans but for some reason they love Kilimanjaro, a passion that I can only ascribe, maybe, to the 'Hemingway effect', his books doing much to publicise the mountain in his native country. Brits, of course, have a colonial connection to East Africa and are great travellers, and the same description can be applied to the Germans.

The emergence of the new economic superpowers, in particular China, appears to be reflected in their figures, too, and is one of the few countries to have increased the number of people it sent to Kili (from 772 in 2012). It's noticeable, too, that Russia feature for the first time, sending 712 people to Kili. This can be ascribed, we believe, both to the country's increasing economic performance and, perhaps more importantly, the work of Altezza, the first Russian-speaking trekking agency for Kili and one that does much to advertise the mountain in that country.

Incidentally, you'll notice that, apparently, 905 people came from 'British Indian Ocean'. These are a tiny huddle of islands in the middle of the sea halfway between Tanzania and Indonesia. The only inhabitants these days are US and British military personnel and associated contractors – a total population of about 2500; as such, we believe that – unless a third of the people moved en masse to Tanzania to try to conquer Africa's highest mountain – this is a mistake, and the people who declared that they are from British Indian Ocean are actually just British. It doesn't alter the UK's position in the above table either way.   *(continued overleaf)*

(continued overleaf)

BOOKING YOUR TRIP

ed almost 200 climbs on Kilimanjaro with Moshi's Keys Hotel, see p249, as the local supplier. The climb – seven days on Machame – is the only one offered though other routes can be used on request if booking a private trek. An American tour leader-cum-high-altitude expert accompanies every trek and safaris are offered after the trek too.

Intrepid Travel (☎ 800-970-7299, 🖳 intrepidtravel.com/us) US branch of Australian conglomerate and KPAP partner, using their own company, Peak Tanzania, as their ground operators (see p93).

Journeys International (☎ 734-665-4407, toll-free ☎ 1-800-255-8735, 🖳 journeys.travel) Offers six-day treks on the Rongai Route as part of a larger tour that

also encompasses a safari and a few days on Zanzibar, with African Walking Company (see p76), according to their Africa desk, their ground operators.

Journey to Africa (☎ 888-314-7232, 🖳 journeytoafrica.com) Agent for Marangu Hotel (see p90), though they also use African Environments (p75) if people want to take the Lemosho Route.

Kensington Tours (☎ 1-888-903-2001, 🖳 kensingtontours.com) Agent offering fairly luxurious tailor-made trips and cruises and well as three routes on Kili – Rongai, Machame and, refreshingly, Umbwe – as well as a 12-day Machame climb-safari combo.

Madison Mountaineering (☎ 844-526 3629, 🖳 madisonmountaineering.com) Big

---

❑ WHICH NATIONS CLIMB KILI?
(*continued from p109*)

Which route do they all take?
So which routes do all these climbers use? Once again, my gratitude goes to KINAPA for supplying the following figures for 2016:

Machame	20,339	**Rongai**	4088	**Marangu**	12,289
Umbwe	589	**Shira/Lemosho**	9927		

The thing that leaps out at you about these figures is that Machame is still, quite significantly, the most popular route, a position it has held since 2006/7 when it first knocked Marangu into second place. This won't surprise anybody who's trekked on this trail for the past few years – but will come as a blow to those many foreign agents who still try to hype the 'Whiskey Route' as a wild and untrammelled path. Remember, too, that the Marangu Route gets trekkers all year-round, because people on this route sleep in dormitories in huts rather than under canvas so it still gets trekkers during the rainy season, while the Machame Route is virtually deserted at that time; which means, of course, that during the rest of the year they must get many, many more people than the Marangu Route.

Other points to note? Well, it's interesting how much the Lemosho/Shira Route has grown in popularity to become the third busiest route (from 7807 in 2012). That may have something to do with this book, which has always sung its praises, as well as an increasing awareness amongst trekkers that a longer route is better for acclimatisation. We're pleased it's doing so well – but there's a part of us, of course, that doesn't want it to get *too* popular – that just leads to overcrowding and a decrease in the magic that made it so special in the first place.

Finally, I do find it a little surprising to see how unpopular the Umbwe Route continues to be. It's a beautiful route and, being close to Moshi, a convenient one for the agencies to use. But its reputation as the 'hardest' route seems enough to deter most people from taking it.

Expeditions are the ground operators here (see p77).

Mountain Madness (☎ 1-800-328-5925, 🖥 mountainmadness.com) Founded by the late Scott Fischer, after whom Kili's (now disused) Fischer Campsite is named, the highly regarded Mountain Madness and their sister company African Environments (see p75) have a long association with the mountain, pioneering Kili's Lemosho Route across the Shira Plateau. These days, while continuing to patronise Lemosho (including an ascent via the Western Breach and a night in Crater Campsite) they also offer an optional jaunt to the Serengeti. One of the best.

Mountain Gurus (☎ 425-749-7421, 🖥 mountaingurus.com) Offer six-day treks on the Rongai Route, seven days on Machame and eight on Lemosho. More extensive trips that take in a Serengeti safari are available too, with Big Expeditions (see p77) the ground operator.

Mountain Travel Sobek (☎ 1-888-831-7526, 🖥 mtsobek.com) Upmarket trekking company that claims to have been the first in the States to lead commercial treks up Kilimanjaro. Offer ten-day hikes on the Machame/Western Breach trail (with eight days actually on the mountain), including a night at Crater Campsite. Cost is over five grand before you even add on park fees. Uses African Environments (see p75) as their local supplier.

Piper & Heath Travel (☎ 1-858-598-5559, 🖥 piperandheath.com) Uses

And how many people make it to the top?
We were provided with one more table by the park authorities, but whereas we are inclined to believe the other figures that they gave us, we are less inclined to trust these ones:

Point reached	Number of climbers	Percentage
Stella Point	1367	3.33%
Gillman's Point	12,784	31.14%
Uhuru Peak	26,685	65%
Unsuccessful	218	0.53%
TOTAL	41,054	100%

Why are we so sceptical about these figures? Well, firstly, they are incomplete: according to the above tables, 47,232 people climbed in 2016, yet only 41,054 are recorded on this table. Secondly, their claim that only 0.53% fail to get even to the Crater rim (ie either Stella or Gillman's), is, to be blunt, ludicrous. Thirdly, 31.14% got to Gillman's, yet only 3.33% got to Stella – even though they are at approximately the same altitude and more people access the Crater rim via Stella than via Gillman's. And lastly, at the risk of sounding cynical, if there's one set of statistics that KINAPA has an incentive to manipulate, it's the success rate – they want to make the mountain as appealing as possible, of course, and displaying a high rate of success for people attempting to get to the summit is one way of doing that.

Given that this table suggests only 41,054 people climbed in 2016 rather than the full 47,232, we could, I suppose, assume that the 6178 people *not* recorded in this table (ie 47,232 less 41,054) *all* failed to reach the Crater rim. This would give us a total of 218 + 6178 = 6396 who failed to get to either Gillman's or Stella, or approximately 13.5% of the total, which to us looks a lot more believable. But this is just guesswork on our part and as such is no more reliable than KINAPA's own figures on this matter.

Summits Africa (see p97) as their local operator.

Rainier Mountaineering Inc Expeditions (RMI; ☎ 1-888-892-5462, 🖳 rmiguides.com) These mountain experts operate on all 'seven summits'; on Kili they follow the (over-)popular Machame Route for their seven-day treks, though you get a Western tour leader accompanying you on the trek and a four-day safari on the Northern Circuit at the end. Currently uses Dik Dik Tours (see p79) as their local supplier though we have heard rumours this may change.

REI Adventures (☎ 800-622-2236, 🖳 rei.com/adventures) Large and established outfit that's half camping shop, half travel agency with Kili treks on offer on both Marangu and Lemosho routes. Uses Tanzanian Journeys (p98) as their ground operator.

RMI Expeditions (☎ 888-892-5462, 🖳 rmiguides.com) Organises treks on the Machame Route with the obscure Barking Zebra as their local trek provider.

Thomson Safaris (☎ 800-235-0289, 🖳 thomsontreks.com) Highly regarded and multi-award-winning outfit that's been operating for more than 30 years. Indeed, they were the first US tour company in Tanzania and one that was recommended by David Breasher, the director of the IMAX film *Kilimanjaro: To the Roof of Africa* (see p395). Their trekking partner, Nature Discovery (see p92), boasts a great reputation for looking after their porters. There are three routes on offer: Umbwe, Lemosho Route (with a night at Crater Campsite) and the great ten-day Grand Traverse that starts on the Shira Plateau and heads east towards Mawenzi Tarn before looping back to School Hut.

Tusker Trail (☎ toll free 1-800-231-1919, 🖳 tusker.com) American contacts for Tusker Trail/Tembo Trails of Moshi – see p100.

Ultimate Kilimanjaro (☎ 312-278-1008, 🖳 ultimatekilimanjaro.com) Yet another company with a rather boastful site, though essentially they are agents for TDMC (p98), having moved from Zara a few years ago.

Urth Expedition (☎ 512-787-4628, 🖳 urthsafari.com) Texas-based company offering Lemosho, Machame, Rongai and Northern Circuit treks arranged with East Africa Voyage (see p81) as their local partner.

WHOA Travel (☎ 347-875-0338, 🖳 whoatravel.com) Boutique agency run by women, for women, with Trek2Kili as the local ground operator (see p100).

Wild At Heart Journeys (☎ 925-631-7978, 🖳 wildatheartjourneys.com) Offers all routes using both African Environments (see p75) and Summits Africa (see p97) as their ground operators.

Wildland Adventures (☎ 800.345.4453, 🖳 wildland.com) Machame route climbs advertised with Africa VIP (see p75) as the local partner.

Wilderness Travel (☎ 1-800-368-2794, 🖳 wildernesstravel.com) Offers an 11-day Lemosho/Western Breach Route (including a night at Crater Campsite) preceded by a couple of nights in a camp at Arusha National Park for acclimatisation. Uses African Environments (see p75) as their local supplier.

Zephyr Adventures (☎ 888-758-8687, 🖳 zephyradventures.com) Hiking, cycling, skating and multi-sport agency that also does Lemosho treks on Kili, with lodging at Planet Lodge and the trek organised by Good Earth (see p84).

TREKKING AGENCIES IN CANADA

Canadian Himalayan Expeditions (☎ 800-563 8735, 🖳 himalayanexpeditions.com) Run private treks (minimum four people) on the five-day Marangu and six-day Machame routes.

Club Aventure Voyages (☎ 481-687-9043, 🖳 clubaventurequebec.com) Uses East African Voyage as their ground operator (see p81).

Contact Amerique (☎ 450-227-7207, 🖳 cavoyage.ca) Again, East African Voyage (see p81) are the ground operator here.

Esprit d'Aventure (☎ 514-564-8288, 🖳 esprit-daventure.com) Agents for Nature Discovery (see p92).

G Adventures (☎ 416-260-0999, 🖳 gadventures.com; also Vancouver ☎ 1-604 694 6669) Huge outfit that seems to hoover up almost all of the Canadian market, using agents to sell their tours (rather than their own offices); offer treks on all routes, using Easy (see p82) as the local outfitters.

Good Earth (☎ 888-776-7173, 🖳 goodearthtours.com) Vancouver branch of Arusha-based KPAP partners.

The Heritage Safari Co (☎ 888-301-1713, 🖳 heritagesafaris.com; also Calgary ☎ 844-860-3530) Offers Rongai and 'Northern Circuit' routes.

The Safari Partners (☎ 888-717-2327, 🖳 thesafaripartners.com) Offers all routes using Marangu Hotel (see p90) as their local operator.

Trek2Kili (☎ 418-894-8217, 🖳 trek2kili.com) Canadian contacts for this excellent joint North American-Tanzanian venture offering all the routes (see p100).

Wanderlust Adventures (☎ 905-783-3384, 🖳 wanderlustadventures.ca) Use Everlasting Tanzania Travel (see p82) as their ground operator.

World Expeditions (toll free ☎ 1-800-567-2216, ☎ 613-241-2700, 🖳 worldexpeditions.com/ca); also Montreal (toll free ☎ 866-606-1721, ☎ 514-844-8144, 🖳 expeditionsmonde.com). See below (Australia) for more details.

TREKKING AGENCIES IN AUSTRALIA

East Africa Safari Experts (🖳 eastafricasafariexperts.com) Offers the Lemosho and Machame routes with African Scenic Safaris as the ground operator (see p75).

Inspired Adventures (☎ 1300 905 188, 🖳 inspiredadventures.com) Agents for African Scenic Safaris (see p75).

Intrepid Travel (☎ 1300 797 010, 🖳 intrepidtravel.com/au) Head office of agency with branches in the UK. Has its own ground operator (see p93).

Majestic Kilimanjaro (☎ 02-481 241 320, 🖳 majestickilimanjaro.com) Australian contact details of promising Arusha-based outfit (see p90).

No Roads Expeditions (☎ 03-9598 8581, 🖳 noroads.com.au) Offers routes on Rongai and Lemosho routes. Use highly rated Marangu Hotel (see p90) for their treks and also offer expeditions led by an Australian guide.

Peregrine Adventures (☎ 1300 854 445, 🖳 peregrineadventures.com) One of Australia's larger agencies, offering Marangu Route with optional Zanzibar/safari add-ons.

World Expeditions (☎ 02-8270 8400, 🖳 worldexpeditions.com/au, Sydney. Also in Melbourne (☎ 03-8631 3300); and Brisbane (☎ 07-3003 0954) This company offers a challenging 15-day Twin Peaks Trekking trip encompassing both Mount Kenya and Kilimanjaro (Rongai Route) or simple Rongai/Shira treks. They also organise a 16-day 'Tanzania on Foot' (A$4990) tour, a combination of safari and trekking including climbs of Meru and Kili. Uses African Walking Company (see p76) for their treks.

Yomads Travel (🖳 yomads.com) Agency specialising in tours for people in their 20s and 30s with Snowcap as the local outfitter (see p96). Recently merged with World Expeditions (see above).

BOOKING YOUR TRIP

TREKKING AGENCIES IN NEW ZEALAND

Adventure Consultants (☎ 03-443 8711, 💻 adventureconsultants.com) Uses Nature Discovery (see p92) for their climbs and currently offers a Machame trek (and optional safari) half a dozen times a year as well as a 'luxury' option. Also offer a Kili-Elbrus combo so you can tick off two of the Seven Summits in one three- to four-week package. Full of knowledge, humour and good intentions, they are a cracking outfit doing really good stuff. Highly, highly recommended.

Adventure World (☎ 0800-238 368, 💻 adventureworld.co.nz) Offers treks on the Marangu and Lemosho routes.

World Expeditions (☎ 09-368 4161, toll free ☎ 0800 350 354, 💻 worldexpeditions.com/nz). See p113 (Australia).

TREKKING AGENCIES IN SOUTH AFRICA

Acacia Africa (☎ 21-556 1157, 💻 acaciaafrica.com) See p104.

AfricanFlamboyance (💻 africanflamboyance.com)

Climbing Kilimanjaro (☎ 087 230 8421; 💻 climbingkilimanjaro.com) Website is one of the most bombastic on the web – quite surprising, given that they're only another agent for Zara (see p101).

Wild Frontiers (☎ 11-702 2035, 💻 wildfrontiers.com) Organises regular trips up Kili and are involved in the annual Kilimarathon. Offers all the routes and special climbs, including some for single trekkers – and the occasional women-only trek too. We think they still use Keys Hotel as their local supplier (see p86 for more).

Other activities

There are plenty of other things you can do with Kili apart from just climbing it.

Cycling around the northern side of Kilimanjaro

As the upper slopes of Kilimanjaro get ever busier, the desire to get a different perspective on the mountain – to step away from the hordes and take a less crowded path – grows ever stronger. Recognising this, several of the more creative trekking agencies – companies such as Summit Expeditions and Nomadic Experiences (SENE; see p97), and Ahsante Tours (p77) – have now added cycling trips to their roster. The composition of these cycling trips varies widely and may include itineraries to Tanga on the coast, down to the legislative capital of Dodoma and even to the parks of the Northern Circuit, where you swap two wheels for four to enjoy a game drive. (Thanks to a relaxation in the park rules, it is also now possible to cycle to the summit too.)

For us, however, the best route is currently that which takes in Kilimanjaro's little-visited northern side. For those interested in the culture of the people who call the mountain their home – a culture that, on this side of the mountain, remains largely untouched by the trespasses of the tourist – this trip has no equal.

It's in the small things that you notice just how little the outside world has infiltrated into this sunny corner of Africa. For example, the children here ask not for 'chocolate', 'school pen' or 'money' – requests that you'll hear pretty

much everywhere else in Northern Tanzania; instead, the kids here just want the chance to say 'Jambo' to the sweating middle-aged *mzungu* wobbling past on his bike. It's very lovely and very, very refreshing.

Such an unexpected reception emphasises the fact that you are now in a different sort of Tanzania, one that has so far been left pretty much untouched by outsiders. Which is why we need to make the following request: don't spoil it. In particular, please do not give out gifts to locals you meet on the way. We know the children are cute and the locals look both friendly and, often, quite poor. But all it takes is one thoughtless act of 'kindness' by a visitor and suddenly that innocent interaction between tourist and local will be much harder to come by; for no matter how well-intentioned the hand-out, the local recipient of your largesse could for evermore look upon foreigners as a potential source of gifts. Inevitably, one day, the Maasai and Chagga of northern Kilimanjaro will come to view the tourist in the same light as people in most other parts of Tanzania, and friendly greetings will be replaced by requests for material goods, or simply hard cash. I recognise that. But let's try not to accelerate that process.

We must also add a word of warning: cycling round here can be tough. Admittedly, regular cyclists, the fit and the under-thirty may find it a breeze. Those, however, who have, ahem, lived a little, carry a paunch, and whose normal idea of an exercise regime is to walk the dog for an hour a day round the gentle hills of Sussex, may find themselves wobbling in the wake of the rest of the team. If that sounds like you, you can always extend the expedition by a day or two to allow yourself to cycle for shorter distances each day. After all, this is a trip that needs to be savoured, and the peace and stillness that can be experienced round Kili's northern side is one that's best enjoyed without the perpetual screaming of one's calf muscles.

So how long does it take? Well, from our own experience of this 'Tour de Kili', we were able to pedal **from Marangu**, on the south-eastern side of the mountain, **to Simba Farm**, on Kili's western flank, in two and a half days. That's not going at a frenetic pace at all, and for more experienced cyclists that's really quite slow going. But it does give you plenty of time to take in the scenery and visit the markets on the way.

On such a trip you'll quickly notice that each side of the mountain has its own character. On the eastern side, for example, the newly built road has made cycling much more straightforward but it also means that the traffic is greater. This is also, interestingly, the hardest side, particularly the long haul up to **Useri** – a climb that cyclists have dubbed, not inaccurately, Heartbreak Hill. It's a relentless climb, guaranteed to make you sweat and swear while uniformed schoolchildren shout cheerful insults that are addressed to you, though in all honesty are intended more for the amusement of their classmates. If you have begun your trip in Marangu and this first day reduces you to tears, don't despair: the cycling on subsequent days is more straightforward, the gradients less severe and what you see is more diverting too.

Approaching the north-eastern corner of the mountain, you'll pass through patches of virgin forest, where turaco shout encouragement from the trees, huge blue butterflies flit between the members of your convoy, and the occasional

BOOKING YOUR TRIP

colobus monkey will stop eating for a second to peer through the branches at this strange and colourful pedalling parade. And by the time you move around the northern side, and leave the tarmac behind at **Kamwanga**, a tranquillity settles on the landscape that is just lovely. Few are the cars that drive along this stretch and your fellow road-users will, on the whole, be pedestrians travelling to and from the local markets, together with the occasional motorcycle hired to transport those travellers with heavier loads or further to go.

The lively village of **Kigielli** is a venue for one such market, where you can pick up a pair of Maasai sandals (the ones made out of old tyres) for about US$3-5. Thereafter, the scenery of neat, fertile farmland gives way to a dusty wilderness of acacia and savannah, where the tyres on your bike squelch through the dung of buffalo and elephant that occasionally cross the road. Maasai children sometimes appear out of the bushes at the side of the road, herding their precious cattle, but otherwise humanity seems a long way away.

Further on, the village of **Kitendeni** signals some sort of return to civilisation and the next village, **Lerangwa**, is big enough to require its own school. Many of the cycle groups camp for the night in the school grounds, much to the amusement of the pupils who arrive for lessons at 7am the next day.

By the time you reach the mountain's western side, the slopes of Kili have been divided up among several huge farms, including Mountainside Farm, where eland and antelope can still be seen roaming. (You can read about the experiences of the farmer, David Read, who established Mountainside, in his memoir *Another Load of Bull*, see p390.) Their neighbours are **Simba Farm**, where rooms and hospitality await (see p246). From here, it's another couple of hours down to the main Arusha-Moshi road and **Boma N'gombe**, a ride that's described (in reverse) in the introduction to the Lemosho and Shira Routes on p326. Of course, there's nothing to stop you from completing an entire circumnavigation of Kili by cycling along the road via Moshi and all the way to Marangu – a distance of around 65km in total. But for many, the main highway between Arusha and Moshi is a poor substitute for what has gone before, and they are happy to hang up their helmets and give their aching limbs some time off.

Endurance events

How about entering the **Kilimanjaro Marathon** (🖳 kilimanjaromarathon.com)? Taking place in late February or early March, the race is run over the standard 26 miles/42.2km and starts by heading out along the road to Dar before returning to Moshi via a climb to Mweka. As such, it doesn't actually enter into the national park at all – though given the levels of exhaustion suffered by your average marathon participant, it's probably just as well that they don't have to climb a mountain too. A half-marathon, a 10km disabled wheelchair and handcycle race and a fun run are also held at the same time, and with prizes of Ts4 million each to the winners of the men's and women's full marathon (Ts2 million for the half-marathon, plus prizes for the various disabled categories) this is turning into one of the biggest events in Northern Tanzania's social calendar.

For those for whom a marathon is not testing enough, there is always the **Kiliman Challenge** (🖳 kilimanjaro-man.com). This particular brand of

masochism begins with a six-day saunter up the Machame Route to Uhuru Peak, followed by a two-day circumnavigation of the base of Kilimanjaro by mountain bike (around 190km in total), before rounding it all off with the marathon described above. The organisers are at pains to point out that only the last two events are competitive; with the climb, of course, it's too dangerous to race up. If it all sounds too much, you can opt to join just one or two of the activities.

Still not exhausted? Then sign up to the annual **Kilimanjaro Trail Run** (🖥 kilimanjarostagerun.com), an eight-day, 260km (approximately 160 miles) slog around the mountain. Led by Simon Mtuy – record holder for a speed ascent on Kili (see p168), founder of the highly regarded SENE trekking agency (see p97) and all-round good egg – the trail runs along dirt tracks and footpaths, taking you past lush rainforest and waterfalls. The scenery is breathtaking, of course – which is a bit unfortunate when you're spending most of your time running – and your encounters with the locals living on the northern slopes of Kili, where few tourists venture, are usually memorable. Simon is at pains to point out that this is a run, *not a race*, so the competitive aspect of the trip is reduced to a minimum, allowing a strong *esprit de corps* to develop amongst the participants instead. It's not cheap – the 2017 price was US$2195 per person – but for a true adventure you'll be hard-pushed to find a better one.

Horseriding

Makoa Farm (🖥 makoa-farm.com) near Machame Gate organises horseback safaris in the West Kilimanjaro Wildlife Management Area, where you stay in permanent luxury camps, mobile camps, farmhouse accommodation next to Kilimanjaro Forest Reserve or at the guesthouse on Makoa Farm. They also run horseback safaris in Arusha National Park and ride from the slopes of Mount Meru to the slopes of Kili. Some experience is necessary for most of these rides. Costs are €1680-3220 per person for three to six days on the Wilderness Trail in the West Kilimanjaro region, while for the eight-day trek around Kili the prices are between €1990 and €3500pp. Various other options, including a ride in Arusha National Park (2-6 days, €1260-2790), are also offered. It's certainly a unique experience and being on horseback allows you to go where four-wheel drives and mountain bikes never could.

❏ Lap up some luxury or tie the knot

If all of the above sounds just too, well, energetic, then there are a couple of more sedentary options. A few years ago the previous boss of KINAPA, Mr Lufungulo, revealed that he had plans to build a couple of luxury lodges on Kilimanjaro, for those who want to be on the mountain without actually doing anything so exhausting as trekking. To be honest we've yet to see much in the way of progress in this field but should this plan ever come to fruition, the TANAPA website will probably be the best place to look for details (🖥 tanzaniaparks.com).

They have also started to allow people to marry at the summit of Kilimanjaro – though we know of one couple who had to arrange to have the local bishop carried to the top to conduct the ceremony as he was too unfit to walk himself; and those involved should be prepared to get hitched lower down the slopes should any of the participants be unable to make it to Uhuru Peak.

3

TANZANIA

'Strange country isn't it?'
'Yes. It seems so cruel one moment, then suddenly kind and very beautiful.
Maybe there are parts God forgot about – he meant it all to be like this.'
Robert Taylor and **Anne Aubrey** discuss the land we now call
Tanzania in the 1959 swashbuckling classic *Killers of Kilimanjaro*

Although this book concentrates specifically on Kilimanjaro, some
background knowledge of the country in which it stands, Tanzania,
is necessary. For the chances are that climbing Kilimanjaro forms
only one part of your trip to Tanzania, and as such you are going to
need to know what this beautiful country is like and how to travel
around it. With this in mind, the following chapter is divided into
two parts. The first provides a background of the country by looking at the history, economy, culture etc. This should both increase
your enjoyment of visiting Tanzania and serve to put Kilimanjaro
in its national context. The second half deals with the more practical side of things, offering advice and tips to help the visitor.

Facts about the country

GEOGRAPHY

Tanzania occupies an area of 945,087 sq km – a little over twice the
size of California – made up of 886,037 sq km of land (including the
offshore islands of Pemba, Mafia and Zanzibar) and 59,050 sq km of
water. This makes it the largest country in the geo-political region of
East Africa. It is bounded to the north by Uganda and Kenya, to the
west by the Democratic Republic of Congo (DRC), Burundi and
Rwanda, to the south by Mozambique, Malawi and Zambia, and to the
east by the Indian Ocean. The terrain in that 886,037 sq km of land
includes a wide, lush coastal plain and a large and dusty central plateau
flanked by the eastern and western branches of the **Great Rift Valley**
(see p138). There are highlands in both the north and south of the
country and in the centre of the plateau are some volcanic peaks which
again owe their existence to the Rift Valley. Interestingly, over a quarter of the country is given over to national parks or nature reserves.

Tanzania is also a land of extremes, housing Africa's largest
game reserve, the **Selous** (covering 54,600 sq km), and the **Serengeti**,
the park with the greatest concentration of migratory game in the

world. Its borders also encompass a share in the continent's largest lake, **Lake Victoria**, and part of **Lake Tanganyika**, the longest and, after Lake Baikal in Siberia, deepest freshwater lake in the world. The third largest lake in Africa, **Lake Malawi**, also forms one of Tanzania's borders. These lakes were formed when the Great Rift Valley, which runs through the heart of the country, opened up about 30 million years ago. As a direct result of the formation of this valley, Tanzania contains Africa's lowest point, the floor of Lake Tanganyika, some 350m below sea level. It is also, of course, the proud owner of Africa's highest.

Beautiful as this country undoubtedly is, it is also beset by enormous environmental problems, from deforestation to desertification, soil degradation, erosion and reef bombing. Significant damage has already occurred, and is still occurring, with added pressures on the land caused by the meteoric rise in tourism over the past couple of decades. For details of how you can minimise your impact on the environment of Kilimanjaro, see p272.

CLIMATE

Tanzania's climate varies greatly, and you'll be encountering just about all of the variations in the four or five days it takes you to walk to the top of Kilimanjaro. For more about this, see the Kilimanjaro climate section on p15.

Away from the mountain, the narrow coastal strip tends to be the hottest, most humid and tropical part of the country, with the inland plateau being of sufficient elevation to offer some cooler temperatures and respite from the heat. On the coast the average temperature during the day is a sticky 27°C; luckily the sea breezes temper this heat and make it bearable. On the inland plateau you're looking at an average temperature of around 20-26.5°C during the cooler months of June to August, up to a roasting 30°C between December and March.

The **rainy seasons** extend from November to early January (the short rains), and from mid March to May (the long rains). On the coast the average annual rainfall is around 1400mm; inland it is a much drier 250mm, though in mountainous areas it can be a magnificent 2000mm; unsurprisingly, flooding can be a problem at this time.

HISTORY [For a detailed history of Kilimanjaro, see p147]

We, the people of Tanganyika, would like to light a candle and put it on the top of Mount Kilimanjaro, which would shine beyond our borders, giving hope where there was despair, love where there was hate, and dignity where before there was only humiliation.
Julius Nyerere in a speech to the Tanganyika Legislative Assembly in 1959. Following independence in 1961, his wish was granted and a torch was placed on Kili's summit.

The discovery of the 1,750,000-year-old remains of an early hominid, **Australopithecus (Zinjanthropus) boisei**, at Olduvai Gorge in the Ngorongoro Crater (near hominid footprints that could be as much as three-and-a-half million years old), suggest that Tanzania has one of the longest histories in the world. We are now going to cram these three and a half million years into the next three and a half pages – a task made considerably simpler by the fact that this history has, until the last 200 years or so, been unrecorded.

We know that **Khoisan speakers** (from southern Africa) moved into the area of modern Tanzania around 10,000 years ago, to be joined between 3000BC and 1000BC by Cushitic speakers from the Horn of Africa (Ethiopia and Eritrea), who brought with them more advanced agricultural techniques. Over the next few hundred years **Bantu speakers** from West Africa's Niger Delta and Nilotic peoples from the north and Sudan also migrated to the area we now know as Tanzania.

By 400BC merchants from Classical Greece knew about and traded with the coast of East Africa, which they called **Azania**. Some of them eventually settled here to take advantage of the trading opportunities, to be joined later by **traders from Persia** and, by the end of the first millennium AD as trade routes stretched into China, merchants from **India**. The majority of immigrants, however, proved to be the seafaring **traders from Arabia**, and soon the Swahili language and culture, an amalgamation of the cultures of Arabia and the Bantu speakers who had also settled on the coast, began to emerge there.

Portuguese, Arabs, Germans and British

Life on the coastal strip of what is now Tanzania continued, as far as we know, pleasantly enough for a number of centuries, a fairly idyllic existence that was rudely shattered by the arrival of the **Portuguese** following Vasco da Gama's legendary expedition at the end of the 15th century. As greedy as they were intrepid, they built the coastal village of Kilwa Kisiwani into a major trading port which, in typical Portuguese style, they later sacked. Understandably unpopular, the Portuguese nevertheless held on grimly and gamely to their East African possessions for almost 200 years until the end of the 17th century. That they managed to survive for so long is largely due to a lack of a united opposition, which didn't arrive until 1698 in the form of **Omani Arabs**, summoned to help by the long-suffering traders of Kilwa Kisiwani. Unlike the Portuguese, the Omani Arabs were keen to forge trading links with the interior. They pushed new routes across the plains to Lake Tanganyika, thereby facilitating the extraction of gold, **slaves** and ivory from deep within the continent. The Arabs grew inordinately wealthy from the fat of Africa's land to the extent that the Omani sultan decided to pull up his tent pegs from the desert sands of Arabia and relocate, establishing his new capital at Stonetown on Zanzibar.

While this was going on, the Europeans returned to Africa. Initially it was just a trickle of **missionaries** and **explorers**, hell-bent (if that's the right term) on making converts and mapping continents respectively. Indeed, one man who famously combined both vocations, Dr David Livingstone, spent a while in Tanzania searching for the source of the Nile, and it was at Ujiji, on the Tanzanian side of Lake Tanganyika, that Henry Morton Stanley is believed to have finally caught up with him and uttered those immortal words 'Dr Livingstone, I presume'.

With intrepid, independent Europeans now roaming all over the continent, it could only be a matter of time before one European country or another would come up with the idea of full-scale colonisation. By the late **1880s** Britain had already secured a dominant role on Zanzibar. But over on the mainland it was Germany who was making the most progress.

Or rather, one German, for it was **Carl Peters** who, acting independently of his government, established German influence on the mainland at this time, negotiating treaties with local chiefs in order to secure a charter for his **Deutsch-Ostafrikanische Gesellschaft** (DOAG, the German East Africa Company). A few years later and with his homeland's government now supporting his work, Peters' DOAG was formally given the task of administering the mainland. This left the British on Zanzibar fuming – and not a little scared – at the German's impertinence, and war was averted between the two superpowers only with the signing of an accord in 1890 in which Britain was formally allowed to establish a protectorate over her Zanzibar territories. One year and further negotiations later and the land we now know as Tanzania (Zanzibar excluded) officially came under direct German control as **German East Africa**.

The Germans brought a Western education, a rail network, and a higher level of healthcare with them to Africa. They also brought harsh taxes, suppression, humiliation and no small amount of unrest. They were eventually replaced as colonial overlords after World War One by the **British** following a League of Nations mandate. The territory was renamed Tanganyika at this time. After World War Two a near bankrupt Britain clung on to administrative control, though officially Tanganyika was now a 'trust territory' of the fledgling United Nations.

Independence

Life under the British was marginally better than under the Germans, with greater political freedom and an improved economy thanks to the cultivation of export crops; but it was only marginal and soon political groups were springing up all over the country with each campaigning for the same thing: independence. The most important of these was the Dar es Salaam-based Tanganyika Africa Association which, in 1953, elected teacher **Julius Nyerere** as its president. Pressure from Nyerere and his party (now known as TANU, or the Tanganyika African National Union) forced Britain to agree to the formation of an internal self-government. Indeed, so impressed was Britain with Nyerere that the only condition they placed on the establishment of this new regime of self-government was that he should be its first chief minister.

Such a vote of confidence by the British was well founded, for Nyerere seemed to have the necessary intelligence, courage and popularity to ensure a smooth transfer of power. The following extract is from Nyerere's radio broadcast in September 1960, following his accession to Chief Minister, as quoted in Ranford Pratt's *The Critical Phase in Tanzania 1945-68: Nyerere and the emergence of a socialist strategy*. It typifies his wisdom and good sense, and gives a decent indication, I think, of the calibre of the man:

I know the people of this country have already earned the admiration of millions of other people abroad through the way in which the struggle for freedom has been conducted. Militant nationalism has been combined with a smile and humour. Temptation to violence and lawlessness as a means of independence has been resisted. The people of Tanganyika became fervently nationalist without becoming racialists (sic). Colonialism was hated but the hatred did not spread to the people who represented colonialism. Bad laws were resented but

there was no resort to lawlessness in order to remove them. This is maturity. I know this maturity has a firm foundation in our character as a people.

Now a mere formality, **independence** for Tanganyika was eventually declared on 9 December 1961, with Nyerere, just as Britain had hoped, as prime minister. Exactly one year later it was formally established as a **republic**, with Nyerere promoted to president.

On **Zanzibar**, meanwhile, things were going less smoothly. Whilst the Zanzibaris won their independence not long afterwards (December 1963), the two parties that formed the first government did not enjoy popular support but instead had been thrust into power by the departing British because of their pro-British leanings. With a tenure that was decidedly shaky, it came as no surprise when they were toppled in a revolution just a month later. In their place came the popular, radical Afro Shirazi Party (ASP).

Less than a year after independence, on 26 April 1964 the ASP leader, Abeid Karume, was signing an act of union with his mainland neighbours and the **United Republic of Tanganyika** was formed. In October of the same year the name was changed to the **United Republic of Tanzania**, the name being a neat combination of the two former territories. The two maintained separate governments, however, even after 1977 when ASP and TANU were combined by Nyerere to form **Chama Cha Mapinduzi** (Party of the Revolution), or **CCM**, the party which maintains political control of Tanzania to this day.

Modern history

From 1967 to the late 1980s Nyerere and his party followed a socialist course; the economy was nationalised, the tax regime was deliberately aimed at redistributing wealth and new villages were established in order to modernise the agricultural sector and give the rural poor greater access to social services. Unfortunately, the 20-year experiment was eventually deemed a flop, with the economy in seemingly perpetual decline. By 1992 things had got so desperate that the CCM took the unprecedented step of legalising opposition parties after pressure from Western donors for more democracy in the country.

Curiously, this move seems to have done little to achieve this. Three years after the legalisation of political opponents, the first democratic elections were held and the CCM, now under the leadership of **Benjamin Mkapa** following Nyerere's resignation in 1985, emerged once again as the major force in Tanzanian politics. The elections in late 2000 confirmed their dominance with over 95% of parliamentary seats won by CCM candidates. While they undoubtedly remain Tanzania's most credible political party, the scale of the victory suggests that proper political debate is all but impossible; an assumption that the election of **Jakaya Kikwete** in 2005 and 2010 and, in 2015, John Magufuli, both CCM candidates, did little to dispel.

On semi-autonomous **Zanzibar**, things, as usual, have been a little more explosive. Throughout the 1990s and into the 21st century the elections have consistently been marred by accusations of ballot rigging and intimidation of the opposition leaders. These 'voting irregularities' have often brought about a violent response from the people, such as in January 2001 when 27 protesters were shot dead in Pemba as they marched through the streets. Even as recently as 2015 the election was cancelled after the opposition CUF party was said to have prematurely announced their victory. When the vote was rerun the following March the CUF urged its followers to boycott it in protest at the way they had been denied victory the last time round. As a result, the CCM candidate, the incumbent President Ali Mohamed Shein, who first came to power in 2010, was returned with a jaw-dropping 91% of the votes cast.

The future

In some ways Tanzania is a model African nation, garnering international acclaim for its fight against corruption and its efforts to reform itself peacefully – as exemplified by the move towards democracy in the 1990s. That said, given that the ruling CCM party was the only legally permitted party prior to the restoration of the multi-party system in 1992 and has won every election since, one must wonder at the quality of democracy practised in the country.

The current president, John Pombe Magufuli, came to power on his birthday in 2015 in one of the more closely contested elections of recent years. Former Prime Minister Edward Lowassa, having been overlooked for his own party's nomination, decided to leave the CCM and provided the main opposition. Magufuli's reputation for being incorruptible, however, (he has been one of the few public figures in Tanzania about which there hasn't been the whiff of scandal) was enough to see him win through with 58.5% of the vote.

The outlook for the economy seems rosy: in 2010 Tanzania joined its neighbours in forging an East African Common Market. In 2012 huge gas reserves were discovered off the Tanzanian coast. The Chinese, too, have invested heavily in the country, as anybody who has witnessed the growth of Arusha over the last few years, with its gleaming new towers and tarmac roads, will testify.

It remains, however, a nation beset by problems. The usual African ailments – poverty, AIDS, and a lack of clean water, basic healthcare and decent education – are as prevalent in Tanzania as they are over much of the continent. Though the election of Magufuli may seem a step in the right direction, corruption remains rampant too.

In addition to those pan-African ailments, however, Tanzania has other local problems to contend with, from a lack of credible opposition to the main autocratic CCM party to the secessionist grumblings of many on Zanzibar who were never happy with the union with the mainland – a dissatisfaction that four subsequent decades and more of turmoil have done little to dispel. The influx of refugees from neighbouring Burundi and Congo has also put added pressure on the country, particularly in the west around lakes Victoria and Tanganyika. It remains to be seen whether the moderate line Tanzania has taken throughout its independence will continue into the future; and whether this thoughtful, con-

servative (with a small 'c') attitude will be enough to help it to overcome the enormous difficulties it still faces.

ECONOMIC AND POPULATION STATISTICS

Tanzania is one of the world's poorest countries, in the bottom 10% of nations in terms of per capita income. Its per capita GDP stands at a modest US$865 (2015 estimate) and just over 28% live below the poverty line. Nevertheless, these are significant improvements on the figures recorded in the first edition of this book back in 2001 when GDP per capita was US$264 and over 50% lived below the poverty line. Other statistics also suggest that Tanzanians are better off than they were in 2001. Infant mortality stands at a level of 41.2 per 1000 births (down from 85 per 1000 in 2001), and life expectancy is now 62.2, up from 49. Presumably some of this improvement can be put down to the decrease in HIV infection, with 4.7% of the population now estimated to be infected, down from 8.38% of the population in 2001 (though that 4.7% still represents over 1.4 million people).

It's early days yet but the economy is starting to show some positive signs too. Growth in real GDP, for example, hovers around the 7% mark, though this has in turn led to inflationary pressures, with the inflation rate rising to a worrying 6.5% in March 2017. These figures are a bit surprising given that Tanzania is still largely an **agricultural** country. The style of agriculture is mainly traditional, the large collective farms introduced under Nyerere's socialist experiment having been rejected on the whole in favour of the age-old system whereby each farmer cultivates a small plot of land called a *shamba*. The most popular home-grown crops are cotton, rice, sorghum, sugar, bananas and coconuts; sisal, coffee and tea are produced principally for the export market, while cloves and other spices are still grown on Zanzibar and the coast. Agriculture accounts for over a quarter of Tanzania's GDP and employs 80% of the workforce.

Tanzania also has a solid **mining** base with oil, tin, iron, salt, coal, gypsum, phosphate, natural gas, nickel, diamonds and, of course, tanzanite all extracted in the country. Tourism is now a major contributor to the GDP too and is a vital source of much-needed foreign currency, particularly in the north.

THE PEOPLE

With around 53.5 million people split into more than a hundred ethnic groups, numerous local languages and dialects and three main religions, Tanzania is something of an ethnic and cultural hotchpotch. It is a credit to the country that they exist largely in harmony, without succumbing to the sort of ethnic hatred that has riven many other countries around these parts. Native Africans make up 99% of the population; of these, the vast majority (estimated at 95%) are of Bantu origin, though even here there are over 130 tribes. The other 1% are of European, Arabian or Indian origin. Around Kilimanjaro it is the Chagga people, one of the more wealthy and powerful groups in Tanzania, who dominate.

A 2010 Pew survey – the latest figures we have – found the **religious divi-**

sion in Tanzania to be 19.8% Muslim, 74.2% Christian, while 3.2% profess traditional indigenous beliefs, 2.7% are unaffiliated, and 0.1% are Hindu. These last are undoubtedly a highly visible presence in Tanzania with some large, ostentatious Hindu temples in Dar, Arusha and Moshi.

The Chagga people around Kilimanjaro are largely Christian; you can read more about them, their culture and their beliefs on pp185-91.

❏ Language

The first and most common language in Tanzania is **Swahili**, the language originally used by traders on the coast and thus based on Arabic and various Bantu dialects. Zanzibar is still known as the home of Swahili, where the purest form of the language is spoken. A few words of Swahili (**below**) will go a long way in Tanzania; although the prefixes and suffixes used in the language can be a little tricky to grasp, any efforts to speak a few words will endear you to the local people. There are plenty of Swahili dictionaries around: street vendors sell little green versions in Arusha or you can pick one up in souvenir stores for about a sixth of the price they charge.

Around Kilimanjaro, however, it is not Swahili but the language of the **Chagga** people, a tongue sometimes known as **Kichagga**, that dominates, though there are several different dialects. See p186 for a brief introduction.

Swahili – Basics

Yes	*Ndiyo*
No	*Hapana*
Good morning	*Jambo*
My name is...	*Jina langu ni...*
How are you?	*Habari gani?*
Please...	*Tafadhali...*
Thanks (very much)	*Ahsante (sana)*
Do you speak English?	*Unasema Kiingereza?*
Help!	*Saidia!*
How much is it?	*Kiasi gani?*
Slowly, slower	*Pole, pole-pole*
Let's go!	*Twendai!*

Travel

bus station	*kituo cha mabasi*
airport	*kiwanja cha ndege*
port	*bandari*
train station	*stesheni*
ticket office	*wanapouza tikiti*
When will we arrive at...?	*Tutafika...jini?*
Is this the direct way to...?	*Hii ni njia fupi kwenda...?*

Places

bank	*banki*
launderette	*kufulia*
post office	*posta*

Food and drink

beans	*maharagwe*	meat	*nyama*
bread	*mkate*	orange	*chungwa*
chicken	*kuku*	pork	*nyama ya nguruwe*
coffee	*kahawa*	vegetables	*mboga*
cold	*baridi*	venison	*nyama ya porini*
eggs	*mayai*	water	*maji*
fish	*samaki*		

Days of the week

Monday	*Jumatatu*
Tuesday	*Jumanne*
Wednesday	*Jumatano*
Thursday	*Alhamisi*
Friday	*Ijumaa*
Saturday	*Jumamosi*
Sunday	*Jumapili*

Numbers

1	*moja*	7	*saba*	21	*ishirini na moja*	90	*tisini*
2	*mbili*	8	*nane*	30	*thelathini*	100	*mia*
3	*tatu*	9	*tisa*	40	*arobaini*	200	*mia mbili*
4	*nne*	10	*kumi*	50	*hamsini*	1000	*elfu*
5	*tano*	11	*kumi na moja*	60	*sitini*	2000	*elfu mbili*
6	*sita*	12	*kumi na mbili*	70	*sabini*		
		20	*ishirini*	80	*themanini*		

Practical information for the visitor

DOCUMENTS AND VISAS

Rumours are once again afoot – as they periodically are – that there will soon be a visa that covers the five East African countries (Kenya, Uganda, Tanzania, Rwanda and Burundi). But for the moment separate visas still need to be bought for each country.

For Tanzania

Visitors from most countries (including pretty much every country in Europe, as well as Canada, Australia and New Zealand) must pay US$50 for their visa; visitors from the United States, however, must fork out US$100.

A visa is typically valid for 90 days from the **date of issue** (and not the day you arrive in Tanzania, though I have to say many officials don't seem to recognise this). It used to be the case that, unless you were coming from a country without Tanzanian representation, officially you had to buy your visa at the consulate/embassy beforehand. That law was never really enforced, however, and these days **everyone can buy their visa at the airport on arrival in Tanzania** *except* **for citizens of**:

Afghanistan, Abkhazia, Azerbaijan, Bangladesh, Chad, Djibouti, Equatorial Guinea, Eritrea, Ethiopia, Kazakhstan, Kyrgyzstan, Lebanon, Mali, Mauritania, Morocco, Niger, Nigeria, Palestine, Senegal, Somalia, Sierra Leone, Sri Lanka, Tajikistan, Turkmenistan, Uzbekistan.

For those who need or want to buy their visa beforehand a quick web search will bring up contact details for their local embassy. With all **applications** you will need to present a **passport that's valid for at least six months** together with two passport photos (though photos are not usually required at the airport).

You can pick up a visa at one of the following **border controls**: Dar es Salaam International Airport, Kilimanjaro International Airport, Zanzibar International Airport and the Namanga and (so we've been told) Tarakea border crossings between Tanzania and Kenya. (With the upgrading of the road between Marangu and the border crossing at Loitokitok, by the start of Kilimanjaro's Rongai Route, there is some hope that this too will become an official crossing point. But for the moment, though a few adventurers – after some pretty intense negotiations – are getting through, this crossing remains officially closed to Westerners.)

Yellow-fever vaccination certificate It seems that once again it is compulsory for visitors to Tanzania to show evidence that they have been vaccinated against yellow fever if coming from a country where the disease is endemic and assuming that they actually left the airport in that country rather than just transited for less than 12 hours. Given that airport staff in Tanzania have in the

past asked to see proof of inoculation whether you require the jab or not, it's probably best to play it safe and get one anyway. The certificate can be picked up from your doctor after you have received the inoculation and is usually free, though the jab itself is not.

Visas for Kenya

Remember that, if you're flying in and out of Kenya rather than Tanzania you will need a **Kenyan visa** (typically US$50) as well as a Tanzanian one. In 2015 the Kenyan government announced that everyone must apply for their Kenyan visa beforehand by visiting www.ecitizen.go.ke. Visitors are advised to register their application in advance of travel as approvals may take up to 7 days to grant. It's also a very time-consuming process as you have to scan and send various documents, and if you delay for any reason the website throws you out and you have to start all over again! Mercifully, the rule has never been properly enforced and currently it's still straightforward to pick up your visa at the airport. Nevertheless, do check on the latest situation before flying out.

MONEY AND BANKS

Currency

The **Tanzanian shilling (Ts)** is the national currency. It's fairly stable but cannot be imported except by residents of Tanzania, Kenya and Uganda, and cannot be exported.

Cash Foreign currency can be imported and exported without limit. **Dollars** and, to a lesser extent, **sterling** and **euros** are the best currencies to bring.

The question is: in what form should you take your money to Tanzania, ie: should you just bring cash? Or should you rely solely on your credit/debit cards and use the latter to get money out of cashpoints in Tanzania? We advocate bringing

❑ Exchange rates

To get the latest exchange rates visit 🖥 www.xe.com. At the time of writing they were:

UK£1	Ts3000
€1	Ts2649
US$1	Ts2244
Can$1	Ts1745
A$1	Ts1721
NZ$1	Ts1573
SwissFr1	Ts2277
KenyaS1	Ts21.7
Japan ¥1	Ts19.9
S Africa R1	Ts175.4
Norway NOK1	Ts268.2
Sweden SEK1	Ts266.1
Poland PLN1	Ts630.6

credit/debit cards, with a few hundred US dollars in cash as back-up in case you can't find a cashpoint that will take your card.

Dollars are also very useful for those occasions when the Tanzanian shilling is not accepted, such as when paying for upmarket hotel rooms and air tickets, both of which, officially at least, must be paid for in hard currency. The downside of cash is, of course, that it is also the riskiest way to carry money. How many dollars you bring, of course, depends on how much of your trip you've paid for in advance, how long you're staying, and what you hope to do while there.

You will need cash for **tipping**. For a rough guide as to how much you should take, see p23 – then add a few dollars, just in case.

One more thing: when it comes to bringing dollars, **make sure they are new notes** – notes printed before 2003 are seldom accepted.

Credit/debit cards Credit cards are useful in major tourist hotels, restaurants, gift shops and airline offices and their usefulness is increasing. Both **debit and credit cards** enable you to withdraw cash from an ATM; Visa is probably the more useful card in that you can withdraw money from more ATMs than with MasterCard. Credit cards tend to be more expensive as you get charged interest from the moment that you withdraw money (unless you 'pre-load' your card so it is in credit and remains so even after you've withdrawn money). Of course, you run the risk that the cash machines will reject your card or, worse, swallow it, leaving you stuck in Africa with no means of support. Bring some cash as well.

Banks, ATMs and moneychangers
Banking hours are typically 8.30am-4pm Monday to Friday, and 8.30am-1pm on Saturday. However, these days many banks no longer change money and if they do the queues for a cashier can be long. As such, most people visit a moneychanger to swap their currencies. **Moneychangers** are fairly ubiquitous (though less so now that ATMs are increasing in number) and we have pointed out some of them in the city/town guides.

As a general rule, you get a better rate for large denomination bills (US$50 and $100 bills) than small ones. Keep your **exchange receipts** so that when you leave the country you can change your spare shillings back into hard currency. They rarely check, but you never know.

There are **ATM**s in every town in Tanzania and Kenya. Not only are they getting more numerous, they are also becoming more reliable and these days tales of cashpoints swallowing cards or giving out the wrong amount are rare. Alas, **Tanzanian ATMs have started charging for withdrawals**. The cost varies according to how much you want to take out and which bank's cashpoint you are using. The only banks we found that were still offering fee-free withdrawals were **Stanbic** and the **Kenyan Central Bank** (KCB) – though I should imagine there's a good chance that they, too, will have started charging by the time you read this. Trying to withdraw Ts400,000, we found that Barclays were the worst, charging a ridiculous Ts15,400; Standard Chartered were only slightly less venal, charging Ts10,500; while NBC, Exim and most of the others shouldn't feel any sense of pride just because their charges were slightly lower at Ts9000; they are, after all, still charging you to get your hands on *your* money.

GETTING AROUND

Public transport in Tanzania is unreliable, uncomfortable, slow, and not recommended for those with either long legs or haemorrhoids. It is also dangerous. A little-known but highly pertinent fact about Tanzania's transport system is that 3% of total deaths in Tanzania are road-accident victims. Reckless driving is by far and away the biggest cause of most of these accidents, with poor maintenance of roads and vehicles also significant contributors.

That said, Tanzanian transport is cheap, convenient and, it must be said, cheerful: conversation usually flows pretty easily on a bus or dalla-dalla (providing you can make yourself heard above the noise of the stereo). And while some roads are little more than a necklace of potholes strung together with tyre tracks, the main roads between towns are splendid, well-maintained tarmac strips – with speed ramps to deter drivers from going too fast.

By bus
The most luxurious form of ground transport is provided by the **express bus** companies. A few of them, such as Dar Express, deserve their reputation for safety and comfort; you may want to ask your hotel or a local which bus company is currently the most reliable. These express buses run to a fixed timetable and will leave without you if you're late. Buy your ticket in advance.

The cheaper alternative is the ordinary buses or **Coasters** – minibuses which leave when full. These are cheap but you definitely get what you pay for. As with all forms of local transport, ask your fellow passengers what the correct fare is before handing any money over to the 'conductor'; rip-offs are the rule rather than the exception on many journeys. In addition there are the indigenous **dalla-dallas**: minibuses (smaller than Coasters) plying routes around and between neighbouring towns. They're usually a tight squeeze as drivers pile in the customers to maximise their takings. If you're being pushed into one that looks full-to-bursting, simply refuse to enter; there'll be another along in a minute. In Kenya these minibuses are known as **matatus**.

Finally, there are the **shuttle buses** that convey passengers from Nairobi to Arusha/Moshi and back. Comfy and reasonably priced, they're by far the best way of crossing the border overland. See the relevant chapter for more details.

By car
You can **hire a car** in Dar es Salaam and from many of the bigger tour and trekking agencies in Moshi and Arusha – usually with driver included. Make sure you choose a vehicle that is suitable for your requirements. Don't, for example, be tempted to conduct your own off-road safari in a two-wheel drive.

You can **hitch** around the country, though payment will often be expected from a Western tourist; it is, of course, wiser not to hitch alone.

By train
Tanzania *currently* has only a skeleton train service; services to Arusha and Moshi stopped running years ago, though the stations and tracks are still there in both towns and are interesting places to look around if you're very bored. The current administration, however, has plans to revive the railway network – it'll be interesting to see if anything actually materialises from these ambitions.

By air
Flying is an efficient way to cover the vast distances of Tanzania and there are several small chartered and scheduled airlines including Coastal Air, Precision Air, Air Excel, ZantasAir, ZanAir, Tropical Air, Auric Air and the budget airline Fastjet. For details of airlines flying to Kilimanjaro, see p387.

ACCOMMODATION

Tanzania's guesthouses and hotels can be split into three sorts: those that welcome tourists, those that accept them, and those that refuse them altogether. These last are usually the cheapest, double as brothels, have minimum security and advertising and can safely be ignored.

Room rates for the other two start at about Ts10,000/15,000 per night for a single/double; dorms are a rarity (though where you can find them they start at about US$6/Ts15,000 per night). Bear in mind that many hotels still have two tariffs, one for locals and people living in Tanzania (commonly known as the '**residents' rate**') and a more expensive one for foreigners. If business is slow, it doesn't take much effort to persuade some of the smaller hotels to charge you the residents' rate, regardless of whether you live in Tanzania or not.

Take your time when choosing a hotel, particularly in the towns featured here where there are lots of options. **Standards** vary widely but you'll probably be surprised at how pleasant some of them can be, with mosquito nets and attached bathrooms and maybe even a telly.

In Nairobi, safety is a concern in some of the hotels, though the ones we have chosen to recommend in this book were fine. Accommodation on Zanzibar, incidentally, is generally much more expensive. Note, too, that in Swahili *hotel* or *hoteli* sometimes means restaurant rather than accommodation (*mazate*).

For details of **accommodation on the mountain**, see p288.

ELECTRICITY

Tanzania is powered by 250V, 50 cycles, AC network. Those bringing electrical items from home may wish to invest in a power breaker: Tanzania's electricity supply can be erratic on occasions and power surges could seriously impair the efficacy of your electrical instruments, if not melt them altogether. Plugs and sockets vary in style, though by far the most common are the British three-square-pin or, less common, European two-round-pin style.

TIME

Tanzania is **three hours ahead of GMT** and thus, ignoring any Daylight Savings Time, Tanzania is two hours ahead of Western Europe, three hours ahead of the UK, eight ahead of New York, eleven ahead of San Francisco, one ahead of Johannesburg, seven hours behind Sydney and nine behind Wellington.

A point of endless confusion for travellers, and with the potential to cause major problems for the uninitiated, is the concept known as **Swahili time**, used throughout much of East Africa where Swahili is the *lingua franca*. Swahili time begins at dawn, or more precisely at 6am. In other words, 6am is their hour zero (and thus equivalent to our midnight), 7am in our time is actually one o'clock in Swahili and so on.

To add further confusion, this system for telling the time is not prevalent everywhere in Tanzania, with most offices, timetables etc using the standard

style for telling the time. Whenever you're quoted a time it should be obvious which clock they are using but always double check.

BUSINESS HOURS

These are typically 8am-noon and 2-4.30pm Monday to Friday, and 8am-12.30pm for some private businesses on Saturdays.

POST AND TELECOMMUNICATIONS

Telephone

The incredible rise in popularity of **mobile phones** in Tanzania means that the old Yellow TTCL **cardphones** are obsolete these days, though the offices still exist as

> The telephone country access code for Tanzania is ☎ 255.

do, occasionally, the booths themselves. Instead, if you're staying in Tanzania for some time you'll find it far easier and often cheaper to invest in a Tanzanian mobile phone or at least a **Tanzanian SIM card** (Ts2000).

The process of getting a SIM card is straightforward enough: simply visit the store of the network provider you wish to patronise (Vodacom, Airtel etc), and they'll guide you through the process; if you're unsure, ask a member of your trekking agency to accompany you to the store. You may have to show some ID, so bring along your passport/driving licence etc. It's probably not worth getting a local SIM card if you're only visiting Tanzania for a week or two but if you're staying longer than a month it's definitely worth considering. Topping up on credit is simple too – you'll find credit vendors on most street

---

❏ HOLIDAYS AND FESTIVALS

The following are **public holidays** in Tanzania; note that some (eg Zanzibar's Revolutionary Day) are not held nationwide but are celebrated locally only.

1 Jan	New Year	7 July	Industrial Day
12 Jan	Zanzibar Revolutionary Day	8 Aug	Farmers' Day
April	Good Friday/Easter	9 Dec	Independence/Republic Days
26 April	Union Day (National Day)	25 Dec	Christmas Day
1 May	International Labour Day	26 Dec	Boxing Day

Islamic holy days

The dates of the following holidays are determined according to the Islamic lunar calendar and as such do not fall on the same date each year. Their **approximate dates** for the next few years are given. The extent to which these days are celebrated and whether these celebrations will impact on your holiday depends to a great extent on where you are in Tanzania; remember that around Kilimanjaro the people are largely Christian so the impact tends to be minimal, though some shops and businesses close.

● **Id al Fitr** (End of Ramadan – a two-day celebration) approx dates: 15 June 2018, 5 June 2019, 24 May 2020

● **Eid El-Hajj** (also known as Eid El-Adha or Eid Al-Kebir) approx dates: 22 August 2018, 12 August 2019, 31 July 2020

corners and hopefully they would have explained to you when you bought your SIM card what you need to do.

In the book we mark the offices of the various network providers in Arusha on the map.

If your existing phone is unlocked you can put the SIM card straight in; if not, you can pick up a phone cheaply in Tanzania or **get your phone unlocked**. Bensons in Arusha offer this service – see p219 – but when I checked they were asking for at least Ts100,000 to unlock a phone and said it would take anywhere from 24 hours to 20 days (the exact cost and time depending on the make of the phone and the network).

Buying a SIM in Tanzania can save you a small fortune in bills compared to using a mobile and SIM from your home country. That said, telephoning in Tanzania has always been a hit-and-miss affair, and sometimes it's an illogical one too. Phone a Tanzanian landline from a Tanzanian mobile, for example, and you often still have to dial Tanzania's international dialling code (☎ +255). Furthermore, if you are having trouble ringing home, try tacking an extra '0' on to the front of the international dialling code: for example, if you wish to ring the UK but the phone continues to bar your call, dial ☎ 00044 rather than just ☎ 0044. But even if you follow these rules, there are still occasions when it's impossible to get any sort of connection.

Of course the best and cheapest way of ringing abroad is **via Skype and the internet**; most hotels now offer some sort of internet service and if the speed is fast enough it's possible to have a reasonably fluent conversation. If you've brought your Iphone/Android/Windows Phone/Blackberry 10 then WhatsApp will enable you to make free calls over the internet – again assuming you can find a fast enough connection.

Internet access

Most restaurants and nearly all hotels now advertise wi-fi. If your hotel internet is sub-standard then the quickest internet can be had at those cafés which advertise raha wi-fi, for this service is probably the easiest to join and currently the most reliably rapid.

If you didn't bring your own smartphone, laptop or ipad then you'll probably have to resort to Tanzania's **internet service cafés** to get online. They're efficient and good value, charging about Ts1000 per hour. Some of the equipment is a little dated, as you'd probably expect, and the speed of the connection can be a little slow – though since the arrival of broadband the situation has improved markedly.

Post

Thanks to the presence of the English missionaries, matters have already advanced so far in Jagga that the Europeans stationed there get their letters and newspapers not more than a month old. **Hans Meyer** *Across East African Glaciers* (1891)

The postal system in Tanzania has improved since Meyer's day but not massively. Reasonably reliable and reliably sluggish, things do occasionally get 'lost in the post' but most gets through... eventually. You should allow about a

week for postcards to reach their destinations from Dar, a day or two longer
from regional post offices.

MEDIA

Tanzanian television holds little appeal to the average tourist. Sure, BBC and
CNN can be found on many TV sets, but the locally produced fare is of a fairly poor quality. Many Tanzanians are happy to pay the US$80 per month in sub-
scription fees that it costs to watch Premier League football from the UK, and
those locals that can't afford this amount can often be found at one of the local
bars that can and do.

If it's not football, then more often than not the telly in your restaurant will
be showing **music videos**. At a rough guess, I'd say that about 90% of these
videos are promoting the latest **bongo flava** artist – a genre that's spread like
wildfire across the country. It's possible to spend the next couple of pages defin-
ing exactly what is – and isn't – bongo flava, but suffice to say, if you're watching a pop video and in it there's a young man in a cap prancing around a huge
mansion somewhere or driving a very flashy convertible, while at one point a
voluptuous female dancer turns away from the viewer to jiggle her impressive
buttocks vigorously at the camera, then you can be fairly certain that bongo
flava is the category under which this particular video can be filed.

For **newspapers**, *The Daily News* is Tanzania's oldest newspaper, while
The Guardian is, in our opinion, of a better quality and provides better coverage of world events. The weekly *Arusha Times* covers local news stories in its
own inimitable fashion. There are a couple of Kenyan publications too, including the *East African*, which feels more professional and sophisticated. Freedom
of speech is enshrined in the Tanzanian constitution, though journalists are
encouraged to practise self-censorship and journalists who criticise the authorities have in the past been threatened or attacked.

FOOD

*The native foods do not offer much variety, though they do differ widely in different dis-
tricts; but if the traveller is not too dainty and is prepared to make the best of what is to be
had, it is wonderful what can be done.*   **Hans Meyer** *Across East African Glaciers* (1891)

Tanzanian food is, on the whole, unsubtle but tasty and filling. If there's one
dish that could be described as quintessentially East African, it would be
nyama choma – plain and simple grilled meat. If the restaurant is any good
they'll add some sauces – often curry and usually fiery – to accompany your
meat and the whole lot will usually come with rice, chips, plantains or the
ubiquitous *ugali* (a stodgy cornmeal or cassava mush). Usually served in a single cricket-ball-sized lump that you can pick up with your fork in one go, ugali
has the consistency of plasticine and gives the impression of being not so much
cooked as congealed. A bit bland, it nevertheless performs a vital role as a
plate-filler and acts as a soothing balm when eating some of the country's more
thermogenic curries.

The food of the dominant tribe of the Kilimanjaro region, the Chagga, is dominated by bananas, which you'll see growing all over the lower slopes of the mountain. Not only do they brew their own beer from them (see below) but the fruit (and its cousin the plantain) crop up in dishes such as *mchemsho*, a kind of banana and meat stew. Aside from the Chagga's bias for the banana, the indigenous cuisine of Tanzania caters mainly for carnivores, allowing the country's significant Indian minority to corner the market for vegetarian fare. Indian restaurants abound in Dar, Moshi, Arusha and Nairobi, catering mainly for the budget end of the market; that said, the cuisine at a top-notch Indian restaurant in Tanzania is amongst the best served outside Britain or India.

A good website that includes a section on Tanzanian dishes is ⌨ www.foodbycountry.com. For details about food on the trail, see p289.

DRINKS

The usual world-brand **soft drinks** are on sale in Tanzania. Juices are widely available and pretty cheap, though be warned: a lot of upset stomachs are caused by insanitary juice stalls. Coconuts are far safer and are ubiquitous at the coast and on Zanzibar. **Beers** include the tasty Serengeti (our favourite), Ndovu (a pretty close second), Safari and Kilimanjaro from Tanzania, Tusker from Kenya, and the potent Chagga home-brew *mbege*, or banana beer. You'll usually be offered this if you take a stroll around Marangu (or indeed any Chagga village), particularly if it's market day when the world (or at least the male half of it) seems to be intent on obliterating itself by imbibing vast quantities of the stuff from jerrycans.

THINGS TO BUY

kíRìmíyà – A Chagga term meaning a treat brought home by mother to kids upon completion of a successful day at market From **University of Oregon's** *Word of the Week* website

Tanzania has the usual supply of weavings and woodcarvings, T-shirts, textiles and trinkets. Amongst the T-shirts are a number of variations on the 'I climbed Kili' motif. Witchcraft items, battle shields, Maasai beads and necklaces as well

❏ **About bargaining**
I promise this is the first and last time I will lecture you on how to behave. But I just have one simple message: **please don't bargain too hard**.

I used to take a certain amount of pride in how cheaply I could obtain various goods and services when travelling and how tenaciously I would stick to my price until, out of sheer desperation (and probably to get rid of me as much as anything else) the vendor would relent and give me the price I demanded. Not asked, note, but demanded.

It is only recently, having now spent a fair bit of time here, that I am able to see the living conditions of many people in this country – and I realise how wrong my approach to bargaining has been. Sure, nobody wants to get ripped off and if you think you're being taken for a sucker it's important that you stand up for yourself. Furthermore, it is the culture to haggle in this country and you will be expected to engage in some sort of a discussion about how much you're willing to pay for something. But do it with a smile and treat the process as a bit of a game rather than a war to be fought to the death. Because if you've just spent 20 minutes haggling over some item in order to save yourself the equivalent of 40p, it's not just the price that will have been reduced – you'll probably find your dignity will have diminished too.

as bows and arrows are up for grabs in the high streets of Moshi and Arusha. Kilimanjaro **coffee** makes for a good and inexpensive present for the person who's been feeding your cat while you've been away; buy it in a wooden box or velvet bag in a souvenir store, or pick a simple bag of it for a third of the price in a supermarket. Though not grown on the slopes of Kilimanjaro, the organic Africafé has been described by one enthusiastic reader as the best instant coffee in the world and makes an affordable souvenir.

Another popular souvenir is the *kanga*, the traditional Tanzanian woman's dress that usually has a message or motto running through the print, or the similar but smarter and message-less *kitenge*. Also popular are those cloth **shoulder-bags**, dubbed 'volunteer bags' by locals as they are said to be popular with women working for charitable causes.

It depends on your taste, of course, but Zanzibar is widely reckoned to have a better selection and higher quality of souvenirs (though I think the shops of Arusha are catching up; check out Blue Heron Café, for example, or the souvenir/furniture outlets in the TFA complex). Some of the items in Zanzibar, particularly the carved door jambs and furniture, are lovely, though difficult to get home; furthermore, these people are extremely tough negotiators, know the true price of everything and bargains are few.

In the afternoon I bought some small capes made of hyrax skins, of a style formerly much in vogue, and two long spears of the most modern narrow-bladed pattern, which were quite works of art. **Hans Meyer** *Across East African Glaciers* (1891)

SECURITY

Tanzania is a pretty safe country, at least by the standards of its neighbours. That said, the standards of its neighbours are very, very low indeed – as anybody who

has already been to Kenya's capital, known to many travellers as 'Nairobberi', will testify – so do take care. Violent crime is relatively rare during the day but not unknown, especially in Dar es Salaam and Arusha, while pickpockets are common throughout the country and reach epidemic proportions in busy areas such as markets and stations. The best (if somewhat contradictory) advice is:

● Keep a close eye on your things.
● Don't walk around after dark but take a taxi.
● Wear a moneybelt and don't flaunt your wealth.
● Be on your guard against scams and con merchants...

... but at the same time don't let a sense of paranoia ruin your holiday and remember that the vast majority of travellers in East Africa spend their time here suffering no great loss beyond the occasional and inevitable overcharging. If you are unfortunate enough to become the victim of a mugging, remember that it's your *money* they're after, so hand it over – you should be insured against such eventualities anyway. Report the crime as soon as possible to the police, who are generally quite helpful, particularly when the victim is a tourist. This will help to back up your claim from the insurers and may prevent further crimes against tourists in the future.

HEALTH

Diarrhoea is often symptomatic of nothing more than a change of diet rather than any malignant bacteria, so if you get a vicious dose of the runs and your sphincter feels like a cat flap in the Aswan Dam, don't panic and assume you've got food poisoning. That said, there are problems with hygiene in Tanzania, so it's wise to take certain precautions. Take heed of that old adage about patronising only places that are popular – so food doesn't have a chance to sit around for long – as well as that other one about eating only food that has been cooked, boiled or peeled. Stick to **bottled**, **purified** or **filtered water** and avoid ice unless you're certain it has been made from treated water. Washing fruit, vegetables and your hands and ensuring food is thoroughly cooked can all prevent food poisoning. Shellfish, ice cream from street vendors and under-cooked meat should all be avoided like the plague, or you could end up feeling like you've got it. Slathering yourself in an **insect repellent** to prevent you from being eaten alive by the smaller members of Tanzania's animal kingdom is a good idea too.

We could go into a detailed examination here of all the dreadful diseases you could catch in Tanzania. But the truth is that for most of the worst ones you should have already had an inoculation or be taking some sort of prophylactic. Besides, it's unlikely that you'll suffer anything more in Tanzania than a dose of **the runs**, some **altitude sickness** or, if you're careless, a touch of **sunstroke**. If you've got the first, just rest up and take plenty of fluids until you recover; to protect against the last wear a high-factor sun lotion and a hat and again drink a lot of fluids. As for altitude sickness, which the majority of trekkers on Kili suffer from to some extent, as well as other ailments that you may contract on the trail, read the detailed discussion on pp260-72.

KILIMANJARO

Geology

Our geological work was especially delightful... Every rock seemed to differ from another, not only in form but in substance. In half-an-hour it was no uncommon thing for us to pick up specimens of as many as two-and-twenty different kinds. **Hans Meyer** *Across East African Glaciers* (1891)

Rising 4800m above the East African plains, 270km from the shores of the Indian Ocean and measuring up to 40km across, Kilimanjaro is a bizarre geological oddity, the tallest freestanding mountain in the world and one formed, shaped, eroded and scarred by the twin forces of fire and ice. It is actually a volcano, or rather three volcanoes, with the two main peaks, **Kibo** and **Mawenzi**, the summits of two of those volcanoes. The story of its creation goes like this:

About three-quarters of a million years ago (making Kilimanjaro a veritable youngster in geological terms) molten lava burst through the fractured surface of the **Great Rift Valley**, a giant fault in the earth's crust that runs through East Africa (see box p138; actually, Kilimanjaro lies 50 miles from the East African Rift Valley along a splinter running off it, but that need not concern us here). The huge pressures behind this eruption pushed part of the Earth's crust skywards, creating the **Shira volcano**, the oldest of the volcanoes forming the Kilimanjaro massif. Shira eventually ceased erupting around 500,000 years ago, collapsing as it did so to form a huge *caldera* (the deep cauldron-like cavity on the summit of a volcano) many times the size of its original crater.

Soon after Shira's extinction, **Mawenzi** started to form following a further eruption within the Shira caldera. Though much eroded, Mawenzi has at least kept some of its volcanic shape to this day. Then, 460,000 years ago, an enormous eruption just west of Mawenzi caused the formation of **Kibo**. Continual subterranean pressure made Kibo erupt several times more, forcing the summit ever higher until reaching a maximum height of about 5900m. A further huge eruption from Kibo 100,000 years later led to the formation of Kilimanjaro's characteristic shiny black stone – which in reality is just solidified black lava, or **obsidian**. This spilled over from Kibo's crater into the Shira caldera and around to the base of the Mawenzi peak, forming the so-called Saddle. Later eruptions created a series of distinctive mini-cones, or **parasitic craters**, that run in a chain south-east and north-west across the mountain, as well as the

KILIMANJARO

❑ The Great Rift Valley

According to the theory of plate tectonics, the Earth's exterior is made up of six enormous plates that 'float' across the surface of the planet. Occasionally they collide, causing much buckling and crumpling and the creation of huge mountain ranges such as the Himalayas. At other times, these plates deteriorate and break up because of the massive forces bubbling away in the earth's interior. When this happens, valleys are formed where the Earth fractures.

The Great Rift Valley, whose origins are in Mozambique but which extends right across East Africa to Jordan in the Middle East, is a classic example of a fracture in the Earth's surface caused by the movement of these plates. The same monstrous internal forces that two million years ago caused the disintegration of the tectonic plate and the formation of the Rift Valley are also responsible for the appearance of volcanoes along the valley, as these forces explode through the surface, pushing the Earth's crust skywards and forming – in the case of Kilimanjaro – one huge, 5895m-high geological pimple.

Of Africa's sixteen active volcanoes, all but three belong to the Rift Valley. Kili was just one of a number of volcanic eruptions to hit the valley; others included Ol Molog (to the north-west of Kilimanjaro), Kilema (to the south-east) plus, of course, the jaw-dropping Ngorongoro Crater.

By the way, don't be misled into thinking that these kinds of major tectonic shifts happened millions of years ago and have little relevance to the present day: the earthquake in Arusha in 2007 shows that this 'active rifting' is still occurring, and even minor movements can have major repercussions.

---

smaller **Reusch Crater** inside the main Kibo summit. The last volcanic activity of note, just over 200 years ago, left a symmetrical inverted cone of ash in the Reusch Crater, known as the **Ash Pit**, that can still be seen.

Today, **Uhuru Peak**, the highest part of Kibo's crater rim and the goal of most trekkers, stands at around 5895m. The fact that the summit is now around five metres shorter than it was 450,000 years ago can be ascribed to the simple progress of time and the insidious glacial erosion down the millennia. These glaciers, advancing and retreating across the summit, created a series of concentric rings like **terraces** near the top of this volcanic massif on the western side. The Kibo peak has also subsided slightly over time, and about 100,000 years ago a landslide took away part of the external crater, creating **Kibo Barranco**, or the **Barranco Valley** (see p316). The glaciers were also behind the formation of the valleys and canyons, eroding and smoothing the earth into gentle undulations all around the mountain, though less so on the northern side where the glaciers on the whole failed to reach, leaving the valleys sharper and more defined.

While eruptions are unheard of in recent times, Kibo is classified as being dormant rather than extinct, as anybody who visits the inner **Reusch Crater** can testify. A strong sulphur smell still rises from the crater, the earth is hot to touch, preventing ice from forming, while occasionally *fumaroles* (a small hole or opening through which sulphurous gases escape) emerge from the Ash Pit that lies at its heart. Indeed, according to the 2003 Nova documentary *Volcano Above the Clouds*, scientists say that Kibo is actually becoming more active again and that,

using estimates based on the temperature of some of the fumaroles, magma lies only 400m below the surface and a cataclysmic landslide, similar in magnitude to the one that led to the formation of the Western Breach, could happen any day!

THE GLACIERS

It is now time to consider the discovery on which Mr Rebmann particularly prides himself, namely, that of perpetual snow.   **W D Cooley** *Inner Africa Laid Open* (see box p153)

At first glance, Kilimanjaro's glaciers look like nothing more than big smooth piles of slightly monotonous ice. On second glance they pretty much look like this too. Yet there's much more to Kili's glaciers than meets the eye, for these cathedrals of gleaming blue-white ice are dynamic repositories of climatic history – and they could also be providing us with a portent for impending natural disaster.

You would think that with the intensely strong equatorial sun, glaciers wouldn't exist at all on Kilimanjaro. In fact, it is the brilliant white colour of the ice that allows it to survive as it reflects most of the heat. The dull black lava rock on which the glacier rests, on the other hand, *does* absorb the heat; so while the glacier's surface is relatively unaffected by the sun's rays, the heat generated by the sun-baked rocks underneath leads to glacial melting.

As a result, the glaciers on Kilimanjaro are inherently unstable: the ice at the bottom of the glacier touching the rocks melts, the glaciers lose their 'grip' on the mountain and 'overhangs' occur where the ice at the base has melted away, leaving just the ice at the top to survive. As the process continues the ice fractures and breaks away, exposing more of the rock to the sun... and so the cycle begins again. The sun's effect on the glaciers is also responsible for the spectacular structures – the ice columns and pillars, towers and cathedrals – that are the most fascinating part of the upper slopes of Kibo.

You would have thought that, after 11,700 years of this melting process, (according to recent research, the current glaciers began to form in 9700BC) very little ice would remain on Kilimanjaro. The fact that there are still glaciers is due to the prolonged 'cold snaps', or ice ages, that have occurred down the centuries, allowing the glaciers to regroup and reappear on the mountain. According to estimates, there have been at least eight of these ice ages, the last a rather minor one in the 15th and 16th centuries, a time when London's River Thames frequently froze over and winters were severe. At these times the ice on Kilimanjaro would in places have reached right down to the treeline and both Mawenzi and Kibo would have been covered. At the other extreme, before 9700BC there have been periods when Kilimanjaro was completely free of ice, perhaps for up to 20,000 years.

The woes of Kilimanjaro – where have all the glaciers gone?

Of the 19 square kilometres (7¹/₃ sq miles) of glacial ice to be found on Africa, only 2.2 square kilometres (just less than 1 square mile) can be found on Kilimanjaro. Unfortunately, both figures used to be much higher: Kili's famous white mantle shrunk by a whopping 85%-plus between the first survey of the

summit, in 1912, and 2011. Even since 1989, when there were 3.3 square kilometres (1¼ sq miles), there has been a decline of over 33%; and indeed in the seven years between 2000 and 2006 the mountain lost a quarter of its remain-

❏ So how high is it then?

Ever since Hans Meyer ambled down from the summit of Kibo and told anybody who'd listen that he'd reached 19,833ft above sea level (**6045m**), an argument has been raging over just how high Africa's highest mountain really is. For though Meyer's estimate is now unanimously agreed to be a wild over-estimate (an inaccuracy that can be ascribed to a combination of the imprecise 19th-century instruments that he had at his disposal, and perhaps a touch of hubris), finding a figure for the height of Kili that meets with a similar consensus of opinion has proved altogether more difficult.

For years the accepted height of Kilimanjaro was **5892m** (19,331ft), that being the figure set by the colonial German authorities some five years after Meyer's ascent. You'll see this figure crop up time and again in many a 20th-century travelogue as well as on pre-World War Two maps of the Kilimanjaro region. Not many people at the time bothered to question this estimate; the few dissenting voices almost invariably belonged to climbers whose own estimates (which were, perhaps unsurprisingly, nearly always over-estimates, ranging from 5930m to 5965m – 19,455½ft to 19,570ft) are today regarded as even more inaccurate than the Germans' figure.

Under British rule the figure was revised to **5895m** (19,340½ft) following the work of the cartographers of the Ordnance Survey (OS), who mapped Kilimanjaro in 1952; it is this figure that those trekkers who reach the summit will find written on the sign at the top, as well as on the certificates they receive from KINAPA and on the souvenir T-shirts on sale back in Moshi. The trouble was, of course, that whereas the OS's techniques and equipment may have been state of the art in the 1950s, so were vinyl records and the transistor radio. Technology has moved on a couple of light years since then. The OS's readings for Kilimanjaro had been taken from a distance of over 55km (34 miles) away from the mountain; as such, the probability that the OS's figure was not entirely accurate was rather high.

So in 1999 a team of specialists at University College of Land and Architectural Studies in Arusha, together with experts from Karlsruhe University in Germany, set out to measure the precise altitude using a technique involving GPS (Global Positioning Satellites) that had previously been used on Everest, and which resulted in that mountain shrinking by a couple of metres to 8846.10m (29,022½ft).

The result of their findings in Africa? Kilimanjaro was now a full 2.45 metres shorter than the traditionally accepted figure, at **5892.55m** (19,332½ft).

That wasn't the end of the story, however, for in 2008 a team of 19 boffins from six countries decided that even this measurement wasn't accurate enough, for reasons too complicated for a layman to understand (and I include myself in this category), and by combining GPS data with gravimetric observations (where variations in a gravitational field are measured) they came up with a figure of **5890.79m** (19,326½ft) for the orthometric height (ie the distance above the mean sea level).

So is Kilimanjaro shrinking? Or was the old estimate of 5895m just plain inaccurate? Unfortunately, the scientists have yet to tell us that. And while they have every confidence in the accuracy of their latest readings, the old figure of 5895m is still the official figure and the one you'll hear bandied about by tour operators, guides, porters and anybody else you care to speak to; and until we are told otherwise, 5895m is the one we're using in this book too.

ing ice. At that rate, say the experts, Kili will be completely ice-free in just a few decades.

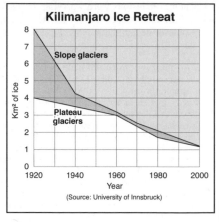

Kilimanjaro Ice Retreat

(Source: University of Innsbruck)

'We found that the summit of the ice fields has lowered by at least 17 metres [almost 56 feet] since 1962,' said Professor Lonnie Thompson of Ohio State University. 'That's an average loss of about a half-metre (a foot and a half) in height each year.' Since then, the Uhlig Glacier, to the north-west of the Western Breach, has disappeared completely, while the famous Furtwangler Glacier – named after the first person to ski down the mountain, and usually visited by those staying at Crater Camp – is vanishing fast. Other scientists and academic institutions have waded into the fray since Professor Thompson's initial studies. Most recently Pascal Sirguey, research scientist at New Zealand's University of Otago, has suggested that Kili's Credner Glacier will be gone by 2030, and the entire mountain will be completely free of ice by about the middle of the century. Even the summit's mighty Northern Icefield, where the glaciers are over 40m tall (131¼ft), is not immune. According to Sirguey, the icefield has lost about a third of its volume since the start of the millennium, and has even split in two, exposing parts of the summit that haven't seen the sun for several thousand years.

The big question, therefore, is not whether they are shrinking, but why – and should we be concerned? Certainly glacial retreats are nothing new: Hans Meyer, the first man to conquer Kilimanjaro, returned in 1898, nine years after his ascent, and was horrified by the extent to which the glaciers had shrunk. The ice on Kibo's slopes had retreated by 100m on all sides, while one of the notches he had used to gain access to the crater in 1889 – now called Hans Meyer Notch – was twice as wide, with the ice only half as thick. Nor are warnings of the complete disappearance of the glaciers anything new: in 1899 Meyer himself predicted that they would be gone within three decades and the top of Kili would be decorated with nothing but bare rock.

What concerns today's scientists, however, is that this current reduction in the size of Kili's ice-cap does seem to be more rapid and more extensive than previous shrinkages. But is it really something to worry about, or merely the latest in a series of glacial retreats experienced by Kili over the last few hundred years?

Professor Thompson and his team attempted to find answers to all these questions. In January and February 2000 they drilled six ice cores through three of Kibo's glaciers in order to research the history of the mountain's climate over the centuries. A weather station was also placed on the Northern Icefield to see how the current climate affects the build-up or destruction of glaciers.

Their conclusions were worrying. In a speech made at the annual meeting of the American Association for the Advancement of Science in February 2001, the professor declared that while he cannot be sure why the ice is melting away

❏ Another inconvenient truth

About a decade ago Kilimanjaro's disappearing glaciers became *the* symbol of global warming when it featured in Al Gore's film *An Inconvenient Truth*. His use of Africa's highest mountain seemed both an obvious and potent choice: everybody marvels at Kilimanjaro's snowy summit and the thought of it being bare by 2020 is a distressing one. Indeed, Al Gore wasn't the only one to use Kilimanjaro's glaciers as a classic example of man's deleterious effect on the environment: Greenpeace even held a satellite news conference from the summit in order to highlight the decline of Africa's largest collection of glaciers due to climate change.

However, there are several groups who think that it is wrong to use Kilimanjaro as a poster child for global warming. Among their number are those who deny altogether that anything is wrong. Indeed, more than one minister for tourism in Tanzania has claimed that the snows of Kilimanjaro will be with us in perpetuity. While these sentiments can perhaps be dismissed as the illogical ramblings of someone who clearly had a vested interest in telling the world that the snows aren't melting, there are others, even among those who believe in climate change, who remain uneasy at Kilimanjaro being used by the green lobby in this way.

The main concern is that the mountain is a bad example to use when discussing global warming. As we said earlier, Kilimanjaro's glaciers have been shrinking for the best part of a century, long before humans began pumping large amounts of carbon dioxide into the atmosphere. Indeed, it is believed that they have been expanding and contracting regularly over the past few thousand years – and separating this natural contraction from the reduction caused by man's effect on the climate is no simple matter. Furthermore, recent data from Kilimanjaro show temperatures never rise above freezing on the summit – so how can a warmer climate be responsible for melting glaciers?

The Austrian Georg Kaser, who has studied the glacial decline on Kilimanjaro for several years (see p143), is one who believes that global warming is *not* melting the ice on Kilimanjaro. Instead, he concluded that the loss of ice is driven by a lack of snowfall and sublimation (this is when ice essentially skips the melting step and simply evaporates, and is caused by exposure to sunlight and dry air), with melting having only a negligible effect. And while climate change could have led to a decline in precipitation (snowfall) that replenishes the glaciers – after all, there have been droughts in much of Tanzania in the past few years – contrary to popular wisdom the glaciers, while undoubtedly shrinking by about a metre a year, aren't actually melting. Indeed, if the current climate models are correct, global warming should actually *increase* rainfall in Eastern Africa, which should mean greater snowfall on the summit of Kilimanjaro, and thus, perversely, could be the thing that saves Kilimanjaro's snows!

And it is this last point that worries those who believe in the reality of global warming but are uneasy about Kilimanjaro being used by the climate change movement in this way: that global warming *is* responsible for the decline of many other glaciers in the world – but *not* on Kilimanjaro. And that by citing Kilimanjaro's shrinking glaciers as an example of the effects of global warming, they are allowing climate-change sceptics the chance to prove, justifiably, that it isn't so – which could then open the door to them dismissing other climate-change trends that *are* true, thereby diluting the climate change lobby's arguments.

so quickly, what is certain is that if the glaciers continue to shrink at current rates, the summit could be completely ice-free by 2015. Thankfully this prediction has proved to be inaccurate, of course. Other, later calculations have estimated that the first ice-free year will be around 2040: Austrian scientist Georg Kaser, who together with Thomas Moelg has been studying new glacial data, said in 2007 'We have done different kinds of modelling and we expect the plateau glaciers to be gone roughly within 30 or 40 years from now, but we have a certain expectation that the slope glaciers may last longer.'

But whatever estimates you believe, there can be no doubt that the glaciers are in serious trouble. This doesn't surprise locals who live in the shadow of Kilimanjaro, some of whom believe they know why the ice is disappearing. According to an AllAfrica.com news report, a 50-year-old native of Old Moshi, Mama Judith Iyatuu, reckons that it's the evil eyes of the white tourists which are melting the ice, while 65-year-old Mzee Ruaici Thomas from Meela village believes that the ice is disappearing because God is unhappy with mankind.

Whatever the reasons, if Kilimanjaro were to lose its snowy top, the repercussions would be extremely serious, particularly for those villagers who live on the mountain slopes and for whom the glaciers are a source of water.

But many reckon it is more than just a local problem. For if the scientists are to be believed, what is happening on Kilimanjaro is a microcosm of what could face the entire world in the future. Even more worryingly, more and more scientists are now starting to think that this future is probably already upon us.

For an excellent (and refreshingly readable) summary of the latest on Kilimanjaro's glaciers, do check out ⌨ kiboice.blogspot.co.uk, the website of the University of Massachusett's Climate System Research Center.

Climate

Kilimanjaro is big enough to have its own microclimates. The theory behind this pattern is essentially very simple. Strong winds travel across the oceans, drawing moisture up as they go. Eventually they collide with a large object – such as a mountain like Kilimanjaro. The winds are pushed upwards as they hit the mountain slopes, and the fall in temperature and atmospheric pressure leads to precipitation or, as it's more commonly called, rain and snow.

In one year, there are two rain-bearing seasonal winds buffeting Kilimanjaro. The south-east trade wind bringing rain from the Indian Ocean arrives between March and May. Because the mountain is the first main obstacle to the wind's progress, and by far the largest, a lot of rain falls on Kili at this time and for this reason the March-to-May season is known as the **long rains**. This is the main wet season on Kilimanjaro. As the south-east trade winds run into the southern side of Kili, so the southern slopes tend to be damper and as a consequence more fertile, with the forest zone much broader than on the northern slopes.

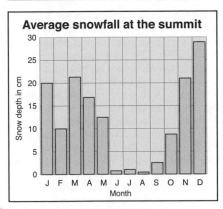

Average snowfall at the summit

y-axis: Snow depth in cm (0, 5, 10, 15, 20, 25, 30)
x-axis: Month (J F M A M J J A S O N D)

Adapted from DR Hardy's *Kilimanjaro snow*
in: AM Waple & JH Lawrimore (eds.)
State of the Climate in 2002,
Bull. Am. Meteorol. Soc., 84, S48

Then there are the dry **'anti-trade' winds** from the north-east which carry no rain and hit the mountain between May and October. These anti-trade winds, which blow, usually very strongly, across the Saddle (the broad valley between Kilimanjaro's two peaks), also serve to keep the south-east trade winds off the upper reaches of Kilimanjaro, ensuring that the rain from the long monsoon season stays largely on the southern side below 3000m, with little falling above this. Which is why, at this time of year, the first day's walk for trekkers

KILIMANJARO

❑ **Trekking in the rainy season**

For those who have absolutely no choice but to walk during the rainy season, don't get too downhearted. For one thing, it's not uncommon for the rains to fail altogether – devastating for the local farmers, of course, but good news for your average trekker. (We were on the mountain in late November once and didn't see a drop of rain the whole time we were there.) And even when there is rain, it doesn't necessarily make for a dreadful trek. We have had letters from several readers who positively recommend the experience. For example, take Jack Hollinghurst from the UK who wrote to us with the following:

'...I do think that you don't give enough encouragement to walking in the rainy season. I was forced to walk at this time by holiday dates and thought it excellent. Due to the hugely reduced numbers of trekkers on the mountain me and my friend were given our own room at all of the huts (including Kibo, where it is about 12 beds to a room) and [your] advice about having dinner early at Horombo is irrelevant as there were about five other groups there at the most.

'...the walking is [also] much more enjoyable when you have some peace and quiet...Maybe you should advise walkers to wear waterproof trousers at this time of year (although I didn't take any and was fine) but otherwise I wouldn't walk at any other time of year.'

His sentiments were endorsed by Martin Fehr from Denmark, who wrote to me of his experience a few years later:

'Don't be afraid to recommend climbing the mountain [at the end of] April. Our porters were so happy to have work in low season, we didn't get a lot of rain, and there were absolutely no climbers on the mountain besides us, which made our climb exceptionally great! Plus the top of the mountain was all covered in snow – a challenge, but soooo beautiful (and it was great to be able to "sleigh" down the mountain as well).

on the Marangu, Umbwe or Machame routes is usually conducted under a canopy of cloud, while from the second day onwards they enjoy unadulterated sunshine.

A second seasonal rain-bearing wind, the north-east monsoon, having already lost much of its moisture after travelling overland for a longer period, brings a **short rainy season** between November and December. While the northern side receives most of the rain to fall in this season, it is far less than the rain brought by the south-east trade winds and as a result the northern side of Kili remains on the whole drier and more barren than the southern side. Once again, the rain falls mainly below 3000m.

This theory seems fine in principle but it does pose a tricky question: if the precipitation falls below 3000m, how did the snow and ice on the summit of Kibo get there in the first place? The answer, my friend, is blowing in the (anti-trade) wind: though these winds normally blow very strongly, as those who walk north across the Saddle will testify, they occasionally drop in force, allowing the south-east trade winds that run beneath them to climb up the southern slopes to the Saddle and on to the summit. Huge banks of clouds then develop and snow falls.

This, at least, is the theory of Kilimanjaro's climate. In practice, the only predictable thing about the weather is its unpredictability. What is certain is

KILIMANJARO

However, Martin does go on to warn: *'Of course, by climbing the mountain during the low season you are very much at the mercy of the elements – and conditions can be quite extreme at this time.'*

Martin's experience – and his opinion of walking in the low season – seems similar to that of Tom Stoa, another reader and Kili conqueror who sticks up for the rainy season:

'I went in April despite the recommendations of you and everyone else to avoid April due to weather, simply because that is when I could go. No regrets. I chose the Marangu route, six days, because of the huts – I figured that despite the rain, we would be warm, dry and comfortable in the huts at least. And that was correct (and we were lucky, it mostly just rained at night). Being the off season, my son and I had a hut to ourselves each night, and the big dining hut was also nearly empty.

We made the summit just fine. My only regret was not having crampons for the big icy snowfield between Hans Meyer Cave and before Gillman's Point. We were gingerly kicking steps in the snow, or trying to step in the steps of others. Having some alpine climbing experience, I know that a slip would have resulted in a nasty, long slide with a crash onto the rocks below. I know that crampons are not customary on Kili, but for that route, on that day, they would have made all the difference between a very sketchy and slow slog, versus an "easy" and safe walk up.'

So there you have it. It would seem that if you have an adventurous spirit, maybe consider the Marangu Route (the only route on the mountain where you sleep in huts rather than under canvas), have crampons and/or ice axes, can put up with some pretty extreme conditions and are prepared for some possibly treacherous walking – the low season is a fine time to climb!

that, with rain more abundant the further one travels down the mountain slopes, life, too, becomes more abundant – as the Fauna and Flora section on p178 illustrates.

The temperature at the summit: bikinis – or brass monkeys?

It's a question many trekkers want to know the answer to: just how cold is it on the summit of Kilimanjaro? Well, there is an old mountaineer's saw that says that once you climb above 4000m, for every 150 metres you ascend the temperature drops by 1°C. Given that the average temperature at around 4000m is 0°C, by the time you reach the summit you would have ascended through about 13 lots of 150m. In other words, the temperature would be around -13°C. Pretty chilly you may think, but bearable. But this, of course, fails to take into consideration the wind-chill factor which can push that figure even further downwards, to around -30°C – though these extremes are rare, as you can see in the graph. This shows the aver-

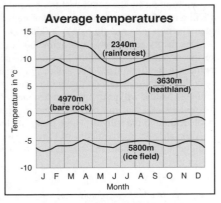

Temperature graph adapted from *General Characteristics of Air Temperature and Humidity Variability on Kilimanjaro, Tanzania* by WJ Duane, NC Pepin, ML Losleben and DR Hardy

age monthly air temperatures over the year at weather stations at 2340m, 3630m, 4570m and 5800m. It gives you an idea of how much the temperature drops as you ascend through the various vegetation zones: montane rainforest (2340m, 7677ft), heathland (3630m, 11,909½ft), alpine desert (4570m, 14,993½ft), and on an icefield at 5800m (19,029ft), just 95m /311½ft below Uhuru Peak. You can see that even in the warmest month the mean temperature doesn't rise above -5°C at the top; the mean temperature at the summit, by the way, is -7.1°C. We have also mapped mean precipitation (ie rain – or, at this altitude, snow) at this higher weather station.

It is beyond the scope of this book to go into Kili's climates and weather patterns in any further detail, so instead I'll just point you in the direction of the University of Massachusetts' geoscience website 🖳 geo.umass.edu/climate/kibo.html which summarises data from their summit weather station. Do also track down the fascinating *General Characteristics of Air Temperature and Humidity Variability on Kilimanjaro, Tanzania* by WJ Duane, NC Pepin, ML Losleben and DR Hardy, from which much of the material in this section was taken. While for the latest on the readings from the weather stations and other news, do visit University of Massachusetts' blog at 🖳 kiboice.blogspot.co.uk.

The history of Kilimanjaro

EARLY HISTORY

Thanks to several primitive **stone bowls** found on the lower slopes of Kilimanjaro, we know that man has lived on or around the mountain since at least 1000BC. We also know that, over the last 500 years, the mountain has at various times acted as a navigational aid for traders travelling between the interior and the coast, a magnet for Victorian explorers, a political pawn to be traded between European superpowers who carved up East Africa, a battlefield for these same superpowers, and a potent symbol of independence for those who wished to rid themselves of these colonial interlopers. Unfortunately, little is known about the history of the mountain during the intervening 2500 years.

It's a fair bet that Kilimanjaro's first inhabitants, when they weren't fashioning bowls out of the local terrain, would have spent much of their time hunting and gathering the local flora and fauna, Kilimanjaro being a fecund source of both. Add to this its reputation as a reliable region both for fresh drinking water and materials – wood, stones, mud, vines etc – for building, and it seems reasonable to suppose that Kilimanjaro would have been a highly desirable location for primitive man and would have played a central role in the lives of those who chose to take up residence on its slopes.

Unfortunately, those looking to piece together a comprehensive history of the first inhabitants of Kilimanjaro rather have their work cut out. There are no documents recording the life and times of the people who once lived on the mountain; not much in the way of any oral history that has been passed down through the generations; and, stone bowls apart, little in the way of archaeological evidence from which to draw any inferences. So, while we can *assume* many things about the lives of Kilimanjaro's first inhabitants, we can be certain about nothing: and if Kilimanjaro did have a part to play in the pre-colonial history of the region, that history, and the mountain's significance within it, has, alas, now been lost to us.

And so it is to the notes of foreign travellers that we must turn in order to find the earliest accounts of Kilimanjaro. These descriptions are usually rather brief, often inaccurate and more often than not based on little more than hearsay and rumour rather than actual first-hand evidence.

One of the first-ever descriptions of East Africa is provided by *Periplus of the Erythraean Sea*, written anonymously in 45AD. *Periplus* – a contender for the title of the world's first-ever guidebook – is a manual for seafarers to the ports of Africa, Arabia and India and includes details of the sea routes to China. In it the author tells of a land called Azania, in which one could find a prosperous market town, Rhapta, where 'hatchets and daggers and awls ... a great quantity of ivory and rhinoceros horn and tortoise shell' were all traded. Yet inter-

estingly, there is no mention of any snow-capped mountain lying nearby; indeed, reading *Periplus* one gets the impression that the author considered Rhapta to be just about the end of the world:

Beyond Opone [modern-day Ras Harun on the Somalian coast] *there are the small and great bluffs of Azania ... twenty-three days sail beyond there lies the very last market town of the continent of Azania, Rhapta ...*

Just over a hundred years later, however, **Ptolemy of Alexandria**, astronomer and the founder of scientific cartography, wrote of lands lying to the south of Rhapta where barbaric cannibals lived near a wide shallow bay and where, inland, one could find a '**great snow mountain**'. Mountains that wear a mantle of snow are pretty thin on the ground in Africa; indeed, there is only one real candidate – and that, of course, is Kilimanjaro.

How exactly Ptolemy came by his information is unknown, for he almost certainly never saw Kilimanjaro for himself. Nevertheless, based on hearsay though it may have been, this is the earliest surviving written mention of Africa's greatest mountain. It therefore seems logical to conclude that the outside world first became aware of Africa's tallest mountain in the years between

---

❑ Kilimanjaro – the name

The meaning of the name Kilíma Njáro, if it have any meaning, is unknown to the Swáhili... To be analysed, it must first be corrupted. This has been done by Mr Rebmann, who converts Kilíma Njáro into Kilíma dja-aro, which he tells us signifies, "Mountain of Greatness." This etymology... is wholly inadmissable for the following reasons: 1st. It is mere nonsense...

So said **W D Cooley** (see p153), leading British geographer during the mid 19th century in his book *Inner Africa Laid Open*. Nonsense Rebmann's suggestion may have been but in the absence of better alternatives the translation is as valid as any other. For the fact of the matter is that despite extensive studies into the etymology of the name Kilimanjaro, nobody is sure where it comes from or exactly what it means.

When looking for the name's origin, it seems only sensible to begin such a search in one of the local Tanzanian dialects, and more specifically, in the language spoken by those who live in its shadow, namely the Chagga people. True, the name Kilimanjaro bears no resemblance to any word in the Chagga vocabulary; but if we divide it into two parts a few possibilities present themselves. One is that Kilima is derived from the Chagga term *kilelema*, meaning 'difficult or impossible', while *jaro* could come from the Chagga terms *njaare* ('bird') or *jyaro* ('caravan'). In other words, the name Kilimanjaro means something like 'That which is impossible for the bird', or 'That which defeats the caravan' – names which, if this interpretation is correct, are clear references to the sheer enormity of the mountain.

Whilst this is perhaps the most likely translation, it is not, in itself, particularly convincing, especially when one considers that while the Chagga language would seem the most logical source for the name, the Chagga people themselves do not actually have one single name for the mountain! Instead, they don't see Kilimanjaro as a single entity but as two distinct, separate peaks, namely Mawenzi and Kibo. (These two names, incidentally, are definitely Chagga in origin, coming from the Chagga terms *kimawenzi* – 'having a broken top or summit' – and *kipoo* – 'snow' – respectively.)

the publication of *Periplus* in 45AD, and that of Ptolemy's work, written some-time during the latter half of the 2nd century AD.

THE OUTSIDERS ARRIVE
Arabs, an anonymous Chinese man and some Portuguese
Following Ptolemy's description, almost nothing more is written about Kilimanjaro for over a thousand years. The Arabs, arriving on the East African coast in the 6th century, must have heard something about it from the local people with whom they traded. Indeed, the mountain would have proved essential to the natives as they travelled from the interior to the markets on the East African shore: as one of the few unmissable landmarks in a largely featureless expanse of savannah and scrub, and with its abundant streams and springs, the mountain would have been both an invaluable aid for navigation and a reliable source of drinking water for the trading caravans. But whether the merchants from the Middle East actually ventured beyond their trading posts on the coast to see the mountain for themselves seems doubtful, and from their records of this time only one possible reference to Kilimanjaro has been uncovered, writ-

KILIMANJARO

Assuming Kilimanjaro isn't Chagga in origin, therefore, the most likely source for the name Kilimanjaro would seem to be Swahili, the majority language of the Tanzanians. Rebmann's good friend and fellow missionary, Johann Ludwig Krapf, wrote that Kilimanjaro could either be a Swahili word meaning 'Mountain of Greatness' – though he is noticeably silent when it comes to explaining how he arrived at such a translation – or a composite Swahili/Chagga name meaning 'Mountain of Caravans'; *jaro*, as we have previously explained, being the Chagga term for 'caravans'. Thus the name could be a reference to the many trading caravans that would stop at the mountain for water. The major flaw with both these theories, however, is that the Swahili term for mountain is not *kilima* but *mlima* – *kilima* is actually the Swahili word for 'hill'!

The third and least-likely dialect from which Kilimanjaro could have been derived is Maasai, the major tribe across the border in Kenya. But while the Maasai word for spring or water is *njore*, which could conceivably have been corrupted down the centuries to *njaro*, there is no relevant Maasai word similar to *kilima*. Furthermore, the Maasai call the mountain *Oldoinyo Oibor*, which means 'White Mountain', with Kibo known as the 'House of God', as Hemingway has already told us at the beginning of his – and this – book. Few experts, therefore, believe the name is Maasai in origin.

Other theories include the possibility that *njaro* means 'whiteness', referring to the snow cap that Kilimanjaro permanently wears, or that Njaro is the name of the evil spirit who lives on the mountain, causing discomfort and even death to those who climb it. Certainly the folklore of the Chagga people is rich in tales of evil spirits who dwell on the higher reaches of the mountain and Rebmann himself refers to 'Njaro, the guardian spirit of the mountain'; however, it must also be noted that the Chagga legends make no mention of any spirit going by that name.

So we are none the wiser. But in one sense at least, it's not important: what the mountain means to the many thousands who walk up it every year is far more mean-ingful than any name we ascribe to it.

ten by a 13th-century geographer, **Abu'l Fida**, who speaks of a mountain in the interior that was 'white in colour'.

The Chinese, who traded on the East African coast during the same period, also seemed either ignorant or uninterested in the land that lay beyond the coastline and in all their records from this time once again just one scant reference to Kili has been found, this time by an anonymous chronicler who states that the country to the west of Zanzibar 'reaches to a great mountain'.

After 1500 and the exploration and subsequent conquest of the African east coast by Vasco da Gama and those who followed in his wake, the Arabs were replaced as the major trading power in the region by the Portuguese. They proved to be slightly more curious about what lay beyond the coast than their predecessors, perhaps because their primary motive for being there was as much colonial as commercial. A vague but once again unmistakable reference to Kilimanjaro can be found in a book, *Suma de Geographia*, published in 1519, an account of a journey to Mombasa by the Spanish cartographer, astronomer and ship's pilot **Fernandes de Encisco**:

West of Mombasa is the Ethiopian Mount Olympus, which is very high, and further off are the Mountains of the Moon in which are the sources of the Nile.

Amazingly, in the 1400 years since Ptolemy this is only the third reference to Kilimanjaro that has been found; with the return of the Arabs in 1699, it was also to be the last for another hundred years or so. Then, just as the 18th century was drawing to a close, the Europeans once more cast an avaricious eye towards East Africa.

THE 1800s: PIONEERS . . .

With British merchants firmly established on Zanzibar by the 1840s, frequent rumours of a vast mountain situated on the mainland just a few hundred miles from the coast began to reach their ears. British geographers were especially intrigued by these reports, particularly as it provided a possible solution to one of the oldest riddles of Africa: namely, the precise whereabouts of the source of the Nile. Encisco's 16th-century reference to *the Mountains of the Moon in which are the sources of the Nile* (above) is in fact a mere echo of the work of Ptolemy, writing 1400 years before Encisco, who also cites the Mountains of the Moon as the true origin of the Nile.

But while these Mountains of the Moon were, for more than a millennium, widely accepted in European academia as the place where the Nile rises, nobody had actually bothered to go and find out if this was so – nor, indeed, if these mountains actually existed at all.

Interest in the 'Dark Continent' was further aroused by the arrival in London in 1834 of one Khamis bin Uthman. Slave dealer, caravan leader and envoy of the then-ruler of East Africa, Seyyid Said, Uthman met many of Britain's leading dignitaries, including the prime minister, Lord Palmerston. He also met and talked at length with the leading African scholar, **William Desborough Cooley**. A decade after this meeting, Cooley wrote his lengthy essay *The Geography of*

N'yassi, or the Great Lake of Southern Africa Investigated, in which he not only provides us with another reference to Kilimanjaro – only the fifth in 1700 years – but also becomes the first author to put a name to the mountain:

The most famous mountain of Eastern Africa is Kirimanjara, which we suppose, from a number of circumstances to be the highest ridge crossed on the road to Monomoezi.

Suddenly Africa, long viewed by the West almost exclusively in terms of the lucrative slave trade, became the centre of a flurry of academic interest and the quest to find the true origins of the Nile became something of a *cause célèbre* amongst scholars. Long-forgotten manuscripts and journals from Arab traders and Portuguese adventurers were dusted off and scrutinised for clues to the whereabouts of this most enigmatic river source. Most scholars preferred to conduct their research from the comfort of their leather armchairs; there were others, however, who took a more active approach, and pioneering explorers such as Richard Burton and John Hanning Speke set off to find for themselves the source of the Nile, crossing the entire country we now know as Tanzania in 1857. This was also the age of Livingstone and Stanley, the former venturing deep into the heart of Africa in search of both knowledge and potential converts to Christianity, and the latter in search of the former.

... AND PREACHERS

Yet for all their brave endeavours, it was not these Victorian action men but one of the humble Christian missionaries who arrived

David Livingstone preaching near Lake Tanganyika. (HG Adams, 1873)

in Africa at about the same time who became the first European to set eyes on Kilimanjaro. **Johannes Rebmann** was a young Swiss-German missionary who arrived in Mombasa in 1846 with an umbrella, a suitcase and a heart full of Christian zeal. His brief was to help **Dr Johann Ludwig Krapf**, a Doctor of Divinity from Tubingen, in his efforts to spread the Christian faith among East Africa's heathen. Krapf was something of a veteran in the missionary field, having previously worked for the London-based Church Missionary Society in Abyssinia. Following the closure of that mission, Krapf sailed down the East African coast to Zanzibar and from there to Mombasa, where he hoped to found a new mission and continue his evangelical work.

Instead, his life fell apart. His wife succumbed to malaria and died on 9 July 1844. His daughter, born just three days previously, died five days after her mother from the same disease, while Krapf too fell gravely ill with the same; and though he alone recovered, throughout the rest of his life he suffered from sporadic attacks that would lay him low for weeks at a time.

But though his body grew weak with malaria, his spirit remained strong, and, following the death of his wife, over the next six months Krapf both translated the New Testament into Swahili and devised a plan for spreading the gospel throughout the interior of Africa. Estimating that the continent could be crossed on foot from east to west in a matter of '900 hours' (37½ days), Krapf believed that establishing a chain of missions at intervals of one hundred hours right across the continent, each staffed by six 'messengers of peace', would be the best way to promulgate the Christian religion on the dark continent.

Unfortunately for Krapf, Islam had got there first, which made his job rather tougher; indeed, in the six months following his arrival in Mombasa, the total number of successful conversions made by Krapf stood at a nice round figure: zero. Clearly, if the faith was to make any inroads in Africa, fresh impetus was required. That impetus was provided by the arrival of Rebmann in 1846. Having recovered from the obligatory bout of malaria that all but wiped him out for his first month in Africa, Rebmann set about helping Krapf to establish a new mission at Rabai-mpia (New Rabai), just outside Mombasa. The station lay in the heart of Wanika territory, a tribe who from the first had proved resistant to conversion. Even the founding of a mission in their midst did little to persuade the Wanika to listen to their preaching: by 1859, 14 years after Krapf first arrived, just seven converts had been made.

It was clear early on that they would have little success in persuading the Wanika to convert. So almost from the start the proselytising pair began to look to pastures new to find potential members for their flock. In 1847 they founded a second mission station at Mt Kasigau, three days' walk from Rabai-mpia – the first in their proposed chain of such stations across the African continent – and later that same year they began to plan the establishment of the next link, at a place called **Jagga** (now spelt Chagga). Rebmann and Krapf had already heard a lot about Jagga from the caravan leaders who earned their money transporting goods between the interior and the markets on the eastern shore and who often called into Rabai-mpia on the way. A source of and market for slaves, Jagga was renowned locally for suffering from extremely cold temperatures at times, a reputation that led Krapf to deduce that Jagga was probably at a much higher altitude than the lands that surrounded it. This hypothesis was confirmed by renowned caravan leader Bwana Kheri, who spoke to Krapf of a great mountain called 'Kilimansharo' (this, incidentally, being the sixth definite reference to Kilimanjaro). From other sources, Krapf and Rebmann also learned that the mountain was protected by evil spirits (known in the Islamic faith as *djinns*) who had been responsible for many deaths, and that it was crowned with a strange white substance that resembled silver, but which the locals simply called 'cold'.

Following protracted negotiations, Bwana Kheri was eventually persuaded to take Rebmann to Chagga in 1848 (Krapf, being too ill to travel, remained in Rabai-mpia). The parting caused great distress to both parties, as detailed in Krapf's diary:

Here we are in the midst of African heathenism, among wilful liars and trickish men, who desire only our property... The only earthly friend whom I have, and whom he has, does at

once disappear, each of us setting our face towards our respective destinations while our friends at home do not know where we are, whither we go and what we are doing.

Rebmann's journey and the discovery of snow

And so, armed with only his trusty umbrella – along a route where caravans typically travelled under armed escort – Rebmann, accompanied by Bwana Kheri and eight porters, set out for Chagga on 27 April 1848. A fortnight later, on the morning of 11 May, he came across the most marvellous sight:

*At about ten o'clock, (I had no watch with me) I observed something remarkably white on the top of a high mountain, and first supposed that it was a very white cloud, in which supposition my guide also confirmed me, but having gone a few paces more I could no more rest satisfied with that explanation; and while I was asking my guide a second time whether that white thing was indeed a cloud and scarcely listening to his answer that **yonder** was a cloud but what that white was he did not know, but supposed it was **coldness** – the most delightful recognition took place in my mind, of an old well-known European guest called **snow**. All the strange stories we had so often heard about the gold and silver mountain Kilimandjaro in Jagga, supposed to be inaccessible on account of evil spirits, which had killed a great many of those who had attempted to ascend it, were now at once rendered intelligible to me, as of course the extreme cold, to which poor Natives are perfect strangers, would soon chill and kill the half-naked visitors. I endeavoured to explain to my*

❏ **WD Faulty? – The great snow debate**

The most relentless critic was a redoubtable person, for long years a terror to real explorers, Mr Desborough Cooley, a kind of geographical ogre, who used to sit in his study in England, shaping and planning out the map of Africa (basing his arrangements of rivers, lakes and mountains on ridiculous and fantastic linguistic coincidences and resemblances of his own imagination), and who rushed out and tore in pieces all unheeding explorers in the field who brought to light actual facts which upset his elaborate schemes. **HH Johnston** *The Kilima-njaro Expedition – A Record of Scientific Exploration in Eastern Equatorial Africa* (1886)

Though Rebmann's accounts of Kilimanjaro caused a minor sensation amongst the wider reading public when first published in the *Church Missionary Intelligencer* of May 1849, the response it elicited from academic circles back in Europe was initially as cool as the top of Kibo itself. Leading the sceptics was one **William Desborough (WD) Cooley**. Cooley was widely regarded in his day as one of Britain's leading geographers and something of an expert on Africa (though he never actually ventured near the continent throughout his entire life). Indeed, Cooley had already added to the stock of knowledge about the mountain way back in 1845, a full four years before Rebmann's essay was published, by providing the world with a description of Kilimanjaro that he had managed to construct from details furnished to him by the slave-dealer-cum-ambassador Khamis bin Uthman (see p150).

But if he is remembered at all today it is as the man who refused to believe that Kilimanjaro could be topped with snow, as this response to Rebmann's first account (see pp152-3) makes clear:

I deny altogether the existence of snow on Mount Kilimanjaro. It rests entirely on the testimony of Mr Rebmann... and he ascertained it, not with his eyes, but by inference and in the visions of his imagination. *Athenaeum*, May 1849

(continued overleaf)

people the nature of that 'white thing' for which no name exists even in the language of Jagga itself...   **Johannes Rebmann** from his account of his journey, published in Volume I of the *Church Missionary Intelligencer*, May 1849

An extract from the next edition of the same journal continues the theme:

The cold temperature of the higher regions constituted a limit beyond which they dared not venture. This natural disinclination, existing most strongly in the case of the great mountain, on account of its intenser cold, and the popular traditions respecting the fate of the only expedition which had ever attempted to ascend its heights, had of course prevented

---

❏ WD Faulty? – The great snow debate   *(continued from p153)*

Absurd as it seems now, Cooley's reputation in intellectual circles at that time was as high as Kili itself and such was the reverence with which his every pronouncement was received in the mid 19th century that it was his version of reality that was the more widely accepted: as far as people in Europe were concerned, if Cooley said Kilimanjaro did not have snow on it, it did not have snow on it.

A second report by Rebmann, following his trip to the Chagga lands in November 1848, did little to stem the scepticism, even though he – perhaps now aware of the controversy his first account had caused back home – went to great lengths to back up his earlier report:

.. during the night, I felt the cold as severely as in Europe in November; and had I been obliged to remain in the open-air, I could not have fallen to sleep for a single moment: neither was this to be wondered at, for so near was I now to the snow-mountain Kilimandjaro (Kilima dja-aro, mountain of greatness), that even at night, by only the dim light of the moon, I could perfectly well distinguish it.

If Rebmann hoped to persuade his critics, however, he was sadly mistaken: if he was capable of making a mistake once, they countered, then surely he could be wrong a second and third time too. And so for much of the next two years Rebmann's account of his time on Kili was treated with equal parts suspicion and derision.

Indeed, it wasn't until 1850 and the publication of an account by Rebmann's friend and mentor, Dr Krapf, that doubts began to be cast on Cooley's ideas. In an edition of the *Church Missionary Intelligencer* in which he recounts his own experiences working in the Ukamba region immediately to the north of Kilimanjaro, Krapf baldly states that:

All the arguments which Mr Cooley has adduced against the existence of such a snow mountain, and against the accuracy of Rebmann's report, dwindle into nothing when one has the evidence of one's own eyes before one; so that they are scarcely worth refuting.

Suddenly it became that much harder to deny the existence of snow on Kili: after all, there were now two Europeans who had seen the mountain for themselves – and both of them had insisted that they'd seen snow there.

Yet Cooley remained adamant in his convictions and, thanks to the support of some pretty influential friends to back up his arguments, enjoyed popular public support. No less a figure than the President of the Royal Geographical Society, **Sir Roderick Murchison**, said that the idea of a snow-capped mountain under the equator was to *'a great degree incredulous'* (even though there are other snow-capped mountains in the Andes and Papua New Guinea that fall 'under the equator', and which were already known about by the mid 19th century).

them from exploring it, and left them in utter ignorance of such a thing as 'snow', although not in ignorance of that which they so greatly dreaded, 'coldness'.

Still bent on spreading Christianity, and undeterred (indeed ignorant) of the scepticism with which his reports in the *Intelligencer* were about to be met back in Europe (see the box below), Rebmann returned to Rabai-mpia but continued to visit and write about Kilimanjaro and the Chagga region for a few more years.

His second trip, made in November of the same year, was blessed by favourable weather conditions, providing Rebmann with his clearest view of

Even those who *had* been to Africa for themselves had serious reservations about the missionaries' claims. The esteemed Irish explorer **Richard Burton**, for example, having listened to Krapf give a talk on Kilimanjaro in Cairo, declared that *'These stories reminded one of a de Lunatico'*; while **David Livingstone**, recently returned from his latest adventures in Africa, lent further weight to Cooley's arguments during an address to the Royal Geographical Society. In it, Livingstone related a story about some mountains in the Zambezi Valley which were described to him by locals as being of a *'glistening whiteness'*. Livingstone initially believed that these mountains must be covered by snow, until, having seen the mountains for himself, he realised that they were in fact composed of *'masses of white rock, somewhat like quartz'*.

As if to drum home the point of the tale, Sir Roderick Murchison later declared at the same meeting that Livingstone's account:

... may prove that the missionaries, who believed that they saw snowy mountains under the equator, have been deceived by the glittering aspect of rocks under a tropical sun.

The next broadside fired by either side occurred in 1852 and the publication of Cooley's grandly (but inaccurately) titled *Inner Africa Laid Open*. This, Cooley clearly hoped, was to be his masterpiece: the culmination of a lifetime's armchair studying, this was the opus that would secure his reputation during his lifetime and ensure his name lived on in perpetuity as one of the great intellectual heavyweights of the 19th century. As it transpired, the book did indeed serve to preserve Cooley's name for posterity – though presumably not in the way that he had hoped.

To read the book now, it is clear that Cooley hoped it would once and for all dismiss all this nonsense about snow on Kilimanjaro. Within the first few pages almost every part of Rebmann's account is called into question, with the claim of snow on Kilimanjaro being treated with particularly vehement derision:

... it is obvious that the discovery of snow rests much more on 'a delightful mental recognition' than on the evidence of the senses... But in his mind the wish was father to the thought, the 'delightful recognition' developed with amazing rapidity, and in a few minutes the cloudy object, or 'something white,' became a 'beautiful snow mountain', so near to the equator.

Later in the book Cooley forgets the conduct becoming of an English gentleman and the attacks on Rebmann border on the personal, starting with an attack on his eyesight:

Various and inconsistent reasons have been assigned for this failure [by Rebmann to see Kilimanjaro from a nearby hill], *but the only true explanation of it is contained in Mr Rebmann's confession that he is very short-sighted. He was unable to perceive, with the aid of a small telescope, Lake Ibe, three days distant to the south, which his followers could discern with the naked eye; nor could he even see the rhinoceroses in his path.*

(continued overleaf)

Kilimanjaro, and the outside world with the most accurate and comprehensive description of the mountain that had yet been written:

There are two main peaks which arise from a common base measuring some twenty-five miles long by as many broad. They are separated by a saddle-shaped depression, running east and west for a distance of about eight or ten miles. The eastern peak is the lower of the two, and is conical in shape. The western and higher presents the appearance of a magnificent dome, and is covered with snow throughout the year, unlike its eastern neighbour, which loses its snowy mantle during the hot season.

❏ **WD Faulty? – The great snow debate**   *(continued from p155)*
And he goes on to finish his onslaught with this rather uncompromising, hysterical summary of Rebmann's accounts:

... betraying weak powers of observation, strong fancy, an eager craving for wonders, and childish reasoning, could not fail to awaken mistrust by their intrinsic demerits, even if there were no testimony opposed to them.

To further back up his argument, Cooley was able to point out a number of inconsistencies between Rebmann's and Krapf's accounts, such as the postulation by Krapf that the mountain is 12,500ft (3810m) high – this after Rebmann had estimated the height to be closer to 20,000ft (6096m, a pretty good guess by the myopic Rebmann).

Cooley's desire to prove Rebmann wrong was fuelled by more than just a desire to crush a young upstart in a field in which he considered himself the ultimate authority. He was also frightened that the existence of snow on Kilimanjaro would provide support for his rivals' theories at the expense of his own. In the big debate that raged in academic circles in the mid 1800s on the exact location of the source of the Nile, Cooley was firmly of the opinion that the river started from a large lake in Central Africa called Lake N'yassi. (Indeed, in the 1830s he even organised an expedition to prove his theory, though unfortunately it failed abysmally for reasons that remain rather obscure.)

Aligned against Cooley were opponents such as the geographer **Charles Beke**, who preferred the idea that the Nile had its source in a mountain range in the interior – possibly, as Encisco (p150) had stated in the 16th century, the legendary Mountains of the Moon – and looked upon the discovery of snow on an East African mountain as evidence to back up their theories. Indeed, when Rebmann and Krapf's accounts first reached Britain, Beke was only too keen to accept their every word as gospel and even went so far as to suggest that Kilimanjaro was now the most likely source of the Nile.

And that, for the next decade or so, was that: Rebmann and Krapf continued to visit Kilimanjaro and continued to see snow, while Cooley and the gang back in England continued to refute their every utterance and enjoy the majority of public opinion.

Then in 1862, **Baron Carl von der Decken** made his second and more successful attempt on Kilimanjaro (see p158), this time with his friend Dr Otto Kersten who had replaced Thornton for this second expedition. In reaching a reported 14,200ft (4328m) von der Decken and Kersten came as close to the snow as any European ever had, and the brave baron's subsequent account of the expedition exploded Cooley's theories once and for all:

During the night it snowed heavily and next morning the ground lay white all around us. Surely the obstinate Cooley will be satisfied now.

On this second trip Rebmann was also able to correct an error made in his first account of Kilimanjaro: that the local 'Jagga' tribe were indeed familiar with snow and did have a name for it – that name being 'Kibo'!

A third and much more organised expedition in April 1849 – at the same time as the account of his earlier visits to Kilimanjaro was rolling off the presses in Europe – enabled Rebmann, accompanied by a caravan of 30 porters (and, of course, his trusty umbrella), to ascend to such a height that he was later to boast that he had come 'so close to the snow-line that, supposing

There was now a third eyewitness claiming to have seen snow on Kilimanjaro, and a baron at that; Cooley's position as a result began to look increasingly untenable, and his support began to ebb quietly away.

If the baron really believed his testimony alone would persuade Cooley, however, he was much mistaken:

So the Baron says it snowed during the night...In December with the sun standing vertically overhead! The Baron is to be congratulated on the opportuneness of the storm. But it is easier to believe in the misrepresentations of man than in such an unheard-of eccentricity on the part of nature. This description of a snowstorm at the equator during the hottest season of the year, and at an elevation of only 13,000 feet, is too obviously a 'traveller's tale', invented to support Krapf's marvellous story of a mountain 12,500 feet high covered with perpetual snow.

But the redoubtable Cooley was fighting a lonely battle now. The Royal Geographical Society withdrew their backing, with Sir Roderick Murchison – presumably between mouthfuls of humble pie – finally admitting that Rebmann and Krapf were probably right after all. As if to add insult to Cooley's injured pride, the Society even awarded their Gold Medal in 1863 to von der Decken for his contributions to the sum of geographical knowledge of Africa. (Incidentally, in addition to his account of Kilimanjaro, von der Decken was also the first European to see and describe Mount Meru.)

Fourteen years after Rebmann had first announced that there was snow on the equator, the world was finally listening to him. Cooley meanwhile, resolutely refused to believe in the existence of snow on Kilimanjaro, carrying his scepticism with him to the grave and leaving behind a reputation for stubbornness and ignorance that has survived to this day.

In Cooley's defence, one has to remember just how little was known about the continent at that time: few people from Europe had ever visited Africa; fewer still had penetrated beyond the coast; and of those who had, even fewer had survived to tell the tale. So the armchair scholars of Europe were forced to rely upon the sketchy mentions of Kili in historical records for their information; and of those descriptions, none since Ptolemy mentions anything about snow.

As some compensation, perhaps, Cooley at least had the satisfaction of knowing that, while defeated in this particular battle, he had gained a partial victory in the wider war: in 1858 a large body of water in the heart of Africa was discovered and was named **Lake Victoria** after Britain's sovereign. This lake would later be proved to be one of the sources of the Nile. Cooley may have got the name and location of this body of water wrong, but his supposition that the Nile had a lake as its source, and not a mountain, had been proved correct after all.

KILIMANJARO

no impassable abyss to intervene, I could have reached it in three or four hours'.

After Rebmann's pioneering work it was the turn of his friend Krapf, now risen from his sickbed, to see the snowy mountain his friend had described in such detail. In November 1849 he visited the Ukamba district to the north of Kilimanjaro and during a protracted stay in the area Krapf became the first white man to see Mount Kenya. Perhaps more importantly, he was also afforded wonderful views of Kilimanjaro, and was able to back up Rebmann's assertion that the mountain really was adorned with snow (see box p154 for quote).

FIRST ATTEMPTS ON THE SUMMIT

Baron von der Decken and Charles New

After the missionaries came the mountaineers. In August 1861 Baron Carl Claus von der Decken, a Hanoverian naturalist and traveller who had been residing in Zanzibar, accompanied by young English geologist Richard Thornton, himself an explorer of some renown who had accompanied (and been sacked by) Livingstone during the latter's exploration of the Zambezi, made the first serious attempt on Kilimanjaro's summit. Initially, despite an entourage of over fifty porters, a manservant for von der Decken and a personal slave for Thornton, their efforts proved to be rather dismal and they had to turn back after just three days due to bad weather, having reached the rather puny height of just 8200ft (2499m). Proceeding to the west side of the mountain, however, the pioneering baron did at least enjoy an unobstructed view of Kibo peak on the way:

Bathed in a flood of rosy light, the cap that crowns the mountain's noble brow gleamed in the dazzling glory of the setting sun... Beyond appeared the jagged outlines of the eastern peak, which rises abruptly from a gently inclined plain, forming, as it were, a rough, almost horizontal platform. Three thousand feet lower, like the trough between two mighty waves, is the saddle which separates the sister peaks one from the other.

Von der Decken also provided the most accurate estimate yet for the height of both Kibo – which he guessed was between 19,812 and 20,655ft (6038.7m to 6295.6m) – and Mawenzi (17,257 to 17,453ft, or 5259.9 to 5319.7m). Thornton, for his part, correctly surmised that the mountain was volcanic, with Kibo the youngest and Shira the oldest part of the mountain.

The following year von der Decken, now accompanied by Dr Otto Kersten who had replaced Thornton as the baron's travelling and climbing companion, reached a much more respectable 14,200ft (4328m) and furthermore reported being caught up in a snowstorm (see box p156). On his return to Europe, the baron described Kibo as a 'mighty dome, rising to a height of about 20,000 feet, of which the last three thousand are covered in snow'.

Following this second attempt, von der Decken urged **Charles New** (1840-75), a London-born missionary with the United Free Methodist Church in Mombasa, to tackle the mountain, and in 1871 New made a laudable attempt to reach the summit. That attempt failed, as did a second attempt in August of the same year; nevertheless, by choosing on the latter occasion to climb on the south-eastern face of Kibo where the ice cap at that time stretched almost to the

base of the cone, New inadvertently wrote himself into the history books as the first European to cross the snow-line at the African Equator:

The gulf was all that now lay between myself and it [the snow line], *but what an all! The snow was on a level with my eye, but my arm was too short to reach it. My heart sank, but before I had time fairly to scan the position my eyes rested upon snows at my very feet! There it lay upon the rocks below me in shining masses, looking like newly washed and sleeping sheep! Hurrah! I cannot describe the sensations that thrilled my heart at that moment. Hurrah!*

On this second expedition New also discovered the crater lake of Jala, the mountain's only volcanic lake, to the south-east of Mawenzi.

New's experiences on Kilimanjaro fanned his passion for the mountain and two years later he was back preparing for another assault on the still-unconquered peak. Unfortunately, the volatile tribes living at the foot of the mountain had other ideas and before New had even reached Kilimanjaro he was forced to turn around and head back towards the coast, having been stripped of all his possessions by the followers of the Chief of 'Moji' (Moshi), a highly unpleasant man by the name of Mandara (see pp294-5). Broken in both health and spirits, the unfortunate New died soon after the attack.

As rumours of New's demise trickled back to Europe, enthusiasm among explorers for the still unconquered Kilimanjaro understandably waned and for the next dozen years the mountain saw few foreign faces. Those that did visit usually did so on their way to somewhere else; people such as **Dr Gustav A Fischer** in 1883, who stopped in Arusha and visited Mount Meru on his journey to Lake Naivasha and declared Kilimanjaro to be fit for 'European settlement', a statement that would have greater resonance later on in the century. There was also the Scottish geologist, **Joseph Thomson**, who became one of the first to examine properly the northern side of the mountain during an attempt to cross the Maasai territories. He also attempted a climb of Kili, though having allowed himself only one day in which to complete the task his attempt was always doomed to failure; in the end he reached no higher than the tree-line at about 2700m. (Failure though he may have been in this instance, his name lives on as a species of gazelle.)

The first European to venture back to the region with the specific intention of visiting Kilimanjaro arrived in the same year, 1883. In an expedition organised by the Royal Geographical Society, **Harry Johnston** arrived in East Africa with the aim of discovering and documenting the flora and fauna of Kilimanjaro. Though his work did little to further our understanding of the mountain, Johnston's trip is of anecdotal interest in that he later claimed in his biography that he was actually working undercover for the British Secret Service. No documentary evidence has ever turned up to back this claim (though there is a letter written by him to the Foreign Office in which he asks for 40 men and £5000 for the purpose of colonising Kilimanjaro). Much doubt has been cast, too, upon his boast that he reached almost 5000m during his time on the mountain; while his suggestion that Kilimanjaro was 'a mountain that can be climbed even without the aid of a walking stick' was widely ridiculed when first broadcast later that year.

But, whatever the inaccuracies and falsehoods of Johnston's recollections, his journey did at least assure other would-be Kilimanjaro visitors from Europe that the region was once again safe to visit. His visit also served to bring the mountain to the attention of European powers...

COLONISATION

... a country as large as Switzerland enjoying a singularly fertile soil and healthy climate, ... within a few years it must be either English, French or German ... I am on the spot, the first in the field, and able to make Kilima-njaro as completely English as Ceylon.
HH Johnston *The Kilima-njaro Expedition – A Record of Scientific Exploration in Eastern Equatorial Africa* (1886)

In describing the mountain thus, HH Johnston brought Kilimanjaro to the attention of the world's leading powers. Soon the two great colonisers in East Africa, Germany and Britain, were jockeying for position in the region. British missionaries were accused of putting the temporal interests of their country over the spiritual affairs of their flock, while for their part certain German nationals made no secret of the fact they wished to colonise Kilimanjaro. In 1884, the **Gesellschaft für Deutsche Kolonisation** (GDK), a political party founded by the 28-year-old **Dr Carl Peters** with the ultimate goal of colonising East Africa, persuaded a dozen local chiefs to throw off the rule of the (British controlled) **Sultan of Zanzibar** and, furthermore, to cede large sections of their territory to the German cause; one of Dr Peters' envoys, Dr Juhlke, even managed to establish a protectorate over Kilimanjaro in 1885. The British fought fire with fire, forcing two dozen chiefs (including some of those who had sided with the Germans) to swear allegiance to the sultan – and therefore indirectly to them.

The situation was becoming dangerously volatile, with war looking increasingly likely. After further bouts of political manoeuvring, in October 1886 the two sides met in London and Berlin to define once and for all the boundary between British- and German-controlled East Africa and head off the possibility of war: the border between British-ruled Kenya and German East Africa was now in place.

The first period of German rule over Kilimanjaro proved to be exceptionally harsh, and many Germans soon felt uneasy about the excesses of Dr Peters and his followers. In 1906 an enquiry opened in the Reichstag into the conduct of the doctor and his men, in which an open letter by a Herr Eltz (about whom very little is known) was read out to the court. Its contents give an idea of the hatred that the doctor and his men aroused in the locals:

What have you achieved by perpetual fights, by acts of violence and oppression? You have achieved, Herr Doctor, I have it from your own mouth in the presence of witnesses – that you and the gentlemen of your staff cannot go five minutes' distance from the fort without military escort. My policy enables me to make extensive journeys and shooting trips in Kilimanjaro and the whole surrounding country with never more than four soldiers. You have cut the knot with the sword and achieved that this most beautiful country has become a scene of war. Before God and man you are responsible for the devastation of flourishing districts, you are responsible for the deaths of our comrades Bulow and Wolfram, of our brave soldiers and of hundreds of Wachagga. And now I bring a supreme charge against

you: Necessity did not compel you to this. You required deeds only in order that your name might not be forgotten in Europe.

Soon German soldiers were being attacked and killed and, with opposition to their rule growing stronger and more organised, they suffered a massive defeat at Moshi at the hands of the Chagga, led by Meli, Mandara's son (see p294).

Though the Germans soon regained control, it was clear to them that a more benevolent style of government was required if they were to continue ruling over their East African territories. This new 'caring colonialism' paid off and for the last few years of their rule the Germans lived largely at peace with their subjects and even forged a useful alliance with the Chaggas during the Germans' push against rebellious Maasai tribes. The Germans also started the practice of building public huts on Kilimanjaro, establishing one at 8500ft (2591m), called **Bismarck Hut**, and one at 11,500ft (3505m) known as **Peters' Hut**, after Dr Carl.

KILIMANJARO CONQUERED

While all this was going on, attempts to be the first to conquer Kilimanjaro continued apace. In 1887, **Count Samuel Teleki** of the Austro-Hungarian Empire made the most serious assault on Kibo so far, before 'a certain straining of the membrane of the tympanum of the ear' forced him to turn back. Then the American naturalist, **Dr Abbott**, who had come primarily to investigate the fauna and flora of the mountain slopes, made a rather reckless attempt. Abbott was struck down by illness fairly early on in the climb but his companion, Otto Ehlers of the German East African Company, pushed on, reaching (according to him) 19,680ft (5998.5m). Not for the first time in the history of climbing Kilimanjaro, however, this figure has been sceptically received by others – particularly as it is over 100m above the highest point on the mountain! (By way of compensation, however, it was on Kilimanjaro that Abbott first identified

---

❏ **The biggest present ever?**

There is a widely believed story that the kink in the border between Kenya and Tanzania near Kilimanjaro was created to satisfy the whim of Queen Victoria, Britain's reigning monarch at the time the border was first defined. According to the story, she magnanimously decided to give Kilimanjaro to her grandson, the future Wilhelm II, as a birthday present, following a complaint from him that while Britain had two snowy mountains in her East African territories (Mounts Kili and Kenya), Germany was left with none. In order to effect the transfer of such a generous gift, the border had to be redrawn so that Kili fell to the south of the boundary in German territory, which is why the border has a strange kink to the east of the mountain.

Alas, however romantic the story, it is simply not true. The kink is there not because of Victoria's largesse, but as part of the agreement struck between Germany and Britain, and it exists not because of Kili, but Mombasa. Britain's territories in East Africa needed a port: the Germans already had Dar, and if the border between the two was to continue on the same bearing as it had taken to the west of Kilimanjaro the Germans were going to end up with Mombasa too. So a kink was placed in the border to allow Mombasa to fall in British territory.

and collected the species of duiker that now bears his name.) In spite of their relative failures, both Teleki and Abbott played a part in the success of the eventual conqueror of Kilimanjaro, **Dr Hans Meyer**: Teleki, by providing information about the ascent to Meyer in a chance encounter during Meyer's first trip to the region in 1887; Abbott, by providing accommodation in Moshi for Meyer and his party during their successful expedition of 1889.

Hans Meyer was a geology professor and the son of a wealthy editor from Leipzig (he himself later joined his father's editorial board and became its director, retiring in 1888, one year before the conquest of Kili, to become professor of Colonial Geography at Leipzig University). In all he made four trips to Kilimanjaro. Following the partial success of his first attempt in 1887, when he managed to reach 18,000ft (5486.4m), Meyer returned the following year for a second assault with experienced African traveller and friend Dr Oscar Baumann. Unfortunately, his timing couldn't have been worse: the **Abushiri War**, an Arab-led revolt against German traders on the East African coast, had just broken out and Meyer and his friend Baumann were captured, clapped into chains and held hostage by Sheikh Abushiri himself, the leader of the insurgency. In the end both escaped with their lives, but only after a ransom of ten thousand rupees was paid.

However, on his third attempt, in 1889, Meyer finally covered himself in glory. Though no doubt a skilful and determined climber, Meyer's success can largely be attributed to his recognition that the biggest obstacle to a successful assault was the lack of food available near the top. Meyer solved this by establishing camps at various points along the route that he had chosen for his attempt, including one at 12,980ft (3956.3m; Abbott's camp); one, Kibo camp, 'by a conspicuous rock' at 14,210ft (4331.2m); and, finally, a small encampment by a lava cave and just below the glacier line at 15,260ft (4651.2m). Thanks to these intermediary camps, Meyer was able to conduct a number of attempts on the summit without having to return to the foot of Kili to replenish supplies after each; instead, food was brought to the camps by the porters every few days.

He also had a considerable back-up party with him, including his friend and climbing companion, Herr Ludwig Purtscheller – a gymnastics teacher and alpine expert from Salzburg – two local headmen, nine porters, three other locals who would act as supervisors, one cook and one guide supplied by the local chief, Mareale, whom he had befriended during his first trip to the region. These men would help to carry the equipment and man the camps, with each kept in order by Meyer's strict code of discipline, where minor miscreants received ten lashes and serious wrongdoers twenty.

The size of his entourage, however, shouldn't detract from the magnitude of Meyer's achievement: as well as the usual hardships associated with climbing Kilimanjaro, he also had to contend with deserters from his party, the lack of a clear path, elephant traps (large pits dug by locals and concealed by ferns to trap the unwary pachyderm), as well as the unpleasant, rapacious chief of Moshi, Mandara (see p294). Furthermore, Meyer did not begin his walk *on* the

mountain, as today's visitors do, but in Mombasa, 14 days by foot, according to Meyer, from the town of Taveta (which lies to the south-east of Kilimanjaro, in Kenya, and is still a day's walk from the mountain village of Marangu)!

Then there was the snow and ice, so much more prevalent in the late 1800s on Kili than it is today. Above 4500m Meyer had to trek upon snow for virtually the whole day, even though his route up Kibo from the Saddle is not too dissimilar to that taken by thousands of trekkers every year – and today there is no snow on the route. The added difficulties caused by the snow are well described in Meyer's book *Across East African Glaciers*. Rising at 2.30am for their first assault on the summit, Meyer and Purtscheller spent most of the morning carving a stairway out of a sheer ice-cliff, every stair laboriously hewn with an average of 20 blows of the ice axe. (The cliff formed part of the now extinct Ratzel

---

❏ **Meyer's route to the top and the modern trails: a comparison**

While no modern path precisely retraces Hans Meyer's original route to the summit, some of today's paths do occasionally coincide with the trail he blazed. For instance, Meyer and his climbing partner, Purtscheller, began their assault on Kilimanjaro, on 28 September 1889, from **Marangu** village. From there they headed due north up through the trees, arriving two days later at the very upper limits of the forest, where they made camp.

Trekkers on the Marangu trail follow a similar itinerary today, though their starting point is a good deal higher than Meyer's at Marangu Gate rather than Marangu village – which explains why trekkers today need only one day to reach the upper edge of the forest, while Meyer took two. It is also worth noting that, according to the beautifully drawn maps by Dr Bruno Hassenstein in Meyer's book *Across East African Glaciers*, his camp on this second night lay to the south-west of Kifunika Hill at an altitude of 8710ft (2654.8m), whereas the Mandara Huts lie a couple of hours' walk to the east of Kifunika, at a loftier 2743m.

On the third day, Meyer struck a westerly course, crossing the Mdogo (lesser) and Mkuba (greater) streams before making camp at an altitude of 9480ft (2889.5m). This was the all-important **Halfway Camp**, the intermediate station that Meyer would use as his base for tackling Kibo. In the history of climbing Kibo, no single spot on the entire mountain, save Uhuru Peak itself, has played a more prominent role: Harry Johnston had built some huts nearby during his reconnaissance mission of 1883; Meyer himself had camped here during his first expedition on the mountain, with Baron von Eberstein in 1887, and Abbott and Ehlers had also camped nearby in 1889, just a few months before Meyer and Purtscheller arrived. There's even evidence to suggest Count Teleki had also stopped here in 1887; in his account of their attempt on Kili in *Discovery by Count Teleki of Lakes Rudolf and Stefanie*, Lieutenant Ludwig von Höhnel speaks of making camp at 9390ft (2862m) by a brook, near some old huts built originally by HH Johnston.

So where is this spot? There are plenty of clues. It is no coincidence, for example, that all these different parties chose to make camp at this site. Then, as now, campsites would have been chosen largely for their proximity to water and other amenities, so we can guess that a mountain stream or brook must run nearby. We also know that Meyer headed almost due west from his camp of the night before, and that the spot lies at around 2862m (9389¾ft), above the tree-line. No modern campsite exactly fits this description – the Horombo Huts, the second night's accommodation on the Marangu trail, are too high up at 3657m/11,998ft. *(continued overleaf)*

❏ Meyer's route to the top and the modern trails: a comparison

(*Continued from p163*) Rau Campsite, however, on the sadly now defunct Alternative Mweka/Kidia Route, seems a more plausible candidate: though this campsite is too high at 3260m/10,695½ft, just below it is a glorious stretch of grassland bordering the forest and near a mountain stream that would appear to fit the description given by Meyer. If the 19th-century explorers really did camp around there, they are to be congratulated on choosing one of the most beautiful places on the mountain.

Leaving most of his porters behind at this site – it would be their duty from now on to ferry supplies up to the camp from Marangu – Meyer struck due north up to the Saddle, past the **Spring in the Snow**, or Schneequell (12,910ft/3935m) and on to **Abbott's Camp** at 12,980ft (3956.3m), so-called by Meyer because he found an empty Irish stew tin and a sheet of the Salvation Army newspaper *En Avant* at this spot and guessed that this must have been where his missionary friend Dr Abbott had camped a few months previously. As to their location, according to the maps in Meyer's book the Schneequell lies almost exactly due south of East Lava Hill, the easternmost of the parasitic cones on the Saddle, and would seem to tie in fairly neatly with the Last Water Point, the Maua River, that lies below Zebra Rocks on the Marangu Route (see p299). Abbott's Camp, meanwhile, lies to the north-north-west of here, at a point between the two Marangu Route paths to the Saddle.

From here, Meyer's path and the Marangu Route diverge for good. Where Marangu trekkers head roughly north across the Saddle, keeping Kibo to their left, in 1889 Meyer and his two companions, the alpine expert Purtscheller and Mwini Amani, their guide, set off directly for the summit in a more westerly direction, stopping for the night by a prominent rock at 14,200ft (4328.1m). This is **Viermannstein**, the Rock of Four Men, a place popular with Kili explorers in the 19th century. Unfortunately, because it lies far from any trail today, the site rarely features on modern trekking maps; for an approximate location, draw a line running east from Barafu Campsite, and a second due south from the easternmost Triplet: the rock stands near to where they coincide.

Meyer's aim in 1889 was **Ratzel Glacier**, on the south-eastern rim of Kibo. The glacier has now, alas, disappeared, though we know from maps where it was: if walking up to the summit from Barafu Campsite, it would have been on your right when approaching Stella Point. In Meyer's day the glacier covered the entire south-eastern lip of Kibo; it was into this glacier that Meyer and Purtscheller, on 3 October, carved a series of steps that led all the way to the crater rim and a height of 19,260ft (5870.4m).

On this occasion, considerations of time and weather forced them to withdraw back down to camp, having seen – but not scaled – the highest point on Kibo. After a day's rest and contemplation, however, and having decided to bivouac at **Lava Cave** on the slopes of Kibo at 15,960ft (4864.6m), the duo were ready for another assault on the summit. From there, at 3am on a cold October morning, they set off. At dawn they were at the foot of the glacier where, to their delight, they found the glacial stairway that they'd built two days previously was still there. By 8am they had reached and crossed a large crevasse, the only serious obstacle on the way to the summit. Just 45 minutes later they were back standing on the crater rim, the limit of their achievements two days previously.

On this occasion, however, both time and weather were on their side. Walking around the southern rim of Kibo, they climbed three small hillocks, the middle of which they found by aneroid to be the highest by some 40ft (12¼m) or more. Thus at 10.30am on 6 October 1889, Meyer and Purtscheller wrote themselves into the history books as the first to make it to the highest point in Africa.

So where exactly did they gain **access to the crater**? According to Dr Hassenstein's maps, the 'Lava Cave' lies at the northern end of the large South-East Valley, due west of the middle of the three triplets. That puts it somewhere to the north-east of Barafu Campsite, and more than 150m (492ft) higher, on one of the rocky spurs that run south-east down from Kibo. Where it certainly is *not*, though many a guide will tell you otherwise, is Hans Meyer Cave on the Marangu Route, which at 5151m (16,899½ft) is simply too high and too far north. The notch by which they gained access to the crater lay almost exactly north-west of this Lava Cave Camp.

Though again this is largely guesswork, all the evidence does seem to point to the fact that Meyer and Purtscheller on this particular occasion passed into the crater rim from a spot very near to **Stella Point** (5745m, 18,848½ft); the difference in height (Meyer estimated the height at this point on the crater to be 5778m/18956¾ft) can possibly be ascribed to the fact that Meyer's estimates tend to be over-estimates (his height for Uhuru Peak, for example, is over 6000m) – perhaps because in Meyer's day there was a lot more ice at the summit, which would have raised the altitudes.

Having christened the summit after their Kaiser and taken the topmost stone from the summit as a souvenir (a stone that Meyer later gave to the Kaiser, who used it as a paperweight), the pair then hurried back to Abbott's camp on the Saddle. The next few days were spent trying to conquer **Mawenzi** but with no success, the mountain peak defeating them wholly on the first occasion on 13 October, and an attack of colic brought on by some over-ripe bananas stalling their second attempt two days later. Before returning to civilisation, however, they spent five more days revisiting Kibo: on 17 October they headed to the crater's northern side. There they reached 5572m before confronting a sheer wall of ice that forced them to retreat; and then finally, on the 18th, they approached the crater from the east.

The path Meyer took up to the crater on this occasion is not too dissimilar to the trail up to Gillman's from the Kibo Huts. Meyer and Purtscheller on this final climb bivouacked at a location they called **Old Fireplace** because, to their considerable surprise, they found the remains of a recent campfire there, along with the bones of an eland and some pieces of banana matting. This camp, according to Meyer, sat at an altitude of 15,390ft (4690.9m). It's just possible, therefore, that the Old Fireplace is in fact the site we now call **Jiwe La Ukoyo**, which many local mountain guides insist was once a popular hunters' campsite. From the Old Fireplace, Meyer and Purtscheller climbed up the snow-clad slopes of Kibo once more, gaining access into the crater via a cleft in the rim that is now known as **Hans Meyer Notch**, and which lies just a few hundred metres to the north of Gillman's Point. Though they failed in their attempts to reach the inner cone of the volcano, they were at least able to confirm that the floor of the crater was made up of a mixture of mud and ashes. They were also startled when, peering into the first cone, they came across the carcass of an antelope (which possibly explains what the leopard, whose frozen body was found up here many years later, was doing at this altitude).

After one more unsuccessful attempt on Mawenzi, Meyer and Purtscheller finally decided to call it a day and, on 22 October, they said goodbye to the Saddle for the last time. According to Meyer, the pair had spent 16 days between 15,000 and 20,000ft (4572-6096m, though we know this last figure is an over-estimate of course as the height of Kili is only 5895m/19,341ft). During this time they had made four ascents of Kibo, reaching the crater three times and the summit once, and three sorties on Mawenzi, reaching the 5049m summit of Purtscheller's Spitze (Point) but failing to reach the very top.

KILIMANJARO

The conquest of Kilimanjaro
Taking out a small German flag, which I had brought with me for the purpose in my knapsack, I planted it on the weather-beaten lava summit with three ringing cheers, and in virtue of my right as its discoverer christened this hitherto unknown and unnamed mountain peak – the loftiest spot in Africa and the German Empire – Kaiser Wilhelm's Peak [now known as Uhuru Peak]. *Then we gave three cheers more for the Emperor, and shook hands in mutual congratulation.*

Hans Meyer
Across East African Glaciers

Glacier, named by Meyer after a geography professor in his native Leipzig.) As a result, by the time they reached the eastern lip of the crater, the light was fading fast and the approach of inclement weather forced them to return before they could reach the highest point of that lip.

On their second attempt, however, three days later on 6 October 1889, and with the stairs in the ice still intact from the first ascent, they were able to gain the eastern side of the rim by mid-morning; from there it was but a straightforward march to the three small tumescences situated on the higher, southern lip of the crater, the middle one of which was also the highest point of the mountain.

AFTER MEYER

Mawenzi, Pastor Reusch and a frozen leopard

In the decades following Meyer's successful assault on Kili, few followed in his footsteps. Meyer climbed again in 1898, though this time he got only as far as the crater rim. In 1909 surveyor M Lange climbed all the way to Uhuru Peak, and in doing so became only the third (after Meyer and Purtscheller) to reach the summit of Kilimanjaro – a full 20 years after the first two.

The conquest of the last remaining summit on Kilimanjaro, that of Mawenzi (called, somewhat perversely, Hans Meyer Peak), was achieved by the climbers **Edward Oehler** and **Fritz Klute** on 29 July 1912. Thus, 64 years after the first European had clapped eyes on Kilimanjaro, both of its main summits had been successfully climbed. As an encore, Oehler and Klute made the third successful expedition on Kibo and the first from the western side. In the same year, **Walter Furtwangler** and **Ziegfried Koenig** achieved the fourth successful climb and became the first to use skis to descend. Two more successful assaults occurred before the outbreak of World War One, and **Frau von Ruckteschell** kept up the German's impressive record on Kilimanjaro by becoming **the first woman to reach Gillman's Point and the rim of the crater**.

Fresh attempts on Kilimanjaro were suspended for a while during World War One. The countryside around Kilimanjaro became the scene of some

vicious fighting, including Moshi itself, which was attacked by British forces in March 1916. Paul von Lettow Vorbeck, the German commander, went down in military history at this time as the man who led the longest tactical retreat ever. But with the Germans' defeat, Kilimanjaro, along with the rest of German East Africa, reverted to British rule.

After the war, attention turned away from Kibo to the lesser-known Mawenzi. In 1924 **George Londt** of South Africa became, by accident, the first to climb South Peak (he was aiming for Hans Meyer Peak but got lost); the peak (4958m), was named after him. Three years later three English mountaineers climbed Mawenzi, including 22-year-old **Sheila MacDonald**, the first woman to do so; the trio then climbed Kibo, with Ms MacDonald writing her name into the record books again as **the first woman to complete the ascent to Uhuru Peak**. In 1930 two British mountaineers, HW Tilman and Eric Shipton, names more usually associated with Everest, climbed Mawenzi's Nordecke Peak – again, like Londt, by accident.

While all this was happening on Mawenzi, over on Kibo another man was writing himself into the history of Kili: **Pastor Richard Reusch**. Missionary for the Lutheran Church, former officer in the Cossack army and long-time Marangu resident, Reusch is said to have climbed the mountain on no fewer than 65 occasions. During his first assault on the summit in 1926 he found the frozen leopard on the crater rim that would later inspire Hemingway (see p172; Reusch cut off part of an ear as a souvenir), while on another sortie the following year he became the first to gaze down into the inner crater, a crater to which he would later give his name. Later work by mountaineer **HW Tilman** and vulcanologist **JJ Richard** led to confirmation, in 1942, that Kilimanjaro was still active, and while this led to some local panic, in 1957 the Tanganyika Geological Survey and the University of Sheffield were able to allay fears by declaring the volcano to be dormant and almost extinct.

KILIMANJARO TODAY

The 20th century witnessed the inevitable but gradual shift away from exploration towards tourism. The most significant change occurred in 1932 with the building of Kibo Hut; name plates and signs were put up too as the mountain was gradually made more tourist-friendly. With a ready base for summit assaults now established, tourists began to trickle into Tanzania to make their own attempt on Africa's greatest mountain.

In 1959 the mountain became the **focus for nationalist feelings** and a symbol of the Tanganyikans' independence aspirations following Julius Nyerere's speech to the Tanganyika Legislative Assembly (see p119 for quote). Nyerere eventually got his wish and, after independence was granted in 1961, a torch was indeed placed on Kilimanjaro (though it is said that bad weather prevented them from actually reaching the summit itself!). Independence also provided Tanganyika with the chance to rename many of the features of the mountain; in particular, the very summit, dubbed Kaiser Wilhelm Peak by Hans Meyer, was

renamed Uhuru Peak – Uhuru meaning, appropriately, 'Freedom' in Swahili.

Since this mountain's moment of patriotic glory, the story of Kilimanjaro has largely been about **tourism**. The early trickle of tourists of 70 years ago is nowadays more akin to a flood, with visitor numbers increasing exponentially from fewer than 1000 in the late 1950s to 11,000 in the 1990s, to the 50,000-plus we see today. What has been an economic boon to the people of Kilimanjaro, however, has brought little benefit to the mountain itself. With the increase in the number of trekkers comes commensurately greater numbers of pressures and problems. Its soil is being eroded, its vegetation is being

❑ **For the record**

● **Fastest ascent of Kilimanjaro** As discussed in the introduction to this book, on 13 August, 2014, Karl Egloff of Switzerland, ran to the 5895m summit in 4 hours 56 minutes, thereby becoming the first (and so far the only) man to get to Uhuru Peak from a park gate (in this instance, Umbwe Gate) in under five hours. His feat eclipsed the four-year-old record of Spanish runner Kilian Jornet, set in September 2010, by almost half an hour.

● **Fastest ascent and descent** That's not the end of the story, however, for Karl then trotted back down to Mweka Gate in a total time of 6 hours 42 minutes, thus also beating Kilian's record for the fastest ascent and descent and becoming the first man to break the seven-hour mark.

● **Fastest ascent and descent – unaided** It's good to see that a local man holds one of these records. On 22 February 2006, Simon Mtuy, born and raised on the slopes of Kilimanjaro near Marangu Gate at Mbahe, climbed from Umbwe Gate to the summit and back to Mweka Gate in 9 hours 19 minutes. In doing so, he achieved the fastest ever unaided ascent and descent (by unaided, they mean that he carried his own food, water and clothing). This he managed despite suffering from a nasty bout of diarrhoea, as well as taking a three-minute break at the top to video himself, plus two further breaks to vomit! According to Simon, to prepare for his record-breaking attempt he spent a total of two weeks on the mountain beforehand – including five days at Barranco, four spent at Arrow Glacier and three days on the Crater itself.

● **Fastest ascent (female)** On 27 July 2015 Anne-Marie Flammersfeld, a 37-year-old German currently living in St Moritz, Switzerland, set a new record for the fastest ascent and descent by a woman on Kilimanjaro, climbing to the summit via the Umbwe Route in a time of 8 hours 32 minutes and thus smashing the record set in September 2011 by Debbie Bachmann of Zimbabwe by over three hours! Anne-Marie then turned round and made it back to Mweka Gate for a total time on the mountain of 12 hours 58 minutes, destroying Ms Bachmann's record by over six hours!

Nor was this the only impressive feat by Anne-Marie, a Sports Scientist with her own company. The climb was part of her attempt to conquer the seven highest volcanic summits in the world by setting off from the lowest point in that country and getting to the highest point without any 'mechanical' help. So, for example, in Tanzania Anna-Marie set off from the coast at Tanga and cycled for four days to reach Mount Kilimanjaro. They then climbed Umbwe in four days as preparation for her record attempt two days later.

● **Youngest person to reach the summit** On 21 January 2008 Keats Boyd from Los Angeles successfully hauled his 7-year-old body up to the summit of Africa's highest mountain – and in doing so became the youngest person ever to reach the top of

burnt or chopped, its wildlife is disappearing and its glaciers are melting. Along with these environmental pressures come challenges to its dignity, as climbers dream up ever more bizarre ways of climbing to the top, whether riding up by motorcycle or walking in fancy dress, as discussed in the introduction to this book.

Then there's the problem of **fire**. In February 1999, fires raged for five days and 70 hectares were destroyed, the blaze finally being brought under control thanks to the combined efforts of 347 villagers, park rangers and 40 soldiers of the 39th Squadron of the Tanzanian People's Defence Force. Further fires on

Kilimanjaro. An impressive feat, not least because in breaking the record Keats must also have broken all sorts of rules, including the one that says you have to be at least 10 to climb Kili! That record was challenged in 2013 by Aaryan Balaji, a Grade 2 student of Mahatma Gandhi International School in Port Blair, India, who was also seven; however, despite extensive research we have been unable to find out his *exact* age and thus determine who was the youngest. The youngest person to climb Kilimanjaro who *was* above the minimum age was Jordan Romero of Big Bear Lake, California, who achieved the summit on 23 July 2006 at the tender age of 10 years and 11 days.

● **Oldest person to reach the summit**: Perhaps surprisingly, this is the record that has changed hands most frequently over the past few years. On July 20th 2017 Dr Fred Distelhorst, a retired orthodontist from Vail, Colorado, became, at 88, the oldest person ever to climb Kilimanjaro. His achievement eclipsed the previous record set by Russian octagenarian Angela Vorobeva on October 29th 2015, who took the popular Machame Route to the top at 86 years, 267 days. (Impressive, but it's fair to say that it's not the toughest challenge that Ms Vorobeva has faced, having survived of the Siege of Leningrad in 1944!).

Her achievement in turn beat the record set by Anne Lorimor, of Arizona, who climbed in August 2015 with her niece and nephew to the summit aged 85. A few months before that, on 2nd October 2014, Robert Wheeler, from the USA, reached the summit after five days of trekking aged 85 years 201 days. His climb thus trumped Martin and Esther Kafer, from Vancouver, who reached the summit in September 2012 aged 85 and 84 respectively. Esther was just a year older than Bernice Buum, who reached the summit aged 83 in September 2010; while Martin's achievement pipped that of farmer Richard Byerley from Washington, USA, who in October 2011 reached the summit of Africa's highest mountain at the ripe old age of 84 years and 71 days – and who in turn had eclipsed British grandad George Solt, a retired professor from Olney, Buckinghamshire, who the previous summer had summited at the age of 82.

Thankfully, Dr Distelhorst's achievement also beats the unofficial record set by the mysterious Valtee Daniel, a Frenchman whom I only read about once while researching the first edition of our guidebook way back in 2001, and whom I have never heard anything else about since. Mr Daniel's climb at the age of 87 has never been recognised by the Guinness Book of Records, who insist that any record attempt is verified by independent witnesses and must be filmed, photographed and meticulously documented in a log book. With Dr Distelhorst becoming the first person to climb Kili above the age of 87, we can finally put Monsieur Daniel's unofficial record to bed.

Waterfall at the foot of Kilimanjaro. Engraving by Alexandre Le Roy from *Au Kilima-Ndjaro (Afrique Orientale)* published in 1893.

Shira Plateau in 2001, on the Rongai Route before Kikelelwa Campsite in 2007, in October 2008 on the Marangu Route between the Mandara and Horombo Huts, and on the northern side of the mountain in July 2013, have caused yet more damage. Depressingly but unsurprisingly, human activity is believed to have been behind the fires. Some point an accusing finger at local farmers who like to clear their farms by fire before the start of the annual rains. Other possible culprits include honey collectors, who make fires to smoke out the bees; we've even heard accusations that those in charge of the park, KINAPA, start fires in order to extract more money from TANAPA, the body that oversees the administration of all of the country's reserves and parks – though we think this has more to do with the Tanzanians' love of a good conspiracy theory than any basis in reality.

Yet no matter what indignities are heaped upon it, Kilimanjaro continues to inspire both awe and respect in those who gaze upon it. And while man will continue to visit in droves and in his clumsy way will carry on defacing and demeaning it, setting it ablaze and covering it with litter, the mountain itself remains essentially the same powerful, ineffably beautiful sight it always was; perhaps because, while we throw all that we can at it, the Roof of Africa does what it always has done – and what it does best: it simply rises above it all.

Fauna and flora

Kilimanjaro is often called 'The Island Above the Clouds' because it boasts more unique species than many small countries. Many happy years could be spent studying and writing about this mountain's fascinating flora and fauna. The following, therefore, is but the briefest of introductions to the nature of Kilimanjaro.

FAUNA

'The survival of our wildlife is a matter of grave concern to all of us in Africa. These wild creatures amid the wild places they inhabit are not only important as a source of wonder and inspiration but are an integral part of our natural resources and our future livelihood and well being.

In accepting the trusteeship of our wildlife we solemnly declare that we will do everything in our power to make sure that our children's grandchildren will be able to enjoy this rich and precious inheritance.

The conservation of wildlife and wild places calls for specialist knowledge, trained manpower and money. And we look to other nations to cooperate with us in this important task – the success or failure of which not only affects the continent of Africa but the rest of the world as well.'
Julius Nyerere, in a speech made soon after he became the country's first president, in September 1961. The quote that can be found on a bust of him that stands at the entrance to the Tanzanian National Park Office, Arusha.

In order to see much in the way of fauna, you have to be either very lucky or, it would seem, an author of a book on Kilimanjaro. When Hans Meyer was coming down from the mountain in 1889 he spotted an elephant on the slopes. He also found a frozen antelope in the crater. In 1926 a leopard was found frozen in the summit ice by Pastor Richard Reusch (see p167) near a place we now call Leopard Point – providing Hemingway with the inspiration for *The Snows of Kilimanjaro*. The mountaineer, HW Tilman, saw 27 eland on the Saddle when he passed this way in 1937, with each, according to him, especially adapted for the freezing conditions with thicker fur. In 1962, renowned travel writer Wilfred Thesiger and two companions were accompanied to the summit by five wild dogs (aka African hunting dogs). Though the dogs then turned round and disappeared after the three men made the summit, paw-prints in the ice proved that this wasn't the first time they had climbed to the top. More recently, Rick Ridgeway claimed he saw a leopard on his ascent, as did Geoffrey Salisbury while leading his group of blind climbers to the summit; and in 1979 a local guide called David was savaged by a pack of wild dogs above the Mandara Huts and lost a finger.

We mention these stories to demonstrate that the more exotic fauna of East Africa does occasionally venture onto the mountain. It just doesn't happen very often, with most animals preferring to be somewhere where there aren't 40,000-plus trekkers (and their crews) marching around every year.

The decline of fauna on Kilimanjaro is perhaps best illustrated by these random quotes I have drawn from *Tanganyika Notes and Records: Kilimanjaro*, an excellently informative book published in March 1965. It's depressing to see how abundant the wildlife appeared even then, just over fifty years ago.

'Millard considers that the elephant population of Kilimanjaro is of the order of 1,500 and from personal observation this appears to be a very reasonable estimate.'

'Giraffe have been seen by Millard in heavy forest within the montane forest belt.'

'Up to about 1950, Rhinoceros were often encountered in the forest above Marangu...They are still to be found from West Kilimanjaro where their position is fairly good around to Kitenden where their numbers have been considerably reduced.'

'Wild Dogs have been seen in the Mandera [sic] *(Bismark) hut area and in the country to the south of Mawenzi (Forest Division).'*

Baboons in the branches of a Dum palm
(from *Across East African Glaciers*, Hans Meyer, 1891)

Just for the record, elephants do still wander up the slopes of Kilimanjaro, particularly from Amboseli and from the

❏ **Protecting Kilimanjaro**

Kilimanjaro has enjoyed some form of protection since the early years of the 20th century under German rule, when the mountain and surrounding area were designated as a game preserve. In 1921 this status was upgraded to become a forest and game preserve, thereby protecting the precious cloud forest that beards Kili's lower slopes.

Another change in 1957 saw Tanganyika National Parks Authority propose that the mountain become a national park, though this wasn't actually realised until 1973, when **Kilimanjaro National Park (KINAPA)** was formed; a park that, for simplicity's sake, the authorities decided would include all land above 2700m. KINAPA didn't actually officially open until 1977; 12 years later, in 1989, the park was declared a **World Heritage Site** by UNESCO. In 2013 it was also honoured as **one of the Seven Natural Wonders of Africa**, along with its neighbours the Ngorongoro Crater and Serengeti migration. Thus Northern Tanzania plays host to three of the seven natural wonders (the Serengeti migration being shared with Kenya), with the others being the Nile River, Sahara Desert, Red Sea Reef and the Okavango Delta.

West Kilimanjaro corridor, though in nothing like the numbers recorded above; giraffe are seldom if ever recorded on the mountain now, though it's feasible that they too may wander up the northern and western slopes; the total population of rhino in the whole of Tanzania is now less than fifty, with the nearest to Kilimanjaro now well over 100km away in Ngorongoro Crater to the west or Mkomazi National Park to the south-east; while wild dogs are so rare now in Tanzania that a website has even been set up so that those fortunate enough to spot one can tell the world about it!

So in all probability you will see virtually nothing during your time on the mountain beyond the occasional monkey or mouse. Nevertheless, keep your mouth shut and your eyes open and you never know...

Forest and cultivated zones

Animals are more numerous down in the forest zone than anywhere else on the mountain; unfortunately, so is the cover provided by trees and bushes, so sightings remain rare. The mountain is reputed to be the home of the world's largest population of **Abbott's duiker**, a small and very endangered forest antelope of which there are supposed to be only 2500 left on the planet. Rare, shy and mainly nocturnal, it's not difficult to see why sightings of this duiker are so uncommon.

As with the four-striped grass mice of Horombo (see p175), it tends to be those few species for whom the arrival of man has been a boon rather than a curse that are the easiest to spot, including **blue monkeys**, which appear daily near the Mandara Huts and which are not actually blue but grey or black with a white throat. These are the plainer relatives of the beautiful **colobus monkey**, which has the most enviable tail in the animal kingdom; you can see a troop of these at the start of the forest zone on the Rongai and Lemosho routes, and near the Mandara Huts, where a couple are semi-tame. Strangely, despite their beauty, their name is actually derived from the Greek for 'mutilated' as unlike other primates they don't have a proper opposable thumb but a mere stump. This

❑ *'URGENT MESSAGE:*
Location: Amboseli Game Park, Kenya
Human population: 150
Baboon population: 90,000
Meteorological conditions: Severe drought
Water supplies: Nil
Situation: Mutilated bodies discovered. Baboons have turned into man-eating primates – POSITION DESPERATE!'

Taken from the back cover of terrible 1980s' horror film *In the Shadow of Kilimanjaro*, supposedly based on a true story. You may like to consider this when walking past a troop of them on your Meru climb.

'deformity' is even more bizarre when one considers that they are amongst the most arboreal of monkeys; in other words, they very rarely drop down to the ground, preferring instead to spend their time in the trees – where you would have thought a proper opposable thumb would be an advantage for grabbing hold of branches etc. Indeed, so rarely does the colobus drop down to the ground that it would normally be rather difficult to spot were it not for its flamboyant coat and its strange, frog-like croak.

Olive baboons, **civets**, **leopards**, **mongooses** and **servals** are said to live in the mountain's forest as well, though sightings are extremely rare; here, too, lives the **bush pig** with its distinctive white stripe running along its back from head to tail.

Then there's the **honey badger**. Don't be fooled by the rather cute name, for as well as being blessed with a face only its mother could love, these are the most powerful and fearless carnivores for their size in Africa. Even lions give them a wide berth. You should too: not only can they cause a lot of damage to your person but the thought of having to tell your friends that, of all the blood-thirsty creatures that roam the African plains, you got savaged by a badger, is too shaming to contemplate. Of a similar size, the **aardvark** has enormous claws but unlike the honey badger this nocturnal, long-snouted anteater is entirely benign. So fear not: as the old adage goes, aardvark never killed anyone. Both aardvarks and honey badgers are rarely, if ever, seen on the mountain. Nor are **porcupines**, Africa's largest rodents. Though also present in this zone, they are both shy and nocturnal and your best chance of seeing one is as road-kill on the way to Nairobi.

Further down, near or just above the cultivated zone, **bushbabies** or galagos are more easily heard than seen as they come out at night and jump on the roofs of the huts. Here, too, is the **small-spotted genet** with its distinctive black-and-white tail, and the noisy, chipmunk-like **tree hyrax**.

One creature you definitely won't see at any altitude is the rhinoceros. Over-hunting has finally taken its toll of this most majestic of creatures – Count Teleki (see p161), for example, is said to have shot 89 of them during his time in East Africa, including four in one day – and, as we said earlier, there are none on or anywhere near Kilimanjaro today.

Heath, moorland and above

Just as plant-life struggles to survive much above 2800m (8858¼ft), so animals too find it difficult to live on the barren upper slopes. Yet though we may

see little, there are a few creatures living above the treeline on Kilimanjaro. The prime example is the **four-striped grass mouse**, which clearly doesn't find it a problem eking (or should that be eeking?) out an existence at high altitude; indeed, if you're staying in the Horombo Huts on the Marangu Route, one is probably running under your table while you read this, and if you stand outside for more than a few seconds at any campsite you should see them scurrying from rock to rock. Other rodents present at this level include the **harsh-furred** and **climbing mouse** and the **mole rat**, though all are far more difficult to spot. (Your best chance of seeing the harsh-furred mouse is probably on Shira Plateau, particularly amongst the heather by the toilets near the caves at Shira Caves Campsite and, less often, at Shira 1 Campsite on the Lemosho Route.)

For anything bigger than a mouse, your best chance above 2800m/9186¼ft is either on the Shira Plateau, where **buffalos and other grazers** roam occasionally, or on the northern side of the mountain on the Northern Circuit and Rongai Route. Kenya's Amboseli National Park lies at the foot of the mountain on this side and many animals, particularly **elephants**, amble up the slopes from time to time in the search for minerals that they can extract from the rocks. **Grey** and **red duikers**, **elands** and **bushbucks** are perhaps the most commonly seen animals at this altitude, though sightings are still extremely rare.

None of these larger creatures lives above the tree-line of Kilimanjaro permanently, however, and as with the **leopards** that occasionally make their way up the slopes, they are, like us, probably no more than day-trippers.

On Kibo itself the entomologist George Salt found a species of **spider** that was living in the **alpine zone** at altitudes of up to 5500m. What exactly these high-altitude arachnids live on up there is unknown – though Salt reckoned it was probably the flies that blew in on the wind, of which he found a few, and which appeared to be unwilling or unable to fly. What is known is that the spiders live underground, better to escape the rigours of the weather. We've also seen a white butterfly on the way up to Mawenzi Tarn Huts at 4122m; once again, we can only assume that it has been blown up the slopes from the moorland or forest zone.

Hartlaub's turaco

AVIFAUNA

Kilimanjaro is great for birdlife. The cultivated fields on the lower slopes provide plenty of food, the forest zone provides shelter and plenty of nesting sites, while the barren upper slopes are ideal hunting grounds for raptors.

In the **forest**, one of the easier birds to spot is the dark green **Hartlaub's turaco**, partly because of its noisy, monkey-like call, and partly because when it flies, viewers are treated to flashes of bright red under-wings. If you're lucky you may also come

Tropical boubou

across black and white **tropical boubous** (bell shrikes) and **silvery-cheeked hornbills**, though to be honest you're more likely to see hornbills on Meru, and even in Arusha near Jacaranda Hotel, than on Kilimanjaro.

Montane white-eyes – small green birds with distinctive white circles around their eyes – can be found around Machame Huts and occasionally elsewhere on the mountain; another habitué of the Machame Huts is the **common stonechat**, a relative of the more common alpine chat but slightly more striking in appearance, with a white stripe on its black wings and a chestnut patch on its breast.

Other small birds said to live in the forest include the **speckled mousebird** that hang around the fruit trees, and the **trogon** which, despite a red belly, is difficult to see because it remains so motionless in the branches. Smaller birds include the **Ruppell's robin chat** (black and white head, grey top, orange lower half) and the **common bulbul**, with a black crest atop its head and yellow beneath the tail.

Further up the slopes, the noisy, scavenging, garrulous **white-necked raven** is a constant presence on the mountain during the day, eternally hovering on the breeze around the huts and lunchstops on the lookout for any scraps. Smaller but just as ubiquitous is the **alpine chat**, a small brown bird with white side feathers in its tail, and the **streaky seed-eater**, another brown bird (this time with streaks on its back) that often hangs around the huts. For some reason, over the past few years the campsites have been invaded by **dusky turtle doves**, bronze of feather and brazen in character. The **alpine swift** also enjoys these misty, cold conditions.

The prize for the most beautiful bird on the mountain, however, goes to the dazzling **scarlet-tufted malachite sunbird**. Metallic-green save for a small scarlet patch on either side of its chest, this delightful bird can often be seen hovering above the grass, hooking its long beak in to reach the flies sheltering in the lobelias.

Climbing further, we come to raptor territory. You'll rarely see these birds up close as they spend most of the day gliding on the currents looking for prey. **Augur buzzards** are very occasionally spotted hovering in the breeze; these are impressive birds in themselves – especially if you're lucky enough to see one up close – though not as large as the **crowned eagle** and the rare **lammergeyer**, a giant vulture with long wings, a wedge tail and a tufty beard beneath the beak.

Speckled mousebird

White-necked raven

Streaky seed eater

Malachite sunbird

Four-striped grass mouse

Blue monkey

Skink or grey lizard

Colobus monkey

Vervet monkeys (Meru)

Two-horned chameleon

Lammergeyer

FLORA

It is said that to climb up Kilimanjaro is to walk through **four seasons in less than a week**. It is true, of course, and nowhere is this phenomenon more apparent than in its flora. The variety of flora found on Kilimanjaro can be ascribed in part to the mountain's tremendous height and in part to its proximity to both the equator and the Indian Ocean. Add to this the variations in climate, solar radiation and temperature from the top of the mountain to the bottom (temperatures are estimated to drop by 1°C for every 150m gain in altitude), and you end up with the ideal conditions for highly differentiated and distinctive vegetation zones. In all, **Kilimanjaro is said to have between four and six distinctive zones**, or 'seasons', depending on whom you read.

Cultivated zone and forest (800m-2800m)

The forest zone, along with the cultivated zone that lies below it, together receive the most rainfall – about 2300mm per year – of any part of the mountain. The forest also houses the greatest variety of both fauna (see p171) and flora.

For the layman, it may be difficult at first to identify the individual species of **tree**, though some do stand out. On the Marangu Route the first trees you'll possibly notice – and Antipodeans should recognise – are actually non-native: the pale-barked **eucalyptus** was planted by the first park warden of Kilimanjaro, though it is now a tree that his successors are trying to eradicate as it takes so much water from the land. Enormous **camphor trees** (*Ocotea usambarensis*) also flourish at this altitude, as do **fig** trees, **avocado** and *talamontana*, or **wild mango**. On the Umbwe Route in particular you'll also find, in the lower reach of the forest, **coffee** growing in abundance. Further up the slopes towards the

Seradoxus
Fireball lily

Trifolium usambarensis

upper limit of the zone, the smooth grey **African holly** (*Ilex mitis*), with its characteristic red and yellow fruit, becomes the dominant tree. **African redwood** (*Hagenia abyssinica*), though nothing like as common, is perhaps more recognisable with its enormous, blousy, pink-flowered panicles – it's quite the campest tree on the mountain.

Another instantly recognisable species is the giant fern, also known as a **tree fern**, *Cyathea sp*, which clearly enjoys the damp conditions, as does **old man's beard** (*Usnea sp*), which lies draped over most of the branches at the upper limit of the forest zone. At about the same altitude is the **podocarpus**, with

Podocarpus (left) and *juniper* (right)

its slender-finger leaves, and the **juniper** whose leaves, at least when gazing up at the canopy, look similar; put examples of each side by side, however, and you can clearly see the difference between them (see photo, p178). With the drier climate the trees of the northern slopes are slightly different, with **olive trees** now abundant and one species, ***Olea kilimandscharica***, indigenous to the mountain.

Incidentally, a report in late 2016 in the *New Scientist* magazine announced that a group of scientists from the University of Bayreuth in Germany have discovered that Africa's tallest indigenous tree lives on Kili! Measuring a whopping 81.5 metres, the tree is of the species ***Entandrophragma excelsum***, a member of the mahogany family, and a stand of them was found thriving in the mountain's cloud forest. In addition to being the tallest on the continent, the tree is also a contender for being one of the oldest, with each tree in the stand estimated to be around 500-600 years old! While it may seem a surprising coincidence that the continent's highest mountain should also be the home of Africa's highest tree, upon reflection it does make sense. The combination of lush, moist conditions and nutrient-rich volcanic soil is quite rare on the continent.

What catches the eyes of most trekkers is not these giants, however, but the small splashes of colour that grow in their shade: the **flowers**. The star of the montane forest zone is the beautiful ***Impatiens kilimanjari***, an endemic fleck of dazzling red and yellow in the shape of an inch-long tuba. The guides on Kili have christened them **elephant's trunk flowers**, a nickname that makes a lot of sense when you view the flower from side-on. You'll see them by the edge of the path on the southern side of the mountain. Vying for the prime piece of real estate that exists between the roots of the trees are other, equally elegant flowers including its relatives, *Impatiens pseudoviola* and

Impatiens kilimanjari

Impatiens pseudoviola

Begonia meyeri-johannis

Impatiens digitata

Lobelia gibberoa

Polystachyus (orchid)

Parochaetus communis

Kniphofia thomsonii
Red hot poker

Hypericum revolutum
St John's Wort

Protea kilimandsharica
(with malachite sunbird)

Impatiens digitata, and the beautiful **African violet**, *Viola eminii*. Hanging from the trees is the ***Begonia meyeri johannis***, with sweet-smelling white and pink flowers that often litter the path like confetti. There's a **lobelia**, too, with blue or pink, distinctive, three-lobed flowers, that thrives in both the forest and the heath zone above. It's very similar to the ones you'll find in the hanging baskets of Europe (though it bears very little resemblance to the lobelias you will see further up the mountain). For that matter, it also bears little resemblance to *Lobelia gibberoa*, or forest lobelia, a giant plant almost 5m tall with a whorl of large leaves at its top and a very tall flower spike; these tend to love water and you'll usually find them growing on the banks of streams. **Orchids** also enjoy the dark moist conditions of the montane forest, in particular *Polystachyus*, with flowers that always resemble, to me at least, insects in flight.

Perhaps the most unusual aspect of Kilimanjaro's forest zone, however, is not the plants and trees that it *does* have but one that it doesn't. Kili is almost unique in East Africa in not having any bamboo at the upper limit of the forest zone, possibly because it is one of the driest mountains and cannot support bamboo stands the way other African mountains can. As a result, the forest zone ends suddenly, with little warning, throwing us immediately into the less shady trails of the ...

Heath and moorland (2800m-4000m)

These two zones overlap, and together occupy the area above the forest from around 2800m to 4000m – known as the **low alpine zone**. Temperatures can drop below 0°C up here and most of the precipitation that does fall comes from the mist that is prevalent at this height.

Immediately above the forest zone is the **alpine heath**. (And when we say immediately above, we mean it: it's almost possible to draw a line in the ground on the footpath to mark where the forest ends and the heath starts.) Rainfall here is around 1300mm per year. Both the **giant heather** *Erica excelsa* and the similar but less bushy *Erica arborea* grow in abundance. The latter also exists in the upper part of the forest zone, where it can grow to 10 metres or more; the higher you go, however, the less impressive the specimens, with many refusing to grow beyond 2.5-3m. **St John's wort**, *Hypericum revolutum*, with its distinctive yellow flowers, also grows at this

level and occasionally in the upper reaches of the forest too. Most people will know this flower thanks to its anti-depressant properties.

Grasses now dominate the mountain slopes, picked out here and there with some splendid wild flowers including the white- or yellow-flowered *Protea kilimandscharica*, an indigenous rarity that can be seen on the Mweka and Marangu trails and, so we've been told, around Maundi Crater – the best place for botanists to spot wild flowers. A whole raft of *Helichrysum* species make their first appearance here too, though certainly not their last; see box p182.

A plant that most readers will recognise instantly is the back-garden favourite *Kniphofia thomsonii*, better known to most as the **red-hot poker**. Climbing higher, you'll begin to come across **sedges** such as *Mariscus kerstenii* with, like most sedges, a triangular stalk. If you're extremely lucky you may also spot an orchid, *Disa stairsii*, a short flower with a spike of small pink flowers. Also growing in the grass here is a pretty, delicate **anemone**, *Anemone thomsonii*, with white flowers; a **scabious**, *Scabiosa columbaria*; and, occasionally, a vivid red **gladiolus** that's simply gorgeous, *Gladiolus watsonides*, which you can also find in the upper reaches of the forest belt.

The shrubs are shrinking now: *Philippia trimera* is the most common, along with the gorse-like *Adenocarpus* beside

Gladiolus watsonides

Anemone thomsonii

Carduus keniensis

Adenocarpus mannii

Disa stairsii (orchid)

Bidens kilimandsharica

Thunbergia alata

Lobelia deckenii

Bearded lichen

which it often grows; the prettiest shrub in the upper reaches of the heath zone is the pink-flowered *Blaeria filago*. Growing in abundance in patches at this altitude is **African wormwood** (*Artemisia afra*), a waist-high plant that is more eas-

---

❏ Identifying helichrysums (everlastings)

Perhaps the most prolific plants on the mountain, and ones that make their appearance just above the forest and continue up to the foot of Kibo (and even, on occasions,

Helichrysum meyeri-johanis

Helichrysum kilimanjari

on it), are the helichrysums, also known as everlastings; those dry-looking flowers that resemble living pot pourri and grow in clumps all over the moorland (as well as above and below it).

Members of the daisy family, the identification of individual helichrysums is complicated by three factors: firstly there are many **different subspecies**; secondly they change their appearance the further up the mountain they go in order to adapt to the conditions; and thirdly they all look much the same. So how do you distinguish between different types of helichrysums? Well, the easiest one to recognise is *Helichrysum meyeri-johanis*, named after the first man to climb Kilimanjaro, which has a pinkish tinge to its petals. The others, however, require a little more detective work. *Helichrysum kilimanjari* differs from *H. meyeri-johanis* in that its flowers are yellowy/brown, and when you crush its leaves they give off a distinctive lemon smell.

Helichrysum citrispinum

Helichrysum splendidum

Helichrysum cymosum

Helichrysum newii

Those two tend to remain in the moorland zone, but as you move up to the high desert other species appear. *Helichrysum cymosum* and *Helichrysum splendidum* both bear tight clusters of small yellow flowers, the former being distinguishable by its leaves that hug the main stem tightly in order to protect it from the cold. *Helichrysum citrispinum* also has leaves that perform this function, though its flowers are larger, white, dry, and don't grow in tight clusters. Also present at this altitude is *Helichrysum newii*, named after Charles New, the first man to reach the snowline on Kilimanjaro. A truly remarkable plant, this was the helichrysum that was found surviving at 5670m near the eastern fumarole in the crater – a record on the mountain. It is believed that the heat from the fumarole allowed this plant to survive the extreme cold.

ily distinguished by its pungent aroma which perfumes the air for entire sections of the trail than by its rather dreary grey-green leaves. Known to the Chagga as *kichachayia* (my spelling), the wormwood, when placed in hot water and drunk as tea, is said to have medicinal properties and is a good cure for a bad stomach.

Artemisia afra
African wormwood

Lobelia deckenii
flowers

Climbing ever further, you'll soon reach the imperceptible boundary of the moorland zone, which tends to have clearer skies but an even cooler climate. Average per annum precipitation is now down to 525mm. At this altitude, perhaps the weirdest plant on the mountain is the strange *lobelia deckenii*, another endemic species. These curious, phallic- and cabbage-shaped plants take eight years to flower (the purple-blue flowers are hidden inside the leaves to protect them from frost), and enjoy a symbiotic relationship with *Nectarinia johnstoni*, the dazzling green malachite sunbird. It is said that any insects at this altitude are attracted by the flowers of the lobelia and by the warmth and shelter that the velvet leaves supply. This in turn attracts the sunbirds who feed on the flies – and in doing so pollinate the flower. The lobelias are at their best in February and March.

Sharing the same cold, bleak environment are the most distinctive plants on the entire mountain: the giant **tree groundsel**, or **dendrosenecio** (until recently called simply 'senecio', a name that you will see crop up in most books and is used by all the guides too). Even without the name change the literature on these plants is most confusing so I am grateful to Mr Eric Knox, director of Indiana University Herbarium and the leading authority on these plants, for his help here.

There are two main dendrosenecio species on Kilimanjaro. The first is *Dendrosenecio kilimanjari*, which has two subspecies: *D. kilimanjari ssp cottonii* is found only above 3600m and has dull, mustard-coloured flowers. They

Dendrosenecio kilimanjari (tree groundsel)
ssp kilimanjarii

Dendrosenecio kilimanjari (tree groundsel)
ssp cottonii

Leonotis nepetifolia

Dierama pendulum

cleverly protect themselves from the cold by using their dead leaves (which are like felt) to insulate their trunk. These groundsels are slow growers; according to some guides, you can estimate the age of a groundsel by counting the number of 'cabbages' or rosettes, with each 'cabbage' representing about 25 years growth. They tend to favour the damper, more sheltered parts of the mountain, which is why you'll see them in abundance near Barranco Campsite as well as other, smaller valleys and ravines. The second subspecies, *D. kilimanjari ssp kilimanjarii*, thrives further down the slopes, can grow up to 5m high, and on the rare occasion it flowers the petals themselves are yellow and grow from a one-metre-long spike. Even further down, at a range of between 2750 and 3350 metres at the fringes of the montane forest, we get the second dendrosenecio species, *Dendrosenecio johnstonii*. Your best chance of seeing these giants is along the Machame Route where they form surprisingly big trees.

Ranunculus oreophylus
Yellow star

Haplocarpha rueppellii

Arabis alpina
Alpine rock cress

Alpine desert (4000m-5000m)

At this altitude, only three species of tussock grass and a few extraordinarily rugged flowering plants can withstand the extreme conditions. This is the alpine desert, where plants have to survive in drought conditions (precipitation here is less than 200mm per year), and put up with both inordinate cold and intense sun, usually in the same day. The **everlastings** continue to dominate, though they are shorter and stumpier now, presumably huddling nearer to the ground to protect themselves from the wind. At this altitude flowers need special strategies to cope. The striking **yellow star**, *Ranunculus oreophylus*, and *Haplocarpha rueppellii* both do so by hugging the ground, better to avoid the wind and feed on what little warmth the ground can provide. The other yellow flowers at this altitude are the straggly **senecio species**, usually found surviving – if not exactly thriving – in the lee of the rocks and boulders. The shy white *Arabis alpina* or **Alpine rock cress** also clings on to survival at this chilly altitude by sheltering behind rocks.

Ice cap (5000m-5895m)

On Kibo, almost nothing lives. There is virtually no water. On the rare occasions that precipitation occurs, most of the moisture instantly disappears into the porous rock or is locked away in the glaciers. That said, specimens of *Helichrysum newii* (see p182), an **everlasting** that truly deserves its name, have been found in the crater, and **moss and lichen** are said to exist almost up to the summit. While these mainly orange lichens may not be the most spectacular of plants, it may interest you to know that their growth rate on the upper reaches of Kilimanjaro is estimated to be just 0.5mm in diameter per year; for this reason, scientists have concluded that the larger patches of lichen on Kilimanjaro could be amongst the oldest living things on earth, being hundreds and possibly thousands of years old!

The People of Kilimanjaro: the Chagga

With regard to the Chagga people, they are a fine, well-built race. Their full development of bone and muscle being probably due to the exercise they all have to take in moving about on steep hills: they seem intellectually superior to the general run of coast Natives, and despite their objectionable traits (almost always present in the uneducated Native), such as lying, dirty habits, thieving, &c., they are certainly a very nice and attractive race.
Rev A Downes Shaw *To Chagga and Back – An Account of a Journey to Moshi, the Capital of Chagga, Eastern Equatorial Africa*, 1924

Kilimanjaro is the homeland of the Chagga people, one of Tanzania's largest ethnic groups. It is fair to say that when you are in Moshi, Marangu or Machame, there is little indication that you are in a 'Chagga town'. Yet in the smaller villages, though waning year by year, traditional Chagga culture remains fairly strong and occasionally a reminder of the past is uncovered by today's tourist, particularly when passing through the settlements on the less-visited eastern side of Kilimanjaro. Such finds make visits to these villages truly fascinating.

Do not, however, come to Kilimanjaro expecting to witness some of the more extreme practices described in this section. This point needs emphasising: the Chaggas' traditional way of life has been eroded by the depredations of Western culture and, as far as we know, is now largely extinct. Indeed, much of the material on which the following account is based is provided by the reports of the 19th- and early 20th-century Europeans who visited the area; in particular, Charles Dundas's comprehensive tome, *Kilimanjaro and its People*, which was first published way back in 1924. (Incidentally, you can see a portrait of Dundas in Moshi's Union Café, where he's celebrated as the first boss of the Kilimanjaro Native Cooperative Union, KNCU; see p250.)

This, of course, begs the question: why have we included in a modern guide to Kilimanjaro descriptions of obsolete Chagga practices and beliefs that were largely wiped out almost 100 years ago? Well, research revealed the relevance of this inclusion since there are still faint echoes of their traditional way of life that have survived into the present day. Reading this admittedly brief account of the Chagga and how they lived and thought could provide you with a better understanding – and thereby some insight – into the mind, beliefs and behaviour of the people who live in Kilimanjaro's shadow today.

ORIGINS

The Chagga are believed to have arrived between 400 and 250 years ago from the north-east, following local upheaval in that area. Logically, therefore, the eastern side of the mountain would have been the first to have been settled. Upon their arrival these new immigrants would have found that the mountain

❏ Chagga/Kichagga language – a quick introduction

The language of the Chagga, Kichagga, is classified as a Niger-Congo language and has various **dialects** including Vunjo, Rombo, Machame, Huru and Old Moshi. The following is a very brief introduction to that dialect spoken in Marangu. As Chagga is rarely written down, compiling this 'phrasebook' wasn't easy; indeed, many of the spellings below are nothing more than phonetic guesswork. For their help with this box I am indebted to my Chagga chums, Amina Malya and Vincent Munuo; and especially Frank Mtei, who came up with the first draft of the translations below, and Alex Minja for his expert help too.

1	*kimu*	2	*shiwi*	3	*shiraru*	4	*shina*	5	*shitanu*
6	*shirandaru*	7	*mfungare*	8	*nyanya*	9	*kenda*	10	*ikumi*

Yes / No	*Ye'e / Ote*	I have a headache	*Ngiwawiyo mrue*
Please	*Ngakuterewa*	I feel sick	*Ngiwawiyo*
Thank you	*Aika*	I am very cold	*Ngiichoo mbeo*
How are you?	*Shimbonyi shapfo?*	Will you carry me?	*Ochirima ingiira*
Very well, thank you	*Nashicha kapisa, aika*	I do not like porridge	*Ngikundi msopfo*
How old are you?	*Nuore maka inga?*	I cannot feel my fingers	*Ngiichue shimnue shewaawaa*
I am British	*Inyi nyimwingeresa*		
I am American	*Inyi nyimwamerikany*	There is an elephant sleeping in my tent	*Kuwore njofu eela itentiny lyako*
Don't mind	*Molaswe*		
How far is it to the camp?	*Ngeshika masaa yenga handun gendelaa?*	A leopard is biting my leg	*Kuwore rung'we ilya kurende koko*
How many times have you climbed the mountain?	*Ni mara tsinga ulemro msari?*	We are together!	*Luilose!*

was already inhabited. An aboriginal people known as the Wakonyingo, who were possibly pygmies, were already living here, as indeed were the Wangassa, a tribe similar to the Maasai, and the Umbo of the Usambara mountains. All of these groups were either driven out or absorbed by the Chagga.

Initially, these new immigrants were a disparate bunch, with different beliefs, customs and even languages. With no feelings of kinship or loyalty to their neighbour, they instead settled into family groups, or **clans**. According to Dundas, in his day some 732 clans existed on Kilimanjaro; by 1924, however, when his book was published, some of these clans were already down to just a single member.

These family ties were gradually cut and lost over time as people moved away to settle on other parts of the mountain. Thus, in place of these blood ties, people developed new loyalties to the region in which they were living and to the neighbours with whom they shared the land. Out of this emerged 20 or so states or chiefdoms, most of them on a permanent war footing with the other 19. Wars between the tribes and indeed between villages in the same tribe were commonplace, though they usually took the form of organised raids by one village on another rather than actual pitched battles. Slaves would be taken during

these raids, cattle rustled and huts burned down, though there was often little bloodshed – the weaker party would merely withdraw at the first sign of approaching hostilities and might even try to negotiate a price for peace.

Eventually the number of groups was whittled down to just six tribes, or states, with each named after one of the mountain's rivers. So, for example, there are the Wamoshi Chaggas (after the Moshi River) and the Wamachame Chaggas who settled near Machame River. With all this intermingling going on, a few words inevitably became used by all the people living on the mountain – and from this unlikely start grew a common language, of which each tribe had its own dialect. Similar customs developed between the tribes, though as with the language they differed in the detail. However, it was only when the Germans took control of the region during the latter part of the 19th century and the local people put aside their differences to present a united front in disputes with their colonial overlords that a single ethnic group was identified and named the Chagga. From this evolved a single, collective Chagga consciousness.

Today the Chaggas, despite their diverse origins, are renowned for having a strong sense of identity and pride. They are also amongst the richest and most powerful people in Tanzania, thanks in part to the fertile soils of Kilimanjaro, and in part to the Western education that they have been receiving for longer than almost any other tribe in East Africa, Kilimanjaro being one of the first places to accept missionaries from Europe. Take a tour around Tanzania and you will also find the Chagga people to be one of the most widespread of all the tribes, seemingly able to settle in even the furthest-flung corners of the land, and – thanks to their talent for trade and politics – to thrive and prosper too.

SOCIAL STRUCTURE AND VILLAGE LIFE

Hans Meyer notes in his book that the biggest Chagga settlement when he visited in 1889 was Machame, with 8000 people. 'Moji' (Moshi) had 3000, as did Marangu. Each family unit, according to him, lived in two or three extremely simple thatched huts in the shape of beehives, with a granary and small courtyard attached. There are several examples of these **'beehive' huts** still dotted around Kilimanjaro's slopes. Only the **chief**, the head of village society and its lawmaker, lived in anything more extensive. The chief of every village was often venerated by his subjects and to meet him required going through an elaborate ceremony first. According to his report in the *Church Missionary Intelligencer*, Johannes Rebmann, the first white man to see Kilimanjaro, had to be sprinkled with goat's blood and the juice of a plant and was then left waiting for four days before being granted an audience with Masaki, the chief of Moshi. While modern society has reduced his role to a largely ceremonial one, the chief is still a widely respected person in village life today – though thankfully there is now less ceremony involved when paying him a visit.

There are other similarities between the Chagga society of yesterday and today. The economy was, then as now, largely agricultural, using the environmentally destructive slash-and-burn technique for clearing land. **Bananas** were once the most common crop, and though banana bushes were largely replaced

by **coffee** plantations in the early 20th century, both are still grown today, usually side by side.

When it came to trading these bananas and coffee in former times, instead of the Tanzanian shilling people used red and blue glass beads as currency, or lengths of cloth known as *doti*. One hundred beads were equal to one *doti*, with which you could buy, for example, twenty unripe bananas; twelve *doti* would get you a cow.

RELIGION AND CEREMONIES

Unsurprisingly for a people that has been subjected to some pretty relentless missionary work for over a century, most Chagga are today **Christian**. Traditional beliefs are still held by some, though the intensity of the beliefs and the excesses of many of the rituals have largely disappeared. Superstition played a central role in traditional Chagga religion: witchcraft (*wusari* in Chagga) formed a major part, **rainmakers** and rain-preventers were important members of society and dreams were infallible oracles of the future; indeed, many Chagga were said to have dreamt of the coming of the white man to Kilimanjaro.

The traditional faith was based around belief in a god called **Ruwa**. Ruwa was a tolerant deity who, though neither the creator of the universe nor of man, nevertheless set the latter free from some sort of unspecified incarceration. Ruwa had little to do with mankind following this episode, however, so the Chagga instead **worshipped their ancestors**, whom they believed could influence events on Earth. Chagga mythology had many parallels with stories from the Bible, including one concerning the fall of man (though in the Chagga version, a sweet potato was the forbidden fruit, and it was a stranger rather than a serpent that persuaded the first man to take a bite); there are also stories that bear a resemblance to the tales of Cain and Abel, and the great flood.

The Chagga faith also had its own **concept of sin** and their own version of the Catholic practice of confession. In the Chagga religion, however, it is not the sinner but the person who is sinned against who must be purified, in order that the negative force does not remain with him or her. This purification would be performed by the local medicine man, with the victim bringing along the necessary ingredients for performing the 'cleansing'. These included the skin, dung and stomach contents of a hyrax (the small tree-dwelling mammals that live on Kilimanjaro); the shell and blood of a snail; the rainwater from a hollow tree and, as with all Chagga ceremonies, a large quantity of banana beer for the medicine man. These ingredients would then be put into a hole in the ground lined with banana leaves and with a gate or archway built above, which the victim would then have to pass through. This done, the victim would be painted by the medicine man using the mixture in the hole. This entire ceremony would be performed twice daily over four days.

Medicine men did more than care for one's spiritual health; they looked after one's physical well-being too. For the price of a goat and, of course, more banana beer, the medicine man would be able to cure any affliction using a

❏ The Chagga view of Kilimanjaro

The summit of Kilimanjaro is and always has been as enchanting to the Chagga as it has been to visitors. According to Dundas, the Chagga view the Kibo summit as something beautiful, eternal and strengthening, its snows providing streams that support life, while the clouds that gather on its slopes provide precious rainfall. By comparison, the plains that lie in the opposite direction are seen as oppressively hot, where famine stalks, drought and malaria are rife and large creatures such as crocodiles and leopards prey on man. Indeed, so venerated is Kilimanjaro that the Chagga dead are traditionally buried facing towards Kibo, and the side of the village facing the summit is known to be the honourable side, where meetings and feasts are held and chiefs are buried. Furthermore, when meeting somebody, he who comes from higher up the slopes of Kilimanjaro should traditionally greet the other first, for it is he who is coming from the lucky side.

Intriguingly, some Chagga myths about Kilimanjaro are remarkably accurate. In particular, the Chagga traditionally believed that the mountain was formed by a volcano – even though the main eruption that formed Kibo occurred around half a million years ago, way before the arrival of man. What's more, there is a story in Chagga folklore concerning the twin peaks of Mawenzi and Kibo, in which Mawenzi's fire burns out first, and the Mawenzi peak is forced to go to Kibo, whose fire was still burning. Parallels between this story and what scientists now believe really happened – with Kibo continuing to erupt long after Mawenzi expired – are remarkable.

Did the Chagga climb to the top of Kilimanjaro before the Europeans?

The answer is: probably not. The quote on p154 by Rebmann in which he talks about '*the popular traditions respecting the fate of the only expedition which had ever attempted to ascend its heights*' suggests that he had information that they had tried only once – and failed. True, they definitely seem to have reached the snow-line before the *mzungu* (white man) arrived: their belief that Kibo was covered in a magic silver which melted on the way down suggests as much. Furthermore, Rebmann's guide refers to the snow on the summit of Kilimanjaro as 'coldness' (see p153), and later on Rebmann discovers the Chagga have a word for snow: Kibo. What's more, Meyer found traces of a hunting expedition on the Saddle. All of which seem to confirm that they had climbed Kilimanjaro and had some experience of snow. But the fact that Charles New's entourage of porters and guides were buck naked when they climbed up to the snow-line suggests that they were, on the whole, unused to the conditions on Kibo; that, and the fact that the name Kilimanjaro, if it is of Chagga origin (about which, see box p148), roughly translates as 'That which is impossible for birds', suggests they thought that it was therefore impossible for man to reach the top.

Charles Dundas is equally sceptical of the notion that the Chagga climbed Kilimanjaro before Meyer:

It is inconceivable that natives can ever have ascended to the crater rim, for apart from cold, altitude and superstitious fears, it is a sheer impossibility that they could have negotiated the ice. Nor is there any tradition among the natives that anyone went up as high... Rebmann tells us that Rengwa, great-grandfather of the present chief of Machame, sent an expedition to investigate the nature of the ice, which descends very low above Machame, but is impossible to scale. Only one of the party survived, his hands and feet frozen and crippled for life; all the rest were destroyed by the cold, or by evil spirits, as the survivor reported.

whole host of methods – including spitting. If you were suffering from a fever, for instance, you could expect to be spat upon up to 80 times by the medicine man, who would finish off his performance by expectorating up your nostrils and then blowing hard up each to ensure the saliva reached its target. For this particular method, the traditional payment was one pot of honey – and probably some more banana beer.

The Ngasi

The Ngasi was a brutal rite-of-passage ceremony that marked the passing of boys into adulthood. The ceremony was presided over by the so-called King of Ngasi, a man who had the authority to viciously flog any boy taking part in the ceremony who displeased him.

Chagga warriors
(from *Across East African Glaciers,* **Hans Meyer**, 1891)

Before the Ngasi started, boys who were to take part were summoned from their houses by the singing of lugubrious songs at the gate of their homes. From there they were taken to the place of ceremony deep in the forest and the proceedings began. **Hunting** formed a large part of the Ngasi; boys were tested on their ability to track down and kill game, the animals caught being smeared with the novices' excrement. Another test they had to undergo was to climb a tree on the riverbank and cross the river by clambering along its branches to where they intertwined with the branches of the trees on the other side. After this, a chicken would be sacrificed and the boys ordered to lick the blood.

The final part of the initial stage was the most horrific, however: orders were secretly given to the boys to slay a crippled or deformed youth amongst their number. Traditionally, the victim was killed in the night. The parents were never actually told what had happened to their son and, as all present at the Ngasi ceremony were sworn to silence, they rarely found out the whole story. The boys then moved to a new camp. They were now called Mbora, and were free to collect the old clothes that they had shed at the start of the Ngasi (one set of boy's clothes, of course, was left unclaimed). They then repaired to the chief's house for a feast, from where they headed home.

After the tribulations of the ceremony, the boys were allowed a month's holiday, before they returned to the chief's house to participate in the sacrificing of a bull. They were then free to head back to their homes, raping any young women they chanced to meet on the way; the poor women had no redress. The Ngasi was now at an end; the boys who successfully completed the ceremony were now men.

Matrimony

Ver hard on Wachaga to get wife, but when he get her she can make do plant corn, she make wash and cook and make do work for him. Ingreza [English] man very much money to spend. She wife no can wash, no plant corn, herd goats or cook. All money, much merkani (cloth), heap money, big dinner. She eat much posho. She no can cook dinner. She only make 'Safari' and look. Porr, porr Ingreza man. A local's view of matrimony as recorded in
Peter MacQueen's book *In Wildest Africa*, published in 1910

After the Ngasi, boys were free to marry. **Marriage** was arranged by the parents, though the boy and girl involved were allowed to voice their opinions – and unless the parents were particularly inflexible, these opinions would count for something. Furthermore, in order for the boy to stand a chance with his potential suitor, he had to woo her. The Chaggas' **courtship** process involved, as elsewhere in the world, a lot of gift-giving, though the gifts followed a strict set of rules: spontaneity played little part in this process. The first gift, for example, from the man to the woman, was always a necklace. The Chagga male would be well rewarded for his generosity, for traditionally in return the girl would dance naked all day with bells attached to her legs. Over the following days other gifts were exchanged until the time came when the girl, having visited all her relatives, would be shut away for three months. No work would be done by the girl during this time and she would be given fattening food and kept in a cage. At the end of this period a **dowry** would be paid, the marriage ceremony performed and the bride would be carried on the back of the Mkara (the traditional Chagga equivalent of the best man) to her new husband's house.

KILIMANJARO ECONOMY

Tourism is the biggest earner in the region, though **agriculture** is still very much part of the local economy. The volcanic soil of the mountain slopes, so rich with nutrients, is amongst the most fertile in East Africa. Thanks to the regular and reliable rainfall blown in from the Indian Ocean (see p143) and the proliferation of springs trickling forth from the bare rock, Kilimanjaro is also one of the damper parts of the region, and the south-eastern slopes particularly so, thus increasing still further the agricultural fecundity of the mountain.

On the lower slopes of Kilimanjaro annual staple crops such as beans, maize and millet are grown, while cash-crops such as Arabica coffee are planted in the *kihamba* land further up the mountainside. Bananas are also grown at this altitude, their leaves and stems providing both a nutrient-rich mulch for the coffee trees and fodder for the livestock that are traditionally grazed at this height. In Chagga society it is customary for a farmer's land to be divided between his sons on his death; whilst this may seem a fair way of dividing land, it also means that a farmer's landholdings diminish in size with every generation, and many farms are now less than a hectare in size.

The Chagga are also keen bee-keepers, the hives being hollow sections of a tree trunk closed at both ends and left to hang in trees; you may see these hives placed (illegally) in Kilimanjaro's forests or by the side of the Arusha–Marangu road. Once the swarm has taken possession and completed the combs, the bees are smoked out and the honey collected.

ARRIVING IN EAST AFRICA: DAR ES SALAAM & NAIROBI

The following chapter is devoted to helping you take your first few steps in East Africa. It contains guides to the two cities you are most likely to fly into if you're not flying straight into Kilimanjaro Airport — namely **Dar es Salaam** (Tanzania) and **Nairobi** (Kenya). The guides to the two cities are deliberately rather brief but they should be adequate for finding your way around and for choosing somewhere to sleep and eat, as well to experience something of metropolitan East Africa.

We explain, at the end of each description, how to get to Kilimanjaro. **Kilimanjaro International Airport** is, of course, the most convenient airport for the mountain and with more and more airlines flying there this chapter is getting less and less relevant and may be surplus to requirements in the future; for more details see p210.

Dar es Salaam

Dar es Salaam (commonly just called Dar) is a city with a bit of an identity crisis: a large metropolis which behaves as if it were a small and sleepy seaside town; a city that was at the forefront of the country's struggle for independence in the 1950s yet still contains the finest collection of dusty old colonial buildings in possibly the whole of East Africa; and a place that everybody thinks is the administrative capital of Tanzania – but isn't.

It *is* the commercial heart of the country, however, and has been almost since its inception in the 1860s by Sultan Sayyid Majid of Zanzibar. Intended as a mainland port for many of the goods and spices being traded on his island, the sultan, clearly a man of poetic bent, named his new city Dar es Salaam (Haven of Peace). And peacefully was how it spent its first few years, as the sultan died soon after founding the city, allowing Bagamoyo, a dhow port to the north, to emerge as the pre-eminent harbour on this particular stretch of the east coast.

Missionaries from Europe added fresh impetus to Dar with their arrival in the 1880s but it was the coming of the Germans in 1891 that really gave this city a fillip, the colonials feeling that the harbour here was more suitable to their steam-powered craft than Bagamoyo. Having made Dar their seat of power, it remained the capital until 1973 when the Tanzanian government decided to move the legisla-

ture to Dodoma, smack in the geometric heart of the country – which probably seemed like a good idea at the time, until somebody pointed out the shortage of water and other basic amenities there.

So while the capital may be Dodoma, much of the politicking and indeed everything else of importance takes place here in Dar. It's also a city with ambition, with shiny high-rises sprouting up throughout the centre and the country's first mass transport system, the DART, introduced at the start of 2016. The population, currently 4.5 million, is said to be the fastest growing in sub-Saharan Africa too. For tourists, there's nothing particularly special to warrant a long stay in this city; but by the same token, don't fret too much if you do have to spend some time in Dar: it's pleasant, it's laid back and, compared to Nairobi, it's a whole lot saner too.

A TOUR OF THE CITY

None of Dar's attractions is going to make your eyes pop out on springs from their sockets but the following half-day tour is fine for those with time to kill in the city and a cursory interest in the place. For those in a hurry, the **National Museum** (see box below) at least is worth seeing, being the most absorbing and, for Kili-bound trekkers, the most relevant attraction in Dar.

Your tour begins around the back of the **Azania Front Lutheran Church**,

---

❏ National Museum of Tanzania

It still holds true that the National Museum (daily 9.30am-6pm; Ts6500), Tanzania's best, fares badly when compared to Kenya's version. Nevertheless, the exhibits themselves remain mildly diverting at times and the buildings are a cool escape from the heat of the day. And if you manage to avoid the marauding school parties you may well have the entire complex to yourself, with only the cleaner for occasional company.

Most of the more interesting exhibits can be found in the first couple of rooms, located upstairs from the ticket desk. The **Hall of Human Origins** is absorbing, describing as it does our evolution through the millennia, with the help of some apposite replicas of Leakey's discoveries at **Olduvai Gorge**. Next door, the **History Gallery** maps out in pretty concise and thorough detail the story of Tanzania, including some interesting articles on the early explorers as well as – inevitably – a lengthy discourse on Tanzania's fight for independence. The third room is even more interesting, an exhibition devoted to **African Rock Art** with detailed descriptions and photographs of primitive and prehistoric carvings and paintings from all over the continent, from the Sahara to southern Africa. Take your time wandering around – it's fascinating.

Returning downstairs, a small courtyard plays host to half-a-dozen **historic cars** and a small **memorial garden** dedicated to the 12 victims who perished in the US Embassy bombing in Dar on 7 August 1998. Similar in style to the one in Nairobi (see p201), the **sculpture** here includes twisted metal, a rusting motorbike and a window pane shattered by the blast.

The **original museum building** that stands beyond is now all but empty, though I'm pleased to see that one of the weirdest exhibits to be found in any museum anywhere in the world, namely the country's first ATM, established in 1997 and looking pretty much like any other ATM you see today, is still in situ. It's not plugged in, by the way, so don't try feeding your card into it.

built on the seafront at the turn of the century by German missionaries. Heading east along the promenade past many old **colonial buildings** now used by the Tanzanian authorities to house various **ministries**, walk round the south-eastern tip of the peninsula past **Kigamboni Ferry Terminal** and on to the **fish market**, Dar's most vibrant attraction. Having ensured all your money and valuables are securely tucked away, feel free to take a wander around – it's at its best early in the morning – and see what the local fishermen have managed to catch overnight.

Returning to the main road, take the first turning on the left (west) up Magogoni St. Surrounded by spacious, peacock-filled grounds, **State House**, built by the British in the years following World War One, stands to your right; you will get your best view of the house at the junction with Luthuli St. Hurdling the chains lining the road, cross this junction and continue straight on along Shaban Robert St where, to your right, you come to the **National Museum** (see the box on p193).

A right turn after that will land you on one of the prettier roads in central Dar, the eastern end of Samora Avenue, with the **botanical gardens** to your left and, on the opposite side towards the end of the street, steeple-topped **Karimjee Hall**, where Julius Nyerere was sworn in as Tanzania's first president.

Facing the end of the street and hidden behind high walls is the now-defunct **Ocean Road Hospital**, another German building dating back to the last years of the 19th century. Stroll round to the sea-facing front of the hospital to study the rather curious architecture, a hybrid of Arab and European styles, and to view the curious spiked mace that sits atop the hospital roof.

From here you have two choices: one is to continue your walk along the coast road back to the fish market and on to the church; the other is to return to the junction behind the hospital, turn south for 100m then right and amble along attractive, tree-shaded Sokoine Drive back to the cathedral.

ARRIVAL

By air

Though safer than arriving in Nairobi, it still pays to be on your guard when landing in Dar: like a recently hatched turtle taking to the ocean for the first time, you are at your most vulnerable when you land in a new country – and even in the 'Haven of Peace' there are still plenty of sharks out there.

Julius Nyerere International Airport is about 12km south-west of the city centre. There are a couple of ATMs (CRDB and NBC – both charge around Ts8000 for withdrawals), several moneychangers and a

taxi counter which has a set rate of Ts40,000 to take you into the centre. You could try to negotiate a lower rate with the drivers themselves; or you could walk a few hundred metres to the main road, cross over and take a **bus** into town for Ts450, or hail a cab for about Ts30,000.

Overland

If arriving by bus you'll fairly certainly be dropped at Ubungo Bus Station. A taxi to the centre will cost around Ts15,000-20,000. Alternatively, head out onto the main road where you'll find one of the new Dart bus stations; a bus (No 1 and No 2) into the centre, via Kisutu (the station that's

Dar's area code is ☎ 022. If phoning a landline from outside Tanzania dial ☎ +255-22. We have included the area code in the phone numbers of this chapter.

best for several of the cheap hostels) will cost Ts650.

ORIENTATION & GETTING AROUND

Navigating your way around central Dar is no easy task. Things are fairly straightforward on the coast, where Kivukoni Rd/Ocean Rd (now called Barack Obama Drive) follows the shore from the railway station to Ocean Road Hospital and beyond. But step back from the shore and you find yourself in a labyrinth of small streets, many of which curve imperceptibly but dramatically enough to confuse and disorientate.

Keep the map on p197 with you, using it first to help you find your way to the tourist office where they sometimes hand out a photocopied map of the city. They will also be able to help you out with the city's public transport system, which can also be rather confusing. In 2016 the city said hello to the **Dar Rapid Transit**, or DART; fares are just Ts650 and the buses travel along lanes exclusively set aside for them. The most useful route for most people is the Number 1 and 2 services which

run between the Ubungo Bus Terminal and the centre of town.

Regular buses (Ts450) also ply all the main routes, though finding where they start and stop can be difficult. Ask locals, your hotel, or take a cab. Fortunately, central Dar is compact enough to walk around.

SERVICES
Tourist information
There's a tourist information office (Mon-Fri 8am-4pm, Sat 8.30am-12.30pm; ☎ 022-211 1244/5) in Matasalamat Building on Samora Avenue. It depends who is working there when you call in but we found the staff to be helpful and patient, if not always particularly knowledgeable.

Banks
There are **cashpoints** everywhere. To change cash, try the moneychangers down Samora Avenue west of Ohio St.

Communications
The main **post office** (Mon-Fri 8am-4.30pm, Sat 9am-1pm) is on Maktaba/ Azikiwe St. You won't have any trouble finding a

---

❏ **Diplomatic missions in Dar es Salaam**
- **Belgium** 5 Barack Obama Rd; ☎ 022-211 2688; 🖳 tanzania.diplomatie.belgium.be
- **Canada** Umoja House, 26 Garden Ave & 38 Mirambo St; ☎ 022-216 3300
- **Denmark** 1 Ghana Ave; ☎ 022-216 5200; 🖳 tanzania.um.dk
- **Finland** Umoja House, Garden Ave & Mirambo St; ☎ 022-221 2400; 🖳 finland.or.tz
- **France** 7 Ali Hassan Mwinyi Rd; ☎ 022-219 8800, 🖳 ambafrance-tz.org
- **Germany** Umoja House, Garden Ave & Mirambo St; ☎ 022-211 7409/15; 🖳 daressalam.diplo.de
- **Ireland** 353 Toure Drive, Masaki; ☎ 022-260 2355; 🖳 dfa.ie/irish-embassy/tanzania
- **Italy** Lugalo Rd (Upanga); ☎ 022-211 5935/6; 🖳 ambdaressalaam.esteri.it
- **Japan** Plot 1018, Ali Hassan Mwinyi Rd; ☎ 022-211 5827/29; 🖳 tz.emb-japan.go.jp
- **Kenya** Harambee Plaza, Ali Hassan Mwinyi/Kaunda Drive Junction, Oysterbay; ☎ 022-266 8285
- **Norway** Umoja House, Garden Ave & Mirambo St; ☎ 022-216 3100; 🖳 norway.go.tz
- **Russian Federation** Plot 3&5 Ali Hassan Mwinyi Rd; ☎ 022-266 6046
- **South Africa** Corner Garden Ave & Shabani Robert St; ☎ 022 221 8500
- **South Korea** 19th Floor, Golden Jubilee Towers, Ohio St; ☎ 022-211 6086
- **Spain** Plot 99B Kinondoni Rd; ☎ 022-266 6018
- **Sweden** Umoja House, Garden Ave & Mirambo St; ☎ 022-219 6500
- **Switzerland** Plot 79, Kinondoni Rd; ☎ 022-266 6008
- **Uganda** 25 Msasani Rd, Oysterbay; ☎ 022-266 7391
- **UK** Umoja House, Hamburg Ave; ☎ 022-229 0000
- **United States** 686 Old Bagamoyo Rd, Msasani; ☎ 022-229 4000; 🖳 tz.usembassy.gov

ARRIVING IN EAST AFRICA

restaurant or hotel with wi-fi in Dar; they are everywhere. We found the wi-fi at Mokka City Café (see p198) to be the best.

Airline offices

This list is far from complete but has the most useful airlines for Kili trekkers. See also p386.

● **Air Tanzania** Ohio St (☎ 022-211 7500, 0782-737730; Mon-Fri 8am-5pm, Sat 9am-2pm)

● **Coastal Aviation** Upanga Rd (☎ 022-2602 430; Mon-Fri 7.30am-5pm, Sat 8.30am-1pm)

● **Egyptair** Viva Towers, Ali Hassan Mwinyi Road (☎ 0658-583000; Mon-Fri 9am-5.30pm, Sat 9am-1pm)

● **Emirates** 6th Floor, Haidery Plaza, Ali Hassan Mwinyi Rd (☎ 022-2116100)

● **Fastjet** Ground Floor, Samora Tower, Samora Ave (☎ 0784-108900; Mon-Fri 8am-4.30pm, Sat 8.30am-1pm)

● **Flightlink** 1st Floor, Golden Tulip Hotel, Jamhuri Street (☎ 0782 354 448/9/50)

● **Kenya Airways** Viva Towers, Ali Hassan Mwinyi Road (☎ 022-216 3914; Mon-Fri 8.30am-5pm, Sat 8.30am-12.30pm). Shares its office with...

● **KLM** Viva Towers, Ali Hassan Mwinyi Road (☎ 022-216 3914; Mon-Fri 8.30am-5pm, Sat 8.30am-12.30pm)

● **Precision Air** NIC building ground floor, Pamba Rd (☎ 022-212 1718; Mon-Fri 8am-5pm, Sat 9am-1pm)

● **Qatar Airways** Diamond Plaza, 4th floor, corner of Samora Avenue and Mirambo Street (☎ 022-219 8301; Mon-Fri 8.30am-5pm, Sat 8.30am-1pm)

● **Rwandair** Diamond Plaza, 4th floor, corner of Samora Avenue and Mirambo

Street (☎ 0689-394706; Mon-Fri 8am-5.30pm, Sat 9am-noon)

● **South African Airways** Raha Tower, corner of Bibi Titi Mohamed St & Maktaba St (☎ 022-211 7044; Mon-Fri 8.30am-4.30pm, Sat 8.30am-12.30pm)

WHERE TO STAY (see map p197)

The following are listed in **price order**, with the **cheapest first**. As is usual, the more expensive places don't tend to publish rack rates anymore, for their prices change constantly according to demand. For details of the abbreviations, see box below.

● **YWCA** (☎ 022-212 2439; just off Azikiwe St; sgl/dbl Ts20,000/30,000) Perhaps the most popular budget hostel currently operating in Dar, the YWCA has pretty basic accommodation but it's clean and has a good location by the central post office. It's not perfect – the plug socket in our room didn't work and the included breakfast consisted of two slices of bread (no butter) and a boiled egg. There's supposed to be wi-fi too, but we failed to get any in either the room or the restaurant. However, it's safe, cheap and the rooms come with a sink and mosquito net. Oh, and in case you're wondering, you needn't be young, female or a Christian to stay here, as this agnostic middle-aged male can verify.

● **YMCA** (☎ 022-213 5457; Upanga Rd; sgl/dbl/tpl Ts25,000/28,000/39,000) The fallback place should the above be full, the YMCA is only a minute's walk from its sister and offers similar accommodation at slightly more expensive rates, though with a better bar and restaurant. Reasonably cheap by Dar standards; clean-ish and safe-ish too.

● *Safari Inn* (☎ 022-213 8101; 🖳 safari-

❏ Abbreviations

Throughout this book we have used the following abbreviations when writing about accommodation: **pp** means per person; **s/c** is short for self-contained, a local term meaning that the room comes with a bathroom (ie the room is en suite or a bathroom is attached); while **sgl/dbl/tpl** means single/double/triple rooms. So, for example, where we have written 's/c sgl/dbl/tpl US$35/40/45', we mean that a self-contained single room costs US$35 per night, a self-contained double costs US$40 and a self-contained triple costs US$45.

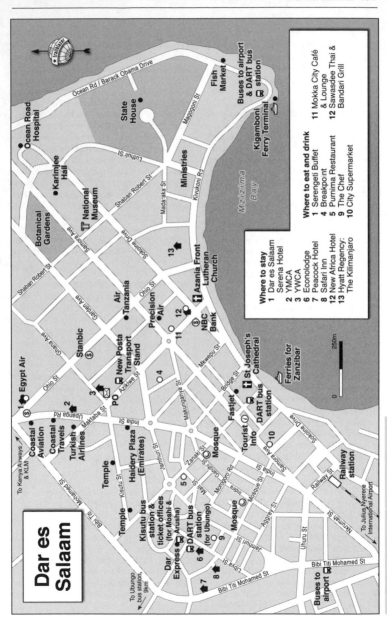

Dar es Salaam

Where to stay
1 Dar es Salaam Serena Hotel
2 YMCA
3 YWCA
6 Econolodge
7 Peacock Hotel
8 Safari Inn
12 New Africa Hotel
13 Hyatt Regency: The Kilimanjaro

Where to eat and drink
1 Serengeti Buffet
4 Breakpoint
5 Purnima Restaurant
9 The Chef
10 City Supermarket
11 Mokka City Café & Lounge
12 Sawasdee Thai & Bandari Grill

Ocean Rd / Barack Obama Drive
Fish Market
State House
Buses to airport & DART bus station
Kigamboni Ferry Terminal
Ocean Road Hospital
Karimjee Hall
National Museum
Botanical Gardens
Luthuli St
Ministries
Shaban Robert St
Mzizima Bay
Madaraka St
Kivukoni Rd
Sokoine Drive
Samora Ave
Garden Ave
Ghana Ave
Shaban Robert St
Azania Front Lutheran Church
Air Tanzania
Precision Air
Stanbic
Egypt Air
Ohio St
New Posta Transport Stand
NBC Bank
St Joseph's Cathedral
Ferries for Zanzibar
250m
Coastal Aviation
Coastal Travels
Turkish Airlines
To Kenya Airways & KLM
Upanga Rd
Makabe St
India St
PO
Azikiwe St
Makunganya St
Mkwepu St
Bridge St
Fastjet
DART bus station
Haidery Plaza (Emirates)
Jamhuri St
Kisutu St
Temple
Zanaki St
Gerezani St
Mosque
Tourist Info
Samora Ave
10
Mchafukoge St
Bibi Titi
Temple
Mali St
5
Morogoro Rd
Mosque St
India St
Railway station
To Julius Nyerere International Airport
Kisutu bus station & ticket offices (for Moshi & Arusha)
Dar Express
DART bus station (for Ubungo)
6
9
Jamhuri St
Mosque
Aggrey St
Libya St
Uhuru St
Nkrumah St
Bibi Titi Mohamed St
Buses to airport
7
8
To Ubungo bus station, 9km
Bibi Titi Mohamed St

inn.co.tz; Band St, off Libya St; s/c sgl/dbl Ts28,000/35,000, or Ts35,000/45,000 with air-con; Ts60,000 for the suites with television). Still a popular budget choice and all the rooms are en suite, though some are a bit gloomy and lack windows.

● *Econolodge* (☎ 022-211 6048; 🖳 econolodge@raha.com; Libya St; s/c sgl/dbl/tpl Ts28,000/38,000/48,000, or with air-con Ts38,000/48,000/55,000) Not quite as 'Econo' as it makes out, this is the smartest of the hotels around Libya St. All rooms are spacious and come with a bathroom. Pretty good value, if a little characterless.

● *Peacock Hotel* (☎ 022-211 4126; 🖳 peacock-hotel.com; Bibi Titi Mohamed St; s/c sgl/dbl US$100-110/133-150) Refreshingly free of any pretension, this ugly but friendly establishment is seeing more and more tourists. It's perfectly OK, with all the facilities you'd expect from a hotel of this class and it's so nice to be welcomed by receptionists who seem genuinely glad you've dropped in.

● *New Africa Hotel* (☎ 022-211 7050; 🖳 newafricahotel.com; corner of Azikiwe St & Sokoine Drive; s/c sgl/dbl from US$200/220) In a better location than the Serena Hotel (see below), its nearest rival, though not with quite the same level of sophistication, the New Africa stands on the site of the Germans' original Kaiserhof. Home to one of Dar's oldest casinos as well as a host of bars and restaurants, the New Africa's rooms have everything you'd expect from a hotel of this calibre, including mini-bar, satellite TV, telephones with internet hook-up and so on.

● *Dar es Salaam Serena Hotel* (☎ 022-221 2500; 🖳 serenahotels.com; Ohio St; s/c rooms start from sgl/dbl US$223/228 up to US$880-plus for the presidential suite, depending on demand) This Middle-Eastern/Zanzibari-style place has changed hands a couple of times since the first edition of this book and used to be the top place in the town centre before the arrival of The Kilimanjaro (see below). It's still a fine establishment, however, boasting a swimming pool, gym and all mod-cons.

● *Hyatt Regency Dar es Salaam: The Kilimanjaro* (☎ 0764-701234; 🖳 dares-

salaamkilimanjaro.regency.hyatt.com; Kivukoni Rd; rooms sgl/dbl US$260/295, rising to US$2500 for the Regency Executive Suite) Yet another luxury hotel that's changed hands (it was previously called the Kilimanjaro Kempinski), you won't find a more refined or, given its name, *appropriate* place to stay. Actually, the hotel's association with Kili is tenuous, other than the fact that you need a bank balance the size of a mountain to be able to stay here. However, it *is* a supremely comfy, fountain-filled haven, sophisticated and shiny and the rooms feature what they describe as 'elegantly tropical' interiors, wood floors, high-speed internet access and wi-fi, international satellite LCD TV with movie channels, multilingual telephone voicemail and all the other bits 'n' bobs you'd expect of a hotel of this standard. The location overlooking the Indian Ocean is great too.

WHERE TO EAT AND DRINK
Many eateries in Dar close on Sundays. One that doesn't, and which has for many years been the most popular place in town amongst travellers – and indeed just about everyone else to judge by the frenetic 'busyness' of the place – is *The Chef* (daily noon-11pm) on Chagga St. It is a popularity that is well deserved: tasty, huge portions of food, fair prices (mains Ts4000-22,000, with most Ts7000-12,000), a location close to the cheaper hotels and English football on the telly is a combination that for some is hard to resist, and many travellers, having eaten here once, venture nowhere else in the city. Just be prepared to share a table, however – it gets that busy.

Another place that's winning over the travellers, particularly those staying at the YWCA or its brother and who are seeking a good wi-fi/internet connection, is the swish *Mokka City* (🖳 mokkacity.co.tz; daily 7am-8.30pm), a café in the centre with a great selection of breakfasts (Ts8000-18,000), including everything from a simple fruit salad to the full fry-up, as well as fast food, sundaes and waitresses who smile (though the service can be a tad tardy). Recommended.

For truly cheap-eats the Indian quarter of central Dar, particularly around the temple-laden Kisutu St (and its extension Pramukh Swami St) and the junction of Indira Gandhi and Zanaki streets, is as good a place as any to start looking. *Purnima* (Mon-Fri 9am-6pm, Sat & Sun 8am-1pm), on Zanaki St, is a great little place, reputedly the oldest Indian restaurant in the country (est 1958) where a vegetarian thali will make you poorer by only Ts7000. There are plenty of other similar places around here – follow your nose to find them.

For more African offerings, the lively *Breakpoint Outdoor Catterers* (sic) is a large and hugely popular al-fresco joint serving cold beer and Tanzanian staples such as *nyama choma* (grilled meat), all accompanied by a music system thumping out the latest African tunes and a screen showing the latest Hollywood blockbuster. Four *mishkaki* (kebabs), a plate of chips and a cold beer is only Ts11,500 and it's always fun watching the locals at play.

For more refined cuisine in plusher surroundings, try the restaurants in some of the upmarket hotels, including *Sawasdee Thai* or the Indian *Bandari Grill*, both at the New Africa (see p198), and *Serengeti Buffet Restaurant* at the Serena (see p198). Your bank manager might not thank you for dining at them but your stomach certainly will.

MOVING ON – TO KILIMANJARO

By bus to Moshi and Arusha
The **Dar Express** office is located in the old Kisutu bus station in the heart of downtown on Libya St. A couple of other bus companies also have their offices here. Tickets cost pretty much the same whichever company you choose, at around Ts30,000-35,000 to either Moshi or Arusha; the journey is around 10 hours to Moshi, 13-14 hours to Arusha.

Unfortunately, the actual **buses do not depart from Kisutu but from Ubungo bus station, (9km) out of town**. A taxi from Kisutu to Ubungo will set you back about Ts15,000 (though they'll try for Ts25,000). Alternatively, catch the DART (see p195) No 1 or No 2 that starts at the

Kigamboni fish market, on the seafront to the west of the Azania Front Lutheran Church, continues through the centre of town (including stops behind the tourist office and at Kisutu for Ts650) and on to Ubungo – it's a painless and cheap way of getting there.

If you don't want to travel with Dar Express for some reason, do at least choose your bus company carefully: despite the presence of speed ramps and traffic police, the Dar to Moshi highway is notorious for accidents and often it's the same few bus companies that are involved. Unfortunately, the number of touts operating at both of Dar's stations means that it can be difficult to buy the ticket you want. Be persistent and insistent and take anything the touts say with a pinch – no, make that a huge bucket – of salt.

By air
For the addresses of airline offices in Dar, please see p196. The best and most reliable bet for flights to Arusha or Kilimanjaro Airport is **Precision Air**, who fly three times daily to Kilimanjaro from Dar and a couple of times a day to Arusha Airport too. **Fastjet** have two flights daily to Kilimanjaro Airport. The national carrier **Air Tanzania** have their main office on Ohio/Garden St and operate a six-times-a-week flight (every day except Wednesday) to Kilimanjaro Airport.

Of the smaller airlines, **Air Excel** have a flight daily to Arusha Airport (currently at 4.20pm; 2hr 10 mins flying time as they go via Zanzibar), while **Coastal Aviation**, on Upanga Rd, have a daily direct flight from Dar to Arusha at 4.30pm, arriving at 5.40pm, and a couple of less direct ones earlier in the day via Saadani, Pangani and Moshi that takes three hours to reach Arusha.

Going to the airport, look for the bus at the fish market signed Gongo La Mboto (or, more likely, an abbreviated version of this); it also stops just south of the junction of Mohamed and Uhuru streets (see map p197) – useful for those staying at this side of town. Leave in plenty of time – it can take over an hour depending on traffic and it's a 5-minute walk from the road to the terminal. The bus is Ts450; a taxi is around Ts25,000-30,000 for the same journey.

ARRIVING IN EAST AFRICA

Nairobi

As rough as a lion's tongue and as raw as a baboon's backside, East Africa's largest city has come quite a long way since its inception in May 1899 as a humble railway supply depot on the Mombasa to Kampala line. It is a city that has suffered much from plagues, fire and reconstruction – and that was just in its first 10 years – yet it has obstinately continued to prosper and grow, rising from a population of approximately zero in 1898 to around three and a half million today.

Official recognition of the city's increasing importance arrived in 1907 when the British made it the capital of their East African territories, and you can still find the occasional colonial relic in the city, from the Indian-influenced architecture of a few downtown buildings (shipped over from the subcontinent, Indians supplied much of the labour force used to build the railway) to some distinctly elegant hotels and orderly public gardens (including one, just to the north of Kenyatta Avenue, which still bears a statue of Queen Victoria). But if you came with the specific purpose of seeing a faded colonial city you'd be disappointed because as the capital of the Kenyan republic and the UN's fourth official 'World Centre', Nairobi is East Africa's most modern, prosperous and glamorous metropolis. It is also, first and foremost, black Africa at its loudest and proudest.

A TOUR OF THE CITY

The number one sight in Nairobi is the **National Museum**; details of it can be found in the box opposite.

As for Nairobi's other sights, they can be seen as part of a half- to full-day walking tour. This is best done on a Sunday morning, when the hassle from touts is at its lowest and the gospel choirs are out in force on the streets and in the parks. The tour begins at the **Railway Museum** (🖥 nrm.co.ke; daily 8am-5pm; Ks800). To reach it, from the railway station head west for five minutes along the road running parallel to the tracks. The museum is a gem. If it's possible to feel nostalgia for a time that one never knew and a place one has never visited before, this is the museum that will prompt those feelings with its fading photos of British royalty riding in the cow-catcher seats at the front of the train and its old posters advertising the newly opened Uganda Railway. Not to everyone's taste, of course, but nevertheless we found this an endearing little museum.

Returning to the station, head north along Moi Avenue. At the junction with Haile Selassie Avenue is the **former site of the American Embassy**, blown up on 7 August, 1998, by Al-Qaeda. The site has now been landscaped into a very small **remembrance garden** (daily 8am-6pm; Ks30), at the back of which is a **Visitor Centre** (Mon-Sat 9am-5pm, Sun 1-5pm; Ks150) which explains in

greater detail what happened that day including a video reconstruction of the events, *Seconds From Disaster*. The garden is worth a visit; you'll find a memorial bearing the names of the Kenyan victims (who constituted all but 12 of the 263 who died), while at the back of the enclosure is a pyramid sculpture containing some of the debris from that day, namely some twisted metal, a lump or two of concrete and a door handle. It's a busy junction, and the Co-op building behind – also badly damaged in the blast – is from the eyesore school of architecture; yet still the park is suffused with an atmosphere of the deepest poignancy. Sadly, one presumes a similar memorial will be built in the near future for the victims of the 2013 Westgate Shopping Mall atrocity (see p203).

Continuing north along Moi, City Hall Way runs parallel to Haile Selassie Ave, two blocks north. The **City Hall** after which the road is named lies about 400m along the road on the right (north). Before it, on the southern side, you'll pass the **Supreme Court**, in front of which is the curious **statue of a naked boy**, carrying a fish, wearing a judge's wig and peeing into a fountain. The idea, apparently, is to remind us of how justice can be naked, blind, slippery like a fish but as brave as a child; it's a curious metaphor and, if I'm being honest, I'm not 100% sure I entirely understand it. The statue's official title is the **Hamilton Fountain**, and was erected in honour of lawyer Alexander George Hamilton, having been commissioned by his wife. This is actually the third statue; the original was lost at sea on its journey from England, while a replica was then stolen, despite its prominent location outside the highest court in the land.

Moving west, opposite City Hall is a **statue** of first president Jomo

---

❏ Nairobi National Museum

If you have time to see only one sight in Nairobi, the **National Museum** (🖥 museums.or.ke; off Museum Hill, near Uhuru Highway; daily 8.30am-5.30pm; Ks1200, Ks1500 including entrance to the Snake Park) is definitely the one to head for, an institution that is not only almost as old as the city itself (having been established way back in 1910) but which effortlessly manages the difficult feat of justifying the rather cheeky entrance fee.

Virtually every gallery in the museum holds something of interest for the visitor. True, the first couple of rooms, where many of Kenya's creatures – including every species of Kenya's avifauna – has been stuffed and put on display, may feel a little anachronistic in this day and age; though even here there are some highlights, including the skeleton (and, in the courtyard, a model, faithfully cast in fibreglass) of **the nation's favourite pachyderm**, Ahmed, an elephant so huge its tusks alone weighed an incredible 68kg each. The next couple of galleries are our favourites, however. They study in great detail (but never tediously so) the different theories behind the evolution of man, illustrated by many of the actual skulls and other fossils that helped to shape these theories.

Heading upstairs, more treats await including a room devoted to the history of Kenya and another that studies the cultures, art and festivals of the nation's tribes, with particular focus on how they celebrate the various rites of passage of their members' lives. This floor is also where you'll find rooms that are mainly given over to contemporary photographic and art exhibitions which we find are usually well worth seeing and a pleasant respite from the more serious, educational exhibits elsewhere.

Kenyatta, sitting regally overlooking the city square with his back, pointedly, to the courts. To Kenyatta's left, rising imperiously from fountains, are the **Kenyatta International Conference Centre**, like a giant water-lily bud on the verge of opening, and the vertiginous **KANU Tower**, once the tallest building in the city and still one of the ugliest – though most locals would probably take issue with this opinion. KANU, incidentally, are the most powerful party in Kenya and have dominated the political arena since independence.

Strolling along City Hall Way – past **Holy Family Cathedral**, neatly juxtaposed with the casino directly opposite – you'll find to the left of the road, lined with flags and guarded by two black lion statues and several bored-looking guards in ceremonial livery, the object of the Kenyatta statue's gaze: his **mausoleum**. Next door and adorned with a rather quaint clock tower is the Kenyan **Parliament**.

Heading back north along Uhuru Highway, in a few minutes you'll come to a large roundabout and the junction with Kenyatta Ave. On the roundabout's south-eastern side is the **Nairobi Gallery** (daily 8.30am-5.30pm; Ks1000), kept in a small administrative building dating back to 1913. The gallery is not, as you might expect, a celebration of the artistic output of the country, but more a repository for the breathtaking collection of Joseph Morumbi, one-time foreign minister in the Kenyatta government and an avid art collector who specialised in works from all over the continent. The exhibition is supposed to be temporary but the display has a permanent feel about it – and justifiably so, for it's a fascinating overview of African crafts and traditions, as well as rooms dedicated to the Murumbis' book and stamp collections.

On the same junction are two memorials, standing across from each other on Kenyatta Avenue but hidden from the Uhuru Highway by hedges. The first you'll come to, to the south-west of the roundabout opposite the Gallery, is a memorial to those who suffered and were killed during suppression of the **Mau Mau uprising**, 1952-60; the second, to the north-west of Kenyatta Avenue, is the **Nyayo Monument** erected in 1988 to commemorate 10 years of former president Moi's rule and 25 years of independence. A few hundred metres further west of the Mau Mau monument is **All Saints Cathedral** with its distinctive crenellated towers. The main Anglican church in the country, the cathedral celebrated its 100th year in 2017.

The cathedral may be the oldest church in the capital but as the centre of worship in the city the roundabout five minutes to the north is a worthy rival, surrounded as it is by a **synagogue** (to the north-east) and no fewer than **four churches** (St Paul's Catholic Chapel to the north-west, with St Andrew's behind it up the hill, the First Church of Christ Scientist further along the same road and the city's main Lutheran church on the roundabout's south-western edge).

From the roundabout you can continue north for 15 hot, dusty minutes along the highway to the **National Museum** (see box p201), or turn east along University Way, taking a right turn south through the business heart of Nairobi along Muindi Mbingu St. On the way you might wish to take a short detour to see the relaxing and shaded square known as **Jevanjee Gardens** (named after another Independence hero, and one whose statue now graces the park), the **indoor**

market, **Jamia Mosque** (Nairobi's most impressive mosque but closed to infidels), and the **McMillan Memorial Library**, a grand colonnaded building dating back to the early 1930s that sits at the opposite end of Wabera Street from the Hamilton Fountain. Heading south to rejoin Kenyatta Avenue, take a left here, and after a couple of hundred metres you'll come to the final port of call on this walk, the **Thorn Tree Café**, with its overpriced but wonderfully cold beer.

PRACTICAL INFORMATION

Security

Nairobi has been the venue of a couple of horrific terrorist attacks in recent years, with 2013's atrocity at the Westgate Mall, when 72 people were killed by Somali fundamentalists, coming on top of the 1998 attack on the US Embassy (see p200) in which 263 people perished. There is little you can do to avoid these – thankfully rare – tragedies. However, these major events are not the only dangers facing tourists in Kenya's capital. A few years back some inspired wag dubbed Kenya's capital 'Nairobberi', and less-inspired wags have been retreading that joke ever since. Tired as the gag may be, however, it does still have relevance, for Nairobi's reputation as East Africa's Capital of Crime is well founded.

To be fair, the authorities are trying to improve matters, at least in the centre, blocking off many of the darker backstreets. There seem to be fewer beggars and touts populating the centre too. There is also a 'beautification' programme going on, which seems to involve a lot of tree-planting.

Nevertheless, the need to be wary when out on the streets of Nairobi remains paramount. The **most notorious hotspot** is the area immediately to the east of Moi Avenue, including River Rd and the bus stations, a popular location with travellers because of its cheap hotels. During the day violent robbery is rare though certainly not unheard of, simply because it's so packed with people; pickpocketing, on the other hand, is rife at this time, probably for the same reason. At night, both techniques are common.

To avoid becoming another victim, **be vigilant**, leave valuables at your hotel (having first checked their security procedures) and make sure they give you a receipt for any goods deposited. Furthermore, tuck moneybelts under your clothing and don't walk around at night but take a taxi, even if it's for just a few hundred metres.

It can only be to your advantage if you are over-cautious for your first couple of days in the capital. After that, if you're still staying here, you can begin to appreciate Nairobi's charms – which do exist, and are not entirely inconsiderable – and can begin to moan, like the rest of the travellers here, about how unfair guidebook writers are about Kenya's capital.

ARRIVAL

By air

Jomo Kenyatta Airport (also known as Nairobi International Airport), situated 18km from the centre of Nairobi, is still struggling to come to terms with the fire in

---

❏ **Diplomatic missions in Nairobi**
Australia Riverside Drive, 400m off Chiromo Rd; ☎ 020-427 7100; ⌨ kenya.embassy.gov.au; **Belgium** Limuru Rd, Muthaiga; ☎ 020-712 20 11; ⌨ countries.diplomatie.belgium.be/en/kenya; **Canada** Limuru Rd, Gigiri; ☎ 020-366 3000, ⌨ canadainternational.gc.ca/kenya; **Denmark** 13 Runda Drive, Runda; ☎ 020-425 3000; ⌨ kenya.um.dk; **France** Barclays Plaza, 9th Floor, Loita St; ☎ 020-277 8000; ⌨ www.ambafrance-ke.org; **Germany** 113 Riverside Drive; ☎ 020-4262 100; ⌨ nairobi.diplo.de; **Japan** Mara Rd, Upper Hill; ☎ 020-289 8000; ⌨ ke.emb-japan.go.jp; **South Africa** 3rd Floor, Roshanmaer Place, Lenana Rd; ☎ 0709-127000; **UK** Upper Hill Rd; ☎ 020-284 4000; ⌨ gov.uk/government/world/kenya; **United States** United Nations Av; ☎ 020-363 6000; ⌨ ke.usembassy.gov.

August 2013 that destroyed a large number of buildings including the international terminal. As a result, international flights are arriving at several different terminals. British Airways, for example, arrives at Terminal 1E, which appears to be little more than a pre-fab hangar with a couple of x-ray machines inside. The procedure at each terminal is pretty similar, however: alighting from the aircraft, make your way to passport control. If you are one of the majority who didn't have a spare couple of hours to apply for a **visa** online, you should be able to get one here. Payment is accepted in US dollars (currently US$50/€40/£30 for all nationalities). Note that **even if you're just changing planes you may have to fork out US$20 for a transit visa**.

Having passed through immigration you should then collect your luggage. Once again be vigilant and, having retrieved your bags, check that they don't look to have been opened: when climbing Kilimanjaro, there are few things more annoying than finding that the thermally insulated mountain hat you thought was safely tucked away in the side-pocket of your rucksack had in fact been taken by a light-fingered baggage handler and is now being used as a makeshift tea cosy in the staffroom of Jomo Kenyatta Airport. Depending on which terminal you arrived at the Arrivals' Hall may be free of facilities, though wander around the airport and you'll find moneychangers and ATMs, the latter being your best bet for a fair rate at the airport, though you could

---

❏ Nine useful things to know about Kenya

● Citizens of most countries need a **visa**, including Britain and the US. You can get yours before leaving home by applying at the following website: 🖳 evisa.go.ke/evisa.html. That said, we found this procedure infuriating, with the website forcing you to restart your application from the very beginning if you leave it for ten minutes, which you'll probably need to do given the amount of documentation required (passport scan, hotel booking confirmation and a scan of a recent passport photo). Given that the last time I arrived at Nairobi's Jomo Kenyatta Airport, those without visas were not subjected to any more delays than those who had secured one beforehand (and by paying £30, I got it cheaper than the US$51 I was being charged online), I think it may be best just to turn up and buy one at the airport – at least until they sort out their online application process.

● One thing to remember: as long as you remain in East Africa there is no need to buy a multiple-entry Kenyan visa if you are flying into Kenya but wish to visit Tanzania or Uganda too, as long as you stay in those countries for less than two weeks and providing, of course, your Kenyan visa has not expired by the time you return to Kenya.

● The official **language** is Swahili. For a quick guide to Swahili, see p125. In addition, many Kenyans speak both their own tribal language and English, which is widely spoken everywhere.

● As with Tanzania, Kenya is **three hours ahead of GMT**. Note that, in addition to standard time, many locals use **Swahili time**, which runs from dawn to dusk (or 6am to 6pm to be precise). See p130 for details on how to convert between East African time and Swahili time.

● The Kenyan **currency** is the shilling (Ks). At the time of writing, €1=Ks121.8, US$1=Ks103.1, UK£1=Ks137.8. Don't change money on the street.

● Kenya's **electricity supply** uses the British-style three-pin plugs on 220-240V.

● The **international dialling code** is ☎ 254; the Nairobi code is 020 and numbers starting 07 are for mobiles.

● The **emergency telephone number** is ☎ 999.

● **Opening hours** are typically 8am to 5 or 6pm with some establishments shutting on Sundays. Banks, post offices etc have their own hours, see p128.

pay for your cab in dollars and wait to change money in town.

You have a number of choices in tackling the journey from the airport to the centre of Nairobi. Taxis cost about Ks1300-2000, the exact amount depending on the time of day and your bargaining skills, or before 8pm you can take the No 34 bus that runs down River Rd with a stop on Moi Avenue (Ks40). Remember to be careful of pickpockets on this route.

If you think you might struggle with the whole process of getting through the airport and into town, or even just to change planes, then **Nairobi Airport Transfers** (🖳 www.nairobiairporttransfers.com) have been recommended to us. Their taxi prices are a little higher than other providers but when it comes to negotiating the procedures at the airport they could prove invaluable: for around US$25 someone will meet you just inside the immigration line and sweep you through the whole process as painlessly as possible; if you've had a long flight and aren't at your sharpest, they could prove a godsend.

By bus
Arrive in Nairobi by **shuttle bus** from Arusha/Moshi and, if they don't drop you off at your hotel, you'll probably be dropped off by Jevanjee Gardens right in the heart of the action. The exception to this is passengers on the Impala Shuttle, see p209, who will be dropped off at Silver Springs Hotel – useful for those staying there or at either Upper Hill or Wildebeest Eco Camp (though to be honest you've still got a fair way to go to get to either of these) before heading to Jevanjee Gardens in the city centre. Arrive by **'ordinary' bus**, on the other hand, and you could well be dropped off near the infamous River Rd, home to several hotels but also a significant minority of ne'er-do-wells – take care!

ORIENTATION & GETTING AROUND

Despite decades of unplanned growth, a mass of sprawling suburbs and a wholesale aversion to street numbers, central Nairobi is actually very easy to navigate, with nearly everything of interest to the traveller within walking distance of Kenyatta Avenue.

A couple of obvious landmarks are the enormous **KANU Tower**, to the south of City Hall, and the even more enormous **Nation Centre**, a red Meccano-type structure nestling between two giant cylindrical towers just off the eastern end of Kenyatta Avenue. Central Nairobi is fairly compact and the fit will be able to walk everywhere. Buses and *matatus* (Kenyan minibuses) run from early morning to late at night, though **we strongly advise you to take taxis after dark**. During the day things are much safer, though keep your wits about you.

SERVICES
Banks
Banks are usually open Monday to Friday 9am-3pm, Saturday 9-11am. Foreign exchange bureaux open later, though on Saturday they, too, often close early (usually noon). Many of the banks have **ATM**s (cash machines) as well, with most accepting Visa cards. Be on your guard for onlookers when withdrawing money from an ATM.

Communications
Big, bright and gleaming, the **post office** (Mon-Fri 8am-6pm, Sat 9am-12pm) occupies a fairly large slice of valuable real estate at the western end of Kenyatta Avenue. Registered, recorded and normal deliveries can be made here.

If you're staying a while in Kenya, the best way to use a **phone** is to get hold of a local SIM card – visit the Orange shop one block south of the post office or similar outlets around town. The card costs around Ks60, you need to go through the two-minute registration process (bring some form of ID), and insert it into your existing phone; you'll find you save yourself a fortune this way, particularly if you are phoning abroad, though if you're heading to Tanzania it's better to wait and get a local SIM card there (see p131). Just make sure you get the right-sized card for your phone (newer iPhones, for example, use smaller SIM cards called nano-SIMs and there's a micro-SIM too) and that your phone is unlocked and can

take other cards. If you're staying only for a night or two, it's probably not worth the hassle and instead use the (more expensive) hotel phone, **Skype** – or remain incommunicado until you leave Kenya.

Wi-fi is available in most hotels now and is usually free.

WHERE TO STAY

(For details of abbreviations see box p196). The following list of hostels and hotels is arranged with the cheapest first. Those intending to **camp** should check out Wildebeest Eco Camp (Ks1250pp, Ks1500 if using one of their tents), listed below. River Rd remains the cheapest area in the centre.

In Nairobi, safety is a concern in some of the hotels, though the ones we have chosen to recommend in this book are fine.

● *Wildebeest Eco Camp* (☎ 0734 770733; 🖳 wildebeestecocamp.com; Moko-yeti Road West, Langata; rates are Ks1750 in a dorm, Ks6300/8000 sgl/dbl with shared facilities; tents Ks8000/10,000 sgl/dbl with shared facilities, luxury tents Ks10,000/13,500/16,000 sgl/dbl/tpl) Simply put, this is a wonderful place. The private rooms are clean and pleasant but it's the fragrant, bird-filled tropical grounds and frog-filled pond that truly steal the show, bordered as they are by deluxe en suite safari tents that provide some of the most appealing accommodation in the capital, with cotton sheets and full electricity. There are also dorms, a campsite and a restaurant with wi-fi too. All in all it's worth the very lengthy trip out of town (it lies about 15km from the centre, or about an hour given the usual traffic), whatever your budget.

● *New Kenya Lodge* (☎ 020-222 2202; River Rd opposite the end of Latema Rd; rates are Ks750 in a dorm, Ks1000 sgl, Ks1500 dbl) Another scruffy, old-style backpacker place with a few private rooms and reasonable wi-fi. It's pretty much the cheapest place that readily accepts tourists, though with a nearby nightclub that thumps away 'til 4am every weekend and doors that can't be locked from the inside, this place is saddled with some drawbacks that not even the friendliness of Nicholas the receptionist can quite redeem. Like most

such places, New Kenya also has a safari operation which is cheap and not bad.

● *Manyatta Backpackers* (☎ 0799-122166, 🖳 manyattabackpackers.com; Milimani Rd; dorm Ks1500 sgl/dbl Ks2500/4000) Scruffy but central and cheap hostel with a capacity of 30, though it's seldom busy. Rooms (including 6- and 8-bed dorms as well as singles and doubles) all come with mosquito nets and there's wi-fi and a small al-fresco restaurant.

● *YMCA* (☎ 020-272 4116/7; 🖳 kenyaymca.com; State House Rd; non s/c dorm/sgl/dbl Ks1400/1500/2800; s/c dorm/sgl/dbl Ks1800/2000/3200; add Ks500 per person for half-board, Ks1000 full-board) Despite the name, women, atheists and the elderly are all welcome at this friendly, secure hostel, a fair choice for those on a budget who don't fancy their chances in the hurly-burly of the River Rd area but still want to be reasonably close to town. The real clincher, however, is the pool.

● *Hotel Kipepeo* (☎ 0710 207162; 🖳 hotelkipepeo.com; River Rd; s/c sgl/dbl/tpl Ks3400/4100/5400) Probably the best of the places left in the River Rd area, the safe and friendly Kipepeo boasts clean self-contained rooms with hot water, mosquito nets, TV and wi-fi – and the rates are fair.

● *Kenya Comfort Hotel* (☎ 0720 608866; 🖳 kenyacomfort.com; Jevanjee Gardens; rack rates start at US$20/40/60 for dorm/sgl/dbl rising to US$60/80 sgl/dbl if you want air-con and TV; breakfast is another US$5 per person) Superbly situated just five minutes north of Kenyatta Avenue – and, more importantly, right next to where the shuttle buses pull in, which could be very handy if you've taken the afternoon shuttle and arrived after dark. Though it looks fairly petite, features include a sauna and steam room, internet and 95 en-suite bedrooms. All in all this represents pretty good value for central Nairobi – particularly if you find a good deal online, which may save you US$10 or so – and one of the better lower mid-range choices. Note that the hotel has a second branch, the *Kenya Comfort Suites* (☎ 0733 608867; 🖳 kenyacomfort.com; junction of Milimani and Ralph Bunch Rd), with

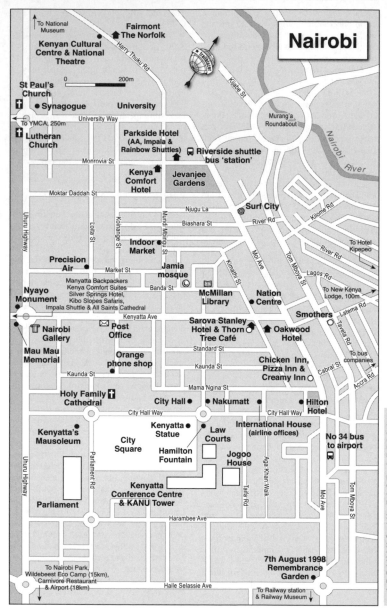

Nairobi

To National Museum

Fairmont The Norfolk

Kenyan Cultural Centre & National Theatre

Harry Thuku Rd

Kijabe St

St Paul's Church

Synagogue

University

University Way

To YMCA, 250m

Lutheran Church

Murang'a Roundabout

Nairobi River

Parkside Hotel (AA, Impala & Rainbow Shuttles)

Riverside shuttle bus 'station'

Monrovia St

Kenya Comfort Hotel

Jevanjee Gardens

Moktar Daddah St

Njugu La

Biashara St

Surf City

River Rd

Kilome Rd

Uhuru Highway

Lolta St

Koinange St

Mundi Mbingu St

Indoor Market

Precision Air

Market St

Jamia mosque

Banda St

Kimathi St

Moi Ave

Tom Mboya St

To Hotel Kipepeo

River Rd

Lagos Rd

To New Kenya Lodge, 100m

Manyatta Backpackers Kenya Comfort Suites Silver Springs Hotel, Kibo Slopes Safaris, Impala Shuttle & All Saints Cathedral

Nyayo Monument

McMillan Library

Nation Centre

Smothers

Latema Rd

Kenyatta Ave

Nairobi Gallery

Post Office

Sarova Stanley Hotel & Thorn Tree Café

Oakwood Hotel

Tavela Rd

To bus companies

Mau Mau Memorial

Orange phone shop

Standard St

Kaunda St

Chicken Inn, Pizza Inn & Creamy Inn

Cabral St

Accra Rd

Kaunda St

Mama Ngina St

Holy Family Cathedral

City Hall

Nakumatt

Hilton Hotel

City Hall Way

City Hall Way

Kenyatta's Mausoleum

City Square

Kenyatta Statue

Law Courts

International House (airline offices)

Aga Khan Walk

No 34 bus to airport

Hamilton Fountain

Jogoo House

Taifa Rd

Moi Ave

Tom Mboya St

Uhuru Highway

Parliament Rd

Kenyatta Conference Centre & KANU Tower

Parliament

Harambee Ave

To Nairobi Park, Wildebeest Eco Camp (15km), Carnivore Restaurant & Airport (18km)

7th August 1998 Remembrance Garden

Haile Selassie Ave

To Railway station & Railway Museum

0   200m

slightly bigger and better rooms and a swimming pool, though it's a 20-minute walk from the city centre in the district of Milimani. Don't get the two confused, particularly if booking online.

● *Oakwood Hotel* (☎ 0735 478294; 💻 madahotels.com; Kimathi St; s/c sgl/dbl/tpl US$65/75/85 inc breakfast; US$10 discount at weekends) Wooden floors, wooden walls, wooden ceiling and wooden doors – spending a night at the Oakwood can make you feel like Charles II hiding from Parliament. The Oakwood's strengths are its location opposite Thorn Tree Café, its elegant antique lift, the cable TV and wi-fi in each room and the vague whiff of colonial charm. Its main drawback is the casino that occupies much of the ground floor, desecrating the once-charming façade. Nevertheless, though not spectacular this 1940s' hotel is convenient and reasonable enough value.

● *Silver Springs Hotel* (☎ 020-272 2451; 💻 silversprings-hotel.com; 3km out of town near the hospital on Valley Rd; rates start at sgl/dbl US$145.50/184, rising to Ks100,000 – US$970 – for the two-bedroomed penthouse, all inclusive of breakfast) This is a fine choice, popular in particular with tour groups and is the main stop for the Impala shuttle bus. Facilities include a pool, gym and hot-stone massages – perfect post-Kili therapy.

● *Sarova Stanley* (☎ 020-275 7000; 💻 sarovahotels.com; corner of Kenyatta Avenue and Kimathi St; US$420/470 for s/c sgl/dbl, room only, though significant discounts are available online and the prices vary according to demand, meaning you could pay as little as US$140). A luxury hotel with a bit of character, the Stanley first opened its doors to the very well-heeled in 1902 – making it just a few years younger than the city itself. Edward, then Prince of Wales, Ernest Hemingway, and Hollywood's finest from Ava Gardner to Clark Gable have all rested their eminent heads on the Stanley's sumptuously stuffed pillows. Victorian elegance still abounds, though the demands of the modern client have led to the introduction of a shopping arcade, swimming pool and gymnasium.

The hotel also plays host to Thorn Tree Café (see below).

● *Fairmont The Norfolk* (☎ 020-226 5000; 💻 fairmont.com; room-only prices start at sgl/dbl US$189 plus 28% tax though again cheaper rates of about US$150 are available online) Nairobi's *other* historic hotel, and younger by two years, the Norfolk has been oozing class from its premises since it first opened its doors on Christmas Day 1904. Boasts the same facilities as the Stanley plus a fine collection of rickshaws and old tractors in the central courtyard and a more peaceful, out-of-town feel.

WHERE TO EAT AND DRINK

Kenya's cuisine is virtually indistinguishable from Tanzania's, being hearty, meaty and with an emphasis firmly on quantity rather than quality.

Embodying this description is the legendary tourist-attraction-cum-restaurant, *Carnivore* (💻 tamarind.co.ke/carnivore; Langata Rd, near Nairobi National Park; take a taxi from the town centre), designed specifically for those people whose first thought upon seeing the playful gambolling of a young impala for the first time is to wonder what it would taste like coated in a spicy barbecue sauce. Actually, the menu has had to be severely reduced in recent years though you can still find ostrich, crocodile and even camel migrating across the pages most nights. Game meat, however, is no longer allowable by law. There are a few vegetarian options too. Vying with the celebrity of Carnivore is *Thorn Tree Café*, something of a Mecca for travellers. Now on its third acacia, the original idea behind planting a tree in the middle of the courtyard was so that travellers could leave messages for other travellers on its thorns. Unfortunately, trees being trees, the roots of the previous two eventually started to undermine the building itself and had to be destroyed. Furthermore, Health & Safety has intervened and the tree is now encircled by noticeboards where you pin your messages – which reduces the romance (and indeed the raison d'être) of the tree some-

what. And when we looked, few of the messages were by travellers, for travellers, but were mainly announcements of people's birthdays etc. All most disappointing. Anyway, enough moaning: the food here is great, particularly for a post-climb breakfast feed-up (Ks2500).

For cheaper and more mundane fare, there are any number of **fast-food places** around River Rd and Tom Mboya St, where lunch shouldn't cost more than Ks200 or so (though be warned, 'kebab' is usually a battered sausage containing meat of unknown origin, and not the kind of kebab you'd enjoy on a Friday night after the pubs have closed back in your home country. For that, you need to ask for a *shwarma*.) More upmarket fast-food restaurants include *Chicken Inn* and *Creamy Inn*, branches of which can be found throughout the city. Our local favourite was *Smothers*, on the corner of Latema Road and Tom Mboya St. Big and busy, they serve a vast range of African dishes including some reasonably fiery curries (around Ks370), while the large number of waiting staff ensure the service is smooth and fast.

MOVING ON – TO KILIMANJARO

By air
Precision Air (☎ 020-327 4282, Barclays Plaza, Loita St, 🖥 precisionairtz.com) fly at least twice daily between Nairobi and Kilimanjaro International; they are pretty much the only reliable operator between the two airports at this time. **To get to Nairobi International Airport**, take bus No 34 (Ks40) which leaves from virtually opposite the Hilton Hotel. Leave plenty of time as this service frequently gets snarled in heavy traffic. Alternatively, a taxi will cost you about Ks1300-2000.

By coach or shuttle bus
Though there are plenty of **coach** operators willing to take you to Arusha, few can be recommended without hesitation. The best are perhaps Simba or Horizon, each leaving about three times a day and costing about Ks1300; their offices are near Latema Road. Far more convenient for most people are the **shuttle buses**. There are two main

companies operating shuttles to Arusha (and several smaller, newer ones). **Riverside** (☎ 0725-999121), on the first floor of Lagos House, Monrovia St, right on Jevanjee Gardens, is the most established, though we prefer **Impala Shuttle** (☎ 0722-506061) whose main office is at the Silver Springs Hotel – their service and vehicles are the best. Other companies with offices at Jevanjee Gardens include AA Shuttle and Rainbow Shuttle. All of these companies advertise two buses a day, at 8am (which continues on to Moshi) and 2pm (though note that this will probably not arrive in Arusha until after dark). The fare for non-residents is US$30 to Arusha, US$35 to Moshi.

Crossing the border between Kenya and Tanzania
The drive between Nairobi and Arusha is fascinating, not least because you may find yourself sharing the road with camels, zebras, impalas, giraffes and Maasai tribesmen on bikes. Despite the chaos of hawkers, warriors and travellers that surrounds the **Namanga crossing**, the border formalities are straightforward enough. On the Kenyan side you'll doubtless have to queue to have your passport stamped (it's quieter on a Sunday) at their smart new offices; while up the hill, on the Tanzanian side, you'll be asked to present your yellow fever certificate, then sent to the next office to show your passport and get a visa. There maybe a little wait while customs officials cast a cursory eye over your belongings – though these days even that formality is seldom observed and your bags may go through completely unchecked.

There's an **ATM** just after passport control (although it charges Ts9000 for withdrawals) and a moneychanger in a shack just beyond that, its signboard displaying the kind of lousy rates that you find only at borders. Don't change anything if you don't have to, for even those who have to catch one of the **dalla dallas to Arusha** from here may be able to pay in Kenyan shillings (the Tanzanian shilling price is Ts7000).

ARUSHA, MOSHI & MARANGU

Kilimanjaro International Airport

Is Kilimanjaro the only mountain to have its own international airport? The airport is situated roughly equidistant between Moshi (43km away) and Arusha (50km away), just under 6km to the south of the main road running between the two. The airport is currently undergoing a major revamp, so the following information may be a little out-of-date by the time you read this – though the essential layout and facilities of the airport will, we think, be largely unchanged.

ARRIVAL AND DEPARTURE
Arriving
Arriving is straightforward. The terminal is small and you'll instantly be ushered into Immigration and Passport Control where you fill out a blue arrival form. If you arrived from a country where yellow fever is prevalent – even if you were only changing planes there – you will probably have your **yellow fever certificate** (see p53) checked too. Fail to have it and you may have to pay something in the region of US$20-50 and you could be given the jab there; or you could, in theory, be refused entry into the country altogether (though we've never heard of this actually happening).

The immigration formalities are usually easily negotiated, especially as Kilimanjaro is also one of only four places in the country where you can pick up a visa on arrival. Once you've made your way through passport control and having collected your baggage, the only thing now separating you from Tanzania is customs from which, safely negotiated, you emerge into the Arrivals Hall. There are a couple of ATMs in their own separate booths to your right outside the hall: Bank Exim, whose machine charges Ts7000 for a Ts300,000 withdrawal (the maximum they allow) and NMB (Ts9000 for the maximum of Ts400,000). Again, if you can wait until you get into town there are ATMs that currently don't charge a fee at all (see p217). The post office at the airport is occasionally open but don't count on it being so when you arrive.

To get to Moshi or Arusha, about 40 or 50 minutes away respectively, costs US$50 in a taxi (locals pay Ts50,000 but I've not heard of a tourist paying this price) or you may be lucky enough to

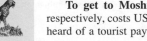

get a shuttle bus depending on which airline you flew in with: KLM passengers have the chance to catch a shuttle to Arusha with Impala (US$15), their minibuses leaving when full. Precision Air operate their own shuttle service (Ts10,000) for internal flights, as do Air Tanzania for their five-times-a-week service between Kilimanjaro Airport and Zanzibar via Dar es Salaam. Fastjet passengers are also met by shuttle bus drivers offering to take them to either Arusha or Moshi for Ts10,000. Fly in with any other airline, however, such as Ethiopian, Qatar or Turkish, and you'll have to take a taxi, there being no public transport to and from the airport.

If you were expecting to be picked up and your lift hasn't arrived, there's a nice drinks stall outside. The stall also serves up the odd samosa, though for something more substantial there's a reasonable canteen, *Delicious Meals Restaurant*, two minutes away just outside the airport grounds, that does a decent *kuku na chipsi* (chicken and chips).

Departing

Leaving Tanzania, things are just as simple. Having completed the initial X-ray that you and your luggage have to undergo before you're even allowed in the terminal building, the check-in desks are the first thing you see. Tickets sorted and bags checked in, from there you turn right to Passport Control (don't wander past it unless you're taking a domestic flight). Don't be in too much of a hurry to get through to the Departure lounge, for there's even less to do there. Instead, peruse the small string of souvenir shops, have a coffee from the café and check your email using the airport's free wi-fi.

Arusha

Arusha may only be Tanzania's third largest city but it is, nevertheless, one of considerable consequence. During the days of British rule, Arusha was the symbolic halfway point between Cairo and Cape Town – the two termini of the old British Empire in Africa. (It should be noted, by the way, that the *actual* midpoint between Cape Town and Cairo lies not here but somewhere in central Congo.)

It was also in Arusha that Britain officially gave Tanzania its independence – and it maintains a central role in African affairs today. It is, for example, the home of the brand new Headquarters of the East African Community – a union between Tanzania, Kenya, Rwanda, Burundi and Uganda that was originally forged in the '70s and has recently been revived. It is also the venue for sorting out issues from all over Africa – including the Tanzanian-brokered peace talks on Burundi and, most famously, the Rwanda War Crimes Tribunal in the Arusha International Conference Centre (AICC), which finished in 2015. And there's no sign of Arusha's momentum ending any time soon as an enormous amount of investment, much of it from China, floods the city, leading to the construction of several spanking-new high rises and some much-needed road-improvement schemes. This has led to an atmosphere of excitement – and a real sense that this is a city

that's going places. Arusha can also boast some of the best tourist amenities in the country, a chaotic and occasionally fascinating central market and several pretty quarters filled with jacaranda and bougainvillea blossoms (not to mention the occasional wooded grove where vervet monkeys and silver-cheeked hornbills can still be spotted crashing through the branches). However, despite these attractions, with the call of the wild from Kilimanjaro, Ngorongoro and the Serengeti beckoning, it's a rare tourist who stays long enough to savour them.

WHAT TO SEE AND DO

Very little is the short answer. There are a couple of museums. By **Arusha Monument** there's the **Arusha Declaration Museum** (daily 9am-5pm; Ts8000) that could conceivably be worth visiting – but only if you're absolutely sure

you've finished preparing for your trek, have written all your postcards, bought all your souvenirs, sent all your emails, cut all your toenails and done all your laundry. Consisting in the main of a few photos and a number of traditional tools and weapons, perhaps the most interesting part is the building itself which is where Nyerere and chums met to hammer out the details of the Arusha Declaration (26-29 January 1967), the announcement that set out the central tenets of African socialism and was adopted by the government in the following years; that, and a torch that was carried around the country every year to promote unity and patriotism among folk (and which is a copy of the torch that was placed on Kili following independence). We suppose some might find this place provides a useful though patchy précis of Tanzanian history from

Arusha Monument

palaeolithic times to the death of Nyerere, and the authorities are to be commended for trying. Overall it's worthy, if not exactly worthwhile.

The **Natural History Museum** (Mon-Fri 9am–6pm, Sat & Sun 9.30am–6pm) is better thanks in large part to an influx of photos of local wildlife by Swedish ex-pat Dick Persson. The photos are, in general, very good and tend to concentrate on the more 'unsung' creatures of Tanzania – the frogs, otters, lizards and hyraxes – and the less-visited parts of the country. Add to this a detailed rundown of the history of the Boma and overall this museum provides a fairly diverting way to spend an hour or so, though the entrance fee of Ts10,500 (or US$5) is a bit too high.

The **African Cultural Heritage Complex** (⌨ culturalheritage.co.tz; Mon-Sat 9.30am-5pm, Sun 9.30am-2pm; free) lies to the west of town on the way to Arusha Airport. The most interesting thing about the first, smaller building is the

roof, which has been designed to resemble the Kibo summit. Inside, however, you'll find little more than a market for woodcarvings and while there's no denying the artistry that's gone into the sculptures on sale, the designs themselves may be a bit too elaborate to appeal to Western tastes. Behind it are more units selling fine quality souvenirs and gifts, though at US$100 for a cushion cover this is definitely stuff that you'd buy only for people you actually care about.

This place, however, has been rather overshadowed by the huge construction next-door, the design of which has been based on those potent African symbols: the spear, the shield and the drum. The reason for these architectural inspirations can be found inside, where a spiral ramp leads you through gallery after gallery of African art, including some fantastic antique bronze sculptures from Benin and wooden totems from all over West Africa on the lower ground floor. Most of the other galleries contain more modern exhibits, largely paintings and photos of various African scenes. As all of the exhibits (including the antiques) are for sale, this giant art gallery could be seen as little more than an upmarket version of the souvenir shop next door. But we think a gentle meander around is a great way of spending an hour or so – and you don't, of course, get any hassle from vendors.

With such a dearth of formal attractions in town, perhaps the most educational and entertaining thing you can do in Arusha is visit a **football game**; it will teach you more about Tanzanians (or at least the male half of the population) and what makes them tick than any papier maché diorama or reconstructed Maasai dwelling. Some of the games are rather low-key but attend a big league match and you're in for a treat.

If football's not your game you can always **play pool** (see p233), or go **swimming** (Ts10,000) in the pool at Impala Hotel (see p227).

❏ **Organised tours and courses around Arusha**

Via Via (see p232) organises tours around the city and neighbouring hills. None of these sights will take your breath away, nor is that their intention: they are simply very pleasant escapes from the city and a refreshing way of discovering the country that exists outside the national parks. All prices are per person. Destinations include **Sapuk Waterfall**, on the slopes of Meru, which involves at least a couple of hours' walking each way (US$50); Lake Duluti (US$50) which includes a walk in the nearby forest and the chance – for an extra fee – to paddle in a canoe on the water; and a visit to the **hot spring at Chemka village** (US$60), north of Boma N'gombe.

They also operate a number of courses including a **cookery course** (US$30), where you spend the morning shopping for ingredients at the local market and the afternoon making something tasty out of them. Or you can take a **batik workshop** (US$30), take part in an **African drum-making workshop** (US$50) or learn to **dance like a local** (US$20 for an hour).

For local tours that take you further afield, the Tanzanian Tourist Board, with help from Dutch development organisation SNV, have created **Cultural Tourism Programmes** where you can visit the rural areas of Tanzania and experience 'real' African life, with all profits going towards various development projects. Prices are around U$15-35 per day depending on the group size. Amongst the many tours they organise country-wide are trips to **Machame** (🖳 machameculturaltourism.com) to see the waterfalls, caves, old churches, a market, and local coffee farms.

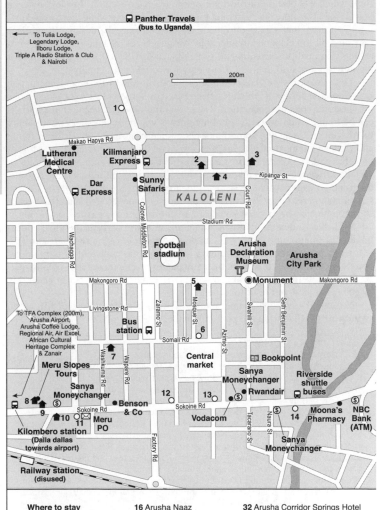

Panther Travels
(bus to Uganda)

← To Tulia Lodge,
Legendary Lodge,
Ilboru Lodge,
Triple A Radio Station & Club
& Nairobi

0   200m

1

Makao Hapya Rd

Lutheran
Medical
Centre

Kilimanjaro
Express

Dar
Express

Sunny
Safaris

Colonel Middleton Rd

2

4

3

Kipanga St

Court Rd

KALOLENI

Stadium Rd

Wachagga Rd

Football
stadium

Arusha
Declaration
Museum

Arusha
City Park

Makongoro Rd

Livingstone Rd

5

Arusha
Monument

Makongoro Rd

To TFA Complex (200m),
Arusha Airport,
Arusha Coffee Lodge,
Regional Air, Air Excel,
African Cultural
Heritage Complex
& Zanair

Bus
station

Zaramo St

Mosque St

6

Somali Rd

Swahili St

Seth Benjamin St

Central
market

Bookpoint

Sanya
Moneychanger

Riverside
shuttle
buses

Meru Slopes
Tours

Washkuma Rd

Wapare Rd

7

Sanya
Moneychanger

8

Benson
& Co

12

13

Rwandair

Azimo St

9

10

11

Meru
PO

Sokoine Rd

Sokoine Rd

Vodacom

Tacarano St

Naura St

14

Moona's
Pharmacy

NBC
Bank
(ATM)

Kilombero station
(Dalla dallas
towards airport)

Factory Rd

Sanya
Moneychanger

Railway station
(disused)

Where to stay

2 Monjes B 3 Monjes C	16 Arusha Naaz	32 Arusha Corridor Springs Hotel
4 Monjes A	18 Arusha Hotel	33 Gold Crest Hotel
5 Arusha Crown Hotel	23 Hotel Equator	34 The African Tulip
7 Venus Premier Hotel	24 The New Safari Hotel	36 Lush Garden Business Hotel
8 Arusha Tourist Inn	25 Palace Hotel Arusha	37 Flame Tree
9 Meru House Inn	27 Naura Springs Hotel	41 The Eight
10 Arusha Backpackers	28 Pepe One	44 Spices & Herbs
	31 Kibo Palace	45 Impala Hotel

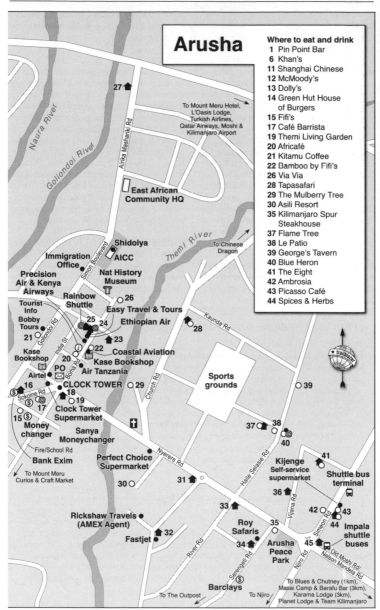

Arusha

Where to eat and drink
1 Pin Point Bar
6 Khan's
11 Shanghai Chinese
12 McMoody's
13 Dolly's
14 Green Hut House of Burgers
15 Fifi's
17 Café Barrista
19 Themi Living Garden
20 Africafé
21 Kitamu Coffee
22 Bamboo by Fifi's
26 Via Via
28 Tapasafari
29 The Mulberry Tree
30 Asili Resort
35 Kilimanjaro Spur Steakhouse
37 Flame Tree
38 Le Patio
39 George's Tavern
40 Blue Heron
41 The Eight
42 Ambrosia
43 Picasso Café
44 Spices & Herbs

To Mount Meru Hotel,
L'Oasis Lodge,
Turkish Airlines,
Qatar Airways, Moshi &
Kilimanjaro Airport

Naura River

Goliondoi River

Arika Mashariki Rd

East African Community HQ

Themi River

To Chinese Dragon

Shidolya
AICC
Immigration Office
Simon Boulevard
Precision Air & Kenya Airways
Nat History Museum
Rainbow Shuttle
Tourist Info
Bobby Tours
26
Easy Travel & Tours
Ethiopian Air
25 24
23
Kaunda Rd
21
Goliondoi Rd
India St
20
22
Coastal Aviation
Kase Bookshop
Boma Rd
Kase Bookshop
Air Tanzania
28
Airtel
PO
CLOCK TOWER
29
Sokoine Rd
16
18
19
Clock Tower Supermarket
15
Money changer
Sanya Moneychanger
Church Rd
Sports grounds
39
Fire/School Rd
Bank Exim
Perfect Choice Supermarket
Nyerere Rd
37
38
40
To Mount Meru
Curios & Craft Market
30
31
Haile Selasie Rd
Kijenge Self-service supermarket
41
Shuttle bus terminal
36
Vijana Rd
33
42
43
Rickshaw Travels (AMEX Agent)
Roy Safaris
35
44
Impala shuttle buses
Fastjet
32
34
Arusha Peace Park
45
Simeon Rd
River Rd
Serengeti Rd
Njiro Rd
Old Moshi Rd
Nelson Mandela Rd
Barclays
To The Outpost
To Njiro
To Blues & Chutney (1km),
Masai Camp & Barafu Bar (3km),
Karama Lodge (3km),
Planet Lodge & Team Kilimanjaro

ARRIVAL

By air

Arusha Airport (or 'the little airport' as it's commonly called locally to distinguish it from Kilimanjaro International) lies to the west of the city and serves internal flights only. There's not much to the place other than a tiny 'departure lounge', a great little bookshop crammed with English titles, a souvenir shop or two and a couple of cafés (Msumbi Coffees have a concession here). A taxi into town will set you back about Ts20,000 (though they'll ask for Ts30,000), or you can walk or catch a *boda boda* (motorbike taxi; Ts1000) to the main junction (about one hot, dusty kilometre) and wait for a dalla-dalla to pass by (Ts500); you shouldn't have to wait more than a minute or two. Those who've arrived with Precision Air can catch their shuttle bus (Ts5000).

Not to be confused with Arusha Airport, **Kilimanjaro International Airport** (for details, see p210) lies to the other (eastern) side of town, 44km along

and 6km to the south of the road to Moshi. For details on **getting to the airports** see the box below.

By bus

Arriving in Arusha by **public bus**, expect to be dumped (sometimes literally) at the bus station at the southern end of Colonel Middleton Rd in the western half of town, reasonably close to the budget hostels.

If you reach Arusha by **shuttle bus**, on the other hand, tell the driver where you wish to jump out in the town centre and he should drop you there; if not, the chances are you'll be dropped off at the terminal on Simeon Rd just north of Impala Hotel, or at the Impala itself if you took their shuttle. From here you'll have to catch a cab, motorbike or walk to your destination.

ORIENTATION & GETTING AROUND

Arusha is bisected by the **Goliondoi River Valley**, a narrow and shallow dip in the town's topography. The division is more than just geographical: to the west is down-

---

❏ GETTING TO KILIMANJARO AND ARUSHA AIRPORTS

To Kilimanjaro International

Impala (☎ 027-250 7197) run a **shuttle bus** from their base in the Impala Hotel car park, the shuttle leaving around three hours before the KLM flight – thus allowing passengers who are joining the KLM flight enough time to check-in – and returning when the bus is filled with KLM passengers who've just landed (US$15 each way). Note that they need a minimum of two passengers in order to run the service.

Precision Air/Kenyan Airways also offer a shuttle service to and from KIA for their flights for a very reasonable Ts10,000. **Air Tanzania** offer a similar service and for the same price for their passengers. Remember with all shuttles to phone or call in at the airline office beforehand to see if you need to book your place.

A **taxi** to the airport officially costs US$50, though with bargaining this can be reduced slightly.

To Arusha Airport

Precision Air operate a service (Ts5000) for their flights from Arusha Airport. If you're not flying with them, however, you'll have to rely on taxis or public transport. Virtually opposite the TFZ complex is the Kilombero bus station, a muddy and chaotic patch of land from where dalla-dallas head west towards Arusha Airport (listen out for the touts shouting 'Kisongo'), dropping passengers off by the junction a kilometre from the terminal for Ts500; from there you can walk or catch a boda boda (Ts1000). If you're carrying all your luggage, you've got to be seriously tightfisted to opt for this rather than take a taxi from town (Ts15,000 minimum, though Ts20,000-30,000 is more normal).

town, the busier, noisier and more fun part of Arusha, where most of the cheap lodgings can be found. To the east of the valley lies the tourist centre, where most hotels, safari companies and better restaurants are located. This eastern section is further divided by a second river, the **Themi**, that runs along the back of such major landmarks as Arusha Hotel, the Via Via Café and the AICC.

Arusha is not a big place, most things are within walking distance of each other and **getting around** is not a major hassle, though to get from one half of town to the other it's a good idea to take a **dalla-dalla**; they charge Ts400 for short trips around town or Ts500 for destinations further afield. **Taxis** are distinguishable by their white number plates (other vehicles have yellow ones); they charge around Ts5000 for a trip within the town centre.

Thanks to a flood of cheap motorbikes from Asia there's a two-wheeled alternative to the taxi. **Boda boda**, or **Toyo** (also very commonly called '**piki piki**'), is the local term for these motorbike taxis; there's no arguing that they are both cheap (Ts7000 will get you from the far east of the city to the far west, even late at night) and the best form of transport for slicing through the traffic. Before hopping eagerly onto one, however, bear in mind that there's already a special wing at Meru Hospital devoted to victims of Toyo accidents – drivers, passengers and bystanders – with passengers by far and away the largest contingent, probably because few if any boda boda drivers supply their customers with a crash helmet. As with taxis, the drivers will come and find you, though they can usually be found outside the main hotels and restaurants.

SERVICES
Tourist information
The tourist information office (Mon-Fri 8am-4pm, Sat 8.30am-1pm) is on Boma Rd. Full of brochures, the office is the best source of information on the city and the safari circuit. They keep a list of licensed tour agencies in both Moshi and Arusha, have a list of local markets that you can visit and even have a rundown of bus, train

and boat services from Tanzania to East African destinations. They also have a noticeboard where some people advertise for trekking companions. They didn't have much useful info on Kilimanjaro when we called in but, in spite of this, in our opinion it's the best tourist office in East Africa.

Banks and changing money
There are **cashpoints** (ATMs) all over the city, particularly towards the eastern end of Sokoine, down from the Clock Tower, and in the TFA Complex, where you'll find most banks represented. For the banks that currently aren't charging commission for withdrawals from their ATMs, try the Stanbic on Sokoine next to the DHL office; they also have a cashpoint in the TFA Complex; Ecobank, another bank that at the moment doesn't charge commission, also have a cashpoint in the parking lot here. If you're staying on the eastern side of town and don't mind paying a fee for withdrawing money, then Barclays have a branch with an ATM on the way down to The Outpost on Serengeti Rd.

As for changing money, the **bureaux de change** are far more efficient than the banks. The five Sanya outlets (daily 7am-8pm) are reliable and are also about the only bureau to open on Sunday. One lies to the east of Fifi's, on the short cut between Fire Road and Sokoine, while four are on Sokoine itself: one about 50m down from Café Barrista, one just down from Green Hut House of Burgers, a third lying about 100m further west of there and a fourth near Meru House Inn to the west.

The **AMEX** agent in Arusha is Rickshaw Travels (☎ 027-254 5955) at 184 Engira Rd, the road running down the hill from the Kibo Palace Hotel.

Communications
The **post office** (Mon-Fri 8am-4.30pm, Sat 9am-noon) is by the Clock Tower, hidden away behind the electronic advertising board, There's a second branch, Meru Post Office (Mon-Fri 8am-1pm, 2-4.30pm, Sat 9am-noon), at the western end of Sokoine near the backpacker hotels.

For phoning, the TTCL offices still

exist but you can no longer place a call there. If you've brought your mobile from home then it should work though it'll be expensive to make a call or send a message. See our advice about buying a local SIM card (p131) and remember you can always use Skype and other internet-based communication services which will be cheaper still (or free).

Most hotels now offer free **wi-fi** to their guests but if you don't have your own computer finding an **internet** café in Arusha isn't difficult, especially as most of the big hotels have one. All charge much the same with Ts2000 per hour being the norm; the New Safari charges Ts3000 but offers a little more peace and privacy. Of the wi-fi services provided by the cafés and restaurants, *Fifi's* (see p229) and, at the other end of town, *Msumbi Coffee* in the TFA (see p229), seem to be the most reliable and popular.

Airline offices (see also p386)

● **Air Excel** Arusha Airport (☎ 0732 102546; ⌨ airexcelonline.com; Mon-Fri 8.30am-1pm & 2-5pm, Sat 8.30am-1pm). The offices sit in the big blue-roofed building at the far end of the parking lot.

● **Air Tanzania** Boma Rd (☎ 027-250 3201; ⌨ airtanzania.co.tz; Mon-Fri 8am-1pm & 2-5pm; Sat & Sun 9am-1pm) Currently Air Tanzania operate just one flight from Kilimanjaro Airport, to Zanzibar via Dar, a service that operates five times per week (daily, Thurs-Mon). They operate a shuttle service to take passengers to and from the airport.

● **Auric Air** TFA Complex (☎ 0783 233334; ⌨ auricair.com) One of several companies flying small planes to mainly tourist destinations, in this case from Arusha Airport to Serengeti, Dar, Zanzibar, Dodoma, and Lake Victoria (Mwanza nd Bukoba).

● **Coastal Aviation** Boma Road (☎ 0769 386732; ⌨ coastal.co.tz; Mon-Fri 9am-5pm, Sat 9am-2pm).

● **Ethiopian Air** Boma Rd (☎ 027-250 4231/250 6167; ⌨ ethiopianairlines.com; Mon-Fri 8.30am-5pm, Sat 8.30am-1pm).

● **Fastjet** (☎ 0783 540540, ⌨ fastjet.com)

Corridor Springs Hotel, Mon-Sat 8am-5pm, Sun 9am-4pm.

● **Kenya Airways** See Precision Air, below.

● **Precision Air** Boma Rd (☎ 0784-402026; ⌨ precisionairtz.com; Mon-Fri 8am-5pm, Sat 9am-1pm).

● **Qatar Airways** Plot 40, opposite Mount Meru Hotel (☎ 0767-004374/78/79/80, ⌨ qatarairways.com; Mon-Fri 8am- 5pm, Sat 8am-1pm).

● **Regional Air** Sable Square Shopping Village, beyond Arusha Airport (☎ 0784 28575, ☎ 0754 285754; ⌨ regionaltanzania.com). Tanzanian division of AirKenya and, as with Auric and Coastal, a useful company to contact if you want to fly to one of the parks on the Northern Circuit, as well as Dar and Zanzibar.

● **Rwandair** Swahili St (☎ 0732-978558; ⌨ rwandair.com; Mon-Fri 8am-5pm, Sat 9am-1pm). Currently has four flights per week to Kigali, on Tues, Wed, Fri & Sun.

● **Tropical Air** (☎ 0687 522886, ⌨ tropicalair.co.tz) Flies between Arusha, Dar and Zanzibar.

● **Turkish Airlines** Plot 40, opposite Mount Meru Hotel (☎ 0785-111849, ⌨ turkishairlines.com; Mon-Fri 9am-5.30pm, Sat 9am-1pm); also at Kilimanjaro Airport (daily 11pm-3am).

● **Zanair** Summit Centre, Sokoine Rd (⌨ zanair.com; Mon-Fri 9am-1pm, 2-5pm, Sat 9am-1pm).

Immigration office

The immigration office (Mon-Fri 7.30am-3.30pm) is across the road from the AICC on Afrika Mashariki Rd.

Shopping

You can get most things in Arusha; it's just a question of knowing where to look. Some of the shops seem to have been deliberately set up with tourists and expats in mind, particularly those at the **TFA complex** at the western end of Sokoine, where you'll find: a couple of safari operators; **TSM Outdoor Adventure**, a well-stocked camping/ trekking shop; several bars, cafés and restaurants; the best English-language bookshops in the city (see opposite); and

even a **massage** parlour, **Ai Care** (☎ 0629 141981; US$35 for an hour's shiatsu, US$40 for Swedish deep tissue and US$55 for a hot-stone massage). These arcades may lack charm and feel a little sterile; but that's probably the point of them, and if you're missing home these places are unrivalled in Arusha.

● **Books** The two branches of chaotic **Kase Bookshop** (Mon-Fri 9am-5.30pm, Sat 8am-2pm), on Boma Rd by the Air Tanzania office and to the west of the Clock Tower, are long established and convenient; **Bookpoint** is fair too and has recently opened a second branch in one of the more obscure corners of the TFA Complex. At the other end of the TFA, **A Novel Idea** (Mon-Sat 9am-5.30pm) is fine but starting to look a little faded.

● **Electrical goods/cameras** **Benson & Co**, now occupying almost an entire block on Sokoine, should be your first port of call for electrical goods, camera batteries, repairs and so forth. Note, however, that they're not cheap! Across the road is their technical department where they can unlock phones – again, for a hefty fee.

● **Pharmacy Moona's** (Mon-Fri 8.45am-5.30pm, Sat 8.45am-2pm) lies near the eastern end of Sokoine, a few hundred metres down from the Clock Tower. The staff speak good English.

● **Souvenirs** You won't have any trouble finding souvenirs in Arusha – indeed, often they come and find you. Some of the stuff is of a poor quality, however. The best place for an overview of what's on offer can be had at **Mount Meru Curios & Crafts Market**, a vast collection of souvenir stalls collected into one handy site on School Rd (aka Fire Rd, as the fire station is at the bottom of the street) about 300m south of the Clock Tower. Manage to make it out of here alive and with some money still in your

---

❏ The International Criminal Tribunal for Rwanda

In 1994 the Hutu people of Rwanda slaughtered en masse their hated Tutsi rivals. It is believed that over the course of 100 horrifying days around 800,000 people were murdered – a figure that represented about 20% of the total population of Rwanda at that time. In addition, over two million people were displaced and became refugees. This appalling episode has become known as the Rwandan genocide.

In the aftermath, the International Criminal Tribunal was set up at the Arusha International Conference Centre (AICC) to hear the trials of some of the ringleaders of the massacre. Over 21 years the four small courtrooms heard reams of harrowing evidence – and made some extraordinary rulings as a result. Amongst those convicted were Jean-Paul Akayesu, a former mayor, who was convicted of nine counts of genocide and three crimes against humanity – the first time a court has ever passed judgement on genocide. Further convictions followed, including that of the former Rwandan prime minister, Jean Kambanda, who became the first head of government to be convicted of genocide by an international court. The tribunal was also the first to recognise rape as a means of perpetrating genocide.

Yet in spite of all the precedents that the tribunal achieved, it's not without its critics. In particular, they point to the hefty US$2 billion price tag and the relatively paltry return on this investment, with only 93 individuals convicted over those 21 years.

Nevertheless, supporters argue that the tribunal has blazed a trail, providing as its main legacy a powerful deterrent to those considering committing similar crimes in the future.

Today, with the AICC returning to its former function as a conference centre, the only reminder of the momentous trials that took place in the city is a small peace park established by the Impala Roundabout; there, in the park's centre, is a small memorial that lists the achievements of the trial.

pocket and perhaps you can try **A&G**, in the TFA complex, which specialises in women's printed garments known as *kitenge* or *kanga*, or **Ethnic Secret Design**, on the other side of the TFA, which sells similar. A third shop here, **Fine Artz Gallery**, is also very good and sells a lot of items that I haven't seen elsewhere.

Adjacent to and affiliated with the Natural History Museum is the **Museum Art Centre** (Fri-Wed 9am-6pm, Thurs to midnight), where about a dozen painters, dressmakers, jewellers and other craftsmen and women beaver away in little huts. All of the stuff is for sale, supposedly at a cheaper price than if bought elsewhere.

Moving east of town, the Curio Hand Craft Industry Shop, just above the Asili Resort on a dirt track running south off Nyerere Rd, claims to have the cheapest prices in town. There's also a very good variety of excellent quality goods at **Blue Heron Café** (see p231), which has a couple of rooms of souvenirs stuffed with fabrics, wooden toys, rattan mats and wooden furniture etc; note that this place has fixed prices.

● **Supermarkets** As we go to press the East African chain Nakumatt has closed its branch in the TFA Complex at the western end of Sokoine. Conveniently situated, the shop may reopen under another owner but it was never the cheapest place and most of the customers, unsurprisingly, were expats. If you're staying at the other end of town, **Kijenge Self-Service Supermarket** by the Spices & Herbs hotel/restaurant and the **Perfect Choice Supermarket** on Nyerere Road are both OK, while most central of all is **Clock Tower Supermarket** (Mon-Fri 6.30am-9.30pm, Sat 8.30am-9pm, Sun 8.30am-8.30pm) on the main roundabout; it enjoyed a degree of fame in the 1960s as the location for a scene in John Wayne's *Hatari!* (see p395) where an elephant runs amok through the aisles.

WHERE TO STAY [see map p214]

As with much of the rest of Tanzania, the hotels in Arusha officially charge different rates for locals and foreigners, particularly for mid-range and high-end hotels. For the prices listed below, we have opted to list the **non-residents' rate** only; the residents' rate is usually lower by 5% or more though not always; sometimes it's just the shilling equivalent of the non-resident price. Note that you may be able to get a cheaper rate for your hotel by booking online through 🖳 booking.com or 🖳 airbnb.com – local hotels often advertise through these sites; if you have the time, it's worth checking the online rates to see if they are lower.

We have divided the hotels in approximate price order and, within each category, have **ordered them approximately from west to east** (see map pp214-5).

Budget: under US$20 for a double

The focus for budget travellers these days is the western end of Sokoine Rd. The management of *Arusha Backpackers* (☎ 0715-377795; 🖳 arushabackpackers.co.tz), the sister of the Kindoroko and Backpacker hotels in Moshi, are to be congratulated for introducing some sort of standards to a traveller's hostel. All rooms are meticulously cleaned daily and come with soap, towels and wi-fi (though the connection is patchy at best and you'll seldom achieve a connection in your room), while the showers are spotless and there's hot water in the taps. They also throw in a reasonable buffet breakfast in their charming rooftop café, where you can feast on muesli, toast and fruit while your eyes feast on great views over the city towards Meru. As for drawbacks? Well its location adjacent to the forecourt of a petrol station is an unpromising one, and there are no self-contained rooms. It's also right on the very busy Sokoine Road so you'll be woken up at 5.30am every morning; invest in some heavy-duty earplugs for your best chance of sleeping beyond dawn. Still, we think it's very good value indeed with rates for B&B beginning at just US$9pp for a spot in a four-bed dorm or US$8-12/18-22/27-36 sgl/dbl/tpl (the higher prices are for the bigger rooms with better views; note that a small single is cheaper than a bed in a dorm). Be warned, however, that sometimes, in the summer high season at least,

you have to book in advance to stand a chance of staying here.

Surviving largely on the overspill from Arusha Backpackers, *Meru House Inn* (☎ 027-250 7803; 🖳 meruhouseinn@hotmail.com; Ts25,000/35,000 sgl/dbl B&B, less Ts5000 if breakfast not required) has been around for a while and is another hotel often patronised by foreign tourists, which is surprising given that it makes little effort to attract them. Still, it's pleasant, relaxed, the manager and his staff are friendly, the rooms have wi-fi and mosquito nets and there are bathrooms with hot water. But do avoid the rooms overlooking either the central courtyard or the road if you want a good night's sleep.

In the first edition of the book the main backpackers area was Kaloleni, a small cluster of streets to the north of the stadium and a few metres east of Colonel Middleton Rd, though with the migration of tourists to the above establishments this area has fallen on hard times and the hotels that remain now have either closed or found alternative clients, some of whom want to hire the room by the hour only. Nevertheless, for those backpackers who don't like other backpackers, and who would rather stay somewhere authentically African – with all that entails – this area is perfect. With each built on or just off Levolosi Rd, the three *Monjes Guest Houses* (☎ 0754 462308, 🖳 monjestz.com), labelled A, B and C, are perhaps the most reliable, with some very pleasant little rooms with televisions and mosquito nets. Monjes A and B charge sgl/dbl/ Ts25,000, with Monjes C and its brighter, bigger rooms charging Ts5000 extra per room.

Mid-range: US$20-75 for a double
Arusha Tourist Inn (☎ 0754-583455, 🖳 arushatouristinnhotel.com; dbl US$55, B&B, US$40 single occupancy), on Sokoine Rd, is hidden away behind the much tattier Meru House Inn, with which it shares an owner. The 29 en suite rooms come with all the facilities including satellite TV and wi-fi but do lack views; indeed its location verges on the claustrophobic. Still, it's a safe, decent choice.

The *Arusha Crown Hotel* (☎ 027-250 8523; 🖳 arushacrownhotel.com), on Makongoro Rd by the south-eastern corner of the stadium, is very much a hotel for local businessmen. It's smart and comfy enough, with rooms all equipped with wi-fi, TV and bathroom, though it's a little bland and the walls cannot entirely block out the noise from the streets below. That said, you do at least get a grandstand view of the football across the road from some rooms. Rates start at US$60/74 s/c sgl/dbl for B&B, which in our opinion is fair. Another one that sees few foreign faces is *Arusha Naaz* (☎ 0754 282799; 🖳 arushanaaz.net; s/c sgl/dbl/tpl US$45/60/75), situated right in the centre of town at the eastern end of Sokoine. The façade looks unpromising but the rooms are squeaky clean, en suite and all come with TV; there's also a (dazzlingly bright) roof terrace. Try to get a room away from the road if possible.

L'Oasis Lodge (☎ 0757-557802; 🖳 loasistanzania.com; off map to the northeast) is in an obscure location, a 15-minute walk north of the town, with accommodation in 27 huts, rondavels and 'boma-style' rooms all hidden behind a high wall. The rooms themselves are fine, the food is said to be great and they've got wi-fi and a small pool. In fact, the only quibble we have is that more than one reader has written to say that they've failed to get any sleep due to the barking of the neighbourhood dogs – particularly true for those who've opted for the cheaper Backpackers Lodge, across the dirt track, which has shared amenities and lacks some of the charm of the main lodge. Rates: sgl/dbl/tpl US$48-66/66-93/90-129; Backpackers Lodge US$28pp B&B in one of 12 twin-bedded rooms.

Over the east side of town are two establishments that are more renowned as restaurants, but which both have a few neat rooms attached. Neither seems to do much business and both rely on the restaurants to keep them afloat, though we found all the rooms perfectly fine and pleasant. On Kenyatta Rd, *Flame Tree* (☎ 027-254 5780, or ☎ 0783-940802; 🖳 flametree.reservation@gmail.com) has simple rooms though still with TV, wi-fi and hot water; rates are sgl/dbl US$35/40. *(continued on p226)*

ARUSHA, MOSHI & MARANGU

❑ ACCOMMODATION AROUND ARUSHA

Whilst we have spent pages describing the accommodation in Arusha, the fact of the matter is that most of you will have booked your trek before you arrive and your agency in turn will have arranged your hotel; and it's more than likely that this accommodation won't even be in Arusha but outside of it, where several swish, smart and salubrious lodges are situated, surviving on the patronage of foreign travel companies and their local agents. It's hard to criticise these places except that they do tend to be in the middle of nowhere.

Arusha Coffee Lodge (☎ 027-250 9279; 🖥 elewanacollection.com) consists of 30 luxury chalets (or 'plantation houses') that are just gorgeous. Unlike the other hotels in this section, it lies to the west of Arusha on the way to the local airport but is still being used by a couple of trekking companies, particularly those who combine their treks with a safari afterwards. The private chalets on the plantation are served by a pool and they also offer a massage service. Another thing in its favour is its renowned restaurant. Owned by the Elewana chain, prices start at s/c sgl/dbl US$193/386 in the low season, high season sgl/dbl US$413/550.

Legendary Lodge (☎ UK +44 207 096 1287, ☎ South Africa +27 21 876 2153; 🖥 classic-portfolio.com) is a highly rated luxurious property, smart and relatively new, incorporating 12 huge cottages (including two with two bedrooms), each with their own lounge and fireplace, set on a former coffee farm in lush gardens 5km north-west of the city on way to Nairobi, with good views of Meru. Rates, including laundry service and transfers between Arusha Airport, are US$406-580 full board per cottage, the exact price depending on season. Note that despite the eye-watering rates, there is no pool on the premises; for that you have to go to a nearby member's club. It is often used by Abercrombie & Kent (p104) to house their clients.

Tulia Lodge (☎ 0755-700001; 🖥 tuliahotelandspa.com) north of town on the way to Nairobi is popular with a couple of trekking and safari companies. You'll find 20 lovely relaxing rooms (Tulia is Swahili for 'Relax') with a spa to treat those post-trek aches and pains. Price-wise, their rack rates are US$80-100 sgl/dbl.

Firmly in the luxury bracket, *Onsea House* (☎ +31 622 744 340; 🖥 onsea-house.com) is a delight. Everything, from the locally made furniture to the outdoor pool with views across to Meru, the friendly and conscientious staff and the tranquil setting on Namasi Hill, 7km east of Arusha, is spot on. And I haven't yet mentioned

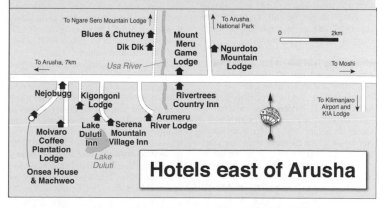

Hotels east of Arusha

the food, overseen by the Belgian manager who's been working in Michelin-starred restaurants since he was 16. The rates – s/c sgl/dbl US$162.50/325 – are not cheap even by Arusha's standards but they are very fair value. It's our favourite.

Once upon a time the only problem with Onsea was one of availability, its four double rooms (plus two in the separate cottage by the pool) frequently booked up well in advance. They have alleviated that problem, however, by building a new establishment next door. Linked by a bridge and with the same sense of understated style, *Machweo Wellness Retreat & Fine Dining* (see contact details above) is nevertheless also quite a different entity to its elder sister. For where Onsea House is more homely, cosy and intimate, Machweo, while still exquisitely tasteful, is slightly more 'showy', with rooms boasting satellite TVs and even bathtubs in the Honeymoon suites; there's also a spa here too. Rates are the same as at Onsea House.

On the way to Onsea, but much nearer the main road, *Nejobugg* (☎ 0756 710000; 🖳 nejobuggpalacehotel.com) is currently in the process of expanding its premises to include a gym and swimming pool. It's a flashy hotel, all air-con and electronic keys, shiny and opulent. The rooms are antiseptically clean and smart, and there's nothing wrong with it, but we do think the taste is more for the local businessman than the average tourist. Rates: sgl/dbl/ US$75-120/85-150.

Not too far away at the end of a bumpy dirt track about 7km east of Arusha, 2km south of the road to Moshi, is *Moivaro Coffee Plantation Lodge* (☎ 0754324193, 🖳 moivaro.com), consisting of 40 cottages, each hidden away amongst the lush vegetation of the verdant grounds. Each room is en suite and has a veranda; the lodge also boasts a swimming pool and bar. A massage service is available, too, which will enable you to while away the hours when you're not on the mountain. Rates: s/c sgl/dbl/tpl US$160-228/200-317/260-428 for B&B.

Kigongoni Lodge (☎ 027-255 3087, ☎ 0732-978 876, 🖳 kigongoni.net) is located in a beautiful hilltop location on an old coffee estate about 11km from Arusha. The 19 rustic cottages are simple but wonderful, with fireplaces, four-poster beds and lovely wooden verandas overlooking the monkey-filled forest below, while Meru and even Kibo loom in the background. The Dutch family who run it are jolly and helpful, the food is good and, to top it all, part of the profit goes to the nearby Sibusiso Foundation, a centre for mentally and physically handicapped children. Throw in the usual facilities, including wi-fi and a swimming pool, and you have a very, very pleasant lodge indeed. Rates in the self-contained rooms are around US$90 per person.

Serena Mountain Village Inn (☎ 027-255 3313, ☎ 0787-444015, 🖳 serenahotels.com) is one of many Serena properties in Tanzania and yet another lodge that is situated on a coffee plantation, though this time at Tengeru and with the added attraction of Lake Duluti behind. This gorgeous location and the grand, almost baronial reception/restaurant area aren't quite matched by the 42 rooms in concrete bungalows but nevertheless some have full sunken baths and lake views and all have wi-fi. Rates are s/c sgl/dbl US$105/220 low season, up to US$265/365 in peak season.

Before you get to Serena, on the right-hand side as you drive down the dirt track is a much newer lodge with absolutely no pretensions towards antiquity at all. *Lake Duluti Lodge* (☎ 0769 356 504, 🖳 dulutilodge.com) is around four years old now, its nineteen rooms built, as is usual, on an old coffee farm (though one, refreshingly, where they've not ripped up all the plants but have let them continue to flourish between the chalets). The rooms themselves are modern and comfortable, with plenty of natural light streaming in through their large windows and a roomy bathroom with modern fittings. *(continued overleaf)*

❑ ACCOMMODATION AROUND ARUSHA

(*continued from p223*) There's also a pool and massage facilities, and plenty of other activities available including the chance to go canoeing on the lake. Rates are around sgl/dbl US$236/413.

Arumeru River Lodge (☎ 0785-555131, 🖳 arumerulodge.com) consists of 29 large, comfortable chalets and a huge, high-roofed makuti reception-cum-restaurant, all standing amongst neatly trimmed gardens amidst the bushes of a coffee estate 20km along and 1km south of the road to Moshi. All the usual facilities are here, including wi-fi (US$5 in the chalets, free in the suites), a small solar-heated pool, satellite TV (on request only) and a highly regarded restaurant; there's even some guinea fowl and a dik dik running around the grounds, supervising everything. Rates are s/c sgl/dbl/tpl US$150-200/200-290/255-375 for the garden chalets depending on the season, rising to US$235-270/260-340/330-450 for the suites. Overall, safe and satisfactory without being spectacular.

Now under new management, *Dik Dik* (☎ 027-255 3499, 0732-979943; 🖳 dikdik.ch) is homely and in a good location north of the highway. The hotel is named after one of Africa's smallest antelopes and is appropriately petite, particularly when compared to the nearby Ngurdoto (see opposite). The high-roofed reception is a tribute to the woodcarver's art and the 20 rooms, divided between 10 bungalows, all come with a fireplace, veranda, wi-fi, hammock and mini-bar; there's a small pool here too and even a viewing tower – from the top of which you can see Kilimanjaro. All in all a pleasant, cosy option. Rates: s/c sgl/dbl US$190/280 for B&B. Dik Dik also runs a trekking agency, see p79.

Further up the track are two more very good choices. The unusually named *Blues & Chutney* (☎ 0732-971668; 🖳 bluesandchutney.com; rates s/c sgl/dbl US$130/175; meals US$18-20) has moved from its old location near the centre of Arusha to the much quieter Usa River area. Established by the same people running the excellent Rivertrees (see below), the six rooms here are a delight, all self-contained and with wi-fi, and simply but exquisitely decorated with panache and style. It's a pleasant and tastefully decorated B&B, and our only issue is with the enormous suite upstairs, which is a joy to behold but also, with its low tin roof, really hot.

A little further along, *Ngare Sero Mountain Lodge* (☎ 073-2978931; 🖳 ngaresero-lodge.com) is one of my favourites. A really lovely choice, it's reachable only by crossing a small footbridge over a tranquil pond where cormorants sunbathe and colobus monkeys peer through the branches. The lodge started life as a colonial farmhouse in the early twentieth century though the original building (which has now been divided into two rooms) has been amended and added to, with twelve tasteful self-contained chalets (with walk-in wardrobes) spread around the perimeter of the lawned grounds, in the middle of which is a 'massage tower'. Those who have booked with Summits Africa (see p97), Nature Discovery (see p92) or one of the other more expensive trekking outfitters may end up here – and there's nothing to complain about if you do. Rates are sgl/dbl US$225-255/290-330 depending on the season.

The delightful *Rivertrees Country Inn* (☎ 0732-971667; 🖳 rivertrees.com) sits on the banks of the Usa River, 22km east of Arusha. It's a stylishly rustic inn, the cosy, slightly 'shabby chic' reception and lounge making good use of old reclaimed wood, while the 34 self-contained guestrooms, two cottages and large thatched River House – which contains two double rooms – are similarly understated and tasteful. But it's the grounds that, for this author at least, are the biggest draw, the Inn's many great old trees offering both welcome shade for residents and a perfect habitat for birds; indeed, the whole place comes alive with magnificent birdsong throughout the morning.

Add to this such facilities as wi-fi, a kitchen that bakes its own bread and an attentive, conscientious staff and you have the ideal option for those looking for a little luxury but who aren't bothered about being close to the town. After all, if it's good enough for both a football-club-owning, London-based Russian oligarch and the heir to the British throne – both of whom have stayed here – it'll probably be good enough for you too. Rates for their standard rooms are s/c sgl/dbl US$137-211/189-279 B&B, or it's US$672-753 for the River House, which can accommodate up to six guests, and US$856-1228 for the exclusive use of the Far House, accommodating up to ten guests.

Opposite is another establishment that's full of character. *Mount Meru Game Lodge & Sanctuary* (☎ 027-255 3885; ☐ merugamelodge.com) was established back in 1959 (the founder's son is now in charge) although its colonial style harks back to an earlier era. The 17 large, en suite rooms with wi-fi (for which they charge) in wooden bungalows are comfortable and the restaurant is renowned among expats who flee Arusha to dine here at weekends; but it's the **animal sanctuary** (Ts3000 for non-residents) that really sets this lodge apart, with water buffalo, zebra, crocodile, tortoises, porcupine, monkeys and storks all roaming the adjacent grounds. Rates are s/c sgl/dbl US$30 per person for B&B.

Continuing east, *The Ngurdoto Mountain Lodge* (☎ 0784 226165; ☐ thengurdotomountainlodge.com) is a massive hotel owned by the same people behind Arusha's Impala and Naura Springs hotels. Located just off Moshi Rd on the way to Arusha National Park, the rooms and chalets at this lodge are en suite and come with TV and mini-bar; some even have their own Jacuzzi. With two restaurants, coffee shop, tennis and badminton courts, swimming pool, health club and even its own golf course, this is just about as good as it gets facility-wise – though it must be said that it's not so much a lodge as a full-on hotel. Probably geared more towards the business client than the tourist, to be fair they've kept their rates the same for a few years now at s/c sgl/dbl US$110/150 rising to US$1200 for the presidential villa.

KIA Lodge (☎ 027-250 6315; ☐ kialodge.com) is another link in the Moivaro chain and is recommended by more than one reader as a great place to spend one's last night in Africa before flying out from neighbouring Kilimanjaro International Airport (to and from which it offers free shuttles). It's decorated in a smorgasbord of Tanzanian styles, too, from the Zanzibar-style reception, the Tinga-Tinga paintings in the restaurant and the Makonde woodcarvings in the rooms. Their hilltop location also allows you unequalled views of both Kili and Meru, as well as distant glimpses of the Pare Mountains and Maasai plains. Lovely. Rates are the same as Moivaro Coffee Plantation's at s/c sgl/dbl/tpl US$160-228/200-317/260-428 for B&B.

It should be noted that Planet Lodge are in the process of building a second hotel on the way to the airport. Even if you're not staying here overnight the idea is that you can shower and relax here for US$10. Contact *Planet Lodge* (see p227 for details) for more information – it'll probably be the cheapest accommodation near the airport.

❏ Abbreviations
Throughout this book we have used the following abbreviations when writing about accommodation: **pp** means per person; **s/c** is short for self-contained, a local term meaning that the room comes with a bathroom (ie the room is en suite or a bathroom is attached); while **sgl/dbl/tpl** means single/double/triple rooms. So, for example, where we have written 's/c sgl/dbl/tpl US$35/40/45', we mean that a self-contained single room costs US$35 per night, a self-contained double costs US$40 and a self-contained triple costs US$45.

(*continued from p221*)   Further east, on Simeon Rd, the Ethiopian *Spices & Herbs* (☎ 0754-313162, ☎ 0754-818533; ☐ axum_spices@hotmail.com) is better, with 20 en-suite rooms built around a central courtyard at the back of their premises. The rooms are simple but clean and airy, with box nets, *some* have TV, and rates are sgl/dbl US$45/55 including breakfast.

Moving south-east of the Clock Tower, *Lush Garden Business Hotel* (☎ 0715-801140, ☐ lushgardenhotels.com) is very smart, swish and hi-tech, with 24 self-contained rooms and an impressive array of facilities including satellite TV, air-con and even slippers. Amazingly, it's also very reasonably priced at sgl/dbl US$55/65-75. True, you probably weren't dreaming of staying somewhere quite so 'untraditional' when you booked your accommodation in Arusha – but if you can get over that, this is a lovely, comfortable hotel.

Upper-range: US$75-150 for a double

With many similarities to L'Oasis, including a location in the dusty suburbs north of town and a layout consisting of brick and thatch rondavels built round a pool, *Ilboru Lodge* (☎ 0754-270357; ☐ ilborusafarilodge.com; off map to the north-west) is nevertheless a superb option. The whole lodge feels more spacious, its rooms bigger, brighter and smarter, and its grounds well maintained by the Dutch owner and his smiling staff. The pool is very large, there is wi-fi in the grounds and reception, while the upstairs restaurant has a large menu. They also offer massage sessions, Swahili cookery and Tinga-Tinga painting lessons. All in all, very impressive, though you do pay for the privilege (sgl/dbl/tpl US$73.50-109.50/103-146/147-195 depending on season).

The *Venus Premier Hotel* (☎ 027-254 7174, ☐ venushotels.co.tz) is a shiny new high-rise that has recently opened in the most unlikely of locations for a semi-luxury hotel, in the grid of narrow shopping streets to the west of the market. Rooms are very comfortable and it's great looking over the sweaty hubbub below from your air-conditioned room with flat-screen TV. Rates start at US$79/99 for sgl/dbl. We like it.

Standing both literally and metaphori-cally in the shadow of the huge Palace Hotel Arusha right in the centre of town, just up from the Clock Tower, *The New Safari Hotel* (☎ 027-254 5940/1, ☐ newsa-farihotel.com; s/c sgl/dbl/tpl/suites US$100/125/180/200-220) was once the pre-eminent place in this part of town, though now it squats sulking and skulking in the lee of its new neighbour. There are stories that Hemingway stayed here, though I doubt he'd do so these days as it's now owned by the Lutheran Church and there's no alcohol to be seen anywhere. To be fair, the comparisons with its neighbour are a tad unfair, for it remains a decent hotel, with the gleaming, polished nature of the lobby mirrored by the spotless en suite rooms with TV, wi-fi and mini-bar. Incidentally, the baby elephant that ran amok in the Clock Tower Supermarket (see p220) also careered through the lobby here during its rampage, with John Wayne still in bow-legged pursuit.

Across the road from – and sister to – the New Safari, hidden away behind the old phone office is the *Hotel Equator* (☎ 027-250 8409; ☐ equator-hotel.com). With every room fitted out with a shower, private balcony, satellite TV, wi-fi, phone and fan, this hotel must also have been hit rather hard by the arrival of the gleaming Palace Hotel Arusha, nearby – which makes it such a pleasant surprise whenever we visit to find no visible signs of decline whatso-ever. The price is fair too, at s/c sgl/dbl/tpl US$65/85/100 including buffet breakfast.

Moving onto Nyerere Road and the roads that run off it, the great lump of gleaming blue glass and concrete down Engira Rd (the road that runs down the side of Kibo Palace) is *Arusha Corridor Springs Hotel* (☎ 027-254 5074; ☐ corri-dorspringshotel.com) housing 96 beds in self-contained rooms, air-con, TV, wi-fi and all the other essentials of a luxury hotel. It's actually fairly well priced at just US$90/110 for sgl/dbl, with twins for US$140, and all for B&B. Alas, it can be deathly quiet here, and the staff don't do much to cheer the place up.

Further east, *The Outpost* (☎ 027-254 8405; ☐ outpost-lodge.com; off map to the south-east) lies down Serengeti Rd to the

south of Nyerere Rd, a lane so exclusive that Arusha's usual noise of traffic and touts is replaced by the soothing sound of birdsong and the gentle rhythm of people brushing the dust from the street. Popular with tour groups, The Outpost has its own wi-fi and laundry service and a lovely lounge area kitted out, as with the rooms, in a spartan but relaxed, comfy style. The rooms have TV, are all en suite and there's a small pool and attractive bar/restaurant area. B&B here costs US$65/85/102 s/c sgl/db/tpl; pretty good value and a reliably nice hotel.

Another hotel that's undergone a bit of a rebrand recently, *The Eight* (☎ 0758 777 333, 🖳 info@theeight.co.tz), was once known as the Bay Leaf. It's pleasing to see that the highest standards of the former are still being observed at the latter, with each blade of grass on the lawn individually measured and manicured so it is no bigger or smaller than its neighbours – or at least that's how it looks. This lovely boutique style B&B had only opened for a couple of months when we dropped by but already seems to have found its niche, its five rooms all boasting a supremely, sumptuously comfortable feel. Such luxury comes at a price, however, and at The Eight that price is sgl/dbl US$120-150 for B&B.

Continuing east along Nyerere to the Impala Roundabout, one can only guess at the number of forest creatures that were made homeless in order to furnish *Impala Hotel* (☎ 027-254 3082, 🖳 impalahotel .com) with its wood-heavy reception. It's one of the main business centres in Arusha, with all the trimmings one would expect – a plethora of bars and restaurants (Indian, Chinese, Italian), a pool and conference facilities, and the rooms, all en suite, come equipped with colour television and hot water. Strangely they are all actually quite reasonably priced at s/c sgl/dbl/tpl US$100/130/155 with breakfast, suites US$230.

Still further east, *Karama Lodge* (☎ 0754-475188, 🖳 karama-lodge.com) lies 3km south-east of town along Old Moshi Rd/Nelson Mandela Rd. An unusual lodge, the Karama is tucked quietly on a hillside facing away from Arusha; it boasts 22 stylish en suite rooms housed in log cabins on stilts, with views of Meru from many. A

sauna, pool, massage and yoga room complete the facilities. Rates start as low as sgl/dbl/tpl US$80/124/160 in low season, rising to US$111/149/215 in the high season. There's been a bit of concern about the change in management and the subsequent drop in standards that is supposed to have happened because of it, though when we called round (and had a group staying there) we could see no evidence of this. But perhaps check online first before booking to see what the latest reviews say.

A couple of kilometres further along Old Moshi Rd/Nelson Mandela Rd is *Planet Lodge* (☎ 0686-141670, 🖳 planet-lodge.com) which is maturing nicely. Readers tend to rave about this place. We still think the concrete 'bandas' look a little plain but that's more than offset both by the comfort of the large en-suite rooms themselves, which each have air-con, television, phone, the hottest showers in town (which are just lovely after a Kili trek) as well as the lovely grounds in which they sit. The service, too, is faultless. There's a pool as well. Rates: sgl/dbl/tpl US$68-106/94-138/132-180 depending on season.

Expensive: US$150 and above for a double

Naura Springs Hotel (☎ 027-205 0001, 🖳 naurasspringshotel.com; rates sgl/dbl US$120-170/160-210, rising to US$1200 for the Presidential Suite) is a soaring, shiny blue-glass landmark north of the AICC. It's not a bad option – a bit dazzling, but the open-air reception is a nice touch and the rooms have all the features you'd expect of a hotel this size (internet access, satellite TV, safes, bathrooms with jacuzzis); but there are others that have sprung up since its opening about five years ago that are even bigger and shinier. One of these stands just a few hundred metres to the south. There are few more potent symbols of the upturns in Arusha's fortunes – and the massive investment pouring in from China – than that bloody great erection known as the *Palace Hotel Arusha* (☎ 027-554 5800, 🖳 palacehotelarusha.com), a giant glass-and-steel monolith that reaches skywards, dazzling in the African sunlight. I hardly need tell you that the rooms within are all self-

contained and have every sort of modern convenience, from wi-fi to air-con, satellite TV and safe deposit box. Price-wise it's not as eye-watering as one might expect, with sgl/dbl US$145-250/155-260 per room, rising to US$400/420 for the suites.

Perhaps the largest hotel in this category is *Mount Meru Hotel* (☎ 027-297 0256, 🖳 mountmeruhotel.com; off map to the north-east), once upon a time the Holiday Inn though now fully renovated, restored and reopened by the president of Tanzania after years of being mothballed. It's a bit impersonal, as you may expect from a building this size (it has 178 rooms), but it's extremely well maintained, everything is manicured to within an inch of its life and the rooms are supremely comfy and feature all the usual facilities including air-con, wi-fi, satellite TV, mini-bar and so on. Rates start at sgl/dbl US$195/235 and go up to US$560/600 for the Presidential Suite.

No review of Arusha's hotels would be complete without mention of the oldest of the lot, *The Arusha Hotel* (☎ 027-250 7777; 🖳 fourpointsthearushahotel.com) which is actually fairly anonymous despite its location in the very heart of the action by the Clock Tower. Formerly known as the New Arusha, the name change was only sensible considering it opened in 1894 (though the current building dates 'only' from 1927). That said, having been taken over by the Sheraton the hotel now looks like it's being rechristened again, this time to the (rather ridiculous) *Four Points By Sheraton Arusha, The Arusha Hotel*. Assuming that nobody not on Sheraton's payroll will actually call it that, however, we imagine it will still be referred to as simply *The Arusha Hotel*. Despite all the changes, it remains amongst the swishest and plushest of all the town-centre hotels, and there is still the vague whiff of colonial charm. The restaurant is, of course, very good, the swimming pool heated and the rooms sumptuous and kitted out with television, wi-fi and, of course, a bathroom. Surprisingly, this luxury isn't jaw-droppingly expensive, with rooms costing as little as US$100 per night; whether it remains such good value in the long term, however, only time will tell.

Because of these renovations, many people are now migrating a few hundred metres east along Nyerere Rd to *Kibo Palace Hotel* (☎ 027-254 4472; 🖳 kibopalacehotel.com), with rooms from sgl/dbl US$200/230 rising to US$480/520 for the suites. With every room en suite and boasting wi-fi, a TV, telephone and safe, this is a great addition to the hotel scene in Arusha, particularly as the service is consistently praised by guests. There's even a small gym and pool for that last-minute Kili workout. A few metres further along Nyerere Rd, *Gold Crest Hotel* (☎ 027-254 5300; rooms from sgl/dbl US$120/150) is quite a new construction but one that's already undergone a name change (it was formerly called the East Africa Hotel). At the moment it seems to survive largely on the patronage of East African businessmen, despite similar facilities to Kibo Palace.

Still further east, *The African Tulip* (☎ 027-254 3004; 🖳 theafricantulip.com) is yet another fine establishment in this neck of the forest. Named after the bright orange flowers that grow on the trees along this lane, the Tulip is owned by Roy Safaris (see p95). The rooms are huge and kitted out with every possible modern convenience including flat-screen TVs, remote-controlled air-con, phone and the fastest wi-fi in Arusha. Aside from all this high-tech gadgetry, it's worth mentioning that it's also a very comfortable hotel in a shiny, glamorous sort of way, and the buffet breakfast spread is the largest in the city, with both Marmite and Vegemite available! Rates are sgl/dbl US$190/250, rising to US$550 for the two-bedroom suites.

WHERE TO EAT AND DRINK
[see map pp214-15]

Arusha is a good place for foodies, with African, Oriental and Indian eateries abounding. Some also advertise 'Continental food', which basically means any dish that doesn't fit into one of the categories above.

Cafés and breakfast spots

Note that pretty much all of the eateries listed in this section also serve lunch and dinner, and pretty good at it they are too. But

they have been listed in this category because they advertise themselves as coffee houses and it is coffee for which they are primarily known. Do peruse the menus, however, or you'll be missing out on some real treats. Amongst our favourite cafés is *Fifi's* (Mon-Fri 7.30am-9pm, Sat & Sun 8.30am-9pm) on Themi Rd, just off Sokoine. They serve some of the best food in the city centre and the drinks list includes a huge coffee, milkshake and smoothie selection while for food the menu offers Western favourites (sandwiches, burgers and salads etc) as well as some decent mains (Ts12,500-16,500, though the rump steak and chips is Ts21,500), all well prepared and served with a smile. It also boasts **raha wi-fi**, which was pretty much the fastest and most reliable internet service in the city at the time of writing.

On Boma Rd by the tourist office, *Africafé* (Mon-Sat 7.30am-9pm, Sun 8am-9pm) is a comfy coffee house catering to crowds of caffeine-crazy consumers. The coffee menu is indeed lengthy but what makes this place well worth a visit is once again the food, with great platefuls of some very tasty – though expensive – grub; best value, we think, is the country-friend steak and (two) eggs with toast and fries for Ts14,500, though their Spanish omelette with masala potatoes and toast at Ts9500 is not totally unfair either. Be warned, however, that when they say 'large coffee' on the menu, they mean it; my latte came in a beer mug! So if you fancy spending an afternoon downing a pint of coffee from a vessel so huge that, when you eventually manage to heave it to your lips, it makes you feel like you have a really tiny face, then this is the café for you.

If the prices there are making your eyes water, there's a new café opened to the west of the Clock Tower on Goliondoi. *Kitamu Coffee* (daily 7am-10pm) is a friendly little diner with a decent line-up of coffees (some of it in cloth bags for sale) and a great selection of cakes and African dishes (Ts5000-11,000 for mains) all made on the premises. Try the *kuku makange*, for instance – chicken chunks, mixed veg with a touch of lemon and pili-pili sauce (Ts11,000).

The *Barrista* (Mon-Sat 7am-6.30pm, Sun to 3pm), was, in its former guise as *The Patisserie*, once the main internet café in town and, once upon a time, travellers would turn up by the overland truck-load for the chance to reconnect with folks back home. Alas, nowadays of course every shop, pub and eatery has wi-fi, which is probably why currently it feels like a café in search of both a USP and customers. Food-wise they've pretty much covered the globe, with Chinese, Indian, Mexican and Italian all featuring on the menu but even that hasn't attracted the masses back and, when we dropped in, the place was deserted save for a dozing kitten – and even he got up and stalked out without paying. We've always had a soft spot for Barrista but the bottom line is that there are now other places that do the same stuff, only better. Furthermore, though we can understand the reasons behind it, charging people for wi-fi unless they order lunch or dinner is, in our opinion, a wrong turn.

Finally, in the TFA Complex, of the two cafés standing opposite each other across the parking lot we prefer *Msumbi Coffees* (daily 7.30am-8pm, Sun 8am-4pm) to *Stiggbucks* (Mon-Sat 9am-5pm), with the former boast-

---

❏ **The top six places to celebrate a climb in Arusha**
In no particular order:
● **Spices & Herbs** (p232) Classy Ethiopian food, good for sharing.
● **Onsea** (p233) Posh nosh for the smarter summiteer.
● **Via Via** (p232 & 233) For those wanting a party afterwards without changing venue.
● **George's Tavern** (p232) New but hugely popular, with an extensive bar and a menu to please everyone.
● **Le Patio** (p232) Good food, extensive drinks menu, pool tables – lots of fun.
● **Chinese Dragon** (p232) Large venue, large menu, large bar and huge food portions.

ing better coffee (just) and more comfy seats. That said, if you want something more substantial than just coffee and cake then the better option is probably Stiggbucks, which boasts super-fast raha wi-fi and a more imaginative menu, with a lengthy selection of filling sandwiches (Ts7000-10,000) and salads (Ts8000-10,000).

Lunches and snacks

As with the category above, the definition here is rather loose: most of the places below also serve dinner; furthermore, most of the eateries in the categories above and below also serve snacks and lunches, of course. Nevertheless, in our experience the following tend to be more popular during the day and for this reason we've put them here.

Starting with the establishments in the **TFA complex**. The first is *Ciao Gelati* (Mon-Sat 8am-6.30pm, Sun 10am-5.30pm), ostensibly an ice-cream parlour (Ts4000 per scoop) but one that also serves some of the biggest and tastiest salads in Arusha. The best burger we found in the city was actually at *Alpha Burger* (Mon 10am-2pm, Tues-Sun 10am-11pm) at TFA Complex. The place looks unpromising, with few clients and an expression on the waitress that could curdle milk. But the food came fast, was bloomin' delicious and reasonable value too with burgers Ts8000-12,000, and it's just an extra Ts3000 for chips and a soda.

Moving east on Sokoine Rd, *McMoody's* (daily 10.30am-9.30pm) has opened again after a lengthy hiatus. Though from the exterior it looks like a burger bar, the menu is actually one of those 'please-everyone' lists with pizzas, Chinese and Indian dishes also cropping up. It's OK but I am not sure quite how they managed to earn the large Tripadvisor banner they put in their window – my burger being both a little dry and rather tasteless. Still, it gets a fair share of custom so they must be doing something right.

Still further east, *Dolly's* (Mon-Sat 7am-7pm, Sun 10am-2.30pm) is a curious place, ostensibly a patisserie though with a few Indian dishes Ts7500-11,000), a couple of pizzas (around Ts5000) and a few burgers (Ts5500-7000) on offer too. It does all

seem a little half-hearted but they've been going forever, the place is always spotlessly clean and the chocolate croissants are great (Ts2500).

A little way along the street, *Green Hut House of Burgers* is a bit of a misnomer, for burgers feature but seldom on the menu. This is a great little place for lunchtimes, however, with cheap, simple but filling local fare the order of the day including *maandazi* (a sort of fried bread; Ts500), *mishkaki* (meat – usually lamb/goat – skewers; Ts1800), *kitumbua* (a sort of rice cake or pattie; Ts600) and several dishes featuring that tasteless Tanzanian staple, *ugali* (a stodgy cornmeal or cassava mush). Note that both locals and tourists have found out about this place so you may find yourself sharing a table with strangers – come before 12.30pm if you'd rather not. Note, too, that this place is shut in the evenings.

Opposite the tourist office, *Bamboo by Fifi's* (daily 11.30am–10pm) was once quite a lovely little place with reasonable prices, eccentric decor and good food. The take-over and makeover has, we think, done it no favours, sucking both the charm (and, it seems, much of the custom) completely out of the place. Still, you can't fault the food, though the prices can make you wince (with mains from Ts20,000).

Moving across the Themi River, there's a new place opened up behind the church on Nyerere which we've become very fond of. Quiet and peaceful, but still just a couple of minutes from the action, *The Mulberry Tree* (Mon-Wed 8.30am-9pm, Thu-Sat to 11pm, Sun 11am-7pm) boasts a great selection of *mezze*, ie tapas-style snack food, all around the Ts2000-5000 range, including salt-and-pepper squid, chicken satay and chicken wings, mini-fried rice bowl, fish cakes etc. More conventional lunch items are available too including burgers and wraps, sandwiches and salads (Ts7000-9000), all of which can be washed down with one or two items from their extensive cocktail list. Across Nyerere road, *Themi Living Garden* (12.30-2.30pm) is a lovely lunchtime-only organic vegetarian eatery that's part of an important social project that aims to empower Tanzanian women through busi-

ness and social inclusion. It also clearly aims to provide a healthy alternative to much of the restaurant fare on offer in Arusha! If that's not reason enough to visit then the food is both delicious and cheap (Ts10,000 should easily cover it) and the setting, by a part of the river that's been cleaned up and given over to growing many of the restaurant's ingredients, is lovely; highly recommended!

Blue Heron (Mon-Thurs 10am-5pm, Fri & Sat 10am-10pm) occupies, in our opinion, the best grounds in Arusha, a sweet 1950s house set in the middle of some lovely manicured gardens, complete with fountains and some gorgeous mature trees between which pretty yellow birds flit. This place is also notable for its fine souvenir emporium as well as some of the comfiest sofas in East Africa. As such, it's a great place to come and write postcards, send emails (they have wi-fi) or, given how long the food takes, write your first novella. The food's great and occasionally delightfully hearty, with pizzas from Ts12,500 and more interesting items such as red snapper fillet (Ts25,000) and cream of salmon spaghetti (Ts32,000) also available.

Also in this corner of Arusha, this time over on Simeon Rd, there's ***Picasso Café*** (Mon-Sat 9am-11pm, Sun 9am-5pm), yet another smart café and one with a good pizza/burger menu. Relaxed and unpretentious, we like it here.

Dinner
This isn't a comprehensive guide to dining in Arusha but it does include most of the most popular eateries – at least amongst tourists – in the city.

Asian food, local barbecues... and an Ethiopian
Travellers staying in one of the cheap hostels at the western end of Sokoine (ie the Arusha Backpackers or Meru House Inn) are ill-served by restaurants nearby now that Meru House's Noble Juice Parlour has closed. Indeed, the nearest choice is probably the ***Shanghai Chinese*** (daily 11.30am-3pm, 6-10.30pm), though at least it's a good option. Huge platefuls of food accompanied by a year's harvest of rice is always popular with

trekkers looking to replace the weight they lost on Kili. With mains Ts11,000 up to around Ts17,500 it won't break the bank either – though perhaps ask them go a little easy on the Soy sauce as some dishes can be a bit too salty.

There are several hangouts specialising in Tanzania's hearty, cheap and simple brand of spicy local and Indian cuisine, of which ***Khan's*** stands out as a favourite with locals and ex-pats alike. Operating for well over 25 years, Khan's is a garage by day but at around 5pm transforms itself into a barbecue to serve up their take on the chicken-in-a-basket theme, namely 'chicken-on-a-bonnet' (Ts15,000, or Ts7500 for a small plate). They also do lamb or beef mince kebabs (Ts8000), with chips Ts2500 or Ts5000, naan bread Ts1500, and a serve-yourself table full of salads and spicy sauces all included. It's just to the north of the Central Market on Mosque St; be careful around here after dark – take a cab.

East of Themi River, on or near Nyerere Rd and its continuation, Old Moshi Rd (now renamed Nelson Mandela Rd after the college that's been built further along it out of town), there are several large-scale restaurants that are possibilities as venues for that post-Kili celebration (or commiseration) meal. The newest and perhaps biggest of the lot is the ***Asili Resort*** (☎ 0766 684126, ☎ 0784 199890; daily 8am-11pm), a colourfully painted place with a couple of bars, wi-fi, sport on the telly and a huge range of alcohol of every shade and strength. Food-wise they're probably most famous for their barbecues (where the meat comes with a couple of plantains and you buy it by the kilo, with beef Ts12,000, goat Ts16,000 and chicken Ts20,000 per kg). Other dishes are available and are well priced at Ts10,000-12,000.

To the north of Nyerere Rd are several fine places hidden amongst the jacaranda trees. ***Flame Tree*** (☎ 0754-377359; daily 10.30am-10.30pm) on Kenyatta Rd is now under Chinese management, so what was once the smartest and most tasteful restaurant in town is now an enormous Asian restaurant with an equally large menu. Nevertheless, some of the dishes are still very tempting with a Kenyan T-bone steak

(served in a range of sauces) for Ts27,000, fish dishes for Ts18,000-19,000 (including a delicious prawn pili-pili) and some truly indulgent puddings including a Moshi brownie served with chocolate sauce for Ts7000 and chocolate pithivers (warm puff pastry stuffed with chocolates and nuts ands served with a scoop of vanilla ice cream) for the same price. Some may shudder at the loss of refinement, though to be fair it still pays close attention to detail and the food is good.

About 500m further north, by the entrance to the Gymkhana Club, is *Chinese Dragon* (☎ 027-254 4107; Mon-Fri 11.30am-2.30pm & 6-10.30pm, Sat & Sun 11.30am-10.30pm). It is, as you've probably guessed, a Chinese restaurant and is widely regarded as the best one in town, with a large menu of authentic and generous dishes and a healthy list of alcoholic drinks too. With mains generally in the Ts11,000-18,000 range (though anything with lobster in it is more likely to be nearer Ts42,000), and rice extra, don't expect much change from Ts30,000 per person once you've added drinks.

Moving south towards the Impala Hotel, on Simeon Road is another eatery with enormous grounds. *Ambrosia* is a welcome new addition to the restaurant scene, largely because the last few years has seen the demise of several Indian restaurants in town. Ambrosia aims to plug the gap they left and seems to be doing a good job, with an extensive menu of subcontinental fare (Ts15,000-28,000 for mains). Just to make sure they cater for everyone they also serve a few Mexican and European dishes, a Thai red curry (Ts18,000-24,000), a Moroccan tagine (Ts16,500-24,000) and even a Swiss fondue (Ts28,000).

Virtually opposite, for something out of the ordinary a trip to *Spices & Herbs*, the blossom-laden Ethiopian restaurant in the hotel of the same name, could be in order. With vegetarian dishes for Ts13,500-15,500 as well as meat dishes (around the Ts18,500 mark), this place has been garnering praise from hungry travellers for years. Try the *yebeg tibs* – lamb cooked in Ethiopian butter with onions, green peppers and rosemary (Ts18,500) – and you'll see why.

Western food

With branches in Honduras, Java and Zanzibar, *Via Via* is a chain of 14 travellers' cafés which is renowned for the good work it does in introducing travellers to the local culture. Situated by the old German Boma, it offers live local music every Thursday (see p233), movie night on Tuesday and an African buffet on Saturday, as well as an array of daytime activities from drum-making and batik workshops to cookery and Swahili courses (see p213). And if you don't give a cuss about the culture there's always the food, which includes burgers (Ts12,000-15,000), sandwiches (Ts10,000-12,000), pasta and pizzas (Ts10,000-12,000) and a few steak, chicken and fish dishes (Ts12,000-16,000).

Further east on Haile Selassie Rd, and relatively new on the scene, *George's Tavern* (☎ 0782 943690) is located on a lovely shaded patch of ground and has making quite a name for itself. It is certainly a great place for a post-trek feed-up with a large and lovely **Greek menu** (George himself is Cypriot) including meat and fish mezze (three-course set menus for Ts45,000 and Ts54,000 respectively), an entire page of vegetarian main courses, which is very good to see, and wood-fired oven pizzas from Ts14,000 up to Ts37,000 for the Vittorio triple decker, which seems to have everything they could find in the kitchen thrown on top of it including chicken, prawns and cheese. It ain't cheap but how many other chances are you going to get to celebrate climbing Africa's highest mountain!

Moving down the hill, virtually opposite the Blue Heron on Haile Selassie Rd, *Le Patio* (☎ 0759 222555) is a large place divided into two, with one side converted into an open-sided lounge and bar area (with pool table), while the other side is the restaurant where they serve some fairly simple but intriguing mains from the refreshingly small menu, including grilled king fish (Ts18,000), beef *mishkaki* (Ts18,500) and pizzas (Ts13,500-20,000).

Still further down the hill and onto the main road, *Kilimanjaro Spur Steakhouse* is a vast, garish place near the Impala Roundabout at the eastern end of Nyerere, though in atmosphere and decor its spiritu-

al home would be, we feel, the Njiro Mall. Part of a chain, this meat house ain't cheap, with burgers from Ts12,000 for a simple veggie-burger up to a wallet-exploding Ts38,500 for a cheese, bacon and guacamole multi-stacked number; their steaks, too, range from Ts25,000 up to Ts57,000 for the T-bone. What's more, the cheeseburger (Ts18,000) we had was only so-so. Indeed, we wouldn't recommend this place at all if it wasn't for the fact that they show sport on their many televisions, have fast (raha) wi-fi, and also boast a large play area of slides and climbing frames and thus is good for those who brought a small child with them. Not exactly the most charming of places, then, and not somewhere to come for a romantic tête-à-tête – but presumably if you've got a child then those days are behind you anyway.

Finally, the best food in town (or, rather, just outside it) is at *Onsea*, where the chef used to work in Michelin-starred restaurants in London. It's food with finesse – they describe it as Belgian and French brasserie-style with an African touch – and usually exquisite, with the menu changing daily. Count on spending about US$70 per head for three courses plus wine.

NIGHTLIFE

Arusha is the **nightclub** and **live music** capital of northern Tanzania, attracting rastas and ravers from far and wide. Unfortunately, as with any large city, the scene changes rapidly and what's recommended here may well be out of date by the time you arrive.

One place that's almost certain to remain, however, is *Triple A* (just northwest off the map on p214), a radio station and also one of Arusha's most popular nightspots. Open Fridays and Saturdays (Ts10,000), the action begins at about 8pm and carries on 'til dawn.

Way out east of town is *World International Garden* (🖥 worldgarden tz.com), a new place that is actually quite family orientated – they've even got a playground and fairground rides outside for the little'uns. But the centrepiece of the complex is the nightclub itself, *Club D*. 'Classy,

clean and loud' is how they describe a night there on their website and, while I am not too sure I would agree with two thirds of that, there's no doubt they've thrown a lot of money at the place. Attracting more tourists than either of these, *Via Via* have live performances on a Thursday evening (Ts5000, or Ts10,000 after 10pm); visit them during the day to find out what they've got lined up. *Empire Sports Bar,* at the TFA Complex, takes over on a Friday, while their karaoke night is on Wednesdays. If you'd rather just drink with the locals, two places seem particularly popular at the moment: *Pin Point Bar* in Plaza Le Manyatta, north of the bus station, is lively (sometimes intimidatingly so); and there's *Babylon Club* by Green Hut House of Burgers, on Sokoine, which is equally vibrant.

The mall out at **Njiro** hosts the city's best **cinema**. The Institut Français (🖥 www.aftarusha.org) offers free French films every Wednesday evening, while *Via Via* (see p232) have a film and karaoke night on Tuesdays, with participants in the latter being given a free shot of tequila.

For a game of **pool**, the *Empire*, *Le Patio* and *Flame Tree* all have tables.

Finally, for those who can't live without their weekly dose of English Premier League football, *Kilimanjaro Spur*, *Picasso Café*, *City Park*, *Asili Resort* and *Empire Sports Bar* in the TFA Complex show most games.

MOVING ON
By bus or shuttle

To Moshi Those heading towards Kili will find the **local 'Coaster' buses** are the most convenient way to travel the 81km to Moshi. They run throughout the day from the main bus station, with the last one around 5pm (Ts2500-3000). Always an intimidating place to go, negotiating the bus station is actually fairly straightforward and there'll usually be a tout on hand to point you to the right bus as soon as they see you. Once you're aboard sellers will come to your window with sunglasses and sunhats, papers and perfumes, cake and Coke; everything, in fact, to keep you cool, comfortable, fed and fragrant for the journey. True, using a Coaster bus is not a particularly pleasant

❏ **Dangers and annoyances in Arusha**

Unfortunately, the ban on **flycatchers** (ie safari touts) that was issued a few years ago no longer seems to be holding, and tourists are once again subjected to a lot of hassle from those working for the safari companies, as well from the souvenir-, newspaper- and dope-sellers hawking their wares, which can make a visit to Arusha a pretty excruciating affair. They have a job to do and a need to earn money like the rest of us, but there's no doubting how tiring it can be dealing with them on such a frequent basis. Be polite but firm, don't stop walking and they soon get the message. Hopefully, in time the city will once again realise that, despite all the Chinese money coming in, tourism remains the bedrock on which this town is built and the ban will be reinstated.

Pickpocketing is rare but does happen, particularly in those busy places such as the bus station and central market. Keep any valuables out of sight and safely tucked away, preferably in the safe back at the hotel. If you have to bring them with you then use a money-belt and keep a close eye on everything. This is particularly true if someone does something unusual – tugs at your arm or even spits at you – as this maybe a distraction technique while his partner steals from you.

As for potential dangers, well **it's always hazardous stepping out in Arusha after dark**. Between 7-9pm, while the streets are still fairly busy, you should be OK, as long as you stick to the main streets where people are still milling about – and assuming those streets are well lit. But don't even think about going out after dusk east of the Themi River (ie east of the Arusha Hotel). Dark, quiet, and full of hotels where Westerners are staying, if I was a mugger this is where I would hang out. To be safe, the golden rule you should follow is that once the sun disappears, take a cab. The extra expense is something you'll quickly forget; get attacked, however, and that is something that could stay with you forever.

way to travel but other options are thin on the ground, with Moshi ill-served by the **shuttle bus** companies. **Riverside** (☎ 027-254 5993 or ☎ 027-254 6088; 🖳 riverside-shuttle.com), with its office in a chemist on Sokoine Rd, have one bus per day at 2pm (US$10), as do **Rainbow Shuttle** (☎ 0754 204025 or ☎ 0753 648895), in the back of New Safari Hotel. The services for both these companies depart from the parking lot up from Impala Hotel on Simeon Rd, though if you book in advance you might get picked up from your hotel – depending on the state of the traffic. The car park at Impala Hotel is home to **Impala Shuttle** (☎ 0784-550012 or ☎ 0754 678678). They, too, operate a daily bus to Moshi (US$10) that calls in at Arusha at around 2pm on its way from Nairobi to Moshi.

Note that, at the time of writing, the new upgraded road to Voi was in the process of being built. If there are still road-works by the time you visit, it will add about 20 minutes onto any journey heading

east (eg to Moshi, Marangu and Dar). Once the works have finished, however, expect journey times to decrease considerably.

To Nairobi and Kampala Of the **bus** companies, **Dar Express** (3pm; Ts25,000), in offices on Wachagga Rd, offer a good and safe service to Nairobi. **Panther Travels**, who have their offices on the Nairobi-Moshi Road, east of Colonel Middleton Rd, also head to Nairobi and continue onto Kampala (daily, 2pm, Ts65,000 to Kampala).

As for the **shuttles**, **Riverside** run two daily to Nairobi, at 8am (arrive 2-3pm) and 2pm (it's the one from Moshi and is supposed to arrive in Nairobi at 7pm). They charge US$25 for foreign tourists. **Rainbow Shuttle** and **Impala** (see above) operate identical times and prices. As with all shuttles, they *should* pick you up from your hotel. However, thanks to the massive rise in traffic in the city and the consequent jams and delays to any journey, these days

many of the shuttles pick up passengers only if they are staying at hotels near the shuttle bus car park.

To Dar es Salaam There are several companies plying this route, the most experienced and reliable being **Dar Express** (see above; 6/day between 5.50am and 8.30am; Ts30,000, though the 6.30am and 7.30am 'luxury' buses are Ts33,000) and **Kilimanjaro Express** (7/day; same prices and roughly the same times). 'Luxury' in this case usually just means that there's a toilet on board. Kilimanjaro Express's office is in Kaloleni, while Dar Express are a few hundred metres to the west (a plot they share with several other operators); see map pp214-15.

By air
Arusha effectively has two airports: **Arusha Airport** is only about 20 minutes from the centre of the city and **Kilimanjaro International Airport** (see p210) is less than an hour away. See p218 for details of the airline offices in Arusha and p387 for details of flights.

In our experience the **departure tax** (US$7 for domestic flights, US$40 for international destinations) is always included in the fare nowadays.

Moshi

Cheaper, quieter, nearer and prettier, Moshi sits in the shadow of Kilimanjaro and, for climbing the mountain, is perhaps a superior base to neighbouring Arusha, 81km away to the west. As the unofficial capital of the Chagga world, most visitors find Moshi a little more interesting too. The missionaries who followed in the wake of Rebmann gave the Chaggas the advantage of a Western education and this, combined with the agricultural fecundity of Kilimanjaro's southern slopes, has enabled the Chaggas to become one of the wealthiest, most influential and most securely self-aware groups in the country. Moshi has reaped the benefits too, prospering to the point where it is now one of the smartest towns in Tanzania (though grim poverty is still not difficult to find, as anybody who has walked around Moshi at night, stepping over the sleeping bodies of the dispossessed lying on the pavements as they do so, can testify).

Though the Chaggas are the dominant force in town, Moshi is a cosmopolitan place, with a large expat community (as well as a huge number of short-term teenage volunteers) and a highly visible Indian minority; this colourful ethnic mixture is reflected in the architecture, with a huge Hindu temple abutting an equally striking mosque and with dozens of small churches and chapels scattered in the streets thereabouts. There also seems to be more civic pride in Moshi than in other parts of the country. Indeed, the only dark cloud for tourists here is the inordinate amount of hassle they suffer from trekking agency touts, 'artists' and the like. Look beyond this, however, and you're sure to find Moshi charming, friendly and a lovely place for a stroll. Take an amble any afternoon and you'll pass sewing machinists stitching shirts on sun-baked sidewalks, blade sharpeners spraying sparks from their cycle-powered grinders and smiling schoolkids shouting salutations to the sweaty *mzungu*. It can also boast enough facilities to enable you to organise a trek – and enjoy some long nights of celebration at the end.

ARRIVAL

The (sometimes unreliable) Precision Air shuttle is *usually* there to pick up passengers from **Kilimanjaro Airport** and take take them to Moshi for Ts10,000. Air Tanzania also operate a shuttle (Ts10,000), leaving about three hours before their flights from their office at Kibo Tower. Fastjet run a similar service at the same price for their flights to and from Dar. However, if you arrive on KLM (which has a shuttle to Arusha but not Moshi), Ethiopian, or other internal airlines, you'll have to catch a cab to Moshi (US$50).

Flights to **Moshi Airport** are so seldom that hopefully you'll already have your transport from there sorted; you'll be lucky to find a taxi waiting at the airport. Coastal Air, the main airline serving this airport, have an office in town by the Union Café.

Arrive **by bus** and you'll be dropped off at the terminal on Mawenzi Rd, 200m south of the Clock Tower, within walking distance of most hotels.

ORIENTATION & GETTING AROUND

According to Harry Johnston (see p159), Moshi could simply mean 'town' or 'settlement', though as with everything Johnston wrote, this could well be wrong. Indeed, Moshi also translates as 'smoke' – a reference, perhaps, to its situation at the foot of a volcano? What is certain is that Moshi is compact but expanding fast, and where once upon a time almost everything of interest to the holidaying visitor lay on or near the main thoroughfare, **Mawenzi Rd** (aka Nyerere Rd, which is also more commonly known as Double Rd), these days there's no real focal point to the town and the best restaurants, hotels and other tourist amenities are scattered around all four corners of Moshi. However, it still helps to think of Mawenzi Rd, and its northern extension, **Kibo Rd** (the two names borrowed from the two main peaks of Kilimanjaro), as the main spine of the town, for together they run all the way from the market at Moshi's southern end to the roundabout on the main road to Arusha at its northern end adorned with the statue of a soldier facing north towards Kilimanjaro. Separating Mawenzi Rd from Kibo Rd is a second roundabout adorned with a **Clock Tower** (or should that be 'Coke tower', given the soft-drink sponsorship of the roundabout), which if Moshi has to have one is, I suppose, the best candidate for the spiritual centre of town. There is a second road running parallel to Double Rd, officially christened **Market St** though known by most people as Single Rd, which terminates at the Clock Tower.

To the north lies the suburb of **Shanty Town** (see map p248), home to some great restaurants, a few fine hotels and some massive houses.

Dalla-dallas drive up and down the main Mawenzi and Market streets for Ts300, though it doesn't take long to walk anywhere. The one exception to this rule is Shanty Town: a **taxi** to KCMC (the hospital on the far edge of Shanty Town) will cost Ts6000 from the town centre; **motorbikes** (also called boda boda, Toyo or piki piki) cost around Ts2000 and rickshaws (Bajaj) – which are very popular here – T2500.

SERVICES
Banks

The banks don't change money. In their place, **moneychangers** such as the wonderfully named God Hates Corruption – Join Him Executive Bureau de Change, which is in Voda House, stay open later, their rates are fine and they don't charge commission. The moneychanger with the best rates is currently Trust (spelt 'Trast' on the sign), which also happens to be the most convenient for most of the tourist-friendly hotels.

❏ **New bus station**

A new bus terminal is in the pipeline. The old one in the heart of town is due to close, with all inter-city buses using a new terminal north of the main Arusha/ Marangu Road, just east of the Kilimanjaro Grand Hostel. The tarmac has been laid on the approach roads so this is one scheme that may actually get off the ground. Kilimanjaro Grand will be one of the bigger beneficiaries, as it will be the nearest hostel to the bus station.

There are **ATMs** everywhere including, conveniently, one at Barclays that's on the main drag near most of the budget hotels, and another one block west next to Moshi Leopard Hotel. The only two ATMs we've found that don't charge commission in Moshi are Stanbic, on Boma Road, and, very nearby, the KCB.

Communications
The **post office** (Mon-Fri 8am-4.30pm, Sat 9am-noon) is by the Clock Tower at the junction with Boma Rd. There's also a DHL office (Mon-Fri 8am-5pm, Sat 9am-noon) down near the Clock Tower. **Wi-fi** is commonplace in Moshi with even some of the cheapest hotels offering it as well as many cafés, restaurants and bars. If you need a terminal, **internet** places aren't too hard to find. The internet service at Easycom, in the basement of Kahawa House by the Clock Tower, has long been highly regarded (Ts1000 per hour), though Buffalo Hotel's internet centre is probably more convenient for most people and has longer opening hours – 8am-10pm – and a pretty fast connection too.

Airline offices
Precision Air (☎ 07846 86418, 🖥 precisionairtz.com; Mon-Fri 8am-5pm, Sat, Sun & hols 9am-1pm) are in KNCU Building. **Fastjet** (☎ 0652 938611; Mon-Sat 8am-5pm, Sun to 4pm) are in the Kili Crane Hotel and **Coastal** (☎ 0785 500729l; Mon-Sat 8am-5pm), which uses Moshi Airport, have a small office tucked alongside the Union Café. **Air Tanzania** (☎ 0754 829827, 🖥 airtanzania.co.tz; Mon-Fri 8am-5pm, Sat 8-11am) is now in Kibo Tower by Nyumbani Hotel. For other airlines, including KLM and Qatar, visit **Emslies** (☎ 027-275 2701 or ☎ 275 1742; Mon-Fri 8.30am-12.30pm & 2-5pm, Sat 8.30am-noon only) on Old Moshi Rd.

Medical facilities
Jaffery Charitable Medical Services (☎ 027-275 1843; Mon-Fri 8.30am-5pm, Sat to 12.30pm & Sun closed) should be your first port of call if you have anything more than a slightly dickie tummy; they can provide malaria tests and other examinations and treatment. If your illness inconsiderately coincides with a time when it's shut then try **St Joseph Hospital** down in Soweto, or, as a last resort, the **KCMC**, though the bureaucracy required before you even get seen may make you feel even worse than when you entered.

Laundry
Your hotel will probably have some sort of laundry service or you can visit Quick Laundry (Mon-Sat 8am-6pm, Sun 8am-2pm) on School St (it shares the same doorway as Materuni Tours).

Swimming pools
The YMCA, Sal Salinero and Keys Hotel all charge to use their pools (usually around Ts4500-5000); in all of these places hotel guests can use the facilities for free. Officially you need to be a member of Ameg Lodge to use their pool, though this doesn't seem to be rigorously enforced and we've met people who just turn up and pay Ts12,000 per day.

Massage
Lala Salama (which translates as 'Sweet Dreams'; ☎ 0754 030071, 🖥 lalasalamaspa.strikingly.com; Tues-Sun 10am-6pm) are a small, NGO-sponsored spa in the YWCA building on Boma Rd offering a one-hour massage service for Ts45,000 and a foot massage for Ts30,000. Most of the big hotels also offer some sort of massage service.

Shopping
● **Trekking equipment** Finally, Moshi can boast a decent trekking equipment supplier. Indeed, they've now got two! **Gladys Adventure** (Mon-Sat 8am-6pm, Sun 8am-2pm) is run by the enterprising, eponymous Gladys, who started out trading souvenirs from her curio shop in return for hard-to-come-by bits of trekking equipment with tourists coming off the mountain. Having built up an extensive collection over the decade, Gladys has now moved her operation from her former base 5km out of town to Hill St in the heart of Moshi, just down from the Coffee Shop and round the corner from her trekking agency (see p84). Her collection is extensive, her stuff is good

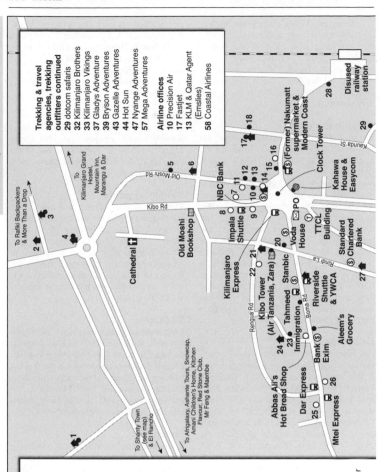

Moshi

Where to stay
1 Hostel Hoff
2 Hub Hill
3 Keys Hotel
4 YMCA
6 Moshi Urban
14 New Coffee Tree Hotel
17 Kilimanjaro Crane Hotel
21 Nyumbani Hotel
24 Nyota B&B
27 Bristol Cottages
30 Parkview Inn
38 Aa Hotel
42 Zebra Hotels
46 Backpackers Paradise
51 Buffalo Hotel
53 Kindoroko Hotel
54 Haria Hotel
56 Moshi Leopard Hotel
57 We Travel Hostel
59 Big Mountain Inn
60 Osy Grand Hotel
61 Panama Hotel
62 Umoja Lutheran Hostel
63 Kilimanjaro Backpackers

Where to eat & drink
7 Black Diamond
8 Story Lounge
9 Pub Alberto & Chrisburger
11 Kilimanjaro Ice Cream Parlour

Trekking & travel agencies, trekking outfitters continued
29 dotcom safaris
32 Kilimanjaro Brothers
33 Kilimanjaro Vikings
37 Gladys Adventure
39 Bryson Adventures
43 Gazelle Adventures
44 Hot Sun
47 Nyange Adventures
57 Mega Adventures

Airline offices
10 Precision Air
17 Fastjet
13 KLM & Qatar Agent (Emslies)
58 Coastal Airlines

Kilimanjaro Grand Hostel, Mountain Inn, Marangu & Dar

To Rafiki Backpackers & More Than a Drop

To Kilimanjaro Grand Hostel, Mountain Inn, Marangu & Dar

Cathedral

To Shanty Town (see map) & El Rancho

To Afrigalaxy, Ashante Tours, Snowcap, Amani Children's Home, Kitchen Flavour, Red Stone Club, Mr Feng & Maembe

Old Moshi Rd

Kibo Rd

NBC Bank

Old Moshi Bookshop

Impala Shuttle

Kilimanjaro Express

Kibo Tower (Air Tanzania, Zara)

Tahmeed

Stanbic

Immigration

Bank (\$) Exim

Aleem's Grocery

Riverside Shuttle & YWCA

Voda House

TTCL Building

Standard Chartered Bank

PO

Kahawa House & Easycom

Clock Tower

(Former) Nakumatt supermarket & Modern Coast

Disused railway station

Rengua Rd

Bonna Rd

Rindi La

Kaunda St

Abbas Ali's Hot Bread Shop

Dar Express

Mtei Express

ARUSHA, MOSHI & MARANGU

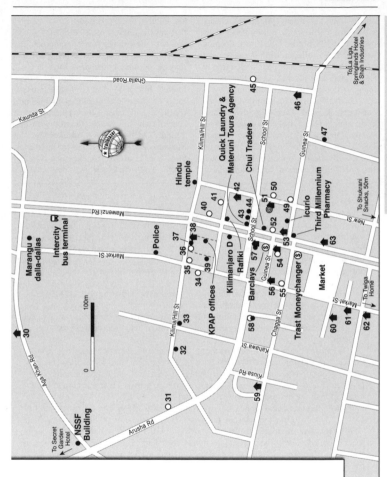

14 New Coffee Tree Café
16 Kilimanjaro Coffee Lounge
    & Restaurant
22 Malindi Club
25 Jay's Kitchen
26 Aroma
31 Mimosa
34 Moeen's
35 Deli Chez
36 Coffee Shop
40 East African Pub
41 Milan's
45 Peppers
49 Pamoja Café
50 Indoitaliano
52 Taj Mahal
54 Haria Hotel
55 Chagga Bar & Grill
58 KNCU/Union Café

Trekking & travel agencies,
trekking outfitters
1 African Scenic Safaris
3 Keys
4 Trans-Kibo Travels
5 Tanzania Joy
12 Kessy Brothers
15 MEM Tours
18 Kili Heroes Adventures
20 African Spoonbill Tours
23 Tin Tin Tours
28 Pristine Trails

quality and her rental prices are cheap: US$10 for a head torch, pillow US$5, thermarests US$25, bottles US$10 and sleeping bags US$25 – all per trip! Perhaps most usefully of all, she also does a nice line in fleeces and base layers – items that can be really difficult to source in Tanzania.

Gladys's success has inspired a second outfitters, **Ascend Tanzania** (daily 7am-6pm; sample prices: trekking poles US$10, sleeping bags US$25, waterproof trousers US$10, all for a 5- to 7-day trip), to open up on New St, nearly opposite Zebra Hotel. Just one word of caution: while these places

are indubitably a godsend, do remember that your agency should be able to supply you with most major bits of equipment that you might have forgotten to bring and they may be included in the price too.

Other items you may well have overlooked but will find extremely useful include: chapsticks (along with mosquito repellent and most other pharmaceutical needs), which can be bought from the **Third Millennium pharmacy** on Mawenzi Rd; and bin liners (or large shopping bags), useful for keeping clothing within your rucksack dry and available

---

❏ Amani Children's Home

Like many children in Tanzania, Peter was driven to the streets because of extreme poverty and neglect. Born to alcoholic parents who struggled to keep a roof over the family's head and food on the table, Peter was malnourished and sick from an early age. Although Peter was nine when he came to Amani, his physical size alone made him look years younger. With the help of Amani's dedicated team, Peter is healthy and growing fast. He is doing well in school and is looking forward to a positive and happy future.

Despite the Chaggas' reputation among Tanzanians for prosperity and power, the region is not immune to the problems afflicting the rest of the country and that includes the malaise of street children. And while the stories of each child are unique, the general themes of neglect, poverty and desperation are a common theme with all of them.

Whatever the reason is for ending up on the streets, the door is always open to them at Amani Children's Home. Founded in 2001 by dedicated Tanzanians, the centre has grown to become the largest in the region, caring for around 80 children at any given time. Most are boys, though around a dozen are girls. Their ages range from 7 to 16, though the majority are between 10 and 14.

Most children come to the centre with the social workers who are employed full time by Amani to meet and rescue children living on the streets. Some are orphans who've lost both their parents, in many cases to AIDS, while others have run away from home because of the physical, mental or sexual abuse they faced there. Once on the streets it's a precarious existence. Boys can try to graft a living by collecting scrap metal, begging or stealing; for girls, a life on the streets is even more dangerous, with many ending up as prostitutes.

Once in the Amani Centre, they are washed, fed and given new clothes. Social workers interview the children to learn about their backgrounds, hear how they ended up on the street and assess what their chances are of potential reunification with immediate family or relatives. Children quickly adapt to the daily routine, making beds and cleaning the dormitory. They have responsibilities such as washing their clothes and, after each meal, their own dishes. After breakfast most attend school either externally or in Amani's on-site primary education programme, which ranges from the Starters class for those who have never been to school or are deemed too old to join the first grade, to Classes A, B and C which are accelerated programs to get children to the educational level they should be attaining at their age. School ends mid-afternoon and then it is free-time for art, games, practising acrobatics, playing

from the market or one of the supermarkets mentioned below.

● **Maps and books** about Kili can be bought from **Old Moshi Bookshop** (Mon-Fri 8.30am-12.30pm, 2-4.30pm, Sat 8.30am-12.30pm) on Rindi Lane at the junction with Kibo Rd, from **Kilimanjaro Market** on the ground floor of Kibo Tower, or, perhaps best of all, from the **souvenir shop** by Marangu Gate.

● **Supermarkets and other possibly useful stores** As we go to press, the useful supermarket Nakumatt, just down from the Clock Tower, has closed down but it may soon be replaced by another supermarket here. Up the hill to the west of the Clock Tower on Boma Rd is **Abbas Ali's Hot Bread Shop** (Mon-Fri 8.30am-7pm, Sat 8.30am-3pm), a very pleasant place with great fresh bread and pastries. Opposite is **Aleem's** (Mon-Fri 8.45am-1pm, 2-5pm, Sat to 4pm only), which seems to have been going forever and has a loyal ex-pat following. A convenience store that truly deserves the description is **Kilimanjaro D**, just up from Barclays, and there are branches of **Rafiki Supermarket** opposite as well as by the Moshi Leopard Hotel.

with a skipping rope etc; but for many children, the highlight of the day is the afternoon football match.

Despite the security and comparative normality provided by the home – at least compared to their life on the streets – the aim is to eventually reunify the children with their parents or extended family, having first evaluated that such a move would be appropriate. Indeed, at Amani they create a place for healing with the Upendo Programme (*upendo* is Swahili for 'love'), where each staff member serves as a 'parent' to several children, supervising them and listening to their problems.

It is both possible and worthwhile to visit the orphanage. One of the most heartwarming aspects of visiting the children is seeing how the older ones look after the newcomers and the more vulnerable. For example, Daudi, an autistic child, is looked after without complaint and treated with both kindness and respect by the other children at the orphanage.

In 2007 Amani made the move from the family house in which it began to a purpose-built centre. At one time in the old house 65 children shared a bedroom but in the new facility each child has his or her own bunk bed. The growth of Amani is due to the dedication of the staff and careful management of funds. As an essentially secular organisation (respecting the children's beliefs and values of Christian and Muslim faiths) the centre is not supported by any one institution or organisation but instead relies on donations – the majority of Amani's support comes from individuals and families who visited the centre or heard about its good work and wanted to help.

Amani welcomes new volunteers and needs those who either have a good working knowledge of Swahili or are willing to learn. Volunteers must be willing to commit to stay for six months or more (by which time Amani reckons your Swahili will be of an acceptable level). But if you can't commit that kind of time, don't despair. The home welcomes foreigners to come and look around the centre and spend some time with the kids. Many tourists find that turning up to join in the afternoon football (soccer) game (daily around 3pm) is a good idea, being an easy way to mix and bond with the kids without the need for a common language.

Whether you want to arrange a visit, make a donation or merely find out about their work, have a look at their website (🖳 amanikids.org) or call them (☎ 0752-220637, or during office hours ☎ 0732-973579).

Trust us, if you've got a day to spare in Moshi, there's no more rewarding a way to spend it.

The **central market** does, of course, also sell food – and you'll probably be eating some of it on your trek. Out in Shanty Town (see map p248), **Woodland Shoppers** is just above 10210 Pizzeria.

● **Souvenir shops** There are plenty of souvenirs to buy in Moshi and many places willing to flog them to you. Two in particular deserve special mention: **Shah Industries** is a leather workshop housed in what used to be a flour mill. It's a strange combination but a beautiful place and a worthy one too: over a third of the workers at Shah Industries have some sort of disability. Definitely worth looking around, it lies to the south-east of town across the train tracks on the way to Springlands Hotel. Up to the west of the Clock Tower, on Boma Road, in the YWCA, is **Moshi Mama's Craft Coop** – again, excellent stuff and a worthy cause behind it.

Of the 'regular' souvenir shops, the best in terms of choice and quality is **iCurio**, just round the corner from Kindoroko Hotel, with the widest array of stock including a fine line in Kilimanjaro Beer T-shirts. Also worth a nose around is **Chui Traders**, near New Castle Hotel on Nyerere Rd, and the large Kilimanjaro Market in Kilimanjaro Tower, which sells pretty much the same stuff you've seen everywhere else, just lots more of it.

WHERE TO STAY   [see map p238]
The following is not an exhaustive list but whilst there are some cheaper places at the southern end of town, many refuse to accept Westerners. Manage to persuade one to let you stay and you can expect to pay around Ts10,000 per night, though the chances are it'll be assumed you want bed and broad rather than bed and board. Those looking to **camp** are advised to head out of town to Weru Weru Lodge (US$15 per night, or US$25 if using their tents; see p247) or Rafiki Backpackers (US$6 per night, or US$5 with your own tent). Or you can go to Marangu, where virtually every hotel allows camping in their grounds.

As with Arusha, you may be able to get a cheaper rate for your hotel by booking online through 🖳 booking.com or 🖳 airbnb .com.

As for hotels that definitely do welcome tourists, they are as follows:

Below US$20 per double
Occupying a shady, peaceful spot along from the old Sikh Club (now Peppers Restaurant), **Backpackers Paradise** (☎ 0759 744974) is satisfactorily tidy and clean and there are self-catering facilities as well as free wi-fi – making this pretty good value at Ts12,000/Ts15,000 in a large/small dorm, or en suite sgl/dbl/tpl for Ts35,000/ 40,000/45,000; breakfast is Ts5000 extra. The only thing missing is an atmosphere, despite the management's best efforts with their brightly painted walls and cheerful staff.

Nearby and a near namesake, **Kilimanjaro Backpackers** (☎ 027-275 5159; 🖳 kilimanjarobackpackers.com; Mawenzi/Double Rd) is a relative of its namesake in Arusha, but while it's around the same price at US$6-8/8-10/18-20/27-30 dorm/sgl/dbl/tpl for B&B (all with common bathroom; the lower prices tend to be reserved for those rooms on the noisier lower floor), it's not quite as smart. Nevertheless, it is still hugely popular though do check out a couple of rooms as they vary in size and quality – it's fair to say, for example, that cats could happily enter into the single rooms without fear of ever being swung around. It boasts wi-fi, fan and mosquito nets and I like the place; the staff too, in particular the new lad, Peter, are lovely. Indeed, everything looks smashing ... until you realise there are just two showers for up to 38 guests. Still, as with its Arusha sibling, you won't find a cheaper private room in town.

Now under new management, **Haria Hotel** (☎ 0656 318841, 🖳 hariahotel.com), on the other side of Double Rd, has undergone a bit of a revolution since the days when it was the cheapest but scruffiest hotel on the street. The rooms are OK and boast wi-fi, mossy net and fans. However, the prices (dorm bed US$10, sgl/dbl with bathroom US$25/35, or US$25 in a double with common bathroom) are too high in our opinion, though if you are staying here and paying that money then you can console yourself with the fact that 100% of the prof-

its goes to support a charity. Their rooftop bar and restaurant is great too. Note that breakfast is not included, however.

Still in the same area, *Buffalo Hotel* (☎ 027-275 3736; 🖥 buffalocompanyltd@yahoo.com), on New St, has clean bright rooms with mosquito nets as well as

a fairly popular bar and restaurant downstairs. The hotel has installed cable TV into the rooms (sgl/dbl/suite Ts30,000/35,000/ 45,000, all en suite); all rates include breakfast. Note there is no wi-fi – presumably because they want you to use their internet place next door. I can't help feeling this

---

❏ Accommodation for volunteers and long-term residents

It seems a little ironic, perhaps, that what is traditionally one of the wealthiest and most developed parts of Tanzania is also the one area that receives more interest from NGOs, charities and the like. As a consequence, Moshi is flooded with volunteers working on any number of projects in the town and surrounding area. This has led in turn to the establishment of several hostels designed specifically to cater for these longer-term residents. And as many of these volunteers will, understandably, want to climb Kili at some point while they're here, it is our duty to cater for them in this book too and look briefly at these hostels.

To begin, we must mention *Hostel Hoff* (☎ 0787-225908; 🖥 hostelhoff.com). Run by an Australian lady who married a local, such is the success of this place that there's now a *Hoff 2* near Maembe that houses 20 guests, adding to the 28-guest capacity of the original building that lies just two minutes to the east. In both houses only long-term guests (ie those staying a minimum of one month) can stay unless there is availability in the low (rainy) seasons. As such they are hugely popular with volunteers, a situation that the owner encourages by actively finding volunteer positions for those who email her before arriving. Accommodation is largely in gender-divided **dorms** (with mosquito nets and lockable drawers) though there are a couple of double/twin **rooms** in each place, all of which are clean and *usually* tidy (though the possessions of long-term residents inevitably tend to sprawl out over time onto every available surface). There are even a couple of **safari tents** in the back garden of the original hostel though these are very popular and tend to be taken by those residents who are staying the longest. The price is very reasonable at US$19-21pp per day including buffet breakfast, dinner and laundry (the exact price depends on how long you're staying), which is one reason why it regularly receives rave reviews from its residents. They also now run a successful trekking agency, African Scenic Safaris (see p75). All in all, a nice place run by nice people.

Twiga Home (☎ 0762-035030; 🖥 moshi-hostel.com) is located to the south of town, beyond the airport, a half-hour walk to the centre. The bar is good, there's wi-fi and satellite TV, the restaurant's decent, the garden pleasant, the staff amiable and the rooms clean and come complete with mosquito nets. It's all very reasonable too at sgl/dbl US$16/32 for rooms with fan (though you may be able to find a double for as little as US$18 online), US$20/40 for those with air-con (or US$26 if booking a double/twin online; prices may vary according to how long you stay). Indeed, my only gripe *is* the location, for it can feel a bit lonely if you're staying here by yourself. Still, if you can overcome this then you've got yourself a bargain.

Rafiki Backpackers (☎ 0714 422500; 🖥 rafikibackpackers.com) is located out in peaceful Rao, 20 minutes' walk north of town and east of Shanty Town. This hard-to-find hostel (ask for Uhuru Museum – which most locals know, and which is actually a bar – as it's by there) is for those who want to stay in a village while still being close enough to the town centre. The place itself is clean and cheap at US$8-10 for a dorm bed or US$20/30/45 for sgl/dbl/tpl with breakfast, wi-fi and use of the kitchen and a fridge. Overall, it's a nice, safe and friendly option – albeit a fair distance from town.

place is going downhill, however, and really needs a makeover.

Just south of the market is **Umoja Lutheran Hostel** (☎ 0769-239860); look for the sign 'KKKT Umoja Hostel'. There's nothing wrong with this place. It's clean, well-run and the al-fresco eating area is certainly pleasant and popular with locals. The rates, too, are decent, at Ts15,000/25,000 sgl/dbl for rooms with shared bathrooms, or s/c sgl/dbl Ts30,000/40,000, all with breakfast. Nevertheless, I rarely see tourists staying here. Similarly failing to appeal to the *mzungu* market is **Big Mountain Inn** (☎ 027-275 1862; ⌨ p.mtitos@hotmail.com), on Kiusa St, where some very smart en suite rooms with air-con and fan are squashed together around a small garden (Ts30,000-40,000 sgl/dbl, including breakfast).

Occupying a great central location, **Aa Hotel** (☎ 027-275 3919) is a surprisingly somnolent sort of place – indeed, even the receptionist was asleep when we visited, which at least allowed us to look around unhindered. What we found was a spotless place with murals on the walls of each room, each of which also contained a fan and mosquito net. The prices seem fair too at s/c sgl/dbl Ts20,000/25,000. There could be one obstacle to your staying here, however, as is made clear with a sign on the way in, saying unmarried couples aren't allowed to share a room. Still, we know of at least one budget agency, Gladys Adventure, that uses this place for their clients, possibly because they have their offices just downstairs – and despite the misgivings generated by the scruffy exterior, this seems a decent place.

At the northern end of town by the roundabout, **New Coffee Tree Hotel** (☎ 0752-388311) is a place for those for whom every *shilingi* matters. I've always had a soft spot for this place but, in all honesty, I think I'm pretty much the only *mzungu* who does. Nevertheless, I like the staff, I like the location right next to the Clock Tower and I like the café (see p251) on the top floor. Admittedly, the rooms are basic but they're only Ts15,000 for a single with shared facilities (and no fan) or Ts20,000-30,000 for en suite twins and doubles (again, no fan or a/c), all including breakfast.

Continuing northwards, the **YMCA** (☎ 027-275 1754) on the main roundabout has always felt a little rundown. To be fair, the prices of US$15/18 sgl/dbl B&B in rooms with a mosquito net but no fan and with shared bathroom are just about reasonable and guests say it's functional, fine and the pool is lovely. However, just a little way along Uru Road is one of those surprising finds that both delights you – and makes you worried for their future. **Hub Hill Budget Lodge** (☎ 0716-276606) has 10 really surprisingly lovely rooms, all en suite and with fan and mosquito net, for which they charge an even more surprisingly low price (US$10, or US$15 for the bigger rooms with a sofa in them). I say surprisingly because the outside of the lodge is unpromising, and its history as former accommodation for students doesn't exactly speak of cleanliness or luxury. But I also worry for them, because they're not on the usual tourist forums, and it must be difficult to sustain the place when you charge so little and offer so much, including breakfast and, so it is promised, wi-fi.

US$20-60 per double

Beginning in the south of the town, **Osy Grand Hotel** (☎ 0754-421220; ⌨ osygrandhotel.com) and **Panama Hotel** (☎ 027 275 3691, 0756-206615; ⌨ panamahoteltz.com) stand close to each other to the west of the market. Both are proud of their facility-stuffed rooms (wi-fi, TV, hot water etc etc) and both are fine – though they seldom cater to the foreign tourist. Prices are s/c sgl/dbl US$45/60-70 in the Osy Grand and sgl/dbl/tpl US$50/60/90 in the Panama.

A few hundred metres north **Moshi Leopard Hotel** (☎ 027-275 0884; ⌨ leopardhotel.com), on Market St, is an old favourite with tour groups and independent travellers alike. Boasting an excellent terrace bar, the rooms are en suite, very comfy and include a fridge, TV, wardrobe, air-con and balcony. As for the rates, the foreigner prices are US$50/60 s/c sgl/dbl, which is fair value but not exceptional. Shame about the staff, who often can't seem to muster a smile between them. On Mawenzi Road, **We Travel Hostel** (☎ 0715 820280, ⌨ wetravelhostel.com) has seven rooms,

including two spick-and-span dorms (usually divided between the sexes though not always) with enormous bunk-beds, each with mosquito net, fan, wi-fi and hot water showers and only US$10 per night including breakfast. Private rooms (sgl/dbl/tpl US$20/25/30, s/c sgl/dbl US$30/35) are also available and there's a pleasant restaurant terrace. The owners also run Mega Adventures from the same building.

The *Kindoroko Hotel* (☎ 027-275 4054; 🖥 kindorokohotels.com) has long been one of the mainstays of the hotel scene in Moshi, bridging that gap between backpacker places and mid-range hotels. It's good to see, too, that despite a few fallow years it has bounced back and is once again a popular choice, thanks in part to some renovations and a renewed effort on the part of the management (the others in this chain, the backpackers hostels in Arusha and here in Moshi, are also reaping the benefits of this rejuvenation). It's a very reasonably priced place, too (sgl/dbl/tpl US$15-20/25-30/30-45 including a decent breakfast) with a good little bar/restaurant (with wi-fi) on the ground floor and some smart rooms with towel/soap, fan and mosquito net.

Zebra Hotel (☎ 0766-998648, 🖥 zebrahotelstz.com) is a large but fairly commonplace hotel in the middle of Moshi. Features of their facility-heavy en suite rooms include air-con, satellite TV, direct-dial telephone and room service. We've had several complaints about the water pressure once you climb above the first floor, so do check this before committing to stay – and the wi-fi rarely stretches this far either. The prices are very fair, however, at US$35/40/60 s/c sgl/dbl/tpl. If your trekking company has booked a room for you, it's neither a reason to rejoice nor rebel because, unlike a zebra, there's nothing particularly black and white about this hotel; more a fairly unspectacular grey.

Moving to the Clock Tower area but staying in the same price bracket, to the west on Rengua Rd, the old Philip's Hotel has been bought up, spruced up and converted to another link in the *Nyumbani Hotel* (☎ 027-2754432; 🖥 nyumbanihotels.com) chain. Mercifully, the rooms are more elegant than the rather overcrowded

reception (complete with a hotchpotch of giant Chinese vases, a head of an eland and a stuffed zebra) would have you fear. Rates for these air-conditioned, self-contained rooms with satellite TV and wi-fi start at Ts85,000-100,000/100,000-150,000 for sgl/dbl B&B.

Across the other side of the Clock Tower, *Kilimanjaro Crane Hotel* (☎ 027-275 1114; 🖥 kilimanjarocranehotel.com) seems to be more of a local businessmen's hotel. It's a decent-enough place, however, with 30 smart rooms, sauna and even a very small pool. Singles, which have showers, TV and telephone, are US$50; doubles and triples have both bathtubs and showers and go for US$60, or it's US$75 for a triple.

The *Lutheran Uhuru Hotel* (☎ 027-275 4512; 🖥 uhuruhotel.org) sits in fairly vast grounds in leafy **Shanty Town** (see map p248); don't get this hotel confused with Lutheran Umoja Hostel in central Moshi. It's a quiet, relaxed place, the only activity coming from the team of gardeners and cleaners maintaining the neat-and-tidiness of it all. The rooms are very pleasant – particularly those in the new Kibo or Kilimanjaro wings – and all are self-contained with mosquito nets and wi-fi. The tariff, in our opinion, is a little high at US$50/60 s/c sgl/dbl in the Mawenzi Wing (where there's air-con and TV), US$45/55 in the Kilimanjaro and Kibo wings and Uluru Annex (with TV and fan). Despite this moan, it maintains a healthy trickle of customers and if you don't mind catching some form of transport or walking a fair distance to get to Moshi – or are happy doing nothing all day except watch a battalion of gardeners watering the grass – it's fine.

Not far away, one of our very favourite B&Bs in Moshi is *The Hibiscus* (☎ 0754-245000, 0759-597202, 🖥 thehibiscus-moshi.com). It's a lovely place to the north of the Uhuru Roundabout. With an artistic hand behind the decor (one senses the English owner was involved in styling the rooms), smiling staff and a lovely peaceful location down from St Margaret's Church, this really is a lovely place. The twelve rooms with mosquito nets and fans are light and airy and all en suite, while the communal areas are very relaxing, including a fire

❏ Accommodation near Moshi and around Kilimanjaro

The foothills, lower slopes and surrounding plains of Kilimanjaro are dotted here and there with some very pleasant accommodation; it is unlikely you will stay at any of them *unless* your trekking agency puts you up in one as part of your Kilimanjaro package. And if you do then congratulations – I think that on the whole they offer some of the most pleasant and interesting accommodation in the region. Note that we haven't included all hotels or lodges, of course; almost every village has some sort of accommodation so we have narrowed our survey down to just those that market themselves to tourists. Note, too, that we have not included the hotels in Marangu; you can find these on pp258-9.

The following hotels are ordered from west of Moshi round to the east.

House of West Kili (☎ 0753-462 668, 🖳 houseofwestkili.com) Located in **Lawate, Sanya Juu**, this place is probably the most suitable candidate if you're looking to cut the travelling time to Londorossi Gate and the start of the Shira or Lemosho routes. Eight huge rooms sit about 20 minutes' drive from Boma N'Gombe. Very comfy, there are no TVs but instead the owner hopes you'll participate in a couple of local activities, including bird-watching at the nearby swamp or visiting a local sacred Maasai hill. Rates start at about US$99 per room.

Ndarakwai Ranch (☎ 027-250 2713, 🖳 ndarakwai.com) Set in 11,000 acres in the **Siha District**, on the lower western slopes of Kilimanjaro, unlike the others in this section – with the exception of Simba Lodge, below – this ranch is less a stopover on the way to the mountain than a destination in itself: 15 en suite, wi-fi-connected tents on raised wooden platforms, each located on land that teems with 70 species of mammal and 350 species of birds. Beautiful, if above the budget of most trekkers at US$450-500 for sgl/dbl/tpl, with game drives extra.

Simba Farm Lodge (☎ 0784-687335 or ☎ 0787-904580, 🖳 simbafarm lodge.com) Originally owned by Swiss-German settlers, and with one of its buildings dating back to 1910 – making it one of the oldest constructions in the region we think – the 7500-acre Simba Farm is certainly one of the more historical lodges in the area and one of the more charming too. Nine rooms, all individually decorated and with much of the furniture designed by the owner, are dotted amongst the flower beds, with a children's play area, pool and five roaming tortoises. It's a lovely relaxed place and pretty fair value at sgl/dbl US$65-80/90-120, with lunch US$10 extra, dinner US$20. Well worth it, we think!

Millie Lodge (☎ 027-275 2240), just 500m down from Machame Gate, is the sister lodge of one of Moshi's smartest addresses, Sal Salinero (see p249). As you'd expect, Millie maintains the standards of its sibling, with 22 very smart self-contained rooms, some with balconies and views of Kibo. At the time of writing the place had only just opened so they were still in the early stages of attracting business, but groups from Big Expeditions and Tanzania Experience have already used them. Rates are currently US$112/171/214 for B&B, but given the paucity of eateries around here you'll probably want the full-board option at sgl/dbl/tpl US$160/214/278.

Hotel Aishi Machame (☎ 0758 170 254; 🖳 aishi-machame.com) lies in the village several kilometres down from Kili's Machame gate. Now under new ownership, the hotel boasts 30 en suite rooms with wi-fi and telly in each. It's a nice if slightly odd-looking place with a pool and some very precisely manicured grounds; but like many in this section it survives mainly – indeed, almost exclusively – from the business of tour groups; as a result, if you aren't part of a group you may feel a little isolated and lonely. Rates are sgl/dbl/tpl US$100/120/140 B&B; add US$15 per person per meal for half- and full-board; if booking for yourself they ask you use 🖳 booking.com.

Kaliwa Lodge (☎ 255 762 620 707, 🖳 kaliwalodge.com) consists of several

simply furnished concrete, glass-fronted box bungalows nestled between eucalyptus and banana trees on the way up to Machame Gate. We're not sure about the style of the bungalows – they're a bit too 'brutalist' for our tastes – but the direct views of Kibo from the terrace are lovely. Rates are US$99 per person, with dinner US$20 and lunch US$15.

Stella Maris Lodge (☎ 0686-663244, 🖥 stellamarislodge.com) Located on the outskirts of Moshi just south of the road to the airport, in a village that goes by the name of **Mailisita**, blancmange-coloured Stella Maris is a not-for-profit hotel stuffed with facilities (wi-fi, air-con, satellite TV, conference facilities, balconies on all the rooms) where all profit goes to paying the teachers at the attached primary school and buying food for the children under the auspices of Mailisita Foundation (🖥 mailisita.org), a US initiative. Accommodation is fair, though the food when we stayed was below standard. Prices are US$75/85/95 for sgl/dbl/two-room suite.

Weru Weru River Lodge (☎ 0736-502488, 🖥 weruweruriverlodge.com) Also in **Mailisita** and owned by successful Moshi trekking agent Ahsante (see p77), this is their latest venture; a huge, semi-luxury, facility-filled place with 32 air conditioned veranda-fronted rooms, bar, coffee lounge, swimming pool, wi-fi and two conference halls. The charming wooden fittings and stone floors more than compensate for the slightly plain nature of the buildings but all in all it's very impressive and rates are fair at US$85-135/142-84 for sgl/dbl B&B; add US$15 per person for half-board, and another US$20 per person on top of that for full board. The bar, by the way, is large, well stocked and a terrific place to celebrate reaching Uhuru. **Camping** is also available for US$15 or US$25 if hiring one of their tents (US$25/35 half-board, US$35/45 full board).

Kili-konka Holiday Home (☎ 0758-842917, 🖥 kilikonka.com) The ultimate in luxury in the region, Kili-konka is a new, private four-bedroom bungalow that you can rent out on a sole-occupancy basis for US$792 B&B *a night*, though individual rooms are cheaper at just US$250 per night! Sounds incredibly expensive, which it is, of course, though you do get your own chef, house- and grounds-keeper, security team and on-site manager all included. A fully equipped kitchen, lounge, en suite master bedroom (with two further bathrooms) and wi-fi, iPod docks and microwave are just some of the features. The location is a good one too, just **east of KCMC Hospital** north of Moshi.

Honey Badger Lodge (☎ 0767-551 190, 🖥 honeybadgerlodge.com) An attractive place for those who want to get away from it all. Facilities include a pool and 15 smart en suite rooms – all set in some lush gardens where tortoises roam. The hotel also supports several charitable initiatives and has its own climbing company, Milestone Safaris (see p92). Well worth a look. Prices: sgl/dbl/tpl US$50-60/70-90/90-110 B&B.

Snow Cap Cottages (book through Snow Cap, see p96, in Moshi: ☎ 027-275 4826, 🖥 snowcap.co.tz) Homely little chalets in a pleasant spot by Rongai Gate, simple but cosy, but its the main building with its open fire, TV lounge and a well-stocked bar that's the real draw. Prices are US$60pp in a double, though add US$10pp each for lunch and dinner. A lovely spot.

❏ Abbreviations

Throughout this book we have used the following abbreviations when writing about accommodation: **pp** means per person; **s/c** is short for self-contained, a local term meaning that the room comes with a bathroom (ie the room is en suite or a bathroom is attached); while **sgl/dbl/tpl** means single/double/triple rooms. So, for example, where we have written 's/c sgl/dbl/tpl US$35/40/45', we mean that a self-contained single room costs US$35 per night, a self-contained double costs US$40 and a self-contained triple costs US$45.

pit and plenty of outdoor seating in their lovely garden. Try to get a room upstairs if you can, for they come with veranda – and those at the back have views of Kili too. Highly recommended. Rates sgl/dbl/tpl US$30/45/70, though look on 🖳 booking.com to see if you can get it cheaper.

Something strange happened to the hostel scene in Moshi in 2016. Firstly, the *Kilimanjaro Grand* (☎ 0767-646722, 🖳 kiligrandhostels@gmail.com) arrived in the centre of town, garnered a lot of positive reviews online – then promptly upped sticks and moved north of Moshi to the Rose Garden district. The new place is undoubtedly more pleasant and quieter than the original. Though expensive for a hostel (dbl/tpl US$18-25/27-35, the exact price depending on the season) it's a lovely place nevertheless; five simple but clean self-contained rooms with air-con and mosquito nets, a lovely outdoor space and some very friendly staff, led by the chatty, busy Ghynwine (though he's better known by his nickname of Mandela). Camping (US$10 per tent) and a dormitory room (US$8 per person) are also planned, and some of the profits go towards sponsoring the nearby Komboa Kilimanjaro Organisation,

US$60 and above per double

Bristol Cottages (☎ 027-275 5083; 🖳 bristolcottages.com), on Rindi Lane, describe themselves as 'The countryside hotel in the middle of town', and though the noise from the buses revving up the hill outside rather shatters that boast, it's true that this is a little blossom-filled idyll and the most convenient upper-bracket hotel in Moshi. The smart cottages, all with large TV and mosquito net, go for US$70/100/130 s/c sgl/dbl/tpl; the new wing, a little noisier due to its proximity to the road, is consequently slightly cheaper at US$60/90 s/c sgl/dbl, while there are some suites with a mountain view that will set you back US$80/110/140 s/c sgl/dbl/tpl.

Just a few metres up the hill on Aga Khan Rd is another smart place. *Parkview Inn* (☎ 027-275 1341, ☎ 0754 052000; 🖳 pvim.com) was once a bijou B&B boasting just 12 rooms or so but these days it's a fairly enormous monolith with 49 rooms of

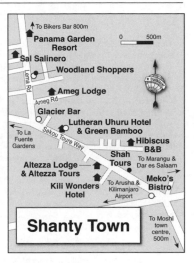

elegant (if monotonous) uniformity and the facilities – TV, telephone, wi-fi, air-con and bath or shower – of a large chain hotel. Thankfully, however, it still retains its friendly informality. Rates are US$75/85/120 for s/c sgl/dbl/suite.

However, for the top places in Moshi you have to go to the north of the Arusha-Moshi road to **Shanty Town** – a smart area of jacaranda-lined avenues that's quite unlike any shanty town you've seen or heard about. While the Kilimanjaro Impala Hotel is closed for renovations, and possibly permanently, four new places have sprung up nearby to fill the gap. The first, the huge *Kilimanjaro Wonders Hotel* (☎ 027-275 1984; 🖳 kiliwonders.com), is quite a gargantuan place, its sheer size a bit incongruous in the normally discreet, understated Shanty Town. Still, there's no arguing with the quality of the place nor the sumptuousness of its 44 rooms (with satellite TV, wi-fi, air-con and safe), its gardens, spa and pool. Despite the high standards, rooms aren't actually too extortionate, with B&B rates sgl/dbl/tpl starting at just US$90/110/130, rising to US$180/215/250 in the June-October high season; these rates may, however, be some sort of introductory offer and in future we expect them to rise. Best of all, however, is the rooftop bar

where you can stare eye-to-eye at Kili (well, more like eye-to-ankle if we're being honest, but it's still a good view).

If you head north-west on Lema Rd then east off that onto Ameg Rd you come to something of a curiosity. Maybe it's the high concrete walls surrounding the place, maybe it's the uniform whitewashed, green-roofed chalets, or maybe the popular pool where everybody seems to congregate – whatever it is, there's something about *Ameg Lodge* (☎ 0754-058268; ☐ ameglodge.com) that's reminiscent of a 1950s' British seaside holiday camp. Thankfully, the rather bland, shadeless exterior belies some quite stylish – though now dated – rooms, each with shower, satellite TV, aircon, wi-fi, veranda and phone. Prices (all rooms are doubles) start at sgl/dbl US$82-135/106-159. In addition to the pool, guests are also entitled to use the hotel gym.

On Lema Road, another vast, gleaming monolith has just opened its gates to well-heeled customers. Not to be confused with its namesake in town, *Panama Garden Resort* (☎ 027-275 2566, ☐ panamagardenresort.com) boasts 45 shiny rooms with balconies as well as 25 cottages with all the facilities you'd expect (air-con, TV etc) plus such surprises as a coffee maker in each room. The grounds include a lovely pool with a bar and BBQ area. Once more, the prices are perhaps not as wince-making as you might expect at US$100/120 sgl/dbl for B&B; once again, we are impressed by what good value this represents, though fear it may just be a special low introductory offer, to be removed when the hotel becomes more established. I'm sure both will find favour with the trekking agencies and they'll have no trouble filling their rooms.

Nearby, *Sal Salinero* (☎ 027-275 2240; ☐ salsalinerohotel.com) is a conglomeration of cottages and standard rooms hidden behind high hedges to the west of Lema Rd. All accommodation comes with air-con, TV and fridge, with many boasting bathtubs too; the executive rooms also have hairdryers. Guests seem to have enjoyed the place, with the cottages getting the best reviews. The sparkling sun-kissed pool is very inviting too. With the prices at sgl/dbl/tpl US$112/171/214 and suites

US$246, this may be one of the more expensive places in town but it's also one of the smartest.

Accommodation connected with the trekking companies

Several tour companies in Moshi have decided to sink some of their hard-earned profits into property and, in particular, hotels. It makes perfect sense, of course, enabling the companies to fulfil their clients' requirements from the moment they arrive in Tanzania to the moment they leave – and to make a profit at every step too. It's worth noting here that even if you aren't a client of the trekking company you can still stay with them, though you'll have to pay the prices given below; whereas those who have booked a trek with them will find their accommodation is included in the package.

On Uru Rd, *Keys Hotel* (☎ 027-275 2250 or ☎ 275 1875; ☐ keys-hotel-tours.com) is a traditional-looking family-run hotel and one of the smartest addresses in Moshi. In the main building it's doubles only, all coming with TV, telephone, mini-bar, toilet, shower with hot/cold running water and air-con. There are also 15 small thatch-and-cement cottages in the grounds which are quite fun. All rates (sgl/dbl/tpl US$86/99/132) include continental breakfast.

The relatively new *Nyota* (☎ 0754 481672), on Rengua Rd, is the latest enterprise from Tin Tin Tours. It's a small but light and airy place divided into two, with simple but pleasant rooms, four triples and a 4-bed dorm, all equipped with mosquito nets and fan. All but one of the rooms come with a veranda overlooking the sleepy street-life below. The rooms aren't self-contained but there are plenty of bathrooms to go around, as well as a communal kitchen, and overall we like this B&B as much as we like Tin Tin. Climbers will probably get a couple of nights for free here, otherwise the rates are US$20 per person for B&B, with dinner just US$5 extra.

The Moshi Urban Hostel (☎ 0767 100788) is currently anonymous – look for the pink building with Amed Affer Dhanji written on it; the hostel is through the large glass door, the last one on Bath Road

(though they're planning to move reception to next-door and put a sign out too). It's owned by Pristine Trails though again is not exclusively for their clients. We like this place, particularly the size of the rooms (massive), and the kitchen/dining area and outdoor terrace with glimpses of Kibo. Currently the hostel has only four rooms though they are planning to expand if they can obtain the building next door. All rooms share the facilities. A spot in one of their two eight-bed dorms is US$10, while the family room is just US$12 per person and the double is US$20 per person, all including a decent breakfast. Facilities include (rapid) wi-fi, mosquito nets and solar-heated showers. Overall, very good.

Secret Garden (☎ 0768-611840, 🖳 secretgardentz@gmail.com) is aptly named, hidden away as it is to the west of Moshi Airport in the southern suburb of Soweto. It is not actually finished yet, though several of the rooms are now habitable and the communal areas seem complete too. And quite charming it is too, with the walls painted a subtle shade of green adding to the tranquil, natural feel of the ten smart, clean, self-contained rooms. The bathrooms could do with a makeover – they're looking a bit grungy compared to the rest of the place – but the wi-fi-enabled bar, with views over Moshi towards Kibo, is lovely. Prices are US$20-25 in the single, US$30-35 in the doubles, with a dorm just US$10 per night or US$12 with breakfast.

Up in Shanty Town, *Altezza Lodge* (☎ 027-275 5557, 🖳 altezza-lodge.com) is now owned by one of the more popular trekking agencies on the mountain. And just like Altezza the trekking agency, the clientele is made up almost entirely of Russians. The nine air-conditioned rooms are supremely comfy and the pool's a beauty too, and it's reasonable value at sgl/dbl US$85/95 – though it's very unlikely you'll stay here, with the whole place usually booked out by our Russian friends.

Mountain Inn (☎ 0716 264427, 🖳 mountaininn.co.tz) lies 4km from town, a 24-room establishment owned and run by Shah Tours (see p96 for contact details). A buffet breakfast is included and a pool, wi-fi, sauna and a pretty garden are just some of the attractions here. The staff are nice too, though some of the bathrooms could do with a clean. Prices are around US$75 for a double though you may be able to find cheaper if booked online. Finally there's Zara-run (see p101) *Springlands Hotel* (☎ 027-2750011; 🖳 zara.co.tz/springlands), 2km to the south of Moshi, with the hotel providing shuttle buses throughout the day to and from the town centre. Most people who stay here are happy with what they find, the pool being the main attraction.

WHERE TO EAT AND DRINK
[see map pp238-9]
Five great cafés
As befits a town that grew wealthy on the back of the bean with the caffeine, Moshi has some rather decent little coffee houses. Indeed, there has been a fierce rivalry between them for several years now, though all of them have been rather swept away by a café that manages the difficult feat of being both the newest on the scene – and yet the one with the longest heritage. *KNCU Café* (Kilimanjaro Native Coffee Union, better known as *Union Café*; daily 7am-8.30pm) is named after and run by Africa's oldest surviving cooperative, an organisation that represents some 60,000 farmers who grow coffee on the lower slopes of Kilimanjaro. It's a history that it is clearly proud of, with the walls adorned with portraits of previous chairmen of the co-op and the building itself, once the HQ of KNCU, retaining many original features, as well as an industrial coffee roaster – so presumably the smell of coffee is wafting over Moshi as you read this, luring yet more customers to their premises. It's great to see Africa's history being celebrated in this way; this is coffee with a conscience, too, for much of the profit generated is ploughed back into the farming community. As for what you can actually consume here, the coffee (Ts4500 for a latte) is, of course, both organic and fantastic (the best in Moshi, by common consent), there's a lengthy list of teas too (all Tanzanian) and the menu is Western and covers salads, sandwiches, quesadillas and the inevitable pizzas. The décor is simple and tasteful and the veranda is a lovely place to watch the world go by and enjoy

that caffeine buzz. Its faults? Well, I always think it a little cheeky when a café charges for wi-fi – but doubtless they'd argue otherwise; oh, and they served my latte in a glass, which does of course go against the laws of Nature and suggests that they may have embarked on some sort of relationship with Satan himself. Other than that, this place is great – don't miss it.

It must be rather galling for the *grande dame* of Moshi's cafés, the *Coffee Shop* (Mon-Sat 7.30am-9.30pm), on Kilima/Hill St, to be upstaged by a place that has, after all, only just celebrated its fifth birthday. But it shouldn't be too concerned for it still has plenty of which it should be proud and they're half the price of the other cafés in this review, there's heaps of local information on the noticeboards and, perhaps best of all, the little garden out back is wonderfully tranquil. Nevertheless, you can't ignore the fact that the crowds are drifting away. This is possibly because, while they claim to have wi-fi, I have never actually seen any evidence of this; but it could also be that they've changed the menu and now serve mainly Chinese food, which, no matter how good or tasty the dishes (Ts3500-9000), does rather detract from the traditional coffee shop ambience that this place had before.

Now occupying large grounds at the Clock Tower end of town, *Kilimanjaro Coffee Lounge* (Mon-Sat 8am-9pm, Sun 10am-8pm) continues to hold its own despite the change of location, probably because it seems to be going out of its way to supply everything a *mzungu* could want, from internet (Ts500 for thirty minutes) to salads and sandwiches. They also serve some pretty decent attempts at Mexican food including burritos (Ts13,500) as well as the usual role call of pizzas (Ts12,500-14,000) and pastas. It's a pleasant, shady spot and a lovely place to hide from the relentless pounding of the sun.

A fourth coffee lounge, *Aroma* (Mon-Sat 6am-8pm) is a pleasant escape for those looking to evade the tourist hordes, for this feels like more of a local's place and, though they serve little except drinks and the odd snack, is a great choice for those who find themselves at this end of town.

Finally, with terrific scenery, but tardy service, *New Coffee Tree Café* (daily 6am-10pm), on the top floor of the eponymous hotel (see p244), is a light, airy place with sumptuous views towards Moshi in one direction and Kili in the other; they don't seem to be doing much in the way of food these days but it remains a good place to get away from the heat, hassle, touts and tourists.

Local food

On the northern end of Uhuru Park, with the entrance on Aga Khan Road, is a food court with several outlets serving some fairly lip-smacking local fare. A bit quiet sometimes, come at a weekend and it's a pleasant place to sit on a park bench and chew away on some *nyama choma* while watching the sun sink below the horizon.

At the southern end of town, one steadfastly African joint lies hidden behind a mosque on New St. *Shukrani Snacks* (noon-8pm) is a Somali-run establishment that's popular and cheap. A meal with a soft drink won't come to more than Ts5000. For more homegrown East African cooking there are several choices. Currently the most popular amongst *mzungu*, and not just for its location, *Taj Mahal* (daily 7am-10pm) sits right by Kindoroko Hotel and despite the Indian name is actually a great place for local fare such as meat skewers (Ts500 each) and Zanzibar pizza (a sort of omelette filled with mince, onions and an egg and a great way to fill up for just Ts1000). A couple of blocks away, *Chagga Bar and Grill* (daily 8am-10pm) near Moshi Leopard Hotel has a small menu but it includes a huge mountain of *mchemsho kuku* (boiled chicken, vegetables and bananas) for just Ts5000 for a quarter of a chicken.

Further up Market St is *Moeen's* (Mon-Sat 7am-10pm), a quieter and perhaps more likeable venue with tasty and huge portions of African food; nothing on the menu costs more than the Ts4000 you'd pay for chicken and chips and Moeen himself is a friendly soul.

Thai, Indian, Chinese, Korean – and a burger joint

The ageless *Indoitaliano* (daily 11am-9.30pm) continues to pack 'em in night after

night. Its popularity can be ascribed to two factors: a) a good location amongst the hotels near the market, and b) some great food. The name may conjure up all sorts of unappealing fusions but really it's just a straightforward Indian restaurant that happens to make some delightful pizzas too (from Ts11,000). A block or two away, **Peppers** (Mon-Fri 11am-3pm & 6-10pm, Sat & Sun 10am-3pm & 6-10pm) provides welcome sanctuary, a lovely peaceful spot with a small but delicious Indian menu (veggie mains Ts7000, others Ts8000-12,500) and views across a hockey pitch to the hills beyond. Even though there was a Moshi-wide power-cut when we visited they still managed to rustle up a fantastic kauai chicken (Ts9000) and for subcontinental sustenance their food is without compare in town; their bar is very well stocked too. Just one word of warning: the streets around here are particularly dark and it's best not to wander around alone at night.

Nearby is perhaps our favourite place in Moshi. Half of **Milan's** (daily 11am-9.30pm) is taken up with a typically scruffy snack café of the kind you find all over the country. The other half, however, is rather different: a cute little lilac-painted eatery with hand-stitched place mats that boasts an extensive menu of cheap and delicious Indian vegetarian food, including dosas, samosas, bhajis and thalis. No dish is over Ts9500. There are just a couple of minor drawbacks: the service can be fairly desultory, for one thing, and secondly another guidebook has finally discovered it too, so it's not as quiet as it once was. Nevertheless, to my mind this is still a good-value place, and their masala dosas (Ts7500) and thalis (Ts7500-8500) provide proof that God loves us and wants us to be happy.

While we thought that the rooms at the **Haria Hotel** were overpriced, the same can't be said of their excellent menu. The format is simple: local food, with a nightly special (usually about Ts8000), all well cooked and served in a lovely rooftop dining area lit by a hundred fairy-lights. Their Ts2000 charge for wi-fi is a bit steep but otherwise this place is spot on.

Some people may be put off by the appearance of **Deli Chez** (Wed-Mon 9.30am-9.30pm), which from the outside looks like a fast-food café, though the ground floor décor owes more to the aesthetics of a wedding reception. But upstairs you'll find a very pleasant shaded terrace where the food is fine and fair value, with a huge menu encompassing good value Chinese (Ts7000-9000 for mains), curries (Ts7000-9000 for mains), sizzle plates (Ts10,000) and a charcoal grill (Ts3000-8000).

Moving up Arusha Road and occupying an enviable place at the western end of Uluru Park, **Mimosa** (daily 8am-11pm) is another place that tries to cater for everyone, its menu encompassing pizzas, burgers, curries, Mexican and Thai food – as well as **vegan and gluten-free options**. There's no doubting the quality of the food, making it one of our favourite places in the centre of town; even if you don't actually eat here – and with most mains upwards of Ts12,500 it may be beyond a volunteer's budget – do treat yourself to one of their delicious mango smoothies (Ts5500) while enjoying their speedy wi-fi.

On Boma Road **Jay's Kitchen** is a Korean eatery with a menu like no other in Moshi. Not only are the dishes refreshingly unfamiliar – you won't find pizzas or pasta here – but Jay helpfully both describes the food, so you know what you're getting, and tells you how to make it, too! Even if you don't fancy a Korean meal (mains are Ts10,000-25,000) while you're in Tanzania, do drop in to try their vinegar juice and banana drink – it's one of the most refreshingly zingy things I've ever tried.

Just north of the Clock Tower roundabout, **Chrisburger** (see also p254) claims to stay open 24 hours and offers very good-value dishes; if you can get a seat on its leafy veranda it's a good place to hide away and watch the world go by. Once again it's great value, with nothing over Ts7000 (for simple meals such as steak and chips) and their 'humburgers' just Ts2500-5000.

Kilimanjaro Ice Cream Parlour (Mon-Sat 8am-8pm), also known as the **Food Palace Café**, charges Ts1500 per scoop, though they also do a few simple meals such as chicken and chips (Ts4000), or pilau (Ts3000). A friendly, simple, and largely *mzungu*-free place, I've met more than one

❏ **The top six places in Moshi and Shanty Town to celebrate a climb**
● **Indoitaliano** (p251) The old favourite and convenient for many hotels. Book in advance if planning to arrive after 8pm or you're a large group.
● **Green Bamboo** (p254) Don't be put off by the fact it's part of a religious hostel; this is a decent place with great food.
● **Mimosa** (p252) Large place, varied menu, good food, large drinks menu – what more do you want?
● **Maembe** (see below) Huge grounds, great cocktails and fine cooking; a great choice – unless it's raining!
● **Kitchen Flavour** (see below) Has a varied menu that spans the globe and we found it one of the best places for Chinese food in Moshi.
● **La Fuente Gardens** (p254) Obscure location but what a lovely place with some great Mexican grub.

ex-pat who says it's their favourite eatery in town, probably for those very reasons.

Proving that she's as adept at running a kitchen as she is at arranging a trek, *Kitchen Flavour* (Mon-Sat 8am-10pm) is owned and run by Gladys of Gladys Adventure fame. This is a lovely retreat from the heat with some of the best Chinese food we've had in Africa (mains Ts12,500-18,000); their beef cashew (Ts14,000), in particular, was delicious and served with a surprising (and welcome) degree of spicy heat. Indian, local and continental dishes are also available – but it's Chinese that is their forte, and what we heartily recommend, particularly if washed down with one of their pineapple and orange juices. Wi-fi is available here too.

Dining out on a petrol station forecourt may not be everyone's idea of a romantic night out but *Meku's Bistro* certainly makes a decent fist of providing a lovely, shaded restaurant in the most unpromising of locations. Open-sided, but with a canvas roof to protect diners from the heat and sun, it's a colourful place with brightly-painted furniture and paper lampshades that dance in the breeze as you eat. As usual, however, this would all count for nought if the food was no good but thankfully there's a magician in the kitchen conjuring up large portions of particularly tasty local food, including a ridiculously tasty *makange ya mbuzi* (goat stew) with chips. For those who don't want to eat what the locals eat then there's the usual collection of 'continental' dishes (pizzas Ts9000-12,000,

sarnies Ts10,000-18,000). True, the service could be friendlier – but I guess that all adds to the authenticity of this quintessential Tanzanian experience.

Maembe (Mon-Sat 8am-10pm, Sun 10am-10pm) was set up by several people who used to work at the small Pamoja Café in the town centre (which we think has gone downhill and is no longer included here), and has been receiving ecstatic reviews ever since. Their departure seems to have been a less than amicable one and certainly there appears to be some rancour between the two. By all accounts it's Maembe that's the winner, however, for two ex-pats were gushing in their praise for this place on the first day I arrived back in town. And I can see why: boasting spacious open grounds with a kids play area, a (very expensive) souvenir shop and, best of all, an imaginative menu of sandwiches, Swahili food and other dishes rarely seen in this part of the world (eg spicy Thai octopus stew, Ts10,000), and with some of the income generated going towards the Pamoja Tunaweza Women's Centre, it's a great place.

Down from Maembe on the Moshi-Arusha Road, *Mr Feng* (Mon-Fri noon-3pm, 6-10pm, Sat & Sun 11am-10pm) is a large joint hidden behind high walls and with only a discreet sign revealing its location. The service can be a little slow and the choice limited, but you can't deny the quality of the food when, several epochs after you've ordered it, it finally arrives; try the douban fish or double-cooked pork (Ts22,000).

In Shanty Town (see map p248)

A new Mexican has opened in town and it's kicking up quite a storm. Gaily painted, and with a lovely neat garden including a children's play area, *La Fuente Gardens* (Tues-Sat 9am-9pm) maybe European-owned and set in the suburbs of Moshi but the experience of eating here is as Mexican as you can get, with authentic dishes and even mariachi music emanating from the speakers. Admittedly, a friend who's half-Mexican said their tortilla shells were troublesome, being insufficiently rigid enough – but I notice that didn't stop him from eating there fairly regularly. You can enjoy the experience right throughout the day, too, with huge breakfasts served from 9am (including *huevos rancheros* – two fried eggs served on tortilla and smothered with a black bean and salsa sauce) and all your favourite Mexican dishes (tacos Ts10,000, fajitas Ts12,000, enchiladas Ts11,000 and quesadillas Ts10,000) served throughout the rest of the day. The location of the restaurant is fairly obscure but not difficult to find – where Lema Rd turns sharp right, just continue straight on and keep going beyond the tarmac to another sharp-right bend; La Fuente is on that bend.

Green Bamboo is a massive place, open all day (8am-late) and specialising in set menus, including a meat-heavy version (including lamb, steak, spare ribs, chicken wings, beef sausages etc) for Ts27,000, and a less indigestion-inducing vegetarian version for Ts15,000. Other dishes are available for those who don't fancy all that meat-munching, and there are salads to balance all that protein. The main attraction, however, is the lovely (and huge) garden where you can feast on flesh while listening to the strains of 'Bringing in the Sheep' on the Hammond organ being piped through the speakers – the restaurant is, after all, located in the Lutheran Hotel.

NIGHTLIFE

The most popular place in town (or, rather, just outside it) is probably the *Biker Bar*, particularly their busy Friday night karaoke sessions. Its location on the northern edge of Shanty Town ensures it grabs the majority of the expats working in the KCMC.

Their popularity has badly hit *Glacier Bar*, on Sekou Toure Way, though it can still pack 'em in occasionally.

On the main Moshi-Arusha road, *Red Stone Club* (entrance Ts5000-10,000) is a proper, purpose-built nightclub with plenty of outdoor seating and a large indoor dancefloor. On a good night you'll get a good mix of locals and ex-pats/tourists here. The food here is provided by Chrisburger, which is slightly surprising given that they have their own nightclub, *Pub Alberto*, which can still gather a reasonable crowd at the weekends, though it's now under serious pressure from several places very nearby: *Black Diamond*, just up the road a little way, is run by the same people who used to run the huge La Liga club to the south of town; and, a few metres west of Nyumbani Hotel, *Malindi Club*. The entrance here is through a set of concrete elephant legs, while inside you'll find a cavernous, friendly place serving food and beer and showing **premier league football** on the telly; it can, however, get a little too raucous at times. A similar experience, though this time nearer most of the hotels, is provided by *East African Pub*, a real rowdy locals' hangout that lovers of English football will adore, with live premiership matches the main entertainment. They also serve a decent plate of *nyama choma* (grilled meat). If you prefer your premier-league football served in more sophisticated surroundings, *Peppers Sports Bar and Restaurant* (see p252) is the place to go.

A couple of local places are now trying to put on regular **live music (usually zouk)**, including *Local Bar*, opposite the Moshi Bookshop on Kibo Road, which advertises bands on a Saturday night; and the *River Nile Restaurant* on Thursday, down from the Union Café along an alleyway behind the NMB bank.

For those who prefer a less frenetic end to their trip, there are few activities more pleasant than sitting at a **rooftop bar**, sipping a cold beer, staring at Kibo, and thanking God you're not up there. Kilimanjaro Crane Hotel, Kindoroko and, best of the lot, Kilimanjaro Wonders Hotel in Shanty Town, can all help here (and you don't need to be staying at any of them to enjoy the privilege).

MOVING ON

By bus – Arusha, Marangu and Tarakea

Heading to **Arusha**, 'Coaster' buses (the small 30-seat minibuses) leave regularly throughout the day from the bus terminal on Mawenzi (Ts3000; remember that the bus station is due to move soon; see p236). Big buses are usually a little cheaper at Ts2500. For **Marangu** catch one of the dalla-dallas from the adjacent terminal (Ts1500) labelled to 'Mwika' or 'Kilema'. If you've arrived early in the morning and nothing seems to be leaving from here, try round the corner on the Double/Mawenzi Road – they often wait here too.

Now the road round this side of the mountain has improved all the way to the Kenyan border you can catch public transport to the start of the **Rongai** trek; take a Noah van (one of the sleeker, smarter 'dalla dalla' vans) for Ts4000-5000 to Tarakea, from where you get a boda boda for 15 minutes (Ts3000) to the start of the trail. Remember, of course, that if you've booked a trek on the Rongai Route then transport to the start of the trail is included in the price.

The **shuttles** – Impala, Riverside – charge US$10 for the two-hour journey to Arusha. Services tend to leave at 6.30am and 11am. Riverside (☎ 0754 885521) are now in the YWCA building on Boma Road. Impala (☎ 0754 293119) are next to Pub Alberto. If you book in advance, you should get picked up from your hotel, though emphasise this when buying your ticket.

By bus – Nairobi and Mombasa

Shuttle buses to Nairobi leave from outside their respective offices (see above). Both Riverside's (☎ 0754 885521) and Impala's (☎ 0754 293119) services leave at 6.30am and 11.30am and cost US$35. Cheaper are the big **buses**, though for travel to Nairobi they're not recommended due to lack of comfort and the fact that they arrive at the bus terminal there after dark. Contact Modern Coast, near the Clock Tower, if you want a seat on their 3pm bus to Nairobi (Ts26,000). The same company also operates a bus to **Mombasa** (8.45am, Ts20,000), as do Tahmeed on Boma Road (8am, Ts18,000).

By bus – Dar es Salaam

There are plenty of **bus** companies plying the route to Dar. Be careful, however: as we've already stated, this route is notorious for speeding and, as a result, horrific crashes; the traffic-calming measures installed along the road's length have reduced – but not eliminated – these, and have also helped to increase the total journey time from Moshi to something like 10 hours.

The cheaper companies are best avoided; even though they could save you Ts5000 or more it's simply not worth it.

Several have managed to garner a reputation for safety, however: **Dar Express**, on Boma Rd, are still the best in our opinion with buses at 7.15am, 8.15am and 9.30am (Ts30,000). Opposite are **Mtei Express**, with an 8.30am bus (Ts28,000). They are adequate but the main rivals to Dar Express are **Kilimanjaro Express**, with six buses between 7am and 10am (Ts33,000, or Ts36,000 for the 8am one which features a toilet and air-con); their big new office-cum-waiting-room can be found opposite the Clock Tower. A fourth competitor is **Modern Coast**, near the Clock Tower, charging Ts28,000 for a seat on its 1pm bus to Dar.

By air

For details of flights out of **Kilimanjaro International**, see p386.

Getting to Kilimanjaro airport takes about 45 minutes from Moshi. There is no public transport and while you can take an Arusha-bound bus from Moshi and jump off at the junction, that still means you have to hitch or get a boda boda (Ts5000) for the final 6km to the airport itself.

Precision Air and Fastjet both run shuttle services (Ts10,000) to coincide with their domestic flights; the bus leaves from outside their offices 2-3hrs prior to departure (though do check first). A **taxi** costs US$50; bargaining can reduce this but you'll struggle to get much of a discount at night.

Moshi does actually have its own airport and Coastal (🖳 coastal.co.tz) do occasionally call in to connect with most of their extensive East African network, as well as a couple of other, smaller airlines – but only if there's demand.

Marangu

According to legend, Marangu got its name when the first settlers in this part of Kilimanjaro, astonished by the lush vegetation, well-watered soils and the countless waterfalls they found here, cried out in delight 'Mora ngu! Mora ngu!' ('Much water! Much water!'). It remains a verdant and extremely attractive place, at least once you move away from the small huddle of shops and hustlers by the bus stop (situated in a part of the town called Marangu Mtoni, which literally translates as 'Marangu in the River') and start to climb up the hill towards Marangu Gate. The town, 14km along the Himo–Taveta highway, is extremely elongated but is in reality little more than two roads running up the mountain, with a filigree of dusty paths running off both.

WHAT TO SEE AND DO

Always one of the prettiest villages on Kili's slopes, for some reason over the past couple of years Marangu has become the unofficial centre of Chagga culture – and it's really fascinating. You can try to find many of the attractions yourself – they're all pretty well signed – but it's much nicer and easier to hire one of the local kids who'll doubtless come up to you to offer themselves as guides (give them around Ts5000 per day). And while none of these 'Chagga' sights is going to have you rushing to your phone in order to tell your nearest and dearest back home of the wonders you have seen, nevertheless it's good to see some sort of revival of a fascinating culture that would otherwise be confined largely to the history books. What's more, though your interest in Chagga culture may be slight, the chance to walk around one of the prettiest, homeliest parts of Tanzania should not be passed up; it's a lovely way to spend a day.

The first port of call is usually **Kinukamori Falls** (daily 8am-5pm; US$5), just 10 minutes' walk up from the bridge. As lovely as these are, we feel that this is one sight that maybe should have been left as it was, for the addition of a **Hall of Chagga Culture** – an open-air series of statues or dioramas lining the eastern path down to the falls, each depicting some aspect of Chagga culture or history – seems unnecessary and adds nothing to the beauty of the place. Indeed, with that god-awful statue of a woman about to plunge to her death that's now been installed at the top of the falls, this is one 'enhancement' that is anything but.

Still, some of the other sights are really absorbing. Falling into this category is **Chagga Living Museum**. The museum is right next to Kilimanjaro Mountain Resort, 10 minutes beyond the market place. There's a reconstruction of a thatched Chagga house complete with livestock inside, a reproduction of a chief's chair (modelled on a real chair owned by one of the local chiefs), as well as displays of traditional Chagga tools, farm implements, rope made from the

Marangu

Car park
Marangu Gate

Small
dirt track

Coffee Tree
Campsite &
Alpine Tours

To Mbahe
Farm

Hotel
Nyumbani

The
Capricorn
Hotel

To Chem Chem
Campsite

Kinukamori Waterfalls &
Hall of Chagga Culture

Village Craft Shop

Peter's Lodge

Market

Kilimanjaro
Mountain
Resort

Chagga
Living
Museum

Marangu Mtoni
football pitch

PO

To Chagga,
blacksmiths,
caves &
Rombo

To Kilema &
Ngango Hill

Kibo
Hotel

Bus
stop

Telephone
office and
internet

Bridge

To the
Kilasiya
Falls

Market
place

Lutheran
Church

Itosi
Caves

Marangu
Hotel

To Himo, Moshi,
Taveta & Dar

0   1km

bark of the *mringaringa* tree, a genealogical look at the history of the Chagga,
some drums and a bugle made of kudu horn.

Just before the museum is a turn-off to many people's favourite attraction
in Marangu, the delightful **Kilasiya Falls**. The waterfalls are just part of the
attraction, for it's the local flora that really catches the eye and many of the
plants have been labelled. Reached via a steep muddy path, the falls are exquisite; there are even a couple of natural swimming pools in the gorge for those
who fancy a cold dip. It's a great place to have lunch. Like most waterfalls,
there's a negotiable entrance fee.

Those who've really got a taste for all this Chagga culture may also like to
venture east to the village of Mamba Kua Makunde. Walking up the hill from
the main road you'll soon hear the sound of the **Chagga blacksmiths**, making
anything from weapons to farm implements, often with little children working
the bellows to keep the fires hot. It's free, though they'll sting you if you want

to take a photo. Nearby, there are some underground **caves** once inhabited by the Chagga. Claustrophobic, dark and difficult for anyone bigger than a smurf to negotiate, they're not the most pleasant of attractions though they are, in their own way, fascinating. There are some other caves, **Itosi**, signposted from the Marangu Hotel.

Finally, for modern-day Chagga culture look no further than the twice-weekly **markets** (Monday and Thursday) in the main village square by the junction, which are lively and, by the end of the day, often quite drunken too.

And once you've done all of that? Well don't miss the chance to rest your weary limbs at the **Village Craft Shop** (Mon-Sat 9am-6pm), just behind the market above the river. Part of the Village Education Project Kilimanjaro, you can buy souvenirs made by some of the pupils who have benefitted from the charity and there's a decent *café* here too.

PRACTICAL INFORMATION
ARRIVAL
Marangu is reached by **dalla-dalla** from Moshi (Ts1500) in about 60-90 minutes. Passengers are dropped at the junction next to the bridge in Marangu Mtoni. A ride in a **shared taxi** (six people on seats made for four) from the bridge to Marangu Gate costs Ts1000 – make sure you specify you don't want a private hire.

SERVICES
There's a **post office** (Mon-Fri 8am-1pm & 2-4.30pm, Sat 9am-noon) close to the bridge. Across the main road is a CRDB bank with ATM (currently Ts8000 fee).

WHERE TO STAY
Accommodation in Marangu is fairly luxurious and survives by catering to the tour-group trade. As such, it tends to be quite upmarket and expensive. One way to avoid the high price of staying in a hotel is to camp. All the main hotels provide a space for **camping** and there's also one purpose-built place: *Chem Chem* (contact Dilly Mtuy, ☎ 0754-312086), which is run by the Village Education Project Kilimanjaro charity. The site lies 1.5km up from the market past Kinukamori Waterfalls; a taxi there will cost Ts6000-7000, or a motorcycle taxi Ts3000. Another option is *Kilimanjaro Mountain Resort* (see opposite); the grounds are gorgeous, the facilities spotless and huge and they charge US$20, or US$35 including tent hire – plus

you get to enjoy the bar/restaurant facilities of one of Marangu's most charming and luxurious hotels. Camping is also available at *Nyumbani Hotel* (see below; US$20pp), *Kibo Hotel* (see below; US$10pp including use of kitchen and pool) and *Marangu Hotel* (US$10 per night including use of bar and pool).

And that, alas, is it for 'cheap' accommodation here. Some of the other places in the village, however, while not 'budget', do at least offer some sort of value for money. A new place that's opened up on the road to Marangu Gate is *Peter's Lodge* (☎ 0717 344977), with very smart self-contained rooms going for sgl/dbl Ts50,000/70,000 per night B&B; not excellent value but cheap by Marangu standards.

Near Coffee Tree Campsite is the friendly *Nyumbani Hotel* (☎ 0754-277300; ⌨ nyumbanihotels.com) a sister of the place in Moshi. Formerly Hotel Nakara – you can still see the original signs on the way up – presumably the Nyumbani will, like its predecessor, aim to grab its share of the tour-group trade, though independent trekkers are welcome if there's space (rack rates sgl/dbl US$70/100 B&B).

On the main road, *The Capricorn Hotel* (☎ 0784 994248) is made up of a number of buildings, some older (and therefore cheaper) than others, and charges US$70/90 sgl/dbl, or US$150/190 in the (overpriced) new executive rooms.

No hotel review of Marangu would be complete without mentioning *Kibo Hotel*

(☎ 0754-038747) which, whilst it cannot compete with most of the others here in terms of luxury or comfort, can at least rival the Marangu Hotel when it comes to character and history. The hotel still displays a sign welcoming former US president Jimmy Carter above the entrance – it's a perfect symbol of the faded yet fascinating grandeur of the place, and of the time-warp it appears to be living in now. Indeed, rather comfortingly, the place has changed little since we first visited in 2001, with antique German maps and other paraphernalia from the last two centuries adorning reception. If you want to stay, try to get a room in the main building as those in the garden are starting to look very faded. Rooms are overpriced at sgl/dbl/tpl US$45/55/65 but I think it's worth it just to wallow in this much nostalgia; it remains an absorbing place to wander around even if you don't intend staying. Lunch (currently US$15) and dinner (US$20) are also available.

Further up the road, 10 minutes past the market and right by Chagga Living Museum, is a relatively new place (by comparison) that's doing very well. *Kilimanjaro Mountain Resort* (☎ 0754-999755, 🖳 kilimountresort.com; sgl/dbl/tpl US$147/220/323, full board US$197/310/473) is luxurious and lovely, with sumptuous rooms that boast huge bathrooms with powerful, multi-jet massage showers, digital TVs and their own balconies facing towards Kili's summits. The grounds are gorgeous (with a resident tortoise roaming around), the bar is beautiful, there's internet access (US$1 for 15 mins), a gym, jacuzzi and massage service (US$40) and the roof terrace is terrific, with views of Kili and Lake Jipe to boot.

On the road back to Moshi there's another old favourite – and we mean '*old*'. The *Marangu Hotel* (☎ 0717 408615, ☎ 0754 886 092; 🖳 maranguhotel.com) was once a farmhouse dating back to the early 1900s, and has been providing accommodation for climbers and travellers since the 1930s. The hotel is a couple of kilometres south of town (about a 10-minute walk) on the way to Himo and it stands in 12 acres of gardens (with pool and weaver birds chattering away in the trees). The food is great too; rates are sgl/dbl/tpl US$85/150/225 in the low season, US$120/200/275 in the high. Their main claim to fame, however, is not the hotel, as venerable and delightful though it may be, but their treks – about which, see p90.

Mbahe Farm is set in 13 acres in the Marangu 'suburb' of the same name, a couple of kiliometres west of Marangu Gate. Owned by one of the top trekking companies on the mountain, SENE (see p97), and used by them (though not exclusively) to house their clients either side of their trek, Mbahe Farm consists of eight lovely rustic rooms plonked amidst the vegetable patches on this busy little farm. Coffee is amongst the myriad of crops grown here and Simon, the boss of SENE, provides demonstrations of the process of making coffee from bean to cup and sells the stuff too. Costs for those who aren't climbing with SENE is US$70 full board – well worth it.

MOVING ON
Dalla-dallas back to Moshi (Ts1500) leave when full from the main junction at Marangu Mtoni; don't worry about finding one – they'll find you.

❏ **Abbreviations**
Throughout this book we have used the following abbreviations when writing about accommodation: **pp** means per person; **s/c** is short for self-contained, a local term meaning that the room comes with a bathroom (ie the room is en suite or a bathroom is attached); while **sgl/dbl/tpl** means single/double/triple rooms. So, for example, where we have written 's/c sgl/dbl/tpl US$35/40/45', we mean that a self-contained single room costs US$35 per night, a self-contained double costs US$40 and a self-contained triple costs US$45.

7

SAFE AND MINIMUM IMPACT TREKKING

Safe trekking

Came to cave. Men cold. Passed two corpses of young men who died of expo-sure, a short time ago. The vultures had pecked out their eyes, the leopards had taken a leg from each.

From the diary of **Peter MacQueen** as recorded in his book
In Wildest Africa (1910)

Because of the number of trekkers who scale Kilimanjaro each year, and the odd ways in which some choose to do so, many people are under the mistaken impression that Africa's highest mountain is also a safe mountain. Unfortunately, as any mountaineer will tell you, there's no such thing as a safe mountain, particularly one nearly 6000m tall with extremes of climate near the summit and ferociously carnivorous animals roaming the lower slopes. Your biggest enemy on Kilimanjaro, however, is likely to be neither the weather nor the wildlife. KINAPA are shy about revealing how many trekkers die on Kili each year, though we reckon it's about six or seven (see p262). The main culprit behind these fatalities is nearly always the same: the altitude.

The authorities do try to minimise the number of deaths: guides are given some training in what to do if one of their group is show-ing signs of acute mountain sickness (AMS) and trekkers are required to register each night upon arrival at the campsite and have to pay a US$20 (plus VAT) 'rescue fee' as part of their park fees (though what this actually gets you is unclear). But you, too, can do your bit by avoiding AMS in the first place. The following pages dis-cuss in detail what AMS actually is, how it is caused, the symptoms and, finally, how to avoid it. Read this section carefully: it may well save your life. Following this, on p269 you'll find details of other ail-ments commonly suffered by trekkers on Kilimanjaro.

(Incidentally, for those climbing Meru the above introduction and the following advice are all relevant. Of course, given Meru's lower altitude, the risks of AMS are consequently lower; though this is offset by the slightly higher risk of attack by wildlife!)

WHAT IS AMS?

AMS, or **acute mountain sickness** (also known as **altitude sick-ness**), is what happens when the body fails to adapt in time to the lack of available oxygen at altitude. The atmospheric pressure drops

by about one tenth for every 1000m of altitude you gain. Thus the air pressure at the top of Kilimanjaro is approximately 40% of that found at sea level. As a result, every time you breathe on Kibo you take in only about half as much air, and thus oxygen, as you would if you took the same breath in Dar es Salaam. This can, of course, be seriously detrimental to your health; oxygen is, after all, pretty essential to your physical well-being. All your vital organs need it, as do your muscles. Your lungs load your red blood cells with oxygen and then your heart pumps them round your body delivering oxygen to your muscles and organs as they go.

Fortunately, your body is an adaptable piece of machinery and can adjust to the lower levels of oxygen that you breathe in at altitude. Unconsciously you will start to breathe deeper and faster, your blood will thicken as your body produces more red blood cells and your heart will beat faster. As a result, your essential organs will receive the same amount of oxygen as they always did. This process is known as **acclimatisation**. But your body needs time before it can effect all these changes. Though the deeper, faster breathing and heart-quickening happen almost as soon as your body realises there is less oxygen, it takes a few days for your blood to thicken. With Kilimanjaro, of course, a few days is usually all you have on the mountain, and the changes may simply not happen in time. The result is AMS.

There are **three levels of AMS**: mild, moderate and severe. On Kilimanjaro, it's fair to say that most people will get some symptoms and will fall into the mild-to-moderate categories. Having symptoms of mild AMS is not *necessarily* a sign that the sufferer should give up climbing Kili and descend immediately. Indeed, most or all of the symptoms suffered by those with **mild AMS** will disappear if the person rests and ascends no further that day; assuming they make a full recovery while resting, the assault on the summit can continue. The same goes for **moderate AMS**, though here the poor individual and his or her symptoms should be monitored far more closely to ensure they are not getting any worse and developing into **severe AMS**. This is a lot more serious and sufferers with severe AMS should always descend immediately, even if it means going down by torchlight in the middle of the night.

The following describes the symptoms of the various levels of AMS, while **there's a more comprehensive and more scientific summary of acute mountain sickness on p400**.

What are the symptoms?

The symptoms of **mild AMS** are not dissimilar to the symptoms of a particularly vicious hangover, namely a thumping headache, nausea and a general feeling of lousiness. An AMS headache is generally agreed to be one of the most dreadful you can get, a blinding pain that thuds continuously at ever-decreasing intervals; only those who have bungee-jumped from a 99ft building with a 100ft elasticated rope will know the intense, repetitive pain of AMS. Thankfully, the usual headache remedies should prove effective against a mild AMS headache though do be careful as they can also mask any worsening of symptoms; and do tell your guide as he needs to know your symptoms and what you have taken to ease them

in order to judge how well you're faring. As with a hangover, mild AMS sufferers often have trouble sleeping and, when they do, that sleep can be light and intermittent. (**NB: do <u>not</u> take sleeping tablets** to counter this as they suppress breathing and thus will worsen your condition.) Sufferers can also experience a lack of appetite. Given the energy you've expended getting to altitude in the first place, both symptoms can seem surprising if you're not aware of AMS.

Moderate AMS is more serious and requires careful monitoring of the sufferer to ensure that it does not progress to severe AMS. With moderate AMS, the sufferer's nausea will lead to vomiting and the headache will not go away

❏ Deaths & injuries on Kilimanjaro

It is almost impossible to ascertain with any degree of accuracy the number of people who die on Kilimanjaro each year. The one organisation that knows the exact body count, KINAPA, the park authorities, doesn't want to release them, for fear that it would impact negatively on the number of people who climb the mountain each year, resulting in a loss of revenue. Similarly, the companies are understandably reluctant to advertise when a client dies on one of their climbs.

Luckily, a few years ago a study by Markus Hauser addressed precisely this topic. In the paper, *Deaths due to High Altitude Illness among Tourists Climbing Mount Kilimanjaro*, Hauser studied autopsies from 1996 to 2003 and found that over those eight years only 25 people died. Ranging in age from 29 to 74, with 17 male and 8 female, the reports tell us that 14 of the deceased were victims of High Altitude Illness (HAI), of which five had HAPO (see p264), one HACO (see p264), while eight had symptoms of both. Causes of death amongst the other 11 victims include two who died of pneumonia, three to trauma (ie a fall) and one from appendicitis.

Extrapolating from these figures, given that there are over twice as many people who climb the mountain each year now, so **we estimate the number of people who die on Kili each year to be about six or seven**.

It should be noted that the study does not include the death of porters, for whom a post-mortem is not compulsory and thus the number of fatalities they suffer is more difficult to quantify with any degree of accuracy. Remember that more porters climb Kili than tourists, at a ratio of about three to one on every trek – so you would think perhaps there would be three times as many deaths amongst them. They also put their bodies under extra stress because of the heavy loads they are carrying, and the fact that the food they eat and the conditions in which they sleep are far inferior. Many of them also still turn up on Kili with insufficiently warm clothing. But of course they seldom climb up Kibo to the summit unless the trek includes a night at Crater Camp, so the highest altitude they reach is usually about 4600m. So given all these factors, **the best educated guess we have is that about the same number of porters and other mountain crew die on the mountain each year too**.

The conclusion that one can draw from all these statistics is that climbing Kilimanjaro, as with any ascent of a seriously big mountain, is inherently a risky undertaking; one that is made all the more dangerous by the rapidity with which one is expected to reach the summit (as we mention elsewhere in the book, if the standard guidelines for ascending a mountain were followed on Kilimanjaro, people would take twelve days to reach the summit from 12,000ft, (3658m) not the usual 24 hours that is taken on Kili!).

Problems are exacerbated by the fact that it is possibly the easiest mountain of such a size to scale, with no actual climbing involved – which attracts more people

even after pain-relief remedies; in addition the sufferer will appear to be permanently out of breath, even when doing nothing.

With moderate AMS, it is possible to continue to the summit **but only after a prolonged period of relaxation** that will enable the sufferer to make a complete recovery. Unfortunately, treks run to tight schedules and cannot change their itineraries mid-trek. Whether you, as a victim of moderate AMS, will be given time to recover will depend largely upon how fortunate you are and whether the onset of your illness happens to coincide with a scheduled rest day or not.

of all levels of fitness, whether they are of a suitable physicality to climb such a large mountain or not

And yes, for sure, measures such as making sure your trek is equipped with supplementary oxygen, carrying Diamox (acetazolamide), drinking plenty, going slowly, taking as many days as you can afford on the mountain....all of these can help to mitigate your chances of something serious or fatal happening to you on Kili. But they can't modify the biggest risk factor of them all: the fact you chose to put yourself on the mountain in the first place.

A senior member of staff at KCMC had a rather neat analogy for it, comparing it to someone standing on a motorway reciting poetry. That person can put on a hi-vis jacket, can position himself between the lanes rather than in the middle of one, and maybe choose to stand on the motorway at a time when it's not so busy. All of which can help to reduce his or her chances of being killed; but the bottom line is that by standing on the motorway in the first place, that person has put himself or herself in danger. And so it is when you decide to climb Africa's highest mountain. Because it is estimated that about 50% of people will get mountain sickness of some sort or another on Kili; and of those, about one in fifty will go on to develop something serious.

Further investigation suggests that KCMC, the hospital at the foot of Kilimanjaro, sees a trekker every two to three weeks – and more in the rainy season when hypothermia, an injury from slipping or altitude sickness are all, according to the statistics, more likely.

Perhaps even more disconcerting than the deaths, however, are the cases of those who survived their climb but were never quite the same again: of the ship's captain who climbed Kilimanjaro, got into trouble, came down unconscious and, though he pulled through, was not able to continue working due to the permanent effect climbing the mountain had on his cognitive powers. Or the people who end up blind in one or even both eyes following a Kili climb (it is estimated that 1-2% of people who climb Kili will get some sort of bleeding at the back of the eye). As we've already written, deaths on Kilimanjaro are seldom publicised; but those who suffer some sort of permanent injury or disability following their climb never receive any attention, and it is concerning to think how many of them there may be...

We never want to put anyone off climbing Kili. We have seen how happy people are after a successful climb, and we've received many letters and emails from people over the years saying how it has completely changed their life, giving them a confidence and self-assurance that was previously lacking. Getting to the top of Africa's highest mountain is a wonderful experience. But in order to climb safely, you need to be fully aware of the risks and do everything you can to make sure you minimise them as much as possible because the last thing we want is for you to end up as just another statistic.

SAFE & MINIMUM IMPACT TREKKING

With **severe AMS**, on the other hand, there should be no debate about whether or not to continue: if anybody is showing symptoms of severe AMS it is imperative they **descend immediately**. These symptoms include a lack of coordination and balance, a symptom known as **ataxia**. A quick and easy way to check for ataxia is to draw a 10m line in the ground and ask the person to walk along it. If they clearly struggle to complete this simple test, suspect ataxia and descend. (Note, however, that this lack of coordination can also be caused by hypothermia or extreme fatigue, so ensure the sufferer is suitably dressed in warm clothing and has eaten well before ascertaining whether or not he or she is suffering from ataxia.)

Other symptoms of severe AMS include mental confusion, slurred or incoherent speech, and an inability to stay awake. There may also be a gurgling, liquid sound in the lungs combined with a persistent watery cough which may produce a clear liquid, a pinky phlegm or possibly even blood. There may also be a marked blueness around the face and lips, and a heartbeat that, even at rest, may be over 130 beats per minute.

These are the symptoms of either HACO and HAPO, as outlined below, while ways to treat somebody suffering from AMS are given on p268.

HACO AND HAPO

Poor Mapandi, a carrier whom I had noticed shivering with fever for the last day or two, stiffened, grew cold and died beside me in the mud.
Peter MacQueen *In Wildest Africa* (1910)

HACO (High Altitude Cerebral Oedema) is a build-up of fluid around the brain. It's as serious as it sounds. It is HACO that is causing the persistent headache, vomiting, ataxia and the lack of consciousness. If not treated, death could follow in as little as 24 hours, less if the victim continues ascending.

Just as serious, **HAPO (High Altitude Pulmonary Oedema)** is the accumulation of fluid around the lungs. It's this condition that causes the persistent cough and pinkish phlegm. Again, the only option is to descend as fast as possible. In addition, one of the treatments outlined on p268 should also be considered.

GO *POLE POLE* IF YOU DON'T WANT TO FEEL POORLY POORLY – HOW TO AVOID AMS

Haraka haraka haina baraka 'Great haste has no blessing' – a common Swahili saying.

'Pole pole' is a phrase you'll probably hear more than any other on Kili. It's Swahili for 'slowly slowly' and is usually uttered by guides to dissuade their charges from ascending too fast.

AMS can be avoided, but the only surefire way to do so is to **take your time**. Opting to save money by climbing the mountain as quickly as possible is a false economy: the chances are you will have to turn back because of AMS and all your efforts (and money) will be wasted. According to one respected agency, their average success rates based on the number of days their clients' took in getting to the top are as follows:

6 days: 75% of clients made it to the top
7 days: just over 80%
8 days: 90%
9 days or more: over 98%.

As you can see, the longer you take the greater your chance of getting to the top.

According to the Expedition Advisory Committee at the Royal Geographical Society, the recommended acclimatisation period for any altitude greater than 2500m is to sleep no more than 300m higher than your previous night's camp, and to spend an extra night at every third camp. But if you were to follow this on Kilimanjaro's Marangu Route, for example, from Mandara Huts you would have to take a further *eight* nights in order to adjust safely to the Kibo Huts' altitude of 4713m – whereas most trekkers take just two days to walk between the two. The EAC realise that the short distances and high per diem cost of climbing Kilimanjaro make this lengthy itinerary impractical, so instead they recommend a pre-trek acclimatisation walk up Mount Meru (4566m at the summit) or Mount Kenya (4895m to Point Lenana, the third highest peak on the mountain and the highest point that non-climbing 'trekkers' can reach). This is an excellent idea if you have the time and money and are feeling fit; providing you do one of these walks *immediately* before you climb Kili, these treks can be beneficial – and the views towards Kilimanjaro from Meru are delightful too (see pp274-85 for a description of this route).

But what if you don't have the time or money to do other climbs? The answer is to plan your walk on Kilimanjaro as carefully as possible. If you've enough money for a 'rest day' or two, take them. These 'rest days' are not actually days of rest at all – on the Marangu trail, for example, guides usually lead their trekkers up from Horombo to the Mawenzi Hut at over 4500m before returning that same afternoon. But they do provide trekkers with the chance to

---

❏ **If you're farting well, you're faring well — other effects of altitude and acclimatisation on the human body**
In addition to AMS, there are other symptoms suffered by people at high altitude that are not in themselves usually cause for any concern.

The first is the phenomenon of **periodic breathing** (aka sleep apnoea). What happens is that, during sleep, the breathing of a person becomes less and less deep until it appears that he or she has stopped breathing altogether for a few seconds — to the obvious consternation of those sharing the person's tent. The person will then breathe or snore deeply a couple of times to recover, causing relief all round.

Another phenomenon is that of **swollen hands and feet**, more common amongst women than men. Once again, this is no cause for concern unless the swelling is particularly severe. Another one that is far more common among women than men, is **irregular periods**. The need to **urinate** and **break wind** frequently are also typical of high-altitude living and, far from being something to be concerned about, are actually positive indications that your body is adapting well to the conditions. As is written on an ancient tombstone in Dorset:

> *Let your wind go free, where e'er you be,*
> *For holding it in, was the death of me.*

SAFE & MINIMUM IMPACT TREKKING

experience a higher altitude before returning down the slopes, thereby obeying the mountaineers' old maxim about the need to '**climb high**, **sleep low**' to avoid mountain sickness.

The route you take is also important. Some of the routes – the Machame, Lemosho and Shira trails via the Barafu Huts, for example – obey the mountaineers' maxim on the third or fourth days, when the trail climbs above 4500m (around Lava Tower) before plunging down to an altitude of 3986m at Barranco Huts where you spend the night. Some of the shorter trails, however, do not: for example, it is possible for a trekker walking at an average pace on the Marangu, Umbwe or Rongai trails to reach Kibo in three days and attempt an assault on the summit for that third night. This sort of schedule is far too rapid, allowing insufficient time for trekkers to adapt to the new conditions prevalent at the higher altitude. This is why a higher proportion of people fail on these trails and it is also the reason why, particularly on these shorter trails, **it is imperative that you take a 'rest' day on the way up**, to give your body more time to acclimatise.

How you approach the walk is important too. Statistically, men are more likely to suffer from AMS than women, with young men the most vulnerable. The reason is obvious. The competitive streak in most young men causes them

---

❏ Diamox

Acetazolamide (traded under the brand name Diamox) is the wonder drug that fights AMS and the first treatment doctors give to somebody suffering from mountain sickness. It works because it is a **carbonic anhydrase inhibitor**. This means that the kidneys are forced to expel bicarbonate, thus re-acidifying the blood, which stimulates breathing, thereby allowing a greater amount of oxygen to enter into the bloodstream.

A lot of climbers were initially a bit sceptical about Diamox, worrying whether it actually helped to fight AMS or merely masked the symptoms. Indeed, I've spoken recently to an expert in the field of altitude sickness who is still not convinced by Diamox. It was, after all, developed as a treatment for the eye disease 'glaucoma' and its beneficial effects on AMS sufferers were only noticed much later. But these odd lone voices aside, it seems widely accepted that it really is a most effective drug against altitude sickness. That's not to say that it works for everyone, however; for some reason, some people just don't seem to derive any benefit from the drug at all.

It's worth noting that while Diamox is widely regarded as a boon, there are still many questions to be answered about it. It's not unusual for climbers to be given different prescriptions by their doctors: some will have 125mg tablets, for example, and will be expected to take them twice a day; others (the majority) will have 250mg tablets and will be told to take them either once or, more often, twice per day; while still others will be issued with a single 500 or even 750mg tablet and told to take it only if they are feeling ill.

That last prescription leads us neatly onto the second major question about Diamox: Should the drug be used as a cure for when someone starts developing symptoms of mountain sickness? Or should it be used prophylactically, taking it daily from the start of the walk to prevent AMS occurring in the first place? The disadvantage with doing this, according to one doctor serving on the Annapurna Circuit in Nepal, is that by using Diamox prophylactically, you are using up one possible cure. That is to say, should you begin to suffer from AMS even though you've been taking

to walk faster than the group; that, and the erroneous belief that greater fitness and strength (which most men, mistakenly or otherwise, believe they have) will protect them against AMS. But AMS is no respecter of fitness or health. Indeed, many experienced mountaineers believe the reverse is true: the less fit you are, the slower you will want to walk and thus the greater chance you have of acclimatising properly. The best advice, then, is to **go as slowly as possible**. Let your guide be the pacemaker: do not be tempted to hare off ahead of him but stick with him. That way you can keep a sensible pace and, what's more, get to know him better and ask him any questions about the mountain and Tanzania that occur to you along the way.

There are other things you can do that may or may not reduce the chance of getting AMS. One is to **eat well**: fatigue is said to be a major contributor to AMS, so try to keep energy levels up by eating as much as you can. Dehydration can exacerbate AMS too, so it is vital that you **drink every few minutes** when walking; for this reason, one of the platypus-style water bags (Camelbaks), which allow you to drink hands-free without breaking stride, is invaluable (see p43).

Wearing warm clothes is important too, allowing you to conserve energy that would otherwise be spent on maintaining a reasonable body temperature.

Diamox, doctors are going to have to look for another form of treatment to ensure your survival.

At the moment the jury is still out as to what is the best dose and prescription for Diamox, though for what it's worth I find that most people take them prophylactically, either at the very start of the trek or on day three when they are at an altitude of around 3500m or so; 250mg twice a day is the usual regime prescribed from here.

However you decide to take it, there are a couple of **rules you should always follow**: consult your doctor before taking Diamox to discuss the risks and benefits; and secondly, if you do take it, remember to try it out first at home to check for any allergic reaction, as Diamox is a sulfa derivative and some people do suffer from side effects, particularly a strange tingling sensation in their hands and feet.

Are there any other drugs that are as effective as Diamox?

I am grateful to reader Erasmus Schneider for pointing me in the direction of two studies that both suggested that the humble Ibuprofen could also be an effective weapon against altitude illness – and with fewer side effects. The first study, published in 2012 in *National Center for Biotechnology Information* (🖥 ncbi.nlm.nih.gov) concluded that 'Compared with placebo, Ibuprofen was effective in reducing the incidence of acute mountain sickness.' A second study published in the same journal concluded that 'Ibuprofen and acetazolamide were similarly effective in preventing high altitude headache. Ibuprofen was similar to acetazolamide in preventing symptoms of AMS [my underlining], an interesting finding that implies a potentially new approach to prevention of cerebral forms of acute altitude illness.' For the moment I would still recommend Diamox over Ibuprofen all the time – as the second study says, it is effective against the symptoms but not necessarily against the cause of altitude sickness – but it will be interesting to hear what other studies have to say in the future.

SAFE & MINIMUM IMPACT TREKKING

The table below shows the oximeter readings of five trekkers on the Machame Route. You can see how the amount of oxygen in the blood decreases as they ascend the mountain. Perhaps the most interesting feature of the graph, however, is the way that everybody's oxygen saturation declines and climbs at the same places. Despite the differences in each individual's readings, it may interest you to know that all of the climbers made it to the top. For information on pulse oximeters see p401.

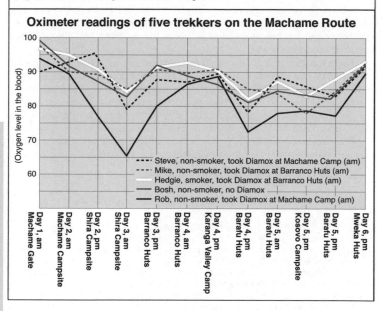

Oximeter readings of five trekkers on the Machame Route

(Oxygen level in the blood)

- ---- Steve, non-smoker, took Diamox at Machame Camp (am)
- --- Mike, non-smoker, took Diamox at Barranco Huts (am)
- — Hedgie, smoker, took Diamox at Barranco Huts (am)
- — Bosh, non-smoker, no Diamox
- — Rob, non-smoker, took Diamox at Machame Camp (am)

Although there hasn't been a serious study on this subject, many people swear that carrying your own rucksack increases your chance of succumbing to AMS. Certainly, in our experience, this is true, so, finally, **hire a porter to carry your baggage** (the agencies will assume you want to unless you specify otherwise).

HOW TO TREAT AMS

Sat down beside P.D. in the mud. Gave him one bottle of champagne. Revived him greatly.
Peter MacQueen *In Wildest Africa* (1910)

It is possible that on your trek you will see at least one poor sod being wheeled down Kilimanjaro, surrounded by porters and strapped to the strange unicycle-cum-stretcher device that KINAPA uses for evacuating the sick and suffering from the mountain. Descent is the most effective cure for AMS but in some severe cases it is not enough. **Diamox** (see box pp266-7) is also usually given, though again, if the victim has been suffering for a while, or Diamox is not available, some other treatment may be used. Such other treatments include:

Dexamethasone is useful for treating severe AMS and, in conjunction with other treatments, in treating HACO. Two 4mg tablets should be given to the HACO sufferer, followed by one tablet every 6 hours until the victim has recovered. Some doctors are horrified at the thought of giving a person a steroid on the mountain (which is what Dexamethasone is), but other mountaineers are convinced of the benefits it can bring.

Nifedipine is useful in treating HAPO though is hard to source in Africa and thus is seldom seen on the mountain. To administer the drug, prick a 10mg capsule many times with a pin before giving to the sufferer who should then chew it thoroughly before swallowing. If the victim then shows signs of breathing more easily, this should be repeated 15 minutes later. The drug has the side-effect of lowering blood pressure but can be most effective in helping treat victims of HAPO; some people even continue to ascend if they respond well to the drug – though we don't recommend this.

Gamow hyperbaric bag This is a man-sized plastic bag into which the victim is enclosed. The bag is then zipped up and inflated. As it is inflated, the pressure felt by the sufferer inside the bag is increased, thus mimicking the atmospheric conditions present at a lower altitude. The disadvantage with this method is one of inconvenience. The cumbersome bag has to be taken up the mountain and, worst of all, in order to work effectively once the patient is inside, the bag must be kept at a constant pressure. This means that somebody must pump up the bag every two or three minutes. This is tricky when at least two other people are trying to manoeuvre the bag (with the patient inside it) down the slopes. Some of the upmarket trek operators carry one with them and KINAPA are trying to make this compulsory for all groups on the Western Breach where descent is very difficult. If you are going to spend some time on the summit or in the crater, or if you know that helicopter rescue is available (so you can wait inside the bag for the helicopter to arrive), then a Gamow bag could prove invaluable; otherwise, a rapid descent should be possible and still the best solution.

Oxygen Giving the victim extra oxygen from a bottle or canister does not immediately reverse all the symptoms, though in conjunction with rapid descent it can be most effective. Two companies, African Travel Resource (ATR), who are agents for African Walking Company, and the Tanzanian ground operator Kili Zone, are now supplying their clients (for a fee) with an **ALTOX** system, where oxygen is fed to the client through cannulas inserted in their nose while they are ascending – the only companies that gives their clients oxygen to help people get to the top. It sounds uncomfortable but for those who are very worried about altitude, or who *know* they are susceptible, this could be the difference between success and failure.

OTHER POTENTIAL HEALTH PROBLEMS
Coughs and colds

These are common on Kilimanjaro. Aspirin can help alleviate some of the symptoms. Lozenges containing anaesthetic are useful for a sore throat, as is gargling with warm salty water. Drinking plenty helps too. A **cough** that produces mucus

has one of a number of causes; most likely are the common cold or irritation of the bronchi by cold air which produces symptoms that are similar to flu. It could, however, point to AMS. A cough that produces thick green and yellow mucus could indicate bronchitis. If there is also **chest pain** (most severe when the patient breathes out), a high fever and blood-stained mucus, any of these could indicate **pneumonia**, requiring a course of antibiotics. Consult a doctor.

Exposure
Also known as hypothermia, this is caused by a combination of exhaustion, high altitude, dehydration, lack of food and not wearing enough warm clothes against the cold. Note that it does not need to be very cold for exposure to occur. Make sure everyone is properly equipped, *including* your porters.

Symptoms of exposure include a low body temperature (below 34.5°C or 94°F), poor coordination, exhaustion and shivering. As their condition deteriorates the shivering ceases, coordination gets worse making walking difficult and the patient may start hallucinating. The pulse then slows and unconsciousness and death follow shortly. Treatment involves thoroughly warming the patient quickly. Find shelter as soon as possible. Put the patient, without their clothes, into a sleeping-bag with hot water bottles (use your water bottles filled with hot water and wrapped in something to prevent burning the victim); someone else should take their clothes off, too, and get into the sleeping bag with the patient: there's nothing like bodily warmth to hasten recovery.

Frostbite
The severe form of frostbite that leads to the loss of fingers and toes rarely happens to trekkers on Kilimanjaro. You could, however, be affected if you get stuck or lost in particularly inclement weather. Ensure that all members of your party are properly kitted out with warm socks, boots, gloves and woolly hats.

The first stage of frostbite is known as 'frostnip'. The fingers or toes first become cold and painful, then numb and white. Heat them up on a warm part of the body (eg an armpit) until the colour comes back. In cases of severe frostbite the affected part of the body becomes frozen. Don't try to warm it up until you reach a lodge/camp. Immersion in warm water (40°C or 100°F) is the treatment. Medical help should then be sought.

Gynaecological problems
If you have had a vaginal infection in the past it would be a good idea to bring a course of treatment in case it recurs.

Haemorrhoids
If you've suffered from these in the past bring the required medication with you since haemorrhoids can flare up on a trek, particularly if you get constipated.

Snowblindness
Though the snows of Kilimanjaro are fast disappearing, you are still strongly advised to wear **sunglasses** when walking on the summit – particularly if you plan on spending more than just a few minutes up there – to prevent this uncomfortable, though temporary, condition. Ensure everyone in your group, including porters, has **eye protection**. If you lose your sunglasses a piece of cardboard

with two narrow slits (just wide enough to see through) will protect your eyes. The cure for snow-blindness is to keep your eyes closed and lie down in a dark room. Eye-drops and aspirin can be helpful.

Sunburn

Protect against sunburn by wearing a hat, sunglasses and a shirt with a collar that can be turned up. At altitude you'll also need high-factor sunscreen for your face.

❏ Toilet etiquette

The toilets at the various camps come in for a lot of stick from trekkers. And rightly so, too, because for the most part they're bloody awful. KINAPA did attempt to improve the facilities a couple of years ago, but the sheer number of trekkers who use them – and the fact that some of these trekkers were never schooled in even the basic skill of cleaning up after themselves – mean that these toilets are in the same parlous state as their old wooden forebears, and smell just as bad too.

But whatever their state and no matter how unpleasant they may be, you still have a duty to use them (unless you've paid for having a private toilet dragged up the mountain for your use, a privilege which usually costs around US$10 per day). There are few sights on Kilimanjaro more depressing than the clods and streamers of used toilet roll hiding behind rocks and hanging from bushes surrounding each campsite. It's hard to understand why some people think it's OK to sleep in a campsite surrounded by their own shit, rather than spending two minutes inside one of the public loos, no matter how disgusting the latter. But if you happen to be one of them, the following tips may help you overcome your terror of the toilet:

● If you're worried about being disturbed by a fellow trekker, on hearing someone approach try coughing, whistling, screaming or otherwise alerting them to your presence *before* they have a chance to invade your space.
● Conversely, when approaching the toilet, give any occupants inside fair warning of your presence by approaching noisily and knocking before entering. It's only polite.
● If it's the smell that worries you, a bandanna round your nose and mouth can help.
● Visiting the toilet in the early morning – when the stuff inside is frozen solid and the stench is reduced – is also a good plan.
● While you're inside the toilets you have a responsibility to keep things tidy. It can be difficult to maintain balance and aim but if you do miss, do the decent thing and tidy up.

Going outside

If you really, really, really can't wait to reach one of the toilets, the least you can do is deliberate before you defecate. Firstly, make sure you're at least 20m away from both the path and any streams – the mountain is still the main source of water for many villages and they would prefer it if you didn't crap in their H$_2$O. Secondly, having done your business, dispose of your toilet paper properly. One way is to try burning it. One reader has written in to say that it's very difficult to burn soggy toilet paper. The editor of a previous edition, however, conducted a controlled experiment and gave this advice: 'If you light the dry corner of partially wet loo paper and twirl it round so the flame dries the wet bit it *does* all burn up'. Give it a go next time you need to, er, go. Even better, why not adopt the 'pack it in, pack it out' method, ie put the used paper in a bag for disposal in the next toilet – the best approach for keeping the mountain clean.

If we all follow these rules maybe, just maybe, Kilimanjaro will remain Earth's most beautiful mountain – rather than resembling one huge, 5895m-high pile of poo.

SAFE & MINIMUM IMPACT TREKKING

Care of feet, ankles and knees

A twisted ankle, swollen knee or a septic blister on your foot could ruin your trek so it's very important you take care to avoid these. Choose comfortable boots with good ankle support. Don't carry too heavy a load. Wash your feet and change your socks regularly. During lunch stops take off your boots and socks and let them dry in the sun. Attend to any blister as soon as you feel it developing.

Blisters There are a number of ways to treat blisters but prevention is far better than cure. Stop immediately you feel a 'hot spot' forming and cover it with a piece of moleskin or Second Skin/Compeed. One trekker suggests using the membrane inside an egg-shell as an alternative form of Second Skin. If a blister does form you can either burst it with a needle (sterilised in a flame) then apply a dressing or build a moleskin dressing around the unburst blister to protect it.

Sprains You can reduce the risk of a sprained ankle by wearing boots which offer good support. Watch where you walk, too. If you do sprain an ankle, cool it in a stream and keep it bandaged. If it's very painful you'll probably have to abandon your trek. Aspirin is helpful for reducing pain and swelling.

Knee problems These are most common after long stretches of walking downhill. It's important not to take long strides as you descend; small steps will lessen the jarring on your knee. It may be helpful to wear knee supports and use walking poles for long descents, especially if you've had problems with your knees before.

Minimum impact trekking

'Manya ulanyc upangenyi cha ipfuve' – 'Do not foul the cave where you have slept' (A Chagga proverb that refers to the habits of the baboon who are said to 'foul their caves' until there comes a point where the stench compels them to find alternative accommodation.)

KINAPA (see p173) does try to keep Kilimanjaro clean. At all huts and camp-sites, trekking groups have their rubbish weighed by the ranger; if there's any evidence that some rubbish has been dumped (ie if the rubbish carried weighs less at one campsite than at the previous camp) the guide could have his licence temporarily revoked and/or have to pay a heavy fine. It's a system that would appear to have loopholes but until recently Kili *was* a very clean mountain, and though it can be frustrating to have to wait for your guide every morning while the rubbish is weighed, it's a small price to pay for a pristine peak. Sadly, standards appear to have slipped recently and there is now serious concern amongst trekking agents and environmentalists about the state of some of the trails. While it's easy to blame the authorities for the sorry state of Lemosho and other routes, trekkers are just as culpable. After all, much of it is our rubbish.

You can help Kilimanjaro become beautiful once more by following these simple rules that apply to almost every mountain anywhere in the world.

SOME GUIDELINES FOR KEEPING THE MOUNTAIN PRISTINE

● **Dispose of litter properly** In theory, all you should have to do is give your litter to your crew: given the stiff punishments they receive for leaving rubbish behind (see opposite), this should ensure all waste is taken off the mountain. Unfortunately, despite all the cleaning crews and the weighing stations at each campsite, some think the litter situation is getting worse. Whatever you decide to do, don't give **used batteries** to porters; keep them with you and take them back to the West where they have the facilities to dispose of them properly (the batteries that is, not the porters).

● **Don't start fires** There's absolutely no need for fires on Kilimanjaro: for cooking, your crew should use kerosene, while for heat, put another layer of clothes on or cuddle up to somebody who doesn't mind being cuddled up to.

● **Use the purpose-built latrines** True, some of them could do with emptying (especially the toilet at the Barranco campsite, which is now so full that the pile of human waste is in danger of developing a snowy summit all of its own), but this is still better than having piles of poo behind all the bushes on the trail and toilet paper hanging from every bough.

● **Leave the flora and fauna alone** Kili is home to some beautiful flowers and fascinating wildlife but the giant groundsels rarely thrive in the soils of Europe and the wild buffalo, though they may look docile when splashing about in the streams of Kili, have an awful temper that makes them quite unsuitable as pets. It's illegal to take flora and fauna out of the park, so leave it all alone. That way, other trekkers can enjoy them too.

● **Boil, filter or purify your drinking water** This will help to reduce the number of non-returnable, non-reusable, non-biodegradable and very non-environmentally friendly plastic mineral water bottles that are used on Kili.

● **Stay on the main trail** The continued use of shortcuts, particularly steep ones, erodes the slopes. This is particularly true on Kibo: having reached the summit, it's very tempting on your return to slide down on the shale like a skier and you'll see many people, especially guides, doing just that. There's no doubt that it's a fast, fun and furious way to get to the bottom, but with thousands of trekkers doing likewise every year, the slopes of Kibo are gradually being eroded as all the scree gets pushed further down the mountain. Laborious as it sounds, stick to the same snaking path that you used to ascend.

● **Wash away from streams and rivers** You wouldn't like to bathe in somebody else's bathwater; nor, probably, would you like to cook with it, do your laundry in it, nor indeed drink it. And neither would the villagers on Kili's lower slopes, so don't pollute their water by washing your hair, body or clothes in the mountain streams, no matter how romantic an idea this sounds. If your guide is halfway decent he will bring some hot water in a bowl at the end of the day's walk with which you can wash. Dispose of it at least 20m away from any streams or rivers.

MOUNT MERU

INTRODUCTION

Mount Meru, which overlooks Arusha from the north, is used by many trekkers as a **warm-up trek** – an *hors d'oeuvre* to the main course of Kili if you like. And a perfect starter it is too: though smaller, it's also quite similar in that to reach its volcanic summit you have first to climb through a number of vegetation zones before embarking on the final night-time march to the highest point on the crater rim and thus the summit itself. What's more, at 4566m (14,980ft) it provides the trekker with the perfect opportunity to acclimatise to Kilimanjaro's rarified atmosphere. In other words, the mountain offers a taste of the challenges that lie ahead on Kilimanjaro, whilst also whetting the appetite for the thrills and beauty of that mountain.

However, Meru is worth doing as much for the differences as for the similarities it shares with its neighbour. In particular, there's the greater abundance of **wildlife**. Lying at the heart of Arusha National Park, a reserve that's teeming with animals, it's an odd trekker who doesn't finish the trek with his or her camera filled with pictures of buffalo, giraffe, elephant, bushbuck, dik dik, suni, colobus, blue monkey and warthog. Luckier ones may also see leopard and hyaena, while twitchers will be more than content with the number of birds on offer, from the noisy Hartlaub's turaco to the silver-cheeked hornbill and black-and-white bulbul.

If all this sounds like your idea of a perfect holiday – a safari-and-trek all rolled into one – then you're probably right, though there is one point that needs to be emphasised: **do not underestimate Meru**. Though it may be more than a thousand metres lower than Kili, it's still well above the height necessary to bring about **altitude sickness** and with almost everybody taking just over two days before reaching the summit, the risks are not small. There is also **more night-time scrambling** to be undertaken on the smaller sibling. Indeed, without a shadow of a doubt our most nerve-racking ascent was a few

Leopard track (Mt Meru)

years ago on Meru and not Kili. True, this had much to do with the fact that there had been heavy rain the evening before the night-time walk to the summit, a downpour which quickly froze and caused the entire trail from Saddle to summit to become covered with a layer of ice. Inconvenient on the first part of that nocturnal ascent, on the second half it became positively dangerous, causing us to scribble hurriedly a last will and testament in our notebooks. Indeed, it was thanks only to the hard work of the guides, who dug out footsteps in the ice with a piece of rock or the back of their heels – footsteps in which, taking our lead from King Wenceslas, we then trod – that we gained the summit at all. And it was only by inching our way back down, bottom pressed into the ice, limbs looking for any piece of rock or other non-slippery material to put our weight on, that we made it back down to write this guide.

So though Meru may not carry the cachet, prestige or the sheer scale of Kili, it's no pushover – and maybe it's no coincidence that the first successful recorded ascent, though still in dispute (being credited to either Carl Uhlig in 1901 or Fritz Jaeger in 1904), occurred at least a dozen years after the conquest of Kilimanjaro. Meru remains an awfully big mountain – the 10th highest peak in Africa in fact – and as such it should be treated with respect.

PRACTICALITIES

The route
There is only one main route up Meru. It begins at Momela Gate, around 15km from the main Ngongongare entrance to the park where you pay your park fees. Having paid up and driven those 15km, past the plain known as Little Serengeti (Serengeti Ndogo) because of its similarity to Tanzania's most famous park, you arrive at **Momela Gate** (altitude 1597m; 5240ft) where you pick up your ranger and possibly hire your porters.

The route from Momela Gate to the summit is punctuated by **two sets of accommodation huts**: the first are the **Miriakamba Huts (2503m, 8212ft)**, a day's walk from Momela Gate; and the second are the **Saddle Huts (3560m, 11,680ft)**, lying a short day's walk from there. From the Saddle Huts it's a further day's walk – or rather, a night's walk – to the summit.

Which path to take Though we just stated above that there's only one path to the summit of Meru, that's not entirely true for, in fact, on this first day there are **two possible paths**, the split between the two occurring just five minutes along the trail. Most trekkers, of course, will want to take both paths, one on the way up and the other on the way down. The question is, therefore, which path to take first?

Regarding these two trails, **the first** is a longer and more circuitous route that follows a 4WD dirt track as it swerves drunkenly and only very approximately along the course of the Ngare Nanyuki (the river you cross on a bridge right at the beginning of the trek) and Jekukumia rivers through the forest before turning north to cross the Crater Plain to the huts. As for the **second option**, this is a much more direct path and, on first sight at least, would appear

to be the more tempting. It includes a crossing of the Meru Plain that's alive with Africa's tallest mammal (the giraffe) and its most bad-tempered (the buffalo), and could also take in a diversion to the beautiful Tululusia Falls (if you haven't already visited them on the way up, of course, which is where we describe them on p278). Weirdly, there's very little forest on this route, the path sticking to the top of a grassy, largely tree-less ridge.

Unless you specify otherwise the chances are your ranger/guide will take you on this shorter, steeper path; and it is indeed a wonderful walk. However, we advise you to leave this option until the end and instead **choose the longer trail for your ascent**. Why? Simply because, in our experience, most trekkers are too tired on the last day of their trek to attempt the longer trail on the way down, whatever their intentions when they began their trek. (Indeed, if you're on a three-day trek you may well not even have time to do the longer trail on the last day.) In other words, if you don't take the longer path now, for the ascent, the chances are you'll miss out on it altogether. There's also the matter of acclimatisation to consider, for taking over four hours to climb the 906m to Miriakamba Huts is more sensible than taking just two or so, as you would on the shorter trail. So don't be too eager to get amongst the animals on the plain at the foot of Meru but instead choose the longer trail for your ascent and save the shorter trail for the way down; and this is how we've described the trek in the route description beginning on p278.

The cost

Trips up Meru are usually offered by the agencies in Arusha (the best place to organise such a trek) for either three or four days. **Don't be misled into thinking that if you book a four-day trek you are more likely to reach the summit because of the extra day's acclimatisation**; that extra day is actually spent on the *way down*, not up. So, while we like to have the extra day to descend – it's a bit too much of a rush otherwise to go from the summit to Momela Gate in one day and we were grateful to spend a second night at Miriakamba – if you're on a tight budget you'll save yourself a small fortune in **park fees** by taking a day less. These park fees tend to be a little cheaper than the equivalent charges on Kili and are as follows (all prices from July 2017):

- Conservation fee (formerly known as Park Entrance fee): US$45 per day (US$22.50 per day for under 16s)
- Hut fee: US$30 per night
- Rescue fee: US$20 per trip
- Guide/ranger fee: US$15 per day

Once again there is **18% VAT** to pay on top of each of these fees.

Thus for a four-day/three-night trip you're looking at a total figure of US$350 plus VAT. On top of this you'll probably need to pay the equivalent **porters/guide fees** to enable them to enter and stay in the park. All these fees will be factored into the total amount the trekking agency charges for your trek so needn't concern you too much here. However, you may have noticed in the above examples that there are in fact two guides in the party: one supplied by

the agency and one by the park (whom we have called a ranger/guide to avoid confusion). The **ranger/guide** supplied by the park **is compulsory**, for it is he who carries the gun that, should any of the local fauna take an unhealthy interest in your party, could come in very handy. However, these rangers in our experience are often better guides, with good English and a greater knowledge of the park, mainly because they spend most of their time in it. Indeed, on one of our treks we didn't even see the guide who had been supplied by the trekking agency until we got to the Miriakamba Huts at the end of the first day!

Trekking with an agency

The trekking agencies in Arusha usually charge from US$700pp for four days. You may want to factor into this fee a night or two at one of the lodges near the park. This will enable you to make an early start in the morning (though treks are officially not allowed to start until 10am anyway, so as not to disrupt the animals' dawn hunt). The top choice is the eccentric *Hatari Lodge* (☎ 0752-553456; 🖳 hatarilodge.de), which has real history and character. The lodge is named after the John Wayne film (see p395) that was shot on the farm. Indeed, one of Wayne's co-stars, a German actor called Hardy Krüger, actually ended up giving up Hollywood for Arusha, and bought the farm on which the lodge is set soon after the film was completed. Lying just outside the park's northern boundary, the only realistic way of getting to it is via the park itself so you have to pay the park fees. With a small library, long bar, breakfast terrace and great views of both Kili and Meru, this is a refreshingly different safari lodge with décor and location that are best described as quirky. Prices start at around US$300 per person full board even in the very low season. If you have the time, come here for a drink even if you're not staying. There are cheaper places near the Ngongongare entrance gate.

❏ **Pressure from guides for a big tip**

One of the uglier aspects of many Meru climbs is the pressure exerted by guide and ranger in tandem on the poor trekker to pay a sizeable tip. Sit in the Miriakamba or Saddle Huts and you'll see them sidle up to their clients, innocently ask them how their dinner was, make a light bit of chit chat – and then launch into a speech about how much they are expecting to receive in gratuities. I have heard tales of people paying fortunes after being subjected to such pressure and of other trekkers being left in tears after being forced to hand over far more than they were initially expecting. Suffice to say, I think it's well within your rights to tell these gentlemen in no uncertain terms to get lost. Furthermore, you could also tell them that if they are to get a tip (which, of course, they are entitled to if they have carried out their job professionally) **it is entirely up to you how much you'll pay**, and that if they don't leave you alone the tip will be reduced in size accordingly. If they continue, report them to both the park authorities and the agency with which you climbed. See p25 for tips on tipping on Kili; on Meru the daily rate should be pretty much the same for porters, cooks and guides, though you'll also have to factor in tips for the ranger who should get the same amount as the guide.

I am a great supporter and admirer of the guides and rangers and the work they do – but this is a disgusting practice and needs to stop.

STAGE 1: MOMELA GATE TO MIRIAKAMBA HUTS
(VIA THE LONGER ROUTE)   [MAP A, p279]

Distance: 13.8km (8½ miles); altitude gained: 906m (2972ft)
Though this longer route avoids the fauna-filled Meru Plain, there's still an abundance of wildlife to be seen on this trail. In addition to the beasts of the savannah that can still be espied behind the screen of acacias, within the first five minutes – no, make that three – of starting one trek up Meru we also encountered dik dik and suni standing motionless in the scrub lining the path, while a little further on a troop of baboons greeted our approach by turning their backs to us and displaying their red-raw fundaments.

It's a hot and dusty start to the trek but a distinctly memorable one; even on this longer route we guarantee you'll see more animals within the first

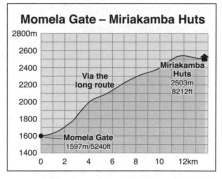

half-hour of your expedition than you would in a month on Kili. If your guide is amenable, you can also take the path off right to visit impressive **Tululusia Falls**.

The scenery changes slightly as you reach the junction with the path to Campsite 3 and the path bends right (west), with both the gradient and the size of the trees increasing. (These campsites, incidentally, are not for the use of trekkers.) The first junipers, bearded with lichen, appear and the whole trail now takes on a lusher, greener aspect. Continuing up the hill, your guide, bored with the repetitive twists and turns of the official trail, may take you on a well-known short-cut, emerging back onto the trail just before a stream with a marshy patch of grassland to the left – nicknamed **Meru's Garden** by the guides and often populated by bushbuck and blue monkey – and the summit beyond. A good opportunity for a photo, methinks. A second photo opportunity occurs just a minute later with the first of several signposted **Kilimanjaro viewpoints**.

Regardless of whether you take photos at these places or not, one sight which we can almost guarantee will have you reaching for your Rolleiflex is the **arched fig tree**, a magnificent strangler fig (*Ficus thonningii*) which has now completely enveloped its host and arches across the track. It is reminiscent of those pictures you see of giant redwoods in California which have cars driving through them – though in this instance it is said to have been elephants who have passed through the tunnel formed by the tree, widening the gap as they do so.

The path, illuminated by popcorn cassia (*Cassia didymobotrya*; incorrectly

MOUNT MERU

For details about the features shown on the trail maps in this guide, please see p286.

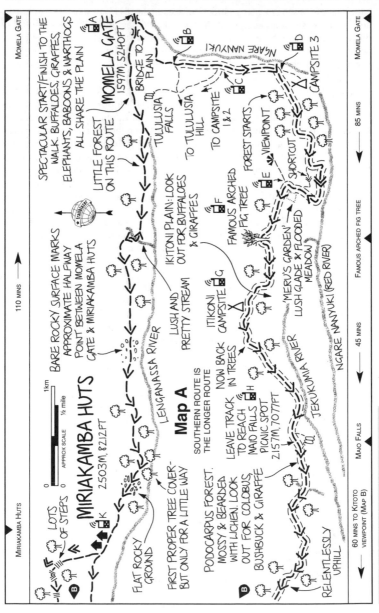

MIRIAKAMBA HUTS

MOMELA GATE

110 MINS

SPECTACULAR START/FINISH TO THE WALK. BUFFALOES, GIRAFFES, ELEPHANTS, BABOONS & WARTHOGS ALL SHARE THE PLAIN

MOMELA GATE 1597M, 5240FT

A

B

C

D

NGARE NANYUKI

BRIDGE TO PLAIN

CAMPSITE 3

TULULUSIA FALLS

TO TULULUSIA HILL

TO CAMPSITE 1 & 2

LITTLE FOREST ON THIS ROUTE

E VIEWPOINT

FOREST STARTS

SHORTCUT

BARE ROCKY SURFACE MARKS APPROXIMATE HALFWAY POINT BETWEEN MOMELA GATE & MIRIAKAMBA HUTS

IKITONI PLAIN: LOOK OUT FOR BUFFALOES & GIRAFFES

F FAMOUS ARCHED FIG TREE

LENGANASSA RIVER

LUSH AND PRETTY STREAM

ITIKONI CAMPSITE G

'MERU'S GARDEN' LUSH GLADE & FLOODED MEADOW

MIRIAKAMBA HUTS

K 2503M, 8212FT

Map A

SOUTHERN ROUTE IS THE LONGER ROUTE

NOW BACK IN TREES

LEAVE TRACK TO REACH MAIO FALLS H PICNIC SPOT 2157M, 7077FT

NGARE NANYUKI (RED RIVER)

JEKUKUMIA RIVER

LOTS OF STEPS

B

FLAT ROCKY GROUND

FIRST PROPER TREE COVER - BUT ONLY FOR A LITTLE WAY

PODOCARPUS FOREST. MOSSY & BEARDED WITH LICHEN. LOOK OUT FOR COLOBUS, BUSHBUCK & GIRAFFE

B

RELENTLESSLY UPHILL

APPROX SCALE

0   1km
0   ½ mile

trailblazer

85 MINS

FAMOUS ARCHED FIG TREE

45 MINS

MAIO FALLS

60 MINS TO KITOTO VIEWPOINT (MAP B)

MOUNT MERU

called candle bushes by many guides) in season, heads north soon after to cross an open area with a good view of the summit and possible sightings of buffalo on the **Itikoni Plain** to the south of the trail. The northerly direction is but temporary, however, the path soon reverting south to acquaint itself with the sweetwater **Jekukumia River** at **Maio Falls**, at 2157m (7077ft) altitude a picturesque spot and a delightful place to break for lunch.

Rested and replete, you now return to the main track as it continues its weaving, wriggling way westwards up the slope. It's a pleasant stroll, the gradient seldom steep and the stands of juniper and podocarpus providing essential shade. The forest is still alive with animals, too, even though they may be more difficult to see. Your ranger/guide, however, should be able to point out the tracks of hyaena, snake, leopard, giraffe or buffalo and your walk will, more than likely, be accompanied by the bark of the bushbuck, call of the colobus monkey (which sounds curiously like a frog) and the broken-klaxon honk of Hartlaub's turaco (which, just to confuse matters, sounds curiously like a monkey). If you're lucky, a crash in the undergrowth or in the branches will give away the precise location of these shy creatures, or indeed of giraffe or buffalo.

The scenery is just as pleasant as before lunch, but by now tiredness and a desire for change will probably have set in, along with a wish that the track, for a few metres at least, would follow a straight line. Thankfully, about an hour after leaving the falls the first red hot pokers (Map B) appear (*Kniphofia thomsonii*), a flower that heralds the imminent arrival of **Kitoto Viewpoint**, with views east-north-east over the Momela Lakes and east-south-east over the fauna-filled Ngurdoto Crater, the original centre and raison d'être of Arusha National Park before it merged with Meru to create the current park you find today.

From now until the end of this first stage the path feels more alpine. It's still upwards, at least until you reach a clearing with unrestricted views of the petrified lava flow that runs down from the ash cone to the plateau on which you stand – the so-called **Crater Plain**. This plain, though more than 2600m (8530ft) above sea level, still attracts an abundance of game including giraffe, hyaena, leopard, elephant and buffalo. On the northern edge of this mini plain is the dry, rocky river-bed of the upper reaches of the **Lenganassa River**, which you follow downhill to your first night's destination.

Miriakamba Huts (Map A) are a smart pair of accommodation huts and

accompanying buildings at an altitude of 2503m/8212ft. The huts are divided into rooms for four people in two bunk beds and are popular not only with tourists but also, if the amount of dung is anything to go by, buffalo and elephant too; for this reason, we advise you to take care when nipping out to the loo at night. There are also good views across to Kilimanjaro from the toilets and the viewing platforms at the back of the dining hut.

The famous arched fig tree

STAGE 2: MIRIAKAMBA HUTS TO SADDLE HUTS
[MAP A, p279; map B, p282]

Distance: 6.1km (3¾ miles); altitude gained: 1057m (3468ft)

Everybody has their favourite section of the Meru trek and the walk from the Miriakamba Huts to the lunch stop at Mgongo Wa Tembo is ours. There's something gentle and gorgeously pastoral about the grassy slopes that puts one in mind of the rolling hills of England for some reason – the exotic flora and piles of buffalo and elephant crap notwithstanding. Indeed, it's the unusual flora – the *Hagenia abyssinica* with its heavy pink/brown blossom, for example, or a species of lobelia (see p183) which resembles in no way the lobelias you'll find in your garden at home – and the continuing presence of the park's larger fauna that add so

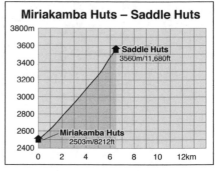

much to the day. Even the path is impressive, a wooden staircase leading west up the slopes of the ridge towards the Saddle. Then, of course, there are the views over your shoulder of Kilimanjaro glowering at its little brother, its white summit glistening in the sun. It's a great morning's walk. Nor does the interest for trekkers wane much after lunch as the path enters the alpine zone. The trees diminish in size before disappearing altogether, to be replaced by the heathers that flourish at this altitude. The only problem with the latter half of this second day is that it can become slightly monotonous after a while and impatience and ennui can set in. But don't be in too much of a hurry: from the moment you set off it's vital you take it *pole pole* because of the altitude.

So, from Miriakamba adopt a funereal speed from the word *Twende* ('Go!'). After a few minutes traversing the ridge, the trail heads off up the steps of the mountain's eastern flanks. The path zig-zags for much of the morning, with juniper and hagenia lining the way together with the occasional stand of *Lobelia gibberoa*, whose younger plants display an impressive phallic brush growing out of their tops. Elephants can occasionally be seen along this stretch, so do make sure you stick close to the man with the gun. The path soon bends in a more northerly direction, with great views of Kili to your right framed by the local vegetation. There are some venerable old fallen trees here with some vivid red mountain gladioli growing from the trunks. Following the zig-zags, **Mgongo Wa Tembo** ('Elephant's Back'; about 3086m, 10,124ft) is reached, the usual lunch-stop on this second stage with views south over the Crater Plain.

The path continues to climb after the break, soon leaving the forest for something altogether more alpine with *Philippia excelsa* and *Erica arborea* now proliferating. If you're lucky, you may also come across chameleons that, despite

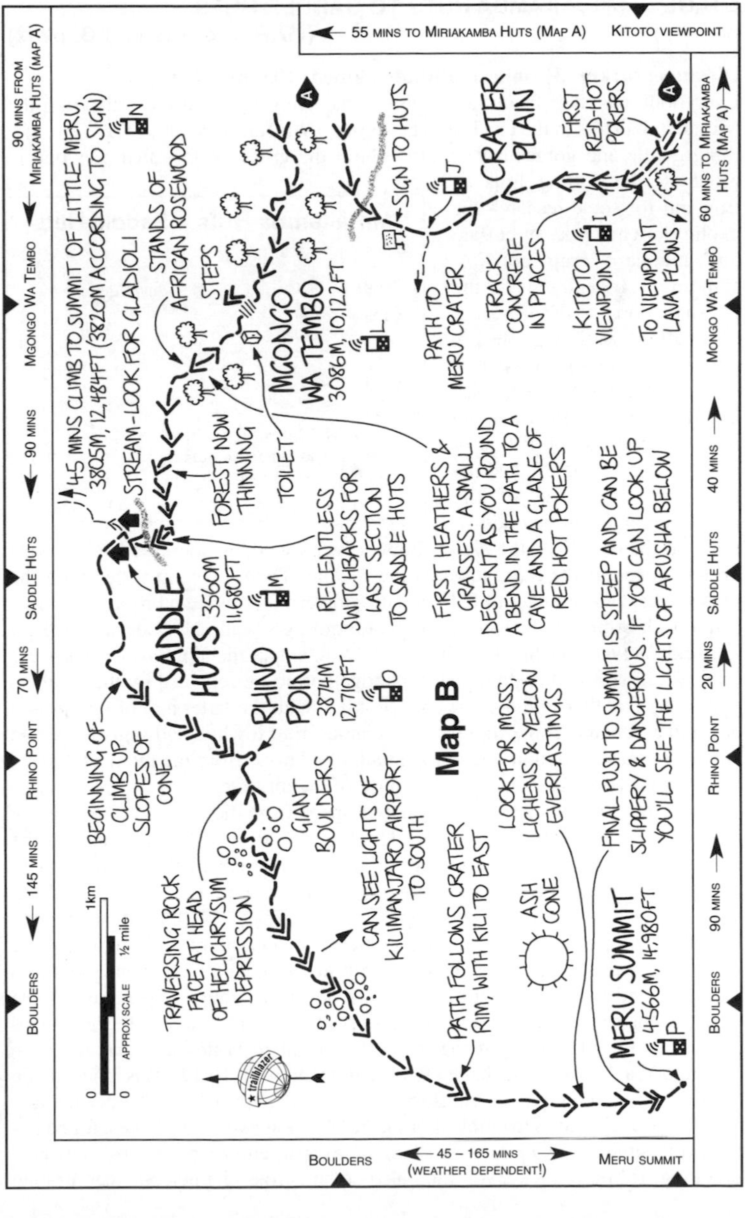

MOUNT MERU

55 MINS TO MIRIAKAMBA HUTS (MAP A)   KITOTO VIEWPOINT

90 MINS FROM MIRIAKAMBA HUTS (MAP A)

90 MINS TO MIRIAKAMBA HUTS (MAP A)

1¼-1½ MINS CLIMB TO SUMMIT OF LITTLE MERU, 3805M, 12,484FT (3820M ACCORDING TO SIGN)

STREAM—LOOK FOR GLADIOLI

STANDS OF AFRICAN ROSEWOOD

STEPS

SIGN TO HUTS

CRATER PLAIN

FIRST RED-HOT POKERS

TRACK CONCRETE IN PLACES

KITOTO VIEWPOINT

TO VIEWPOINT LAVA FLOWS

PATH TO MERU CRATER

MGONGO WA TEMBO 3,086M, 10,122FT

TOILET

FOREST NOW THINNING

RELENTLESS SWITCHBACKS FOR LAST SECTION TO SADDLE HUTS

FIRST HEATHERS & GRASSES. A SMALL DESCENT AS YOU ROUND A BEND IN THE PATH TO A CAVE AND A GLADE OF RED HOT POKERS

BEGINNING OF CLIMB UP SLOPES OF CONE

SADDLE HUTS 3560M, 11,680FT

RHINO POINT 3874M, 12,710FT

Map B

GIANT BOULDERS

CAN SEE LIGHTS OF KILIMANJARO AIRPORT TO SOUTH

LOOK FOR MOSS, LICHENS & YELLOW EVERLASTINGS

FINAL PUSH TO SUMMIT IS STEEP AND CAN BE SLIPPERY & DANGEROUS. IF YOU CAN LOOK UP YOU'LL SEE THE LIGHTS OF ARUSHA BELOW

TRAVERSING ROCK FACE AT HEAD OF HELICHRYSUM DEPRESSION

1km

APPROX SCALE   ½ mile

0

0

ASH CONE

PATH FOLLOWS CRATER RIM, WITH KILI TO EAST

MERU SUMMIT 4,566M, 14,980FT

MGONGO WA TEMBO

SADDLE HUTS

RHINO POINT

BOULDERS

145 MINS

90 MINS

70 MINS

90 MINS

40 MINS

20 MINS

90 MINS

60 MINS TO MIRIAKAMBA HUTS (MAP A)

BOULDERS   45 – 165 MINS (WEATHER DEPENDENT!)   MERU SUMMIT

being cold-blooded creatures, somehow thrive in this region. It's a bit of a relent-less, monotonous trek but it's not long before the **Saddle Huts** (3560m, 11,680ft) are reached. As with Miriakamba, these are smart huts that almost put those on Kilimanjaro to shame. Yet despite the altitude the huts still get the occasional interloper from Africa's animal kingdom, including elephant and buffalo passing through on their way to the grasslands further west. There's little to do up here, allowing you to spend the rest of the afternoon climbing the nearby 3805m (12,484ft) **Little Meru**, a simple 45-minute trudge that the guides will often allow you to do by yourself; it's a climb that takes you to an altitude not far short of Rhino Point which you'll be visiting tonight – so remember to climb *pole pole* even though there maybe no-one to regulate your speed. That done, you can relax and prepare yourself for the exertions of the night to come...

STAGE 3: SADDLE HUTS TO THE SUMMIT
(AND BACK TO MIRIAKAMBA HUTS) [Map B, opposite]
Distance: 5.5km (3½ miles); altitude gained: 1006m (3301ft)

The ascent – Saddle Huts to the Summit
And so to the final ascent, and if the height of Meru is invaluable for acclima-tising, so this night-time march is wonderful preparation for that final push to Kili's Uhuru Peak. True, this walk is shorter and, unlike the relentless zig-zags taking you up Kibo's slopes, more varied and direct. But the experience of waking up at some godforsaken hour to undertake a chilly high-altitude trek up a very big African vol-cano, before contouring around the crater rim to reach the high-est point as the sun rises to the east, is useful training indeed.

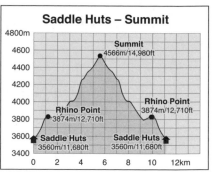

The stage begins with a crossing of the Saddle before bending south to the start of the climb. It's a walk that sees you leave behind the larger vegetation – the ericas and philippias – on a winding path that eventually joins the crest of a ridge that brings you out at **Rhino Point** (3874m, 12,710ft), the climb's first landmark. Thereafter the route bends west and, having descended to cross a **rockface** at the head of a lush (by the standards of this altitude) depression, then climbs to follow the lip of the Meru Crater. For the next couple of hours the path follows the course of the crater rim. Being night, of course, you'll have to wait for views of the crater itself until the morning, though beyond it you should be able to see, in the distance, the lights of various settlements as well as Kilimanjaro International Airport and even, in the far dis-tance, the Mererani tanzanite mine, working away through the night. Eventually, about 3½ hours after setting off, the crater rim begins to bend noticeably south.

On the summit of Mount Meru

As it does, hopefully at the same time the eastern horizon will start to turn pink and orange with the onset of the new day, and the silhouette of Kili can clearly be discerned, with both Kibo and Mawenzi summits visible.

The summit (4566m; 14,980ft) seems tangibly closer, too, so it's disheartening to discover that it's still a minimum of an hour away – or nearer three if it's been snowing and your guides have to create a path in the ice using nothing but the heels of their boots as spades and bits of rocks as shovels! It can be a little terrifying, too, with one false step sending you plummeting down the icy slopes. Take care!

At the summit (which used to be called Socialist Peak, though they've since taken away the sign) there's little save a flag, a sign and a box containing a book where you can sign your name. There are also, of course, great views over Arusha to the west and Kili to the east, with Meru's perfect ash cone below you.

The descent – the Summit to Miriakamba Huts

Photos taken and hands shaken, it's time for the descent – and isn't it wonderful to be able to walk at a speed of your choosing again! It's also interesting to see how different in daylight the path looks. Look back from **Rhino Point**, for

MERU SUMMIT

RHINO POINT

SADDLE HUTS

Mount Meru – Route to the Summit

example, to the climb up to the crater rim – was it really that steep? Notice, too, while renegotiating the descent from the summit, all the mini bumps and craters to the north and west of Meru which were hidden on the way up.

The descent back to the Saddle, though wearying, shouldn't take more than 2½-3 hours. Those who've opted to spend four days on the mountain will take an hour or so back at the **Saddle Huts**, packing their bags, eating some well-earned food and maybe getting a little shut-eye, before the two-hour return stroll down to Miriakamba where they'll be spending the night. Those on the three-day trip will also have an hour to recover at the Saddle Huts, though for them the walk down is, of course, that much longer. If you're reading this at the Saddle Huts after your ascent to the summit, you'll probably appreciate now why we suggested taking the long route on the first stage and saving the shorter route for now.

STAGE 4: MIRIAKAMBA HUTS TO MOMELA GATE
(via the shorter route)   [Map A, p279]

Distance: 6.5km (4 miles); altitude lost: 906m (2972ft)

One of the advantages Meru has over Kilimanjaro is that this last stage, though short, is in no way an anti-climax, whereas the last day on Kili often feels like something to endure rather than enjoy. The descent from Miriakamba is hard on your knees, of course, but by way of compensation there's some unusual flora (check out the pink *Impatiens* growing right on the path and the hardy Sodom's apple trees, *Solanum sodomaeum*, growing by the side of it), a charming little river to cross and, of course, a crossing of the buffalo- and warthog-filled Meru Plain at the very end, with Kili as an awe-inspiring backdrop.

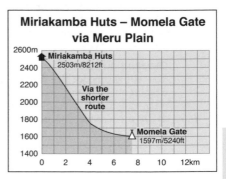

If you haven't already seen them this walk could also include a brief diversion to the impressive **Tululusia Falls**, just a few minutes off the path to the south before the plain. Isn't it curious, by the way, how there's so little forest on this route compared to the dense, dark cloud forest on the first day – even though they both cover the same altitude?

Even with the diversion you should find yourself back at Momela Gate just two hours or so after setting off. There'll just be time to distribute tips, collect your certificates (one for Mount Meru, possibly one for Little Meru too) and say your farewells to your companions. It's been a wonderful walk, hasn't it? You've seen some beautiful birds, flowers and animals, taken in some breath-taking views and through sheer bloodymindedness climbed to the very summit of Tanzania's second highest mountain.

Now it's time for the highest…

TRAIL GUIDE & MAPS

Using this guide

ABOUT THE MAPS IN THIS GUIDE
Scale
Most of the **trekking maps** in this guide are drawn to the same scale, namely 26mm to 1km (1²/₃ inches to the mile). The exceptions are the maps which depict the final ascent to the top, ie the trails up to the Kibo summit (Map Nos 6, 13, 18 & 33), which is usually made at night. On these maps the scale has been doubled (ie 52mm to 1km or 3¹/₃ inches to the mile) to allow for more detail to be drawn on them.

Walking times
The times indicated on the maps should be used only as an approximate guide. **They refer to walking times only and do not include any time for breaks and or food.** Overall you may find you need to **add around 30-50%** to our times depending on your walking speed and the time taken for rest breaks to get an idea of the total time you'll spend on the trail.

Gradient arrows
You will also notice that we have drawn '**gradient arrows**' on the trekking maps in this book. The arrows point uphill: two arrows mean that the hill is steep, one that the gradient is reasonably gradual. If, for example, you are walking from A (at 80m) to B (at 200m) and the trail between the two is short and steep, it would be shown thus: A – – – – >>– – – – B.

The Marangu Route

Because this trail is popularly called the '**Tourist Trail**' or '**Coca Cola Trail**', some trekkers are misled into thinking this 5- or 6-day climb to the summit and back is simply a walk in the (national) park. But remember that a greater proportion of people fail on this route than on any other. True, this may have something to do with the fact that Marangu's reputation for being 'easy' attracts the more inexperienced, out-of-condition trekkers who don't realise that they are embarking on a **36.55km (22¾ miles) uphill walk**, followed imme-

diately by a 36.55km knee-jarring descent. But it shouldn't take much to realise that Marangu is not much easier than any other trail: with the Machame Route, for example, you start at 1811m (5942ft) and aim for the summit at 5895m/19,341ft. On Marangu, you start just a little higher at 1905m (6250ft) and have the same goal, so simple logic should tell you that it can't be that much easier. Indeed, the fact that this route is often completed in 5-6 days as opposed to the 6-7 days it takes to complete Machame would suggest that this route is actually more arduous – and gives you some idea of why **more people fail on this trail** than on the so-called 'Whiskey Route'.

The main reason why people say that Marangu is somehow easier or 'softer' is because it is the only route where you **sleep in huts** rather than under canvas. The accommodation in these huts should be booked in advance by your tour company, who have to pay a deposit per person per night to KINAPA in order to secure it. To cover this, the tour agencies will probably ask you to pay them some money in advance too. This deposit is refundable or can be moved to secure huts on other dates, providing you give KINAPA (and your agency) at least seven days' notice.

(Bear in mind if you're booking with a Tanzanian agency for a trek the next day, you should ask your agency to show you a receipt confirming they have paid a deposit for your accommodation. Otherwise, you may find yourself being turned away at Marangu Gate at the start of your trek because your company didn't book your accommodation and there's no room.)

The fact that you do sleep in huts makes little difference to what you need to pack for the trek, for sleeping bags are still required (the huts have pillows and mattresses but that's all) though **you can dispense with a ground mat for this route**. Regarding the sleeping situation, it does help if you can get to the huts early each day to grab the better beds. This doesn't mean you should deliberately hurry to the huts, which will reduce your enjoyment of the trek and increase the possibility of AMS. But do try to **start early each morning**: that way you can avoid the crowds, beat them to the better beds, and possibly improve your chances of seeing some of Kili's wildlife too. *(continued on p290)*

Kilimanjaro seen from Lake Jipé
(from *The Kilima-njaro Expedition – A Record of Scientific Exploration in Eastern Equatorial Africa* **HH Johnston**, 1886)

(continued on p290)

❏ WHAT'S IT LIKE ON THE MOUNTAIN?

Fun. It really is. Sure, the last push to the summit is hard, as some of the quotes used later in this book clearly indicate, but don't let that put you off. Kilimanjaro is a delightful mountain to climb:

But we had much to compensate us for all we had to give up. The charm of the mountain scenery, the clear, crisp atmosphere, the tonic of 'a labour we delight in' and the consciousness now and again of success achieved, all went far to make our fortnight's arduous toil a happy sequence of red-letter days.

Hans Meyer *Across East African Glaciers*

The days are spent walking through spectacular landscapes which change every day as you pass through different vegetation zones. The pace is never exhausting, as you have to walk slowly in order to give yourself a chance to acclimatise. What's more, at the end of the day, while the guides are cooking your dinner, you are free to wander around the campsite and, as you bump into the same people time and again over the course of the trek, a sense of community soon develops. Then as night falls, and you tuck into the huge plates of food cooked by your crew, the stars come out, stunning everyone into silence. This is the favourite time of day for most people: rested, replete with food and with a day of satisfactory walking behind and a good night's sleep ahead, it's natural to feel a sense of comfort and contentment, with the thought of wild animals possibly lying nearby serving to add a pleasing frisson of excitement.

Bed? It's too early. I feel too good. Aaah, I wonder if there'll ever be another time as good as this.   **Gregory Peck**, in the film version of *The Snows of Kilimanjaro*

Of course, walking up from less than 2000m or thereabouts to 5895m does, as you can probably imagine, take a lot of effort and the night walk to the summit is unarguably tough. But short of actually carrying you up, your crew will do everything in their power to make your entire experience as comfortable as possible. In fact, they'll spoil you: not only do they carry your bag, but at the end of the day's walk you'll turn up at camp to find your tent has already been erected, with a bowl of hot water lying nearby for you to wash away the grime of the day. A few minutes later and a large plate of popcorn and biscuits will be served with a mug of steaming hot tea or coffee.

Accommodation on the trail

I got back in time to see P.D. lying on sloping ground, slipping off the stretcher, and in great pain. Small fire had been made under the root of a great tree. Rain soon came on and wiped out the fire ... tent was not put up and we were all in great misery. Men with tent lost in the darkness. Thought if the rain stopped we could go on in the moonlight. Rain did not stop.   **Peter MacQueen** *In Wildest Africa* (1910)

Unless you are on the Marangu Route, accommodation on the mountain will be in tents brought up by your porters. (Do not be tempted to sleep in any of the caves as that is against park regulations.) On the Marangu Route, camping is forbidden; instead people have to sleep in huts along the route. (You will see people camping on this route but they are trekkers who took the Rongai Route to ascend and are now descending on Marangu.) The sleeping arrangements in these huts are usually dormitory-style, with anything from four to twenty beds per room.

Confusingly, away from the Marangu Route **many of the campsites are actually called 'huts' but don't be fooled**: they are called huts because of the green shacks you'll find at these campsites which are usually inhabited by the park rangers. Trekkers used to be allowed to sleep in these huts too, many, many years ago but no longer.

The only other buildings you will possibly see along the trail are the **toilets**. Most

are of the same design, namely a little wooden hut with a hole in the floor. Some are in better condition than others; all we will say is that some people are terrible shots, while other latrines are in desperate need of emptying before the contents become Kilimanjaro's fourth peak. The 'smart new toilets' that in the last edition we stated were being built at many of the bigger camps have now been finished, and after a couple of years' use are in as parlous a state as their predecessors, with doors off their hinges, the acrid smell of ammonia and faeces all pervasive and shit everywhere. Good luck!

Food on the trail
Remember to tell your agency if you have any special dietary requirements – because meat, nuts, gluten and dairy form a substantial part of the menu on Kilimanjaro.

A typical **breakfast** will involve eggs (boiled or fried), porridge, a saveloy (possibly with some tomatoes too), a piece of fruit such as a banana or orange, some bread with jam, honey or peanut butter and a mug of tea, hot chocolate or coffee.

Lunch is sometimes prepared at breakfast and carried by the trekker in a daypack, though more expensive companies have tables set up and cook food on site. (This practice is supposedly being phased out by the authorities, concerned at the environmental damage it causes.) This packed lunch often consists of a boiled egg, sandwiches, a banana or orange, and some tea kept warm in a flask and carried by your guide.

At the end of the day's walking, **afternoon tea** is served with biscuits, peanuts and, best of all, salted popcorn. The final and biggest meal of the day, **dinner** usually begins with soup, followed by a main course including chicken or meat, a vegetable sauce, some cabbage or other vegetable, and rice or pasta; if your porters have brought up some potatoes, these will usually be eaten over the first few days as they are so heavy.

Drink on the trail
Porters will collect **water** from the rivers and streams along the trail. Some of this they will boil and maybe purify for you at the start of the day to carry in your water bottles. On the lower slopes you can collect water yourself from the many streams and purify it using a filter or tablets. Note, however, that as you climb ever higher water becomes more scarce. On the Machame trail, for example, the last water point is at Karanga Valley, the lunch-stop/campsite before Barafu; on Marangu, it's just before the Saddle. For this reason it is essential you carry enough bottles or containers for *at least* three litres.

In camp, **coffee** and **tea** are served and maybe **hot chocolate** or **Milo** (chocolate with malt) too – all usually made with powdered milk. Remember that caffeine, present in coffee and tea, is dehydrating, which can be bad for acclimatisation. Caffeine is a diuretic too (ie you will want to urinate frequently – something you should already be doing a lot as you adapt to the higher conditions).

What to put in your daypack
Normally you will not see your main backpack from the moment you hand it to the porter in the morning to at least lunchtime, and maybe not until the end of the day. It's therefore necessary to pack everything you may need during the day in the bag you carry with you. Some suggestions, in no particular order:

- sweets
- water and water purifiers
- camera/batteries/film/memory card
- phone plus battery pack
- this book/maps
- sunhat/sunglasses and suncream
- toilet paper and trowel
- plastic bag for rubbish
- rainwear
- walking sticks/knee supports
- medical kit, including chapstick
- packed lunch (supplied by your crew)

TRAIL GUIDE AND MAPS

Note: In the following descriptions, the treks have been divided into stages, with each stage roughly corresponding to a day's trekking. For this reason, throughout the text the words 'stage' and 'day' have been used interchangeably.

(continued from p287) In terms of **duration**, the Marangu Route is one of the shorter trails, and it's possible to complete the climb and descent in just five days. Many people, however, opt to take an extra day to acclimatise at Horombo Huts, using that day to visit the Mawenzi Hut at 4535m/14,879ft. From a safety point of view this is entirely sensible and aesthetically such a plan cannot be argued with either, for the views from the path to the huts across the Saddle to Kibo truly take your breath away – assuming you have some left to be taken away after all that climbing.

One aspect of the Marangu Route that could be seen by some as a drawback is that it is the only one where you **ascend and descend via the same path**. However, there are a couple of arguments to counter this perception: firstly, between Horombo and Kibo Huts there are two paths and it shouldn't take too much to persuade your guide to use one trail on the ascent and a different one on the way down; and there's a Nature Trail alternative on the descent from Mandara Huts to the gate as well. Both of these are described in the book on p373 and p375 respectively. Secondly, we think that the walk back down the Marangu Route is one of the most pleasurable parts of the entire trek, with the gradients more gentle than on other descents and splendid views over the shoulder. Furthermore, it offers you the chance to greet the crowds of sweating, red-faced unfortunates heading the other way with the smug expression of one for whom physical pain is now a thing of the past and whose immediate future is filled with warm showers and cold beers.

STAGE 1: MARANGU GATE TO MANDARA HUTS
[MAP 1, opposite; MAP 2, p295]

Distance: 8.3km (5¼ miles; 8.75km – 5½ miles if taking the Nature Trail); altitude gained: 818m (2684ft)

The woods are lovely, dark and deep,
But I have promises to keep,
And miles to go before I sleep.
Robert Frost as seen on a signwriter's wall in Moshi

As the headquarters of **KINA-PA** (Kilimanjaro National Park), you might expect Marangu Gate (altitude 1905m/6250ft) to have the best facilities of all the gates and it doesn't disappoint. Not only does

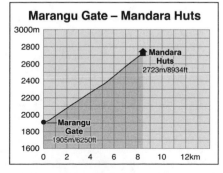

Marangu Gate – Mandara Huts

Mandara Huts 2723m/8934ft

Marangu Gate 1905m/6250ft

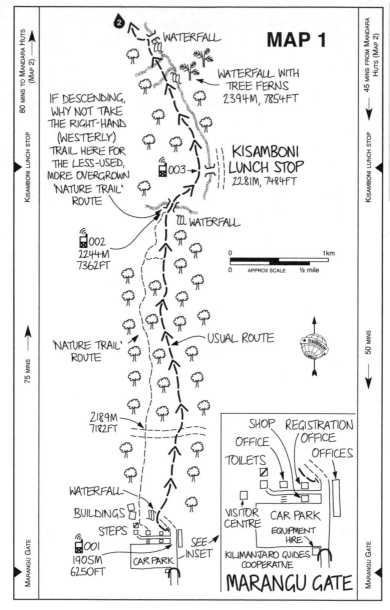

MAP 1

80 MINS TO MANDARA HUTS (MAP 2)

KISAMBONI LUNCH STOP

75 MINS

MARANGU GATE

45 MINS FROM MANDARA HUTS (MAP 2)

KISAMBONI LUNCH STOP

50 MINS

MARANGU GATE

WATERFALL

WATERFALL WITH TREE FERNS 2394M, 7854FT

IF DESCENDING, WHY NOT TAKE THE RIGHT-HAND (WESTERLY) TRAIL HERE FOR THE LESS-USED, MORE OVERGROWN 'NATURE TRAIL' ROUTE

003

KISAMBONI LUNCH STOP 2281M, 7484FT

WATERFALL

002 2244M 7362FT

0   1km
0 APPROX SCALE ½ mile

'NATURE TRAIL' ROUTE

USUAL ROUTE

trailblazer

2189M 7182FT

WATERFALL

BUILDINGS

STEPS

001 1905M 6250FT

CAR PARK

SEE INSET

SHOP   REGISTRATION OFFICE   OFFICE
TOILETS   OFFICES

VISITOR CENTRE   CAR PARK
EQUIPMENT HIRE
KILIMANJARO GUIDES COOPERATIVE

MARANGU GATE

MAPS AND MAPS *(TRAIL GUIDE AND MAPS)*

❏ **Mobile (cell) phone reception on the Marangu Route**
Marangu Route generally has poor reception. It depends which network you're with but I found that there is little to no reception at the Mandara Huts (though I did get reception at the nearby **Maundi Crater**), and the first real chance of getting reception on the trail was at **Horombo Huts**; reception there was patchy but walk around and you should be able to find some places where you can connect with the outside world. After that, reception at Kibo Huts was pretty much non-existent and you'll have to wait until **Stella Point** and **Uhuru Peak** before regaining contact with the outside world again.

---

the gate have the usual **registration office** but there's also a picnic area, a smart toilet block and a **shop** that has a good collection of books and souvenirs. There's also a small booth run by Kilimanjaro Guides Cooperative by the entrance to the car park where you can **hire any equipment** you may have forgotten to bring along, from essentials such as hats and fleeces, coats (US$10 per trip), trekking poles (US$10 per trip) and water bottles (US$5 per trip) to camping stuff that you almost certainly won't need on the trail such as stoves and so forth, which should be provided by your agency.

Having gone through the laborious business of **registering** (a process that usually takes at least an hour, though it can be quicker if you manage to get here before the large tour groups arrive), you begin your trek by following the trekkers' path which heads left off the road (which is now used solely by porters). You may still find the odd eucalyptus tree around the gate, one of the few non-native plants on the mountain. They were introduced, according to the version I've heard, by the first chief park warden of Kilimanjaro, a man who married a relative of Idi Amin – the former despot of Uganda later shooting him in an argument, so the story goes. As an 'alien' species and one that consumes a lot of water, the eucalyptus trees are slowly being eradicated by the authorities from the national park itself. (It has to be a gradual process, however: look through the trees to your right just after you start out and you'll see a big open area – the ugly result of eradicating the trees too quickly.)

This first day's walk is a very pleasant one of just over 8km and though the route is uphill for virtually the entire time, there are enough distractions in the forest to take your mind off the exertion, from the occasional troop of **blue monkeys** to the vivid red *Impatiens kilimanjari*, a small flower that has become the emblem of Kilimanjaro. The path soon veers towards and then follows the course of a **mountain stream**; sometimes through the increasingly impenetrable vegetation to your right you can glimpse the occasional small **waterfall**.

After about 1¼ hours a wooden bridge leads off the trail over this stream to the picnic tables at **Kisamboni** (2281m/7484ft) and a reunion with the 4WD porters' trail. This is the halfway point of the first stage and in all probability it is here that you will be served lunch.

... ferns and heaths were plentiful, the last-named preponderating as we got higher up. At a height of 6,300 feet, however, all these were merged in the primaeval forest, in which old patriarchs with knotted stunted forms stood closely together, many of them worsted in the

❑ TREKKERS' EXPERIENCES

Of course, everybody's experience of climbing Kili is different. The majority of correspondence we get are of the 'had the time of my life' variety, which are particularly lovely to receive, especially as it's great to know other people enjoyed the experience as much as we always do:

What a fab trip! And yes, we all made it to the top (one of us with a humungous, vice-like headache, but our good guide carried her pack on the last leg)!! And best of all, we all came back friends!   Anneliese Dibetta (Canada)

A few letters also contain some useful advice:

If I can make any strong recommendations it is the truth and value of 'pole pole'... I redefined the phrase pole pole and from the first step to the last I went the pace I needed to do to keep my heart rate even and not get out of breath. More often than not I was way behind the group, always had one of the guides or assistant guides with me and not once did I feel pressured to go faster. It was the key to my success.
Clare Wickens (US)

I found the trail up the Western Breach to be tough but not necessarily dangerous. I think the 'toughness' came from being at the altitude we were at – which raised both the level of exertion needed to climb and the fatigue I was experiencing from the trip so far – more than the trail itself. As I watched the porters trot by with large loads (five dozen eggs on one guy or our dining table and chairs) I realised how easy the trail really was even though at the time I was feeling taxed by it.   Patti Wickham (US)

One general observation would be that although everyone said how much it was to do with altitude, I didn't realise the extent of it. I thought I'd tire easily and be breathless, but didn't understand how half the people would have headaches, and people would be running out of the dining hall to vomit. I was mentally prepared for something physically demanding, but not for feeling ill and having a headache for days on end...
    As you come up to Kibo, a few people said they start to get excited and want to get it over with quickly. I'd say it's worth advising them to make sure they keep going slowly, and warn them that a lot of people suddenly feel really tired during the last 5-10 minutes of the walk.   Richard Evans (UK)

One or two of them were quite encouraging too:

Two of us were not really in good enough shape to complete Kili by any route, no scrambling experience, and no strong expectation of summiting, but by taking seven days and by doing the scramble in the daylight, all made it to the summit, and back down to Mweka Gate, happy, safe and sound.   John Wickham (US)

That's not to suggest, of course, that everyone has a pleasant time...

I've had a lovely few days but now I have a headache and feel like shit. Please leave me alone. Thank you. Overheard at Barafu Camp and shouted by an anonymous German hiding inside his tent while his group readied themselves for the final climb.

For a couple of days I thought you must have a great job: travel around the world and write about it. I now know better. I feel sorry for you. I thought climbing Kilimanjaro was hell. I would ask for a big raise in your salary if I were you...
Mark Burgmans (Holland)

perpetual struggle with the encroachments of the parasitical growths of almost fabulous strength and size, which enfolded trunks and branches alike in their fatal embrace, crippling the giants themselves and squeezing to death the mosses, lichens, and ferns which had clothed their nakedness. Everything living seemed doomed to fall prey to them, but they in their turn bore their own heavy burden of parasites; creepers, from a yard to two yards long, hanging down in garlands and festoons, or forming one thick veil shrouding whole clumps of trees. Wherever a little space had been left amongst the many fallen and decaying trunks, the ground was covered with a luxurious vegetation, including many varieties of herbaceous plants with bright coloured flowers, orchids, and the modest violet peeping out amongst them, whilst more numerous than all were different lycopods and sword-shaped ferns.   **Lieutenant Ludwig von Höhnel**
                                  Discovery by Count Teleki of Lakes Rudolf and Stefanie (1894)

Returning to the trail and turning right, you continue climbing north for 30 minutes to another bridge, again leading off to the right of the trail; your path, however, heads off to the left, directly away from the bridge. The trail is a little steeper now as you wind your way through the forest. It is a very pretty part of the walk, with varieties of *Impatiens* edging the path and, draped amongst the trees, the white-flowered *Begonia meyeri-johannis*; though by now you may be feeling a little too tired to enjoy it to its fullest.

Press on, and 15 minutes later yet another bridge appears which you *do* take (see Map 2). Like some sort of botanical border post, the bridge heralds the first appearance of the **giant heathers** (*Erica excelsa*) on the trail, with masses of **bearded lichen** liberally draped over them; though the forest reappears intermittently up to and beyond Maundi Crater it's the spindly heathers and stumpy shrubs of the second vegetation zone, the alpine heath and moorland, that now dominate.

From this bridge, the first night's accommodation, **Mandara Huts** (2723m/8934ft), lies just 35 minutes away. If you have the energy, a quick 15-minute saunter to the parasitic cone known as **Maundi Crater** is worthwhile both for its views east over Kenya and north-west to Mawenzi and for the wild flowers and grasses growing on its slopes. On the way to the crater, look in the trees for the bands of semi-tame monkeys, both blue and colobus, that live here and are particularly active at dusk.

It was a relief to enter the rain forest, and it is a relief to leave it in early afternoon, emerging into an open meadow of grass six feet high. However, by now I am very tired – astonishingly tired and the path up the meadow is steep. I am wondering how much farther I must go. There are no signposts to tell me how I am doing, how far before we reach the huts. Unable to plan, unable to pace myself, I find my fatigue feels extreme. Do I have an hour still to go? Two hours? Then I see, on a ridge above the high grass, the brown geometric A-frames of the Mandara huts. They are very close. It is only four o'clock in the afternoon. I am not really so tired after all.   **Michael Crichton**, *Travels* (1988)

Incidentally, Mandara Huts are the only huts on the mountain to be named after a person rather than a place. Mandara was the fearsome chief of Moshi, a warrior whose skill and bravery on the battlefield was matched only by his stunning cupidity off it. Mandara once boasted that he had met every white man to visit Kilimanjaro, from Johannes Rebmann to Hans Meyer, and it's a fair bet

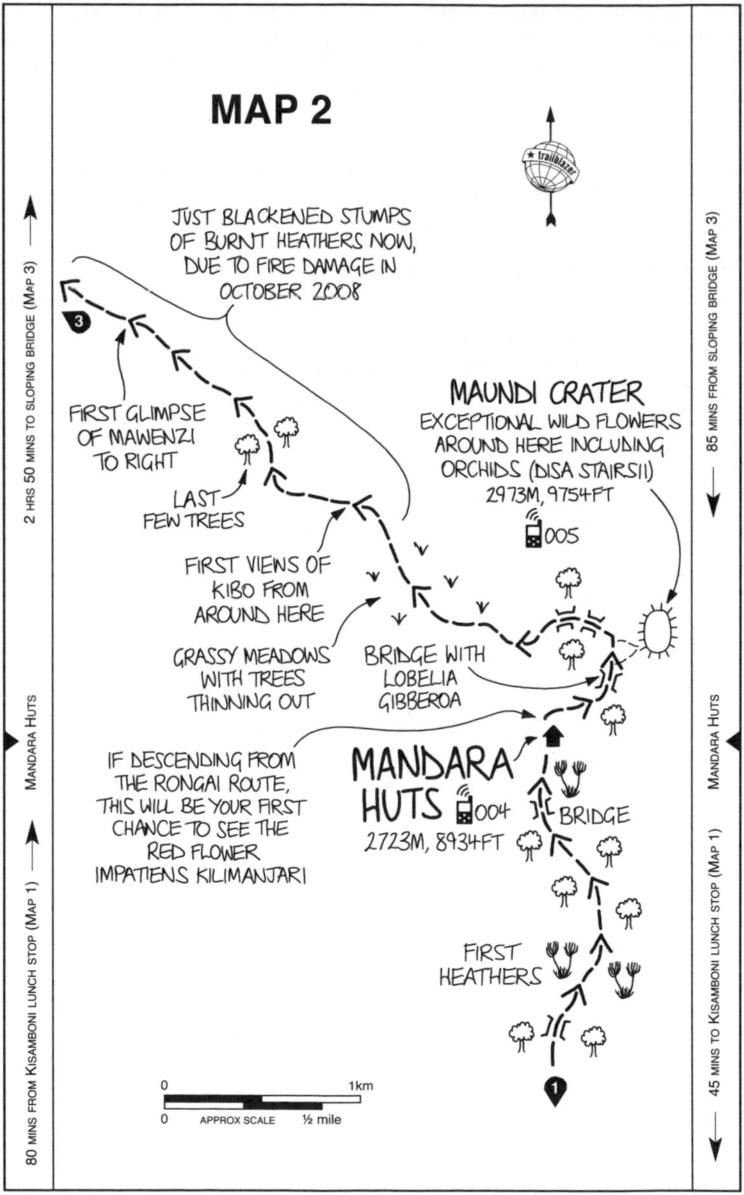

MAP 2

JUST BLACKENED STUMPS
OF BURNT HEATHERS NOW,
DUE TO FIRE DAMAGE IN
OCTOBER 2008

3

FIRST GLIMPSE
OF MAWENZI
TO RIGHT

LAST
FEW TREES

FIRST VIEWS OF
KIBO FROM
AROUND HERE

GRASSY MEADOWS
WITH TREES
THINNING OUT

MAUNDI CRATER
EXCEPTIONAL WILD FLOWERS
AROUND HERE INCLUDING
ORCHIDS (DISA STAIRSII)
2973M, 9754FT
005

BRIDGE WITH
LOBELIA
GIBBEROA

IF DESCENDING FROM
THE RONGAI ROUTE,
THIS WILL BE YOUR FIRST
CHANCE TO SEE THE
RED FLOWER
IMPATIENS KILIMANJARI

MANDARA
HUTS 004
2723M, 8934FT

BRIDGE

FIRST
HEATHERS

1

0   1km
0   APPROX SCALE   ½ mile

2 HRS 50 MINS TO SLOPING BRIDGE (MAP 3)

MANDARA HUTS

80 MINS FROM KISAMBONI LUNCH STOP (MAP 1)

85 MINS FROM SLOPING BRIDGE (MAP 3)

MANDARA HUTS

45 MINS TO KISAMBONI LUNCH STOP (MAP 1)

that all of them would have been required to present the chief with a huge array of presents brought from their own country. Failure to do so was not an option, for those who, in Mandara's eye (he had only one, having lost the other in battle), were insufficiently generous in their gift-giving, put their lives in peril. The attack that led to the death of Charles New (see p159), for example, was said to have been orchestrated by Mandara after New had 'insulted' him by refusing to give the chief the watch from his waistcoat. Read any of the 19th-century accounts of Kilimanjaro and you'll usually find plenty of pages devoted to this fascinating character – with few casting him in a favourable light.

STAGE 2: MANDARA HUTS TO HOROMBO HUTS
[MAP 2 p295; MAP 3, opposite]

Distance: 12.5km (7¾ miles); altitude gained: 998m (3274ft)

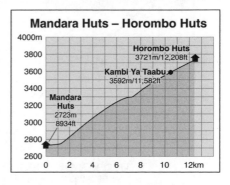

On this stage, in which you gain almost a kilometre in altitude, you say a final goodbye to the forest and spend the greater part of the day walking through the bleaker landscape of Kilimanjaro's moorland. If the weather's clear you will get your first really good look at the twin peaks of Kili, namely spiky Mawenzi and snow-capped Kibo; they will continue to loom large and will doubtless appear in just about every photo you take from now to the summit. The proteas, giant groundsels (*Dendrosenecio kilimanjari*) and phallic lobelias (*Lobelia deckenii*) also make their first appearance, with the groundsels growing in some abundance towards the latter part of the walk and especially around Horombo Huts.

The whole landscape as far as the eye could reach was a medley of dull grey lava slabs, dotted with the red-leafed protea shrub (Protea Kilimandscharica) and stunted heaths, which became smaller and smaller as we rose higher. Not a sound disturbed the silence of this uninhabited mountain mystery; not a sign of life broke the stillness save a little ashy-brown bird that hopped about the boulders, flipping its tail up and down. And to add to the impression created by the eerie scene, huge senecios lifted to a height of 20ft their black stems and greyish-yellow crowns and stood spreading out their arms in the deep moist gullies, like ghostly sentinels of the untrodden wilds.

Eva Stuart Watt *Africa's Dome of Mystery* (1930)

Note: In all the route descriptions, do remember that the times we quote are approximations and, more importantly, refer to **walking times only** with no time spent resting, taking photos etc. Add on 30-50% to get an estimate of the total time spent on the trail.

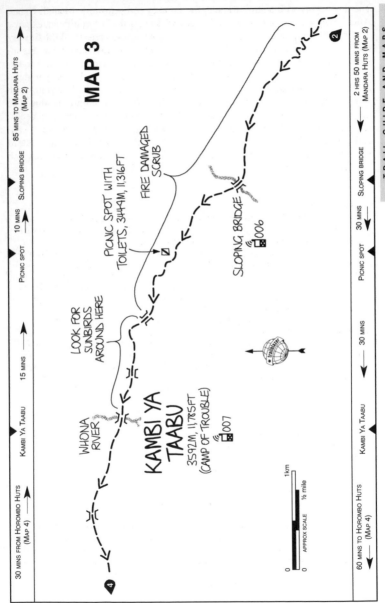

MAP 3

← 85 MINS TO MANDARA HUTS (MAP 2) →

SLOPING BRIDGE

← 10 MINS →

PICNIC SPOT

← 15 MINS →

KAMBI YA TAABU

← 30 MINS FROM HOROMBO HUTS (MAP 4) →

PICNIC SPOT WITH TOILETS, 3449M, 11,316FT

FIRE DAMAGED SCRUB

LOOK FOR SUNBIRDS AROUND HERE

WHONA RIVER

KAMBI YA TAABU
3592M, 11,785FT
(CAMP OF TROUBLE)

SLOPING BRIDGE

📷💾 006

📷💾 007

← 2 HRS 50 MINS FROM MANDARA HUTS (MAP 2) →

SLOPING BRIDGE

← 30 MINS →

PICNIC SPOT

← 30 MINS →

KAMBI YA TAABU

← 60 MINS TO HOROMBO HUTS (MAP 4) →

1km
0
0   ½ mile
APPROX SCALE

2

4

The day begins with a stroll through the monkey forest towards Maundi Crater. After 15 minutes you cross a small bridge and, leaving the last significant expanse of forest behind, enter a land of tall grasses and giant heathers. **Wild flowers** rarely seen elsewhere, such as the pinkish *Dierama pendulum*, abound in this little bumpy corner of the mountain. Crossing bridges over (often dry) water courses, if it's a clear day you may be able to make out, atop one of the many undulations, some **picnic tables** and toilets amongst the heather; this will be your lunch stop, reached after a fairly trying 30-minute climb from the **sloping bridge**. The guides typically call this the halfway point in the day but they're being unnecessarily pessimistic: Horombo Huts lie just 90 minutes away, the path tracing a generally westward course across a number of (dry) stream beds including the head of the Whona River that runs through a valley known as **Kambi Ya Taabu**, which translates, rather melodramatically, as the 'Camp of Trouble'!

❏ Mawenzi

Though less than 8km of nothingness (namely the Saddle) separates the foot of one from the foot of the other, the twin peaks of Kibo and Mawenzi could scarcely be more different. Where Kibo is all gentle slopes and a perfectly circular crater, Mawenzi is spiky, steep, and rises to a series of peaks like the back of a stegosaurus. Furthermore, where the former is at least partially covered in glaciers, the other stands naked, or at least wears no permanent raiment of ice, its sides too steep to allow the glaciers a secure-enough footing. And while Kibo is easily accessible to walkers, any assault on Mawenzi involves some serious preparation, specialist equipment and no small amount of technical skill.

Indeed, the only similarity between the two peaks is their enormity: Mawenzi's **Hans Meyer Peak**, at 5149m, is the third highest in Africa (after Kibo and Mount Kenya, 50m taller). Its smaller size when compared to Kibo can be ascribed to the fact that the Mawenzi volcano died out first, while the forces that formed Kibo continued to rage for a few thousand years after Mawenzi had become extinct, pushing Kibo above the height of its older brother. Erosion then caused the collapse of Mawenzi's entire north-east wall, releasing the waters of a lake that had formed in its crater down into the valley below.

The jagged appearance of its summit is due to the formation of **dykes**. This is where lava, pushed into gaps in the crater rim, solidified over time and, being harder than the original rock, remained while the softer rock eroded. Today, this hardened lava is also rather shattered, which, combined with its steep gradients, makes Mawenzi extremely dangerous to climb. John Reader, in his book *Kilimanjaro*, tells of two Austrian climbers who perished on their descent from the summit of Mawenzi, with the body of one of them found dangling by a rope snagged to the rocks. Such is the difficulty associated with any climb of Mawenzi that, rather than risk clambering up the peak to recover the corpse, the park authorities decided instead to hire a marksman to shoot at the rope with a rifle.

For years the peak was closed to mountaineers but that changed in 2017 when a new (and hopefully safe) route up Kili's second summit opened up to climbers. Before you can tackle it, however, you'll need to prove to the park authorities that you have the necessary climbing qualifications and you'll also need to pay an extra US$750 on top of the regular park fees, presumably to cover the cost of the marksman's bullets in case you, too, should fall.

Horombo Huts (3721m/12,208ft) are generally regarded as the most pleasant of those on the route: small A-frame shelters partitioned down the middle, with each side holding beds for four people. They cater for a transient population of around 160 trekkers plus porters and guides as well as a more permanent population of four-striped grass mice whose numbers are now almost at plague proportions; indeed, some of them have now forsaken their grassy homeland to scavenge in the main dining hall. The huts are also the busiest, catering not just for those ascending the mountain but those coming back down too, as well as those who spend the day here acclimatising.

Speaking of which, if you have opted for an **acclimatisation day** the chances are you'll be led by your guide on the northern route (aka Mawenzi Route, see box p373) past the **Zebra Rocks** and up to the **Mawenzi Hut** at 4535m/14,879ft (see Map 4, p300). Not only will this afford you magnificent views of your ultimate destination across the Saddle but it is also, of course, wonderful exercise to help you to cope with the thin air of Kibo later on. The benefits of taking this extra day may not be immediately apparent but will hopefully manifest themselves later on as you saunter up Kibo with at most a minor headache, while littering the trail around you are the weeping, retching bodies of the AMS-sufferers who opted not to take the extra day. Oh, and the huts are also near enough to allow you to return to Horombo for a late lunch.

STAGE 3: HOROMBO HUTS TO KIBO HUTS
[MAP 4 p300; MAP 5, p301]

Distance: 9.5km (6 miles; 10.3km – 6½ miles on the Mawenzi alternative); altitude gained: 993m (3258ft)

The path to Kibo from Horombo now divides; almost invariably you will be led along the southern (left-hand) route, which we describe now. If your guide is amenable, however, you may like to ask him on the return from Kibo to use the more northerly route, particularly if you did not take a day to acclimatise at Horombo (those who did will be familiar with much of this northerly path, which we

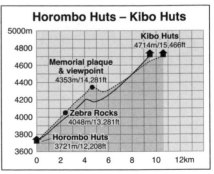

Horombo Huts – Kibo Huts

Kibo Huts 4714m/15,466ft

Memorial plaque & viewpoint 4353m/14,281ft

Zebra Rocks 4048m/13,281ft

Horombo Huts 3721m/12,208ft

have called the Mawenzi Route and describe, starting at Kibo Huts, on p373).

The 9.5km **southern path** seems rather steep at first as it bends left (north-west) and up through the thinning vegetation of the moorland. Looping north, just under 30 minutes after leaving Horombo you come to the tiny mountain stream known as **Maua River** (3914m/12,841ft). You should fill up your water bottles here, for the water from this point on is rather brackish. The terrain climbs steadily after Maua, passing the **junction** with

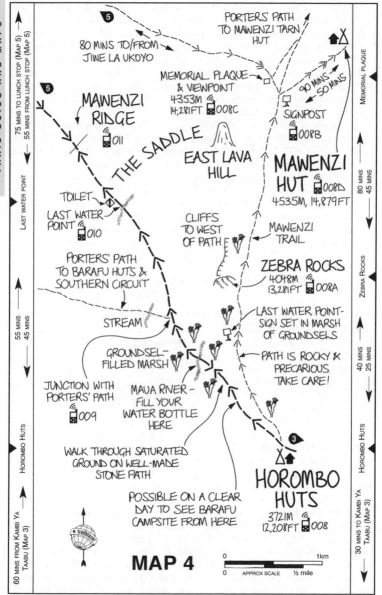

5

PORTERS' PATH
TO MAWENZI TARN
HUT

80 MINS TO/FROM
JIWE LA UKOYO

MEMORIAL PLAQUE
& VIEWPOINT
4353M
14,281FT 008C

90 MINS
50 MINS

5

75 MINS TO LUNCH STOP (MAP 5)
55 MINS FROM LUNCH STOP (MAP 5)

MEMORIAL PLAQUE

MAWENZI
RIDGE
011

SIGNPOST
008B

THE SADDLE

EAST LAVA
HILL

MAWENZI
HUT 008D
4535M, 14,879FT

80 MINS
45 MINS

LAST WATER POINT

TOILET

LAST WATER
POINT 010

CLIFFS
TO WEST
OF PATH

MAWENZI
TRAIL

PORTERS' PATH
TO BARAFU HUTS &
SOUTHERN CIRCUIT

ZEBRA ROCKS
4048M 008A
13,281FT

ZEBRA ROCKS

55 MINS
45 MINS

STREAM

LAST WATER POINT-
SIGN SET IN MARSH
OF GROUNDSELS

GROUNDSEL-
FILLED MARSH

PATH IS ROCKY &
PRECARIOUS.
TAKE CARE!

40 MINS
25 MINS

JUNCTION WITH
PORTERS' PATH
009

MAUA RIVER -
FILL YOUR
WATER BOTTLE
HERE

HOROMBO HUTS

WALK THROUGH SATURATED
GROUND ON WELL-MADE
STONE PATH

3

HOROMBO
HUTS
3721M
12,208FT 008

HOROMBO HUTS

60 MINS FROM KAMBI YA
TAABU (MAP 3)

POSSIBLE ON A CLEAR
DAY TO SEE BARAFU
CAMPSITE FROM HERE

30 MINS TO KAMBI YA
TAABU (MAP 3)

trailblazer

MAP 4

0   1km
0   APPROX SCALE   ½ mile

the porters' path (ie the Southern Circuit), this section being largely used by porters as a short-cut to Barafu.

Soon after, some of Kili's many parasitic cones move into view for the first time. The **Last Water Point**, well signposted and rather incongruously furnished with picnic tables, marks the beginning of the uphill approach to **Mawenzi Ridge**, beyond which lies the **Saddle**, the dry, barren terrain separating Kilimanjaro's two major peaks. With the **Middle Red Hill**, a large parasitic cone, ahead of you to the right, you find yourself descending into a rather flat, extremely windswept and dramatic landscape, the only decoration provided by a few tufts of grass, some hardier floral species such as the aptly named everlastings, and a number of boulders and smaller stones, some of which have been arranged into messages by previous trekkers. It is for these kinds of views that you brought your camera, for the light at this altitude is frequently superb, and while many of your photos may end up in the fire it's a fair bet that a few will be destined for the mantlepiece. The path heads almost due north between the Kibo summit on your left and the Middle Red on your right, whose western

KIBO HUTS 45 MINS → JIWE LA UKOYO 50 MINS LUNCH STOP 55 MINS TO LAST → WATER POINT (MAP 4)

TO SCHOOL HUT

MAP 5

★ trailblazer

015

25

6

JIWE LA UKOYO 014

SIGN FOR
KIBO CIRCUIT 013

KIBO HUTS
4714M
15,466FT 016

TOILETS &
PICNIC TABLE

THE SADDLE
OFTEN EXTREMELY
WINDY

BIG BOULDER

80 MINS
BETWEEN
JIWE LA UKOYO
& MEMORIAL
PLAQUE

4

TRIPLETS

0   1km
0   APPROX SCALE   ½ mile

LUNCHSTOP
& TOILETS 012

**MIDDLE
RED HILL**

FEELS LIKE A ROAD -
A WIDE TREK CROSSING
THE ALPINE DESERT

4

KIBO HUTS ← 75 MINS JIWE LA UKOYO 50 MINS LUNCH STOP 75 MINS FROM LAST WATER STOP (MAP 4)

TRAIL GUIDE AND MAPS

slopes shelter trekkers from the often howling wind and more often than not provide the venue for **lunch**.

Your path for the afternoon continues northwards across the Saddle. It's a bit of a weary trudge on a steadily inclining path to **Jiwe La Ukoyo**, a former campsite with some toilet huts and a huge boulder (*jiwe* means 'rock' in Swahili). It is also the meeting point between the two main paths from Horombo. Thereafter the path turns sharply westwards towards the **Kibo Huts**, which nestle snugly on the lowest slopes of the summit after which they were named. Though the huts look close, you still have around 1¼ hours' walking from Jiwe La Ukoyo; it's a tough walk too, a gradual but relentless uphill slog to round off what has already been a fairly wearying day.

The accommodations at Kibo Hut are reminiscent of a Siberian prison camp. Triple-decker bunks line all four tin walls; in the middle of the room, a central pit for eating. The wind whines through the cracks in the walls; nobody removes any clothing indoors. We have dinner at 5:00 p.m., porridge and tea. Nobody can eat much. We are all thinking about the ascent. We must reach the top before ten in the morning, because after that the weather is likely to sock in, closing off the views and making the summit dangerous. If we climb too slowly, we risk being turned back from the summit because of the weather.

Michael Crichton, *Travels*.

The huts themselves are basic, built of stone and rather chilly. A sign on the door of the main hut tells you that you are now at 4750m (15,584ft; though we think it's a little bit lower than this at 4714m/15,466ft); a second sign warns you that Gillman's Point is still five hours away...

STAGE 4: KIBO HUTS TO GILLMAN'S POINT AND UHURU PEAK
[MAP 6, opposite; MAP 33, p384]

Distance: 6.25km (4 miles); altitude gained: 1181m (3875ft)

And so you come to the testing part of the walk. No matter how tough you have found the trekking so far, it was but a leisurely stroll compared to what lies ahead of you tonight. The path to Gillman's Point on the crater rim has been in your sights since the previous afternoon when you crossed the Saddle and saw it rearing up at an angle of 16° (John Reader's estimate) behind the Kibo Huts.

We think that one of the reasons why this route has a higher failure rate than any of the others is down to the difficulty of this last stretch, which seems steeper and the ground less solid than on other routes. The stretch between Gillman's and Uhuru Peak also sees a high percentage of people giving up, presumably because of the greater distance, even though the gradient is less steep and

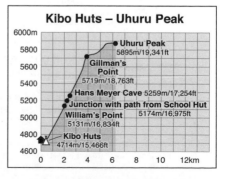

Kibo Huts – Uhuru Peak

- **Uhuru Peak** 5895m/19,341ft
- **Gillman's Point** 5719m/18,763ft
- **Hans Meyer Cave** 5259m/17,254ft
- **Junction with path from School Hut** 5174m/16,975ft
- **William's Point** 5131m/16,834ft
- **Kibo Huts** 4714m/15,466ft

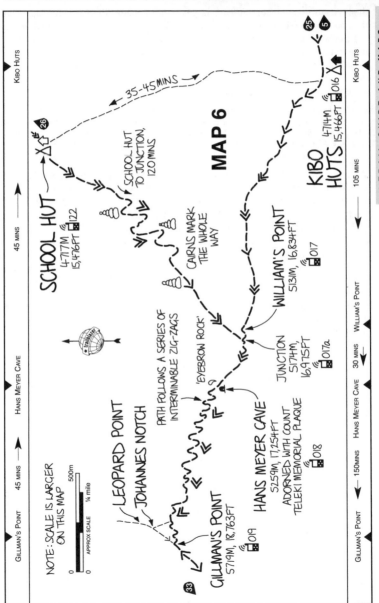

MAP 6

KIBO HUTS ← 45 MINS → ← HANS MEYER CAVE → ← 45 MINS → GILLMAN'S POINT

SCHOOL HUT
4,717M
15,476FT

35-45 MINS

SCHOOL HUT
TO JUNCTION,
120 MINS

CAIRNS MARK
THE WHOLE
WAY

WILLIAM'S POINT
5,131M, 16,834FT

KIBO
HUTS
4,714M
15,466FT

NOTE: SCALE IS LARGER
ON THIS MAP

500m
APPROX SCALE
¼ mile

LEOPARD POINT
JOHANNES NOTCH

PATH FOLLOWS A SERIES OF
INTERMINABLE ZIG-ZAGS

'EYEBROW ROCK'

JUNCTION
5,174M,
16,975FT

GILLMAN'S POINT
5,719M, 18,763FT

HANS MEYER CAVE
5,259M, 17,254FT
ADORNED WITH COUNT
TELEKI MEMORIAL PLAQUE

GILLMAN'S POINT ← 150MINS → HANS MEYER CAVE ← 30 MINS → WILLIAM'S POINT ← 105 MINS → KIBO HUTS

the hard stuff is, in theory at least, largely behind them. All of which means that the chances of failure on this route are comparatively high – and of making it, but throwing up or passing out along the way, are even higher. Just remember the golden rule: when it comes to climbing Kibo, there is no such thing as too slow. The mountain was formed around 500,000 years ago and has remained much the same ever since, so I think it's reasonable to assume it will still be there in the morning, no matter what time you arrive at the top.

I find a rhythm and try to lose my thoughts to it but feel the first pain of a stomach cramp and then another, and I feel the nausea starting and the headache that I recognise all too well ... The pain is sharp in my head and my cramping is still with me; if I feel this way how is Danny doing with no sleep and nothing in his stomach from the vomiting after dinner?
Rick Ridgeway, *The Shadow of Kilimanjaro – On Foot Across East Africa*

What you can't see from Kibo Huts, and yet what is rather good about this path, is that there are a number of landmarks on the way – the main ones being William's Point at 5131m (16,834ft) and Hans Meyer Cave at 5259m (17,254ft) – that act as milestones, helping both to break up the journey and to provide you with some measure of your progress. **William's Point** – or rather, the large east-facing rock immediately beneath it – lies 1¾ hours from Kibo Huts and is usually the first major resting point. **Hans Meyer Cave**, a small and undistinguished hollow adorned with a plaque commemorating the Hungarian hunter, Count and *bon viveur* Samuel Teleki, who is believed to have rested here in 1887, is 30 minutes further on.

From Hans Meyer Cave, it's a case of following the scree **switchbacks**; if you've mastered the art of walking in a zombie-like trance, now is the time to put that particular technique into action.

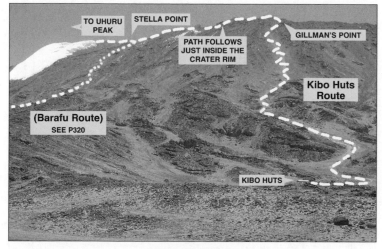

Kibo Huts Route

By some transcendental process I seemed to take on the characteristics of a Shire [horse], my head lowered, resolute, I just plunked one foot in front of t'other, mentally munching nothingness. **Sebastian Snow** *The Rucksack Man*, writing about his attempt to walk from Tierra del Fuego to Alaska across the Americas. It's a good example to follow for your walk to Gillman's Point.

This part, as you pinball back and forth on a stretch of fine scree bounded by two boulder-strewn slopes, is extremely exposed and if there's any wind about, you will almost certainly feel it here. If you bought one in Moshi, now is the time to put on your balaclava: your friends will be too concerned with their own situation to laugh at you. By the way, look behind you and you'll see a line of torches snaking up the slope in a scene that feels almost Biblical; while ahead of you, other torches in the distance ahead are virtually indistinguishable from the stars.

Gradually the zig-zags begin to reduce in size like the audiograph of an echo. You are now entering the final phase of the climb to Gillman's, though it takes an hour to complete and you'll probably be breathless the whole way. It's easy to get lost in the dark on this final stretch, so don't be too surprised to find other trekkers to the left and right of you on a different path. Assuming your guide is at least halfway competent, however, you should find yourself at the crater's edge at **Gillman's Point** (5719m/18,763ft; if, upon arrival at the crater rim, you find no signpost welcoming you to Gillman's, the chances are the guide has got his bearings slightly wrong and has led you to the slightly lower point of **Johannes Notch**. No matter: Gillman's is just a three-minute scramble up to your left.).

Gillman's Point is 960m above Kibo Hut [we actually make it 1005m]*, that is almost the equivalent of three Empire State Buildings standing one on top of another. The horizontal distance between Kibo Hut and Gillman's Point is roughly 3000 metres, so the gradient averages about 1:3.3 and the distance covered on the way up is about 3300m – the equivalent of nine Empire State Buildings laid end to end up the incline.*

John Reader *Kilimanjaro*

If the wind is not too high, Gillman's is a good spot to sit for a few minutes, get your head together, contemplate the star-spangled night with the silhouette of Mawenzi to the east, and congratulate yourself on having earned a nice certificate for making it to the crater rim, having completed the hardest part of the trek. At least, it's the hardest part physically; the hardest part from a psychological point of view now awaits as you try to muster up the energy and enthusiasm to tackle the walk to **Uhuru**. Because if Kilimanjaro is the Roof of Africa, all you've done so far is make it as far as the eaves.

Though the time varies slightly throughout the year, as a rough guide you need to be at Gillman's at around 4.45am in order to have a chance of seeing the sunrise at Uhuru at around 6am. If you've no chance of making it by then, consider seeing the sunrise from somewhere along the way: from Stella Point, for example, or overlooking Rebmann Glacier, or from one of the lesser peaks before Uhuru.

See Map 33 on p384 for details of the summit and the walk around the crater rim. The first part of this walk is undulating as you ride the rim's peaks and troughs; you may well need your head torch as you walk in the moon-shadow. From **Stella Point**, 30-45 minutes to the south of Gillman's, the path begins to climb more steadily. Though nothing like as steep as that which has gone

before, at this stage any incline is a major challenge. Don't be too disheartened by the many false summits you will encounter along the last part; instead, distract your mind from the pain and exhaustion by looking at the huge and beautiful icefields to your left and the sheer, desolate enormity of the crater on your right. A gorgeous dawn at the summit, and a certificate back at Marangu Gate, are the prizes that await...

For details of what you can actually see at the summit, turn to p382, while for a description of the designated descent path, turn to the **Marangu Route descent** on p372.

The Machame Route

Then they began to climb and they were going to the East it seemed, and then it darkened and they were in a storm, the rain so thick it seemed like flying through a waterfall, and they were out and Compie turned his head and grinned and pointed and there, ahead, all he could see, as wide as all the world, great, high, and unbelievably white in the sun, was the top of Kilimanjaro. And then he knew that there was where he was going.
Ernest Hemingway, *The Snows of Kilimanjaro*

For most of the last decade, if you were to ask any guide or tour agent which was their favourite walk on Kilimanjaro, often they would choose this, the Machame-Mweka Route (usually just shortened to the Machame Route, a convention we have adopted here). While today its sheer popularity has led many to reconsider their choice and look at other routes more favourably, it is still not difficult to see why this route remains so in vogue: beginning on the south-western side of the mountain, the path passes through some of the mountain's finest features, including the **cloud forest** of Kili's southern slopes, the dry and dusty **Shira Plateau** and the delightful groundsel-clad **Barranco Campsite**.

Furthermore, you have a choice of ascent routes to the summit with thrill-seekers opting for the daunting **Western Breach Route**, while the majority head for the lengthy, long-winded climb up the **Barafu Trail**, with Rebmann Glacier edging into your field of vision on your left as dawn breaks behind Mawenzi on your right. Furthermore, unlike the Marangu Route, on Machame you don't use the same path to descend but instead you come down via the Mweka Route, a steep but pretty trail encompassing inhospitably dry mountain desert and lush lowland forest in a matter of a few hours.

For all these reasons, Machame is now the busiest trail on the mountain. Another reason could be that while the Machame Route is widely reckoned to be that much harder than the Marangu Route (and is thus nick-

Is it so small a thing
To have enjoy'd the sun,
To have lived light in the spring,
To have loved, to have thought,
* to have done;*
To have advanc'd true friends,
* and beat down baffling foes?*
Matthew Arnold
Empedocles on Etna (1852)

named the Whiskey Route, in opposition to Marangu's softer soubriquet of the 'Coca Cola trail'), the proportion of trekkers who reach the top using this route is marginally but significantly higher. This could be down to a number of factors: the Machame Route allows people to acclimatise better because it's longer (**40.41km/25 miles to the summit via Barafu** as opposed to 36.55km/22¾ miles on Marangu); when it comes to climbing the slopes of Kibo, the Barafu Route is more straightforward than the route from Kibo Huts to Gillman's, as is largely conducted on the firm terrain of a ridge rather than sliding, shifting shale; or maybe the Machame's higher success rate is merely an indication that more experienced, hardened trekkers – ie the very people who are presumably most likely to reach the summit – are more inclined to choose this route.

The following description assumes you will be taking the Barafu Route to the summit. This walk via Barafu traditionally lasts for six days and five nights, though it is now more common for trekkers to opt for an extra night during the ascent, usually at Karanga Camp, halfway between Barranco and Barafu camps. Not only does the extra day aid acclimatisation but it also reduces from almost six to three the number of hours walked on the day that precedes the exhausting midnight ascent to the summit, thereby allowing trekkers more time to recover their faculties, relax and prepare themselves for the final push to the top.

Incidentally, those daredevils wishing to try their hand at the Arrow Glacier/Western Breach Route will leave the regular Machame Route on the third day; the map on p314 and the box on p315 indicate where. You can then find a description of that path to the summit on p338.

STAGE 1: MACHAME GATE TO MACHAME HUTS
[MAP 7, p308; MAP 8, p310]

Distance: 10.75km (6¾ miles); altitude gained: 1210m (3970ft)
Coming from Moshi, the drive to Machame Gate, at an altitude of 1811m, takes just under an hour. On the way to the gate ask the driver to point out the house of the local chief, a simple yet large bungalow on the left-hand side of the road. Passing through **Machame village** you'll soon arrive at the gate itself, a small collection of buildings huddled around a 4WD car park. **Register** in the office and make sure you use the toilet facilities on site – you may not think much of them now but, believe me, compared to some of the latrines on the trail these are heavenly.

Back at the car park, porters are busy haggling over who is going to take what, guides are reporting to KINA-PA reception to wrestle with the red tape, while the trekkers are packing away their lunch-

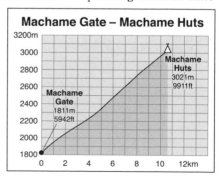

Machame Gate – Machame Huts

Machame Huts 3021m 9911ft

Machame Gate 1811m 5942ft

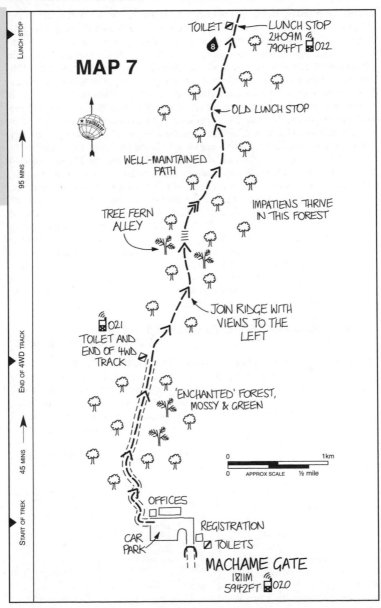

TRAIL GUIDE AND MAPS

LUNCH STOP

95 MINS

END OF 4WD TRACK

45 MINS

START OF TREK

MAP 7

TOILET ☒ ← LUNCH STOP
2409M 📶
🔘8   7904FT 📱022

← OLD LUNCH STOP

WELL-MAINTAINED
PATH

IMPATIENS THRIVE
IN THIS FOREST

TREE FERN
ALLEY

JOIN RIDGE WITH
VIEWS TO THE
LEFT

📱021
TOILET AND
END OF 4WD ☒
TRACK

'ENCHANTED' FOREST,
MOSSY & GREEN

0   1km
0   APPROX SCALE   ½ mile

OFFICES

REGISTRATION
☒ TOILETS

CAR
PARK

MACHAME GATE
1811M 📶
5942FT 📱020

boxes and quietly steeling themselves for the rigours ahead. To one side of this chaos is the beginning of the trail...

This ten-plus kilometre first day is a long and sweaty one. It starts with a 3km (2 mile) amble up a 4WD track, a wide snaking trail that cuts through the kind of deep, dark enchanted forest that Hansel and Gretel would be familiar with. Green moss hangs thickly from the branches that creak and groan in the wind; it's a magical start to a wonderful adventure. After 45 minutes the 4WD road comes to an end, the gentle curves and steady incline giving way to a narrower, steeper but now beautifully maintained pedestrians-only path that continues all the way to Machame Huts. Looking to the side of the path you'll notice that the vegetation is already changing as you progress deeper into the **cloud forest**, the scarlet and yellow *Impatiens kilimanjari* and pink *Impatiens pseudoviola* now flourishing between the roots of the 30-metre tall trees; tree ferns also proliferate here.

About a hundred minutes beyond the end of the 4WD track, the path widens momentarily to form several small **clearings** (one of which has en suite toilet facilities) that make for popular lunch stops. Those who've already drunk their water bottles dry can replenish their supplies from the stream down in the valley to the west. Listen out for the primate-like call of the black (actually very dark green) and red turaco which nests around here, and watch your lunch too: it's not uncommon for the forest rodents to sneak into lunchboxes and drag off a samosa or two.

The post-prandial path varies little from that which has gone before, though the gradient increases slightly the higher you climb. As the forest gradually begins to thin out you'll notice that you are actually walking on a narrow forested spine between two shallow valleys. A stream – more audible than visible – runs to the right of the trail.

Around two hours after lunch a signpost appears, warning against the careless discarding of cigarette butts; as well as dispensing some sound advice, this sign also marks the border between the cloud forest and the heath, where long

---

❏ **Mobile (cell) phone reception on the Machame Route**

It depends which network you're with, of course, but mobile (cell phone) reception on the Machame Route seems to be OK by the standards of Kilimanjaro. There's reasonable reception at **Machame Huts**, and at **Shira Caves** I was told that reception is OK if the weather's good. Often you'll see the porters climb up the rocks surrounding the camp to use their phones here so you may want to follow them; the traditional afternoon 'acclimatisation' walk offers more opportunities to get a connection. At **Lava Tower** there is fair reception, and while you have to wander around the camp to get anything at both **Barranco** (you may well have to wait until you reach the top of the Barranco/Breakfast Wall to get reception here) and **Karanga**, it is good at **Barafu**, intermittent at **Stella Point** and fine, so we are told, at **Uhuru Peak**. The **Millennium Camp**, on the descent, also has good mobile reception. If you are taking the Western Breach Route, please see the box on p327 for a summary of your mobile reception from Lava Tower.

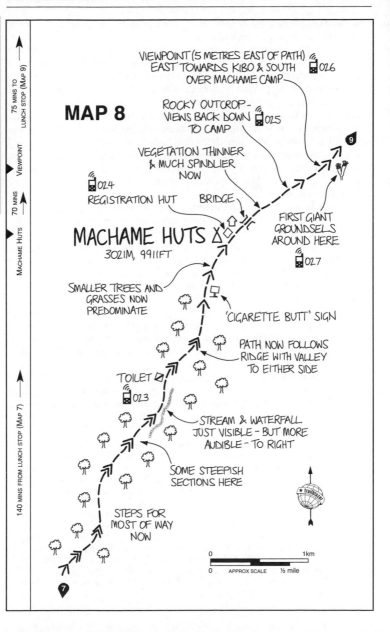

MAP 8

75 MINS TO LUNCH STOP (MAP 9)

VIEWPOINT

70 MINS

MACHAME HUTS

VIEWPOINT (5 METRES EAST OF PATH) EAST TOWARDS KIBO & SOUTH OVER MACHAME CAMP 026

ROCKY OUTCROP - VIEWS BACK DOWN TO CAMP 025

VEGETATION THINNER & MUCH SPINDLIER NOW

024
REGISTRATION HUT

BRIDGE

FIRST GIANT GROUNDSELS AROUND HERE 027

MACHAME HUTS
3021M, 9911FT

SMALLER TREES AND GRASSES NOW PREDOMINATE

'CIGARETTE BUTT' SIGN

PATH NOW FOLLOWS RIDGE WITH VALLEY TO EITHER SIDE

TOILET
023

STREAM & WATERFALL JUST VISIBLE - BUT MORE AUDIBLE - TO RIGHT

SOME STEEPISH SECTIONS HERE

140 MINS FROM LUNCH STOP (MAP 7)

STEPS FOR MOST OF WAY NOW

trailblazer

0   1km
0   APPROX SCALE   ½ mile

grasses dominate and the robust trees of the forest give way to the spindly, tree-like giant heathers. *Kniphofia thomsonii* (known to you and me as red hot pokers) make their first appearance at this altitude at certain times of year, as do several other wild flowers and shrubs such as the bushy *Philippia excelsa*. With the forest thinning, Kibo peak hoves into view for the first time to the east.

It is only 20 minutes from the forest edge to **Machame Huts** (3021m/9911ft), a series of level pitches cut into the grass, each with its own toilet. Make sure you sign your name in the **registration book** and aim to pitch your tent as high as possible for the best views: by the green hut is a good spot, affording views to the east up to Kibo and south-west towards Mount Meru. Look out for the birdlife too, which is abundant round here, with olive thrush, common stonechats and flocks of montane white-eye all resident, in addition to the usual seedeaters and alpine chats that are ubiquitous on the mountain.

By the way, having climbed to 3021m you are now higher than the top of Mawson Peak, at 2745m (9006ft) the highest point in Australia.

STAGE 2: MACHAME HUTS TO SHIRA CAVES
[MAP 8, opposite; MAP 9, p312]

Distance: 5.3km (3¼ miles); altitude gained: 818m (2684ft) This leg of the trek is short but a little strenuous as you ascend from 3021m/9911ft up to the Shira Plateau, finally coming to a halt at the Shira Caves at 3839m/12,595ft. Parts of this walk are a bit steep and the skinny, naked heathers at this altitude provide little shade from the heat; what's more, the path is extremely dusty, particularly towards the end of the dry sea-

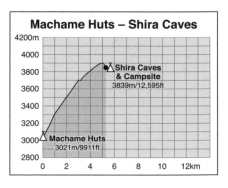

son, so if you have gaiters you'll probably be thankful for the protection they provide (and remember to keep your camera bag tightly closed too to prevent dust inveigling into any valuable equipment). In spite of all this, by taking it slowly, resting frequently and enjoying the en-route views that encompass Kibo, Meru and all points in between, this day needn't be too taxing and if you're on a six-day schedule, this may prove to be the easiest day of them all. Indeed, many guides now try to have the walk finished by one or two o'clock, in the hope of beating the afternoon rains that douse this part of the mountain at certain times of year.

The walk starts as it goes on for much of the morning, with a steepish climb north up through forests of stunted, twisted heather bushes; while ahead of you in the distance is the lip of Shira Plateau. The path winds its way up to the top of a ridge formed by a petrified lava flow, occasionally allowing trekkers some splendid **views** over Machame Huts and the village below as well as the flat

TRAIL GUIDE AND MAPS

Tanzanian plains beyond. Giant groundsels (*Dendrosenecio kilimanjari ssp cottonii*), the squat, chunky trees with the green-leaf crown, begin to dot the path and Kilimanjaro's desiccated **helichrysums**, ubiquitous above 3000m, appear here for the first time, like living pot pourri. Note, too, how most of the vegetation not only diminishes in size as you climb higher but the taller plants seem to bend as one towards the plateau, as if pointing the way.

After passing a number of **viewpoints** and clambering from one side of the ridge to the other, the gradient of the trail increases exponentially towards the **lunch stop**, hidden from view behind a rocky outcrop. The effort expended in

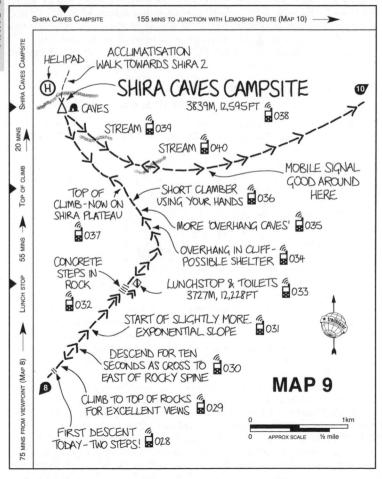

SHIRA CAVES CAMPSITE   155 MINS TO JUNCTION WITH LEMOSHO ROUTE (MAP 10) →

HELIPAD

ACCLIMATISATION WALK TOWARDS SHIRA 2

SHIRA CAVES CAMPSITE
3839M, 12,595FT 📱038

🔟

CAVES

STREAM 📱039

STREAM 📱040

MOBILE SIGNAL GOOD AROUND HERE

TOP OF CLIMB - NOW ON SHIRA PLATEAU 📱037

SHORT CLAMBER USING YOUR HANDS 📱036

MORE 'OVERHANG CAVES' 📱035

OVERHANG IN CLIFF - POSSIBLE SHELTER 📱034

CONCRETE STEPS IN ROCK 📱032

LUNCHSTOP & TOILETS 3727M, 12,228FT 📱033

START OF SLIGHTLY MORE EXPONENTIAL SLOPE 📱031

DESCEND FOR TEN SECONDS AS CROSS TO EAST OF ROCKY SPINE 📱030

MAP 9

8

CLIMB TO TOP OF ROCKS FOR EXCELLENT VIEWS 📱029

FIRST DESCENT TODAY - TWO STEPS! 📱028

0   1km
0   APPROX SCALE   ½ mile

SHIRA CAVES CAMPSITE | 20 MINS | TOP OF CLIMB | 55 MINS | LUNCH STOP | 75 MINS FROM VIEWPOINT (MAP 8)

reaching here is worth it, for while munching on chicken legs and boiled eggs you can savour yet more views of Kibo as well as all points south. You'll also be able to observe the line of porters and trekkers on the path ahead and from them you can pick out the afternoon's trail, which initially continues north and up, before bending fairly sharply to the north-west, cutting a near horizontal line beneath the rim of the plateau. But though the worst of the day's climbing is behind you, don't be fooled into thinking this is an easy section, for the path on this north-westerly trail undulates considerably as it climbs over rocks and boulders and it can be tiring in the searing afternoon heat. As a distraction, the first of Kilimanjaro's celebrated moorland **lobelias** (*Lobelia deckenii*), both phallic and cabbage-shaped and growing to a height of around two metres, appear by the trail.

Just under an hour after lunch the plateau is gained and the path continues northwards. Look out for Shira Plateau's distinctive, shiny black **obsidian** rock (see p137). Your camp for the night is **Shira Caves Campsite** (3839m/12,595ft).

Looking west from the campsite, ask your guide to point out **Shira Cathedral** and **East Shira Hill** which line the southern boundary of Shira Plateau, and, behind them to the far west, **Johnsell Point** and **Klute Peak**, the highest points of the Shira Ridge, the western rim of the oldest of Kili's three craters. Mount Meru, too, is still visible to the west on the horizon. For an afternoon stroll, your guide will probably take you via the helipad and the caves themselves on the path leading towards Shira 2 Campsite, a stroll of less than half an hour in total.

Incidentally, by reaching Shira Caves you are now at a higher altitude than Mafadi (3450m/11,319ft), the highest peak in South Africa.

STAGE 3: SHIRA CAVES CAMPSITE TO BARRANCO HUTS
[MAP 9, opposite; MAP 10, p314; MAP 11, p317]

Distance: 10.3km/6½ miles via Lava Tower (7.1km/4½ miles to Lava Tower, 3.2km/2 miles from there to Barranco); altitude gained: 147m/482ft (788m/2585ft up to Lava Tower, then 641m/2103ft descent to Barranco)

Camp-life on Kilimanjaro is a capital school for the practice of self-denial. **Hans Meyer** *Across East African Glaciers*

During this section of the trek you cover over 10km (6½ miles) as you move from the western to the southern slopes of Kilimanjaro; by the end of it you may feel slightly disappointed to learn that, for all your efforts, you will have gained just 147m/482ft in height, from Shira Caves at

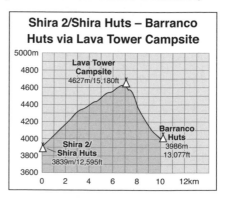

Shira 2/Shira Huts – Barranco Huts via Lava Tower Campsite

Lava Tower Campsite 4627m/15,180ft

Shira 2/Shira Huts 3839m/12,595ft

Barranco Huts 3986m 13,077ft

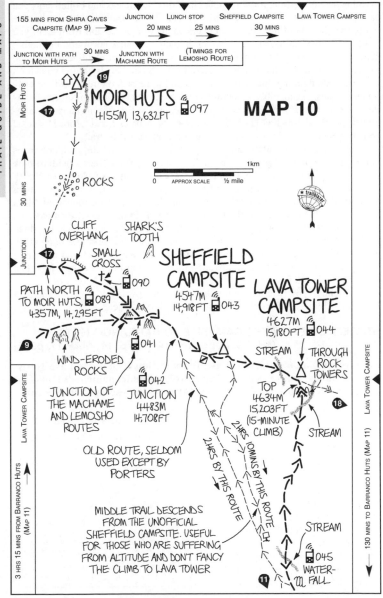

TRAIL GUIDE AND MAPS

155 MINS FROM SHIRA CAVES CAMPSITE (MAP 9) → JUNCTION →20 MINS LUNCH STOP →25 MINS SHEFFIELD CAMPSITE →30 MINS LAVA TOWER CAMPSITE

JUNCTION WITH PATH TO MOIR HUTS →30 MINS JUNCTION WITH MACHAME ROUTE (TIMINGS FOR LEMOSHO ROUTE)

Moir Huts

19

MOIR HUTS 📱097
4155M, 13,632FT

17

MAP 10

30 MINS ←→

°°°° ROCKS

0   1km
0   ½ mile   APPROX SCALE

★ trailblazer

JUNCTION

CLIFF OVERHANG

SHARK'S TOOTH

SMALL CROSS

📱090

SHEFFIELD CAMPSITE
4547M, 14,918FT 📱043

LAVA TOWER CAMPSITE
4627M, 15,180FT 📱044

17

PATH NORTH TO MOIR HUTS, 📱089
4357M, 14,295FT

📱041

STREAM

THROUGH ROCK TOWERS

9

WIND-ERODED ROCKS

📱042

JUNCTION 4483M, 14,708FT

TOP 4634M, 15,203FT (15-MINUTE CLIMB)

18

STREAM

JUNCTION OF THE MACHAME AND LEMOSHO ROUTES

OLD ROUTE, SELDOM USED EXCEPT BY PORTERS

2 HRS BY THIS ROUTE

2 HRS 10MINS BY THIS ROUTE

MIDDLE TRAIL DESCENDS FROM THE UNOFFICIAL SHEFFIELD CAMPSITE. USEFUL FOR THOSE WHO ARE SUFFERING FROM ALTITUDE AND DON'T FANCY THE CLIMB TO LAVA TOWER

STREAM

📱045 WATER-FALL

11

3 HRS 15 MINS FROM BARRANCO HUTS (MAP 11) ↑   LAVA TOWER CAMPSITE

LAVA TOWER CAMPSITE ►   130 MINS TO BARRANCO HUTS (MAP 11) ↓

❏ Ascent of Kibo via the Western Breach/Arrow Glacier Route

The Western Breach Route is a harder, shorter, more dangerous and less popular alternative trail than the standard Machame Route to the summit that travels via Barafu Huts. But it's also a great walk that allows you to explore the crater floor and all its features – the Furtwangler Glacier, Reusch Crater and Ash Pit, to name but three – as well as affording supreme views of the Shira Plateau, Barranco Valley and the summit of Mount Meru. The route starts at the Lava Tower Campsite. You can find a full description of the Arrow Glacier/Western Breach Route starting on p338.

3839m/12,595ft to Barranco, situated at an altitude of 3986m/13,077ft. Nevertheless, this leg of the trek is vital for acclimatisation purposes, for during the day you will climb to a respectable **4627m/15,180ft** if taking the path via Lava Tower. (There's another path which breaks off from this path at the little-used and unofficial **Sheffield Campsite**, 4547m/14,918ft, which is great for those who can't quite manage the climb up to Lava Tower; and a third and older trail which is lower still.) Don't be surprised, therefore, if by the end of it you have a crashing headache: this is normal and is only cause for concern if it is accompanied by other symptoms of mountain sickness, or if the pain hasn't disappeared by the morning.

The day begins with a steady, gentle ascent through the dry, boulder-strewn terrain of Shira Plateau towards the western slopes of Kibo, which appears from here so white and so *huge* that it looks vaguely unreal, as if it's the painted backdrop of a stage. Some trekkers also insist that the summit of Kibo, from this angle, resembles the profile of a Native American Indian chief at rest. (No, I can't really see it either.) At first the path meanders somewhat, rising and falling regularly as it negotiates the gentle folds of the plateau before finally settling on a roughly easterly direction, with a steady, shallow incline for most of the next 6km (3¾ miles). Notice how the vegetation has declined until only a few everlastings and lichen manage to cling to life. Ahead, facing you down, is the brilliant white smear of Penck Glacier.

Soon after the **junction with the Lemosho Route** the path loops to the south-east and divides. Not too long ago it was only those people who opted to tackle the summit on the more difficult Western Breach Route who headed east towards **Lava Tower**; these days, however, most

'...an extraordinary arborescent plant, since named *Senecio Johnstonii*... Its trunk was so superficially rooted and so rotten that, in spite of its height and girth, I could pull it down with one hand. (from *The Kilima-njaro Expedition,* **HH Johnston**, 1886; note that the tree he is talking about and depicting is no longer called *Senecio johnstonii* but *Dendrosenecio kilimanjarii ssp cottonii*).

guides recognise the acclimatisation benefits of taking this climb and also opt for this route, even if they then divert off down to Barranco Huts. As for the more southerly route, this is now largely the preserve of porters and those trekkers who aren't doing so well and need to descend quickly to Barranco. (This more gentle, southerly trail bends round to the right past the **lunchstop** and onto the highest point of *this* walk, 4530m/14,862ft, before descending quickly via a series of zigzags into a gully. It then bends south-east once more, following the contours of Kibo's lower reaches as it crosses two more streams. Less than an hour later the trail meets a proliferation of signposts, from where it's downhill all the way to Barranco.)

Back at Lava Tower the higher route splits again. The route up to Arrow Glacier soars above, while the path to Barranco drops steeply south to a stream, and rises and falls a couple of times before plummeting, finally and fabulously, into the delightful **Barranco Valley**, rich in groundsel and lobelia. A huge gouge in the southern face of Kibo to the south-west of Uhuru Peak, the valley is in places 300m (almost 1000 feet) deep and was formed when a huge landslide swept southwards down from the summit about 100,000 years ago.

From **Barranco Huts campsite** (3986m/13,077ft) and its environs you'll have spectacular views of Kibo's southern face, the Western Breach and the mighty Heim Glacier, with glacial moraine tumbling southwards towards the camp. Few are the trekkers who do not rank this campsite as their favourite on this trail. Indeed, so beautiful is it that it's tempting to linger outside one's tent after dark and savour the sights and scenery of this most spectacular site – though in reality, the cold soon chases most people into their sleeping bags. Unfortunately, there has been a spate of thefts from tents on the mountain recently, and Barranco has experienced more than its fair share of them. Do be careful, make sure your tent is zipped up when you're not in it and keep your valuables on you.

By the way, though you have gained only 147m/482ft since this morning, by climbing to Lava Tower Campsite (4627m/15,180ft) you have reached an altitude that's just 7m (23ft) shy of the highest mountain in Switzerland, the Dufourspitze; bother to climb up Lava Tower itself, which takes about 15 minutes or so, and you'll be 57m (187ft) higher.

STAGE 4: BARRANCO HUTS TO BARAFU HUTS
[MAP 11, opposite; MAP 12, p318]

Distance: 9.2km (5¾ miles); altitude gained: 676m (2218ft)
At this altitude this is a long stage; so long that many trekkers prefer to tackle it over two days, camping for the night above Karanga Valley, the last place to get water on the Machame Route. As you walk along the path the great glaciers of Kili's Southern Icefields – Heim, Kersten and Decken – will appear on your left one after the other. Curiously, although this stage sets you up nicely for the final push to the summit, by the end of the day you will actually be further from Uhuru Peak (as the lammergeyer flies) than you were at the start of the day at Barranco.

The hardest part of the day occurs right at the beginning, with a near-vertical scramble to the east of the campsite up **The Barranco Wall** or **Breach Wall**

TRAIL GUIDE AND MAPS

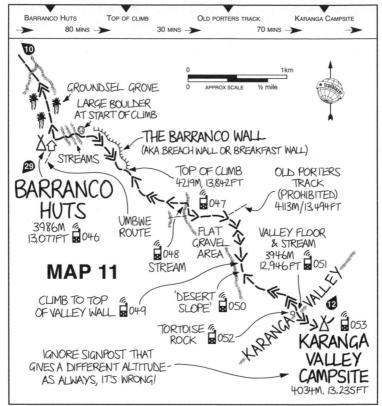

BARRANCO HUTS → 80 MINS → TOP OF CLIMB → 30 MINS → OLD PORTERS TRACK → 70 MINS → KARANGA CAMPSITE →

GROUNDSEL GROVE

LARGE BOULDER AT START OF CLIMB

THE BARRANCO WALL (AKA BREACH WALL OR BREAKFAST WALL)

STREAMS

TOP OF CLIMB 4219M, 13,842FT 047

OLD PORTERS TRACK (PROHIBITED) 4113M/13,494FT

BARRANCO HUTS 3986M 13,077FT 046

UMBWE ROUTE

048 STREAM

FLAT GRAVEL AREA

VALLEY FLOOR & STREAM 3946M 12,946FT 051

MAP 11

CLIMB TO TOP OF VALLEY WALL 049

'DESERT SLOPE' 050

KARANGA VALLEY

TORTOISE ROCK 052

KARANGA VALLEY

053

KARANGA VALLEY CAMPSITE 4034M, 13,235FT

IGNORE SIGNPOST THAT GIVES A DIFFERENT ALTITUDE – AS ALWAYS, IT'S WRONG!

APPROX SCALE

(now more commonly called the **Breakfast Wall**, as it is usually tackled after breakfast). In my experience most trekkers actually get a real kick out of this climb, probably because it provides such a welcome change from the relentless *pole pole* trudge of the previous stages. You'll have to stash your walking poles away for this first section, because at times you'll need to use both hands to haul yourself up the

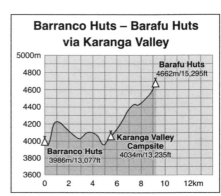

Barranco Huts – Barafu Huts via Karanga Valley

Barafu Huts 4662m/15,295ft

Karanga Valley Campsite 4034m/13,235ft

Barranco Huts 3986m/13,077ft

groundsel-dressed slopes. People talk in hushed, fearful tones about the Wall's main feature, the so-called '**Kissing Rock**', and how it forces you to tiptoe on the very edge of the path, with an almighty fall awaiting those who lose their footing. But in reality it's all rather straightforward and no trekker, as far as we know, has ever plunged to their demise on this section. False summits along the way shouldn't discourage you as you progress up the Wall for after about 80 minutes you'll reach its true summit; here you can sit on the bare rock and enjoy the views west over Mount Meru and on a clear day south-east towards the Pare Mountains, with the great Heim Glacier over your shoulder to the north, and relish the prospect of the relatively gentle descent into the next gully below.

At the bottom of this pretty little gully, and having crossed the small stream that flows through it, you come to a **flat gravel area**, possibly once a camping spot and, by the amount of loo roll hanging from the bushes, a popular pit stop too. Your guide will lead you along an undulating trail cutting south before ascending to surmount the eastern edge of a sheer-sided valley. The path quickly veers away east from the precipice, however, to traverse a **desert slope** where the silence and stillness are positively deafening, before finally descending down the western, lusher slopes of the **Karanga Valley**. Lobelia, heather and other greenery reappear for a while as you descend along the rock-and-mud path, a path that you share in places with a mountain stream.

Karanga Valley is, in the words of John Reader, 'narrow, steep and exquisite' and is a small oasis of green, albeit a cold and windswept one; beautiful shimmering green **malachite sunbirds** nest around here – you may spot them feeding on the lobelias. Those who plan to cover this leg in two days rather than one will camp at the top of the next climb, a very steep 20-minute ascent on a switchback path. This is the somewhat misnamed **Karanga Valley Campsite** (4034m/15,235ft); I

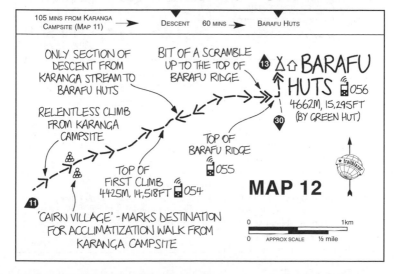

say misnamed because, of course, it's above the valley and not in it; also, *karanga* is Swahili for 'peanut' – yet I doubt nuts have ever grown up here. It's an unlovely place, windswept and ramshackle, with something of the atmosphere of a refugee camp about it. At this altitude it's often hemmed in by clouds which unfortunately obscure its best feature, namely the lovely views it affords of Kibo's southern face. By the way, for those who are staying here the distance from Barranco to Karanga is **5.5km** (3½ miles) and despite all your efforts you will now be just **48m** (157ft) higher than when you set off from Barranco.

At the campsite the trail takes a leftward turn, heading in a north-easterly direction on a steady, relentless incline, with the Kersten and Decken glaciers a permanent presence to your left. The scenery now becomes even more barren as you make your way between the boulders and over the shattered rocks and stones of this misty mountain slope. Even the trail is faint. Only the collection of cairns that mark the destination for those on an acclimatisation walk from Karanga give any an indication that man has passed this way before (unless, of course, some bastard has dropped litter). If George Lucas is looking for somewhere wild, inhospitable and unearthly as a location for his next Star Wars film, he could do a lot worse.

At the top the path bends more to the east and descends into a shallow valley that, if anything, is even drier and more blighted than the previous section. Once again, the Southern Icefields loom ominously to your left, with Rebmann Glacier appearing for the first time.

Barafu Huts (4662m, 15,295ft), your destination for this leg, lies at the end of this valley, reached after a short scramble up the cliff-face and a 15- to 25-minute walk almost due north. Barafu means 'Ice' in Swahili and the camp is probably called this because of its proximity to Rebmann Glacier, away to the northwest. It's an appropriately chilly spot but it has its advantages: the views of the climb that you face are good, and they've installed some new toilets too (and not before time; according to one popular rumour, a woman died at Barafu when the toilet she was sitting in collapsed and slid down the hillside – not the most dignified way of meeting your Maker). By the way, at 4662m you are now higher than Mount Elbert, at 4401m (14,439ft) the highest mountain in the Rocky Mountains.

Try to get some food and rest as soon as possible and sort out your preparations for the next stage before it gets dark: you've got a long night ahead. But don't stress if you don't manage to sleep tonight: in all honesty, few people do.

STAGE 5: BARAFU HUTS TO STELLA POINT AND UHURU PEAK
[MAP 13, p321; MAP 33, p384]

Distance: 4.86km (3 miles); altitude gained: 1233m (4045ft)

But now, apparently, the mountain was inhabited by fiery beings who baffled man's adventurous foot: the mountain receded as the traveller advanced, the summit rose as he ascended; blood burst from the nostrils, fingers bent backwards... even the most adventurous were forced back. **Richard Burton** in *Progress of Expedition to East Africa*, reporting the rumours he had heard about Kilimanjaro while residing in Tanga (circa 1857).

And so you come to the final ascent. For the past five days or so you've enjoyed some wonderful walking and miles of smiles; now it's time to do the hard yards.

The climb itself is a rigorous, vigorous push to Stella Point and the crater rim, followed by a 45-minute trudge up to Uhuru Peak, the highest point in Africa. It's tough, no doubt about it, but if you manage to avoid sickness or injury there's no reason why you shouldn't be clutching a certificate come tomorrow evening.

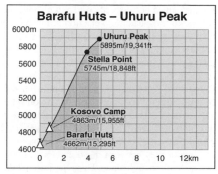

Barafu Huts – Uhuru Peak

- Uhuru Peak 5895m/19,341ft
- Stella Point 5745m/18,848ft
- Kosovo Camp 4863m/15,955ft
- Barafu Huts 4662m/15,295ft

This final stage usually begins at around midnight; this not only allows trekkers the chance to see sunrise from the summit but also leaves enough daylight to allow for the long descent to the next night's campsite, with an hour's recuperation back at Barafu on the way. As such, you can leave most of your **luggage** at Barafu while you tackle the ascent, though you should take any valuables with you (there have been a few robberies from tents left unguarded), as well as your **camera**, spare memory cards/film and batteries and all your **water**, which should be kept in **insulated bottles** or it'll freeze up and be useless on the ascent. Cameras, particularly digitals and feature-heavy SLRs, have been known to freeze in these conditions as well so keep them (or at the very least their batteries) insulated, preferably by putting them in an inside pock-

← TO UHURU PEAK

SEE P304 FOR MORE DETAIL

STELLA POINT

BARAFU HUTS

Barafu Route

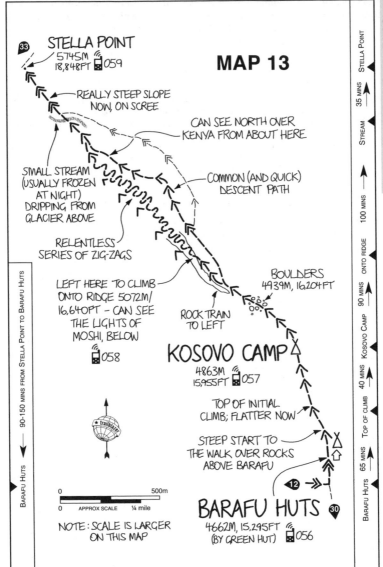

MAP 13

33 STELLA POINT
5745M
18,848FT 059

REALLY STEEP SLOPE
NOW, ON SCREE

CAN SEE NORTH OVER
KENYA FROM ABOUT HERE

SMALL STREAM
(USUALLY FROZEN
AT NIGHT)
DRIPPING FROM
GLACIER ABOVE

COMMON (AND QUICK)
DESCENT PATH

RELENTLESS
SERIES OF ZIG-ZAGS

BOULDERS
4939M, 16,204FT

LEFT HERE TO CLIMB
ONTO RIDGE 5072M/
16,640FT - CAN SEE
THE LIGHTS OF
MOSHI, BELOW
058

ROCK TRAIN
TO LEFT

KOSOVO CAMP
4863M
15,955FT 057

TOP OF INITIAL
CLIMB; FLATTER NOW

STEEP START TO
THE WALK OVER ROCKS
ABOVE BARAFU

12

BARAFU HUTS 30
4662M, 15,295FT
(BY GREEN HUT) 056

★ trailblazer

0   500m
0   APPROX SCALE   ¼ mile

NOTE: SCALE IS LARGER
ON THIS MAP

90-150 MINS FROM STELLA POINT TO BARAFU HUTS

BARAFU HUTS

TRAIL GUIDE AND MAPS

STELLA POINT

35 MINS

STREAM

100 MINS

ONTO RIDGE

90 MINS

KOSOVO CAMP

40 MINS

TOP OF CLIMB

65 MINS

BARAFU HUTS

et or wrapped in clothing in your daypack. Wear most of your **clothes** too – you can always take a layer or two off in the unlikely situation you find yourself getting too hot – and have your **head-torch** readily to hand (with fresh batteries installed) when you wake up so you don't have to spend time and energy looking around for it before you go. Carry your sunhat, sunglasses and suncream as well – you'll need them once the sun is up.

Good luck!

At 4am by the light of a hurricane lamp, and wrapped in everything that could give warmth, I started with Mawala, the headman, and Jonathan, our guide, on the long uphill pull of 4000ft over loose scree and fissured rocks. The cold was intense, and Mawala got two of his toes frost-bitten ... our breathing had become so difficult that we could barely drag ourselves along and had to sit down every few yards to recover breath, now and again sucking icicles and nibbling Cadbury's Milk Chocolate. Yet the steep ascent was mostly over projecting ridges of lava slabs and presented no real obstacle beyond the extreme altitude. Here and there, however, we struck a bed of loose shingle, which mockingly carried us backwards at every footstep almost the whole distance of our tread.

Eva Stuart Watt *Africa's Dome of Mystery* (1930)

The way to the summit starts, as you've probably already observed from Barafu, by scrambling over the **small cliffs** at the northern end of the camp in what is the steepest part of the trek save for the final push to Stella Point. Passing through the unofficial **Kosovo Camp (4863m/15,955ft)** about 1¾ hours into the trek, you may be pleased to know that you are higher than Mont Blanc, the highest mountain in Western Europe (4807m/15,771ft).

Climbing still further, the path now ascends to a rocky ridge, in the shadow of which you initially walk before taking a sharp left to surmount it and walk

Machame village in the late nineteenth century. Engraving by **Alexandre Le Roy** from *Au Kilima-Ndjaro* published in 1893.

along its spine. You are now heading directly for the summit and Stella Point, a direction you will maintain for nearly the entire night. The **switchback path** begins in earnest once you leave the ridge and continues for most of the next two hours or more. It is pointless describing the scenery on this section, for the chances are you won't be able to see much beyond the radius of your torch-beam and you probably won't be keen on surveying the landscape now anyway. If it's a clear night, however, you may be able to see **Rebmann Glacier** ahead of you to your left, with the ice-free Stella Point a little to its right in the distance. Picking your way through the trail of knackered trekkers and exhausted assistants, ignore the sound of people retching and sobbing and remember to keep your pace constant and very slow, even if you feel fine: you've come this far, and now is not a good time to get altitude sickness. This is when you need to take yourself off to your happy place and perhaps, for a little while, forget where you really are. Here's Michael Crichton's account of his tactics when climbing Kili, as recounted in his collection of travel essays entitled, simply, *Travels*:

In the end, what seemed to work is to think of a nice warm swimming pool in California. Or the nice beer and curry dinner I will have when I get back to civilization. Hawaiian palm trees and surf. Scuba diving. Something far from my present surroundings. A pleasant fantasy or daydream.

Though you probably won't notice it, the path actually drifts slightly to the north over these three hours, before crossing a **stream** that is usually frozen at night. You are now just 35 minutes from **Stella Point** (5745m/18,848ft), but it's a painful, tear-inducing half-hour on sheer scree. The gradient up to now has been steep, but this last scree slope takes the biscuit; in fact, it takes the entire tin. In just about everybody's opinion this is the hardest part of the climb, when the cold insinuates itself between the layers of your clothes, penetrating your skin, chilling your bones and numbing the marrow until finally, inevitably, it seems to freeze your very soul. The situation seems desperate at this hour and you can do nothing; nothing except keep going. It's one thing to fail to reach the summit because of altitude sickness; quite another to fail from *attitude* sickness.

The situation was appalling, there was a grandeur and a magnificence about the surroundings which were almost too much for me; instead of exhilarating, they were oppressive.

Charles New, the first person to reach the snowline on Kilimanjaro, in his book *Life, Wanderings, and Labours in Eastern Africa* (1873)

The ground underfoot is just one more obstacle at this stage, the distinctive **shale and gravel slopes** of Kibo causing you to slip back with every step. Everybody has their own way of tackling this, with some trekkers stabbing their poles hard into the ground to aid their balance, while others walk with a Chaplinesque gait, their feet splayed outwards to stem the slide back. Whatever way you choose, you'll find it hard work.

Lift one foot and then the other, just enough to place it higher; don't use any more energy than you need to and breathe deeply between each move. Rhythm is everything, rhythm and pacing, and when you are in it your thoughts go and it is dreamlike, but you are still here

*in the moment, the cone beam of light coming from your forehead tying you through the
blackness to the lava slope of this mountain that in your mind you see rising to a rare glacial height above the acacia-studded plain of Africa.*
Rick Ridgeway *The Shadow of Kilimanjaro – on Foot across East Africa* (1999)

Make it to Stella and you can afford to relax a little. To give you an idea of your
achievement, you are now higher than the summit of Russia's Mount Elbrus, at
5642m/18,511ft the highest peak in Europe.

If you really, absolutely, positively, definitely can't do any more, take comfort from the fact that you have already matched the feat of respected climber
HW Tilman, for whom Stella Point was the highest point reached on his first
attempt on the summit; and you can always use his excuse – he thought that
this *was* the highest point – too. (Mind you, as if to prove that it was ignorance
and not a lack of fortitude that prevented him from reaching Uhuru, he then
went on to conquer the much-harder Mawenzi Peak a few days later.) Take
comfort, too, from the fact that you have also earned yourself a certificate; a
certificate, moreover, that's identical – save for a couple of words – to the one
they give you if you reach the summit. But for most trekkers, those two words
– 'UHURU PEAK' – are everything. Words that are worth all the money, time
and energy one has spent in getting to this point; and which are certainly worth
the extra 45 minutes it takes to stagger around the crater rim (see Map 33,
p384), passing minor pinnacles such as **Elveda** and **Hans Meyer** points before
finally arriving, just as Hans Meyer himself did over a century ago, at **Uhuru
Peak**: the true summit of the mountain and the highest point on the whole continent. You are now enjoying an unrivalled view of Africa – nobody on this
great chaotic, crazy, charismatic continent is currently gazing down from as
lofty a vantage-point as you.

From the summit, it's usual for trekkers who took the Machame Route up
to take the **Mweka Route** back down; and this you'll find described on p375.

The Lemosho & Shira Plateau
routes – an introduction

*Without doubt Kibo is most imposing as seen from the west. Here it rises in solemn majesty,
and the eye is not distracted by the sister peak of Mawenzi, of which nothing is to be seen
but a single jutting pinnacle. The effect is enhanced by the magnificent flowing sweep of the
outline, the dazzling extent of the ice-cap, the vast stretch of the forest, the massive breadth
of the base, and the jagged crest of the Shira spur as it branches away towards the west.*
Hans Meyer *Across East African Glaciers* (1891)

These two treks have been put together simply because they have a lot of features in common, the main one being that both involve a crossing of the expan-
sive Shira Plateau which stretches out for around 13km to the west of Kibo.
This plateau is actually a **caldera**, a collapsed volcanic crater: when you are

❏ **How we have ordered this section**
The difficulty with writing a description of the trails that cross the Shira Plateau is that there is no one official Lemosho Route and no one official Shira Plateau Route either.

So, for simplicity's sake, we have assumed in the following descriptions that from Shira 1 Campsite the **Lemosho Route** will head towards Shira 2/Shira Huts (either straight there or via the Cathedral) and from there to Lava Tower. We have ordered it this way as this is the route most people follow when they book a Lemosho trek. From Lava Tower it's more common to go round the southern side of Kibo and head to Barranco Campsite, a route you can read about on p313. That said, the **Lemosho Route is also the most common trail taken by those who are looking to climb via the Western Breach**, and this is the route we take in the following description.

For the **Shira Route**, on the other hand, we have assumed that from Shira 1 people will head to Moir Huts and from there round the northern side of Kibo on the Northern Circuit, simply because the two major companies that use this route – Nature Discovery and African Walking Company – use this combination.

But do bear in mind that the various stages of these routes are interchangeable; it is just as feasible for you to start off on the Shira Plateau Route, for example, and head round to Barranco Campsite, or begin on the Lemosho Route and head to Moir Huts and the Northern Circuit – or indeed to ignore both options and head up the Western Breach!

The simple fact is, there are **several paths** on the plateau and a number of possible campsites too, and each year the guides slightly alter the routes taken by their trekkers. For these reasons, the descriptions of these routes may not tally exactly with your own experience on the plateau; so look at the itinerary your company has provided and that way you can see which parts are relevant to you.

walking on the plateau, you are actually walking on the remains of the first of Kilimanjaro's three volcanoes to expire, over 500,000 years ago; it was then filled by the lava and debris from the later Kibo eruption.

The plateau also has a reputation for its **fauna**, largely thanks to its proximity to both Amboseli National Park in Kenya and the West Kilimanjaro Wildlife Corridor, from where herds of elephant, eland, buffalo, and big cats such as lion and leopard have been known to wander. Indeed, not so many years ago trekkers on these routes had to be accompanied by an armed ranger to protect them against encounters with predators. That said, to be honest you will be very, *very* lucky to see any evidence of visiting wildlife on the plateau, save for the odd hoofprint or two and the occasional sun-dried lumps of scat and spoor. So, while the proximity of Africa's finest wild beasts adds a certain frisson of excitement to the walk, don't choose either of these trails purely on the strength of their reputation for spotting game: it's an awful long way to come just to see some desiccated elephant shit.

The first thing to know about these two routes is that **it is common for the Lemosho Route to be referred to as the Shira Plateau Route** (or just Shira Route), particularly by foreign agencies keen to promote the fact that you'll be walking across the Shira Plateau. This, of course, is confusing so you should ask your agency to indicate *exactly* which of the two routes you will be taking.

Another way to check is to see where your first night's accommodation will be; if it's Big Tree Campsite (Mti Mkubwa in Swahili), it's the Lemosho Route that you'll be following, regardless of what your trekking agency calls it.

The journey to Londorossi

Getting to the start of the Lemosho/Shira Routes is a bit of a bind. Your immediate destination is Londorossi Gate, the starting point for both treks, but before you get there you first have to suffer a two-hour African massage (the local euphemism for any sort of vehicular ride on a typically rutted African track). As a result of the extra effort and petrol required to get here, these two trails often cost a little more than the more accessible Marangu, Umbwe and Machame trails.

Thus, for much of the first day you won't be walking anywhere but will be strapped into the back of a jeep as it glides along the Arusha–Moshi highway before turning off at **Boma Ya Ng'ombe** ('Cattle Corral'; 26km from Moshi). From there it bounces along for another hour and a half past **Sanya Juu** (22km/13½ miles from the turn-off and virtually the last place to get supplies), **Ngarenairobi** and **Simba Farm** (a huge estate to the left of the road). Your guide will have to alight briefly at a small hut to pay a fee to the Forest Authority before you finally pull up near the village and **gate of Londorossi**. It's a weird place, a Spaghetti Western outpost stuck in the middle of Africa, made entirely of wood, divided up and shut off from the outside world by high wooden fences designed to keep the local fauna at bay. The gate, where you can register and pick up a **permit**, is slightly separate and stands in its own compound.

From here, the two trails divide and are described separately below and on p343.

The Lemosho Route

The Lemosho Route is a relatively new variation on the traditional Shira Plateau Route (described on p343), which is seldom used nowadays. Indeed, though many people book what they think is a trek on the Shira Route – as that is what the trekking agencies often call it – it is usually the Lemosho Route on which they will actually be walking.

The Lemosho Route used to be one of the quietest on the mountain. Once upon a time only the Umbwe Route, which has a reputation for being the most difficult trail, and the Shira Route, which largely follows a road for its first couple of days, were less popular. However, its popularity has grown fast and it's now the third busiest, behind only the Marangu and Machame routes. This is not surprising, for this 7- to 8-day yomp (though some companies take as many as 10 days) takes you through the remote and pristine cloud forest of West Kilimanjaro and across the Shira Plateau to the highest point in Africa and back down again. The assault on the summit is conducted via either the tricky **Western Breach Route** (see p338) or via Barranco, Karanga Valley and Barafu to Stella Point on

the **Barafu Route** (a description of which begins on p315). A few companies also offer a route that utilises the Northern Circuit (see p362), and an ascent to the summit via School Huts and Gillman's Point (see p305). Either way, the usual **descent route is the Mweka trail** (see p375).

It is the first day or so, when you are walking through the forests on Kilimanjaro's western slopes, that is the real reason why this trail has overtaken the old Shira Plateau Route as the main path attacking Kilimanjaro from the west. With the latter you are often driven all the way up to the plateau, thereby missing out on some fine forest, which you experience only through a car window. But by starting in the forest, taking the Cathedral diversion and using the Barafu Route to get to the summit you'll be on the **longest official ascent route on Kilimanjaro at 46.96km/29 miles** (though it can be just 33km/20½ miles if taking the direct route to Shira Huts and then the Western Breach).

Colobus monkey
(from *The Kilima-njaro Expedition,* **HH Johnston**, 1886)

Other advantages with this route? Well from personal experience I think the birdlife is the most diverse and interesting of any on the mountain; though I admit I can't actually back this up with any statistical proof, the fecundity of the forest means many species are able to thrive under its canopy. What's more, the Lemosho Route allows for more variations and diversions from the main route than any other trail. As well as side trips to the minor peaks of Kilimanjaro's third summit, the Shira Ridge – usually done as an acclimatisation walk on the second day – you can also branch off the main path to visit the **Shira Cathedral**, on the southern side of the plateau, on day three. Again, such a side trip is useful for acclimatisation purposes and no extra days need to be taken to do this. Other side trips that *do* require an extra day include a trek to Moir Huts, on the

---

❏ **Mobile (cell) phone reception on the Lemosho Route**

Trekkers with mobile (cell) phones will find little opportunity to use them on the first half of the Lemosho Route. The first place we have ever managed to get reception was after leaving the forest on the second morning, though this happened only once; the first place where it's just about certain you'll get reception is by the **Cathedral** on the third morning. That said, others have managed to get reception near Shira Ridge, the highest point on the second day. **Shira Huts** has reception if you're prepared to search for it on the boulders around the campsite, and reception is OK at **Lava Tower**. Thereafter it depends on which route you're taking. For the Western Breach, reception is fair at **Arrow Glacier**, you can sometimes get it at **Crater Camp** too and, so it is said, at the **summit**.

If you're taking the Barafu Route to the top, see the box on p309 for a summary of mobile reception on this section of the route.

north-western side of the mountain; and, if taking the Western Breach Route to the summit, a diversion to see Reusch Crater and Ash Pit. Indeed, one of the joys of the Lemosho Route is the variety of different trails one can take and itineraries one can build – there is no one standard 'Lemosho Route'.

Though it's a great route, Lemosho is not without its **drawbacks**. For one thing, we reckon it to be the **wettest route**; though meteorology doesn't back us up, in our experience it always seems to rain on this side of the mountain more than anywhere else. Though it varies from month to month, the amount of **rubbish** on the trail and especially at the campsites can be distressing too. How anyone could be stupid enough to drop sweet wrappers in somewhere as lovely as the western forest is beyond me, while those who leave used batteries on the ground at campsites deserve shooting.

STAGE 1: LONDOROSSI GATE TO MTI MKUBWA/BIG TREE CAMP
[MAP 14, opposite]

Distance: 4.8km (3 miles); altitude gained: 396m (1299ft)

Park fees paid and luggage weighed at Londorossi, you jump back on the coach/car as it takes you up the slopes past largely denuded hills and little wooden shacks incongruously furnished with satellite dishes. As these dishes indicate, the inhabitants aren't particularly poor even though the conditions of their houses would indicate otherwise; in fact, the reason why they live in crudely erected wooden shacks is

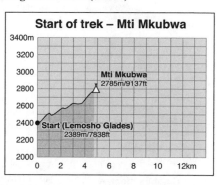

Start of trek – Mti Mkubwa

because they aren't actually allowed to build any permanent construction this high up on Kili. Some of these settlements have actually been dignified with names, including **Gezaulale** and the last 'village' before the forest, **Chaulale**. The authorities have begun a program to remove the inhabitants from this part of Kili, so by the time you get here they may have disappeared altogether.

Eventually, 10 minutes after Chaulale and having entered the forest, your vehicle will give up trying to negotiate the muddy path – either at the official start of the track, marked by a couple of toilets, or some distance before it if the road or your vehicle is in a particularly poor state – and it will be time to alight, grab your daypack and make your own way up the slopes. Even if you aren't having lunch now and have no need for the toilets, do delay setting off just for a few moments to see if the colobus monkeys that hang around here put in an appearance. This starting point, by the way, is sometimes called **Lemosho Glades (2389m/7838ft)**.

It may already be late in the day by the time you start walking, although the

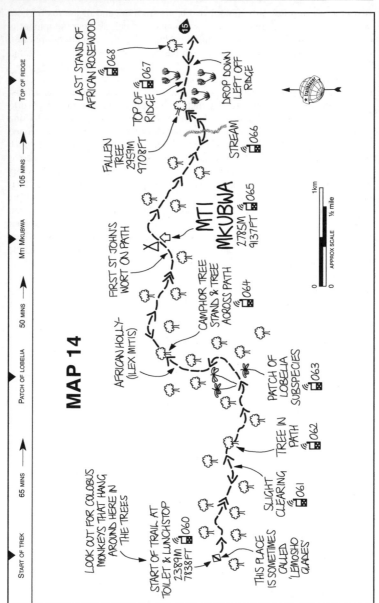

first night's camp lies only around two hours from the end of the road. There are enough steep gradients in these two hours to check all your equipment is comfortable and your limbs are in full working order. The conditions are often misty and cool on this first stage through the forest; ideal weather for walking, if not for taking photos.

As you can tell from the map on p329, landmarks in the forest are few; nevertheless, it's still a splendid start to your trek. At times there is an almost Jurassic quality to the trail, a feeling that you've stumbled into some Lost World – a sense that I can ascribe only to the untamed nature of the forest on this side of the mountain and the complete lack of any evidence that humanity has passed this way. It's just wonderful. It helps too, of course, that throughout today you'll be sharing the forest with colobus and blue monkey and the rarely encountered buffalo, elephant, lion and leopard. Indeed, it wasn't uncommon a few years back for trekkers to be accompanied by armed rangers to ward off any over-curious animals. In addition to the fauna, you'll be sharing the path with many of the celebrities of Kilimanjaro's floral kingdom, including the two most prominent *Impatiens* species, *kilimanjaro* and *pseudoviola*, as well as millions of soldier ants; while watching over the whole shebang are those giants without which there would be no forest, in particular the camphor, podocarpus and hagenia trees. Look out, too, for the *Lobelia gibberoa* and ask your guide to point out the *Dracaena afromontana*, locally known as the *masale*, which though seemingly unimpressive is held in high esteem by the Chagga (see box below).

Your destination for this first stage is the campsite known officially (ie by

---

❑ *Dracaena afromontana* – **the Chagga's constant companion**
Known as *masale* by the locals, the inedible and – at least compared to some of the beautiful plants on Kilimanjaro – rather unedifying *Dracaena afromontana* has nevertheless been cultivated and used by the Chagga since time immemorial, to the extent where it's now almost their tribal emblem. Nobody knows why this should be but it's clear that where the outside world sees an unspectacular green plant of little practical use, the Chagga see a shrub whose spiritual qualities and symbolism are far more important than the practical and nutritional value inherent in other plants.

You'll probably first come across the *dracaena* in one of the mountainside villages where it's still commonly used as a boundary marker, with a row of them planted to form a fence to demarcate the extent of a person's property. According to some Chagga guides, this is because *dracaena* is able to ward off evil spirits which, so it is said, are unable to pass through a line of them. The plant was also traditionally a symbol of contrition and an appeal for clemency. If you were in dispute with a neighbour, for example, or had somehow wronged somebody, the best way to ask for forgiveness would be to give them a *dracaena* plant. Do so, and they'd have to have a very strong reason for not pardoning you.

Indeed, in some Chagga villages it is said that the *dracaena* is a Chagga's constant companion, accompanying a person throughout their life from their first breath to their last. There's some truth to this, too, because in some Chagga villages it was customary to give the sap of the plant to newborns before they took their mother's milk for the first time; while when it came to burying a village chief, the corpse would traditionally have been wrapped in *dracaena* leaves before being interred.

nobody) as the **Forest Camp**, and unofficially (ie by everybody) as **Mti Mkubwa**, or **Big Tree Camp** (2785m/9137ft), for obvious reasons. Lying at the top of a ridge in the shade of a wonderful spreading podocarpus, as with all the campsites on Kili there's little to it other than a piece of flat ground, a couple of long-drop toilets and a ranger's hut. But it's still many people's favourite stopping point on the trail, with the noise of the turaco and colobus in the trees at both dusk and dawn making for a quintessential African night.

STAGE 2: MTI MKUBWA/BIG TREE CAMP TO SHIRA 1 CAMPSITE
[MAP 14, p329; MAP 15, p333]

Distance: 7.9km (5 miles); altitude gained: 719m (2359ft)
You've spent a whole day travelling, registering, walking and sweating and you are still some way short of the plateau, which you will finally reach towards the end of this second stage, leaving the forest for the moorland as you do so. Many trekkers' favourite stage on the trail, this 4hr+ walk (though with all the breaks you'll need it will take a full day) is some-

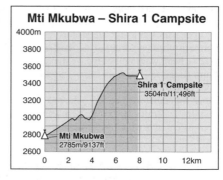

Mti Mkubwa – Shira 1 Campsite

Shira 1 Campsite
3504m/11,496ft

Mti Mkubwa
2785m/9137ft

thing of a red-letter day too. For not only do you forsake forest for moorland and get your first proper views of the Shira Plateau and its accompanying ridges and peaks but it is on this stage that, finally and famously, you get your first views of Kibo.

These rewards are not gained without effort, however; during today you'll be climbing over 700m, taking you above 3500m and into the realm of dastardly HACO and its equally evil twin, HAPO (see p264). So do make sure you go *pole pole* if you don't want to feel poorly poorly.

The day begins just as the last one left off, as you head in a general easterly direction and generally upwards too, though with plenty of minor variations as you negotiate the folds and creases of Kili's forested slopes. Eventually you find yourself heading north-east to climb to the top of a ridge, the point where you actually gain the top being marked by a large **fallen tree**. As with many of the larger trees in this neck of the woods, this giant used to show signs of having been scorched around the trunk – the unmistakable handiwork of honey-seekers who burn the hollow inside the tree in order to smoke out the bees, making it easier to gain access to their produce.

Heading east and up along the ridge, it's not long before the trees start to diminish in size and number to be replaced by their hardier cousins in the heather and stoebe families. These soon begin to crowd you in on both sides but not enough to obscure your view north over the valley. It's a valley you even-

tually join, too, as you continue your eastward and upward progress, contouring gently to the valley floor to reacquaint yourselves with the decorative **African rosewood**, *Hagenia abyssinica*, here making one last stand.

The relentless uphill is finally interrupted by a short descent to what was once a popular lunchstop (Map 15) – popular, that is, until the litter left behind drove guides and their trekkers to find another dining-room to frequent and, in time no doubt, to despoil too. This better **lunch-spot** lies at the top of the next ridge; while there's no water up here (whereas there is in the original picnic site down below) the views are better, particularly to the north over the river known as Ngare Nairobi and the 4x4 road of the Shira Plateau Route beyond. From this new location the path once again points east then bends south, following the ridge, before heading east once more to contour around the slope of what is – though you may not realise it just yet – the northern extremity of the **Shira Ridge**.

The path's gradient, steep since lunch, flattens out as you contour along this northern slope and drops at the **first sight of Shira Plateau**. This is the moment you've been waiting for all day: standing at 3536m/11601ft above sea level, the Shira Ridge to your right, snow-capped Kibo ahead and the plateau unfurled at your feet with your next two days' trekking mapped out for you upon its face. More immediately, beneath you lies the green uniport of **Shira 1 Campsite** (3504m/11,496ft), a spot that's popular with four-striped grass mice, streaky seed-eaters and white-necked ravens as well as the usual foreign itinerants in lurid Gore-Tex.

STAGE 3: SHIRA 1 CAMPSITE TO SHIRA HUTS
[MAP 15, opposite; MAP 16, p336; MAP 17, p338]

Distance: 6.9km (4¼ miles, though it's 10.1km – 6¼ miles – via the Cathedral); altitude gained: 391m (1282ft)
As mentioned in the introduction, one of the advantages of the Lemosho Route is the number of variations one can take. And this third stage is perhaps the one with the greatest number of options, for not only are there are several destinations, there are also different ways of reaching them.

In order to introduce some sort of clarity and simplicity, we've chosen as our destination for this third stage the Shira Huts (also known as Shira 2), simply because it's to there that most people head. But it is not unheard of for some companies, such as Tusker Safaris, to head on to Moir Huts, on the north-western side of Kibo, before dropping back south to Barranco, or even to carry on round the Northern Circuit (as used on Team Kilimanjaro's TK Lemosho Route, AWC's Shira Route and Nature Discovery/Thomson's Grand Traverse) as discussed on p343.

There are **two main ways of getting to Shira Huts** from Shira 1: the regular direct trail slicing north-west to south-east across the plateau or the new and increasingly popular alternative detour via Shira Cathedral on the plateau's southern rim. Though it's not too strenuous, this latter option does provide some useful if marginal acclimatisation as you climb to 3862m (12,671ft) before briefly dropping again. Furthermore, as if the lack of a blinding AMS headache

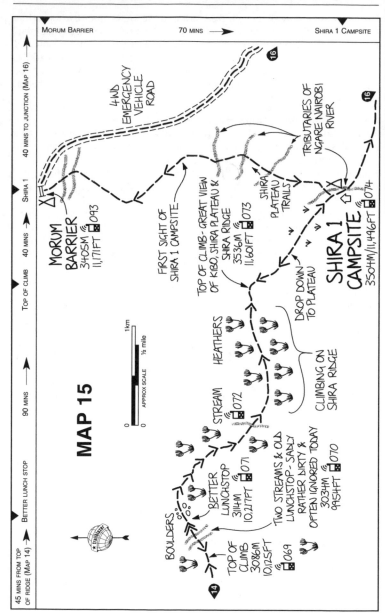

MORUM BARRIER   70 MINS ———→   SHIRA 1 CAMPSITE

4WD EMERGENCY VEHICLE ROAD

TRIBUTARIES OF NGARE NAIROBI RIVER

SHIRA PLATEAU TRAILS

MORUM BARRIER
3405M
11,171FT 📷 093

FIRST SIGHT OF SHIRA 1 CAMPSITE

TOP OF CLIMB - GREAT VIEW OF KIBO, SHIRA PLATEAU & SHIRA RIDGE
3536M
11,601FT 📷 073

SHIRA 1 CAMPSITE
3504M/11,496FT 📷 074

DROP DOWN TO PLATEAU

MAP 15

HEATHERS

STREAM
📷 072

CLIMBING ON SHIRA RIDGE

1km
APPROX SCALE   ½ mile
0

BOULDERS

BETTER LUNCHSTOP
3114M
10,217FT 📷 071

TWO STREAMS & OLD LUNCHSTOP- SADLY RATHER DIRTY & OFTEN IGNORED TODAY
3034M
9,954FT 📷 070

TOP OF CLIMB
3086M
10,125FT 📷 069

40 MINS TO JUNCTION (MAP 16) ———→   SHIRA 1 ———→   40 MINS ———→   TOP OF CLIMB   90 MINS ———→   BETTER LUNCH STOP   45 MINS FROM TOP OF RIDGE (MAP 14) ———→

TRAIL GUIDE AND MAPS

later on wasn't reward enough, there are also the views from the top of the Cathedral across the plateau and towards Kibo; as it takes only a day and thus no more time than the regular route, we recommend you select this option if given the choice. Though if you do choose this variation try to set off early as the clouds often roll in by mid morning, obscuring any decent views. As it is the alternative route to the main trail, we have described the route via the Cathedral second, beginning on p335.

Shira 1 Campsite to Shira Huts: the regular route

This 'traditional' trail may lack the pzazz of the younger alternative but that's not to dismiss it altogether. After all, no stroll across the Shira Plateau could ever be described as dull. Shira Huts is the main campsite on the plateau, equipped with a rangers' office, some smart toilets and a particularly prominent suggestion box, as if to invite criticism from trekkers; given the filthy state of the campsite when we last visited, it's probably going to get it too.

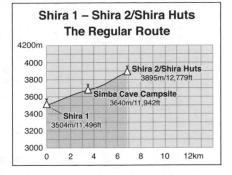

To get to Shira Huts involves just under three hours of steady uphill walking. From Shira 1 you head south-east through the heath and moorland of the plateau; watch out for buffalo tracks and those of other animals – klipspringer, dik dik – that cross the plateau in search of salt and fresh grazing. Come to think of it, watch out for buffaloes themselves – encountering one can seriously ruin your holiday.

Cross the unimpressive trickle of the waterway that will, further down the slopes, become the torrent of the Ngare Nairobi, and about 85 minutes from breaking camp you reach the plateau's crossroads. It is here that the Lemosho Route meets the 4x4 track of the Shira Plateau Route; here too that you meet the deep-ish creek of the Simba River. Shame, then, that such an important landmark should be marked only by a couple of toilets belonging to **Simba Cave Campsite** (3640m/11,942ft), used largely by those on the (old) Shira Route (see p343). The **cave** itself is a rather forlorn effort lying north-east of the junction.

From here it's another 40-45 minutes of marching, past the junction with the path to Moir Huts and to the top of a ridge, from where you can see the green roof of your destination, **Shira Huts** (3895m/12,779ft). It's a fairly direct 35-minute path from the junction that takes you there, crossing a couple of shallow ridges and a stream along the way.

By the way, on arriving at Shira Huts you will be higher than the top of Großglockner, at 3798m (12,461ft) the biggest mountain in Austria.

Shira 1 to Shira Huts: the alternative route, via Shira Cathedral

This route begins by following the regular trail as it heads south-east across the southern half of the plateau, turning off south by a big and distinctive boulder just after crossing the Ngare Nairobi (Map 16). Note that from this boulder you can already see your final destination on this stage, the Shira Huts, in the far distance. It's a long trek across to the foot of the Cathedral, with **Shira Cone** (aka Cone Place) the only major landmark nearby, but it's not a trek that's lacking in interest. In all probability you should see the first *lobelia deckenii* of your trek, standing sentinel-straight as they peer

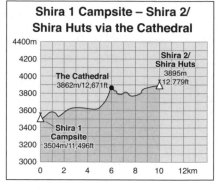

**Shira 1 Campsite – Shira 2/
Shira Huts via the Cathedral**

above the grass to check on your progress. You may also see many animal tracks on the trail, including klipspringer, eland and dik dik, hoofprints that betray this path's origins as a trail used by animals in search of salt, minerals and fresh grazing.

Crossing many (probably dry) **stream-beds**, all of which, when filled with water, feed into the Ngare Nairobi, you start to climb through heather trees to the foot of the rounded hump known as the **Cathedral** (3862m/12,671ft). The summit is gained soon after, the whole expedition from Shira 1 taking just under three hours.

Panorama-wise, not only are there the delights of the plateau ahead, including Moir Huts to the north-east and Kibo to your right, but behind and to the east of the Cathedral your guide should be able to point out the faint traces of the Machame Route etched into the slopes. This is also the most reliable place on the plateau to get **phone reception**.

From the summit you make your way north-east across **East Shira Hill** and the other undulations of the crater rim, eventually arriving at a strange muddy area sprinkled with boulders, the lack of vegetation being due to poor drainage according to one guide. The eastern end of this area has been converted into a makeshift **helipad**, until now used largely by film crews to fly in supplies, including the IMAX crew during the 40 days they spent on the mountain to film their *Kilimanjaro: To the Roof of Africa* documentary. Just a couple of minutes later you come to the **roadhead** – the final termination of the 'rescue road' that emergency vehicles use when ferrying people from the mountain (and the continuation of the road that those on the old Shira Route take to gain access to the plateau, though they alight at Morum Barrier – see p344). It may be the end of the road, but you still have a further 45 minutes up to the **Shira Huts** (Map 17; 3895m/12,779ft) and the day's end.

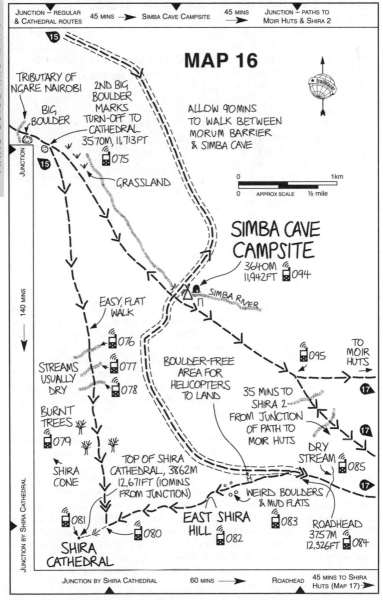

JUNCTION – REGULAR & CATHEDRAL ROUTES 45 MINS → SIMBA CAVE CAMPSITE 45 MINS → JUNCTION – PATHS TO MOIR HUTS & SHIRA 2

MAP 16

15

TRIBUTARY OF NGARE NAIROBI

BIG BOULDER

2ND BIG BOULDER MARKS TURN-OFF TO CATHEDRAL 3570M, 11,713FT

ALLOW 90MINS TO WALK BETWEEN MORUM BARRIER & SIMBA CAVE

JUNCTION

15

075

GRASSLAND

0   1km
APPROX SCALE   ½ mile

SIMBA CAVE CAMPSITE
3640M
11,942FT 094

140 MINS

SIMBA RIVER

EASY, FLAT WALK

076

077

BOULDER-FREE AREA FOR HELICOPTERS TO LAND

095

TO MOIR HUTS

17

STREAMS USUALLY DRY

078

35 MINS TO SHIRA 2 FROM JUNCTION OF PATH TO MOIR HUTS

17

BURNT TREES

079

DRY STREAM 085

17

SHIRA CONE

TOP OF SHIRA CATHEDRAL, 3862M 12,671FT (10MINS FROM JUNCTION)

WEIRD BOULDERS & MUD FLATS

JUNCTION BY SHIRA CATHEDRAL

081

080

EAST SHIRA HILL 082

083

ROADHEAD 3757M 12,326FT 084

SHIRA CATHEDRAL

JUNCTION BY SHIRA CATHEDRAL 60 MINS → ROADHEAD 45 MINS TO SHIRA HUTS (MAP 17) ►

STAGE 4: SHIRA HUTS TO LAVA TOWER CAMP/BARRANCO HUTS
[MAP 17, p338; MAP 10, p314]

Distance: 10.1km (6¼ miles) to Barranco Huts (6.9km/4¼ miles to Lava Tower); altitude gained: 91m/299ft (732m/2402ft to Lava Tower Campsite, then 641m/2103ft descent to Barranco Huts)

If you've spent the last three days marvelling at the silence and solitude of the Lemosho Route and wondering what all those reports decrying the over-crowding on Kilimanjaro were about, today should answer that. For it is on this stage that the tranquil Lemosho Route (where, if you're very lucky, it is still possible to feel as if you're the only group on the mountain) merges with the over-popular Machame Route. Nor is it just solitude you'll be bidding farewell to on this

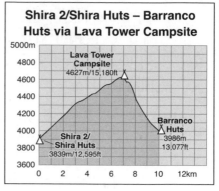

Shira 2/Shira Huts – Barranco Huts via Lava Tower Campsite

Lava Tower Campsite 4627m/15,180ft

Shira 2/Shira Huts 3839m/12,595ft

Barranco Huts 3986m 13,077ft

stage: the Shira Plateau also takes a final bow. As a result of all that relentless ascending you've been doing, you'll also be leaving the World of Heather for the Land of Lichen. True, those opting for the trek round the southern side of Kibo will reacquaint themselves with heathers, stoebes, lobelias and senecios at the magical Barranco Valley. But from now until the summit, the Barranco and other valleys excepted, it is the alpine desert that prevails.

As mentioned on p326, there are two alternative routes to the summit – and it's on this stage that the two paths diverge. You can read about both of them on p315 onwards (regular route via Barranco Valley and the Barafu Route) and p338 onwards (Western Breach Route).

But you have to get to the Machame Route first and that involves about three hours of uphill walking. As you probably expect, it's an easterly climb up the fairly gentle slope of the Shira Plateau, gradually forsaking the heather and moorland for something altogether more barren, where lichen-covered boulders predominate. Look out for the shiny black obsidian rock (see p137) on the trail, not forgetting to look up occasionally to see Meru in the distance over your right shoulder. There are few steep passages to this stage, save for a brief clamber up a narrow gully; 10 minutes more of clambering on a fairly steep gradient and suddenly you find the path flattening out, just before the **junction with the lit-tle-used path to Moir Huts** (Map 10, p314); the hut itself lies about 30 min-utes away (see p346). This junction is a popular place to rest and, if the mist that swirls around Kibo is in a particularly benign mood, a great place for photos too. There's also a path from here to the foot of **Shark's Tooth** (25 mins), the pointy little peak sitting to Kibo's west. The regular trail, however, bends right

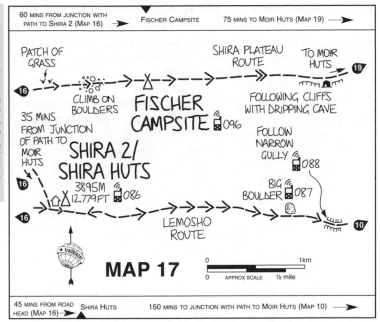

60 MINS FROM JUNCTION WITH
PATH TO SHIRA 2 (MAP 16) → FISCHER CAMPSITE   75 MINS TO MOIR HUTS (MAP 19) →

PATCH OF GRASS

SHIRA PLATEAU ROUTE   TO MOIR HUTS

16

CLIMB ON BOULDERS

FISCHER CAMPSITE 096

FOLLOWING CLIFFS WITH DRIPPING CAVE

19

35 MINS FROM JUNCTION OF PATH TO MOIR HUTS

FOLLOW NARROW GULLY 088

16

SHIRA 2/ SHIRA HUTS

3895M 12,779FT 086

BIG BOULDER 087

16

LEMOSHO ROUTE

10

MAP 17

0   1km
0   APPROX SCALE   ½ mile

45 MINS FROM ROAD
HEAD (MAP 16)→   SHIRA HUTS   150 MINS TO JUNCTION WITH PATH TO MOIR HUTS (MAP 10) →

(south) to chop through a gully, from where it curves again to follow, approximately, a line of overhanging rocks. Arching south again, you now climb up to the top of the neighbouring ridge... and there, marked by some weird mushroom-rock formations, you meet the main Machame Route that has been contouring that ridge from the Shira Caves.

Soon after, the path loops to the south-east and divides, though pretty much everyone these days opts for the left-hand branch that heads off east on a deceptively lengthy and fairly steep trail towards the Lava Tower, passing through the unofficial **Sheffield Campsite** (from where there is a further trail heading south to Barranco) and on to **Lava Tower Campsite** (4627m/15,180ft), squeezed between Kibo and the tower itself. Though not the most direct path to Barranco, this route is useful in order to gain some much-needed altitude that could be vital in the battle against mountain sickness.

If you are taking the longer route to the summit via Barranco, Karanga and Barafu campsites, turn to p315 for a description of your trek; while if you're continuing on the Western Breach, read on.

THE WESTERN BREACH ROUTE TO UHURU PEAK

Over the years the Western Breach Route has acquired a certain aura and a reputation as the hardest of the summit routes. Nor is this reputation entirely unde-

served. Though it's the shortest, time-wise, it's also the steepest (with the mean gradient of the route said to be 26°) and there's a bit of non-technical and very basic scrambling involved. What's more, and most worryingly, this trail is subject to occasional rockfalls and there are a couple of places where your guide should stop and listen out for any heading in your direction. Though more than a decade ago now, following the deaths of three American climbers in a rockslide near Arrow Glacier in January 2006 KINAPA brought in some legislation, and these rules are still in situ to this day. As such, all trekkers are now usually issued with protective helmets during their climb on this route by their agency and KINAPA will ask you to sign a waiver form too. These measures have done little to prevent more deaths, however, with the last one we know of occurring in 2015.

It's interesting to see the reactions of the trekking agencies to the route. Some shy away from it while others, such as SENE and African Environments, positively recommend it. Such reactions are an indication of just how diverse the opinions are about this path.

That said, to hear some people talk about the Western Breach you'd think you'd have to have the climbing capabilities of your average housefly in order to make it to the top. Suffice to say: you don't. Yes, this route is a little trickier in parts. And yes, after snowfall the route up can be icy and an ice axe may be required in extreme conditions. But as with all the routes in this book no technical climbing know-how is necessary – just the ability to haul yourself up with your hands on occasion when required.

So what are the benefits of doing this route? Well, firstly, the Western Breach is the only one that enters directly into the crater as opposed to peaking

Western Breach Route

at the top of the rim that rises above the crater floor. As such, this is the most convenient route to take if you want to explore the Ash Pit, Reusch Crater, Furtwangler Glacier and the other features of the summit. (Though it's possible to visit these features even though you climbed to the summit on other routes, few trekkers actually do so; whatever their intentions before they reach the top of Kibo, by the time trekkers get there via Gillman's or Stella Point they're usually too knackered or in too much pain to spend the two hours-plus necessary to explore the crater.) And the other main benefit of climbing via the Western Breach is, of course, the kudos that comes with having conquered the hardest non-technical route Kilimanjaro has to offer.

Note that once upon a time the Western Breach was the one trail to the summit that was often tackled during the day rather than at night, traditionally by those intending to camp on the summit. Despite this, the general consensus amongst Kili connoisseurs is that it is still much easier to tackle 'The Breach' at night, when the scree, shale and rocks are frozen and thus less likely to move when you step on them. Furthermore, after dark the occasionally vertiginous drops are invisible, which makes climbing for vertigo sufferers much easier. Indeed for safety reasons KINAPA now insist that everybody is away from Arrow Glacier Campsite by 5am, in order that they are clear of the area with the greatest risk of rockfall by 7am (ie the first hour after sunrise). There are still a few groups who tackle it by day but, like both the other routes up Kibo, the Western Breach is now mostly attempted at night.

Do note, finally, that this route, though the shortest way to the top, is often the most expensive if you intend to camp at the summit because it is usual for porters to receive a premium to climb up Kibo. This is understandable; on all other routes they don't go above around 4700m/15,420ft (ie the altitude of the last campsite/huts), whereas here they have to go to the crater (above 5700m/18,700ft) and carry all their load up the trickiest route too.

STAGE 5: LAVA TOWER CAMPSITE TO ARROW GLACIER CAMPSITE
[Map 18, opposite]

Distance: 2.5km (1½ miles); altitude gained: 244m (801ft)
By our reckoning this particular leg, even if taken *pole pole*, lasts little longer than 75 minutes, yet it's not unusual for trekking agencies to set aside an entire day for it. In one respect this seems a little over-cautious and does lead to a situation where, those 75 minutes aside, you'll be spending the rest of your day freezing your butt off inside your tent. On the

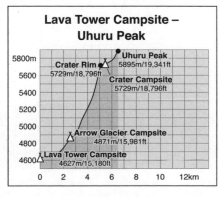

Lava Tower Campsite –
Uhuru Peak

Uhuru Peak 5895m/19,341ft
Crater Rim 5729m/18,796ft
Crater Campsite 5729m/18,796ft
Arrow Glacier Campsite 4871m/15,981ft
Lava Tower Campsite 4627m/15,180ft

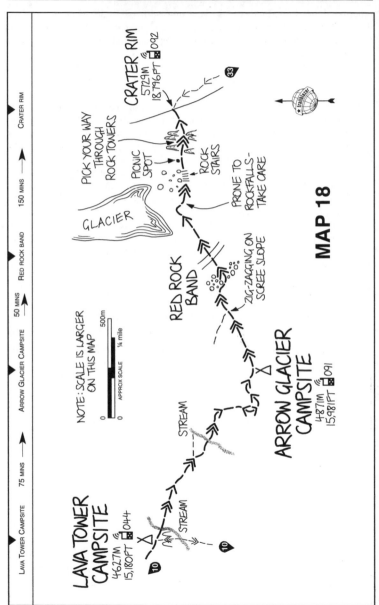

other hand, it's a good idea to take your time at this altitude. After all, save for the Crater Camp this is the highest place where you can pitch your tent on the mountain (the altitude of Arrow Glacier Campsite being 4871m/15,981ft); and that kind of altitude should always be taken seriously.

Furthermore, the walk, though only brief, is still quite exhausting, it being uphill all the way. You begin by crossing a stream or two (one of which, **Bastions Stream**, runs below Lava Tower) before climbing steeply in a south-easterly direction to the top of a ridge. Near the top of the climb you pass an old trail running directly from Lava Tower to the Western Breach Route that bypasses Arrow Glacier Campsite altogether; it's a path that's seldom used these days and unless your guide points it out to you, it's easily missed. Descending for a few seconds to a stream and then climbing to a second ridge, by following the direction of *that* ridge eastwards you soon come to **Arrow Glacier Campsite**. Engulfed by avalanches and often subject to the vagaries of the extreme conditions up here, this place has always been a bit of a mess and little has changed. Whilst the rubbish is depressing, it's the toilets that are the most revolting spectacle, with the ones that haven't been destroyed now home to an entirely new geological form: neither stalactite nor stalagmite, but stalacshite. Console yourself with the thought that if you're not spending a night on the summit, you probably won't be spending a full night here but should be away by 2am. Happy Camping!

Incidentally, you are now just 6m/20ft lower than the summit of the Vinson Massif – at 4877m/16,001ft, the highest point in Antarctica.

STAGE 6: ARROW GLACIER CAMPSITE TO UHURU PEAK
[Map 18, p341; Map 33, p384]

Distance 4km (2½ miles); altitude gained: 1024m (3360ft; see profile p340)

Mungu akipenda, tutafika – If God wants it, we shall arrive

Though we've talked as if there is one set path from campsite to crater rim, this isn't actually the case; the path changes as snow and rockfalls dictate. Every guide has his own way of tackling the ascent, too. As such, the map on p341 and the description that follows may differ from the exact route you end up taking. But whatever route you take, rest assured it will be steep, and it will be exhausting.

Having said that each path up the Western Breach is unique, your guide will doubtless aim for the rocky ridge that you can see from Arrow Glacier Campsite which runs from the rock towers near the crater down towards the camp (and is often called the 'Stone Train'). It will take around 1¾ hours before you properly join this ridge (soon after crossing a second stream), a walk that includes the most dangerous part of the ascent, where **rockfalls** are frequent. Furthermore, this area is often also covered in snow and many a guide has lost the path here. Successfully gain the ridge and about 15 minutes later you'll find yourself at the foot of the so-called **Rock Stairs** – natural steps that, after the shifting scree and rocks of the previous 1¾ hours, come as something of a relief. These stairs are also viewed as a 'Point of No Return' by the porters who, once they see that you've reached here, consider there's no turning back and thus break camp and

march off to Mweka (unless you're planning to sleep at Crater Camp, of course, in which case they'll be right behind you).

The stairs take about 40 minutes to tackle altogether, at the end of which you find yourself on a small, flat space that's often used as a **picnic spot** by those tackling the Western Breach during the day. Dirty and chilly, a more inhospitable picnic spot it would be hard to find, though you do get great views down to Barranco Campsite. Beyond the picnic site the stairs are replaced by a path that's just as steep, though you have to tackle this section without the benefit of any steps. The trail picks its way between the **rocky towers** guarding the crater. Persevere for another 40 minutes and you'll find yourself finally gaining the **crater rim (5729m/18,796ft)**, with **Furtwangler Glacier** on your left the first of many spectacular sights up here. Walking on level ground for a change, it takes around 10 minutes to reach **Crater Campsite** (also 5729m), set amongst boulders at the foot of the climb up to Uhuru. If you're staying here you'll have to pay an extra park fee of US$100 – and you'll also have to pay more to your porters, too, as they will have climbed over 1000m higher than they would on any other route.

The path up to **Reusch Crater** and **Ash Pit Viewpoint** (40 mins) bends north round and behind Furtwangler Glacier. For more on what's up here, see p382.

The **stiff switchback climb** up to **Uhuru Peak**, 50 minutes away, lies to the south of the campsite, clearly etched into the crater wall. It's a hard climb and you'll be cursing every zigzag and switchback on the way. But keep going: the sense of achievement at the top is beyond compare. And it's a feeling that will stay with you all the way down, and all the way back to your home country. Because if you get to the summit, you'll believe you can do anything.

Oh, to be able to bottle that feeling...

The Shira Plateau Route (& Northern Circuit)

This is the older of the two trails that cross the Shira Plateau and, in our opinion, is definitely the inferior. That said, a couple of the biggest companies operating on the mountain – African Walking Company and Nature Discovery/Thomson (who start their Grand Traverse Route on the Shira Trail) – insist this is the better route, for reasons we shall come to in a moment.

Our problems with this route are twofold. Firstly, and in our opinion most importantly, you miss out on the forest zone on the way up (it's a very rare trekker who, these days, begins their walk before Morum Barrier which lies at the start of the Shira Plateau); and it's not just any old forest either, for the jungle on this western side of Kili is the best on the mountain. That, we think, is little short of unforgivable.

The second problem we have is that the Official Shira Route is actually a 4WD track used by emergency vehicles. In other words, you'll be walking on a track that's been designed with vehicles in mind – which can never be as fun as walking on a trail made for pedestrians. Though to be fair to the companies that

do offer this route, most of them these days seem to turn off the 'road' as soon as they can in favour of one of the many other paths that criss-cross the plateau – in effect ending up on one of the Lemosho Route variants – and some don't actually walk on the road at all.

All of which begs the question: why do the companies who patronise this route think it's better than Lemosho? Well from what we can gather, it's simply because they reckon that if you are going to have a 7- or 8-day trek, spending those days at a higher altitude (Morum Barrier is at 3405m), will enable you to acclimatise better and thus have a better chance of reaching the top than if you'd spent one or two of those days at a lower altitude trudging up Kilimanjaro's western slopes. All of which may be true – though to our mind this still doesn't compensate for missing out on the forest of the western slopes, which you now see only through a car window.

So I guess it comes down to a matter of opinion and taste: if your sole reason for setting foot on the mountain is to get to the summit, the Shira Plateau Route *may* be a better route for you. But if you have any interest in the more complete experience, one that includes both ascending and descending via *all* the various vegetation zones, Lemosho wins hands down.

STAGE 1: LONDOROSSI GATE TO MORUM BARRIER, SHIRA 1 OR SIMBA CAVE CAMPSITE   [MAP 15, p333; MAP 16, p336]

Morum Barrier to Shira 1:
Distance: 3.75km (2¼ miles); altitude gained: 99m (325ft)

Morum Barrier to Simba Cave Campsite: 6.5km (4 miles); altitude gained: 215m (705ft)

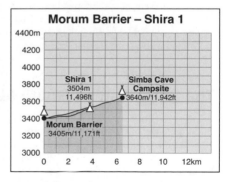

A journey of a thousand miles begins with a single step, said the inscrutable 6th-century BC philosopher Lao-tzu. Thankfully, for those of you who have chosen this route, your own journey will be a lot shorter than 1000 miles and your first step will be onto a bus that will convey you to **Londorossi Gate** (p328). It is a rare trekker who begins his or her walk here, however, so – ramblers registered and permits purchased – you'll rejoin the bus as it conveys you up the slopes, through pine plantations, forest and moorland, with the occasional monkey or baboon crossing your path and the waters of the Ngare Nairobi a capricious companion to your right.

Eventually the twisting track bifurcates in the shadow of Morum Hill. A few metres on from this divide are the remnants of what was clearly some sort of concrete gatepost – the remnants of the old **Morum Barrier** (3405m/11,171ft). Several information boards also stand nearby and there's a toilet here too. It's a lonely place: the landscape windswept, the flora dry and scrubby, the fauna virtu-

ally non-existent. Indeed, it almost feels as if humanity has abandoned this corner of the mountain and coming across the remains of the barrier always puts me in mind of that moment when Charlton Heston comes across the Statue of Liberty at the end of *Planet of the Apes*. Rather than sink to your knees and bewail the demise of Homo sapiens, however, as Charlton did, we advise you to keep your spirits up and get walking. Incidentally, by driving to 3405m you are only 2m short of the *combined* altitudes of the highest points of Scotland, Wales and England – namely Ben Nevis (1344m/4409ft), Snowdon (1085m/3560ft) and Scafell Pike (978m/ 3209ft) respectively – and you haven't even started walking yet!

Morum Barrier marks the start of the Shira Plateau, where you'll be spending the next couple of days. Occasionally, groups turning up late are forced to **camp** here though if everything has gone smoothly thus far it's more usual to walk to one of the campsites on the plateau, with Shira 1 or Simba Cave Campsite being the only realistic choices.

Shira 1 (3504m) is reached via a narrow trail that heads south from the information boards. The trail crosses several streams but the whole walk takes only 70 minutes or so; from Shira 1 you then continue along the Lemosho Route to Shira 2 (possibly via the Cathedral, as described on p335) and Lava Tower (see p337); or your trekking company may have opted to head towards Moir Huts and possibly continue from there round the Northern Circuit, which we describe on p346.

Those who instead opted to stay at **Simba Cave Campsite (3640m)**, reached by walking along the road for about 90 minutes, have essentially the same options. The campsite, adorned with several weatherbeaten old wooden toilets as well as the cave, marks the main junction between the road and the Lemosho Route. (Incidentally, we don't know of any company that still uses the 'road' after Simba Cave, with more easterly footpaths, described as part of the Lemosho Route on p344, being superior alternatives.)

STAGE 2: SIMBA CAVE CAMPSITE TO MOIR HUTS
[MAP 16, p336; MAP 17, p338; MAP 19, p347]

Distance: 6km (3¾ miles); altitude gained: 515m (1690ft)
Around 45 minutes from Simba Cave lies a **junction** marked with little more than a simple sign, with direction arrows usually scraped into the dirt too. Nevertheless, it's quite an important place, where the regular Lemosho Route and the route to Moir Huts divide. Those heading to Shira 2/Shira Huts should see p335; while those heading towards Moir

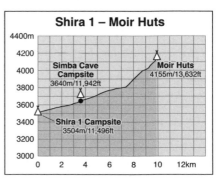

Huts and the Northern Circuit should read on. From the junction with the main trail a 135-minute path picks its way between boulders, around or over petrified

TRAIL GUIDE AND MAPS

> ❏ **Mobile (cell) phone reception on the Shira Plateau Route**
> The Shira Route – or at least the version of it described here – has perhaps the worst reception of all the trails. On my last trek on this trail I failed to get reception pretty much the whole way round. You can sometimes have success at one of the **Pofu Camps** on the Northern Circuit and, before that, you may be lucky enough to get something on the **ridge above Moir Huts** which the guides say is reliable – though I failed. There is little reception at Third Cave so, after that, the next time you'll be able to use your mobile phone will be at **Gillman's** (doubtful), **Stella** (probably) or **Uhuru Peak** (maybe).

lava flows, and through grassy swards. The main 'landmark' is the **disused Fischer Campsite**, named after Scott Fischer who did much to pioneer this route with his company Mountain Madness and who perished on the slopes of Everest. Hunt around for (or get your guide to show you) the small plaque that commemorates him and admire the resplendent giant groundsels that thrive in this chilly location. Just over an hour's schlep afterwards the path curves in the shadow of some **low cliffs** past an impressive **dripping cave** just before the **Moir Huts** (4155m/13,632ft). Set in a lovely sheer-sided valley that sees few visitors, the campsite is more peaceful than almost any other on the mountain; alas, it also means the cleaning crews seldom drop by, so there's often plenty of rubbish around. Furthermore, apart from the three toilets, the only other building is a ruined pyramid-shaped hut, built as a sleeping shelter but now sadly vandalised. As a result, the whole camp does feel a bit cold and bleak. Even the white-necked ravens don't bother scavenging around here, the pickings presumably being too slim, and the silence as a result can be positively deafening. A rare touch of warmth and pleasure, however, is provided by the seedeaters which, lacking the social graces of their brethren at lower altitudes, happily hop into your tent in search of crumbs. There's also a great deal of pleasure to be had in views that take in both the Shira Ridge – where you have just come from – and snow-laden Kibo where, all being well, you hope to be going...

STAGES 3 & 4: THE NORTHERN CIRCUIT (MOIR HUTS TO THIRD CAVE CAMPSITE)   [MAP 19, opposite; MAP 20, p349]

At first sight, the Northern Circuit, which drapes around the northern face of Kibo, appears to offer little to the Kili climber, especially when compared to its counterpart the Southern Circuit. For one thing, the northern trail lacks such attractions as the lovely Barranco Valley and its photogenic campsite, the charm of the sunbird-flitted Karanga Valley, the busy excitement of Barafu Campsite and the scrambling challenge of the Barranco/Breakfast Wall. Furthermore, the Southern Circuit is nearer to civilisation, with Moshi and the neighbouring villages both visible, on occasion, and just a day's walk away, which may prove vital if you run into difficulty and need to descend quickly. In contrast, there is no such descent available on the Northern Circuit; if you need to evacuate from this side of Kibo you'll have to walk to the Shira Plateau or the Saddle and work out how to get back down from there.

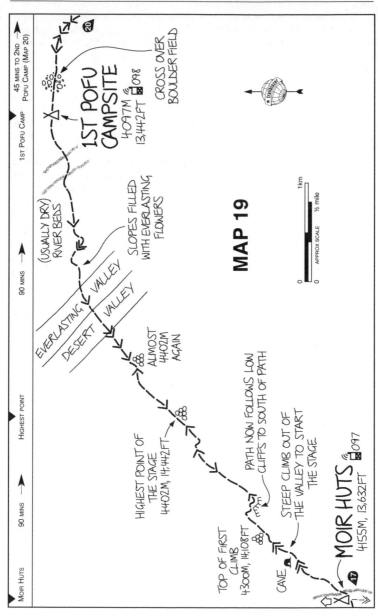

MAP 19

MOIR HUTS | 90 MINS | HIGHEST POINT | 90 MINS | 1ST POFU CAMP | 45 MINS TO 2ND POFU CAMP (MAP 20)

1ST POFU CAMPSITE
4097M 13,442FT [098]
CROSS OVER BOULDER FIELD

(USUALLY DRY) RIVER BEDS

SLOPES FILLED WITH EVERLASTING FLOWERS

EVERLASTING VALLEY

DESERT VALLEY

ALMOST 4402M AGAIN

HIGHEST POINT OF THE STAGE 4402M, 14,442FT

PATH NOW FOLLOWS LOW CLIFFS TO SOUTH OF PATH

TOP OF FIRST CLIMB 4300M, 14,108FT

STEEP CLIMB OUT OF THE VALLEY TO START THE STAGE

CAVE

MOIR HUTS
4155M, 13,632FT [097]

0 — 1km
0 — ½ mile
APPROX SCALE

So far, so unattractive. But there is one quality the Northern Circuit has that its southern neighbour lacks: **solitude**. For while the Southern Circuit resounds to the footfall of just about every trekker who opted for the Machame, Umbwe, Lemosho and Shira routes – not to mention their crews – the Northern Circuit sees very few people. True, visit in the high season and you may bump into trekkers who have signed up to one of the 'alternative' routes offered by the big companies such as Team Kilimanjaro, Nature Discovery/Thomson and African Walking Company plus those companies who, lacking imagination, merely copy them; but even then there's a slight possibility you will have the whole path to yourself. For the Northern Circuit is not part of any of the 'official' routes but instead exists to offer those who want to avoid the crowds the chance to do so.

The path can be completed in one day – though it is more normally divided into two stages, with a night spent at one of three **Pofu camps**. Altitude-wise, and assuming you are going from west to east ie from Moir Huts to Third Cave Campsite, you actually lose a little in altitude – from 4155m to 3936m. This, how-ever, fails to convey the sometimes quite large and sweaty climbs and descents you have to make on your way round and you will in fact climb to 4402m/14,442ft at one point; as such, this route is pretty good for acclimatisation.

Though we have written this from west to east, this is one of those paths which sees walkers heading in both directions. I do apologise but those of you walking from east to west (having come, usually, from the Rongai Route) will have to read this description backwards, as it were...

Moir Huts to Second Pofu Campsite   [Map 19, p347; Map 20, opp]

Distance: 9.2km (5¾ miles); altitude _lost_: 122m (400ft) (247m/810ft up to the high point then 369m/1211ft descent to Pofu)
As mentioned, peace and solitude are the main characteristics of this path. In terms of acclimatisation, you actually achieve the lofty altitude of 4402m/14,442ft today before falling to the Second Pofu Camp at 4033m/13,232ft. It won't be unusual, therefore, for people to feel some symptoms of altitude sickness (often a headache) by the time they arrive at one of the Pofu campsites. So do try to go *pole pole* and to drink lots to avoid this. Furthermore, don't set off from Moir Huts if you're feel-ing any effects of the altitude as you are going to even more remote places.

The walk begins with per-haps the steepest climb of the day, a relentless slog up a barren slope to exactly 4300m (14,108ft). Cairns both mark the top of the ascent and the way forward, as you spend your day making your way around Kibo's northern face, dropping down into the many north–south val-

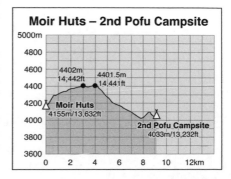

Moir Huts – 2nd Pofu Campsite

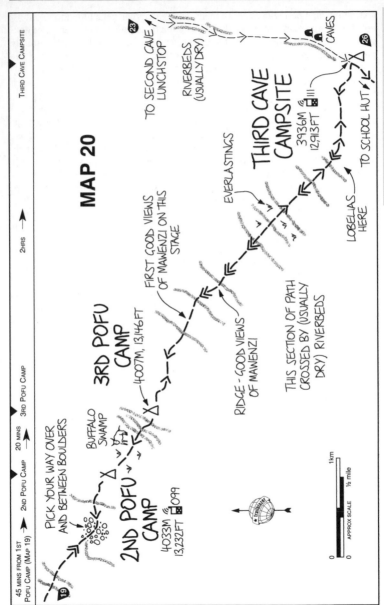

MAP 20

2ND POFU CAMP
4033M
13,232FT

3RD POFU CAMP
4007M, 13,146FT

BUFFALO SWAMP

PICK YOUR WAY OVER AND BETWEEN BOULDERS

FIRST GOOD VIEWS OF MAWENZI ON THIS STAGE

EVERLASTINGS

RIDGE - GOOD VIEWS OF MAWENZI

THIS SECTION OF PATH CROSSED BY (USUALLY DRY) RIVERBEDS

LOBELIAS HERE

THIRD CAVE CAMPSITE
3936M
12,913FT

TO SCHOOL HUT →

TO SECOND CAVE - LUNCHSTOP

RIVERBEDS (USUALLY DRY)

CAVES

APPROX SCALE
0   1km
0   ½ mile

leys before clambering back out of them. Though this can get a little monotonous, note how the character of each valley is different to its neighbours, with some decorated with everlastings, others blanketed in heathers, and still others virtually pure, lifeless desert. Eventually, after three hours, you'll come to the **first of the Pofu Camps** – this one said to be preferred by Nature Discovery/Thomson – followed in short order by some **boulders** that you need to scramble over to reach the **second** (45 mins) and most popular of the three possible Pofu campsites.

It has to be said that these camps are all fairly uncharismatic places, perched on chilly ridges between the valleys and with not a toilet between them (your agency will have packed one for you to use). It will probably come as no surprise to you that we think a cleaning crew is definitely required around here; though the number of trekkers passing this way is small, over time the mess they and their crews have left has built up considerably. Unfortunately, there's not much to distract you from the mess except to sit and watch the mist roll in and, on occasion, clear again, giving you the chance to spot the eland that are said to hang about in these parts and after which the campsites are named. If the skies are clear enough you should get a full frontal view of Kibo, while Mawenzi peers coyly over your shoulder and the lights of Kenya twinkle in the far distance below.

Second Pofu Campsite to Third Cave Campsite [Map 20, p349]

Distance: 6.8km (4¼ miles); altitude _lost_: 97m (318ft)

Unsurprisingly this stage continues in pretty much the same vein as the previous one as the path continues on its merry traverse around the northern slopes. Once again the trekker is asked to negotiate numerous valleys, mostly dry, one or two slightly more fecund, and one at the very start of the day that is, so it is said, favoured by buffaloes in search of water during the dry season. The gradients aren't quite as dramatic on this stage and the day slightly shorter though you'll still find yourself pretty puffed out by the time you reach **Third Cave Campsite** (3936m/12,913ft). The reason for this is clear when you look at the gradient profile and see how much ascending and descending you have to do on this stage. The views, however, provide ample compensation, with Kibo to your right and Mawenzi gradually looming larger and larger ahead of you, though you won't see much of the glorious Saddle that separates them until the next stage.

For details of Third Cave Campsite, please see p359, while for details of your trail from here you'll need to consult this book in conjunction with the itinerary your agency has provided – with School Hut, Kibo Huts and even Mawenzi Tarn just three of the possible destinations.

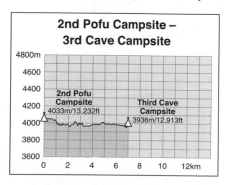

2nd Pofu Campsite – 3rd Cave Campsite

2nd Pofu Campsite 4033m/13,232ft

Third Cave Campsite 3936m/12,913ft

The Rongai Route

Please convey to the seven blind climbers who reached the summit of Kilimanjaro my warm congratulations on their splendid achievement.
Queen Elizabeth II in a telegram to Geoffrey Salisbury who, with his team of young, blind African trekkers, used the Rongai Route for their attempt on the mountain.

Probably due to the improvement in the road heading from Marangu to the Kenyan border that leads to the start of this trek, the Rongai Route has become increasingly popular over the past couple of years. Where once you had a 50:50 chance of having the trail to yourself, these days you'll be lucky indeed to avoid the hordes.

While many will see the Rongai's new-found popularity as a drawback, it can't be denied that it is deserved – even though, at first glance, this trail seems decidedly unattractive. The lower slopes at the very start of the trail have been denuded by farmers and now present a cultivated and unexciting landscape, the 'forest' for the first hour here being nothing more than a pine plantation (though the park authorities are building a new route that will avoid these plantations and start in the native forest once more – see p353). Nor is the 'proper' native forest that you do eventually walk through that spectacular either, being little more than a narrow band of (albeit pretty) woodland which soon gives way to some rather hot and shadeless heathland. Indeed, the parched character of Kili's northern slopes often means trekking parties have to carry water along the way (often all the way from the Second Cave lunchstop to the School Hut if taking the regular Rongai Route without the diversion to Mawenzi Tarn); your agency should have supplied you with enough porters for this. And then there's the expense: if you are booking your trek in Moshi, Arusha or Marangu, the cost of a Rongai trek can be higher than all other trails except Lemosho/Shira Plateau due to the higher transport costs associated with travelling to the start of the trek.

So why, if this route is more expensive, far-flung and barren than all the others, has it become so popular? Well for one thing, there's the **wildlife**.

❏ **What's this route called again?**
The name **Rongai Route** is actually something of a misnomer. It may be the name that everybody uses but, strictly speaking, it's not the correct one. The real, original Rongai Route used to start at the border village of the same name but was closed several years ago by the authorities who decided that two trails on a side of the mountain that few trekkers visit was unnecessary. You will still see this route marked on older maps but nowadays all trekkers who wish to climb Kilimanjaro from the north follow a different trail, also known as the **Loitokitok Route** after the village that lies near the start. Just to confuse the issue still further, this isn't officially the correct name either, for along the trail you'll see various signs calling this trail the **Nalemuru Route** – or, occasionally, Nalemoru – though this name is rarely used by anyone.

Because of its proximity to Amboseli, your chances of seeing the local fauna here are greater than on any other route bar those starting in the far west below Shira Plateau. During the research for the first edition of this book we encountered a troop of colobus monkeys, while later that same day we came across an elephant skull, with elephant droppings and footprints nearby; and at night our little party was kept awake by something snuffling around the tents (a civet cat, according to our guide, though presumably one wearing heavy hobnail boots to judge by the amount of noise it was making). Buffalo and eland also frequent the few mountain streams on these northern slopes (though, as previously mentioned, these streams, never very deep, are almost always dry except in the rainy season and consequently the buffalo choose to bathe elsewhere for most of the year; though occasionally they head up the slopes in search of minerals that they lick off the rocks). The **flora** is different here too, with its juniper and olive trees. And if at the end of the **26.8km/16¾ miles** (37.65km/23½ miles if taking the Mawenzi Tarn Diversion) ascent to Uhuru Peak you do feel you've somehow missed out on some of the classic features of Kili – lobelias, for example, or the giant groundsels, which don't appear regularly on the northern side except near Kikelelwa Camp on the diversion up to Mawenzi Tarn – fear not, as both can be found in abundance on the 36.55km-long (22¾-mile) Marangu Route, **the designated descent** for those coming from Rongai.

Furthermore, opt for the extra day – which we strongly advise, for reasons not only of acclimatisation – and you will spend that extra night at **Mawenzi Tarn Hut**, which not only allows you to savour some gobsmacking views across to Kibo from the top of the ridge above the tarn but also gives you the chance the following day to walk across the Saddle, many people's favourite part of the mountain. And finally, when it comes to the ascent, we found the walk from School Hut to Gillman's Point to be *marginally* easier than that from Kibo Huts (though admittedly the two do share, for the last three or four hours or so to the summit, the same path).

Other advantages include the drive to the start: from Moshi the road passes through a rural Chagga heartland, so giving you the chance to see village life Chagga-style (see p187), which we heartily recommend. Furthermore, if you

---

❏ **Mobile (cell) phone reception on the Rongai Route**
Mobile reception on the Rongai Route is not great, though it's better if you are taking the Mawenzi Tarn variation. As always, reception depends a lot on which network you are with. Guides say you can get reception by the **Hut at Simba Camp** – though I have to say I've never managed it. One place where I do always get reception, however, is at the popular resting place on the large flat rock during the second morning. **Second Caves** also has reasonable reception. Thereafter, however, on the regular Rongai Route the chances to use your phone are limited.

Those taking the trail via Mawenzi Tarn will find reception at **Kikelelwa** comes and goes; while at **Mawenzi Tarn** it is also intermittent, though more reliable by the toilets. Crossing the Saddle there is usually no reception, so the next time you'll be able to use your mobile phone will be at **Gillman's** (possibly), **Stella** or **Uhuru Peak**.

manage to find other trekkers to join you and split the cost, the transport should not be too expensive.

PREPARATION

The journey to Loitokitok and Rongai Gate

What was once one of the more arduous aspects of trekking on the Rongai Route – getting to the start – has since become much easier thanks to the improvement of the road from a muddy, dusty track to a fully fledged tarmac highway. A journey that used to take half a day or more can now be completed in just a couple of hours. But though the journey may be a lot easier it still retains some interest, mainly because it takes you through several Chagga villages.

Until the new gate at Rongai opens (see below), you are still obliged to pick up permits from **Marangu Gate**, from where your vehicle will return down the hill to **Marangu Mtoni** before continuing round the dry, eastern side of the mountain, through the villages of **Mwika** and **Mrere** in the heart of the Rombo District. After them, in order, the villages of **Shauritanga** (site of an horrific tragedy in June 1994, when 42 schoolgirls were burnt to death in a dormitory fire started by a candle), **Olele**, **Usseru**, **Mashima** and **Kibaoni** emerge in fairly rapid succession before, eventually, you arrive at **Tarakea**, the largest settlement. There is also a border post with Kenya in Tarakea; presumably your driver will know *not* to take the road leading to it but instead to keep on following the road which now heads north-west. The wooden settlement of **Loitokitok** lies a few minutes on from Tarakea, where a track on the left branches up to the park gate, situated at around 2000m. From the gate you can see the smart and lovely *Snow Cap Cottages* (see p247 for details), which resemble (from this distance at least) Swiss-style chalets.

STAGE 1: RONGAI GATE TO SIMBA CAMPSITE
[MAP 21, p354; MAP 22, p355]

Distance: 7km (4¼ miles); altitude gained: 638m (2093ft)

At the time of writing, the park authorities are supposed to be opening a new gate at Rongai. This new entrance lies just a couple of minutes to the north of the old one but it is hoped that the few hundred metres that separate the two will make a world of difference. How? Well, at the moment trekkers are frogmarched past a hot and dusty blemish of **pine plantations**, followed by fields of potato and maize that are pockmarked here and there with the

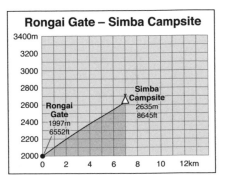

Rongai Gate – Simba Campsite

Rongai Gate 1997m 6552ft

Simba Campsite 2635m 8645ft

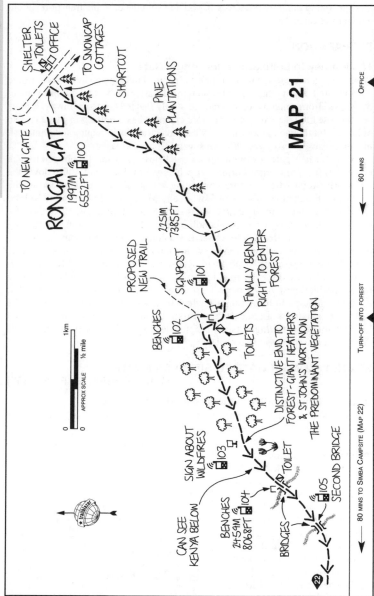

MAP 21

TO NEW GATE

RONGAI GATE
1997M 6551FT 🏠100

SHELTER
TOILETS
OFFICE
TO SNOWCAP COTTAGES

SHORTCUT

PINE PLANTATIONS

2251M 7385FT

PROPOSED NEW TRAIL

SIGNPOST 🏠101

FINALLY BEND RIGHT TO ENTER FOREST

BENCHES 🏠102

TOILETS

DISTINCTIVE END TO FOREST - GIANT HEATHERS & ST JOHN'S WORT NOW THE PREDOMINANT VEGETATION

1km
½ mile
0   APPROX SCALE   0

SIGN ABOUT WILDFIRES

🏠103

CAN SEE KENYA BELOW

BENCHES 2459M 8068FT 🏠104

TOILET

BRIDGES

🏠105 SECOND BRIDGE

22

◀ 80 MINS TO SIMBA CAMPSITE (MAP 22)   TURN-OFF INTO FOREST ▶   ◀ 60 MINS   OFFICE ▶

wooden shacks of those who eke out a living from the soil. Just off to the right, however, and clearly visible from the existing path, is a decent swathe of native, natural forest lining a mountain stream – along which, all being well, the new path will travel, thereby saving tomorrow's trekker the tedium of walking past fields of vegetables for the first hour. The new gate will also have the facility to issue permits, thus saving a diversion in the bus to Marangu Gate as currently happens.

Assuming you're on the old trail, it comes as a blessed relief when the path turns sharply right and crosses a bridge to escape into the lush green haven of the forest and a union with the as-yet-unopened trail. This forest is teeming with wildlife, in particular **colobus monkeys**, with a troop often grazing by the bridge – so it comes as something of a disappointment to find just how quickly the tall trees of the montane forest give way to the more stunted vegetation of the **heathland**, such as giant heathers and St John's wort. Leaving the forest on a trail that slowly steepens, about 50 minutes afterwards you cross a stream and a few minutes later reach the first campsite on this route, known as the **Simba (or Sekimba) Campsite**, at an altitude of 2635m/8645ft. It's always good to get to a campsite, and this one in particular is pleasant: surrounded by heathers, with creatures snuffling about the tent at night and birdsong to wake you in the morning, this spot has a pleasingly wild, isolated ambience.

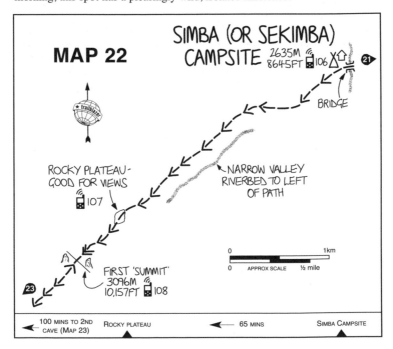

STAGE 2: SIMBA CAMPSITE TO THIRD CAVE CAMPSITE
[MAP 22, p355; MAP 23, opposite]

Distance: 5.8km (3½ miles) to Second Cave Campsite; 3.3km (2 miles) to Third Cave Campsite (9.1km/5¾ miles in total); altitude gained: 852m (2795ft) to Second Cave; Second Cave to Third Cave 449m(1473ft); 1301m (4268ft) in total

This day perhaps lacks the variety of others on the trail. For most of the day you will be walking up slopes flanked with heather with the twin peaks of Kilimanjaro keeping a watchful eye as you progress. If you're on a five-day trek, during this stage you will bid farewell to those lucky trekkers who opted to take the extra day and visit the Mawenzi Tarn Hut; they will go their own way after lunch. (That route is described on p358.) For the

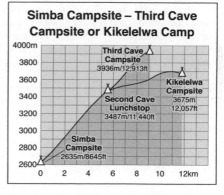

Simba Campsite – Third Cave Campsite or Kikelelwa Camp

Third Cave Campsite 3936m/12,913ft

Kikelelwa Campsite 3675m 12,057ft

Second Cave Lunchstop 3487m/11,440ft

Simba Campsite 2635m/8645ft

'five-dayers', by the end of today you will have ascended more than 1300m. But there's no gain without pain and today is long, involving almost 4½ hours of steady walking on a steep, dusty path. Take comfort from the fact that tomorrow is much easier, and that you have already ascended almost 2000m from the gate, and are now well over halfway to the summit.

If you haven't already been doing so, this is also the time to take things deliberately *pole pole* ('slowly slowly' in Swahili) – you're reaching some serious altitudes now, and mountain sickness stalks the unwary.

The path at the start of this stage is, perhaps surprisingly, a westward one, its goal seeming to be the northern slopes of Kibo rather than the eastern slopes you will eventually climb. The heathers are gradually shrinking in size now too and while some trees still cling on at this altitude, they are few in number and scattered. For these reasons, the first part of this stage is rather shadeless and very hot.

After 45 minutes a **river bed** (dry for the best part of the year) joins you from the left and the path follows its course for most of the next hour. Look back occasionally and, weather permitting, you should be able to see a number of villages on the Kenyan side of the border, the sunlight glinting off the metal roofs. Continuing upwards, the path steepens slightly and begins to turn more to the south. The terrain up here is rather rocky and bumpy. The path continues south-south-west, rounding a few minor cliffs and hills and crossing a number of false summits, before eventually flattening out and arriving at a small, waterless cave. As inviting as the cave and the shade it offers now appear, this is not your lunch stop. That lies 20 minutes further on through lizard country of bare

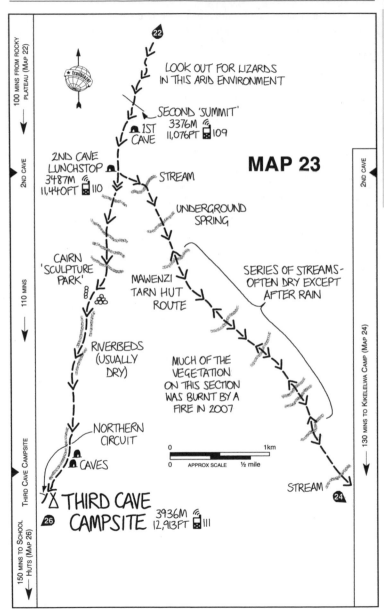

22

LOOK OUT FOR LIZARDS
IN THIS ARID ENVIRONMENT

SECOND 'SUMMIT'
1ST CAVE   3376M   📱109
11,076FT

2ND CAVE
LUNCHSTOP
3487M   📱110
11,440FT

STREAM

MAP 23

UNDERGROUND
SPRING

CAIRN
'SCULPTURE
PARK'

MAWENZI
TARN HUT
ROUTE

SERIES OF STREAMS-
OFTEN DRY EXCEPT
AFTER RAIN

RIVERBEDS
(USUALLY
DRY)

MUCH OF THE
VEGETATION
ON THIS SECTION
WAS BURNT BY A
FIRE IN 2007

NORTHERN
CIRCUIT

CAVES

0   1km
0   APPROX SCALE   ½ mile

STREAM

△ THIRD CAVE
CAMPSITE   3936M   📱111
12,913FT

24

26

100 MINS FROM ROCKY PLATEAU (MAP 22)

2ND CAVE

110 MINS

THIRD CAVE CAMPSITE

150 MINS TO SCHOOL HUTS (MAP 26)

2ND CAVE

130 MINS TO KIKELELWA CAMP (MAP 24)

rocks and long grasses and is known as the **Second Cave** (3487m/11,440ft).

Before setting off in the afternoon, make sure you are on the correct trail, for the path to the Mawenzi Tarn Hut branches off at this point (see below): if your destination is the Third Cave Campsite but you find yourself heading south-east, reconsider.

The path to the Third Cave begins behind and above the caves. Crossing a wide and usually dry riverbed, which in the rainy season is sometimes used as a playground by buffalos, the path continues drifting southwards across increasingly arid terrain, the 'dry flower' helichrysum now interspersed amongst the heathers.

❏ **The Mawenzi Tarn Hut Route**
                                [Map 23, p357; Map 24, p360; Map 25, p361]
This alternative path is wonderful. Great views, lovely scenery and a useful way to acclimatise. If you can afford the extra day on the mountain, don't hesitate.

From Second Cave to Kikelelwa Campsite
Distance: 5.95km (3¾ miles); altitude gained: 188m (617ft)
From Second Cave, the usual lunchstop on the second day, the path takes an abrupt south-easterly turn directly towards the jagged peak of Mawenzi. Traversing open moorland the path meanders and undulates; assuming you've already walked from Simba Camp this morning, you will feel rather drained by the time you stumble into **Kikelelwa Camp** (3675m/12,057ft), situated near a couple of caves by the Kikelelwa River, with giant groundsels and lobelias flourishing nearby. (Incidentally, I don't know why this should be so but whenever I have walked this stretch of the path – which must be a good half-dozen times now – it has always been either raining or very misty. That said, it has always brightened up in the evening to reveal Kibo's snowy summit peaking over the ridge that separates the campsite from the Saddle.) Compared to the morning where you gained over 850m, this afternoon's walk increases your altitude by less than 200m, though the distances of the two parts are about the same and, given the amount of up- and downhills, this latter walk is just as exhausting.

Kikelelwa Camp to Mawenzi Tarn Hut Campsite
Distance: 3.75km (2¹⁄₃ miles); altitude gained: 627m (2057ft)
Though this stage to Mawenzi Tarn is relatively short at less than 4km and is usually completed in a morning (allowing time for a brief acclimatisation trek in the afternoon for those who feel up to it), it's also steep as you gain more than 600m/1969ft, the path shedding the moorland vegetation as it climbs steadily.

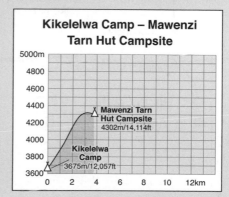

Kikelelwa Camp – Mawenzi Tarn Hut Campsite

Mawenzi Tarn Hut Campsite 4302m/14,114ft

Kikelelwa Camp 3675m/12,057ft

The halfway point between Second and Third Caves is marked, surreally, by a '**cairn sculpture park**' where the more creative trekkers and porters have left dozens of elegantly arranged rocks and stones artfully balanced into pillars, peaks and other forms; a good place to take a break, methinks. As huge rocks begin to appear to left and right, temporarily obscuring Mawenzi and Kibo, the unmistakable outline of toilet huts appear ahead on the trail, a sure sign that the campsite is nearing, this time to your left across another **broad riverbed**. This is the **Third Cave Campsite** (3936m/12,913ft) and the **last water point** before the summit.

For the continuation of this route, please go to p362.

Mawenzi Tarn Hut Campsite (4302m/14,114ft) is situated in one of the most spectacular settings, in a cirque beneath the jagged teeth of Mawenzi. There's a small ranger's hut here and a toilet block.

Assuming the walk here was trouble-free you will have most of the afternoon to go on an acclimatisation climb up the ridge to the west; if you're lucky, the sky will be clear, affording you fantastic views of Kibo, though in all probability you'll merely catch the odd glimpse through the clouds that usually roll in across the Saddle in the afternoon.

But no matter, for you'll get the same views tomorrow morning when the skies should be clearer and the sun will be behind you too. The views back down to the Tarn – which, to be honest, is little more than a puddle with delusions of grandeur – are great too.

Mawenzi Tarn Hut Campsite to Kibo Huts
Distance: 8.9km (5½ miles); altitude gained: 412m (1352ft)
This lovely day begins with a slight retracing of your steps before you strike out westwards, crossing the ridge and dropping down the slope to tiptoe along the beautifully barren Saddle's northern edge. With views like screensavers to east and west, it's a rare trekker indeed who doesn't rate this day as their favourite on the mountain. The

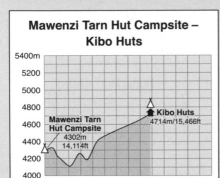

flora is sparse but do look out for eland which are said to stroll up here.

You have two destinations at the end of this third day: School Hut (see Map 6) or, more usually these days, Kibo Huts. Both lie on the lower slopes of Kibo and both are just a few hours' walk away.

Depending on which hut you end up at, see p363 for the continuation of your walk up to Gillman's from School Hut, or p302 for the walk up to Uhuru from Kibo Huts.

TRAIL GUIDE AND MAPS

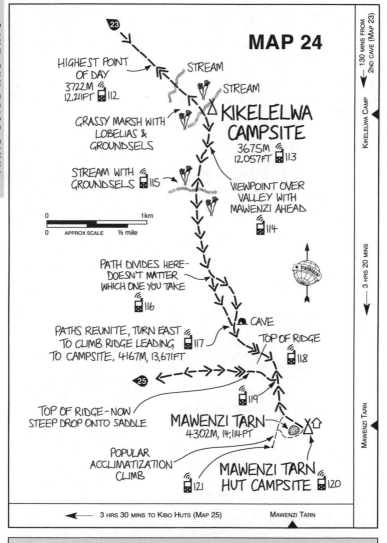

MAP 24

23

HIGHEST POINT
OF DAY
3722M 📶
12,211FT 📱112

STREAM

STREAM

GRASSY MARSH WITH
LOBELIAS &
GROUNDSELS

KIKELELWA
CAMPSITE

3675M 📶
12,057FT 📱113

STREAM WITH 📶
GROUNDSELS 📱115

VIEWPOINT OVER
VALLEY WITH
MAWENZI AHEAD
📱114

0   1km
0   APPROX SCALE   ½ mile

PATH DIVIDES HERE-
DOESN'T MATTER
WHICH ONE YOU TAKE
📱116

★trailblazer

CAVE

PATHS REUNITE, TURN EAST 📶
TO CLIMB RIDGE LEADING   📱117
TO CAMPSITE, 4167M, 13,671FT

TOP OF RIDGE
📱118

25

📱119

TOP OF RIDGE-NOW
STEEP DROP ONTO SADDLE

MAWENZI TARN
4302M, 14,114FT

POPULAR
ACCLIMATIZATION
CLIMB
📱121

MAWENZI TARN 📶
HUT CAMPSITE 📱120

◄ 130 MINS FROM
2ND CAVE (MAP 23)

KIKELELWA CAMP ►

◄ 3 HRS 20 MINS

MAWENZI TARN ►

◄ 3 HRS 30 MINS TO KIBO HUTS (MAP 25)   MAWENZI TARN

In all the route descriptions, do remember that the times we quote are approximations and, more importantly, refer to walking times only with no time spent resting, taking photos etc. Add on 30-50% to get an estimate of the total time spent on the trail.

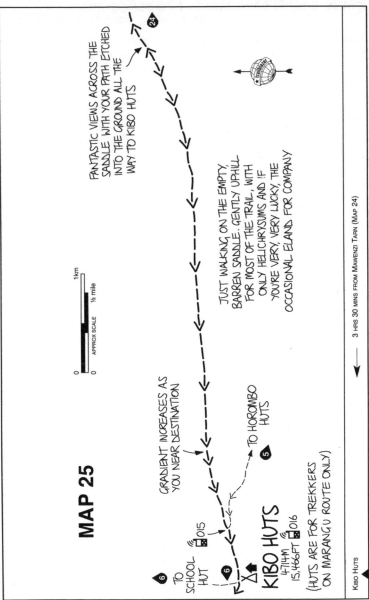

MAP 25

FANTASTIC VIEWS ACROSS THE SADDLE WITH YOUR PATH ETCHED INTO THE GROUND ALL THE WAY TO KIBO HUTS

JUST WALKING ON THE EMPTY, BARREN SADDLE. GENTLY UPHILL FOR MOST OF THE TRAIL, WITH ONLY HELICHRYSUMS AND IF YOU'RE VERY, VERY LUCKY, THE OCCASIONAL ELAND FOR COMPANY

GRADIENT INCREASES AS YOU NEAR DESTINATION

TO HOROMBO HUTS

015

016

TO SCHOOL HUT

KIBO HUTS
4714M
15,466FT

(HUTS ARE FOR TREKKERS ON MARANGU ROUTE ONLY)

0   1km
0   APPROX SCALE   ½ mile

3 HRS 30 MINS FROM MAWENZI TARN (MAP 24)

KIBO HUTS

TRAIL GUIDE AND MAPS

STAGE 3: THIRD CAVE CAMPSITE TO SCHOOL HUT
                    [MAP 23, p357; MAP 26, opposite]

Distance: 4.8km (3 miles); altitude gained: 781m (2562ft)

This stage is little more than an *hors d'oeuvre* for the main course, which will be served at around midnight tonight. Yet it may surprise you to find out that over the course of this stage you climb 781m/2562ft. By the end of it you'll be on the eastern slopes of Kibo, with splendid views across the Saddle to Mawenzi.

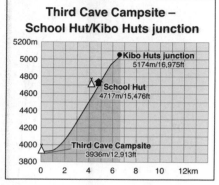

Looking south-west from the Third Cave Campsite, you should be able to see much of today's path snaking over the undulations of Kibo. The path begins by retracing the last few steps of yesterday back to the **river bed**, which forks just a few minutes south of the campsite into two distinct tributaries. The path, too, divides at this junction and is signposted, with your trail heading off to the right (west), crossing the western tributary and continuing on towards the foot of Kibo. It's a slow slog southwards up the hill. Even the heathers struggle to survive up here, disappearing for the last time less than an hour outside camp; only the everlastings and the occasional yellow senecio continue to thrive, providing a welcome relief from the relentless greys and browns of the rocky soil.

After about 75 minutes a summit of sorts is reached, whereafter the path now heads more to the west, directly towards Kibo. A porters' path bisects the trail around here, a path so seldom used that the junction is easily missed. No matter, for your path is clear as it bends more to the south, traversing **Kibo's eastern slopes** with the western face of Mawenzi now in full view to your left. Soon after, your guide may take you off the trail and down the hill a little to see the main sight of the day: a **buffalo carcass**, well preserved by the dry conditions, currently mounted on top of a boulder. Originally the body was found wedged between some nearby rocks and one can only assume that the buffalo was up here looking

for minerals, which they lick off the bare stone, but became trapped between the rocks and couldn't get out again.

The last bit of the walk is steep and the difficulty in getting oxygen into your lungs will leave you feeling quite exhausted. But after just over an hour

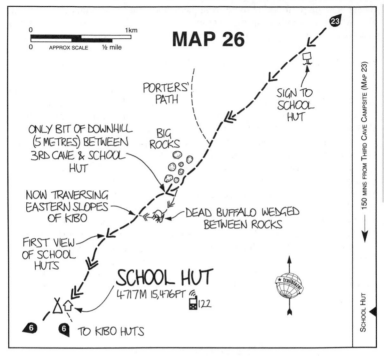

from the western bend in the path you finally reach the **School Hut** (marked as the Outward Bound Hut on some maps, its former name and one that KINAPA would prefer you didn't use), sitting in the shadow of some rather daunting cliffs. The hut sits at an altitude of about 4717m/15,476ft. This, incidentally, is virtually the same height as the Kibo Huts, which are larger, permanently manned by park staff, and the first place to head if you need emergency help. They lie around 35-45 minutes to the south, the path beginning by the southernmost toilet hut.

STAGE 4: SCHOOL HUT TO UHURU PEAK VIA JUNCTION WITH KIBO HUTS ROUTE [MAP 6, p303]

Distance: 1.9km (1¼ miles) to Kibo Huts route, plus 4km (2½ miles) to Uhuru Peak (5.9km/3¾ miles in total); altitude gained: 457m (1499ft) to Kibo Huts route, plus 721m (2365ft) to Uhuru Peak, 1178m (3865ft) total (see p302 for the Kibo Huts to Uhuru Peak profile)

The higher we climbed the rarer grew the atmosphere and the more brilliant the light of the stars. Never in my life have I seen anything to equal the steady lustre of this tropical starlight. The planets seemed to grow with a still splendour which was more than earthly, ... Assuredly, the nights of lower earth know nothing of this silver radiance.

Hans Meyer *Across East African Glaciers* (1891)

There is no direct trekking route from the School Hut to the crater rim. Instead, the path heads south from the huts to join up with the 'Tourist trail' running from Kibo Huts towards Gillman's Point – the trail we have dubbed the Kibo Huts Route. Your trail joins it between William's Point (5131m/16,834ft) and Hans Meyer Cave (5259m/17,254ft). In our experience, it takes slightly – though only slightly – less time from School Hut to this junction than it does from Kibo Huts, so you may wish to start this stage a little later than you would if walking from Kibo Huts – say at 12.15-12.30am rather than midnight.

Finding the start of the path from the School Hut can be a little tricky in the dark so we recommend you or your guide conduct a little reconnaissance while it's still light to ensure he knows where you're supposed to go. Once you're on the path, which starts with a scramble up the rocks behind the School Hut, the trail becomes fairly clear, being marked with cairns the whole way. A repetitive pattern emerges during the walk: generally you are walking in a south-south-westerly direction over scree, but every so often the path turns more westerly and climbs more steeply over solid rock – these being petrified lava flows. At the end, a short descent brings you into the Kibo Huts 'valley' and a union with the path up to Gillman's. After the isolation of the previous two hours, the number of trekkers on this path comes as something of a shock. Hans Meyer Cave lies just 20 minutes above you along a series of switchbacks.

For details of the path up to Gillman's Point from Hans Meyer Cave, turn to p304. For the descent you'll be using the Marangu Route, details of which can be found on p372.

The Umbwe Route

If Marangu is the 'Coca Cola Route' and Machame has the nickname 'The Whiskey Route', what does that make Umbwe, (in)famous as the shortest (**24.7km/15¹/₃ miles**)*, steepest and hardest of the trails on Kili? Sure, Machame is *fairly* steep here and there. But on Umbwe, the gradient is such that in a couple of places on the first two days you can stand upright on the trail and kiss it at the same time. What's more, it's only on the Umbwe Route that you'll be trekking on tree roots for much of the second day. So while Machame is still popularly called 'The Whiskey Route', since its renovation about a decade ago that 'whiskey' has been rather watered down; and when compared to the unadulterated Umbwe Route, Machame starts to seem like pretty small beer.

That said, the Umbwe Route is still **a non-technical climb**. Taxing, but not technical. All you need are an iron will and legs of steel; this is truly a trek to

---

* It should be mentioned that if you don't visit Barranco Camp but head straight from the Umbwe Route to Arrow Glacier – as some speed ascent climbers do – the distance is even shorter at about 21.2km (13¼ miles).

❏ Acclimatising on the Umbwe Route

Having trekked on Umbwe a couple of times now, I have to confess I have properly fallen in love with the tranquillity and beauty of this trail. It's a joy. And I want other people to love it too. But there is one problem that has to be acknowledged: the route is simply too short and too steep to allow many people to acclimatise properly. As a result, the success rate for getting people to the summit is not as high as it is for the nearby Machame Route.

However, there are a couple of simple remedies for this. Firstly, on the third day, having reached Barranco Camp the previous evening, you should then **take an acclimatisation day**. If you use that day to climb to Lava Tower before returning to camp, then the altitude profile you have followed for the first three days almost exactly mimics that of the Machame Route: that is to say, on the first day you climb to around 3000m/9843ft (3021m/9911ft on Machame, 2944m/9659ft on Umbwe), on the second day you make it above 3800m/12,467ft (3839m/12595ft at Shira Cave Campsite on Machame, 3986m/13,077ft at Barranco on Umbwe), while on the third day on both routes you reach 4627m/15,180ft at Lava Tower before sleeping at 3986m/13,077ft. So in theory the success rate should be pretty much identical too. What's more, there are several paths linking Barranco Campsite with Lava Tower – so you can take a different one for the descent than you did for the ascent.

The alternative to taking an acclimatisation day is to **climb Mount Meru first**, before tackling Umbwe over five days immediately afterwards. By tackling Meru, Kili's little brother, first, you will have already reached 4566m/14,980ft – excellent preparation for Umbwe. True, this itinerary will take more time (assuming you have a day off between the two climbs you're looking at around 10 days in total) and cost more money. But in terms of your overall experience of mountain conquering in Northern Tanzania, this is pretty much the best you can get. If I had ten days and a few thousand dollars spare, this would be my choice without a doubt.

test your mettle. The difficulty is that it's so damn relentlessly uphill. Indeed, looking back on the first couple of days we can think of very few places where you actually descend, the longest being the few minutes or so at the end of the second stage when you walk down to Barranco Campsite.

As far as rewards go, while your calves and thighs will curse the day God paired them with somebody who would want to undertake such a climb, your heart and lungs will be thankful for the workout. Your eyes, too, will be grateful you chose Umbwe as they feast upon the scenery, particularly on the second morning as you leave the forest and find yourself walking on a narrow ridge between spindly heathers. The gobsmacking views on either side of the trail here are amongst the most dramatic the mountain has to offer, save for those on the summit itself. Your ears, too, will be glad they're stuck to the side of your head rather than anyone else's for they'll enjoy the break, this being the quietest trail of them all – at least until the end of the second day when you find yourself joining the hordes at Barranco Camp, the busiest on the mountain. Once at Barranco, you can either follow the majority round to Barafu (for a total of **29.06km/18 miles** from gate to summit, thereby making it longer than the standard Rongai Route) and access the summit via Stella Point; or, if you hanker after the quieter, more dramatic option once again, you can join the path up to Lava Tower and continue

TRAIL GUIDE AND MAPS

❏ **Mobile (cell) phone reception on the Umbwe Route**
Mobile reception on the Umbwe Route is good, though as always it depends a lot on which network you are with. I've sometimes managed to get a signal in the forest on this route, and on the second morning after struggling through the giant heathers I do often get reception. At Barranco reception is not good, though on the ridge before entering the camp it's OK. Then up to **Lava Tower** and **Arrow Glacier** it is fine, even up to **Crater Camp** and, so I've been told, the summit.

As for those heading to the summit via Barafu, while it's not great at Karanga I've always got pretty good reception at **Barafu**; while at **Stella**, if you walk around enough, you can get it there too.

---

to the summit via the Western Breach (see p338). This latter option is the connoisseur's choice, no doubt, though be warned that it's an extremely risky strategy unless you take at least one – and preferably two – acclimatisation days en route to Arrow Glacier Campsite (see p342 for more details). Otherwise, the trip from Moshi up to Arrow Glacier Campsite, an increase in altitude of almost 4000m/13,123ft, will have taken you just three days which is far too rapid. Do this and you can kiss your summit certificate – and possibly a lot more – goodbye.

So that's Umbwe: dramatic views, blessed solitude and some terrific, invigorating walking – and all without the clutter and chatter of other trekkers. Those who know the mountain consider it Kili's best-kept secret. It's hard to argue with that.

STAGE 1: UMBWE GATE TO UMBWE CAVE CAMPSITE
[MAP 27, p367; MAP 28, p369]

Distance: 9.9km (6¼ miles); altitude gained: 1293m (4242ft)
As the closest gate to Moshi, getting to the start of the Umbwe Route should be uncomplicated as long as the road is intact. Turning off the Moshi–Arusha road just 10 minutes after leaving the former, you bid farewell to the joys of tarmac by heading north on a mud track to Umbwe. Passing banana and coffee plantations you soon reach the gate, where there's little save for some toilets and a couple of friendly and under-worked rangers.

After the usual faffing around at the gate, you eventually begin your walk by setting off on a 4WD road. With monkeys (blue and colobus) crashing in the trees, turacos gliding above them, chameleons stalking amongst the shrubbery and some of Kilimanjaro's more celebrated flora putting in an appearance, including a profusion of *Impatiens pseudoviola* and, further on, its more glam-

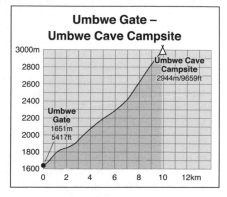

Umbwe Gate –
Umbwe Cave Campsite

Umbwe Cave Campsite 2944m/9659ft

Umbwe Gate 1651m 5417ft

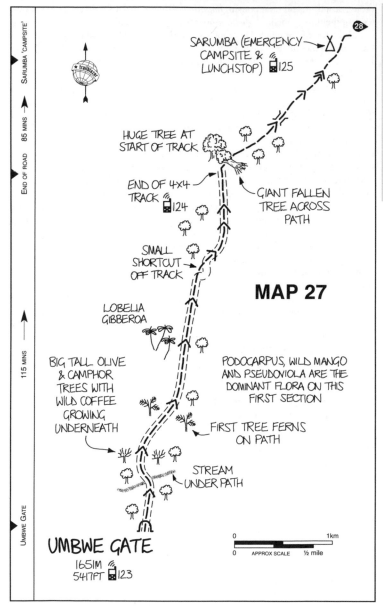

SARUMBA 'CAMPSITE'

85 MINS

END OF ROAD

115 MINS

UMBWE GATE

SARUMBA (EMERGENCY CAMPSITE & LUNCHSTOP) 📱125

HUGE TREE AT START OF TRACK

END OF 4x4 TRACK 📱124

GIANT FALLEN TREE ACROSS PATH

SMALL SHORTCUT OFF TRACK

MAP 27

LOBELIA GIBBEROA

BIG TALL OLIVE & CAMPHOR TREES WITH WILD COFFEE GROWING UNDERNEATH

PODOCARPUS, WILD MANGO AND PSEUDOVIOLA ARE THE DOMINANT FLORA ON THIS FIRST SECTION

FIRST TREE FERNS ON PATH

STREAM UNDER PATH

UMBWE GATE
1651M 📱123
5417FT

0   1km
0   APPROX SCALE   ½ mile

28

orous, beautiful, and rarer cousin, *Impatiens kilimanjari*, it's a fine start. Look out, too, for the forest lobelia, *Lobelia gibberoa*, with its strange phallic brush growing out of the top of the plant. This route is one of the few places where you can find them on the mountain, though they appear in greater abundance on Mount Meru. If it's the weekend, you'll also share the path with locals collecting fodder or firewood from the forest.

No matter how interesting this initial walk is, after almost two hours it comes as something of a relief when the road finally ends and the Umbwe Route 'proper' begins. It's a path that continues the north/north-north-east trend of the road, though in our opinion it's considerably more charming.

Almost an hour and a half after leaving the road you reach **Sarumba**, formerly an emergency campsite for those who set off from the gate very late but now used largely as a lunch stop. Soon after you bend right to **join a ridge**, and a spectacular one at that, with the great forested ravine of the Umbwe River on one side and the more modest dip of the Lonzo Stream on the other. No doubt you've also noticed that the trail is getting increasingly steeper. Indeed, this ridge is one of the steepest parts of the first day and in one or two places you'll be using the tree roots to haul yourself up with your hands. Luckily, there are plenty of tree roots around. The forest around here is rich and dark, the forest canopy minimising the amount of light that filters through to the path. Distract yourself from the muffled screaming coming from your calf muscles by admiring the beauty of the forest here, the trees all knobbled, gnarled and heavy with moss. In between breaths, check out the beautiful red *Impatiens kilimanjari*, too, growing between those same tree roots that are helping you progress along the route.

The gradient relents not a jot as you continue along the ridge and across three bridges, the last of which immediately precedes the **Umbwe Cave Campsite** (2944m/9659ft). More a glorified overhang than a proper cave, the adjacent campsite dribbles up the ridge and is a charming spot; a quiet place hidden in the upper reaches of the forest.

STAGE 2: UMBWE CAMPSITE TO BARRANCO HUTS
[MAP 28, opposite; MAP 29, p370]

Distance: 5.1km (3¼ miles); altitude gain: 1042m (3419ft)
This second stage of the Umbwe Route is a showcase for the weird and wonderful. It's the stage where you move from the forest, past a magical stretch of giant heathers and on to the moorland zone where giant groundsels – surely the strangest plants on Kilimanjaro – grow in abundance. The

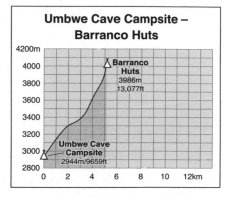

Umbwe Cave Campsite – Barranco Huts

Barranco Huts
3986m
13,077ft

Umbwe Cave Campsite
2944m/9659ft

walking, as with yesterday's stage, is pretty much uphill all the way, and for much of it you'll again be relying on the nearby heathers for hand-holds as you haul yourself up the trail. It's hard work but again it's tiring rather than technical and thus nothing to fear. By the end you will have reached Barranco Huts, a wonderful spot serving a number of routes and on the border of the alpine desert. Note that Machame Route trekkers will have taken three days to get to this camp, and those on the Lemosho Route four. It should remind you, if you didn't know before, of the importance of building in rest days and of taking it *pole pole* from now on. (See p365 for our advice on this.)

The stage starts with a tramp through one of the prettiest sections – no, make that *the* prettiest section – of heathland on the entire mountain, the sunlight penetrating through the giant heathers to dapple the carpet of soft mossy

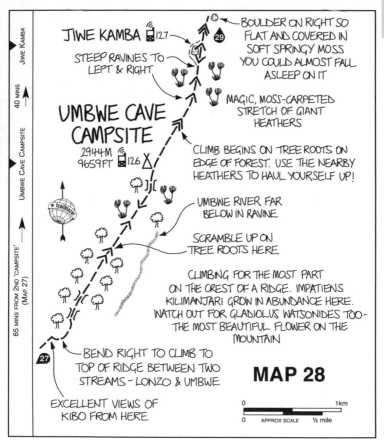

TRAIL GUIDE AND MAPS

JIWE KAMBA

40 MINS

UMBWE CAVE CAMPSITE

65 MINS FROM 2ND 'CAMPSITE' (MAP 27)

JIWE KAMBA 📶 127

STEEP RAVINES TO LEFT & RIGHT

29

BOULDER ON RIGHT SO FLAT AND COVERED IN SOFT SPRINGY MOSS YOU COULD ALMOST FALL ASLEEP ON IT

MAGIC, MOSS-CARPETED STRETCH OF GIANT HEATHERS

UMBWE CAVE CAMPSITE

2944M 📶
9659FT 📱 126 ✕

CLIMB BEGINS ON TREE ROOTS ON EDGE OF FOREST. USE THE NEARBY HEATHERS TO HAUL YOURSELF UP!

★ trailblazer

UMBWE RIVER FAR BELOW IN RAVINE

SCRAMBLE UP ON TREE ROOTS HERE

CLIMBING FOR THE MOST PART ON THE CREST OF A RIDGE. IMPATIENS KILIMANJARI GROW IN ABUNDANCE HERE. WATCH OUT FOR GLADIOLUS WATSONIDES TOO - THE MOST BEAUTIFUL FLOWER ON THE MOUNTAIN

27

BEND RIGHT TO CLIMB TO TOP OF RIDGE BETWEEN TWO STREAMS – LONZO & UMBWE

EXCELLENT VIEWS OF KIBO FROM HERE

MAP 28

0   1km
0   APPROX SCALE   ½ mile

grass. We've never seen heather forest so thick, so uniform, so laden with beard-ed lichen nor so gorgeous. Though normally lumped together with the moorland above it, here, as with the Mweka Route that you'll be tackling on the way down, the heather zone is so very distinct from it. As the path veers to the left you notice you're overlooking the vertiginous valley of the Lonzo Stream (a tributary of the Weru Weru) while veer right and you find yourself staring down the giddying ravine of the Umbwe – and you suddenly realise you're balanced on a knife-edge ridge. Vertigo sufferers should perhaps concentrate instead on Kibo which, if the weather's on your side, glistens magnificently ahead.

Around 40 minutes after breaking camp you reach **Jiwe Kamba**, or 'Rope Rock', the name providing a clue as to how trekkers used to tackle this section. The rope's gone now and the park authorities have built two paths either side of the rock, so there's no need to clamber *over* it at all any more. Even without this obstacle, however, this is still a testing stretch, as the giant heathers that line the path testify, their trunks burnished like the feet of some sacred icon by the hands of trekkers who have struggled up here before you, grasping onto the nearby veg-

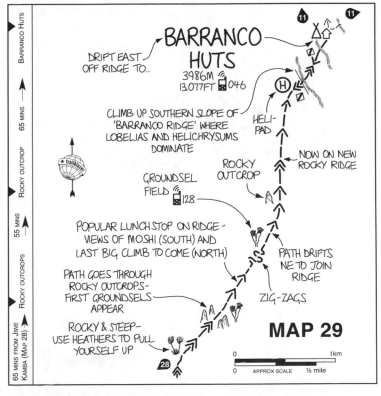

BARRANCO HUTS

DRIFT EAST OFF RIDGE TO...

BARRANCO HUTS
3986M
13,077FT 📱046

CLIMB UP SOUTHERN SLOPE OF 'BARRANCO RIDGE' WHERE LOBELIAS AND HELICHRYSUMS DOMINATE

HELI-PAD

NOW ON NEW ROCKY RIDGE

ROCKY OUTCROP

GROUNDSEL FIELD 📱128

ROCKY OUTCROP

POPULAR LUNCH STOP ON RIDGE - VIEWS OF MOSHI (SOUTH) AND LAST BIG CLIMB TO COME (NORTH)

PATH DRIFTS NE TO JOIN RIDGE

PATH GOES THROUGH ROCKY OUTCROPS - FIRST GROUNDSELS APPEAR

ZIG-ZAGS

MAP 29

ROCKY & STEEP - USE HEATHERS TO PULL YOURSELF UP

28

BARRANCO HUTS

65 MINS

ROCKY OUTCROP

55 MINS

ROCKY OUTCROPS

65 MINS FROM JIWE KAMBA (MAP 28)

0   1km
0 APPROX SCALE ½ mile

etation in order to heave themselves up the slope. As you progress further north the first helichrysums appear, their paper texture and white colour contrasting with the scarlet mountain gladioli, *Gladiolus watsonides*, which survives in both the forest and heathland zones and surely rivals the impatiens and orchids as the most beautiful flower on the mountain. Continue still further and amongst the tussock grass and rocky outcrops the first **groundsels** also put in an appearance, a plant that will dominate the surrounding scenery for the next hour or so.

The ridge which you've been following eventually merges with a new one which you also climb and then follow, still heading north and with Mount Meru now a spectator in the distance to the west. Climbing to yet another rocky ridge, you continue your progress north towards what we will call Barranco Ridge, which you start to climb before turning off right and down to **Barranco Huts** campsite (3986m/13,077ft). For a description, please turn to p316.

It is at Barranco that you have a choice to make: left, north-west and up for Lava Tower Campsite, Arrow Glacier Campsite and the path via the Western Breach to the summit. Or right and east to Karanga, Barafu and the trail up to Uhuru Peak via Stella Point. You will, of course, have already decided one way or the other before you even set foot on the mountain. Whatever route you've opted for, we hope that you factored into your itinerary an acclimatisation day at Barranco. If so, the next stage will be relevant to you too even if you'll be heading in the opposite direction, to Karanga and Barafu, the next day – you can read about this trail on p316. Whereas if you're gunning for the Western Breach, just read on...

STAGE 3: BARRANCO HUTS TO LAVA TOWER CAMPSITE
[MAP 11, p317; MAP 10, p314]

Distance: 3.2km (2 miles); altitude gained: 641m (2103ft)
Many of the trails on Kili started as porters' routes. That is to say, the porters established them before the guides and their clients adopted them and, eventually, the authorities too. Furthermore, it is of course the nature of porters to find the quickest route from A to B, with little thought given as to whether it's a pretty or attractive – or even safe! – route.

So it is with today's trail from Barranco up to Lava Tower, the start of the climb up to the Western Breach. It's a short-cut that was established by porters hurrying down from Arrow Glacier or Lava Tower round to the Mweka Route, in order to meet their clients arriving down from the summit. This trail has become so established as to render the previous route just about obsolete. (That previous route, by the way, continued along the crest of the ridge to

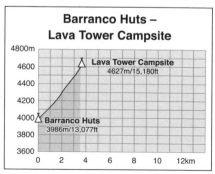

**Barranco Huts –
Lava Tower Campsite**

Lava Tower Campsite
4627m/15,180ft

Barranco Huts
3986m/13,077ft

4800m
4600
4400
4200
4000
3800
3600

0   2   4   6   8   10   12km

the west of Barranco Campsite to the signposted junction at the head of the Barranco Valley and is still marked on most maps though it's a rare guide – indeed, anyone – who'll follow it these days.)

The only problem with this new route is that, as mentioned, it *is* a short-cut, and one moreover used by porters to *descend* from the mountain. As such, as an ascent route many people find it entirely too short and will have succumbed to the pain of altitude sickness by the stage's end. We therefore recommend you take this into consideration and, as discussed several times already, maybe factor two nights at Barranco into your itinerary, with the rest day spent sauntering up to the head of the valley to help you get used to the rarified atmosphere.

The stage begins with a walk up the Barranco Valley. Come here later in the day and you'll find yourself hiking against a tide of trekkers on the Machame, Lemosho and Shira routes all coming the other way down the same path. But assuming you've started walking in the morning it will probably be just you and your crew, allowing you to enjoy undisturbed views of Kibo through the stands of **groundsels**. About 25 minutes after setting off you leave the main path by a **waterfall** as you continue north, eventually crossing the **stream** you've been following since the day's beginning (and, indeed, as further down it turns into the Umbwe River, since the start of the whole trek). Recrossing it further upstream, you'll find yourself on a slightly gentler trail which continues straight ahead over two streams and on, steeply, up to **Lava Tower**. The entire walking, without breaks, would have taken you just 3¼ hours and you'll probably be at Lava Tower by lunch, allowing you plenty of time to savour this grim campsite's uniquely chilly, godforsaken 'charm'.

For details of the rest of the walk from Lava Tower to the summit, see p340.

The descent routes

MARANGU ROUTE

Stage 1: Uhuru Peak to Gillman's Point to the Horombo Huts
[Map 33, p384; Map 6, p303; Map 5, p301; Map 4, p300]

Distance: 15.75km (9¾ miles); (16.55km – 10¼ miles – for Mawenzi alternative); altitude lost: 2174m (7133ft)
Few people remain at the summit for long: weariness, the risk of hypothermia and the thought of a steaming mug of Milo at the Kibo Huts are enough to send most people scurrying back down. There are **two main ways** of doing this: the **first** is to follow exactly the course from Gillman's to Kibo that you took getting up here, carefully retracing every zig and zag like somebody who has dropped a contact lens on the way up but can't quite remember when or where. It is precisely those people who are in greatest need of getting down fast who usually use this slower method to descend.

The **second way** is to cut straight through the switchbacks and simply head

vertically down-
wards in a sort of
ski-style, using the
now defrosted scree
to act as a brake on
your momentum as
you push against it
with the soles of
your boots, heels
first. After the tedi-
um of the previous
night's *pole pole*,
heel-to-toe exercise,
the sheer abandon of
this method and the
rapid progress made
– it takes just over
90 minutes to travel
from Gillman's to
the huts this way –

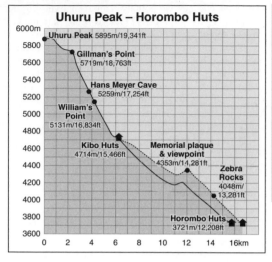

Uhuru Peak – Horombo Huts

- **Uhuru Peak** 5895m/19,341ft
- **Gillman's Point** 5719m/18,763ft
- **Hans Meyer Cave** 5259m/17,254ft
- **William's Point** 5131m/16,834ft
- **Kibo Huts** 4714m/15,466ft
- **Memorial plaque & viewpoint** 4353m/14,281ft
- **Zebra Rocks** 4048m/13,281ft
- **Horombo Huts** 3721m/12,208ft

comes as something of a relief. Take care, however: far more people are injured
going down than going up. Furthermore, do remember that every year at least
20,000 pairs of feet tread on this part of the mountain and, at the risk of sounding like a killjoy, pushing down all that scree cannot be doing the mountain any

---

❏ **Returning via the Mawenzi Route**   **[Map 5, p301; Map 4, p300]**
This is the more interesting path between Kibo and Horombo Huts, encompassing
entire groves of giant groundsels (*Senecio kilimanjari*), Zebra Rocks and perhaps the
best panorama of them all on Kili. It is also seldom used.
    From Kibo Huts the path descends once more to **Jiwe La Ukoyo** (see p302).
Though there appears to be but one path from Jiwe, there is in fact another, much
fainter path heading more directly towards Mawenzi across The Saddle. If you cannot make it out at first don't worry, just aim for Mawenzi and you will soon notice a
faint but distinct path etched into the earth bisecting the Saddle. Ten minutes after
Jiwe a junction with the even-fainter **Northern Circuit** is reached (a signpost is the
only evidence that there is a junction here at all), and 35 minutes after that the path
begins to rise and fall as it follows the contours of Mawenzi's lower reaches.
    After another 35 minutes following this undulating terrain you come to a sum-
mit of sorts, from where you can rest by a **memorial plaque** and gaze back over what
is, in my humble opinion, the finest **panorama** this mountain has to offer: the alpine
desert of The Saddle, with a string of parasitic cones leading from the foreground to
the foot of Kibo and with Mawenzi just over your shoulder. Spectacular. From here,
the path runs due south through heather, past the path leading up to Mawenzi Hut and
on to **Zebra Rocks** (a collection of rockfaces stained by water that resemble the
flanks of a zebra), then down between the groundsel gullies until, 70 minutes from
the unforgettable panorama and 2½ hours since leaving Jiwe La Ukoyo, the roofs of
Horombo Huts appear beneath you.

good. Indeed, may we politely request that you use this faster method only if you need to descend rapidly? Otherwise, stick to the switchbacks which will be far less damaging to the mountain – and safer too!

Upon returning to Kibo Huts, your guide should allow you to rest for an hour at least before moving on again to the **Horombo Huts**. If you ascended on the Marangu Route, heed the advice given at the beginning of Stage 3 (see p299) and ask your guide to take you back via a different route to the one on which you ascended. This usually means returning via the Saddle on the Mawenzi Route, a route we describe in the box opposite. If you return via the southerly, 'usual' route, expect it to take 3¼ hours from Kibo Huts.

If you took the Marangu Route up the mountain, you'll be sleeping in the huts again; while those who took the Rongai Route, which also uses this path to descend, will be camping outside them.

Stage 2: Horombo Huts to Marangu Gate
[Map 4, p300; Map 3, p297; Map 2, p295; Map 1, p291]
Distance: 20km (12½ miles); 20.75km (13 miles) on Nature Trail – see p375;

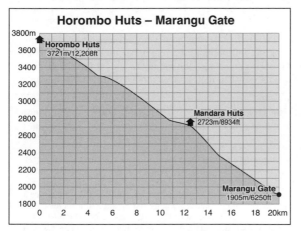

altitude lost: 1816m (5958ft) Don't be in too much of a hurry to finish your trekking, for today holds lots of treats for those who take the time to enjoy them. If you have come from the Rongai Route this is the first time you will have seen forest so thick and vast on Kilimanjaro, and it's worth taking the time to appreciate the different flora on this side of the mountain. But even if you ascended by the Marangu Route, it still warrants a second look on the way down. Much of the scenery may be old hat to you by now but remember you've still paid US$70 in park fees alone for the privilege of walking in the forest today, so you may as well make the most of it. And just as Lee Marvin in *Paint Your Wagon* sang that he'd never seen a town 'that didn't look better looking back', so most people will agree that the forest seems so much more welcoming when you're walking *downhill* through it and the views of Kibo are that much more appealing from over the shoulder, knowing you'll never have to climb it again.

TRAIL GUIDE AND MAPS

❑ **Marangu Nature Trail** [Map 1, p291]

A nice alternative for those who have already climbed via the Marangu Route and don't fancy taking exactly the same route back down is to divert off after one of the trail's many bridges onto the signposted Nature Trail.

Only fractionally longer than the regular route, this trail's main attraction is that it is so rarely used; indeed, when we last walked along this path it was quite overgrown and it was clear it hadn't been trekked in a while. This attraction could also be its main disadvantage – the path does have to divert around the occasional fallen tree and there are places where a number of alternative trails present themselves, so you need a guide whom you trust to know where he is going. Assuming you have one this really is a pleasant alternative to the main trail and possibly for the first time on your entire trek you may get an inkling of just how Meyer, New, Teleki, von der Decken and all the other explorers of the 19th century must have felt as they carved their path through the forest. As a reward for taking the route less travelled the path culminates in a lovely waterfall – though it's only really 'active' during the rainy season. From there it's a simple climb up some steps back to the main trail, with the gate just yards away.

It takes about 2 hours 20 minutes to return from Horombo Huts to the **Mandara Huts** which are, typically, the final lunchstop of the trail. From there, it's back into the forest and down to the **gate**, a journey of some 95 minutes. Name registered, tips dispersed and with certificate clutched close to your bosom (you can actually get it laminated for Ts3000 at the bookshop at the gate), it's time to return to the land of hot showers and flush toilets. Your adventure is at an end – and civilisation will rarely have felt so good.

After we had taken our baths, and Loren had photographed my heels for posterity, we got dressed and walked to the polished dining room. Paul and Jan were eating silently at one table; other climbers at others. We felt a camaraderie as we sat down to eat. We were very tired, far more tired than hungry, but we were also away in some special world reserved for exhausted athletes, a world in which triumph is muted, the gains countered by the costs.
Michael Crichton, taken from *Travels*, a collection of essays about his worldwide wanderings.

THE MWEKA ROUTE

The Mweka Route (21km/13 miles from summit to civilisation) is the designated descent route for the Machame, Lemosho/Shira and Umbwe routes. As such, it is a very busy route. Repair work a few years ago ensured that the latter section through the forest is once more in good condition, though the same cannot be said of the trail down to Mweka Huts, which has treacherous loose rolling stones and other hazards en route. It's awful. Good luck!

Stage 1: Uhuru Peak to Barafu Huts and Mweka Huts
[Map 33, p384; Map 13, p321; Map 30, p377; Map 31, p379]

Distance: 11.5km (7¼ miles); altitude lost: 2789m (9150ft)

What goes up must come down and that includes you. The path back to Barafu is little more than a retracing of your steps of the previous night (assuming you climbed this way and not the Western Breach Route), though there is a slightly

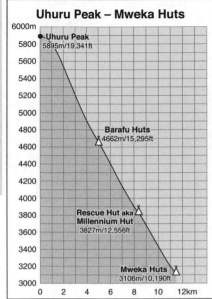

Uhuru Peak – Mweka Huts

- Uhuru Peak 5895m/19,341ft
- Barafu Huts 4662m/15,295ft
- Rescue Hut aka Millennium Hut 3827m/12,556ft
- Mweka Huts 3106m/10,190ft

quicker, if more hair-raising approach: descending from Stella Point, after 10 minutes or so you reach a **boulder** which earlier that morning you would have walked around: it's the same boulder that on the ascent marked the very steep last 30 minutes or so to the crater rim.

This boulder also marks the start of a **straight ski-run down** through the gravel that bypasses the zigzags of the regular route. Some people prefer to make it down as quickly as possible so choose this trail; others find it too taxing on both nerves and knees and opt for the **gentler descent**. Before deciding which is for you, read the advice about erosion on p373 and if possible take the slower option. Note, too, that with the 'faster' descent it's not so easy to find your way back to Barafu: at one point you must turn right to rejoin the main path to camp or you risk ending up being lost in the valley below. A Korean trekker was believed to have done this in 2008 – and has never been seen again. The entire descent takes about two hours from Stella Point, less if you take the 'fast' route.

You probably feel, on returning to camp, that you have earned the luxury of a brief rest at **Barafu**, and indeed you have. But make sure it *is* brief, for you still have another 150 minutes of knee-knackering downhill before you reach Mweka Huts, your probable home for the night. A pretty monotonous 2½ hours it is, too, as you head off due south and down for the entire 6.64km/4 miles. In its defence, the descent is both large (dropping from 4662m/15,295ft to 3106m/10,190ft) and fairly gradual, which can only be good news for AMS sufferers. There is also some interest to be had in seeing how the vegetation changes along the way: at first, only the incredibly hardy yellow senecios are able to survive at the high altitude, but they are soon joined by their dry-looking cousins in the *helichrysum* family. Not long after that the first heathers appear, to be joined a little later by the proteas. However, it must be said that the **actual path is the worst on the mountain**, full of loose rocks that shift when trodden upon, causing already weary trekkers to stumble, fumble, fall and swear their way down.

Around 50 minutes or so from Barafu you come to a **junction**, marked with a signpost or two, with the little-used Southern Circuit: to your left on the slopes

you can see paths from Horombo Huts on the Marangu Route, while to your right are those coming from the Karanga Valley. Another path, an emergency trail from Karanga Campsite for those suffering from altitude, joins the Mweka Route just above the green-roofed hut. This hut was originally established to help out the suffering during the millennium when the mountain was swamped by thousands hoping to see the new era in from the summit. It's remained ever since and, now called the **Rescue Hut** or, more commonly, **Millennium Huts** (though the sign by the warden's hut calls it, rather prosaically, **High Camp**; 3827m/12,556ft), is a campsite for those who prefer something a little quieter than the Mweka Huts; it's also a useful site to use when the Mweka campsite has been flooded by heavy rain. There is also a water source nearby – another advantage over the Mweka Huts and one of the reasons, perhaps, why more and more groups are choosing to stay here.

Immediately afterwards, giant heathers grow for the first time by the dusty path and, further down, the vanilla-coloured **protea** makes its first appearance, and thereafter dominates the pathside vegetation. The protea's presence ensures a healthy population of **malachite sunbirds** live around here too, as well as the little green **montane white-eyes** – so-called because of the distinctive white ring

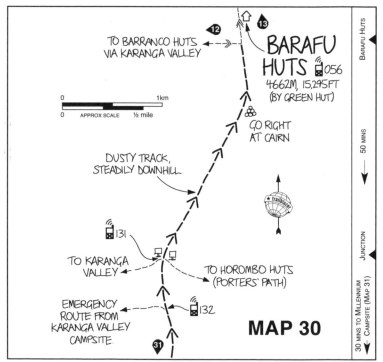

MAP 30

around their eyes. **Chameleons**, surprisingly, also make the heather their home.

You first glimpse **Mweka Huts** (3106m/10,190ft) about 40 minutes before you actually get there as you descend on a ridge between two valleys towards a small heather-clad hill. Rounding this, the path widens and flattens before turning south-west and climbing for a few seconds on the final section to the camp – the only ascent of the entire walk from Barafu. Mweka Huts is unremarkable; the eco-toilets they installed that we raved about in the last edition are now sadly a bit of a blemish on the campsite: malodorous, fly-filled and shit-stained. Nevertheless, Mweka is a happy camp. The porters are happy, for tomorrow is their last day of work, of course, and is pregnant with promises of wages and tips. Those climbers who managed to make it to Uhuru Peak are also happy, of course, and often quite jubilant. But even those who didn't make it to the top will find a happiness of sorts in being here, if only because they'll no longer have to walk on that bloody terrible path from Millennium Camp again. Even the phone reception is pretty good, which cheers up virtually everyone.

By the way, you may wish to share out your tips at Mweka Huts before you depart on this last leg: as porters all walk at different speeds, this may be the last time the whole group is together.

Stage 2: Mweka Huts to Mweka Gate   [Map 31, opp; Map 32, p381]

Distance: 9.5km (6 miles); altitude lost: 1473m (4833ft)

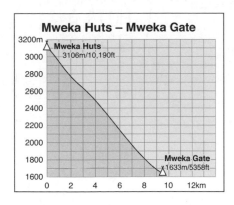

By now you'll probably just want to get off the mountain as quickly as possible. But before you think of cashing in on your helicopter rescue insurance and getting a lift down, we should point out that there's still lots of interest to be had before you bid farewell to the mountain for the last time. This final section of the path has now thankfully been fully restored following years of over-use. The only complaint we have is that the authorities have decided to build steps on the steep parts, which we are sure is good for combatting erosion – but after five days or so of climbing, your knees will be screaming for mercy by the end. This last section follows a very pretty forest trail alive with birdsong and flowers – but whether your mind can concentrate on anything other than the pain in your joints is another matter. Still, if you were having trouble acclimatising to the lack of oxygen available further up the slopes, you'll be delighted by the atmosphere here, which feels so thick and replete with O_2 that you'll wonder why it's not visible.

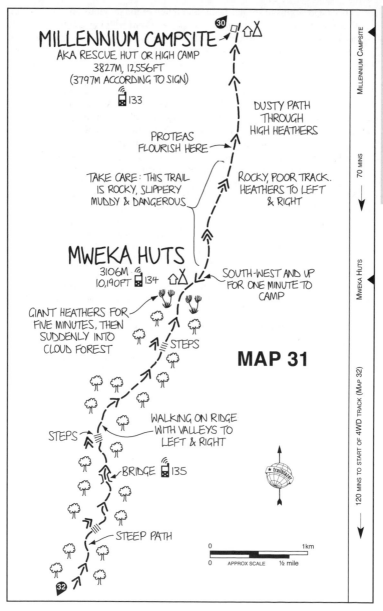

MILLENNIUM CAMPSITE 30
AKA RESCUE HUT OR HIGH CAMP
3827M, 12,556FT
(3797M ACCORDING TO SIGN)
133

DUSTY PATH
THROUGH
HIGH HEATHERS

PROTEAS
FLOURISH HERE

ROCKY, POOR TRACK.
HEATHERS TO LEFT
& RIGHT

TAKE CARE: THIS TRAIL
IS ROCKY, SLIPPERY
MUDDY & DANGEROUS

MWEKA HUTS
3106M 134
10,190FT

SOUTH-WEST AND UP
FOR ONE MINUTE TO
CAMP

GIANT HEATHERS FOR
FIVE MINUTES, THEN
SUDDENLY INTO
CLOUD FOREST

STEPS

MAP 31

STEPS

WALKING ON RIDGE
WITH VALLEYS TO
LEFT & RIGHT

BRIDGE 135

STEEP PATH

★ trailblazer

0   1km
0   APPROX SCALE   ½ mile

32

This stage begins in similar fashion to much of the previous one, by heading south and down. Less than five minutes after you start walking you find yourself in **cloud forest**, the border between this and the giant heather forest so definite and distinct that you could almost draw a line in the ground between the two. Once again walking on a narrow ridge between two valleys, look around and notice how the trees now grow in height and girth, how the moss that grows upon them is thick, green and hearty where before it was stringy and limp, and how flowers such as the *Impatiens kilimanjari* once again make an appearance, and in abundance too. Its cousin *Impatiens pseudoviola* also lines the path, while the occasional, beautiful vivid red mountain gladiolus flourishes here and there, the delicate white flowers of the wild blackberry grow in clusters and the alabaster-white petals of the *Begonia meyeri johannis* litter the trail towards the end.

Around two hours after breaking camp, you'll find yourself walking on the **start of the 4WD track** down to the gate which lies a further 30 minutes away. At **Mweka Gate** (1633m/5358ft) you can usually buy a souvenir T-shirt to advertise the fact you reached the summit (curiously, there are no equivalent T-shirts for those that did not). You must also sign the last **registration book** at the nearby park office, from where those who were successful can collect the appropriate certificate. Those who succeeded in reaching Uhuru Peak can usually be seen standing around, their certificates dangling casually yet deliberately from their hands so they are clearly visible to passers-by, in much the same way that Ferrari owners are wont to display their car keys. Your mountain odyssey is almost at an end: from here, it's a 30-minute drive back to the land of power showers, flush toilets and cold, cold beer. You've earned it – though if you plan to celebrate in Moshi, please take more care than Hans Meyer did upon his return to town in 1889:

In the evening, to show there was no ill-feeling, I treated the natives to a display of fireworks, in the course of which a spark from a rocket set fire to one of the men's huts.

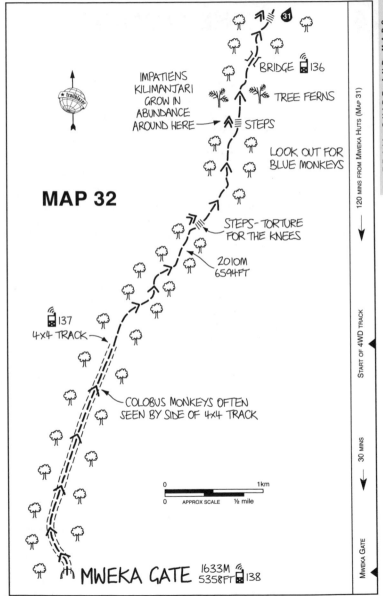

MAP 32

IMPATIENS
KILIMANJARI
GROW IN
ABUNDANCE
AROUND HERE →

BRIDGE 📱136

TREE FERNS

⋀ ≣ STEPS

LOOK OUT FOR
BLUE MONKEYS

STEPS - TORTURE
FOR THE KNEES

2010M
6594FT

📱137
4X4 TRACK →

COLOBUS MONKEYS OFTEN
SEEN BY SIDE OF 4X4 TRACK

0   1km
0   APPROX SCALE   ½ mile

MWEKA GATE   1633M 📱138
              5358FT

120 MINS FROM MWEKA HUTS (MAP 31)

START OF 4WD TRACK

30 MINS

MWEKA GATE

TRAIL GUIDE AND MAPS

THE SUMMIT

What's at the top?

The crater of Kilimanjaro is a primeval place and decidedly uncomfortable, yet I was drawn to it. The idea of spending some days and nights awoke a compelling mixture of reverential fear and wonder; similar, I suspect, to the compulsion which draws some people unquestioningly to church. And like churches, the crater also invites contemplation of the eternal mysteries.
                                                     John Reader *Kilimanjaro* (1982)

It's only when you reach the top of Kibo that you realise the mountain really is a volcano and all you have done is climb onto the crater rim.

The rim itself is largely featureless, though as the highest point on the mountain it has assumed a pre-eminent role and is the focus of all trekkers. Many of the bumps and tumescences on it have been dignified with the word 'Spitze' or 'Point' as if they were major summits in their own right. Heading clockwise around the rim from **Gillman's**, these features in order are: **Bismark Towers**, **Stella Point** (the aim of those climbing from Barafu), **Elveda** and **Hans Meyer points** and **Uhuru Peak**; while just to the north of Gillman's is **Johannes Notch**, **Leopard Point** and **Hans Meyer Notch**. The distance between Gillman's and Uhuru is a little over 2km, with the crater rim rising 176m (577ft) between the two. The floor of the crater, covered in brown shale and rocks and boulders of all shapes and sizes, lies between 25m/82ft (at Gillman's) and 200m/656ft (at Uhuru Peak) beneath this rim.

Trudging around the rim to Uhuru is achievement enough. There are, however, plenty of other diversions to keep you on the summit for longer ...

WALKING ON THE SUMMIT   [Map 33, p384]

For most people the conquest of Uhuru Peak and a nice certificate that says as much is reason enough to climb Kilimanjaro. Some trekkers, however, always want to do just that little bit more and if you still have some energy to burn once you've reached the summit you may care to take a quick tour around the crater itself. **Warn your guide in advance** of your intentions – preferably before you've even started your trek – as some react badly to the idea of spending any longer on the summit than is absolutely necessary; a little gentle cajoling along with a few hints about the size of the tip that awaits them at the end

of the trip should do the trick. Make sure, too, that your guide knows his way around up there: you'll probably be a little short of humour as well as breath on the crater rim and following an ignorant guide while he tries in vain to locate the correct path to the Reusch Crater will do little to lighten your mood.

The standard way to reach **Reusch Crater**, Kibo summit's very own parasitic cone, is to ascend via the Western Breach, where a trail of sorts heads off to the north round Furtwangler Glacier and away from Uhuru Peak to the crater. For this reason, it is common for those who have climbed via the difficult Arrow Glacier/Western Breach Route to visit Reusch than those who ascended by one of the other paths. But those who arrived at the crater rim at either Gillman's or Stella Point needn't despair, for there is also a trail from near Stella Point that crosses the crater floor to join up with the path to Reusch.

The actual climb up to the rim of Reusch Crater is relatively short but surprisingly tiring; if you didn't know you were at altitude before, you will now! This walk can take as little as 30 minutes from the campsite, though that's assuming that you are in fairly good shape; and on the summit this is a very big assumption. Having reached Reusch, check out the bright yellow sulphurous deposits, largely on its western side, and the fumaroles that occasionally puff smoke – proof not only that Kili is a volcano, but that it is also an active one. The smell of sulphur is all-pervasive in this crater and the earth is hot to touch.

Within Reusch Crater is the 120m-deep (394ft) **Ash Pit** which, though it does not conspicuously contain ash, is said to be one of the most perfect examples of this sort of formation in the world. At 360m (1181ft) across it's also one of the largest. If you reach the Ash Pit, you can truly say you have conquered this mountain.

The faces behind the features

Most Kilimanjaro climbers are aware that Uhuru is Swahili for 'Freedom' and the highest point in Africa was christened this after Tanzania achieved independence in 1961. But do you know after what or whom other features of Kibo are named? Some of them are relatively easy: **Rebmann Glacier** is obviously named after the first European to see Kilimanjaro (see p151), while neighbouring **Decken Glacier** is named after another eminent Victorian, Baron von der Decken, the first man to seriously attempt to climb the mountain. His travel partner, Otto **Kersten**, also has a glacier named after him next to the Baron's; while next is **Heim Glacier**, named after Albrecht Heim, world-renowned glacier expert. Hermann **Credner** and Albrecht **Penck** are two other German geologers/geographers who are celebrated in the names of glaciers on Kili; in Penck's case twice, with both a Great Penck and Little Penck Glacier. The Great Penck and Credner Glacier together form the Northern Icefield.

There's also **Furtwangler Glacier**, sadly much reduced recently, which sits on the crater floor and is named after the first man to ski down the side of Kilimanjaro. Herr Furtwangler also has a point on the crater rim named after him, as does the leopard (Leopard Point), which was found frozen in the ice back in the early years of the 20th century.

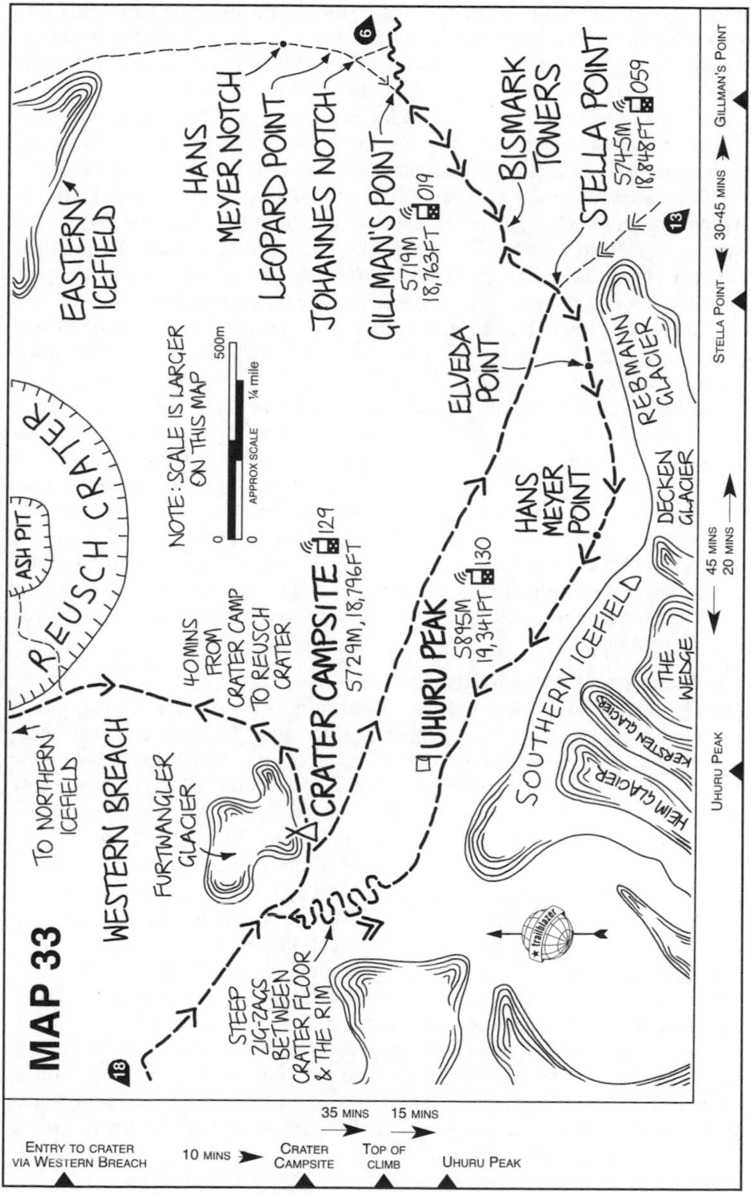

THE SUMMIT

MAP 33

18

To Northern Icefield

WESTERN BREACH

Furtwangler Glacier

STEEP ZIG-ZAGS BETWEEN CRATER FLOOR & THE RIM

REUSCH CRATER

ASH PIT

40MINS FROM CRATER CAMP TO REUSCH CRATER

CRATER CAMPSITE 129
5729M, 18,796FT

EASTERN ICEFIELD

HANS MEYER NOTCH

LEOPARD POINT

JOHANNES NOTCH

6

NOTE: SCALE IS LARGER ON THIS MAP

APPROX SCALE
0   500m
0   ¼ mile

GILLMAN'S POINT
5719M, 18,763FT 014

BISMARK TOWERS

STELLA POINT
5745M, 18,848FT 059

13

UHURU PEAK
5895M, 19,341FT 130

ELVEDA POINT

HANS MEYER POINT

REBMANN GLACIER

DECKEN GLACIER

SOUTHERN ICEFIELD

THE WEDGE

KERSTEN GLACIER

HEIM GLACIER

trailblazer

Gillman's Point ◀ 30-45 MINS ▶ Stella Point

45 MINS ◀——→ 20 MINS

Uhuru Peak

Entry to crater via Western Breach	10 MINS ▶ Crater Campsite	35 MINS Top of Climb	15 MINS Uhuru Peak

Meanwhile, **Hans Meyer**– the first man to the summit, of course – has both a Point and a Notch named after him. Another man who *may* have a Notch named after him is the first European to see Kili, Johannes Rebmann (in addition to the glacier we just mentioned). I say 'may' as there is also a theory that Johannes Notch is in fact named after Hans Meyer's guide Yohani Kinyala Lauwo (see p30) – Johannes being the German 'version' of Yohani. If it is named after Mr Lauwo, it's the only feature on the summit of Kili that's named after a Tanzanian. To the south of Johannes Notch, Bismark Towers are named in tribute to Otto von Bismark (or Bismarck), German chancellor who united the German states and who was in office when Hans Meyer first conquered Kili.

Two of the most well-known points on the crater rim, **Gillman's** and **Stella Point**, are named after quite obscure figures. The former, for example, was *probably* named after the first man to reach the crater rim after the mountain had come under British protection, one Clement Gillman, who reached this point (but no higher) in 1921. As for Stella Point, there's a nice story behind this. It is named after the wife of Dr Kingsley Latham, a member of the Mountain Club of South Africa, and marks the point that they both reached in 1925. It was at this point that Kingsley, who was suffering terribly from altitude sickness, decided to give up in his attempt to the reach the top. He urged his wife, however, to keep climbing; it was, after all, only another forty-five minutes or so to the summit, and if she did so she would become the first woman to the summit of Africa's highest mountain (this being two years before Sheila MacDonald's climb; see p167). Stella, however, clearly a most dutiful wife, refused to go on and demanded to descend with her suffering husband. In tribute, Kingsley forever referred to this point as Point Stella. In subsequent years Kingsley continued to climb (his wife never did) and continued to suffer too. Indeed, he went on to find the frozen leopard mentioned previously, from which Pastor Richard Reusch took an ear as a souvenir (see p167).

Reusch, incidentally, went on to climb the mountain 65 times – a record, we believe, for a non-native – and the inner crater of the Kibo summit was named after him following his 25th ascent of the mountain. His wife is also celebrated on the mountain: **Elveda Point**, which is one of the false summits on the way to Uhuru Peak.

THE SUMMIT

APPENDIX A – FLIGHT SCHEDULES: KILIMANJARO AND ARUSHA AIRPORTS

Of the two main languages you will encounter, **Swahili**, the national tongue, is undoubtedly the more useful and the one you will see written on signs and notices. There are plenty of Swahili dictionaries around: street vendors sell little green versions in Arusha or you can pick one up in souvenir stores for about a sixth of the price they charge.

The other language, **Chagga** and its various dialects, is common around Kili but it is unlikely you'll hear it outside the region. You will, however, curry favour with porters and guides on Kilimanjaro by learning a few words; see the box on p186 for a brief introduction. Chagga dictionaries are rare, though you'll find one mentioned on p393.

FLIGHTS TO AND FROM KILIMANJARO AIRPORT

International flights

The situation regarding flights into Kilimanjaro (JRO) improves with every edition, and there are now seven international airlines flying into JRO. Presumably, once the extensive upgrade of Kili Airport is completed, other airlines will be tempted to fly there too.

Qatar Airways (🖥 qatarairways.com) offer a daily service, particularly useful for those flying from Asia (who've previously always been a little hard done by before now when it comes to getting to Kili), arriving daily and departing an hour later back to Doha.

Turkish Airlines (🖥 turkishairlines.com) fly six times weekly from Istanbul. At the moment they seem to offer the cheapest deals and the service is good too – the only problem being that they often arrive in the middle of the night and depart again an hour later (currently somewhere between 2-4am); thankfully, the trekking agencies and hotels are used to people arriving at this ungodly hour and you can still expect a transfer to your accommodation.

KLM (🖥 klm.com) fly between five and seven times a week in the high season to Tanzania, touching down in Kilimanjaro on their way (usually) to Dar. Flights leave Schiphol (Amsterdam) at around 10am, arriving the same day at Kili at 8.30pm (total travel time approximately 8hrs 30 mins). If you're coming from the UK, where KLM have a great network that links various airports around the country to Amsterdam's Schiphol Airport, they could well be the most convenient airline. Those flying from the US will also find KLM a good option: flights from New York to Amsterdam are around twice daily, or five times if you include their partner Delta Airlines, three of them arriving early enough to enable you to transfer for the flight to Kilimanjaro; they also fly from Los Angeles but any onward connection to Kilimanjaro would currently involve an overnight stop in Amsterdam. KLM's flight leaves Kilimanjaro Airport for Dar at about 8.50pm daily in the high season before returning to Europe.

Ethiopian Airlines (🖥 ethiopianairlines.com) operate a pretty comprehensive pan-African network and are renowned for being one of the most reliable of African airlines and one of the cheapest too. They fly daily from Addis Ababa to Kilimanjaro. From London they have overnight flights to Addis Ababa daily that connect with the flight to Kilimanjaro; from the States, likewise, they have a flight from Washington Dulles Airport daily which connects with the flight to Kilimanjaro as long as everything runs smoothly. Ethiopian Airlines' planes tend to hang around for a couple of hours at Kilimanjaro Airport from the moment they arrive before returning to Addis.

Kenya Airways (🖥 kenya-airways.com) have daily flights to Kilimanjaro via Nairobi and it's a good service, departing in the early evening from London to Nairobi, arriving at JRO around 9am.

Condor Air (🖳 condor.com) re a German outfit flying every Tuesday evening from Frankfurt and returning the following day early in the morning.

Flydubai (🖳 flydubai.com) started flying to JRO in December 2017. They operate six flights a week to Kilimanjaro, three of which are via a stop in Dar es Salaam. As partners of Emirates their total network is already very extensive and should, in time, provide some stiff competition to the established providers.

Regional and domestic airlines to Kilimanjaro Airport

For a good overview of regional airlines – and the chance to book tickets – visit the website 🖳 **alternativeairlines.com**.

Precision Air (🖳 precisionairtz.com), owned by Kenya Airways, are the most reliable and long-standing local airline. They fly four times per day from Nairobi to Kilimanjaro Airport, but just twice per day in the other direction. They also have around three flights from Dar every day, and four going back the other way (with two of those stopping at Zanzibar first).

East Africa's first budget airline, **Fastjet** (🖳 fastjet.com) have flights between Dar and Kilimanjaro (twice a day in each direction). There are rumours that they may be struggling financially and they are earning an unfortunate (but hopefully temporary) reputation for unreliability amongst locals, with flights being occasionally cancelled at the last minute. Still, they are undoubtedly cheap, with fares between Dar and Kili starting at just Ts29,000 if you book far enough in advance (though if you don't you may find their fares are more expensive than the other airlines, and their baggage allowance is less generous too).

Though a small company with small planes, one has to admire the reliability of **Coastal Aviation** (🖳 coastal.co.tz), who now include Kilimanjaro in their journey round Manyara and Serengeti national parks; flights to Nairobi's Wilson Airport and to Dar via Moshi, Tanga and Pangani are also advertised. Another smallish airline serving the safari airstrips is **Regional Air** (🖳 regionaltanzania.com), with their 2.30pm service from JRO visiting Arusha, Manyara and several points in the Serengeti. **Rwandair** (🖳 rwandair.com) currently has four flights per week between Kigali and Kili, on Tues, Wed, Fri & Sun.

The president of Tanzania has decided to invest heavily in getting the old national airline up and running once more – to the chagrin of many locals who think that the country's money would be better spent on more essential items than large jet aeroplanes. Currently there are two planes operating under the **Air Tanzania** (🖳 airtanzania.co.tz) banner, with four more promised by the end of 2018, and flights connect Kilimanjaro Airport with Dar and Zanzibar daily.

FLIGHTS TO AND FROM ARUSHA AIRPORT

Air Excel (☎ 027-254 8429; 🖳 www.airexcelonline.com) have almost daily flights from various destinations in the Serengeti (Grumeti, Kleins, Seronera) as well as Lake Manyara, before finally arriving at Arusha at 12.15pm. Heading the other way, flights tend to leave about 8am. They also have an occasional flight from Dar and Zanzibar to Arusha.

The ever-reliable **Coastal Aviation** (see above) have daily flights from Grumeti, Lobo, Mwanza, as well as the south and Selous. Their flight to Dar arrives at 2.20pm, then continues on to Selous and Mafia. They also serve the Serengeti, Ngorongoro, Tanga and other Tanzanian destinations.

Regional Air (see above) operate flights between Arusha and the Serengeti via Manyara, with another route taking in Zanzibar via Dar.

Zanair (🖳 zanair.com) operate a daily flight from Zanzibar to Arusha, arriving at around 1pm. The plane then returns to Zanzibar about 30 minutes later.

ZantasAir (🖳 zantasair.com) run private charters all over Tanzania and thus are useful if none of the above offers a flight that fits your schedule. They also fly passengers from Northern Tanzania to Western Tanzania twice a week on Monday and Thursdays.

APPENDIX B – RECOMMENDED MAPS, BOOKS, MUSIC & FILMS

MAPS

Maps of Kilimanjaro are available in Arusha, Moshi and probably your own country. The best one we've found, however, is reliably available only online: *Kilimanjaro Kibo* (1:80,000) is written in both English and German and is by some distance the most accurate map available for the mountain. With profiles of a couple of the routes, GPS points, town plans on Arusha and Moshi, descriptions of the vegetation zones and a review of the retreat of permanent ice, this is also the most informative and useful map. You can order a copy by visiting the publisher's website at 💻 climbing-map.com.

The most common map we see is the cartoonish *New Map of the Kilimanjaro National Park*, by Giovanni Tombazzi, which is bright and colourful though in all honesty it's a little inaccurate and the cartoon style means it's of little practical use. Still, it's packed full of information and the flora guide on the reverse is useful. The scale, by the way, is about 1.1cm to 1km (or 1:90,909), with a close-up of the summit on the reverse drawn at a scale of 5.4cm to 1km (about 1:18,518.5). They also publish a similar-style map to Meru. NB Make sure you get the **New Map** as the old one really is out of date. Giovanni also does a map of *Arusha National Park* in a similar style though we think it's inferior to the official map produced by TANAPA called *Arusha National Park – The Tourist Map*.

Back on Africa's highest mountain, *Tourist Map of Kilimanjaro* (1:100,000) by the Ordnance Survey (1989) is the biggest and most beautiful, though once again of little practical use: the routes themselves have been drawn, seemingly, without thought of precision, over the top of what looks an accurate topographical map. It's a little out-of-date, too, and as such it's better in a frame on your wall at home than in your backpack.

Another one that would perhaps be better in a frame – because it is beautiful – is the *Satellite View of Kilimanjaro* (1:90,000), a blue-coloured bird's-eye view of the mountain with contours, roads and routes drawn on top and, unusually but refreshingly, a study of the Chagga people on the reverse as well as gradient profiles.

A third map, *Kilimanjaro* (1:50,000), by Mark Savage, is harder to track down – though the shop at Marangu Gate stocks some. The descriptions of the trails are not brilliant and the map itself is a little ugly, though it is more up to date than the above and the black-and-white drawings of wild flowers are good – though would be far more useful in colour.

The Canada-based ITM (International Travel Maps) series has recently produced *Kilimanjaro*, a colourful 1:62,500 map of the mountain, as well as a separate 1:6,250,000 road map of the area.

Finally, *Original City Map – Arusha and Moshi*, distributed by Toku Tanzania (💻 toku-tanzania.com; last published 2012) offers very good maps of the two cities. There's also *Explore the Slopes of Mount Kilimanjaro*, another cartoon-style affair which also has a (very simple) plan of Moshi centre and some few basic facts about the region. Definitely another that is more decorative than useful – but charming in its own way.

Online maps

A couple of companies have produced GPS maps of the Kilimanjaro region that you can upload to your computer and then plot the waypoints on. The best is by **GPS travelmaps** (💻 gpstravelmaps.com). The basic map itself seems very detailed and it's a useful base for putting on your own GPS readings. Another map producer is **satmap** (💻 satmap.com), though at £37 it's rather expensive.

RECOMMENDED READING

Please note that many of the following are rare and a number are extremely difficult to find. Among those that are readily available are Hemingway's *The Snows of Kilimanjaro* (and the recently published *Under Kilimanjaro*, the rather long-winded novel-cum-memoir-cum-tribute-to-Africa that recounts Papa Hemingway's time in Kenya); the comprehensive and wonderful book-of-the-IMAX-film *Kilimanjaro, Mountain at the Crossroads*, by Audrey Salkeld – possibly the most beautiful and absorbing souvenir of your climb that money can buy (the book that is, not Audrey); and John Reader's excellent (though rather bulky) *Kilimanjaro*. If you're visiting Zanzibar after Kilimanjaro, you may want to wait and buy your reading material for the mountain there: some of the bookshops in Stonetown have fine selections.

Biography and personal accounts

The original editions of many of the following books, particularly those written during the great days of exploration in the 1800s, are very difficult to find and, short of a miraculous discovery in a secondhand bookstore, the only place you're going to find them is at the British Library or a similar institution abroad. The internet is, of course, another source. For example, I've successfully tracked down online the first edition of the English translation of Hans Meyer's account of his conquest of Kili (see first entry below); now all I've got to do is find the US$9000 the dealers are asking for it. The online auction house eBay is a good place to begin your search. The Canadian-based Voyager Press also have some good stuff on Kili, particularly old reports from the Royal Geographic Society.

Thankfully, publishers such as Forgotten Books and Kessinger now republish several of the most well-known. The printing quality of these books is not brilliant and the maps and drawings – the most beautiful parts of the original tomes – are either rendered very poorly or missing altogether from these reprints. Nevertheless, for most of us it's the only way we'll be able to read and own a copy.

For those books that *are* still in print, your best bet is in Tanzania itself, either in the small souvenir shop by Marangu Gate or in the large bookshops in Stonetown, Zanzibar. Failing that, you could always try online bookshops such as Abebooks and Amazon, on which you will usually be able to track down a copy.

The explorers...

● *The Church Missionary Intelligencer* (Seeleys, 1850) Definitely one you'll have to look for in the British Library (or a similar institution elsewhere), this august organ was the first to publish Rebmann's accounts of his three trips to Kilimanjaro as well as Krapf's subsequent visit to the Usambara region. Volume 1, May 1849, contains most of the relevant texts.
● *An Essay on the Sources of the Nile in the Mountains of the Moon* Charles T Beke (Neill and Company, 1848) This short work is of interest not only because it was published at the same time as Rebmann's ground-breaking visit to Kilimanjaro but also, though written around 170 years ago, the author still takes as his starting point the work of Ptolemy written 1800 years before, thus giving an indication of just how little was known about Africa at that time.
● *Life, Wanderings, and Labours in Eastern Africa* Charles New (Cass Library of African Studies, 1971, originally 1873) Charles New set off in 1871 to spread the gospel to Africa's heathen population but it was as an explorer that he is remembered, becoming the first white man to cross the African snow-line during a visit to the Chagga region. This book was written in the months spent in England between his first and second trips, on the latter of which he fell ill and died. Once again, though the account of his time on the slopes of Kili occupies only about a third of the book, it is for the most part fascinating, as much for his description of Chief Mandara and the Chaggas as it is for his climb up the mountain.
● *Discovery by Count Teleki of Lakes Rudolf and Stefanie* Lieutenant Ludwig von Höhnel, translated by Nancy Bell (Longmans, Green and Co, 1894) Lengthy, two-volume

account of the Hungarian count as he shoots and slaughters his way through East Africa's fauna, written by his companion von Höhnel. Only about a sixth of the book deals specifically with Kili, though that sixth is interesting both for the account of their attempt to climb Kili and their dealings with Chagga chiefs Mandara (whom they try to avoid) and Mareale.

● *The Kilima-njaro Expedition – A Record of Scientific Exploration in Eastern Equatorial Africa* HH Johnston (Kegan Paul, Trench and Co, 1886; republished by several publishers including the British Library, 2011) Widely dismissed as exaggeration going on fabrication, this is nevertheless a very entertaining read thanks to Johnston's sense of humour and the scrapes into which he gets. Just possible to find second-hand or pick up the reprint by Kessinger Publishing.

● *Tracts Relating to Missions* (Printed by A Lankester, 1878) Yet another work whose habitat is restricted almost entirely to the British Library these days, this collection of missionary accounts includes one by the Rev A Downes Shaw entitled *To Chagga and Back — An Account of a Journey to Moshi, the Capital of Chagga, Eastern Equatorial Africa*.

● *James Hannington, First Bishop of Eastern Equatorial Africa – A History of his Life and Work* EC Dawson (Seeley and Co, 1887) I have to confess I had never heard of this book – nor indeed the bishop – until I came across a copy on eBay (for a tenner!). And fascinating it is too, for though the bishop's own efforts on Kili are fairly paltry, not getting much above the treeline, his diary entries about the Chagga chief Mandara and the region in general are fascinating, and this book is filled with mentions of the great explorers (Johnston, Thomson etc) he encountered during his time in East Africa before he was speared to death in Uganda on the orders of a local king.

● *Across East African Glaciers – An Account of the First Ascent of Kilimanjaro* Dr Hans Meyer, translated from the German by EHS Calder (George Philip and Son, 1891) Perhaps the most fascinating book ever written about the mountain, Meyer's beautiful work describes his unprecedented ascent of Kilimanjaro, all illustrated with some lovely sketches by ET Compton. Splendid stuff. Now available in a much less-charming – but much more affordable – reprint by Kessinger Press.

...and those who followed in their wake

With the rise of self-publishing you can now find a slew of memoirs written by those who've conquered Kili, both in traditional paper format and, even more so, as ebooks. I have to say I found most a little dull but that could be because I've climbed the mountain a few times now, whereas those who haven't, or who haven't yet, may find them both useful and fascinating. But there are several other books here that I really enjoyed. In alphabetical order:

● *Africa's Dome of Mystery* Eva Stuart Watt FRGS (Marshall, Morgan and Scott Ltd, 1930) Brought up in East Africa, Ms Stuart-Watt describes her life among the Chagga people, including an account of her climb to Kibo's crater rim. Interesting, if only for the fact that there are few accounts of Kibo from this period under British rule.

● *Another Load of Bull* David Read (David Read, 2005) Extracted from the author's diaries, this self-published book, the third in the series, is largely about his successful attempt to run Mountainside, a large farm on the north-eastern side of Kili. It's very detailed and without a doubt Mr Read led a fascinating life; but with its tales of cattle markets, colonialism and sexual incontinence, we finished this book feeling that we'd just spent several hours trapped in the company of a world-class bore. Shame, because in the hands of a more likeable writer there's probably a decent story here.

● *Bicycles up Kilimanjaro* Richard and Nicholas Crane (Oxford Illustrated Press 1985) These two cycled up Kili with Mars Bars taped to their handlebars, to finance the construction of windmills for pumping water in East Africa. The only other person I met who had read this book said he enjoyed it, but I didn't.

● *Climbing Kilimanjaro at 70* Richard A Wolfe PhD (Ingalls Publishing 2011) The title pretty much sums up the contents as septuagenarian nuclear engineer Dr Wolfe manages to

fulfil an ambition that he first dreamed of when a young projectionist at his local cinema and watched *The Snows of Kilimanjaro* about forty times.

● *Duel for Kilimanjaro* Leonard Mosley (Weidenfeld & Nicolson, 1963) Account of the East African campaign during World War I. The fact that I stuck with it to the end, even though my interest in military history is slight, is testament to how well this book is written and what an absorbing story it is. The British, by the way, come across as comically incompetent.

● *A Girl's Guide to Climbing Kilimanjaro – What you need to know and bring to have a wonderful and comfortable climb* Rachel Durchslag & Jackie Payne (CreateSpace, 2012) I don't usually review other guidebooks (or indeed read them) but I thought that the standpoint taken by this book was sufficiently different to mine – I am male, after all – that it would be worth seeing what they had to say without fear of being accused of unfairly slating the competition. That said, I couldn't find much that they say in their book that I don't say in this one. So I asked a female friend who's climbed Kili for her unbiased opinion, though she was even more scathing and summed up the book in one simple word: pointless.

● *Kilimanjaro: Hakuna Matata* Chris Baker (🖥 lulu.com, 2007) There's nothing unusual about this person's climb, nor is there anything special about Mr Baker or his writing style. Nevertheless, as a straightforward account of what it's like to climb Kilimanjaro I really think this book is pretty good.

● *Kilimanjaro – One Man's Quest to go over the Hill* MG Edwards (CreateSpace, 2012) Man on the verge of a mid-life crisis attempts to climb Kili via the Marangu Route. Maybe I'm biased – he got in touch with me to ask if it was OK to use our maps – but I thought this one of the better accounts written recently.

● *Kilimanjaro – One Woman's Journey to the Roof of Africa and Beyond* Deb Denis (Marion Grace Publishing, 2012) Another comprehensive account of one person's climb, covering not only why and when she did it but, most important of all, how she did it. Clearly venturing out of her comfort zone, Deb spent one year preparing for her African adventure, which begins in one of the smallest countries on the continent and ends on its largest mountain. The story of her journey – in both the physical and the personal sense – is an entertaining and thought-provoking one.

● *Kilimanjaro via the Marangu Route: "Tourist Route" my ass* Phil Gray (iUniverse Inc, 2006) This book has had some pretty negative reviews on the internet and it is indeed pretty cynical, but it's not as bad as some people will have you believe. Mr Gray seems an amiable fellow, never one to tell it straight when there's the possibility of a gag, and I found the book a readable account of his climb.

● *Kissing Kibo – Trekking to the Summit of Mount Kilimanjaro via the Lemosho Route* Sheree Marshall (iUniverse, 2011) Though I found it to be the most error-strewn of the titles here, I have to admit that this book wasn't written for a pedant like me and the author, a middle-aged African-American divorcée, is a lot more engaging than the other author who enjoys making out with mountains, Mr Dorr (see below). The book is also, mercifully, a lot more succinct (Ms Marshall is in Tanzania by page seven, for example, while it takes Mr Dorr 49 pages to reach the same point). Also one of the few accounts of a trek on the Lemosho Route, which makes a change, and includes at the end of the book plenty of practical advice – though given the wealth of mistakes that litter this book, I wouldn't necessarily follow them religiously.

● *Kissing Kilimanjaro – Leaving it all on top of Africa* Daniel Dorr (The Mountaineers Books, 2010) Pretty standard account of a pretty standard trek – or rather, treks, for the author returned to climb Rongai having first failed on Machame. Overly thorough and a little too comprehensive, there are too many longueurs to make this an absorbing read. Still, for those seeking a step-by-step account (sometimes literally) of what it's like up there, it's OK – though my goodness the ending is rather melodramatic.

● *Making the Climb: What a Novice Climber Learned About Life on Mount Kilimanjaro* John C Bowling (Beacon Hill Press, 2007) Tedious account of a climb by the president of

Olivet Nazarene University (Chicago, USA) that's reminiscent of the dullest of sermons you used to have to sit through as a child – including a liberal sprinkling of prayers throughout the chapters. Read it if you must, but only as a way to build up stamina; for if you manage to finish it before your own trek then climbing the mountain will feel like a breeze. Very, very dreary indeed.

● *The Road to Kilimanjaro* Geoffrey Salisbury (Minerva Press, 1997) Though mainly autobiographical, recounting Salisbury's busy life, this book includes a heart-warming, humbling account of an expedition in 1969 by the author to the summit of Kilimanjaro on the Loitokitok (Rongai) Route with a group of eight totally blind African youths, all but one of whom made it to the top.

● *The Shadow of Kilimanjaro – On Foot Across East Africa* Rick Ridgeway (Bloomsbury 2006) Well-written account of a walk that begins on the summit of Kilimanjaro and ends at Malindi on the Kenyan coast. Though Kilimanjaro is dealt with in a matter of pages at the front of the book, the narrative style is absorbing and this book is well worth reading.

● *Snow on the Equator* HW Tilman (Bell and Son Books, 1937, republished in 2015 by Tilman publishers) Inaccurate account (Kilimanjaro is not an extinct volcano, for example, but a dormant one) by coffee planter, explorer, mountaineer and all-round show-off Harold William Tilman. Nevertheless a very entertaining read and, for all his bluster, Tilman comes across as an entirely likeable fellow.

● *On Top of Africa – the Climbing of Kilimanjaro and Mount Kenya* Neville Shulman (Element Books, 1995) Tale of the conquering of these two African giants by the author, along with the help of Zen philosophies and his own personal *shin* spirit.

● *In Wildest Africa* Peter MacQueen, FRGS (George Bell and Sons, 1910; reprinted by Forgotten Books, 2012) Account of one of the first tourists to visit Kilimanjaro, coming here during the German occupation. Includes a description of their ascent up Kili, during which some of their porters died, and more were frightened by snow and fled (taking the food with them). MacQueen himself only managed to find his way down by following the trail of porters' corpses left behind from an expedition five months previously. He went on to reach a highly credible 19,200ft, the highest, at that time, by an English speaker.

● *Zombies on Kilimanjaro – A Father/Son Journey above the Clouds* Tim Ward (Changemakers Books, 2012) I was looking forward to reading this book: the praise on the back cover suggested it was going to be a fun read and, unlike many of the other titles reviewed here, the author has some sort of previous experience when it comes to writing. However, the description of the climb gradually takes a back-seat to the author's turgid analysis of his relationship with his son and his obsession with memes until, by the time I finally reached the last page, I felt more drained than I have ever done climbing the mountain. A real test of stamina.

Fiction

● *Bingo Bear was here – A Toy Bear's Climb to the Top of Africa's Highest Mountain* Gwill York Newman (Sunstone Press 2003) It goes against one's nature to criticise a children's book but when the author implies that Kilimanjaro is in Kenya in the preface, thereby insulting an entire nation, I think the gloves are off. Anyway, this is about the adventures of a stuffed koala from Cleveland, Ohio, as he accompanies the author and her husband to the top of Africa's highest mountain – which *is* in Tanzania. The author lives in New Mexico, by the way, and has since climbed with Bingo in other mountainous places including Kashmir and the American Rockies. Which she probably thinks are in France.

● *Home on Kilimanjaro* Margaret Chrislock Gilseth (Askeladd Press, 1998) Novel written by a lady who spent four years teaching in Marangu for the Lutheran Church, written largely from the point of view of her 11-year-old son.

● *Kilimanjaro Burning* John B Robinson (Birch Book Press, 1998) Entertaining enough, but other than in being set in Tanzania it's not really relevant to the mountain. Nevertheless, good at evoking the country, its sights and smells, for those who know the area.

● *The Snows of Kilimanjaro* Ernest Hemingway (Arrow Books, 1994) Short story about a writer plagued by both a gangrenous leg and a rich wife, written by an honorary game warden based in Loitokitok in the early 1950s. Was always regarded as his most autobiographical work until the publication of...

● *Under Kilimanjaro* Ernest Hemingway (Kent State University Press, 2005) Hemingway called it fiction but with himself and his wife as the lead characters and the events that are described presumably pretty close to the truth, this book could just as easily have been pigeonholed in the Biography category above. Long and funereally paced, it has its moments but is probably for fans and aficionados only.

Chagga language, history and lifestyle

● *Chagga – A Course in the Vunjo Dialect of the Kichagga Language of Kilimanjaro, Tanzania* Bernard Leeman and Trilas Lauwo (published in Europe by Languages Information Centre) The best Chagga language book we could find; this tome, written by an Australian who worked as a teacher in the region, deals with the basic structure and grammar and is an ideal introduction to the tongue.

● *History of the Chagga People of Kilimanjaro* Kathleen M Stahl (Mouton & Co, 1964) Highly detailed account of the Chaggas, probably more for those with an academic interest in the subject but proof that contrary to popular opinion the Chagga do have an absorbing – and surprisingly lengthy – history.

● *Hunger and Shame – Child Malnutrition and Poverty on Mount Kilimanjaro* Mary Howard and Ann Millard (Routledge) Comparatively rich by African standards it may be but, as this book proves, the Kilimanjaro region still suffers from more than its fair share of grinding poverty. With views from family members, health workers and government officials, this book discusses the moral and practical dilemmas of malnourishment.

● *Kilimanjaro and its People* The Honourable Charles Dundas OBE (H, F and G Witherby, 1924; reprinted by Routledge, 2014) Probably still the most authoritative account of the Chagga people, this tome is a little dry in places (particularly the rather involved history section) and outdated too (very few of the more extreme Chagga practices, described on pp185-91 of this book, are still conducted today); nevertheless the sections on religion, witchcraft and ritual ceremonies are completely fascinating and offer the most comprehensive insight into how the Chaggas *used to be*, at least, if not how they are today.

Field guides to the fauna

● *Birds of East Africa: Kenya, Tanzania, Uganda, Rwanda, Burundi* Terry Stevenson and John Fanshawe (Helm Field Guides, 2004) Bird guides tend to be amongst the most beautiful books around and this one is no different, with gorgeous drawings by Brian Small, John Gale and Norman Arlott. Reckoned to be *the* authoritative guide.

● *Birds of Kenya and Northern Tanzania* Dale A Zimmerman (Helm Field Guides, 2005) Another in the series, just as beautiful – and only slightly less weighty than the one above.

● *Kilimanjaro – Animals in a Landscape* Jonathan Kingdon (BBC Publications 1983) Born in Tanganyika, Kingdon is an artist specialising in the flora and fauna of his homeland. This book, based on a BBC series, contains examples of his work as well as an extended commentary on the creatures that live on the mountain.

● *Pocket Guide to Mammals of East Africa* Chris Stuart and Mathilde Stuart (Struik, 2009) Around 160 pages of nice photos of animals both fierce and fascinating.

Field guides to the flora

Strangely, there is no comprehensive book on the flora of Kilimanjaro (though I understand the boss of Tusker is in the process of writing one). There is *Field Guide to Common Trees and Shrubs of East Africa* Najma Dharani (New Holland, 2011) but this, alas, has little relevance to the mountain itself.

Coffee-table books
● *Kilimanjaro* John Reader (Elm Tree Books, 1982) Excellent, beautifully written coffee-table book with detailed accounts both of the history and geology of Kili as well as the author's experience of photographing it.

● *Kilimanjaro: The Great White Mountain* David Pluth (Camerapix, 2001) Another tome that will have your coffee-table groaning.

● *Kilimanjaro: To the Roof of Africa* Audrey Salkeld (National Geographic Books, 2002) The best-looking book on Kilimanjaro, this mighty tome includes detailed sections on history and geology as well as some excellent photographs of the mountain. If you only buy one book about the mountain – other than the one you're holding now, of course! – make it this one.

FOR YOUR LISTENING PLEASURE
The following is some appropriate music to take up the mountain with you; appropriate, but not necessarily any good. And we have to wonder: have any of the following artists actually been anywhere near the mountain?

● **Babyshambles** *Killamangiro* Celebrity junkie and Kate Moss's ex is also, apparently, a rock star. This 2005 offering was Pete Doherty's first single with the band Babyshambles following his acrimonious departure from The Libertines.

● **Iration Steppas Meet Dennis Rootical** *Kilimanjaro* A 1995 10-inch single from British dubmasters. Rare; check out the Summit Mix on side two.

● **Lange presents Firewall** *Kilimanjaro* Trance-dance CD from 2004, including 8-minute-long original mix, 9-minute 23-second Lange remix and 7-minute 51-second 'B-side', *Touched*. Not special.

● **Letta Mbulu** *Kilimanjaro* Soulful disco with Afrobeats. Quite groovy but difficult to find except on compilation.

● **Medwyn Goodall** *Snows of Kilimanjaro* 'As uplifting as catching the first sight of the mountain rising up out of the African plains – as inspirational as gazing down from the summit – *Snows of Kilimanjaro* is a perfect musical tribute to the inner strength of those who rise above adversity.' At least, that's what the blurb says and as it was made in support of a charity climb, I'm not going to disagree. Whatever I may really think.

● **Miles Davis** *Filles de Kilimanjaro* Before he went all funky and weird on us with his *Bitches Brew* album – great album cover, unlistenable tunes – Miles Davis recorded this album in 1968 with his 'second great quintet', featuring Wayne Shorter on trumpet and keyboard god Herbie Hancock.

● **Mountain Mocha** *Kilimanjaro* (various titles) This is more like it, an oddball bunch of Japanese funksters from the outskirts of Tokyo named after a mountain in Africa and playing smashing grooves to which, if I could dance, I would. Reminds me most of James Brown's various backing bands – JBs, Maceo & the Macks etc; must be great fun to see live. Their self-titled first album is my favourite (and has a lovely painting of Kili on the cover).

● **Quartette Tres Bien** *Kilimanjaro* Another record that, like Mountain Mocha Kilimanjaro, reminds me that collecting isn't entirely a futile waste of money, the Quartet Tres Bien were a St Louis-based jazz combo who recorded in the mid-60s. This slice of swinging fights a constant battle with cheese throughout both sides, but when they're winning – such as on the brooding title track – they're smashing.

● **The Rippingtons** *Kilimanjaro* Guitarist Russ Freeman's instrumental follow-up to *Moonlighting*, their successful debut. Jazzy, smoothish and with world-music influences.

● **Teardrop Explodes** *Kilimanjaro* One of Britain's loveable oddballs, Julian Cope – last seen in public travelling around Britain to write about stone circles – first came to public attention with the release of this 1980 debut album. Includes their greatest hit, 'Reward', which is bound to stir up memories amongst those who, like me, grew up in the '80s. Described as post-punk by aficionados – shorthand for passionate, angry yet melodious.

● **Toto** *Africa* Bearded '80s crooner's worldwide smash includes the line 'Sure as Kilimanjaro rises like Olympus above the Serengeti'. Which, of course, it doesn't.

● **The Twinkle Brothers** *Kilamanjaro* I so wanted to like this record. I liked the cover; I liked the band's name, and I even liked the deliberate misspelling (it was deliberate, wasn't it?) Besides, apart from a couple of Bob Marley LPs I don't have much reggae in my collection. Thankfully, though a little too reggae-lite for my liking in places, overall it's pretty good and with a bass deep enough to upset the neighbours.

...AND SEVEN RELEVANT FILMS

● *Hatari!* Long on time but short on quality, this 151-minute 1963 epic starring John Wayne in typical derring-do mode as well as Hardy Krüger (see p277) and the preposterously named Red Buttons is not great, though if you can ignore the paper-thin plot, stilted acting, constipated dialogue and questionable attitude towards the wildlife, women and locals, there's some enjoyment to be had in glimpsing the region as it was in the early '60s. The scenes where they hunt and capture the animals (made, of course, without the benefit of CGI) are also very impressive and the score by Henry Mancini is reliably hummable (particularly the signature tune 'Baby Elephant Walk').

● *Kilimanjaro – to the Roof of Africa* The 2002 film of the book – or was it the book of the film? Whatever, this IMAX film recounting the experiences of a group of trekkers on the mountain is beautifully shot by film-maker David Breashears. It's the best documentary if you want to know what it's like to climb the mountain, as well as a gorgeous and evocative souvenir for those who have already done so.

● *Killers of Kilimanjaro* With scarcely a swash left unbuckled, this 1959 tale follows the adventures of trouble-shooter Robert Adamson (Robert Taylor) who, arriving in deepest Africa with Jane Carlton (played by the luscious Anne Aubrey) to oversee the completion of a cross-continental railroad, finds he has all manner of continental clichés to contend with, from slave traders (ruthless) to tribes (savage) and, of course, the local fauna (Grrrr!). Will he make it out alive? And complete the railroad too? And get together with Jane? Probably, yes. It's not great but I quite enjoyed it and it has a certain charm. Usually available on eBay, if you're interested.

● *The Mines of Kilimanjaro* Italian offering from 1986 that's been dubbed into English. Tobias Hoesl stars as Dr Ed Barkely who travels to East Africa in search of his professor's killers. But as Robert Taylor (see *Killers of Kilimanjaro*, above) could have told him, this part of the world is chock-a-block with danger, from savage tribes (in this case, the Gundors), Chinese gangsters (?) and even Nazis (???). And after that, things get *really* weird! And as Robert Taylor could *also* have told him, there are compensations in the form of some lovely scenery and equally comely female company, with Elena Pompei as Eva Kilbrook. All in all, an appalling film but unfortunately not bad enough to be funny – making it possibly the worst couple of hours of cinematic 'entertainment' you will ever experience.

● *In the Shadow of Kilimanjaro* It's 1500 men versus 90,000 flesh-eating baboons that have been driven mad by a drought: the odds look bad but if anybody can find a way out of this 1986 dilemma, John Rhys Davis and Timothy Bottoms can. ... Grab a beer and some chocolate, settle into your favourite armchair, disengage your brain and enjoy this truly rubbish but succulent slice of '80s ham and corn. Available on eBay.

● *Snows of Kilimanjaro* Henry King's 1952 film version of Ernest Hemingway's semi-autobiographical work, with Gregory Peck in the leading role, Susan Hayward as his devoted belle and Ava Gardner as the lost love he pines for – and when you see Ava in this film, you can't blame him. Of course it's the most highbrow film of the seven here and I should like it – but, personally speaking, give me killer baboons any day.

● *Volcano above the Clouds* From the Nova PBS stable comes this hour-long documentary from 2003 about a team climbing the Lemosho/Western Breach Route. Ostensibly it's about the team's attempts to discover how much the glaciers' disappearance will affect the water supply and to see whether the volcano is still active, but really it's just a documentary of a climb – and for that it's OK. Contact Nova direct, or I found it via Amazon marketplace.

APPENDIX C – GPS WAYPOINTS

Each GPS waypoint was taken on the route at the reference number marked on the map as below. Note the position format we are using is known as UTM UPS; the map datum is WGS 84 (37 M); you can change both of these on a Garmin GPS by going to Units Setup on the Settings menu, then changing the Position Format and Map datum where necessary.

Note that by some of the waypoints there is a small 'c', which denotes that the waypoint was not found by us and thus we cannot vouch for its accuracy. Any comments on any of the waypoints and their accuracy will be gratefully received. Thanks.

MOUNT MERU

Map	Ref	GPS waypoint	Description
Map A	A	37M 261065 9642331	Momela Gate
Map A	B	37M 260557 9642021	Turn-off to Tululusia Hill
Map A	C	37M 260452 9641613	Turn-off to Campsite 1 & 2
Map A	D	37M 260430 9640906	Campsite 3
Map A	E	37M 259270 9640892	Turn-off to viewpoint
Map A	F	37M 258686 9641090	Famous arched fig tree
Map A	G	37M 258127 9641264	Itikoni Campsite
Map A	H	37M 256701 9640742	Maio Falls diversion
Map B	I	37M 254592 9641371	Kitoto Viewpoint
Map B	J	37M 254338 9642470	Turn-off to Meru Crater
Map A	K	37M 255495 9642787	Miriakamba Huts
Map B	L	37M 253925 9643310	Mgongo wa Tembo
Map B	M	37M 252564 9644015	Saddle Huts
Map B	N	37M 252628 9644638	Little Meru
Map B	O	37M 251603 9643468	Rhino Point
Map B	P	37M 249943 9641219	Meru summit

KILIMANJARO – ASCENT ROUTES

The Marangu Route

Map	Ref	GPS waypoint	Description
Map 1	001	37M 335295 9641479	Marangu Gate
Map 1	002	37M 335341 9644784	Bridge
Map 1	003	37M 335676 9645120	Bridge to Kisamboni
Map 2	004	37M 334809 9648242	Mandara Huts
Map 2	005	37M 335400 9648732	Maundi Crater
Map 3	006	37M 330631 9651540	Sloping bridge
Map 3	007	37M 328280 9652715	Kambi ya Taabu
Map 4	008	37M 326490 9652894	Horombo Huts
Map 4	009	37M 325328 9654221	Junction with porters' path
Map 4	010	37M 324892 9655246	Last water point
Map 4	011	37M 324379 9655970	Mawenzi Ridge
Map 5	012	37M 323192 9657409	Lunchstop with toilets
Map 5	013	37M 322614 9658810	Sign for Kibo Circuit
Map 5	014	37M 322447 9658958	Jiwe la Ukoyo
Map 5	015	37M 321300 9659306	Junction with path to Mawenzi Tarn
Map 5 & 6	016	37M 320991 9659232	Kibo Huts
Map 6	017	37M 319713 9659625	William's Point
Map 6	017A	37M 319599 9659653	Junction of paths from School and Kibo Huts
Map 6	018	37M 319400 9659750	Hans Meyer Cave
Map 6 & 33	019	37M 318632 9660028	Gillman's Point
Map 33	128	37M 317075 9659821	Uhuru Peak

The Machame Route (via Barafu Huts and Stella Point)

Map 7	020	37M 304266 9649064	Machame Gate
Map 7	021	37M 304409 9650814	Toilet and end of 4WD track
Map 7	022	37M 305373 9654229	Lunch-stop and toilet
Map 8	023	37M 306531 9656282	Toilet
Map 8	024	37M 307321 9657714	Machame Registration Hut
Map 8	025	37M 307748 9658051	Rocky outcrop
Map 8	026	37M 308080 9658257	Viewpoint
Map 8	027	37M 308137 9658337	First giant groundsel
Map 9	028	37M 308233 9658449	First descent of day
Map 9	029	37M 308315 9658560	Climb to top of rocks for views
Map 9	030	37M 308515 9658753	Ten-second descent
Map 9	031	37M 308807 9659087	Start of steep slope
Map 9	032	37M 309122 9659438	Concrete steps in rock
Map 9	033	37M 309123 9659466	Lunchstop and toilets
Map 9	034	37M 309299 9659975	Overhang in cliff
Map 9	035	37M 309192 9660158	Further overhang caves
Map 9	036	37M 309175 9660179	Short clamber using your hands
Map 9	037	37M 308977 9660464	Top of climb – now on Shira Plateau
Map 9	038	37M 308443 9661064	Shira Caves Campsite
Map 9	039	37M 308730 9660835	Stream
Map 9	040	37M 309299 9660600	Stream
Map 10	041	37M 312517 9661462	Junction of Machame & Lemosho routes
Map 10	042	37M 312859 9661292	Lunchstop and toilets
Map 10	043	37M 313415 9661041	Sheffield Campsite
Map 10	044	37M 314131 9660747	Lava Tower Campsite
Map 10	045	37M 313959 9658662	Waterfall
Map 11	046	37M 314325 9657792	Barranco Huts
Map 11	047	37M 315177 9657333	Top of climb ie Barranco/'Breakfast' Wall
Map 11	048	37M 315779 9657062	Stream
Map 11	049	37M 316310 9656600	Top of valley wall
Map 11	050	37M 316315 9656386	Desert slope
Map 11	051	37M 316983 9656046	Valley floor and stream
Map 11	052	37M 316851 9656077	Tortoise Rock
Map 11	053	37M 317089 9655848	Karanga Campsite
Map 12	054	37M 318707 9656657	Top of climb
Map 12	055	37M 319724 9656918	Top of Barafu Ridge
Map 12 & 13	056	37M 319762 9657263	Barafu Huts
Map 13	057	37M 319592 9658015	Kosovo Campsite
Map 13	058	37M 319249 9658326	Turn left to climb on to the ridge
Map 13 & 33	059	37M 318040 9659630	Stella Point
Map 33	128	37M 317075 9659821	Uhuru Peak

The Lemosho Route (via Western Breach Route)

Map 14	060	37M 294046 9667904	Start of Lemosho Route at toilet
Map 14	061	37M 295058 9667784	Slight clearing
Map 14	062	37M 295082 9667762	Tree in path
Map 14	063	37M 295789 9667751	Patch of lobelia
Map 14	064	37M 296078 9668489	Camphor tree stand and tree across path
Map 14	065	37M 297174 9668591	Mti Mkubwa
Map 14	066	37M 298279 9668000	Stream
Map 14	067	37M 299074 9668169	Top of ridge
Map 14	068	37M 299193 9668178	Last stand of African rosewood (left of path)
Map 15	069	37M 299516 9668155	Top of climb

Map 15	070	37M 299765 9668304	Two streams and old lunchstop
Map 15	071	37M 300087 9668487	Better lunchstop
Map 15	072	37M 300897 9667634	Stream
Map 15	073	37M 302211 9667729	Top of climb – first view of Kibo
Map 15	074	37M 303210 9666760	Shira 1 (campsite)
Map 16	075	37M 304514 9665765	Boulder (junction with path to Shira Cathedral)
Map 16	076	37M 304809 9663689	First stream
Map 16	077	37M 304843 9663552	Second stream
Map 16	078	37M 304873 9663387	Third stream
Map 16	079	37M 304884 9662988	Burnt trees
Map 16	080	37M 305059 9661945	Junction with path to Shira Cathedral
Map 16	081	37M 304823 9661850	Top of cathedral
Map 16	082	37M 306091 9662268	East Shira Hill
Map 16	083	37M 306328 9662360	Weird boulders and mud flats
Map 16	084	37M 306876 9662437	Roadhead
Map 16	085	37M 307312 9662331	Dry stream
Map 17	086	37M 308314 9662240	Shira Huts (campsite)
Map 17	087	37M 310497 9662179	Big boulder
Map 17	088	37M 311028 9662077	Narrow gully
Map 10	089	37M 311568 9661987	Path north to Moir Huts
Map 10	090	37M 312105 9661769	Small cross
Map 10	043	37M 313415 9661041	Sheffield Campsite
Map 18	044	37M 314131 9660747	Lava Tower Campsite

Western Breach Route to Uhuru Peak

Map 18	091	c 37M 315109 9660256	Arrow Glacier Campsite
Map 18	092	c 37M 316482 9660666	Crater Rim
Map 33	127	37M 316829 9660194	Crater Campsite
Map 33	128	37M 317075 9659821	Uhuru Peak

The Shira Plateau Route

Map 15	093	37M 303371 9669714	Morum Barrier
Map 16	094	37M 306221 9664795	Simba Cave Campsite
Map 16	095	37M 307186 9663697	Junction with path to Moir Huts
Map 17	096	37M 308711 9663477	Fischer Camp

The Northern Circuit

Map 19	097	37M 311025 9663594	Moir Huts
Map 19	098	37M 316614 9666951	1st Pofu Campsite
Map 20	099	37M 317958 9666354	2nd Pofu Campsite
Map 20	111	37M 323357 9663335	Third Cave Campsite

The Rongai Route

Map 21	100	37M 332794 9672735	Rongai Gate
Map 21	101	37M 330548 9671175	Signpost
Map 21	102	37M 330486 9671195	Benches
Map 21	103	37M 329351 9670985	Sign about wildfires
Map 21	104	37M 328834 9670717	Benches
Map 21	105	37M 328371 9670227	Second bridge
Map 22	106	37M 327535 9670053	Simba (or Sekimba) Campsite
Map 22	107	37M 325494 9668733	Rocky plateau
Map 22	108	37M 324934 9668209	First 'summit'
Map 23	109	37M 324279 9667203	Second 'summit'
Map 23	110	37M 324041 9666423	Second Cave (lunch-stop)
Map 23	111	37M 323357 9663335	Third Cave Campsite

The Mawenzi Tarn Hut Route

Map 23	110	37M 324041 9666423	Second Cave (lunch-stop)
Map 24	112	37M 326938 9662833	Highest point of day
Map 24	113	37M 327477 9662418	Kikelelwa Camp
Map 24	114	37M 327418 9661909	Viewpoint over valley; photo stop
Map 24	115	37M 327332 9661625	Stream with groundsels
Map 24	116	37M 327506 9660758	Path divides; both options OK
Map 24	117	37M 327787 9660261	Paths reunite
Map 24	118	37M 328098 9659970	Top of ridge
Map 24	119	37M 328116 9659841	Junction with path to Kibo Huts
Map 24	120	37M 328485 9659458	Mawenzi Tarn Hut Campsite
Map 24	121	37M 328083 9659117	Top of acclimatisation climb
Map 24	119	37M 328116 9659841	Junction with path to Kibo Huts
Map 25	015	37M 321300 9659306	Junction with path to Horombo Huts
Map 25	016	37M 320991 9659232	Kibo Huts
Map 26 & 6	122	37M 320675 9660736	School Hut
Map 6	017 A	37M 319599 9659653	Jctn of paths from School and Kibo Huts
Map 6	018	37M 319400 9659750	Hans Meyer Cave
Map 6 & 33	019	37M 318632 9660028	Gillman's Point
Map 33	059	37M 318040 9659630	Stella Point
Map 33	130	37M 317075 9659821	Uhuru Peak

The Umbwe Route via Western Breach

(For the route to the summit via Barafu Huts and Stella Point, see waypoints 046-049 & 128)

Map 27	123	37M 308828 9647282	Umbwe Gate
Map 27	124	37M 309943 9651668	End of 4x4 road & signpost
Map 27	125	37M 311278 9652842	Sarumba Emergency Camp
Map 28	126	37M 312330 9654129	Umbwe Cave Campsite
Map 28	127	37M 312630 9654801	Jiwe Kamba
Map 29	128	37M 313428 9656166	Groundsel field
Map 29 & 11	046	37M 314325 9657792	Barranco Huts
Map 10	045	37M 313959 9658662	Waterfall
Map 10 & 18	044	37M 314131 9660747	Lava Tower Campsite
Map 18	091	c 37M 315109 9660256	Arrow Glacier Campsite
Map 18	092	c 37M 316482 9660666	Crater Rim
Map 33	129	37M 316829 9660194	Crater Campsite
Map 33	130	37M 317075 9659821	Uhuru Peak

KILIMANJARO – DESCENT ROUTES

The Marangu Route

See p397 for the Marangu Trail waypoints and use them in reverse until Map 4 where you have the option of doing the Mawenzi Route.

The Mawenzi Route

Map 4	008A	37M 325945 9654684	Zebra Rocks
Map 4	008B	37M 326374 9656687	Signpost and junction
Map 4	008C	37M 326240 9656836	Memorial plaque and viewpoint
Map 4	008D	37M 327617 9657468	Mawenzi Hut

The Mweka Route

Map 33	130	37M 317075 9659821	Uhuru Peak
Map 33 & 13	059	37M 318040 9659630	Stella Point
Map 13 & 30	056	37M 319762 9657263	Barafu Huts

Map 30	131	37M 319091 9654859	Junction with path to Karanga Valley on one side and a porters' path on the other
Map 30	132	37M 319086 9654264	Emergency route from Karanga Valley
Map 31	133	37M 319144 9653675	Rescue Hut (aka Millennium Hut)
Map 31	134	37M 318558 9650985	Mweka Huts
Map 31	135	37M 317765 9649028	Bridge
Map 32	136	37M 317256 9647528	Second bridge
Map 32	137	37M 316526 9645691	Start of 4x4 road
Map 32	138	37M 315727 9644014	Mweka Gate

APPENDIX D – AMS ARTICLES

See p260-9 for AMS information. The first article here was sent in by Gerald (Joe) Power, Director of Cardiac Anaesthesia at Princess Alexandra Hospital, Brisbane, Australia. It is a more scientific – and accurate – summary of altitude sickness, its causes and treatments, and we are very grateful to him for taking the time to write and send this in to us; nice one Joe!

Altitude sickness occurs as a result of there being less oxygen in the air you breathe as you ascend through the atmosphere. Although the percentage of oxygen stays the same, the amount of oxygen, best represented by the pressure it exerts, decreases. At sea level, the atmosphere exerts a pressure of 760 millimetres of Mercury (mmHg) or 101 kilopascals (kPa). Oxygen represents 21% of this total and correspondingly exerts a 'partial pressure' of 152mmHg or 21kPa.

The importance of this pressure can be illustrated by the example of a river – water flowing from a high to a low point under the influence of gravity. The greater the difference in height between these two points will influence how rapidly the water flows. Likewise oxygen has to diffuse (flow) from the lungs, into the blood and then into the tissues. This process is influenced by many factors, the most important being the pressure of the oxygen in the air you breathe into your lungs. Human life has evolved to survive comfortably when that pressure is close to 21kPa.

As one ascends higher in the atmosphere, this pressure decreases and consequently the rate at which the oxygen is able to diffuse from the lungs into the tissues decreases. This, however, is not met with a decreased requirement of oxygen in the tissues.

At the summit of Kilimanjaro, the atmospheric pressure is approximately 349mmHg or 48kPa. This is roughly half the pressure at sea level. The partial pressure of oxygen is 9.2kPa, which represents a significant reduction from that at sea level. If a person were to be exposed to this pressure with no acclimatisation (for example if you flew to the summit of Kilimanjaro in a helicopter), loss of consciousness would most likely be the result.

Altitude sickness comes as a result of the abnormal response of the human body to the oxygen starvation that occurs with altitude. The response of the brain to low oxygen supply is to dilate the arteries supplying blood to it. This results in an increase in the pressure in the brain and if the normal regulation breaks down, swelling (oedema) of the brain occurs and if severe, this can cause death.

The lungs have a normal physiological response to decreased levels of oxygen in the air, whereby the small arteries constrict and decrease the blood supply to an area of the lung. Under normal circumstances, this reflex is essential to allow the correct matching of blood supply and ventilation in the lungs. At altitude, this response can become unregulated and will result in fluid filling the air sacs (alveoli) in the lungs.

Not everyone responds in the same manner to altitude. Research done in the 1980s on Mt Everest, and in low pressure simulators, revealed that certain individuals do not respond appropriately to falling levels of oxygen. Under normal circumstances, the rate at which someone breathes is predominantly controlled by the level of carbon dioxide in the blood. A reserve reflex is to be able to respond to decreasing oxygen pressure by increasing your breathing. Individuals who lack this response appear to be susceptible to developing mountain sickness.

The key element to minimising altitude sickness is through acclimatisation. A gradual ascent of the mountain allows the heart, lungs, brain and blood to adjust to the decreased oxygen pressure. The physiological response includes an increased respiratory rate (made easier by the air being thinner) and increased heart rate to supply more blood to the tissues. Over time, the amount of haemoglobin in the blood will increase as this allows more oxygen to be carried to the tissues.

Factors that will increase the likelihood of developing altitude sickness are those that worsen the supply of oxygen to the tissues – dehydration, hypothermia, fatigue and drugs that depress or interfere with respiration.

Diamox (acetolzolamide) was first proposed as an aid to acclimatisation in the 1960s. In brief, as a person breathes harder with altitude, the levels of carbon dioxide in the blood fall. This has the effect of removing some of the stimulus that a person requires to breathe. This effect is particularly important when one falls asleep. Diamox reduces the impact of the falling carbon dioxide levels and helps to maintain normal breathing.

The treatment of altitude sickness is to restore the oxygen pressures to normal. This is most effectively achieved by descending from altitude. Temporary measures include using bottled oxygen or a Gamow bag (portable pressure chamber). In the event of the development of cerebral oedema, intravenous steroids help to limit the swelling of the brain.

References JF Nunn, *Applied Respiratory Physiology;* JB Wes, *Tolerance to severe hypoxia: lessons from Mt. Everest; Acta Anaesthesiol Scand 1990:34; S94 18-23*

Is pulse oximetry a reliable predictor of who will get AMS?

Over the past few years most of the better trekking agencies have been equipping their mountain teams with a nifty little gadget called a **pulse oximeter**. This matchbox-sized bit of kit, when clipped to a subject's finger, provides, in a matter of seconds, readings for both the pulse (which is normally equivalent to the subject's heart rate) and their blood oxygenation (SaO_2), ie the percentage of haemoglobin that is saturated with oxygen (Haemoglobin is the 'vehicle' that carries oxygen from the lungs to the body tissues; the greater the oxygenation reading, the more efficiently oxygen is being delivered around the body). All very interesting, of course – but what do these figures actually tell us, if anything, about one's chances of suffering from altitude sickness if one continues to climb?

For the answer, I am grateful to Jo Middleton, my teacher on a Wilderness First Responder course, for sending me a highly readable and simple-to-follow article that he found in a 2012 edition of *Wilderness and Environmental Medicine*. The article, entitled *Pulse Oximetry and Predicting Acute Mountain Sickness: Are We Asking the Right Questions?*, summarised the studies that had been done on the link between oximetry readings and altitude sickness.

The first serious study was done in 1998 on Denali (aka Mt McKinley) in Alaska. Surveying 102 climbers at 4200m, they concluded that 84% SaO_2 was their 'cut-off': in other words, the 21 trekkers who went on to develop altitude sickness all recorded an SaO_2 reading below 84%. Unfortunately, there were 56 other people who also registered SaO_2 scores of below 84% and yet did *not* end up with altitude sickness.

Subsequent studies seemed to confirm that oximeters are, at best, unreliable predictors of who will suffer from AMS. In particular, a study on the Mexican volcano Pico De Orizaba (5640m) and published in 2012 found that the average SaO_2 readings (taken at 4260m) of those who subsequently suffered from altitude sickness, when compared to those

who didn't, differed by only 0.3%! All of which would suggest that oximeters are pretty useless when it comes to predicting how well a climber is going to acclimatise. The researchers, however, insist that their science is sound and the link between pulse oximetry and AMS *should* – in theory – be strong. So certain are they of this that instead they think the data collection in the above studies must have been flawed. But until a study is done that satisfies their standards, we have to assume the readings given by pulse oximeters are only of limited use when it comes to guessing who is going to acclimatise well – and who isn't. And for those who record a high oxygenation reading of above approximately 89% when at around 4000m, congratulations – it appears you *should*, according to these studies, acclimatise well; while for those who register a reading below this figure, don't panic – there's a good chance you'll be OK too!

ACKNOWLEDGEMENTS

For this fifth edition I would like to thank those trekkers, locals and expats who kindly offered advice and suggestions. In no particular order (and Tanzanian unless otherwise stated), thanks are due to: Karen Valenti (US) at KPAP, as ever, for all her information and company; Betrita Loibooki, Chief Park Warden at KINAPA, and Charles Ngendo (Warden of Tourism) and Herman Baltazary (Warden for Cleanliness and Tourism Infrastructure) for giving up their time to talk about their plans for the future of the park; Jo Middleton (UK) for providing me with the article on pulse oximetry; Eric Knox (US) of Indiana State University for his help in identifying the various groundsel species; Peter and Valentine, the receptionists at Kilimanjaro and Arusha Backpacker Hotels respectively, for always making me feel so welcome; Cuthbert Swai, Noel Kileo, Hanson Kileo, Abel Edwards & all at Ahsante for sorting out my trek; not forgetting Moses 'lead-us-to-the-promised-land' Cellestine for his guidance on Machame, and Salvatore Josephat Anney for that extraordinary day going down and up the Umbwe Route; Berny Shirima for driving us around the hotels near Arusha for a day; Mr Fredy at Via Via; Tara Mtuy; Cyprian; Joshua Ruhimbi, Simon Kaaya, Shaphiy H Msiru, Donald and everyone at Team Kilimanjaro; Catherine Brown, Angharad Smith, Tammy Trauntner, Carine Roberts, Celine Woods, Victoria Revill-Whelan, Valerie Williams & Linda Salter (all UK or Ire) for their company at Onsea; Jeremie Noel (Fra), Lynn Highland (Alaska, US), Catherine Mauvais, Nicola Spring (Swiss); Edward at Pristine Trails; Narry at Good Earth Tours; Charles Exton (Can) at Ameg Lodge; Sjoerd Venema (Bel) at Kilimanjaro Backpackers; Scott Schoenwaelder (US), Simon Mtuy, Willy Mocha and Francis 'Katunzi' for the excellent if exhausting bike adventure round the northern side of Kili, and to Simon again for the research trip round the western side too; to Seamus, Jackie & Desmond at Marangu Hotel; Zakariah Kessy and Julius Justin Mlay at Marangu Gate; Ollie Brown at the Marangu café; my companions on the Machame trek: Jurjen Munting & Jessica Tsuchiya (Ned), and to Eric Lagerlöf and Daniel Lederberg (Swe), the Crazy Swedes, for being so *odmjuk*. Thanks also to Frank Mtei for his help with the Chagga language guide and Amina Malya and Vincent Munuo for checking it; Ana Grau at Amani Children's Orphanage; Dr Doug Hardy for his help with the climate section of the book; John W. Taylor (US); Tom Hennigan (US) for his help with American insurance companies; Hervé Fagard for his corrections to the Umbwe Route; and Christian Niawiaris & Tristan Zerafa (Can) for their research on the hot springs. I hope you all find that, thanks to your input, this fifth edition is even better than the previous four.

I'd also like to thank Zoe and Henry Jr for all the post-research fun on safari and in Zanzibar – happy days!

At Trailblazer I would like to thank Nick Hill for transforming my childlike scribbles into maps of beauty, Clare Weldon for editing this edition, Daniel McCrohan for proof-reading, Jane Thomas for the index and Bryn, as ever, for making the whole thing possible.

INDEX

Map key

♠ Where to stay	⊠ Post Office	Ⓒ Mosque
O Where to eat	⑤ Bank/exchange office	✝ Church/cathedral
Λ Campsite	ⓘ Tourist Information	🚌 Bus station/stop
⌂ Hut	📖 Library/bookstore	ⓣ Telephone office
☐ Building	@ Internet	▭ Rail line & station
☑ Public toilet	🏛 Museum/gallery	● Other

Main trail	Steep slope	Tree fern
Other trail	Cliff	Heather
4WD track	Bridge and river	Boulders
Road	Trees	📱008 GPS waypoint
Slope	Groundsel	32 Map continuation

TRAILBLAZER TITLE LIST

Adventure Cycle-Touring Handbook
Adventure Motorcycling Handbook
Australia by Rail
Cleveland Way (British Walking Guide)
Coast to Coast (British Walking Guide)
Cornwall Coast Path (British Walking Guide)
Cotswold Way (British Walking Guide)
The Cyclist's Anthology
Dales Way (British Walking Guide)
Dorset & South Devon Coast Path
   (British Walking Gde)
Exmoor & North Devon Coast Path (BWG)
Great Glen Way (British Walking Guide)
Hadrian's Wall Path (British Walking Guide)
Himalaya by Bike – a route & planning guide
Iceland Hiking – with Reykjavik City Guide
Inca Trail, Cusco & Machu Picchu
Japan by Rail
Kilimanjaro – the trekking guide
London Loop (British Walking Guide)
Madeira Walks – 37 selected day walks
Moroccan Atlas – The Trekking Guide
Morocco Overland – a route & planning guide
   (4x4/motorcycle/mountainbike)
Nepal Trekking & The Great Himalaya Trail
Norfolk Coast Path & Peddars Way
   (British Walking Guide)

North Downs Way (British Walking Guide)
Offa's Dyke Path (British Walking Guide)
Overlanders' Handbook – worldwide
   driving guide
Pembrokeshire Coast Path
   (British Walking Guide)
Pennine Way (British Walking Guide)
Peru's Cordilleras Blanca & Huayhuash –
   Hiking/Biking
Pilgrim Pathways: 1-2 day walks on
   Britain's sacred ways
The Railway Anthology
The Ridgeway (British Walking Guide)
Scottish Highlands – Hillwalking Guide
Siberian BAM Guide – rail, rivers & road
The Silk Roads – a route and planning guide
Sinai – the trekking guide
South Downs Way (British Walking Guide)
Thames Path (British Walking Guide)
Tour du Mont Blanc
Trans-Canada Rail Guide
Trans-Siberian Handbook
Trekking in the Everest Region
The Walker's Anthology
The Walker's Anthology – further tales
West Highland Way (British Walking Guide)

UPDATES 2021 *(cont'd from back page)*
Arusha There's a new Indian restaurant near The Outpost: *Tandoor Village*. Veggie mains are Ts9000-14,000, meat and seafood 14,000-18,000. There's nothing wrong with The Outpost but if you fancy a change it's reasonable value and popular with Arusha's Indian community – always a good sign.

Route guide
● **p348 Moir Huts to Second Pofu Campsite** There are now some long-drop toilets at Pofu 2 – the first on the Northern Circuit between Moir Huts and Third Cave campsites. There's also yet another new

campsite on this northern side of Kibo, called **Buffalo Camp**, that sits to the west of the various Pofu campsites.
● **p380 Mweka Gate** Beer/soft drinks stall by the sign by Mweka Gate. Run by Oswald, former ranger who for decades used to dish out the certificates in the office across the yard. He seems much happier in his new role! US$2 for a beer, or Ts5000.
● **p388 Maps** The best map of the mountain, *Kilimanjaro Kibo*, is sadly no longer available.

General For US readers: boiled sweets = hard candy; plasters = band aids.

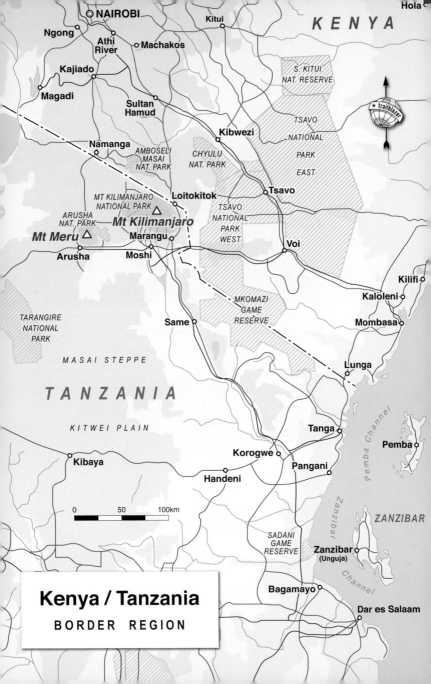

Kenya / Tanzania
BORDER REGION

The summit (see pp382-5) **Above**: Struggling through a snowstorm towards Uhuru Peak.
Below: Marching past the Rebmann Glacier on the Crater Rim.

(Opposite) Top: Sliding on your backside back down to Barafu Camp can be the safest way to descend after a snowstorm (see p376). **Middle**: The joy of reaching the summit! **Bottom**: The Ash Pit at the heart of the Reusch Crater (see p383).